NAVLIPI

A NEW, UNIVERSAL, SCRIPT ("ALPHABET") ACCOMMODATING THE PHONEMIC IDIOSYNCRASIES OF ALL THE WORLD'S LANGUAGES.
VOLUME I, ANOTHER LOOK AT PHONIC AND PHONEMIC CLASSIFICATION: *NAVLIPI*.

By Prasanna Chandrasekhar

with *FOREWORD/APPRECIATION*
by NICHOLAS OSTLER

and additional *FOREWORD*
by CHRISTOPHER MOSELEY

© Copyright 2013, Alternative Book Press

Library of Congress Cataloging-in-Publication Data

Chandrasekhar, Prasanna.

NAVLIPI. A New, Universal, Script ("Alphabet") Accommodating The Phonemic Idiosyncrasies of All The World's Languages.
Volume I, Another Look at Phonic and Phonemic Classification: *NAVLIPI*.

with Foreword/Appreciation by Nicholas Ostler and additional Foreword by Christopher Moseley.

p. cm.
Includes bibliographical references and index.
1. Language and languages--Phonetic transcriptions. 2. Phonetic alphabet. I. Title.

P226.C43 2012
411--dc23
    2013939516

Volume I:
Print Edition ISBN 978-1-940122-00-7
E-Book Edition ISBN 978-1-940122-01-4

Alternative Book Press
2 Timber Lane, #301, Marlboro, NJ 07733, USA.
www.alternativebookpress.com

with FOREWORD/APPRECIATION
by
Nicholas Ostler
[Author, most recently, of *The Last Lingua Franca: English Until the Return of Babel* (Walker & Company, 2010);
of *Empires of the Word: A Language History of the World* (HarperCollins, 2005);
and of several other works in the fields of language and linguistics.]

and additional **FOREWORD**
by
Christopher Moseley
[Editor-in-chief of *UNESCO Atlas of the World's Languages in Danger* (UNESCO Press, 3rd Edition, Paris, 2010- includes online interactive version); Editor of *Encyclopedia of the World's Endangered Languages* (Routledge, 2007); Co-Editor of *Atlas of the World's Languages* (Routledge, 1994); of *Foundation for Endangered Languages*, London, U.K., http://www.ogmios.org/ .]

Dedicated to Yaaska, Paanini and the predecessors they reference, among the world's first linguists; and to the endangered languages of the world.

Yadbhaawi, tadbhaawi, yadabhaawi, na tad anyathaa

Copyright © 2010, 2011, 2012, 2013, Prasanna Chandrasekhar, all rights reserved

TABLE OF CONTENTS

FOREWORD/APPRECIATION

by **Nicholas Ostler**

[Author, most recently, of *The Last Lingua Franca: English Until the Return of Babel* (Walker & Company, 2010); Author of *Empires of the Word: A Language History of the World* (Harper Collins, 2005); and of several other works in the fields of language and linguistics.]

..................................*xxiii*

FOREWORD

by **Christopher Moseley**

[Editor-in-chief of *UNESCO Atlas of the World's Languages in Danger* (UNESCO Press, 3rd Edition, Paris, 2010- includes online interactive version); Editor of *Encyclopedia of the World's Endangered Languages* (Routledge, 2007); Co-Editor of *Atlas of the World's Languages* (Routledge, 1994); of *Foundation for Endangered Languages*, London, U.K., http://www.ogmios.org/ .]

..................................*xxv*

PREFACE AND OBJECTIVES OF THIS BOOK

[PROVIDING A GOOD OVERVIEW OF THE ENTIRE BOOK- READ THIS FIRST!]

..................................*xxxi*

TABLE OF CONTENTS

ii

PART 1:

THE *NAVLIPI* SUMMARY TABLES
.... 1

TABLE OF CONTENTS - PART 1

1. EDITORIAL NOTES, LAYOUT/CONTENT, MATRIX ELEMENTS AND NOTE ON EASE OF LEARNING OF NAVLIPI 5

    1.1 EDITORIAL NOTE 5
    1.2 LAYOUT AND CONTENTS OF PART 1 5
    1.3 MATRIX ELEMENTS IN THE NAVLIPI TABLES 7
    1.4 EASE OF LEARNING NAVLIPI 8

2. THE NAVLIPI VOWEL CLASSIFICATION 9

    2.1 X-AXIS, LIP POSITION 9
    2.2 Y-AXIS, TONGUE'S OR OTHER ARTICULATING ORGANS' POSITION 9
    2.3 Z-AXIS, JAW POSITION 10

3. THE NAVLIPI NON-VOWEL CLASSIFICATION 11

    3.1 ARTITIONS (ARTICULATION POSITIONS) AND PHONOCHROMES ("COLOR" OF THE PHONE) OF NAVLIPI 11
    3.2 THE 15 ARTITIONS OF NAVLIPI FOR NON-VOWELS 11
    3.3 THE 35 PHONOCHROMES OF NAVLIPI FOR NON-VOWELS 12

4. VOWEL MATRICES: THE FULL, 3-DIMENSIONAL NAVLIPI VOWEL CLASSIFICATION MATRIX EXPRESSED IN 14 Y-CROSS-SECTIONS 14

5. NON-VOWEL MATRICES (INCLUDING SEMIVOWELS ("APPROXIMANTS"), CENTRALS AND LATERALS) 31

6. TABLE OF POST-OPS (POST-POSITIONAL OPERATORS) 51

TABLE OF CONTENTS

iii

7. TABLE OF PHONEMIC CONDENSATES **55**

8. SUMMARY OF TONES **58**

9. SUGGESTED DIDACTIC (PEDAGOGICAL) "ALPHABETICAL ORDER" OF NAVLIPI **60**

10. VARIOUS WIDELY-USED WORLD SCRIPTS/ALPHABETS RENDERED IN NAVLIPI **64**

    10.1 THE DEWANAAGARI (DEVANAGARI) SCRIPT RENDERED IN NAVLIPI, INCLUDING VARIANTS THEREOF FOR HINDI/URDU, MARAATHI (ONLY SMALL-PRINT GLYPHS GIVEN, FOR CLARITY) 64
    10.2 THE CYRILLIC SCRIPT (ALPHABET) RENDERED IN NAVLIPI 69
    10.3 THE ARABIC SCRIPT (ALPHABET) RENDERED IN NAVLIPI 72
    10.4 THE TAMIL SCRIPT (ALPHABET) RENDERED IN NAVLIPI 75

11. KEYBOARDING IN NAVLIPI **77**

    11.1 NUMERICAL (m)(n) or (x)(y) MATRIX NOTATION USED BY THE NAVLIPI KEYBOARD 77
    11.2 SCHEMATIC ILLUSTRATION OF THE FOUR (4) REPRESENTATIONS USED BY NAVLIPI FOR EACH KEY, FOR THE NORMAL, SHIFT, CONTROL AND ALTERNATE POSITIONS 79
    11.3 COMBINATION OF THE MATRIX NOTATION AND 4-PART KEYS, TO ARRIVE AT (m)(n)(X) KEY NOTATION, USED CONVENIENTLY TO REFER TO ALL NAVLIPI KEYBOARD KEYS 80
    11.4 NAVLIPI KEYBOARD LAYOUT, FOR THE AMERICAN QWERTY KEYBOARD 81
    11.5 LIST AND LAYOUT OF INDIVIDUAL NAVLIPI KEYS 82
    11.6 LIST OF KEY CHANGES REFLECTING MAJOR REASSIGNMENTS 85
    11.7 CHANGED NUMBER KEYS, AS TO BE USED IN NAVLIPI 87
    11.8 LIST OF KEY CHANGES: KEYS WITH HIGH FREQUENCY OF USE AND SOME MAJOR POST-OPS 88
    11.9 CENTRAL ("R") KEY AND CENTRAL GLYPHS, INCLUDING PHONEMIC CONDENSATES 90
    11.10 MAJOR LATERAL ("L") KEY 93
    11.11 MAJOR VELAR KEYS LANGUAGE-SPECIFIC IN NAVLIPI 94
    11.12 MAJOR PALATAL AND SIBILANT KEYS 97
    11.13 MAJOR DENTAL, ALVEOLAR AND RETROFLEX PLOSIVE ("T-D") KEYS 98

TABLE OF CONTENTS

iv

    11.14 SUMMARY OF THE BILABIAL (11)(3) (P) AND (6)(5), (B) KEYS FOR MAJOR LANGUAGE-SPECIFIC KEYBOARDS 103
    11.15 MAJOR NASAL ("M-N") KEYS 105
    11.16 MAJOR STANDARD-SEMIVOWEL KEYS 106
    11.17 MAJOR VOWEL KEYS 107
    11.18 SPECIAL NON-VOWEL KEYS 108
    11.19 KEYS FOR VERY RARE POST-OPS 109
    11.20 TONE KEYS 110
    11.21 INVENTORY OF LEFTOVER, UNUSED (AVAILABLE) KEYS, REFERENCED BY NAVLIPI KEY NOTATION 115

12. TRANSCRIPTIONS OF THE FIVE (5) MOST WIDELY SPOKEN LANGUAGES IN THE WORLD (IN 2005) IN *NAVLIPI*, LISTED IN ORDER OF DECREASING NUMBER OF SPEAKERS 116

    12.1 NOTES ON THE TRANSCRIPTIONS 116
    12.2 MANDARIN TRANSCRIPTION PASSAGE 117
    12.3 HINDI/URDU TRANSCRIPTION PASSAGE 121
    12.4 ENGLISH TRANSCRIPTION PASSAGE 127
    12.5 SPANISH TRANSCRIPTION PASSAGE 130
    12.6 ARABIC TRANSCRIPTION PASSAGE 133

13. TRANSCRIPTIONS OF SLCTD OTHER LANGUAGES IN *NAVLIPI* 140

    13.1 FRENCH 140
    13.2 GERMAN 143
    13.3 MARAATHI (MARATHI) 147
    13.4 MAAGYAAR (MAGYAR, HUNGARIAN) 152
    13.5 VIETNAMESE 157

PART 2: INTRODUCTION
....163

CHAPTER 1.
NEED FOR A NEW SCRIPT AND "PHONEMIC IDIOSYNCRASY"
..............................165

TABLE OF CONTENTS

1.1 **NEED FOR A NEW SCRIPT** 166

1.2 **AUDIENCE ADDRESSED** 167

1.3 **"PHONEMIC IDIOSYNCRASY"** 169

    1.3.1 THE SIGNIFICANCE OF "PHONEMIC IDIOSYNCRASY" 169
    1.3.2 TWO VIEWS OF PHONEMIC IDIOSYNCRASY 171
    1.3.3 THE HEART OF THE PROBLEM CREATED BY PHONEMIC IDIOSYNCRASY: *HOW DOES ONE ACCOMMODATE AND TRANSCRIBE PHONEMIC IDIOSYNCRASY IN A NEW SCRIPT?* 173
    1.3.4 HOW NAVLIPI TRANSCRIBES PHONEMIC IDIOSYNCRASY; *PHONEMIC CONDENSATES* 174

CHAPTER 2.
OBJECTIVES SET FORTH FOR A NEW SCRIPT, HOW *NAVLIPI* MEETS THESE OBJECTIVES, AND ARGUMENTS *AGAINST* A NEW, UNIVERSAL SCRIPT

............................177

TABLE OF CONTENTS

2.1 OBJECTIVES SET FORTH IN THIS BOOK FOR A UNIVERSAL ORTHOGRAPHY AND HOW *NAVLIPI* MEETS THESE OBJECTIVES 179

2.1.1 TEN (10) REQUIREMENTS FOR A UNIVERSAL ORTHOGRAPHY 179
2.1.2 UNIVERSALITY AND COMPLETENESS (REQUIREMENT #1) 180
2.1.3 RECOGNIZABILITY, DISTINCTIVENESS, SIMPLICITY AND INTUITIVE NATURE (REQUIREMENT #S 2, 3, 4) 180
2.1.4 HIGH AMENABILITY TO CURSIVE WRITING (REQUIREMENT #5) AND THE GAMBLE IN ASSUMING CONTINUED USE OF HANDWRITING BY HUMANS IN THE FUTURE 181
2.1.5 EASE AND RAPIDITY OF TRANSCRIPTION FROM THREE POINTS OF VIEW: CURSIVE, PRINT AND KEYBOARD (REQUIREMENT #5, CONT.) 183
2.1.6 SYSTEMATIC, SCIENTIFIC CLASSIFICATION, AND ACCURACY (REQUIREMENT #6) 185
2.1.7 DISCRETIZATION (REQUIREMENT #7) 188
2.1.8 PRACTICAL PHONEMICS RATHER THAN PHONICS (REQUIREMENT #8) 189
2.1.9 VOICE-RECOGNITION COMPATIBILITY AND A VOICE-RECOGNITION SOFTWARE PACKAGE (REQUIREMENT # 9) 189
2.1.10 ABILITY TO ACCOMMODATE THE PHONEMIC IDIOSYNCRASIES OF ALL THE WORLD'S LANGUAGES (REQUIREMENT # 10) 189

2.2 ARGUMENTS *AGAINST* A NEW, UNIVERSAL, PHONIC OR PHONEMIC ORTHOGRAPHY (SCRIPT) 190

CHAPTER 3.
OTHER PRIOR ART
..............193

TABLE OF CONTENTS

3.1 WHAT IS COVERED IN THIS CHAPTER: *NEW* **SCRIPTS SPECIFICALLY ATTEMPTING SYSTEMATIC, SCIENTIFIC, PHONIC OR PHONEMIC CLASSIFICATION**.. 195

3.2 ASIAN CONTRIBUTIONS... 198

    3.2.1 HAANGUL (HANGUL) 198
    3.2.2 OTHER ASIAN CONTRIBUTIONS: THE VARIOUS MODI'S, JAPANESE, PAHAWH, VARANG KSHITI AND OTHERS 201
    3.2.3 THE INDIAN SCRIPTS 204
        3.2.3.1 SCIENTIFIC AND SYSTEMATIC CLASSIFICATION OF THE INDIAN SCRIPTS AND USE OF THIS AS BASIS FOR EXPANSION... *204*
        3.2.3.2 THE ORIGINAL INDIAN CLASSIFICATION, IN SUMMARY........................... *208*
        3.2.3.3 THE VOWELS... *210*
        3.2.3.4 JAW, LIP AND TONGUE POSITIONS AS INDEPENDENT VARIABLES IN THE INDIAN CLASSIFICATION.. *215*
        3.2.3.5 PROBABLE ORIGINAL SIGNIFICANCE OF SOME ELEMENTS OF THE INDIAN VOWEL CLASSIFICATION: THE WISARGA AS GLOTTAL STOP AND THE DIPHTHONGS AS PURE VOWELS... *216*
        3.2.3.6 THE NON-VOWELS: ARTITION AND PHONOCHROMATICITY AS THE TWO INDEPENDENT VARIABLES.. *218*
        3.2.3.7 ACCURACY OF THE ANCIENT CLASSIFICATION, DESPITE LACK OF MODERN SCIENTIFIC INSTRUMENTATION *220*
        3.2.3.8 INADEQUACIES OF THE ANCIENT CLASSIFICATION EVEN FOR TODAY'S INDIAN LANGUAGES *220*

3.3 EARLY EUROPEAN CONTRIBUTIONS: FROM HART TO MULCASTER 225

3.4 RECENT EUROPEAN AND NORTH AMERICAN CONTRIBUTIONS...... 229

TABLE OF CONTENTS

viii

    3.4.1 "Shorthands" and the Seminal Phonological Classification of Pitman 229
    3.4.2 The Alphabets/Scripts of Pitman, Ellis, Graham, Watt, Lepsius, Bell, Sweet, Jespersen, Janvrin, Story, Johnston, Owen, Pike, and Others 233

3.5 NATIVE NORTH-AMERICAN AND AFRICAN CONTRIBUTIONS 260

    3.5.1 Scripts for Native American Languages of North America: Cherokee, Cree, Inuktitut, Others 260
    3.5.2 New Scripts for African Languages: Vai, N'ko 262

3.6 OTHER RECENT CONTRIBUTIONS 264

    3.6.1 Assorted Other Attempts at New Scripts: Unifon, Shavian, Columbian, Abulhab, Fraser, Pollard 264
    3.6.2 Assorted Other Attempts at New Scripts, cont.: Tolkien, LeGuin, Bloquerst, Wilbur, Arthur, Greenaway, Others 269

3.7 THE IPA (Alphabet of the International Phonetic Association) AND SERIOUS DEFICIENCIES THEREOF 270

3.8 *AMERICANIST* PHONETIC NOTATION (SCRIPT) 279

3.9 BRIEF SYNOPSIS OF DEFICIENCIES OF ALL ALPHABETS/SCRIPTS CITED ABOVE 283

PART 3: PRESENTATION AND DISCUSSION OF *NAVLIPI*:
....287

CHAPTER 4.
THE FULL PHONIC CLASSIFICATION OF *NAVLIPI*: THE "SHELL" MATRICES (TEMPLATES)
..............................289

TABLE OF CONTENTS

4.1 THE CONCEPT OF AN EMPTY "SHELL" MATRIX (TEMPLATE)............ 291

4.2 THE SIX (6) NAVLIPI VOWEL VARIABLES AND THE 5-DIMENSIONAL VOWEL CLASSIFICATION MATRIX... 294

4.3 REDUCTION OF THE 5-DIMENSIONAL VOWEL CLASSIFICATION MATRIX TO THREE (3) DIMENSIONS, ALONG WITH A 4TH VARIABLE FOR VOWEL DURATION, FOR PRACTICAL PURPOSES................................. 303

4.4 SEMI-VOWELS AND THEIR RELATION TO PARENT VOWELS.............. 305

4.5 THE TWO-DIMENSIONAL, (35 X 15), NON-VOWEL MATRIX 310

    4.5.1 TWO PHONOLOGICAL VARIABLES, 15 ARTITIONS, 35 PHONOCHROMES............. 310
    4.5.2 BRIEF DISCUSSION OF THE *UNUSUAL ARTITIONS* 313
    4.5.3 BRIEF DISCUSSION OF THE *UNUSUAL PHONOCHROMES*..................................... 315

4.6 TONES ("MUSICAL" OR "PITCH" ACCENTS) 317

TABLE OF CONTENTS

4.7 MATRIX NOTATION AND USE OF MATRIX ELEMENT NUMBERS WHEN REFERENCING THE NAVLIPI TABLES.. 318

4.8 OUR RESULT: COMPLETE, EMPTY PHONIC CLASSIFICATION "SHELL" MATRICES (TEMPLATES), FOR SUBSEQUENT FILLING-IN WITH A NEW SCRIPT'S GLYPHS (LETTERS, SYMBOLS)... 320

4.9 ALPHABETICAL ORDER, PEDAGOGY, AND SUBSETS OF THE NAVLIPI SUMMARY TABLES 321

CHAPTER 5.
PRELUDE TO *NAVLIPI*:
EXERCISES IN PHONIC CLASSIFICATION, OR "LET'S TRY TO MAKE A NEW SCRIPT". (FILLING IN THE TEMPLATES PRODUCED IN THE PREVIOUS CHAPTER)
..................323

TABLE OF CONTENTS

5.1 INTRODUCTION AND PRINCIPLES 324

5.2 A SCRIPT BASED ON GEOMETRIC SYMBOLS WHICH IS HIGHLY SCIENTIFIC BUT UTTERLY USELESS 325

5.3 A SCRIPT BASED ENTIRELY ON POST-OPS 328

5.4 A VERY BASIC ("*SIMPLE VERSION*") SCRIPT BASED ON DEWANAAGARI WHICH IS ALSO HIGHLY SCIENTIFIC BUT SUFFERS FROM RECOGNIZABILITY AND OTHER PROBLEMS 333

5.5 A MORE REFINED ("*COMPLEX VERSION*") SCRIPT BASED ON DEWANAAGARI WHICH STILL SUFFERS FROM RECOGNIZABILITY AND OTHER PROBLEMS 341

5.6 A SCRIPT BASED ON PITMAN-GRAHAM SHORTHAND-TYPE TRANSCRIPTION 345

5.7 *SHALL WE GIVE UP?!* LESSONS LEARNED 350

CHAPTER 6.
SUMMARY OF ALL POST-OPS USED IN *NAVLIPI*
..................351

TABLE OF CONTENTS

6.1 THE POST-OPS (POST-POSITIONAL OPERATORS) OF *NAVLIPI* 353

6.2 THE FIRST THREE POST-OPS: PO-1 (*ASPIRATE/NON-ASPIRATE PHONEMIC CONDENSATE*), PO-2 (*LENGTH OF VOWELS*), PO-3 (*LENGTH OF TONEMES*) 355

6.3 PO-4 (*ASPIRATION*), PO-5 (*FRICATIZATION*) 357

6.4 PO-6 ((*VOICED* + *UNVOICED*) PHONEMIC CONDENSATE) AND PO-7 (*GENERAL VOICING*) 358

6.5 PO-8 (*NASALIZATION OF VOWELS*) AND PO-9 (*NASAL* + *NON-NASAL*) PHONEMIC CONDENSATE) 360

6.6 PO-10 (*FLAP*) 361

6.7 PO-11 (*UVULARIZATION, SHARED WITH PHARYNGEALIZATION*) 362

6.8 PO-12 (*STOP* + *FRICATIVE*) PHONEMIC CONDENSATE) 364

6.9 PO-13 (*STOP* + *FORWARD FRICATIVE*) PHONEMIC CONDENSATE) 365

6.10 PO-14 (*INGRESSIVE CLICK*) AND PO-15 (*EGRESSIVE CLICK*) 367

6.11 PO-16 (*EJECTIVE*) AND PO-17 (*IMPLOSIVE*) 368

6.12 PO-18 (*STOP* + *SEMIVOWEL*) PHONEMIC CONDENSATE) 369

6.13 PO-19, THE IMPORTANT PHONEMIC CONDENSATE DENOTING A "MOBILE, GENERIC" VOWEL 371

6.14 PO-20, COMBINATION OF PHONES 372

6.15 PO-21, "SILENT" NON-VOWEL 373

6.16 PO-22 AND FURTHER (TONES, TONEMES, ICTUS ACCENTS) 374

CHAPTER 7.
PRESENTING THE FULL, PHONIC *NAVLIPI* SCRIPT, INCLUDING A DISCUSSION OF REASONS FOR SELECTION OF ITS GLYPHS (LETTERS)
..............................375

TABLE OF CONTENTS

7.1 PRELIMINARY NOTES 377

    7.1.1 THE "FULL PHONIC" (NON-PHONEMIC) NAVLIPI... 377
    7.1.2 REDUNDANT AND RE-USED/BORROWED GLYPHS (LETTERS) 377
    AND REASONS FOR SELECTING THEM.. 377
    7.1.3 NEW GLYPHS (LETTERS) AND THE MINIMAL NEED FOR THEM IN NAVLIPI: JUST ONE BORROWED GLYPH, ONE NEW GLYPH AND THREE TRANSFORMED GLYPH IN NAVLIPI (TOTAL FIVE) 380
    7.1.4 DISCRETIZATION AND PHONEMIC IRRELEVANCE.. 382

7.2 THE EMPTY TEMPLATE ("SHELL" MATRIX) AND THE NAVLIPI SUMMARY TABLES 384

    7.2.1 THE TEMPLATE ("SHELL" MATRIX) AND ITS FILLING WITH NAVLIPI GLYPHS (LETTERS)... 384
    7.2.2 NOTATION USED FOR NAVLIPI LETTERS THROUGHOUT THIS BOOK 384
    7.2.3 THE VOWEL SEGMENT OF THE NAVLIPI SUMMARY TABLES 385
    7.2.4 THE NON-VOWEL SEGMENT OF THE NAVLIPI SUMMARY TABLES 386

7.3 THE VOWEL MATRIX AND SELECTION OF NAVLIPI GLYPHS (LETTERS) FOR IT 387

7.4 THE TWO-DIMENSIONAL (35 X 15) NON-VOWEL MATRIX AND SELECTION OF GLYPHS (LETTERS) FOR IT 390

7.5 POST-OPS (POSTPOSITIONAL OPERATORS).. 393

7.6 PHONEMIC CONDENSATES USED AND REASONING 393

7.7 BILABIAL AND MEDIO-PALATAL SEMIVOWELS AND PHONEMIC CONDENSATES THEREOF 394

7.8 CENTRALS (R-SOUNDS) AND SELECTION OF LETTERS FOR THESE. 395

7.9 LATERALS (L-SOUNDS) AND SELECTION OF LETTERS FOR THESE. 396

7.10 TONES ("MUSICAL" OR "PITCH" ACCENTS) 397

7.11 TRANSCRIPTION OF UNUSUAL PHONES 397

CHAPTER 8.
TONES, TONEMES AND ICTUS (STRESS) ACCENTS
..............................401

TABLE OF CONTENTS

8.1 EXTANT SYSTEMS FOR TRANSCRIPTION OF TONES AND THE NEED FOR A NEW SYSTEM.. 402

8.2 VARIATION OF TONES FOUND IN LANGUAGES TODAY 408

8.2.1 TONAL LANGUAGES AND ILLUSTRATIONS WITH MANDARIN, CANTONESE, YORUBA, CASHINAHUA, NAMA................................ 408
8.2.2 "SEMI-TONAL" LANGUAGES AND ILLUSTRATIONS WITH SWEDISH, VEDIC SANSKRIT, HOMERIC GREEK 412
8.2.3 LANGUAGES WITH ICTUS (STRESS) ACCENTS AND ILLUSTRATIONS WITH ENGLISH, SPANISH, EUROPEAN NAMES 417

8.3 THE TRANSCRIPTION OF TONES IN *NAVLIPI*: USE OF FOUR *ATTRIBUTES* OF TONES 420

8.3.1 ATTRIBUTES OF TONES IN NAVLIPI 420
8.3.2 DESCRIPTION OF THE TONE TRANSCRIPTION SYSTEM OF NAVLIPI 423

8.4 EXAMPLES OF TRANSCRIPTIONS OF A VARIETY OF TONAL LANGUAGES IN *NAVLIPI* 426

CHAPTER 9.
PHONEMIC CONDENSATION AND CLASSES OF PHONEMIC CONDENSATES USED IN *NAVLIPI*
...................427

TABLE OF CONTENTS

9.1 SIGNIFICANCE AND PRINCIPLES OF PHONEMIC CONDENSATION 429

9.2 SUMMARY TABLE OF PHONEMIC CONDENSATES 429

9.3 ASPIRATE/NON-ASPIRATE PHONEMIC CONDENSATE, PCON-1, = PO-1 429

9.4 (UNVOICED + VOICED) PHONEMIC CONDENSATE, PCON-2, = PO-6 429

9.5 (STOP + FRICATIVE) PHONEMIC CONDENSATE, PCON-3, =PO-12 430

9.6 (STOP + FORWARD FRICATIVE) PHONEMIC CONDENSATE, PCON-4, =PO-13 .. 430

9.7 (STOP + SEMIVOWEL) PHONEMIC CONDENSATE, PCON-5, =PO-18 430

9.8 (SEMIVOWEL + FORWARD FRICATIVE) PHONEMIC CONDENSATE, PCON-6, DIGRAPH 430

9.9 (STOP + FLAP) PHONEMIC CONDENSATE, PCON-7, DIGRAPH 431

9.10 THE IMPORTANT PHONEMIC CONDENSATE FOR (FLAP + TRILL + SEMIVOWEL) IN APICO-ALVEOLO-DENTAL, CENTRAL ARTITION (THE "COMMON R" PHONEME), PCON-8 432

9.11 THE RARE PHONEMIC CONDENSATE FOR (RETROFLEX) ARTITION, (FLAP + TRILL + SEMIVOWEL) PHONOCHROME, PCON-9 433

TABLE OF CONTENTS

xviii

9.12 ([X] - [R]) COMBINATION: PHONEMIC CONDENSATE COMBINING PCON-8 (FOR THE COMMON /R/-PHONEME) WITH THE UVULAR FRICATIVE, PCON-10, REPRESENTED AS A DIGRAPH 433

9.13 ALVEOLAR-R-L COMBINATION, PCON-11: PHONEMIC CONDENSATE COMBINING PCON-8 WITH THE (APICO-ALVEOLO-DENTAL LATERAL) ARTITION (L-SOUND) 434

9.14 RETROFLEX-R-L COMBINATION: PHONEMIC CONDENSATE COMBINING RETROFLEX CENTRAL SEMIVOWEL (R-SOUND) WITH RETROFLEX LATERAL SEMIVOWEL (L-SOUND), PCON-12 435

9.15 ALVEOLAR-R-L-N COMBINATION, PCON-13: PHONEMIC CONDENSATE COMBINING PCON-8 WITH THE (APICO-ALVEOLO-DENTAL LATERAL) ARTITION (L-SOUND), AND THE (APICO-ALVEOLO-DENTAL NASAL STOP) (N-SOUND) 435

9.16 RETROFLEX-R-L-N COMBINATION: PHONEMIC CONDENSATE COMBINING RETROFLEX CENTRAL SEMIVOWEL (R-SOUND) WITH RETROFLEX LATERAL SEMIVOWEL (L-SOUND) AND THE RETROFLEX NASAL STOP (N-SOUND), PCON-14 436

9.17 SIGNIFICANCE OF R-L-N EQUIVALENCES, EMBODIED IN PCON #S 11, 12, 13 AND 14, TO PHONETIC SHIFTS AND HISTORICAL LANGUAGE DEVELOPMENT 436

9.18 THE IMPORTANT PHONEMIC CONDENSATE DENOTING A "MOBILE, GENERIC" VOWEL, PCON-15, =PO-19 438

9.19 THE RARE (NASAL + NON-NASAL) PHONEMIC CONDENSATE, PCON-16, =PO-9 438

9.20 PCON-17: THE "UNIVERSAL R", TO BE RARELY USED 438

CHAPTER 10.
NAVLIPI KEYBOARDING USING THE *QWERTY, AZERTY* OR OTHER COMMON KEYBOARDS
..............439

TABLE OF CONTENTS

10.1 IMPORTANT FEATURES OF *NAVLIPI* KEYBOARDING 441

10.1.1 KEYBOARD WILL BE LANGUAGE SPECIFIC (FOR BROAD GROUPS OF LANGUAGES), REDUCING NUMBER OF KEYS NEEDED 441
    10.1.1.1 LANGUAGE-SPECIFIC KEYBOARDS FOR BROAD GROUPS OF LANGUAGES *441*
    10.1.1.2 ILLUSTRATION OF LANGUAGE-SPECIFICITY *442*
    10.1.1.3 LANGUAGE-SPECIFIC KEYBOARDS DRASTICALLY REDUCE NUMBER OF GLYPHS, AND HENCE KEYS *443*
    10.1.1.4 REASONING BEHIND LANGUAGE GROUPINGS FOR SOME OF THE LANGUAGE-SPECIFIC KEYBOARDS *443*
10.1.2 NUMERICAL NOTATION (MATRIX NOTATION) USED FOR KEYBOARD KEYS IN NAVLIPI, AND FOUR PART KEY NOTATION ON EACH KEY (FOR NORMAL, SHIFT, CONTROL AND ALTERNATE POSITIONS), ILLUSTRATED HERE FOR THE QWERTY KEYBOARD 445
    10.1.2.1 NAVLIPI'S MATRIX NOTATION FOR THE KEYBOARD AND KEY NOTATION FOR INDIVIDUAL KEYS *445*
    10.1.2.2 EXAMPLES *449*
    10.1.2.3 FOUR-PART NOTATION AND MARKINGS FOR EACH KEY *450*
10.1.3 CONCERNS WITH THE [CTRL], [ALT] AND OTHER KEYS IN RELATION TO UNIX (LINUX), WINDOWS®, OTHER OPERATING SYSTEMS, MOST WORD PROCESSORS, AND OTHER PROGRAMS 450
10.1.4 ONLY MAJOR PHYSICAL CHANGES IN OTHERWISE NEARLY UNDISTURBED QWERTY, AZERTY, OR OTHER COMMON KEYBOARD: MUCH SMALLER SPACE BAR, MUCH LARGER ALT BARS, AND NON-NUMERIC PART OF NUMERIC (NUM LOCK) KEYS CHANGED 452

FOREWORDS

xx

10.1.5 TWO OPTIONS FOR IMPLEMENTATION OF NAVLIPI ON THE KEYBOARD, AND REGISTRATION OF NAVLIPI WITH UNICODE 454

10.2 LIST OF KEYS WITH MAJOR CHANGES 455

10.2.1 MAJOR REASSIGNMENTS 455
10.2.2 MAIN (I.E. NOT NUM LOCK) NUMBER KEYS (ALSO USED FOR TONES, SEE LATER) 457
10.2.3 MAJOR POST-OP KEYS AND KEYS WITH HIGH FREQUENCY OF USE AND KEYS 458
10.2.4 CENTRAL ("R") KEY AND CENTRAL GLYPHS, INCLUDING PHONEMIC CONDENSATES 459
10.2.5 MAJOR LATERAL ("L") KEY 462
10.2.6 MAJOR VELAR KEYS 463
10.2.7 MAJOR PALATAL AND SIBILANT KEYS 466
10.2.8 MAJOR RETROFLEX, ALVEOLAR AND DENTAL PLOSIVE ("T-D") KEYS 467
10.2.9 MAJOR BILABIAL KEYS 473
10.2.10 MAJOR NASAL ("M-N") KEYS 477
10.2.11 MAJOR STANDARD-SEMIVOWEL KEYS 478
10.2.12 MAJOR VOWEL KEYS 479
10.2.13 SPECIAL NON-VOWEL KEYS 480
10.2.14 POST-OP KEYS FOR CLICKS, IMPLOSIVES AND EJECTIVES, THE "MODIFIED-Z" KEYS 481
10.2.15 KEYS FOR VERY RARE POST-OPS 481
10.2.16 TONE KEYS (SEE ALSO NUMBER KEYS, ABOVE) 482

10.3 INVENTORY OF LEFTOVER, UNUSED/AVAILABLE KEYS (FOR POTENTIAL FUTURE USE) 490

10.4 FURTHER NOTES ON PRACTICAL USE OF THE *NAVLIPI* KEYBOARD(S) 491

10.5 THE KEYBOARD PRESENTATION IN PART 1 (*NAVLIPI SUMMARY TABLES*) 492

PART 4: GLOSSARY, LITERATURE CITED, INDEX, ABOUT THE AUTHOR

....493

GLOSSARY

....495

LITERATURE CITED

[INCLUDING 624 REFERENCES, CITED IN ORDER OF THEIR APPEARANCE IN THE TEXT, BUT WITH ADDITIONAL GROUPING AND SUB-GROUPING TO FACILITATE EASY REFERENCE. INCLUDES EDITORIAL NOTE ON METHOD OF LITERATURE CITATION USED.]

....507

INDEX

....565

ABOUT THE AUTHOR

.... 575

FOREWORDS

xxii

FOREWORD/APPRECIATION

by
Nicholas Ostler

[Author, most recently, of *The Last Lingua Franca: English Until the Return of Babel* (Walker & Company, 2010);
Author of *Empires of the Word: A Language History of the World* (Harper Collins, 2005);
and of several other works in the fields of language and linguistics.]

Navlipi (despite its Sanskritic name, which means "new-script") is a systematic extension of Roman script, with a number of aims in view: To be a practical (legible and writable) script for all the world's languages, but at the same time to represent the languages' sounds exactly and consistently, making no compromises on the phonemic principle. In this ambitious goal, it goes beyond existing scripts: Beyond ordinary Roman scripts, because it requires that its symbols are interpreted the same way everywhere; beyond phonetic scripts such as the International Phonetic Alphabet, by representing phonemes singly, rather than as a set of phones; and beyond all the other scripts, by attempting to replace every single one of them without loss of significant phonetic detail. (Chandrasekhar resigns himself to the loss of any historical and etymological traces that may survive in some languages' writing systems.) As such, it aims to be a technical tool for the analysis of languages (for linguists), at the same time as it serves as a practical orthography for every language in the world.

This is a stupendous aim for a single system created by a single scholar, and its author, Prasanna Chandrasekhar, realizes that his chances of success are slim. Nevertheless, the fact that a single human vocal tract is capable - with the right exposure in youth - to articulate any one of the world's languages perhaps encourages us to believe that it would be possible for a single written script - with enough of the right diacritics - to encompass every language, all without compromise in showing all the significant distinctions to be made in the language.

The main obstacle to Chandrasekhar's achievement is the phenomenon of "phonemic idiosyncrasy", whereby the actual speech sounds are organized into different, and cross-cutting, significant sets in various languages: For example, *p*, whether

FOREWORDS

aspirated or unaspirated, is the same phoneme in English, but the two versions belong to contrasting phonemes in Hindi, where (however) *f* is heard as the same sound as aspirated-*p*. By juxtaposing letters, Chandrasekhar conjures up new symbols that represent directly the complex phonemic reality. As a result, no language can be successfully written in *Navlipi* unless its phonemic system has been structurally analysed, which is perhaps no bad thing. Unfortunately, though, phonemic analyses tend to be controversial. This could put a brake on implementation.

The world may well be "too much with us" for *Navlipi* to stand very much chance of widespread adoption as a practical script: One is reminded of the very short-lived success of even Khubilai (Kublai) Khan when he commissioned the brilliant scholar 'Phagspa to create a common script for all the languages of his empire, from Persian and Tibetan to Mongolian and Mandarin. The world tends to set its communication standards for historical reasons, and to suit the powers that be, rather than any academic ideal. But the script is also a dramatic object lesson in the constraints of phonemic analysis, and so may enjoy some popularity among linguists for its technical aims.

The attempt to have all the possible virtues of a phonetic writing system at once - on the basis of single man's ideal - is what makes this a heroic endeavour.

Nicholas Ostler
Bath, England

FOREWORD

by
Christopher Moseley

[Editor-in-chief of *UNESCO Atlas of the World's Languages in Danger* (UNESCO Press, 3rd Edition, Paris, 2010- includes online interactive version); Editor of *Encyclopedia of the World's Endangered Languages* (Routledge, 2007); Co-Editor of *Atlas of the World's Languages* (Routledge, 1994); of *Foundation for Endangered Languages*, London, U.K., http://www.ogmios.org/;]

The name *Navlipi* is one of a number of new terms which are introduced in this unique volume. In it, Dr. Prasanna Chandrasekhar proposes a most ambitious scheme, one which has eluded linguistic science for centuries: A method of reducing all the world's major languages to writing in a uniform way. The name itself derives from Sanskrit, and means 'new script'. It is nothing less than a new script that Dr. Chandrasekhar is offering the world in the pages that follow.

Dr. Chandrasekhar has made a study of all the world's more commonly used scripts and compared their efficiency in rendering the languages they represent. His project was originally a unified script for the languages of India, but he soon extended its mandate to cover all the languages of the world. *Navlipi,* however, is not based on Devanagari or any Indian script, but on Roman, the most widely adapted script in the world. Furthermore, he has devised a scheme where the 26 standard Roman letters are supplemented by only five more. Tones and other suprahonemic features are also catered for, by a system of 'post-ops' (postpositional operators). In other words, it differs from the International Phonetic Alphabet (which aims at the same comprehensive universality) in not attempting to greatly extend the range of distinct graphemes, but rather, aims at the most economic use of the existing inventory, very modestly extended. What is more, its inventor claims and demonstrates that it can be used in a cursive version in handwriting, in addition to the inventory of letters for printing.

Dr. Chandrasekhar's academic background is in chemistry, and his current work is in the defense contracting industry, but his ethnic background places him in a multilingual, multiscriptal society. An idea like *Navlipi* was most likely to arise in India, where numerous scripts compete for the eye's attention in everyday life, and an inquiring mind such as the author's was moved to try to distil them into a single uniform writing system.

The author sets out his alphabet in the form of tables which clearly show the phonemes represented by each letter, grouped by place and manner of articulation, rather like a phonetic chart, He does not comment in the tables on the frequency of each phoneme in the world's languages, except to state where it is negligible. There have been many claims of a perfect fit between the written script and the spoken form of some of the world's languages (such as Hangul and Korean), but so far no claim has been made for a perfect fit of a single script for all the world's languages.

The *Navlipi* script has been put extensively to the test on a wide range of languages, and the test transcriptions make up a large part of the original text of the volumes presented here. Its accuracy in rendering the phonemic distinctions in each language will be weighed, by a native-speaker audience, against the possible sacrifices of etymological transparency. However, it is one of the objects of Dr. Chandrasekhar's project that phonological consistency outweighs etymological or phonemic 'idiosyncrasy', as the author calls it. In terms of phoneme-grapheme correspondence, *Navlipi* is demonstrated to be faithful to the sounds of a language while not being over-complex to write. Dr. Chandrasekhar has made exhaustive comparisons even with scripts which are confined to use with one language (Cherokee, Varang Kshiti and many others).

And what is remarkable about the author's researches is that he has given each of these scripts a rigorous test for universalising it – applying it to the full range (as he sees it) of the world's contrastive phonemes – and in each case he finds them wanting. Their lack of adaptability lies not merely in the impossibility of reassigning redundant graphemes (in other words, a restricted range of possible written signs), but also in less quantifiable, or more 'relative' ways, such as *recognisability* and *intuitiveness*. The primacy of the alphabet in its traditional guise – that is, with upper and lower case letters, and cursive variants – is clearly evident to Dr. Chandrasekhar. However, it is to his credit that he adopts this option only after thoroughly testing the alternatives. What is also attractive to him, one can't help feeling (and this relates to his concept of 'intuitiveness') is the perfectly-balanced degree of contrast between letter-shapes in an alphabet like the Roman one. Perfectly balanced, that is, in terms of visual perception, brain-to-eye co-ordination.

This brings the user of *Navlipi* to the issue of variant letters *vs.* diacritics. Dr. Chandrasekhar has deliberately avoided diacritical marks of the accepted type (cedilla, acute, &c.) above and below the base-letters to indicate a change of phonemic quality from the base. Rather, each letter is to be considered as a complete, separate and organic unit. But that is not to say that the new symbols are not clearly derived from older ones, or that they bear no organic relationship to letters without these extensions. The extensions are of two main types – bars within the letter, and the so-called 'post-ops', which are actually adjuncts written to the right of the base letters. These indicate non-segmental features such as tone, nasalization and the like. This may be taken to be the minimal distinctive variation in an alphabet consisting only of primary symbols, with no secondary or optional members of the inventory. Yet of course these newly created symbols will in some cases be optional – for those languages that do not possess the phonemes in question.

The author's coverage of the range of possible 'post-ops' will give an indication of how comprehensive a range of languages and their contrastive phonemes can be accommodated by this scheme. The 'post-ops' are the simplest and readiest solution to the problem of adapting what is essentially a 31-letter alphabet to all possible phonemic environments. It is interesting to speculate on the effect on literacy in many rarely-written languages that this scheme would have. What looks at first like an attempt at an accurate transcription system for linguists could, the author suggests, be a useful vehicle for everyday writing in any conceivable language.

The author's guiding principle in creating the alphabet and its attendant 'post-ops', then, has been to take note of the frequency of phonemes, in the major languages of the world with which he is familiar, in assigning, reassigning or creating the distinct letters, while allowing for the less frequently occurring ones in his maximally economic system of 'post-ops'. It is, in this sense, primarily an alphabet for practical everyday use with any language. The forms of the new letters themselves have been created bearing in mind their associations with already existing letters.

In dealing with tone, the author has had to be especially thorough. Each language where tone is contrastive (Chinese, Vietnamese, Igbo, to take some obvious examples) has its own set of contrastive oppositions. Dr. Chandrasekhar demonstrates exhaustively the unwieldy nature of the renderings of these contrastive tones (ranging from the mandatory system, in Vietnamese, through the semi-optional marking system of Igbo, to the official and semi-official transcription systems of Mandarin and Cantonese) and posits his own uniform system for showing tone. He goes further, and shows how tone could be marked in *Navlipi* even for languages where tone is predictable but not completely phonemic, such as Swedish. The number of speakers of tone-languages in the world is formidable, and *Navlipi* is presented as lending itself especially well to the rendering on these languages consistently.

Who, then, is the potential 'user of *Navlipi*'? The author contends that his original aim was to bridge the gap, using a Romanized system, between the discrete scripts of India – the Devanagari and its variants that emanate from Braahmi, including the scripts of the Dravidian languages of south India, as well as the smaller scripts such as those for the Munda languages. He soon realised, however, that his invention had potential use, with easy adaptation, to many other non-Roman, or at least non-alphabetic, scripts – Arabic and Chinese for instance – as well as those national alphabets that are still wavering between systems, such as some of the languages of former Soviet Central Asia. Thus he looks forward to adaptation on a national, indeed a multinational, scale, if not a fully international one. He does not use the term 'auxiliary' and does not entertain the notion of a traditional script continuing alongside the use of *Navlipi* for teaching purposes.

Persuading the world to adopt *Navlipi* presents quite a challenge, of course, and the author is well aware of the difficulties he will meet. He presents, in one chapter, both the arguments for and the arguments against its adoption. Who are the actual decision-makers in such cases? The national Academies, where they exist? Governments? Common popular usage? The press? There is no single answer, and the author addresses himself to both the linguistic scientist and the lay reader, and rests his case.

The author's vision stretches both backward and forward in time, as concerns the implications of this script: It can be used to transcribe ancient languages; and on the other hand, it can be adapted to voice recognition technology.

It is refreshing to find this basic issue in linguistics tackled from the point of view of someone versed in the physical sciences. What you find in the following pages and the ensuing volumes is a comprehensive exposition of a theory which is put to rigorous testing. The author does create his own terminology, which might meet with some resistance from those used to the terminological conventions of linguistic science – but he is internally consistent. Some of his terms – such as *phonochromaticity* – are directly analogous with terms in the physical sciences. Where a new term is introduced, it is explained fully.

I commend this book to any reader who is interested in the age-old problem of rendering all languages uniformly in writing. It has been tried before, by Lepsius in the nineteenth century and several others, but the present volume may prove to be the most comprehensive attempt yet made.

Christopher Moseley
Reading, England

PREFACE
AND OBJECTIVES OF THIS BOOK

NEED FOR A NEW SCRIPT AND "PHONEMIC IDIOSYNCRASY" : This book emanated from a direly felt need for a universal orthography (script, "alphabet") capable of representing, systematically and scientifically, every phone (sound) and tone (musical accent, as in the Chinese languages) found in the world's major languages; this is really a minimum requirement for any universal orthography. More importantly, however, it emanated from a need to address what was felt to be an even more urgent issue: The ***phonemic idiosyncrasies*** of the world's languages. This book thoroughly addresses the problem of *phonemic idiosyncrasy* across language families, for the first time ever, to the best of published knowledge.

The term ***phonemic idiosyncrasy*** is defined and discussed in the introductory chapters of this book. However, we may define it very briefly here for the uninitiated reader, within the short space available in a Preface. Before we do, we must also very briefly define some other terms for the reader who may be uninitiated in the terminology of phonetics and linguistics: A *phone* is any sound, here specifically referring to human language. A *phoneme* is a phone with a linguistic value. A quick test for a phoneme vs. a phone is whether substitution changes the meaning of a word in a particular language. Thus, the phones [p] and [ph] are components of the same phoneme in English, designated /p/, since substitution of one by the other does not change meanings of words: E.g. in the word *put*, the *p* can be pronounced with ([ph]) or without ([p]) aspiration. However, [p] and [ph] *are* different phonemes in Hindi/Urdu, since substitution of one by the other *does* change the meanings of words, e.g. *pal*, "an instant", *phal* "fruit". In English, [p] and [ph] are said to be *allophones* of the same phoneme, /p/, whereas in Hindi/Urdu, they are distinct phonemes, designated /p/ and /ph/.

Phonemic idiosyncrasy can then be defined as the existence of very different sets (usually, pairs) of phones *as allophones of the same phoneme in one language, whereas the same phones exist as distinct phonemes in another language*. One example is that cited above: The bilabial stop [p] and its aspirated counterpart, [ph], are allophones of the same phoneme, /p/, in English, whereas they are distinct phonemes in Hindi/Urdu. Another example is the unvoiced and voiced bilabial stops, [p] and [b], which are allophones of the same phoneme in many Chinese languages. That is to say, one can say *Beijing* or *Peijing,* or *pu* or *bu,* without change of meaning, in a Chinese language like

PREFACE

xxxii

Mandarin. On the other hand, [p] and [b] are of course different phonemes in most Indo-European languages. E.g. in English, *pet* and *bet* have entirely different meanings. As yet other examples of peculiar allophones found in some languages, we can cite [x] (uvular/velar fricative) and [r] (trill), two radically different phones of modern French and German. Here, the first phone is a velar or uvular fricative and the second an alveolar tap or trill or semivowel. Nevertheless, these are part of the same phoneme in Parisian French and standard (*hochdeutsch*) German; the [x] allophone is of course the famous "uvular *r*". Other, even more illustrative, examples are the [v]/[w] and [f]/[ph] phone pairs of Hindi/Urdu. These are freely interchanged and have the same phonemic value, although they are obviously very different phones. That is to say, in Hindi/Urdu, one can say *phal* or *fal* and still mean the same thing, "fruit", or *varshaa* or *warshaa*, and still mean "rain".

As this book notes in detailed discussions, there are *two potentially very different views of phonemic idiosyncrasy*:

1) That phonemic idiosyncrasy is indeed a unique phenomenon, as exemplified by the many allophonic examples cited above: The prominent [p]/[ph] allophones of English vs. their clear phonemic distinction in Hindi/Urdu; the prominent [v]/[w] and [f][ph] allophones of Hindi/Urdu vs. their phonemic distinction in nearly all other world languages; and the [x]/[r] allophones of modern French and German. While the first (English) example is only somewhat odd, the latter two (Hindi/Urdu, French/German) examples are truly idiosyncratic!

2) That there is in fact no such thing: What appears to be phonemic idiosyncrasy is simply the total absence of certain phones in certain languages. This may at first glance appear to apply to some languages. For example, the [p] of the bilabial [p]/[b] pair can be said to be simply absent in standard Arabic, the [l] of the [l]/[r] pair can be said to be simply absent in Japanese, and the aspirated stops such as [ph] and [th] can be said to be simply absent in Tamil. However, the English, Hindi/Urdu and French/German examples in (1) above clearly refute this view.

The discussions in the book seek to clearly show that #1) above is correct and #2) is wrong. This is done, e.g., by citing examples from such common languages as English, and showing that, where one phone is supposedly absent in a certain language, it is invariably mistaken *only* for its allophonic counterpart from another language and no other phone.

PREFACE

xxxiii

Why phonemic idiosyncrasy across languages is a serious problem with respect to a system of writing can then be easily appreciated: The expression of phonemic idiosyncrasy across languages must somehow be incorporated into and accommodated by a single writing system, a universal script. For example, an English speaker, when reading Hindi/Urdu in the universal script, should be able to immediately comprehend that the phone [v] can also be pronounced as a [w] although when reading English in the same universal script, [v] and [w] are pronounced quite differently. Similarly, a Hindi/Urdu speaker should immediately be able to comprehend, when reading English in the same script, that [p] and [ph] have the same value in English, unlike the case in his/her own language. An English speaker, when reading Arabic in the same script, should immediately be able to understand that [p] and [b] are not separate phonemes in Arabic, and such bilabial sounds are usually, but not always, pronounced as [b], the [p] being absent in most (but not all) Arabic dialects. Etc. etc.. The universal script must contain and be able to convey this information.

We can briefly cite one example of how *Navlipi* addresses phonemic idiosyncrasy, with the English phoneme /p/. *Navlipi* uses the [$_o$] (subscripted circle *postpositional operator, "postop"* for short), to represent the combined *(aspirated + unaspirated)* phoneme. This postop is very amenable to cursive writing as well as keyboarding, yet very distinct and recognizable. This postop then gives us three sets of glyphs (letters or symbols) for the components of the English phoneme /p/: **[p]** (unaspirated *phone*); **[ph]** (aspirated *phone*); and *p_o* (aspirated/unaspirated *combined phoneme* but generally pronounced [p]). *Navlipi* calls [p_o] a **phonemic condensate**. That is to say, the [p] and [ph] phones are said to be condensed into one *phonemic condensate*, p_o, which is equal to [p] + [ph]. In *Navlipi* transcription, only the p_o would be used for English, i.e. all letters *p* would be written as *p_o*. Thus, the words *spy* and *put* would be written *sp_oy* (actually, *$sp_oae!$*) and *p_out* respectively.

The book also notes that **phonemic idiosyncrasy is a subject that has, to the best of published knowledge, never been addressed by any world script to date. There is as yet no world script that transmits information of phonemic idiosyncrasy of a language to the reader**. For example, reading Mandarin transcribed in virtually any world script, one would not receive the information that voiced and unvoiced phones, [b] and [p] are actually phonemically equivalent and may be mostly interchanged without change of meaning of a word; or, again, that the "r" of French can be pronounced as [r] or as [x], the latter used in Parisian French, without change of meaning of a word.

Additionally, all scripts produced in the world to the present time, including that of the

PREFACE

International Phonetic Association (IPA), suffer from other serious drawbacks as well. They typically lack in one or more of the important requirements of a universal orthography, such as *universality, distinctiveness, recognizability, and ease of keyboarding or cursive transcription*, to name a few. Such prior art is extensively and very comprehensively discussed in this book.

OBJECTIVES SET FORTH IN THIS BOOK FOR A UNIVERSAL ORTHOGRAPHY: This book set for itself the following major requirements for a universal orthography:

(i) *Universality and completeness.*
(ii) *Recognizability.*
(iii) *Distinctiveness:* Distinguishability of one letter of the script from another, especially those representing related phones.
(iv) *Simplicity* and *intuitive nature.* Simplicity is also reflected in *ease of learning.*
(v) *Ease and rapidity of transcription from three points of view: keyboard, cursive, and print. High amenability to cursive writing.*
(vi) *Systematic, scientific classification and accuracy.*
(vii) *Discretization.*
(viii) *Practical phonemics rather than phonics.* A fundamentally *phonemic* system. Thus, e.g., while some scripts (e.g. the IPA) can be used to transcribe the different pronunciations of two individuals speaking the same language, that was not the objective of *Navlipi*.
(ix) *Voice-recognition compatibility and a voice-recognition software package.*
(x) And of course, most important of all, the **ability to accommodate the phonemic idiosyncrasies of all the world's major languages**.

The book devotes an entire chapter to the discussion of prior art, in which it is attempted to demonstrate that all prior scripts are deficient in meeting at least three of the above objectives. For example, in discussing at length the gross inadequacies of the "alphabet" of the International Phonetic Association (IPA), some of the many deficiencies pointed out are the lack of recognizability and distinctiveness: For example, some of the IPA's letters/symbols appear straight from outer space, and many of the inverted, rotated and angled *r*'s, *a*'s, *e*'s etc. are mutually very confusing. Another of the many deficiencies of the IPA cited is the lack of ease of use and intuitiveness: For example, reading the tone symbols almost requires a cipher, with constant referral to the IPA chart, even for an expert. Thus reading an IPA transcription of Cantonese is a nightmare. And of course, the IPA does not even remotely address *phonemic idiosyncrasy*.

Intimately related to the above objectives are the arguments *against* a new, universal orthography, discussed at length in this book. Some of these have much merit, but *Navlipi* nevertheless assumes that the arguments *for* far outweigh arguments *against*.

The first two objectives above (universality/completeness and recognizability) almost mandate a script based on the Roman: Whether one likes it or not, a reality today is that the Roman script is the most recognizable the world over. Needless to say, *Navlipi* is of course based on the Roman script.

Navlipi also has a prominent *cursive* writing component. It thus assumes that handwriting will still be used by humans in the future. This is another big gamble taken by *Navlipi*: As discussed in the book, even as of this writing (2005), scientists have succeeded in implanting chips in human brains that enable paralyzed people to control cursors etc. simply by using their thoughts. By extension, then, such methods could eventually be used for a direct thought-to-orthography system, without the intervention of handwriting or voice communication! (Incidentally, the term "cursive writing" is intended to include the quick, *unjoined*, semi-print handwriting used by keyboard-accustomed kids these days.)

AUDIENCE ADDRESSED: *Navlipi* is humbly addressed not just to situations ripe for its use, one of the most important of which is a *common script for India* that bridges the "Aaryan(Aryan)/-Dravidian" (North/South) divide. This divide (see *PRIMER* and *INTRODUCTION* PARTS) is a prime example of the problems associated with transcription, in the same script, of phonemic idiosyncrasy between languages. Rather, *Navlipi* also humbly seeks to address itself *to existing Romanized transcriptions* which are still not entirely adequate. Examples of these include, but are not limited to, Swaahili (Swahili), Vietnamese, Indonesian/Malaysian (the main Bahasa), Turkish, and the Romanized Mandarin (*pinyin*); the latter was vigorously promoted by the Chinese government many decades ago. And finally, *Navlipi* also seeks *potential new markets*, such as the Turkic languages of the new Central Asian republics. These were originally transcribed in Arabic script, then in Cyrillic under the Soviet Union. Now, many are seeking a Romanization based on the Turkish. With respect to China, it is well recognized that modern China has adapted its ancient ideographic script well to the 21st century. For instance, even computer operating systems such as Windows and Mac OS are entirely in Chinese characters. One might say then that there appears to be absolutely no need for the Roman script in everyday life in China, except when interfacing with non-Chinese. There is also a certain degree of unity that this common ideographic script provides for the Chinese languages. Nevertheless, many of today's Chinese in the science

PREFACE

and literature fields express a desire for a more easily learned and palatable, "Romanized" script, saying that ideographic Chinese is a handicap in intellectual discourse. In earlier times, it was also considered a handicap to universal literacy, since basic literacy required the learning of at least 2,000 characters, and "educated" literacy at least 20,000 characters.

Thus, in a sense, *India and China*, the two most populous countries in the world today (2005), and, potentially, economic powers of tomorrow, represent the two largest potential markets for *Navlipi*. Apart from these, there is of course also the hope that, if a truly capable universal script catches on, it could eventually replace the Cyrillic, the Arabic, the Chinese, the Hebrew, etc.. It could also be used where the Roman script does not do all that well, e.g. for the Slavic languages that use it (Czech, Slovak, Polish, Serbo-Croat, the latter recently further divided into Croatian, Serbian, Bosnian, etc.). On the other hand, this author fully appreciates that attempting to replace existing ways of doing things (here, scripts), is a daunting task, and may be unsuccessful. In this context, replacement of an existing script would make the problems encountered with present (2005) attempts at replacing Microsoft Windows® with Linux pale by comparison! As far as initial propagation in a country such as India, *Navlipi* could perhaps be taught alongside the local script, but not replace it: Kids would learn, along with their standard *"ka kha ga"*, the *Navlipi* equivalents. Books might initially be printed in both scripts. This may be a start for *Navlipi* in India. In China, initially, the new script might be taught wherever the Romanized script is still taught, with the hope that it would catch on from there.

LEVEL OF THE BOOK, FOUR (4) PARTS OF THE BOOK AND THIS BOOK BEING THE FIRST IN THE NAVLIPI SERIES: The present book, called BOOK 1 for convenient reference, is the first volume in a three-part *NAVLIPI* series. In an effort to attract and address *as wide a readership as possible*, the book is written at an extremely basic level. It has a somewhat peculiar organization. For example, to start with, it includes several initial chapters, collectively entitled *INTRODUCTION,* which discuss the *need* for *Navlipi*, and its objectives, as well as other prior art. A complete Glossary of all phonetic, linguistic and grammatical terms is also included (this Glossary even defines "orthography"!). Due to the above organization, there are then *four main parts* to this first volume in the *NAVLIPI* series:

> **PART 1** comprises the SUMMARY TABLES of *Navlipi*, akin to the "Chart" that summarizes the alphabet of the International Phonetic Association (IPA), in the IPA's main publication. It also includes

transcriptions into *Navlipi* of languages as diverse as Vietnamese and Maraathi (Marathi), apart from the five most widely spoken/understood languages in the world as of 2005 (in decreasing order, Mandarin, Hindi/Urdu, English, Spanish and Arabic).
- **PART 2** comprises the INTRODUCTION chapters, which discuss the *need* for *Navlipi*, its objectives, and other prior art.
- **PART 3** comprises the "meat" of the book, and encompasses a detailed discussion and presentation of *Navlipi*.
- **PART 4** includes a Glossary, Literature Cited, Index and the About The Author section.

A useful offshoot of the teaching of *Navlipi* in its innate, "alphabetical" order is that this will also comprise a complete lesson in phonetics, in phonological classification, and in phonemic condensation. This, minus the phonemic condensation, is in fact just as it is for the present-day Indian scripts.

While the inclusion of chapters with subtitles such as "Other Prior Art" is understandable in a book of this nature, the reader may ask why certain other chapters are included as well. The answer is that these other chapters are included simply for *completeness*: To keep the reader as thoroughly informed as possible in discussions which may touch upon these subjects. Without this completeness, this author felt that the book might not be fully appreciated by a lay reader, and its impact thus lessened.

POST-OPS, OTHER NEW TERMINOLOGY, NUMBER OF NEW GLYPHS (LETTERS OR CHARACTERS): *Navlipi* uses *post-ops* (post-positional operators) extensively. Thus, h_o, and h_0, both distinct from the letter h (the glottal fricative), are the post-ops, respectively, for aspiration (as in $[kh_o]$), and fricatization; both these post-ops are easily and distinctively rendered in cursive as well. *Tones* are also represented as post-ops; these are designed in a special way to be both intuitive and extremely easy to render in cursive. This thus avoids the heavy use of diacritics found in almost all Roman tone transcriptions, from Vietnamese to Roman Mandarin to the IPA.

The use of (just a few) post-ops also considerably reduces the number of keyboard keys required. For example, the letter ƶ (z with strikeout) is used as the post-op for ingressive clicks. Using it, *all* ingressive clicks can be written, obviating the need for individual keys for each click. Thus, e.g., the lateral, "giddyap" click is written *lƶ* .

An additional, important result of the use of these few post-ops is that *Navlipi* needs very

PREFACE

few *new* glyphs (letters) outside the standard Roman script. To be precise, *Navlipi* uses: Just *one* borrowed glyph (Greek omega, phone #[33(4)] in *Navlipi* matrix notation); just *one* entirely new glyph (for the *medio*-palatal, unvoiced, unaspirated stop, phone #[1-6] in *Navlipi* matrix notation); and just three transformed glyphs (an inversion of the Roman *c* for the tongue-front-central, lips-stretched, jaw-open-position vowel, as in English *Jack*, denoted #1(1)(4) in *Navlipi* matrix notation; a variant of the Roman *j* for the palatal, voiced, unaspirated stop, *Navlipi* phone #(3-7); and a variant of the Roman *g* for the uvular, voiced fricative, *Navlipi* phone #(7-3)). This makes for a total of ***just five (5) new or transformed glyphs (letters) in Navlipi.***

Besides the term *"post-op"* cited above, *Navlipi* introduces many other new terms along the way. These include, e.g., *phonochromaticity, artition, forward-fricative* and *galatophone*, and the all-important *phonemic condensate*. Most of these terms are self-explanatory. Thus, *phonemic condensate* quite obviously connotes the condensation of two or more phones into a single phoneme peculiar to a particular language and represented by a separate glyph or post-op. As an example, the post-op $[_\infty]$ (subscripted infinity sign) is used to represent the [voiced + unvoiced] phonemic condensate, found e.g., in the combination of the (voiced + unvoiced) bilabial stops in Mandarin. This is then rendered as b_∞, indicating that it is a combination of ([p] + [b]) that is usually but not always articulated as [b].

To give a feel for *Navlipi* for the benefit of the reader, we cite here short passages from the four most widely spoken languages in the world, as of 2005. These are, in decreasing order of number of speakers: Mandarin, Hindi/Urdu, English and Spanish. In the transcription below, the original and a Roman orthography are at left or top, and the *Navlipi* orthography, both print and cursive, at right or bottom; in the case of Mandarin, the tones in the cursive transcription are highlighted by a dotted circle and arrow:

Mandarin:

他 是 谁？
Tā shì shuí?
He is who?

(4) Th₀aa l sh₀qΓ sh₀wii⁄?

(5) *Thaal shql shwii?*

PREFACE
xxxix

Hindi/Urdu (written in Dewanaagari script):

(1) (मिया बिबी, वधुवरे),

(2) *(miyaa biibii, wadhuware),*

(3) (mijaa biibii, vwadh₀u vwarɛ),

(4) *(mijaa biibii, vwadh₀uvware),*

English:

(1) *It is a sunny day.*

(2) Itt₀ iz q sani dtɛi.

(3) *Itte iz q sani dtɛi.*

Spanish:

(1) *a los habitantes de las áreas costeras*

(2) a los haabitaantɛs dɛ laas áarrɛaas kosteerraas

(3) *a los haabitaantes de laas áarreaas kosteerraas*

PREFACE

xl

KEYBOARDING IN NAVLIPI: The very simple, intuitive and "natural" keyboard rendition of *Navlipi* is dealt with at length in this book, in PART 1 as well as in a later, separate chapter devoted solely to this subject. *Navlipi* uses common Roman keyboards, such as the American QWERTY or French AZERTY, with minimal modification.

As a first premise, *Navlipi* starts with *language-specific* keyboards, much like "sub-fonts". This greatly minimizes the need for new keys. For example, for English, the *"p"* key would print as p_o, indicating the ([p] + [ph]) phonemic condensate; however, for Hindi/Urdu or Spanish, it would print just as *p* (the unvoiced, unaspirated bilabial stop only). Similarly, (ALT + k) would print as kh_o (velar unvoiced, aspirated stop) in Hindi/Urdu but *k..* (uvular unvoiced stop currently rendered as *q*) in Arabic. These examples represent three of the many keyboards of *Navlipi* (here for English/West-European-Languages, Hindi-Urdu/-Spanish/-Russian/-Indonesian... and Arabic, respectively). In the Hindi-Urdu/Spanish-etc.. keyboard, the *"r"* key prints as *r*, indicating the alveolar tap/flap/trill phonemic condensate. However, in the English/etc.. keyboard, it prints as r_o, indicating the alveolar semivowel only, since English doesn't use trills.

The keyboarding is *platform-independent*. It is also carried out so that there are no conflicts, e.g. with common CTRL keys used in most word processors (e.g. (CTRL + c), "copy") and UNIX-based operating systems such as LINUX. The (SHIFT + number) keys are also freed up cleverly, so that they are available for the tone post-ops; these tone post-ops are again language-specific for major language groupings (e.g. Mandarin, Cantonese, Yoruba, etc.). Cosmetic modifications include a smaller spacebar key and larger ALT keys, to maximize use of the latter with forefingers. The most common post-ops are assigned common keys, although they may be rarely used in the language-specific keyboards.

VOICE, BRAILLE AND OTHER VERSIONS: It is also planned to issue voice-recognition software for transcription of American English in *Navlipi* shortly after the first publication of the book. The publication of a Braille version of the book has been made contingent upon the success of the standard version.

SCOPE OF THE WORK: The author humbly notes that a single-author work such as this can only be a first basis, a guide for future work. As such therefore, it was his intention only to provide a *maargadarshan* (a Maraathi, Hindi and Sanskrit word somewhat poorly translated as "direction for the way ahead") in devising a new, universal script. The work would thus, hopefully, be refined further by others. A single-person work perhaps cannot, ultimately, compete with the work of a team of savants in the field.

THE NAME "NAVLIPI": The name Navlipi of course means *"New Script"* in Sanskrit and all the major North Indian languages of today, and, through borrowing, Tamil and the other major Dravidian languages of South India. Coincidentally, it is also one of the many words whose transcriptions in Roman script and in *Navlipi* script are very close! (A more accurate transcription is *"Navalipi"* in Roman script and *"Navwqlipi"* or *"Navwlipi"* in *NAVLIPI* script for Hindi/Urdu, but that point is academic!)

HISTORICAL NOTE: On a personal note, the *Navlipi* script portion of this book was completed in substantially its present form in the summer of 1982, when the author had a hiatus between research advisors in graduate school in his main field of study (chemistry), in Buffalo, New York, USA. It was reworked on somewhat in the summer of 1991, but for the most part lay in his attic until he resolved, in Spring 2003, that it must see the light of day. Sporadic work thereafter (a few days in this month, a few days in that month), constrained by the responsibilities of the author's regular, bread-winning occupation, has finally brought it to light and to this publication. The delay since 1982 may however have been beneficial, since the new aspects addressed since 2003, such as advanced keyboarding and voice recognition, would not have been possible in 1982. Additionally, the book may not have been able to foresee, and thus take into consideration, the very rapid demise of cursive writing, and indeed handwriting in general, that we are seeing at the time of the writing of this Preface (around 2005). It may not also have been able to foresee the potential development of direct thought-to-final-transcription technology (whether paper or screen). This is already implemented as of 2005 with a brain chip implant for handicapped persons. This perhaps foretells the demise of writing, keyboarding and *all* other physical methods of transcription *altogether* in the not too distant future!

ACKNOWLEDGEMENTS: The author wishes to express his gratitude to the following for invaluable assistance: April Zay (graphics), Katharine Stanley (editorial), Sarah Murray (some literature search), Carrie Mowbray (Greek/Latin/IE paradigms), Meghana Joshi (language transcriptions) and Ashwin Chandrasekhar (cover design).

Prasanna Chandrasekhar
Holmdel, New Jersey, USA

PART 1:
THE *NAVLIPI* SUMMARY TABLES

PART 1: THE NAVLIPI SUMMARY TABLES

TABLE OF CONTENTS - PART 1

1. EDITORIAL NOTES, LAYOUT/CONTENT, MATRIX ELEMENTS AND NOTE ON EASE OF LEARNING OF NAVLIPI 5

    1.1 EDITORIAL NOTE 5
    1.2 LAYOUT AND CONTENTS OF PART 1 5
    1.3 MATRIX ELEMENTS IN THE NAVLIPI TABLES 7
    1.4 EASE OF LEARNING NAVLIPI 8

2. THE NAVLIPI VOWEL CLASSIFICATION 9

    2.1 X-AXIS, LIP POSITION 9
    2.2 Y-AXIS, TONGUE'S OR OTHER ARTICULATING ORGANS' POSITION 9
    2.3 Z-AXIS, JAW POSITION 10

3. THE NAVLIPI NON-VOWEL CLASSIFICATION 11

    3.1 ARTITIONS (ARTICULATION POSITIONS) AND PHONOCHROMES ("COLOR" OF THE PHONE) OF NAVLIPI 11
    3.2 THE 15 ARTITIONS OF NAVLIPI FOR NON-VOWELS 11
    3.3 THE 35 PHONOCHROMES OF NAVLIPI FOR NON-VOWELS 12

4. VOWEL MATRICES: THE FULL, 3-DIMENSIONAL NAVLIPI VOWEL CLASSIFICATION MATRIX EXPRESSED IN 14 Y-CROSS-SECTIONS 14

5. NON-VOWEL MATRICES (INCLUDING SEMIVOWELS ("APPROXIMANTS"), CENTRALS AND LATERALS) 31

6. TABLE OF POST-OPS (POST-POSITIONAL OPERATORS) 51

7. TABLE OF PHONEMIC CONDENSATES 55

8. SUMMARY OF TONES 58

9. SUGGESTED DIDACTIC (PEDAGOGICAL) "ALPHABETICAL ORDER" OF NAVLIPI 60

PART 1: THE NAVLIPI SUMMARY TABLES

10. VARIOUS WIDELY-USED WORLD SCRIPTS/ALPHABETS RENDERED IN NAVLIPI 64

10.1 THE DEWANAAGARI (DEVANAGARI) SCRIPT RENDERED IN NAVLIPI, INCLUDING VARIANTS THEREOF FOR HINDI/URDU, MARAATHI (ONLY SMALL-PRINT GLYPHS GIVEN, FOR CLARITY) 64
10.2 THE CYRILLIC SCRIPT (ALPHABET) RENDERED IN NAVLIPI 69
10.3 THE ARABIC SCRIPT (ALPHABET) RENDERED IN NAVLIPI 72
10.4 THE TAMIL SCRIPT (ALPHABET) RENDERED IN NAVLIPI 75

11. KEYBOARDING IN NAVLIPI 77

11.1 NUMERICAL (m)(n) or (x)(y) MATRIX NOTATION USED BY THE NAVLIPI KEYBOARD 77
11.2 SCHEMATIC ILLUSTRATION OF THE FOUR (4) REPRESENTATIONS USED BY NAVLIPI FOR EACH KEY, FOR THE NORMAL, SHIFT, CONTROL AND ALTERNATE POSITIONS 79
11.3 COMBINATION OF THE MATRIX NOTATION AND 4-PART KEYS, TO ARRIVE AT (m)(n)(X) KEY NOTATION, USED CONVENIENTLY TO REFER TO ALL NAVLIPI KEYBOARD KEYS 80
11.4 NAVLIPI KEYBOARD LAYOUT, FOR THE AMERICAN QWERTY KEYBOARD 81
11.5 LIST AND LAYOUT OF INDIVIDUAL NAVLIPI KEYS 82
11.6 LIST OF KEY CHANGES REFLECTING MAJOR REASSIGNMENTS 85
11.7 CHANGED NUMBER KEYS, AS TO BE USED IN NAVLIPI 87
11.8 LIST OF KEY CHANGES: KEYS WITH HIGH FREQUENCY OF USE AND SOME MAJOR POST-OPS 88
11.9 CENTRAL ("R") KEY AND CENTRAL GLYPHS, INCLUDING PHONEMIC CONDENSATES 90
11.10 MAJOR LATERAL ("L") KEY 93
11.11 MAJOR VELAR KEYS LANGUAGE-SPECIFIC IN NAVLIPI 94
11.12 MAJOR PALATAL AND SIBILANT KEYS 97
11.13 MAJOR DENTAL, ALVEOLAR AND RETROFLEX PLOSIVE ("T-D") KEYS 98
11.14 SUMMARY OF THE BILABIAL (11)(3) (P) AND (6)(5), (B) KEYS FOR MAJOR LANGUAGE-SPECIFIC KEYBOARDS 103
11.15 MAJOR NASAL ("M-N") KEYS 105
11.16 MAJOR STANDARD-SEMIVOWEL KEYS 106
11.17 MAJOR VOWEL KEYS 107
11.18 SPECIAL NON-VOWEL KEYS 108
11.19 KEYS FOR VERY RARE POST-OPS 109

PART 1: THE NAVLIPI SUMMARY TABLES

4

    11.20 Tone keys 110
    11.21 Inventory of leftover, unused (available) keys, referenced by Navlipi key notation 115

12. TRANSCRIPTIONS OF THE FIVE (5) MOST WIDELY SPOKEN LANGUAGES IN THE WORLD (IN 2005) IN *NAVLIPI*, LISTED IN ORDER OF DECREASING NUMBER OF SPEAKERS 116

    12.1 Notes on the Transcriptions 116
    12.2 Mandarin transcription passage 117
    12.3 Hindi/Urdu transcription passage 121
    12.4 English transcription passage 127
    12.5 Spanish transcription passage 130
    12.6 Arabic transcription passage 133

13. TRANSCRIPTIONS OF SLCTD OTHER LANGUAGES IN *NAVLIPI* 140

    13.1 French 140
    13.2 German 143
    13.3 Maraathi (Marathi) 147
    13.4 Maagyaar (Magyar, Hungarian) 152
    13.5 Vietnamese 157

1. EDITORIAL NOTES, LAYOUT/CONTENT, MATRIX ELEMENTS AND NOTE ON EASE OF LEARNING OF *NAVLIPI*

1.1 EDITORIAL NOTE

The *NAVLIPI* SUMMARY TABLES are presented here, at the beginning of the book, for convenient reference, much like the CHART of the IPA (the International Phonetic Association) is presented at the beginning of the IPA's main publication, the *Handbook of the International Phonetic Association*.

1.2 LAYOUT AND CONTENTS OF PART 1

In this Section, **PART 1**, then, the following are presented in order. Explanations, further descriptions and development of these are found in the text of the book starting at **PART 2**:

1. The *Navlipi* **VOWEL CLASSIFICATION**, which uses three lip positions, 15 tongue or other articulation organ positions and six jaw positions.

2. The *Navlipi* **NON-VOWEL CLASSIFICATION**, which uses 15 *artitions* (articulation positions) and 35 *phonochromes* ("colors of the phone", such as voicing or fricatization).

3. The actual *NAVLIPI* **TABLES**:

    a. The *Navlipi* **Vowel Matrices**, with three (3) x, 15 y and six (6) z variables.

    b. The *Navlipi* **Non-Vowel Matrices**, with 15 x and 35 y variables. These include **Semi-Vowels, Centrals** and **Laterals.**

    c. Summary **Table of Post-Ops** (*Post-positional operators*). There are 20 post-ops in *Navlipi*, some of which are also phonemic condensates.

PART 1: THE NAVLIPI SUMMARY TABLES

      d. Summary **Table of Phonemic Condensates**. There are 17 phonemic condensates in *Navlipi*, some of which are also post-ops.

      e. Summary **Table of Tones** (*musical or pitch accents*), all of which are represented by intuitive post-ops.

4. **SUGGESTED, DIDACTIC (PEDAGOGICAL) "ALPHABETICAL ORDER"** of *Navlipi,* for use in teaching the script.

5. Selected **SCRIPTS/ALPHABETS** rendered in *Navlipi*:

      a. The **Dewanaagari (Devanagari) Script** (Alphabet) in *Navlipi*.
      b. The **Cyrillic Alphabet** in *Navlipi*.
      c. The **Arabic Alphabet** in *Navlipi*.
      d. The **Tamil Script** (Alphabet) in *Navlipi*.

6. **KEYBOARDING** in *Navlipi* on the QWERTY keyboard.

7. **TRANSCRIPTIONS OF THE FIVE MOST WIDELY-SPOKEN WORLD LANGUAGES (as of 2005),** *in order of decreasing number of speakers and significance/importance:*

      a. Mandarin.
      b. Hindi/Urdu.
      c. English.
      d. Spanish.
      e. Arabic.

8. **TRANSCRIPTIONS OF SELECTED OTHER WORLD LANGUAGES:**
      a. French.
      b. German.
      c. Maraathi (Marathi).
      d. Maagyaar (Magyar, Hungarian).
      e. Vietnamese.

PART 1: THE NAVLIPI SUMMARY TABLES

1.3 MATRIX ELEMENTS IN THE NAVLIPI TABLES

In the main body of the actual *NAVLIPI* **TABLES**, each **matrix element** includes the *Navlipi* glyph (letter or character):

- In *lower case* and *capitals ("caps", upper case)*.
- In *print* as well as *cursive*.
- For vowels, the *short duration* and *long duration* forms are also included (only these two durations listed in most cases- see discussion in the sequel).

Each matrix element also includes the keyboard rendition (referenced to the QWERTY keyboard), and a word example, generally from English if possible, otherwise from widely-spoken world languages such as Beijing Mandarin, Hindi, French, etc..

Each matrix element in the **VOWEL** and **NON-VOWEL** portion of the *NAVLIPI* **TABLES** is assigned a **matrix element number** for identification, much like mathematical matrices:

- The matrix element numbers of the final **vowel matrices**, which are *3-dimensional*, have the nomenclature **x(y)(z)**: The need for parentheses for the *y* and *z* variables will become apparent from a reading of the chapters on vowel classification in the second, companion volume in the *NAVLIPI* series (essentially because *y* can have values > 10 and *z* can have (-) values).
- The matrix element numbers of the **non-vowel matrices**, which are *2-dimensional*, have the nomenclature **x-y**.

PART 1: THE NAVLIPI SUMMARY TABLES

1.4 EASE OF LEARNING NAVLIPI

Navlipi is extremely easy to learn, if one knows the Roman script, the most widely used script in the world today. One need only know:

- The 26 glyphs (letters) of the Roman script.
- The five important *additional* glyphs (letters or characters) of *Navlipi*, (these, plus the 26 glyphs of the Roman script, i.e. **31 glyphs in all**, comprise *the entire Navlipi "alphabet"*).
- Plus, finally, no more than about four important *Navlipi* post-ops (post-positional operators, like the *h* in *ph*). These four important post-ops are those for: (1) *Aspiration*. (2) For *uvularization-/pharyngealization*. (3) For the combination *(voiced + unvoiced) phonemic condensate*, (4) And for the combination *(aspirate + non-aspirate) phonemic condensate*. (A *phonemic condensate* is a combination of two or more properties of phones that have the same phonemic value in particular languages; for example the properties *voiced* and *unvoiced*, which have the same phonemic value in many Chinese languages, or the properties *aspirated* and *unaspirated*, which have the same phonemic value in many West Germanic languages.)

In this respect then, *Navlipi* is, in this author's considered opinion, far easier to learn than the IPA script, or for that matter, other adaptations of the Roman script, such as the Polish, Czech, Turkish, Swaahili, etc..

2. THE NAVLIPI VOWEL CLASSIFICATION

2.1 X-AXIS, LIP POSITION

X-AXIS, LIP POSITION

X= 1, Lips stretched
X= 2, Lips flat
X= 3, Lips rounded

2.2 Y-AXIS, TONGUE'S OR OTHER ARTICULATING ORGANS' POSITION

Y-AXIS, TONGUE'S OR OTHER ARTICULATING ORGANS' POSITION

Y= 1, tongue medio-palatal
Y= 2, tongue flat
Y= 3, tongue retracted
Y= 4, tongue central, retroflex
Y= 5, tongue lateral, retroflex
Y= 6, tongue central, palatal
Y= 7, tongue lateral, palatal
Y= 8, tongue central, alveolo-dental
Y= 9, tongue lateral, alveolo-dental
Y= 10, tongue central, interdental
Y= 11, tongue lateral, interdental
Y= 12, nasal, bilabial
Y= 13, nasal, alveolo-dental
Y= 14, nasal, palatal
Y= 15, nasal, velar

PART 1: THE NAVLIPI SUMMARY TABLES

10

2.3 Z-AXIS, JAW POSITION

Z-AXIS, JAW POSITION

(+)Z-axis, jaw vertical position **(jaw horizontal position is "normal", i.e. neither forward nor retracted):**

    Z= 1, close
    Z= 2, close-mid
    Z= 3, open-mid
    Z= 4, open

(-) Z-axis, jaw horizontal position:

    Z= (-)1, jaw forward, close-mid
    Z= (-)2, jaw retracted, close-mid

3. THE NAVLIPI NON-VOWEL CLASSIFICATION

3.1 ARTITIONS (ARTICULATION POSITIONS) AND PHONOCHROMES ("COLOR" OF THE PHONE) OF NAVLIPI

ARTITIONS AND PHONOCHROMES OF NAVLIPI

The **15 *artitions*** (articulation position of tongue or other speech organ(s)) of *Navlipi*, corresponding to the ***y-axis*** of the *Navlipi* 2-d non-vowel matrix presented in the sequel, are, from the back to the front of the speech apparatus:

3.2 THE 15 ARTITIONS OF NAVLIPI FOR NON-VOWELS

THE 15 ARTITIONS OF NAVLIPI FOR NON-VOWELS

1) *Glottal*
2) *Pharyngeal*
3) *Uvular*
4) *Velar*
5) *Retroflex*
6) *Medio-Palatal*
7) *Palatal*
8) *Alveolar*
9) *Apico/Medio-Dental*
10) *Standard Dental*
11) *Pharyngealized Dental*
12) *Interdental*
13) *Infralabio-Supradental*
14) *Supralabio-Infradental*
15) *Bilabial*

PART 1: THE NAVLIPI SUMMARY TABLES

3.3 THE 35 PHONOCHROMES OF NAVLIPI FOR NON-VOWELS

THE 35 PHONOCHROMES OF NAVLIPI FOR NON-VOWELS

The **35 phonochromes** ("color of the phone") of *Navlipi* i.e. its *phonochromaticity* variables, corresponding to the ***x-axis*** of the *Navlipi* 2-d non-vowel matrix, are as below.

Phonochromaticity is the "color of the phone", e.g. whether it is aspirated, voiced, fricatized, clicked, etc., corresponding to each artition.

1) *Unvoiced/unaspirated*
2) *Unvoiced/aspirated*
3) *Voiced/unaspirated*
4) *Voiced/aspirated*
5) *Nasal*
6) *Fricative/unvoiced*
7) *Fricative/voiced*
8) *Flap/unaspirated*
9) *Flap/aspirated*
10) *Flap/nasal*
11) *Flap/fricatized*
12) *Trill/normal*
13) *Trill/fricatized*
14) *Click, ingressive, central, single, unvoiced*
15) *Click, ingressive, central, single, voiced*
16) *Click, ingressive, central, single, nasal*
17) *Click, ingressive, central, trill*
18) *Click, ingressive, lateral, single, unvoiced*
19) *Click, ingressive, lateral, single, voiced*
20) *Click, ingressive, lateral, single, nasal*
21) *Click, ingressive, lateral, trill*
22) *Click, egressive, central*
23) *Click, egressive, lateral*
24) *Ejective, unvoiced*
25) *Ejective, fricative*

PART 1: THE NAVLIPI SUMMARY TABLES

26) *Implosive, unvoiced*
27) *Implosive, voiced*
28) *Semivowel, simple*
29) *Semivowel, pharyngeal*
30) *Semivowel, central*
31) *Semivowel, lateral, unaspirated*
32) *Semivowel, lateral, aspirated*
33) *Semivowel, lateral, fricatized*
34) *Semivowel, lateral, palatalized*
35) *Semivowel, lateral, pharyngealized*

PART 1: THE NAVLIPI SUMMARY TABLES

4. VOWEL MATRICES: THE FULL, 3-DIMENSIONAL NAVLIPI VOWEL CLASSIFICATION MATRIX EXPRESSED IN 14 Y-CROSS-SECTIONS

Y CROSS-SECTIONS OF THE 3-D VOWEL CLASSIFICATION MATRIX

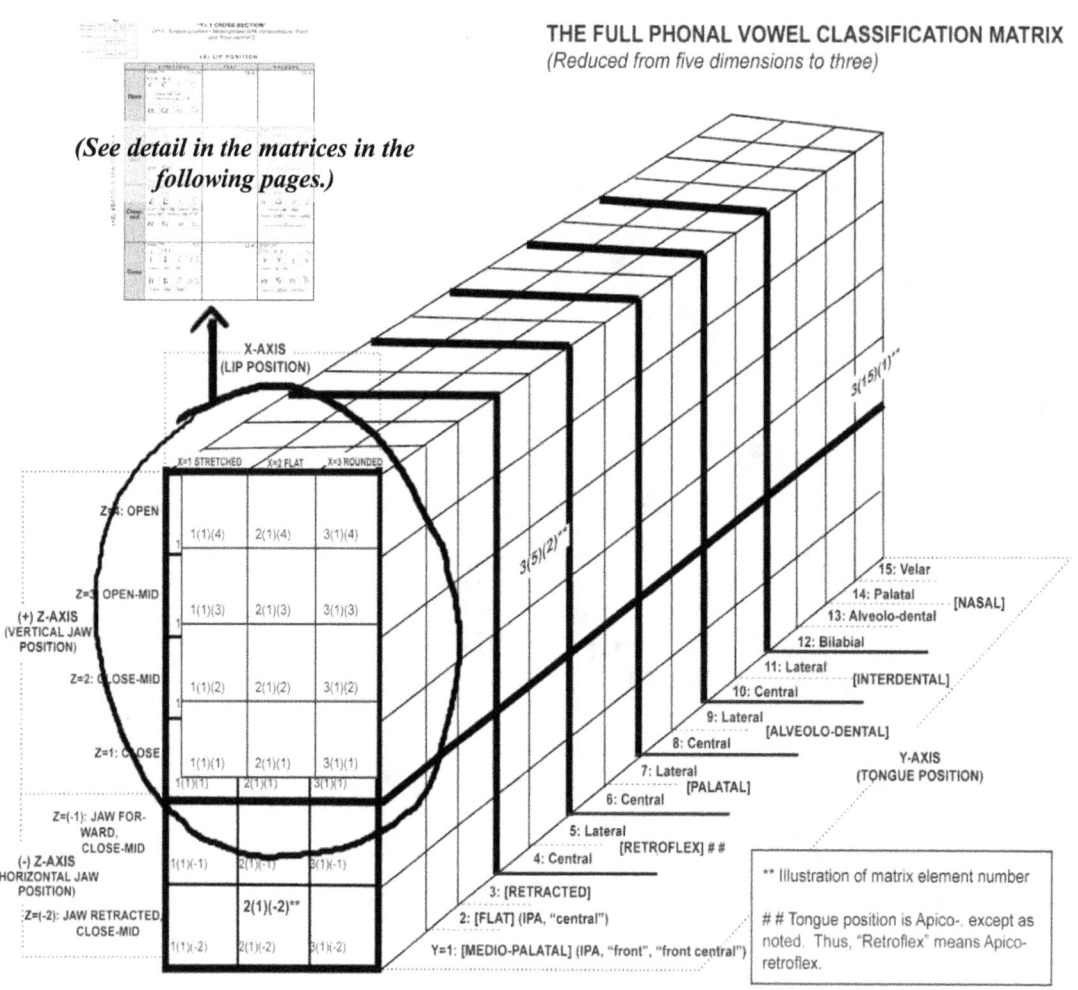

PART 1: THE NAVLIPI SUMMARY TABLES

(4. VOWEL MATRICES, cont)

Key

Matrix number / Dewanaagari	**1(1)(4)**	IPA Symbol	* Asterisk indicates footnote, # (n)	
Short Vowels	Print Small	Print CAPS	Cursive Small	Cursive CAPS
	WORD EXAMPLES			
Long Vowels	Print Small	Print CAPS	Cursive Small	Cursive CAPS
	WORD EXAMPLES			

PART 1: THE NAVLIPI SUMMARY TABLES

"Y= 1 CROSS-SECTION"
(Y=1, Tongue position= Medio-palatal [IPA nomenclature "front", and "front-central"])

(X) LIP POSITION

(+Z) VERTICAL JAW POSITION

	STRETCHED	FLAT	ROUNDED
Open	1(1)(4) IPA: *(1)(6) ॅ ॆ ऍ æ a ɔ ɔ ᴣ ᴣ English [hat] [cat] Hindi/Urdu [mai, "I"] मैं ɔɔ ɔɔ ᴣᴣ ᴣᴣ	*(2,4)	*(2,4)
Open-mid	1(1)(3) IPA: *(2,4) — ɛ e e e e English [bet] [belt] ee ee ee ee English [fair] [dare] Hindi/Urdu [kahanaa] कहना	*(2,4)	3(1)(3) IPA: *(1) (NO NAAGARI EQUIVALENT) œ Œ ɜ o// O// ɤ ɤ French [feuille] [peur] N/A (very rare/ mostly phonemically indistinct)
Close-mid	1(1)(2) IPA: *(1) ए e ə ɛ E ɛ ɛ English [clay] [day] Spanish [eso] French [des] Hindi/Urdu [me, "in"] में ɛɛ Eɛ ɛɛ ɛɛ	*(2,4)	3(1)(2) IPA: *(1) (NO NAAGARI EQUIVALENT) ø θ o/ O/ ɤ ɤ French [peu] [deux] German [schön] Danish [møbel] N/A (very rare/ mostly phonemically indistinct)
Close	1(1)(1) IPA: *(1) इ i I ɨ i I i ɪ I English [bit] [hit] ii Ii ii ɪi Ii English [beat] [heat]	*(2,4)	3(1)(1) IPA: *(1) (NO NAAGARI EQUIVALENT) y, y y Y ɥ ɥ French [tu] [pu] yy Yy ɥy ɥy German [üblich] ("customary")

PART 1: THE NAVLIPI SUMMARY TABLES

"Y= 2 CROSS-SECTION"
(Y=2, Tongue position= Flat [IPA nomenclature "central"])

(X) LIP POSITION

(+Z) VERTICAL JAW POSITION	STRETCHED	FLAT		ROUNDED
Open	*(2,4)	2(2)(4) IPA: ɑ आ aa Aa aa Aa English: *Father* Hindi/Urdu: *laanaa*, "to bring" लाना aa₀ Aa₀ aa₀ Aa₀ This is one of the only two uses of the "little circle" post-op as a vowel lengthening indicator, due to the need to distinguish from the vowel aa.		*(2,4)
Open-mid	*(2,4)	2(2)(3) IPA: ʌ ɜ ɐ अ a A a A	*(1) English: *but* *hut* Hindi/Urdu: *karnaa*, "to do" करना a₀ A₀ a₀ A₀ This is one of the only two uses of the "little circle" post-op as a vowel lengthening indicator, due to the need to distinguish from the vowel aa.	*(2,4)
Close-mid	*(2,4)	*(2,4)		*(2,4)
Close	*(2,4)	2(2)(1) IPA: ə ɐ ɘ q Q q Q English: *about* *hurt* <<schwa>> qq Qq qq Qq	*(1) (3)	*(2,4)

PART 1: THE NAVLIPI SUMMARY TABLES

"Y= 3 CROSS-SECTION"
(Y=3, Tongue position= Retracted [IPA nomenclature "back"])

(X) LIP POSITION

(+Z) VERTICAL JAW POSITION		STRETCHED	FLAT	ROUNDED
	Open	*(2,4)	*(2,4)	3(3)(4) IPA: औ ɔ *(6) Ω Ω ⌒ ⌒ English `talk` `caught` Hindi/Urdu `kaun,` "who?" कौन ΩΩ ΩΩ ⌒⌒ ⌒⌒
	Open-mid	*(2,4)	*(2,4)	3(3)(3) IPA: ओ o ɤ *(1) o O σ O Spanish `doble` French `clos` Hindi/Urdu `ko,` "to" को oo Oo oo Oo
	Close-mid	*(2,4)	*(2,4)	*(2,4)
	Close	*(2,4)	*(2,4)	3(3)(1) IPA: u ʊ *(1)(5) उ ɯ u U ʮ U English `book` `pull` Hindi/Urdu `kintu,` "however" किन्तु uu Uu ʮʮ Uʮ English `boot` Hindi/Urdu `tuu,` "you" तू Spanish `Tu`

PART 1: THE NAVLIPI SUMMARY TABLES

"Y= 4 CROSS-SECTION"
(Y=4, Centrals ("r" sounds), Tongue position= Apico-RETROFLEX)
(X) LIP POSITION

		STRETCHED	FLAT				ROUNDED
	Open	*(2,4)	*(2,4)				*(2,4)
	Open-mid	*(2,4)	*(2,4)				*(2,4)
	Close-mid	*(2,4)	2(4)(2) ɻ (IPA) 𝓃 𝓃 ɻ ɻ American English *purchase*, *hitter*; Mandarin *ii khwər* ("a little")			*(12)	*(2,4)
	Close	*(2,4)	*(2,4)				*(2,4)
	Open-mid Jaw Forward	*(2,4)	2(4)(-1) ɭ (Tamil) (NO IPA SYMBOL) 𝓃o 𝓃o ɻe ɻe TAMIL *pazham, paλam*, "fruit" பழம் NOT USED, NOT APPLICABLE			*(8)	*(2,4)
	Close-mid Jaw Back	*(2,4)	*(2,4)				*(2,4)

(+Z) VERTICAL JAW POSITION

(-Z) HORIZONTAL JAW POSITION

PART 1: THE NAVLIPI SUMMARY TABLES

"Y= 5 CROSS-SECTION"
(Y=5, Laterals ("L" sounds), Tongue position= Apico-RETROFLEX)

(X) LIP POSITION

(+Z) VERTICAL JAW POSITION		STRETCHED	FLAT	ROUNDED
	Open	*(2,4)	*(2,4)	*(2,4)
	Open-mid	*(2,4)	*(2,4)	*(2,4)
	Close-mid	*(2,4)	2(5)(2) IPA ள் l *(7) (9) (12) 𝓛 𝓛 𝓛 𝓛 Vocalic segment of semivowel in TAMIL [pal.l.am, "hole"] பள்ளம் NOT APPLICABLE	*(2,4)
	Close	*(2,4)	*(2,4)	*(2,4)

PART 1: THE NAVLIPI SUMMARY TABLES

"Y= 6 CROSS-SECTION"
(Y=6, Centrals ("r" sounds), Tongue position= Apico-PALATAL)

(X) LIP POSITION

(+Z) VERTICAL JAW POSITION

	STRETCHED	FLAT	ROUNDED
Open	*(2,4)	*(2,4)	*(2,4)
Open-mid	*(2,4)	*(2,4)	*(2,4)
Close-mid	\multicolumn{3}{The "central" variant of this artition is rare and is not phonemically significant in any major language. It is thus not used in NAVLIPI.}	
Close	*(2,4)	*(2,4)	*(2,4)

PART 1: THE NAVLIPI SUMMARY TABLES

"Y= 7 CROSS-SECTION"
(Y=7, Laterals ("L" sounds), Tongue position= Apico-PALATAL)

(X) LIP POSITION

		STRETCHED	FLAT	ROUNDED
(+Z) VERTICAL JAW POSITION	**Open**	*(2,4)	*(2,4)	*(2,4)
	Open-mid	*(2,4)	*(2,4)	*(2,4)
	Close-mid	*(2,4)	2(7)(2) IPA: ʎ *(7) (10) (12) ℒ₀ ℒ₀ ℒ₀ ℒ₀ Vocalic segment of semivowel in Portuguese *pilha* Croation *ljëti* NOT APPLICABLE	*(2,4)
	Close	*(2,4)	*(2,4)	*(2,4)

PART 1: THE NAVLIPI SUMMARY TABLES

23

"Y= 8 CROSS-SECTION"
(Y=8, Centrals ("r" sounds), Tongue position= {Apico} [ALVEOLO-DENTAL]) (Most common "r"-sound)

(X) LIP POSITION

(+Z) VERTICAL JAW POSITION		STRETCHED	FLAT	ROUNDED
	Open	*(2,4)	*(2,4)	*(2,4)
	Open-mid	*(2,4)	*(2,4)	*(2,4)
	Close-mid	*(2,4)	2(8)(2) IPA: ɹ ʇ T ʇ ʇ Vocalic segment of semivowel in British English *(7) (12) red | round NOT APPLICABLE	*(2,4)
	Close	*(2,4)	*(2,4)	*(2,4)

PART 1: THE NAVLIPI SUMMARY TABLES

"Y= 9 CROSS-SECTION"
(Y=9, Laterals ("L" sounds), Tongue position= {Apico} [ALVEOLO-DENTAL]) (Most common "l"-sound)

(X) LIP POSITION

(+Z) VERTICAL JAW POSITION	STRETCHED	FLAT	ROUNDED
Open	*(2,4)	*(2,4)	*(2,4)
Open-mid	*(2,4)	*(2,4)	*(2,4)
Close-mid	*(2,4)	2(9)(2) IPA: ळ 1 l L ℓ ℒ *(11)(12) American English *able* Vocalic segment of Hindi/Urdu *laanaa*, "to bring" लाना Vocalic segment of Tamil *paalam*, "bridge" பாலம் NOT APPLICABLE	*(2,4)
Close	*(2,4)	*(2,4)	*(2,4)

PART 1: THE NAVLIPI SUMMARY TABLES

"Y= 10 CROSS-SECTION"
(Y=10, Centrals ("r" sounds), Tongue position= INTERDENTAL)
(Most common *"l"-sound*)

(X) LIP POSITION

(+Z) VERTICAL JAW POSITION		STRETCHED	FLAT	ROUNDED
	Open	*(2,4)	*(2,4)	*(2,4)
	Open-mid	*(2,4)	*(2,4)	*(2,4)
	Close-mid	*(2,4) — Difficult to Articulate and not phonemically significant in any language. Thus not used. —		*(2,4)
	Close	*(2,4)	*(2,4)	*(2,4)

PART 1: THE NAVLIPI SUMMARY TABLES

"Y= 11 CROSS-SECTION"
(Y=11, Laterals ("L" sounds), Tongue position= {Apico} [SupraDental])

(X) LIP POSITION

		STRETCHED	FLAT	ROUNDED
(+Z) VERTICAL JAW POSITION	**Open**	*(2,4)	*(2,4)	*(2,4)
	Open-mid	*(2,4)	*(2,4)	*(2,4)
	Close-mid	*(2,4)	2(11)(2) IPA: ƚ ḻ ℒl ℒl ℒℓ ℒℓ *(1) (7) (12) Vocalic segment of semivowel in Turkish [la la] ("servant") Irish [Gall] ("foreigner") Also Arabic dialectic pronunciation. NOT APPLICABLE	*(2,4)
	Close	*(2,4)	*(2,4)	*(2,4)

PART 1: THE NAVLIPI SUMMARY TABLES

"Y= 12 CROSS-SECTION"
(Y=12, Nasals ("m" sounds), Tongue position= Nasal/Bilabial)

(X) LIP POSITION

(+Z) VERTICAL JAW POSITION

	STRETCHED	FLAT	ROUNDED
Open	*(2,4)	*(2,4)	*(2,4)
Open-mid	*(2,4)	*(2,4)	*(2,4)
Close-mid	*(2,4)	2(12)(2) IPA: *(13)(15) m_0m_0 M_0m_0 ɱɱ ɱɱ South African name ɱ **M Beki** NOT APPLICABLE	*(2,4)
Close	*(2,4)	*(2,4)	*(2,4)

PART 1: THE NAVLIPI SUMMARY TABLES

"Y= 13 CROSS-SECTION"
(Y=13, Nasals ("n" sounds), Tongue position= Nasal Dental-Aveolar-Palatal-Retroflex)

(X) LIP POSITION

(+Z) VERTICAL JAW POSITION	STRETCHED	FLAT	ROUNDED
Open	*(2,4)	*(2,4)	*(2,4)
Open-mid	*(2,4)	*(2,4)	*(2,4)
Close-mid	*(2,4)	2(13)(2) | IPA: *(14)(15) $n_0 n_0$ | $N_0 n_0$ | ɲ | ɳ Swahili | N Goma N Komo NOT APPLICABLE	*(2,4)
Close	*(2,4)	*(2,4)	*(2,4)

PART 1: THE NAVLIPI SUMMARY TABLES

"Y= 14 CROSS-SECTION"
(Y=14, Nasals Sounds, Tongue position= Velar-uvular)

(X) LIP POSITION

	STRETCHED	FLAT	ROUNDED
Open	*(2,4)	*(2,4)	*(2,4)
Open-mid	*(2,4)	*(2,4)	*(2,4)
Close-mid	*(2,4)	*(2,4)	*(2,4)
Close	*(2,4)	*(2,4)	*(2,4)

(+Z) VERTICAL JAW POSITION

(4. VOWEL MATRICES, cont)

FOOTNOTES FOR MAIN NAVLIPI TABLES (MATRICES)

A. VOWEL MATRIX

1. Due to the need for discretization and practical consideration of actual phonemic distinctions in major languages (the "practical phonemics" aspect of Navlipi), all these IPA phones are taken to be represented by this single Navlipi glyph.

2. Phonemic distinction rare or nonexistent in any major language.

3. Length not phonemically distinct for this vowel in nearly all languages. Shown here for completeness only. Not part of main Navlipi script as presented for teaching.

4. Not used in Navlipi.

5. English examples given do not strictly belong to this phone. However, they are cited here due to the "practical phonemics" aspect of Navlipi.

6. See discussion on the probable original significance of these Dewanaagari letters in Chapter 8 (i.e., pure vowels, not diphthongs).

7. Example words cited use the semivowel derived from this vowel.

8. This central phone, i.e. r-sound, is inexplicably treated as a lateral phone (l-sound) in Maraathi and Tamil orthography.

9. This phone is prominent only in Dravidian languages. In other languages where it is found, e.g. Panjaabi, it is phonemically indistinct from the apico-dental phone.

10. Tongue contact for this phone is actually closer to the medio- position. However, rather than writing "apico-medio-palatal", we retain "apico-palatal" due to phonemic indistinctiveness.

11. American English articulation is strictly with lips rounded, i.e. 2(9)(3) rather than 2(9)(2). But once again, from the "practical phonemics" aspect of Navlipi, it is classed as 2(9)(2).

12. IPA glyphs cited here are for corresponding semivowels.

13. (Supra/infra)-labiodental vowels are phonemically indistinct in all languages, so not treated of.

14. Dental, alveolar and palatal are grouped together here because no major language makes a phonemic distinction between these. Distinction with the other nasal vowel (m0) is that lips are open here.

15. It is important to note that these are true nasal vowels, according to our definition, and do not just represent nasalization of other, non-nasal vowels.

PART 1: THE NAVLIPI SUMMARY TABLES

5. NON-VOWEL MATRICES (INCLUDING SEMIVOWELS ("APPROXIMANTS"), CENTRALS AND LATERALS)

NON-VOWELS, INCLUDING SEMIVOWELS, CENTRALS AND LATERALS

KEY

Dewanaagari	IPA Symbol	Keyboard	1-1	Matrix element number.
			*(n)	Asterisk indicates footnote # n.

PRINT	CURSIVE
Small	Small
Caps	Caps

WORD EXAMPLES

PART 1: THE NAVLIPI SUMMARY TABLES

		PLOSIVES				NASALS
		UNVOICED (SURD)		VOICED (SONANT)		
		UNASPIRATED	ASPIRATED	UNASPIRATED	ASPIRATED	
GLOTTAL	Y=1, X=1	1-1 ʔ 𝔬𝔬 𝔬𝔬 English Cockney pronunciation b*l* ***little*** Arabic *sa*ʔ*ala* "asked"	2-1	3-1	4-1	5-1
PHARYNGEAL		1-2	2-2	3-2	4-2	5-2
UVULAR		1-3 क़ q k.. K..̆ Arabic *qalb* "heart" *qaid* "imprisonment", of Arabic origin क़ैद	2-3 ख़ qʰ k..hₒ K..hₒ Hindi *xilaaf* "against, contrary to", of Arabic origin ख़िलाफ़	3-3 ग़ G g.. G..̆ Hindi *gxaban* "dissolution of inheritance, bankruptcy" ग़बन	4-3	5-3 N n.. N.. Japanese *ban* "turn"
VELAR		1-4 क k K̆ English *sky* Hindi *kitnaa2* "how much?" कितना?	2-4 ख kʰ khₒ Khₒ English *kitten* Hindi *kholnaa* "to open" खोलना	3-4 ग g Ğ English *good* Hindi *gaanaa* "to sing" गाना	4-4 घ gʰ ghₒ Ghₒ Hindi *ghod.aa* "horse" घोड़ा	5-4 ङ nₒ Nₒ Hindi *tang* "trouble" तंग (तङ)
RETROFLEX		1-5 ट t T T̆ or T̆ Hindi *t.uut.aa* "broken" टूटा	2-5 ठ tʰ thₒ Thₒ or Thₒ Hindi *th.iik* "OK, all night" ठीक	3-5 ड d D̆ Hindi *d.aak* "mail, post" डाक	4-5 ढ dʰ dhₒ Dhₒ Hindi *dh.iilaa* "loose" ढीला	5-5 ण ɳ h ɳ h Hindi *gan.atantra* "democracy, people's rule" गणतंत्र

PART 1: THE NAVLIPI SUMMARY TABLES

33

NV_2

		PLOSIVES			NASALS
		UNVOICED (SURD)		**VOICED (SONANT)**	
Y=6	X=1 UNASPIRATED	ASPIRATED	UNASPIRATED	ASPIRATED	
MEDIO-PALATAL	1-6 c 2 2 2 2 Turkish *car* "advantage, profit" Irish *ciall* "sense" Croatian *leća* "beans, lentils"	2-6 No IPA Symbol 2h₀ 2ɦ 2h₀ 2ɦ Hungarian *oss. narancssárgán*	3-6 ɟ i ɓ̈ ɟ̈ i ɓ̈ ɟ̈ Turkish *gem* "horse bit" Irish *giall* "hostage" Croatian *leđa* "back"	4-6 	5-6 ɲ ᵒn ɲ ᵒN ɲ Irish *ngiall* "hostage" Croatian *nyó* "to her"
STANDARD PALATAL	1-7 च No IPA Symbol c c C C English *eschew* Spanish *chaleco* "vest" Hindi *chun-naa* "to chose" चुनना	2-7 छ No IPA Symbol ch₀ cɦ Ch₀ Cɦ English *choose* Hindi *chhaan-naa* "to strain, filter" छानना	3-7 ज No IPA Symbol i ɓ̈ ɟ̈ i ɓ̈ ɟ̈ English *joke* Hindi *jaanaa* "to go" जाना	4-7 झ No IPA Symbol iɦ ɓ̈ɦ Tɦ₀ ɟ̈ɦ Hindi *jhuulaa* "swing" झूला	5-7 ञ n ɲ N ɲ English *inch* Hindi *wyanjana* "non-vowel (consonant)" व्यंजन
ALVEOLAR	1-8 t tt tth Tt Tth or Tth	2-8 tʰ tth₀ tthɦ Tth₀ Tthɦ English *tomorrow*	3-8 d dt dth Dt Dth English *dinner*	4-8 No IPA Symbol dth₀ dthɦ Dth₀ Dthɦ	5-8 n n ɲ N ɲ English *into* *indeed* <<common "n">>
APICO/MEDIO-DENTAL	1-9 English *sty*	2-9 	3-9 	4-9 	5-9
STANDARD DENTAL	1-10 त t̪ t t̪ T t̪ Spanish *tu* "you" Hindi *tuu* "you (singular)" तू	2-10 थ t̪ʰ th₀ t̪ɦ Th₀ T̪ɦ Hindi *thaknaa* "to get tired" थकना	3-10 द d̪ d d̪ D D̪ Spanish *dar* "to give" Hindi *denaa* "to give" देना	4-10 ध d̪ʰ dh₀ d̪ɦ Dh₀ D̪ɦ Hindi *dhonaa* "to wash" धोना	5-10 न n ɲ N ɲ Spanish *andar* "to walk" Hindi *andar* "inside" अन्दर

PART 1: THE NAVLIPI SUMMARY TABLES

	PLOSIVES					NASALS
	UNVOICED (SURD)		VOICED (SONANT)			
Y=6 / X=11	UNASPIRATED	ASPIRATED	UNASPIRATED	ASPIRATED		
PHARYNGEALIZED DENTAL	1-11 t^ε t.. *t* T.. *J* or *T* Arabic **kitaab** "book" Arabic **ktb** "to read"	2-11	3-11 d^ε d.. *d* D.. *Ɖ* Arabic **kidaab** "henna"	4-1		5-11
INTERDENTAL	1-12	2-12	3-12 Not phonemically distinct from Standard Dental in most major languages, so not used.	4-12		5-12
INFRA-LABIO-SUPRADENTAL (NO TONGUE CONTACT)	1-13	2-13	3-13	4-13		5-13
SUPRA-LABIO-INFRADENTAL (NO TONGUE CONTACT)	1-14	2-14	3-14	4-14		5-14
BILABIAL (NO TONGUE CONTACT)	1-15 q p p*p* P*p* English **spy** Hindi **pal** "an instant, a moment" पल	2-15 * फ p^h ph *ph* Ph *Ph* English **put** Hindi **phal** "fruit" फल	3-15 व b b*b* B*B* English **book** Hindi **bolnaa** "to speak" बोलना	4-15 भ b^h bh *bh* Bh *Bh* Hindi **bhuuk** "hunger" भूक		5-15 म m m*m* M*m* English **man** Hindi **man** "mind" मन

PART 1: THE NAVLIPI SUMMARY TABLES

		FRICATIVES		FLAPS				TRILLS	
		UNVOICED (SURD)	VOICED (SONANT)	UNASPIRATED	NORMAL ASPIRATED	NASAL	FRICATIZED	NORMAL	FRICATIZED
GLOTTAL	y=1	6-1 ℏɛ/ h ℏ H ℏ English *hat* *hello*	7-1	8-1	9-1	10-1	11-1	12-1	13-1
PHARYNGEAL		6-2 h ḧ H ḧ	7-2	8-2	9-2	10-2	11-2	12-2	13-2
		Arabic *hurub* 'war' Hebrew *mahar* 'tomorrow'								
UVULAR		6-3 χ χ̈ X̤ χ̤ German *doch* 'but yes' 'however' Hebrew *mahar* 'sold'	7-3 ʁ G̈ Ġ G̈ Ġ French (Parisian) *rouler* 'to roll'	8-3	9-3	10-3	11-3	12-3	13-3
				Phonemically indistinct from fricatives in nearly all languages						
VELAR		6-4 x x̄ X X̄ Arabic *khilaf* 'against' Irish *chaol* 'thin'	7-4 ɣ G̈ G̈ Arabic *ghilaf* 'pillow cover' Farsi *gham* 'sadness'	8-4	9-4	10-4	11-4	12-4	13-4
RETROFLEX		6-5 ṣ t̤h ṭ̈h T̤h T̤̈h	7-5 z̤ d̤h ḍ̈h D̤h D̤̈h	8-5 ṭ ḍ. ḍ D. Ḍ Hindi *kad.ak* 'hard stiff' कड़क	9-5 ṭʰ ḍ.h ḍ̈h Ḍ.h Ḍ̈h Hindi *padh.naa* 'to study' पढ़ना	10-5 r̃ h. ḣ h. ḣ Hindi *gan..atantra* 'democracy' (alternate pronunciation, as flap) गणतंत्र	11-5	12-5	13-5

PART 1: THE NAVLIPI SUMMARY TABLES

	FRICATIVES			FLAPS				TRILLS	
	UNVOICED (SURD)	VOICED (SONANT)		NORMAL		NASAL	FRICATIZED	NORMAL	FRICATIZED
			UNASPIRATED	ASPIRATED					
MEDIO-PALATAL	ç	j							
STANDARD PALATAL	ʃ	ʒ							
ALVEOLAR			ɾ			ɹ̃		r	
APICO/MEDIO-DENTAL	s	z					Phonemically undifferentiated from alveolar in nearly *all* languages.		
STANDARD DENTAL	Phonemically undifferentiated from apico-medio-dental in nearly *all* languages.								

PART 1: THE NAVLIPI SUMMARY TABLES

NV_6

	FRICATIVES		FLAPS				TRILLS	
	UNVOICED (SURD)	VOICED (SONANT)	UNASPIRATED	NORMAL ASPIRATED	NASAL	FRICATIZED	NORMAL	FRICATIZED
PHARYNGEALIZED DENTAL	6-11 th₀·· Th₀··	7-11 dh₀·· dh̬₀·· Dh₀·· Dh̬₀··	8-11	9-11	10-11	11-11	12-11	13-11
INTERDENTAL	6-12 θ th₀ th̬₀ Th₀ Th̬₀ English *thin*/*think*	7-12 ð dh₀ dh̬₀ Dh₀ Dh̬₀ English *the*/*although*	8-12	9-12	10-12	11-12	12-12	13-12
INFRA-LABIO-SUPRADENTAL (NO TONGUE CONTACT)	6-13 f f₀ f̬₀ F₀ F̬₀ English *fat*/*fun* Hindi फीकर/फिर" rare. worry (of Arabic borrowing) हिफ़र <<rare 'f'-common 'f' sound>>	7-13 v v₀ v̬₀ V₀ V̬₀ English *very* Hindi *vinay* ृwmmly, obedience (common colloquial pronunciation) बिनय <<common 'v' sound>>	8-13	9-13	10-13	11-13	12-13	13-13
SUPRA-LABIO-INFRADENTAL (NO TONGUE CONTACT)	6-14	7-14	8-14 <<<< Very very very rare >>>>	9-14	10-14	11-14	12-14	13-14
BILABIAL (NO TONGUE CONTACT)	6-15 φ ph₀ ph̬₀ Ph₀ Ph̬₀ English *phooey* Hausa *phara* 'to begin'	7-15 β bh₀ bh̬₀ Bh₀ Bh̬₀	8-15	9-15	10-15	11-15	12-15 B ph₀ph̬₀ ph̬₀ph̬₀ Ph₀Ph̬₀ Ph̬₀Ph̬₀ Very very rare (imitation of lip sound of horses after feeding)	13-15

Y=11
x=6

PART 1: THE NAVLIPI SUMMARY TABLES

CLICKS - INGRESSIVE

		Central *(7)			Lateral		
		Single Voiced	Nasal	Trill or Continuous	Unvoiced	Single Voiced	Nasal	Trill or Continuous
	x=14 Unvoiced	14-1	15-1	16-1	17-1	18-1	19-1	20-1	21-1
GLOTTAL	Y=1	14-1	15-1	16-1	17-1	18-1	19-1	20-1	21-1
PHARYNGEAL		14-2	15-2	16-2	17-2	18-2	19-2	20-2	21-2
UVULAR		14-3	15-3	16-3	17-3 k..zk..z / K..zK..z	18-3	19-3	20-3	21-3
VELAR		14-4 No IPA Symbol / kz / Kz	15-4	16-4	17-4 No IPA Symbol / kzkz / Kzkz	18-4	19-4	20-4	21-4
RETROFLEX		14-5 / ŧz / Ŧz	15-5 / dz / Dz	16-5 / ŧzn₀ / Ŧzn₀	17-5 / ŧztz / Ŧztz	18-5 Very very rare and phonemically indistinct from alveolar(#8) and palatal(#7) so not used.			

Zulu — very rare

PART 1: THE NAVLIPI SUMMARY TABLES

39

		CLICKS - INGRESSIVE							
		CENTRAL *(7)			LATERAL				
		SINGLE		TRILL OR CONTINUOUS		SINGLE		TRILL OR CONTINUOUS	
	UNVOICED	VOICED	NASAL		UNVOICED	VOICED	NASAL		
	X=14 14-6 Y=6 2z 2ž 2z 𝒟ž̄ ≪common English "tsk tsk"≫	15-6	16-6	17-6	18-6	19-6	20-6	21-6	
MEDIO-PALATAL									
STANDARD PALATAL	14-7 cz cž̌ Cz 𝒞ž̄	15-7	16-7	17-7	18-7	19-7	20-7	21-7	
ALVEOLAR	14-8 ‡z ‡ž̌ ‡z 𝒥ž̄ English click "tut tut" Zulu	15-8 d‡z d‡ž̌ D‡z 𝒟‡ž̄	16-8 ‡zn₀ ‡žn̆₀ ‡zn₀ 𝒥žn̄₀	17-8	18-8 lz lž̌ Lz ℒž̄ English click "horse or "gee-up" Xhosa	19-8 lzoo lž̌ᵤ Lzoo ℒž̄ᵤ Zulu	20-8 lzn₀ lž̌n̆₀ Lzn₀ ℒž̄n̄₀ Zulu	21-8	
APICO/MEDIO-DENTAL	14-9	15-9	16-9	17-9	18-9	19-9	20-9	21-9	
STANDARD DENTAL	14-10 tz tž̌ Tz 𝒯ž̄	15-10	16-10	17-10	18-10	19-10	20-10 Phonemically indistinct from alveolar (#8) in nearly all languages, so not used.	21-10	

PART 1: THE NAVLIPI SUMMARY TABLES

40

CLICKS - INGRESSIVE

	Central *(7)				Lateral		
	Single Voiced	Nasal	Trill or Continuous	Unvoiced	Single Voiced	Nasal	Trill or Continuous
PHARYNGEALIZED DENTAL (Y=11)	14-11	15-11	16-11	17-11	18-11	19-11	20-11	21-11
INTERDENTAL	14-12	15-12 Treated the same as Dental (#10), since phonemically indistinct in most click languages.	16-12	17-12	18-12	19-12	20-12	21-12
INFRA-LABIO-SUPRADENTAL (NO TONGUE CONTACT)	14-13	15-13 Can be articulated, but not phonemically used in any known language.	16-13	17-13	18-13	19-13	20-13	21-13
SUPRA-LABIO-INFRADENTAL (NO TONGUE CONTACT)	14-14	15-14	16-14	17-14	18-14	19-14	20-14	21-14
BILABIAL (NO TONGUE CONTACT)	14-15 ⊙ pz p̥ / Pz p̬	15-15	16-15	17-15	18-15	19-15	20-15	21-15

NV_9

PART 1: THE NAVLIPI SUMMARY TABLES

NV_10

	CLICKS-EGRESSIVE		EJECTIVES		IMPLOSIVES	
	CENTRAL	LATERAL	UNVOICED	FRICATIVE	UNVOICED	VOICED
	x=22 y=1					
GLOTTAL	22.1	23.1	24.1	25.1	26.1	27.1
PHARYNGEAL	22.2	23.2	24.2	25.2	26.2	27.2
UVULAR	22.3	23.3	24.3	25.3	26.3	27.3
VELAR	22.4	23.4	24.4 '(10) K' kz' k'ǧ Kz' K'ǧ Amharic: *k'addada* Hausa *k'aaraa* "to increase"	25.4	26.4	27.4 gz" gǧ" Gz" Gǧ"
RETROFLEX	22.5	23.5	24.5	25.5	26.5	27.5

PART 1: THE NAVLIPI SUMMARY TABLES

	CLICKS - EGRESSIVE		EJECTIVES		IMPLOSIVES	
	CENTRAL	LATERAL	UNVOICED	FRICATIVE	UNVOICED	VOICED
X=22 Y=6	22-6	23-6	24-6	25-6	26-6	27-6
MEDIO-PALATAL						
	22-7	23-7	24-7 No IPA Symbol cz' Cƀ̃ Cz' Cƀ̃	25-7	26-7	27-7 j' ṭz" iƀ̃ ṭz" iƀ̃ Hausa dz"aadz"a 'progeny'
STANDARD PALATAL						
	22-8 ǂz ǂƀ̄ ǂTz Jƀ̄	23-8 ǁz ǁƀ̄ Lz ǁƀ̄	24-8 (12) t' ǂtz' ǂtƀ̃ ǂTz' Jtƀ̃ Hausa t'arraga 'he swept'	25-8	26-8 d dtz" dtƀ̃ Dtz" Dtƀ̃ Hausa d"aana 'to measure' Tukang Besi pid"i 'trash'	27-8
ALVEOLAR						
	22-9	23-9	24-9	25-9 s' Sz' sƀ̃ Sz' sƀ̃ Ethiopian sz'aafa 'he wrote'	26-9	27-9
APICO/ MEDIO-DENTAL						
	22-10 tz tƀ̄ Tz Jƀ̄	23-10 ǁz ǁƀ̄ Lz ǁƀ̄	24-10	25-10	26-10	27-10 IPA: tz" tƀ̃ Tz" Jƀ̃
STANDARD DENTAL						

PART 1: THE NAVLIPI SUMMARY TABLES

NV_12

	CLICKS - EGRESSIVE		EJECTIVES		IMPLOSIVES	
	CENTRAL	LATERAL	UNVOICED (SURD)	FRICATIVE	UNVOICED (SURD)	VOICED (SONANT)
	X=22 Y=11					
PHARYNGEALIZED DENTAL	22-11	23-11	24-11	25-11	26-11	27-11
INTERDENTAL	22-12 Treated the same as dental (#10), since phonemically indistinct in most click languages.	23-12	24-12	25-12	26-12	27-12
INFRA-LABIO-SUPRADENTAL *(NO TONGUE CONTACT)*	22-13 Can be articulated, but not phonemically used in any known language.	23-13	24-13 p' pz' pz̄' Pz' Pz̄'	25-13 f' fz' fz̄' Fz' Fz̄'	26-13	27-13
SUPRA-LABIO-INFRADENTAL *(NO TONGUE CONTACT)*	22-14	23-14	24-14	25-14	26-14	27-14
BILABIAL *(NO TONGUE CONTACT)*	22-15 pᴢ pz̄ Pᴢ Pz̄	23-15	24-15 p' pz' pz̄' Pz' Pz̄' Amharic b'app'as "father/ head priest in church"	25-15	26-15	27-15 b bz' bz̄' Bz' Bz̄' Tukang Besi *ab"a* "prior" Hausa *b" aara* "to peel"

PART 1: THE NAVLIPI SUMMARY TABLES

44

(5. NON-VOWEL MATRICES, cont.)
FOOTNOTES FOR MAIN NAVLIPI TABLES (MATRICES) B. NON VOWEL MATRIX

1. Cursive handwriting of this phone is as shown in the illustration:

2. Should correctly be $\backsix h_0$, i.e. $\backsix$ plus the post-op for fricatives, h_0. However, an exception is made for purposes of recognizability and correspondence to the currently used English sh, German sch, French ch, etc.

3. As for the corresponding unvoiced phone (sh_0), this should correctly be $\mathop{i} h_0$, i.e. $\mathop{i}$ plus the post-op for fricatives, h_0. However, an exception is made again for purposes of recognizability, since zh is the customary phonetic transcription of this phone in Roman script.

4. Common Mandarin articulation of Xie Xie ("thank you") is strictly between alveolar and standard-dental artitions. But once again, from the "practical phonemics" aspect of Navlipi, we place it here.

5. The same glyph (n) is used to represent 5-8 (alveolar nasal) and 5-10 (dental nasal) since these two are phonemically distinct in virtuallyno major languages.

6. (re 8-8) This glyph also represents the phonemic condensate (semivowel + flap) etc. since this is the "common r".

7. For simplicity, and again from the "practical phonemics" aspect of Navlipi, a distinction is not made between a simple click and an affricate click.

8. The English "tsk tsk" click is also articulated as a standard-dental click in some pronunciations, and would thus qualify under this phone as well, i.e. it would be placed here.

9. Zulu also has aspirated variants of the retroflex and alveolar unvoiced clicks listed here. However, closer analysis reveals that these are in fact clicks quickly followed by aspiration. Thus, rather than warranting the use of the aspirate postop (h_0), they are best expressed as simple golttal aspirations, i.e. with h only.

10. The (z plus ') is chosen, rather than the (') alone, to avoid possible confusion with the apostrophe. Since in Navlipi the z, i.e. the post-op for clicks (z with cross-out), will be a rare letter (as opposed to the common z), any transcription with the apostrophe, i.e. z', will be instantly recognized as distinct from the apostrophe alone.

11. This click is used as an obscene articulation in some countries, eg. in Brazil and among the eunuch (*hijra*) community in India.

12. Georgian also has phonemes which are affricate variants of *ttz'*, made by adding the medio-dental fricative, i.e. the common "s", and the palatal fricative (the common "sh", sh_0 in Navlipi). These can be readily transcribed by adding these fricatives to the parent phone, getting *ttz's* and *ttz'sh$_0$*. Thus, they are not treated of separately here.

13. The Mandarin glyph (**X**) is actually post-alveolar with jaw open-mid (vs. pure alveolar with jaw close-mid). However, for "practical phonemics" purposes, characteristic of Navlipi, it is placed here.

PART 1: THE NAVLIPI SUMMARY TABLES

(5. NON-VOWEL MATRICES, cont.: SEMIVOWELS, CENTRALS AND LATERALS)

KEY

| Dewanaagari | IPA Symbol | Keyboard | 1-1 | Matrix element number. |
| | | | *(n) | Asterisk indicates footnote # n. |

PRINT	CURSIVE
Small	Small
Caps	Caps

WORD EXAMPLES

PART 1: THE NAVLIPI SUMMARY TABLES

(5. NON-VOWEL MATRICES, Semivowels, centrals and laterals, cont.)

SIMPLE SEMIVOWELS

		PHONO CHROMATICITY		
		PARENT VOWEL X= (IF APPLICABLE)	SEMI-VOWEL *(1)	PHONEMIC CONDENSATES
ARTITION	**BILABIAL** *(tongue back, lips rounded)*	Y= v [3(3)(1)] u	IPA: ☐ 28-15 *(3) example* w *w* W *W*	
	BILABIAL *(tongue central, lips flat)*		IPA: ☐ 28-15b *(3) example* w° *w°* W° *W°*	
	STANDARD PALATAL	v [1(1)(1)] i	IPA: ☐ 28-7 example* j *j* J *J*	
	PHARYNGEAL		IPA: ☐ 28-2 example* w.. *w..* W.. *W..*	
	(BILABIAL) + (INFRALABIO- SUPRADENTAL)	v [3(3)(1)] u		IPA: ☐ example* vw *vw* VW *VW* [PCON-7]

*(1) A semi-vowel is written as a combination of the parent vowel followed by either a], [i], [u], etc.

*(2) F is used for jaw forward position in the artition. This is the only non vowel for which a jaw forward artition exists within *NAVLIPI*.

PART 1: THE NAVLIPI SUMMARY TABLES

(5. NON-VOWEL MATRICES, Semivowels, centrals and laterals, cont.)

CENTRALS ("r"-SOUNDS)

ARTITION		PHONO CHROMATICITY	
		PARENT VOWEL X= (IF APPLICABLE)	SEMI-VOWEL *(1)
		Y= $v\,[2(4)(2)]$	IPA: ☐ 30-5 *(1)
	RETROFLEX (Jaw Normal)	𝓃	example* 𝓃a 𝓇a / 𝓃a 𝓇a
		$v\,[2(4)(-1)]$	IPA: ☐ 30-5F *(1)(2)
	RETROFLEX (Jaw Forward)	𝓃o	example* 𝓃₀a 𝓇₀a / 𝓃₀a 𝓇₀a
	PALATAL	Not phonemically distinct in any major language. Irish has a palatalized aveolar tap which is probably best described as having two component phones— an aveolar tap [r] and the palatal semi-vowel [j]. It is best transcribed as a digraph [rj].	
		$v\,[2(8)(-2)]$	IPA: ☐ 30-8 *(1)
	ALVEOLO-DENTAL [combining post-alveolo-palatal]	r₀	example* r₀a 𝓇₀a / r₀a 𝓇₀a
	[SUPRA] DENTAL	Very rare, and also not phonemically distinct from neighboring articulation positions (esp. alveolar). Thus not used in NAVLIPI.	
	INTERDENTAL		

*(1) A semi-vowel is written as a combination of the parent vowel followed by either [a], [i], [u], e
*(2) F is used for jaw forward position in the artition. This is the only non vowel for which a jaw forw artition exists within NAVLIPI.

PART 1: THE NAVLIPI SUMMARY TABLES

(5. NON-VOWEL MATRICES, Semivowels, centrals and laterals, cont.)

CENTRALS ("r"-SOUNDS)		PHONO CHROMATICITY		
		PARENT VOWEL X= (IF APPLICABLE) Y=	SEMI-VOWEL	PHONEMIC CONDENSATES
COMBINATION ARTITIONS AND PHONOCHROMATICITIES	ALVEOLO-DENTAL (flap+trill+semi-vowel)			r r r r [PCON-8]
	RETROFLEX (flap+trill+semi-vowel)			Not used, no phonemic significance. Mentioned for completness only.
	ALVEOLO-DENTAL (flap+trill+semi-vowel)+ UVULAR fricative			xr xr Xr Xr [PCON-10]
	(Central flap + central trill + central semivowel + lateral semivowel) in ALVEOLO-DENTAL artition.			₣ ₣ ₣ ₣ [PCON-11]
	(Central semivowel + lateral semivowel) in RETROFLEX artition.			九 九 九 九 [PCON-12]
	(Central flap + central trill + central semivowel + lateral semivowel + nasal) in ALVEOLO-DENTAL artition.			₣ ₣ ₣ ₣ [PCON-13]
	(Central semivowel + lateral semivowel + nasal) in RETROFLEX artition.			九 九 九 九 [PCON-14]
	"UNIVERSAL R"			R R R R [PCON-15]

PART 1: THE NAVLIPI SUMMARY TABLES

LATERALS ("L"-SOUNDS)

ARTITION	PARENT VOWEL (IF APPLICABLE)	PHONO CHROMATICITY					
		SEMI-VOWEL *(1)					PHONEMIC CONDENSATES
		UNASPIRATED	ASPIRATED	FRICATIZED	PALATALIZED	PHARYNGEALIZED	
RETROFLEX, JAW NORMAL	v [2[(5)(2)]	31-5 example: ℓa La / La La	32-5	33-5	34-5	35-5	
PALATAL	v [2[(7)(2)]	31-7 example: ℓa La / ℓa La	32-7	33-7	34-7	35-7	
ALVEOLO-DENTAL	v [2[(8)(2)]	31-8 *(1) example: l a la / La	32-8 *(1) example: lh₀a lh₀a / Lh₀a Lh₀a	33-8 *(1) example: lha lha / Lha Lha	34-8 *(1) example: lja lja / Lja Lja	35-8 *(1) example: l..a l..a / L..a L..a	
INTERDENTAL	—	31-12 *(1) example: ℓla ℓla / ℓla ℓla	32-12	33-12	34-12	35-12	

*(1) A semi-vowel is written as a combination of the parent vowel followed by either [a], [i], [u], etc.

*(2) F is used for jaw forward position in the artition. This is the only non vowel for which a jaw forward artition exists within NAVLIPI

*(3) Multigraph, used only where there is phonemic opposition to other laterals (primarily alveolar, e.g. Irish, Turkish, also some Arabic dialects).

*(5) Multigraph. A detailed analysis of, e.g. the Irish palatalized lateral, orthographed in the IPA as [lʲ], shows that it can easily be repeated as a quick, successive articulation of [l] and [i]; hence the multigraph.

PART 1: THE NAVLIPI SUMMARY TABLES

LATERALS ("L"-SOUNDS)

PARENT VOWEL (IF APPLICABLE)	PHONO CHROMATICITY					PHONEMIC CONDENSATES	PCON #
	UNASPIRATED	ASPIRATED	SEMI-VOWEL *(1) FRICATIZED	PALATALIZED	PHARYNGEALIZED		
$X =$ $Y =$ (Central flap + central trill + central semi-vowel + lateral semi-vowel) in ALVEOLO-DENTAL artition.						ꟻ ꟻ ꟻ ꟻ	PCON-11
(Central semivowel + lateral semivowel) in RETROFLEX artition.						ꟻ ꟻ ꟻ ꟻ	PCON-12
(Central flap + central trill + central semivowel + lateralsemivowel + nasal) in ALVEOLO-DENTAL artition.						ꟻ ꟻ ꟻ ꟻ	PCON-13
(Central semivowel + lateral semivowel + nasal) in RETRO-FLEX artition.						ꟻ ꟻ ꟻ ꟻ	PCON-14

ARTITION

PART 1: THE NAVLIPI SUMMARY TABLES

6. TABLE OF POST-OPS (POST-POSITIONAL OPERATORS)

(Starts overleaf)

PART 1: THE NAVLIPI SUMMARY TABLES

	FUNCTION	DESCRIPTION	EXAMPLES POST·OP	EXAMPLES PRINT	EXAMPLES CURSIVE	CORRESPONDING PCON
PO-1	*Phonemic condensate*, designates (**aspirate + nonaspirate**) generally to be used with nonaspirate letter which is most common in transcription.	**Little circle** (not subscript, just sitting on line.) Cursive is like "little e".	o	*illustrated with (aa)* aa_o	aae	PCON-1
PO-2	Indicates **long length of vowels** when used with vowels. Rare because *Navlipi* uses reduplicated vowels.			*illustrated with (p)* p_o	pe	
PO-3	Length of tones					
PO-4	Indicates **aspiration**	"h" with little circle on or straddling line	h_o	*illustrated with (p)* ph_o	ph	
PO-5	Indicates **fricatization**	"h" with oval. Usually used with root phone (e.g. plosive, central) to indicate fricatization where separate glyph is unavailable. "h" with oval below line is easily distinguishable from little circle. Analogous to "h" in present day English *sh*, French *ch*.	h_o	*illustrated with (ɔ)* $ɔh_o$	$ɔh$	
PO-6	*Phonemic condensate*, designates combination (**voiced + unvoiced**). Generally to be used with most common transcription (e.g. In Arabic with *b* to give *b∞* in Cantonese with *p* to give *p∞*.	*(Print)* **Infinity symbol** straddling or on the line. *(Cursive)* Like two little "e"s.	∞	$p\infty$	pee	PCON-2
PO-7	Indicates **sonant(voicing)**. Used very very rarely, e.g. for clicks.	**Infinity symbol**, same as above, but superscripted.	∞	*illustrated with (lz)* lz^∞	lz^∞	
PO-8	Indicates nasal sound or **nasalization**. Generally used only with vowels (but this includes lateral (l), central (r), vowels etc)	**n with oval, m with oval**, also optional **tilde**	$n_o, \sim$ m_o	$n_o, \sim$ m_o	$\eta, \sim$ m	

PART 1: THE NAVLIPI SUMMARY TABLES

FUNCTION		DESCRIPTION	EXAMPLES			CORRESPONDING PCON
			POST-OP	PRINT	CURSIVE	
PO-9	*Phonemic condensate* indicates a vowel can be **nasal or non-nasal**. Accurately should be used for much American speech, but is impractical.	Same as above but with additional **dot above**. Very very rare.	$\dot{n}_o$	$\dot{n}_o$	$\dot{\eta}\sim$	PCON-16
PO-10	Indicates **flap**. Most flaps have their own separate letters. This symbol used mainly for Indian letters.	**Single dot or period (full stop).** *(Print)* On line. *(Cursive)* Below letter. Distinguished from period by space.	.	illustrated with (t) $t.$	$\underset{.}{t}$	
PO-11	Indicates **uvular or pharyngeal** variant. Mainly Arabic "faucal" letters etc. Mostly used with the velar base plosive (e.g.. (k,g)) also t.. d.. (etc.)	**Double dot** (period). *(Cursive)* Double dot above letter. *(Print)* Double dot (period, full stop) after letter (preferred) or Shift + dot (raised dot). Cursive double dot over letter somewhat emulates some Roman transcriptions today, e.g. of Arabic. Mainly to be used in Arabic, Hebrew. Distinct from period at end of sentence.	..	illustrated with (k) $k..$	$\ddot{k}$	
PO-12	*Phonemic condensate* Indicates **(stop + fricative)**. Usually used with stop.	**h with horizontal infinity sign.** *(Cursive)* Double circle or "double superscript e".	h_∞	h_∞	hee	PCON-3
PO-13	*Phonemic condensate* Indicates **(stop + forward fricative)**. Usually used with stop.	*(Print)* **h with vertical infinity sign** or small "figure 8". *(Cursive)* Same, but infinity sign written like a "figure 8" (Somewhat rare).	h_8	illustrated with (p, į) ph_8 $\underset{.}{i}h_8$	ph_8 $\underset{.}{j}h_8$	PCON-4
PO-14	**Click ingressive.** Used after corresponding stop or semi-vowel (e.g. lateral) to indicate a click in the same articulation position as the operand.	Letter z with crossbar.	ƶ	illustrated with (l) $l\!ƶ$	$l\!ƶ$	
PO-15	**Click egressive.** Used after corresponding stop or semi-vowel (e.g. lateral) to indicate a click in the same articulation position as the operand.	Letter z with double crossbar.	ƶ̄	illustrated with (l) $l\!ƶ̄$	$l\!ƶ̄$	

PART 1: THE NAVLIPI SUMMARY TABLES

	FUNCTION	DESCRIPTION	EXAMPLES			CORRESPONDING PCON
			POST-OP	PRINT	CURSIVE	
PO-16	**Ejective.** Operand is stop, lateral, etc.	**Letter z with crossbar with single apostrophe.** (Very, very rare).	ƶ'	ƶ'	ƶ'	
PO-17	**Implosive.** Operand is stop, lateral, etc.	**Letter z with crossbar with double apostrophe.** (Quite rare).	ƶ"	ƶ"	ƶ"	
PO-18	*Phonemic condensate.* Indicates **(stop + semi-vowel)**	**Vertical "figure 8"** (infinity symbol) on parent stop.	8	*illustrated with (b, j)* b8 j8	b8 j8	PCON-5
PO-19	Denotes a "mobile, generic" vowel where choice of vowel does not appear to matter, e.g. in some Semitic and Chinese languages.	*(Print)* **equals sign.** *(Cursive)* **wave resembling equals sign.** Used as Post-Op. Most difficult amongst phonemic condensates to treat. Found in Arabic dialects and in some Chinese languages. E.g., most Arabic dialects do not have phonemic distinctions between [i] and [u].	=	*illustrated with (a)* a=	a≈	PCON-15
PO-20	Combination of Phones	**Bar-above** *(Print)* To be written as a post-op, thus resembling IPA symbol. *(Cursive)* To be written directly above the phones it acts on. Thus, its use will be much like crossing a t.	‾	*illustrated with (kp)* kp‾ *(Igbo)*	k̄p	
PO-21	"Silent" Non-Vowel	*(Print)* **Empty parenthesis** *(Cursive)* rendered by **circling the relevant glyph.** See description of this unique post-op in the book.	( )	*(Bahasa Malaysia, "No")* Tidak( )	Tidak	

PART 1: THE NAVLIPI SUMMARY TABLES

7. TABLE OF PHONEMIC CONDENSATES

(Starts overleaf)

PART 1: THE NAVLIPI SUMMARY TABLES

	FUNCTION	DESCRIPTION	EXAMPLES			
			P·CON ONLY	PRINT	CURSIVE	RELEVANT EQUIVALENCE
PCON-1	(aspirate + non-aspirate) (non-vowel)	Little circle	o	*illustrated with (p)* p_o	p_o (cursive)	$p_o = [p] + [ph_o]$
PCON-2	(unvoiced +voiced)	Infinity sign	∞	*illustrated with (p)* p_∞	p_∞ (cursive)	$p_\infty = [p] + [b]$
PCON-3	(stop + fricative)	h + (Horizontal infinity sign or double circle)	h_∞	*illustrated with (k)* kh_∞	kh_∞ (cursive)	$kh_\infty = [k] + [x]$
PCON-4	(stop + forward fricative)	h + (Vertical infinity sign or figure 8)	h_8	*illustrated with (p)* ph_8	ph_8 (cursive)	$ph_8 = [ph_o] + [f]$
PCON-5	(stop + semi-vowel)	Vertical infinity sign or figure 8	8	*illustrated with (b)* b_8	b_8 (cursive)	$b_8 = [b] + [w]$
PCON-6	(semi-vowel + forward fricative)	Digraph, starting with forward fricative.	vw	vw	vw (cursive)	vw = [v] + [w]
PCON-7	(stop + flap)	Digraph, starting with stop. (Rare)	ttr	ttr	ttr (cursive)	ttr = [tt] + [r]
PCON 8	(flap + trill + semivowel) in (alveolo-dental central) artition. *("common r")*	The letter "r"	r	r	r (cursive)	$r = [r^0] + [r^0 r^0] + [r_0]$
PCON-9	(flap + trill + semi-vowel) in retroflex artition.	Mentioned for completeness only		Not used no phonemic significance		
PCON-10	[(trill + flap + semivowel) in alveolo-dental artition] + [uvular fricative]	**Digraph:** Corresponds to component phones. Used mainly for French/German "r". No possibility of confusion as individual phones, x, r, almost never occur together. In the very rare instances they do, distinction can be made by context.	xr	xr	xr (cursive)	xr = [x] + [r]

PART 1: THE NAVLIPI SUMMARY TABLES

FUNCTION		DESCRIPTION	EXAMPLES			
			P·CON ONLY	PRINT	CURSIVE	RELEVANT EQUIVALENCE
PCON-11	(central flap + central trill + central semivowel + lateral semivowel) in alveolo-dental artition.	"r" with single bar across. Used mainly with Chinese languages and Japanese and some Southeast Asian languages. Parent phone is actually a lateral, but to avoid confusion with other phones (e.g. Polish palatal L, see above) we use this. The Chinese languages don't normally have a central (r sound) but they typically interchange the lateral [l] and central [r] phones.	ꞓ	ꞓ	ꞓ	ꞓ = $[r^0] + [r^0 r^0] + [r_0] + [l]$
PCON-12	(Central semivowel + lateral semivowel) in retroflex artition.	ⱨ with single bar across. Less common than above, but again used mainly in Chinese, and Southeast Asian languages, some dialects of Maraathi and Tamil also confuse these two component phones and so may need this.	ⱨ	ⱨ	ⱨ	ⱨ = $[ⱨ] + [ɭ]$
PCON-13	(central flap + central trill + central semivowel + lateral semivowel + nasal) in alveolo-dental artition.	"r" with double bar across. Quite rare, but needed for completeness. Also shows up in phonal changes in many language families e.g. Indo-European.	ꞓ̿	ꞓ̿	ꞓ̿	ꞓ̿ = $[r^0] + [r^0 r^0] + [r_0] + [l] + [n]$
PCON-14	(central semivowel + lateral semivowel + nasal) in retroflex artition.	ⱨ with double bar across. Very, very rare. Again done for completeness only.	ⱨ̿	ⱨ̿	ⱨ̿	ⱨ̿ = $[ⱨ] + [ɭ] + [n]$
PCON-15	Denotes a "mobile, generic" vowel where choice of vowel does not appear to matter, e.g. in some Semitic and Chinese languages.	*(Print)* equals sign. *(Cursive)* wave resembling equals sign. Used as Post-Op. Most difficult amongst phonemic condensates to treat. Found in Arabic dialects and in some Chinese languages e.g. most Arabic dialects do not have phonemic distinctions between [i] and [u].	=	*illustrated with (a)* ə=	ɑᴈ	$[a=] = [a] + [e]$ (Mandarin) $[i=] = [i] + [u]$ (some Arabic colloquial dialects)
PCON-16	nasal + non-nasal	Nasal Post-Op, but with dot above	ṅ₀	ṅ₀	ṅ~	
PCON-17	"Universal R"	Uppercase R. To be used to represent ALL centrals when needed. Expected to be rarely used.	R	R	R	

8. SUMMARY OF TONES

(Starting overleaf)

PART 1: THE NAVLIPI SUMMARY TABLES

POINT OF ORIGIN	LEVEL		RISING [EXTENT OF RISE=SMALL]		RISING [EXTENT OF RISE=LARGE]		FALLING [EXTENT OF FALL=SMALL]		FALLING [EXTENT OF FALL=LARGE]	
	PRINT	CURSIVE	PRINT	CURSIVE	PRINT	CURSIVE	PRINT	CURSIVE	PRINT	CURSIVE
1. (HIGH)	▔ [paˉd]	⌐*(1) [ˉpaid]	⌐ [paˉd]	⌐*(2) [ˉpaid]	N/A	N/A	⌐ [paˉd]	⌐ [ˉpaid]	⌐ [paˉd]	⌐ [ˉpaid]
2. (MID)	╱ [pa´d]	⌐*(3) [ˊpaid]	∨ [pa∨d]	⌐ [ˇpaid]	∨ [pa∨d]	⌐ [ˇpaid]	∧ [pa∧d]	⌐ [ˆpaid]	∧ [pa∧d]	⌐ [ˆpaid]
3. (LOW + LOW-MID)	▬*(4) [pa–d]	⌐ [–paid]	⌐ [pa–d]	⌐ [–paid]	⌐ [pa–d]	⌐ [–paid]	⌐*(5) [pa–d]	⌐ [–paid]	N/A	N/A

* (1) Like an uncrossed "t", but taller

* (2) Written like a cursive "x", but circle distinguishes this from an "x".

* (3) The bar or cross at the top is in one direction only (to the left (rising) or right (falling) and is at the very top. This clearly distinguishes it from a "t" and eliminates confusion, as repeated recognizability tests carried out by us have shown.

* (4) Longer than a hypen – seperate key.

* (5) The up (rising) or down (falling) bar is NOT at the end f the hyphen, but cose to the end.

PART 1: THE NAVLIPI SUMMARY TABLES

9. SUGGESTED DIDACTIC (PEDAGOGICAL) "ALPHABETICAL ORDER" OF NAVLIPI

(ILLUSTRATED WITH PRINT, LOWER CASE ONLY, AND INCLUDING MATRIX ELEMENT NUMBERS IN BRACKETS AND SERIAL # IN LEFT MARGIN)

(Starts overleaf)

A. Vowels, Fundamental

001 q [2(2)(1)], qq [2(2)(1)], a [2(2)(3)], a_o [2(2)(3)], aa [2(2)(4)], aa_o [2(2)(4)],

007 i [1(1)(1)], ii [1(1)(1)], u [3(3)(1)], uu [3(3)(1)],

011 $ℏ_o$ [2(4)(-1)], ℏ [2(4)(2)], ₤ [2(5)(2)], $₤_o$ [2(7)(2)], r [PCON-8], l [2(9)(2)], ₤l [2(11)(2)],

081 $m_o m_o$ [2(12)(2)], $n_o n_o$ [2(13)(2)],

B. Vowels, Derivative

020 ɛ [1(1)(2)], ɛɛ [1(1)(2)], e [1(1)(3)], ee [1(1)(3)], ɔ [1(1)(4)], ɔɔ [1(1)(4)],

026 y [3(1)(1)], yy [3(1)(1)], o/ [3(1)(2)], o// [3(1)(3)],

030 o [3(3)(3)], oo [3(3)(3)], Ω [3(3)(4)], ΩΩ [3(3)(4)],

<u>N.B</u>: Total number of vowels: 45 of which 22 have short/long versions (=44) (not all shown in above list) and one of which is a phonemic condensate.

B. Non Vowels, except clicks, ejectives and implosives

034 ^o_o [1-1], h [6-1], h.. [6-2],

037 k.. [1-3], $k..h_o$ [2-3], g.. [3-3], n.. [5-3], x.. [6-3], ɢ.. [7-3],

043 k [1-4], kh_o [2-4], g [3-4], gh_o [4-4], n_o [5-4], x [6-4], ɢ [7-4],

050 t [1-5], th_o [2-5], ɖ [3-5], $ɖh_o$ [4-5] h [5-5], th_o [6-5], $ɖh_o$ [7-5], ɖ. [8-5], $ɖh_o$ [9-5], h• [10-5],

060 ℏ [30-5], $ℏ_o$ [30-5F], ₤ [31-5],

063 2 [1-6], ï [3-6], °n [5-6], $2h_o$ [6-6], $ïh_o$ [7-6],

068 c [1-7], ch_o [2-7], ɟ [3-7], $ɟh_o$ [4-7], ɲ [5-7], sh_o [6-7] zh_o [7-7],

075 j [28-7], ₤ [31-7],

077 tt [1-8], tth_o [2-8], dt [3-8], dth_o [4-8], n [5-8], tth_o [6-8], dh_o [7-8],

084 r [8-8], rh [11-8], rr [12-8], rrh_o [13-8], (***)

PART 1: THE NAVLIPI SUMMARY TABLES

62

B. Non Vowels, except clicks, ejectives and implosives (continued)

088   l [31-8], lh$_o$ [32-8],

090   lh$_o$ [33-8], lj [34-8], l.. [35-8],

093   s [6-9], z [7-9],

095   t [1-10], th$_o$ [2-10], d [3-10], dh$_o$ [4-10], n [5-10] (PCON),

100   t.. [1-11], d.. [3-11], th$_{o..}$ [6-11],

103   dh$_{o..}$ [7-11], th$_o$ [6-12], dh$_o$ [7-12], ɭ [31-12],

107   f [6-13], v [7-13],

109   p [1-15], ph$_o$ [2-15], b [3-15], bh$_o$ [4-15] m [5-15], ph$_o$ [6-15], bh$_o$ [7-15], ph$_o$ph$_o$ [12-15],

117   w [28-15], w° [28-15b],

(***) r$_o$ [30-8], placed here, is very rare, so not used.

D. Phonemic Condensates *(illustrated with examples where appropriate)*

119   p$_o$ [PCON-1] (aspirate + non-aspirate), p$_\infty$ [PCON-2] (unvoiced + voiced), kh$_\infty$ [PCON-3] (stop + fricative)

122   ph8 [PCON-4] (stop + forward fricative),

123   b$_8$ [PCON-5] (stop + semi-vowel), vw [PCON-6] (semi-vowel + forward fricative), ttr [PCON-7] (stop + flap)

126   xr [PCON-10] [((trill + flap + semi-vowel) in alveolo-dental artition) + (uvular fricative)],

127   a= [PCON-15] Denotes a "mobile, generic" vowel where choice of vowel does not appear to matter, e.g. in some Semitic and Chinese languages.

(PCON-11 to PCON-14, PCON-16, PCON-17 not in alphabetical order since they are very rare.)

E. Tones

In the "alphabetical order", tones will be placed here. However, tones will be language specific. Hence, for tonal languages,
each language's tones will be placed here, in the order that they are taught traditionally in that language. Thus, e.g., for Mandarin, the four tones will be placed here in the order they are traditionally taught, with word examples.

PART 1: THE NAVLIPI SUMMARY TABLES

F. Clicks, Implosives, Ejectives*

128 k̤z̤k̤z̤ [17-3], kz̧ [14-4], kz̧kz̧ [17-4], kz̧' [24-4], gz̧" [27-4],

133 tz̧ [14-5], d̃z̧ [15-5], tz̧n₀ [16-5], tz̧tz̧ [17-5],

137 2z̧ [14-6],

138 cz̧ [14-7], cz̧' [24-7], įz̧' [27-7],

141 ʦz̧ [14-8], dʦz̧ [15-8], ʦz̧n₀ [16-8],

144 lz̧ [18-8], z∞ [2-5], lz̧n₀ [20-8],

147 ʦz̧ [22-8], lz̧ [23-8],

149 ʦz̧' [24-8], dʦz̧" [27-8],

151 sz̧' [25-9], tz̧ [14-10], ʦz̧ [22-10], lz̧ [23-10], tz̧" [27-10],

156 fz̧' [25-13], pz̧ [14-15], pz̧ [1-6], pz̧' [24-15], bz̧' [27-15]

*As these are rare in the world's major languages, they are placed last in the "alphabetical order", and are unlikely to be taught at all, except in the languages to which they apply.

PART 1: THE NAVLIPI SUMMARY TABLES

10. VARIOUS WIDELY-USED WORLD SCRIPTS/ALPHABETS RENDERED IN NAVLIPI

10.1 THE DEWANAAGARI (DEVANAGARI) SCRIPT RENDERED IN NAVLIPI, INCLUDING VARIANTS THEREOF FOR HINDI/URDU, MARAATHI (ONLY SMALL-PRINT GLYPHS GIVEN, FOR CLARITY)

(Starting overleaf)

PART 1: THE NAVLIPI SUMMARY TABLES

65

VOWELS

	FUNDAMENTAL (short and long)			DERIVATIVE				
	Dewanaagari	Navlipi		Dewanaagari	Navlipi In current Dewanaagari usage		Navlipi In original (ancient) usage	
		Print	Cursive		Print	Cursive	Print	Cursive
VELAR	अ	V 2-2-3 a	*a*					
	आ	V 2-2-4 aa	*aa*					
PALATAL	इ	V 1(1)(1) i	*i*	ए	V 1(1)(2) ε	*ε*	V 1(1)(2) ε	*ε*
	ई	V 1(1)(1) ii	*ii*	ऐ**	V 2(2)(4) / V 1(1)(2) aaε	*aaε*	V 1(1)(4) ↄ	*ↄ*
BILABIAL	उ	V 3(3)(1) u	*u*	ओ	V 3(3)(3) o	*o*		
	ऊ	V 3(3)(1) uu	*uu*	औ**	V 2(2)(3) / V 3(3)(1) aau	*aau*	V 3(3)(4) Ω	*Ω*
RETROFLEX	ऋ	V 2(4)(2) ℏ	*r*					
	ॠ	V 2(4)(2) ℏℏ	*rr*					
DENTAL	ऌ	V 2(9)(2) l	*l*					
NASAL				ं	n₀	*n₀*	—	—
GLOTTAL				ः ##	h	*h*	NV 1-1 °	
				ऎ	V 1(1)(4) c	*c*		
				ऒ	V 3(3)(4) Ω	*Ω*		

NB: V= from vowel matrix, NV= from non-vowel matrix
**Originally vowels, today articulated as diphthongs.
Originally the glottal stop, today articulated as a "voiceless aspiration".

PART 1: THE NAVLIPI SUMMARY TABLES

(DEWANAAGARI, cont., NON-VOWELS)

ARTITION	PHONOCHROMATICITY														
	Unaspirated Unvoiced			Aspirated Voiced			Unaspirated Unvoiced			Aspirated Voiced			Nasal		
	R	D	N	R	D	N	R	D	N	R	D	N	R	D	N
GLOTTAL															
VELAR	[KA]	क	k (NV 1-4)	[KHA]	ख	kh_o (NV 2-4)	[GA]	ग	g (NV 3-4)	[GHA]	घ	gh_o (NV 4-4)	[¯NA]	ङ	n_o (NV 5-4)
PALATAL	[CA]	च	c (NV 1-7)	[CHA]	छ	ch_o (NV 2-7)	[JA]	ज	j (NV 3-7)	[JHA]	झ	jh_o (NV 4-7)	[ÑA]	ञ	ɲ (NV 5-7)
RETRO-FLEX	[.TA]	ट	ṭ (NV 1-5)	[.THA]	ठ	$ṭh_o$ (NV 2-5)	[.DA]	ड	ḍ (NV 3-5)	[.DHA]	ढ	$ḍh_o$ (NV 4-5)	[.NA]	ण	ɦ (NV 5-5)
DENTAL	[TA]	त	t (NV 1-10)	[THA]	थ	th_o (NV 2-10)	[DA]	द	d (NV 3-10)	[DHA]	ध	dh_o (NV 4-10)	[NA]	न	n (NV 5-8, NV 5-10)
BILABIAL	[PA]	प	p (NV 1-15)	[PHA]	फ	ph_o (NV 2-15)	[BA]	ब	b (NV 3-15)	[BHA]	भ	bh_o (NV 4-15)	[MA]	म	m (NV 5-15)

PART 1: THE NAVLIPI SUMMARY TABLES

(DEWANAAGARI, cont., NON-VOWELS, cont.)

	SEMIVOWELS			FRICATIVES			(CORRESPONDING VOWELS)		
ARTITION	R	D	N	R	D	N	R	D	N
GLOTTAL				[HA]	ह	NV 6-1 h	[A]	अ	V 2(2)(3) a
VELAR									
PALATAL	[YA]	य	NV 28-7 j	[SHA]	श	NV 6-7 sh₀	[I]	इ	V 1(1)(1) i
RETROFLEX	[RA]	र	PCON-8, NV 8-8 r	[RETRO- FLEX- SHA]	ष	NV 6-5 th₀	[R]	ऋ	V 2(4)(2) ℛ
DENTAL	[LA]	ल	NV 31-8 l	[SA]	स	NV 6-9 s	[L]	ऌ	NV 31-8 l
BILABIAL	[WA]	व	NV 28-15 w				[U]	उ	V 3(3)(1) u

PART 1: THE NAVLIPI SUMMARY TABLES

(DEWANAAGARI, cont., NON-VOWELS, cont.)

Selected Adaptations of Dewanaagari Glyphs (Letters).
(Only six are given for simplicity).

Phone (Roman equivalent)	Adapted Dewanaagari rendition in Hindi, Maraathi, etc.	Parent Dewanaagari [Roman equivalents in brackets]	Navlipi
[f]	फ़	फ [ph]	NV 6-13 f
[z]	ज़	ज [j]	NV 7-9 z
[k.] (uvular stop)	क़	क [k]	NV 1-3 k..
[x] (velar unvoiced fricative)	ख़	ख	NV 2-3 k..h$_o$
[g.] (uvular voiced stop)	ग़	ग	NV 3-3 g..
[d..] (retroflex voiced flap)	ड़	ड	NV 8-5 ḓ.

NB: NV= from non-vowel matrix

PART 1: THE NAVLIPI SUMMARY TABLES

10.2 THE CYRILLIC SCRIPT (ALPHABET) RENDERED IN NAVLIPI

(Starting overleaf)

PART 1: THE NAVLIPI SUMMARY TABLES

Cyrillic/Navlipi

CYRILLIC	ENGLISH EQUIVALENTS	NAVLIPI
а	*a* as in c*a*r	aa V 2(2)(4)
б	*b* as in *b*in	b NV 3-15
в	*v* as in *v*an	v NV 7-13
г	*g* as in *g*un	g NV 3-4
д	*d* as in *d*in	dt NV 3-8
е	*e* as in y*e*t	je NV 28-7/V1(1)(3)
ё	*aw* as in *yaw*n	jΩ NV 28-7/V3(3)(4)
ж	*z* as in a*z*ure	zh$_o$ NV 7-7
з	*z* as in *z*inc	z NV 7-9
и	*ea* as in b*ea*t	ii V 1(1)(1)
й	*y* as in *y*es	j NV 28-7
к	*c* as in *c*at	k NV 1-4
л	*ll* as in pu*ll*	l NV 31-7
м	*m* as in *m*an	m NV 5-15
н	*n* as in *n*et	n NV 5-8/5-10
о	*o* as in st*o*ry	o V 3(3)(3)
п	*p* as in *p*in	p NV 1-15

NB: V= from vowel matrix, NV= from non-vowel matrix

Cyrillic/Navlipi (page 2 of 2)

CYRILLIC	ENGLISH EQUIVALENTS	NAVLIPI
р	Scottish trilled r	NV 12-8 rr
с	s as in sink	NV 6-9 s
т	t as in tin	NV 1-8 tt
у	oo as in mooring	V 3(3)(1) uu
ф	f as in fan	NV 6-13 f
х	ch as in German ach or Scottish loch	NV 6-4 x
ц	ts as in bats	NV1-10/6-9 ts
ч	ch as in chins	NV 1-7 c
ш	sh as in harsh	NV 6-7 sh$_o$
щ	shch as in fresh cheese	NV 6-7/1-7 sh$_o$c
ъ		V 1(1)(1)
ы	i as in bit	i
ь		
э	e as in bet	V 1(1)(3) e
ю	ou as in you	NV 28-7/V 3(3)(1) ju
я	e as in bet	NV 28-7/V 2(2)(4) jaa

NB: V= from vowel matrix, NV= from non-vowel matrix

PART 1: THE NAVLIPI SUMMARY TABLES

10.3 THE ARABIC SCRIPT (ALPHABET) RENDERED IN NAVLIPI

(Starting overleaf)

Arabic (Egyptian (Al Azheu) Pronunciations)-Navlipi

NAME IN ROMAN SCRIPT	GLYPH	NAVLIPI
alif	ا	V 2(2)(3) a
baá'	ب	NV 3-15 b
taa'	ت	NV 1-10/2-10 t, th$_o$
ṯaa'	ث	NV 6-12 th$_o$
gim, jiim	ج	NV 3-7/7-7 j, zh$_o$
haa'	ح	NV 6-2 h..
ḥaa'	خ	NV 6-4 x, xx
daal	د	NV 3-10 d
ḏaal	ذ	NV 7-12 dh$_o$
raa'	ر	PCON-8/NV 8-8 r, rr
zaaii	ز	NV 7-9 z
siin	س	NV 6-9 s
shiin	ش	NV 6-7 sh$_o$
saad	ص	NV 6-9/PO-11 s..
daad	ض	NV 3-5/ PO-11 d..

NB: V= from vowel matrix, NV= from non-vowel matrix

PART 1: THE NAVLIPI SUMMARY TABLES

Arabic (Egyptian (Al Azheu) Pronunciations)-Navlipi

NAME IN ROMAN SCRIPT	GLYPH	NAVLIPI
taa	ط	NV 1-5/PO-11 t..
zaa	ظ	NV 7-9/PO-11 z..
'ayn	ع	NV 1-1 $\circ$
gayn	غ	NV 7-4 g
faa'	ف	NV 6-13 f
qaaf	ق	NV 1-3 k..
kaaf	ك	NV 1-4/2-4 k,kh$_o$
laam	ل	NV 31-8 l
miim	م	NV 5-15 m
nuun	ن	NV 5-8/5-10 n
haa'	ه ,هـ	NV 6-1 h
waaw	و	NV 28-15 w
yaa'	ي	NV 28-7 j

NB: V= from vowel matrix, NV= from non-vowel matrix

PART 1: THE NAVLIPI SUMMARY TABLES

10.4 THE TAMIL SCRIPT (ALPHABET) RENDERED IN NAVLIPI

Tamil/Navlipi VOWELS

GLYPH	NAVLIPI
அ	a — V 2(3)(2)
ஆ	aa — V 2(2)(4)
இ	i — V 1(1)(1)
ஈ	ii — V 1(1)(1)
உ	u — V 3(3)(1)
ஊ	uu — V 3(3)(1)
எ	e, je — V 1(1)(3), NV 28-7/ V 1(1)(3)
ஏ	ɛ — V 1(1)(2)
ஐ	aaɛ — V 2(2)(4)/1(1)(2)
ஒ	o — V 3(3)(3)
ஓ	oo — V 3(3)(3)
ஔ	aau — V 2(2)(4)/3(3)(1)

NB: V= from vowel matrix
NV= from non-vowel matrix

PART 1: THE NAVLIPI SUMMARY TABLES

Tamil/Navlipi Non-Vowels

GLYPH	NAVLIPI
க்	k (NV1-4)
ங்	n₀ (NV5-4)
ச்	c (NV1-7)
ஞ்	η (NV5-7)
ட்	ŧ (NV1-5)
ண்	h (NV5-5)
த்	t (NV1-10)
ந்	n (NV5-8/5-10)
ப்	p (NV1-15)
ம்	m (NV5-15)
ய்	j (NV28-7)
ர்	r (PCON-8/NV8-8)
ல்	l (NV31-8)
வ்	w (NV28-15)
ழ்	$\hbar_0$ (V2(4)(-1))
ள்	ℒ (V2(5)(2))
ற்	rr (NV12-8)
ன்	n (NV5-8/5-10)

GLYPH	NAVLIPI
ஜ்	i̠ (NV3-7)
ஷ்	sh₀ (NV6-7)
ஸ்	s (NV6-9)
ஹ்	h (NV6-1)
க்ஷ்	ksh₀ (NV1-4/6-7)
க	ka (NV1-4/V2(2)(3))
கா	kaa (NV1-4/V2(2)(4))
கி	ki (NV1-4/V1(1)(1))
கீ	kii (NV1-4/V1(1)(1))
கு	ku (NV1-4/V3(3)(1))
கூ	kuu (NV1-4/V3(3)(1))
கெ	ke (NV1-4/V1(1)(3))
கே	kε (NV1-4/V1(1)(2))
கை	kaae (NV1-4/V2(2)(3)/V1(1)(3))
கொ	ko (NV1-4/V3(3)(3))
கோ	koo (NV1-4/V3(3)(3))
கௌ	kaau (NV1-4/V2(2)(3)/V3(3)(1))

NB: V= from vowel matrix, NV= from non-vowel matrix

11. KEYBOARDING IN NAVLIPI

11.1 NUMERICAL (m)(n) or (x)(y) MATRIX NOTATION USED BY THE NAVLIPI KEYBOARD

- The notation is *(x,y)*, with x= *columns* and y= *rows*.
- Thus, e.g., the notation for the current QWERTY *s* key is (3,4), and the notation for the *r* key is (5,3).

(Starts overleaf)

PART 1: THE NAVLIPI SUMMARY TABLES

78

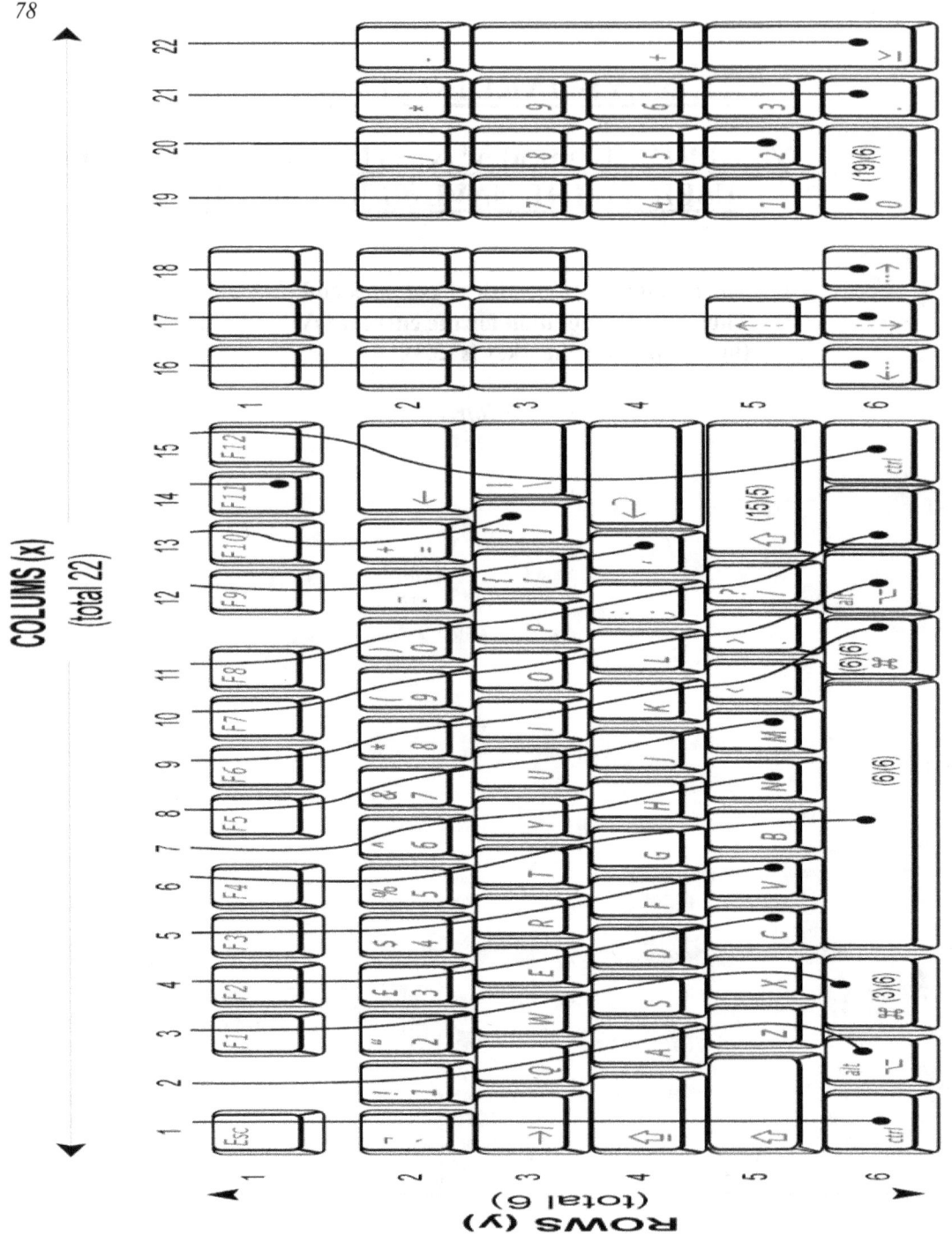

PART 1: THE NAVLIPI SUMMARY TABLES

11.2 SCHEMATIC ILLUSTRATION OF THE FOUR (4) REPRESENTATIONS USED BY NAVLIPI FOR EACH KEY, FOR THE NORMAL, SHIFT, CONTROL AND ALTERNATE POSITIONS

(In the illustration below, the current QWERTY $-4 key is used as an example.)

(5)(2)

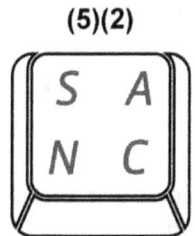

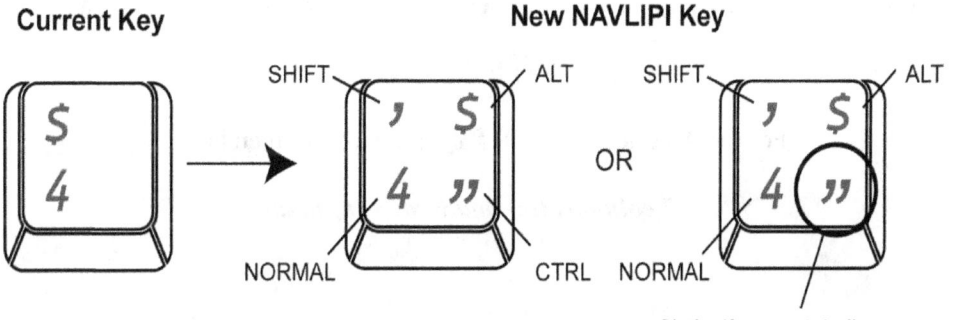

Circle, if present, indicates CTRL + ALT, or (CA) in *Navlipi* notation.

PART 1: THE NAVLIPI SUMMARY TABLES

11.3 COMBINATION OF THE MATRIX NOTATION AND 4-PART KEYS, TO ARRIVE AT (m)(n)(X) KEY NOTATION, USED CONVENIENTLY TO REFER TO ALL NAVLIPI KEYBOARD KEYS

KEY NOTATION

USED FOR REPRESENTATION OF KEYS ON THE NAVLIPI KEYBOARD

(*m*)(*n*)(N,S,C,A)
(*generically referenced as **(m)(n)(X)***)

where **m** is the column number (x-axis, a total of 22), **n** is the row number (y-axis, a total of 6) and **N, S, C** and **A** represent <u>Normal</u>, <u>Shift</u>, <u>Control</u> and <u>Alternate</u>.

When a combination of functions, e.g. CTRL+ALT, is required, then the notation is simply changed accordingly, e.g. as **(C+A)** or simply, and *more preferably*, as **(CA)**.

For the American **QWERTY** keyboard, we then have:

***22 columns (m)** and **6 rows (n)** in all*

PART 1: THE NAVLIPI SUMMARY TABLES

11.4 NAVLIPI KEYBOARD LAYOUT, FOR THE AMERICAN QWERTY KEYBOARD

Layout showing changes to the ALT keys and Spacebar enumerated above. (Only the regular (non-"ergonomic") keyboard is shown for simplicity.)

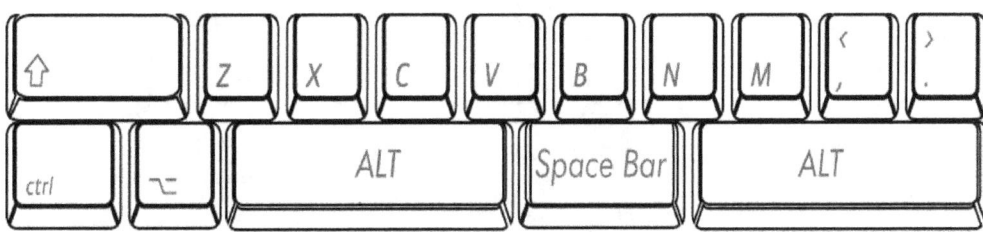

PART 1: THE NAVLIPI SUMMARY TABLES

11.5 LIST AND LAYOUT OF INDIVIDUAL NAVLIPI KEYS

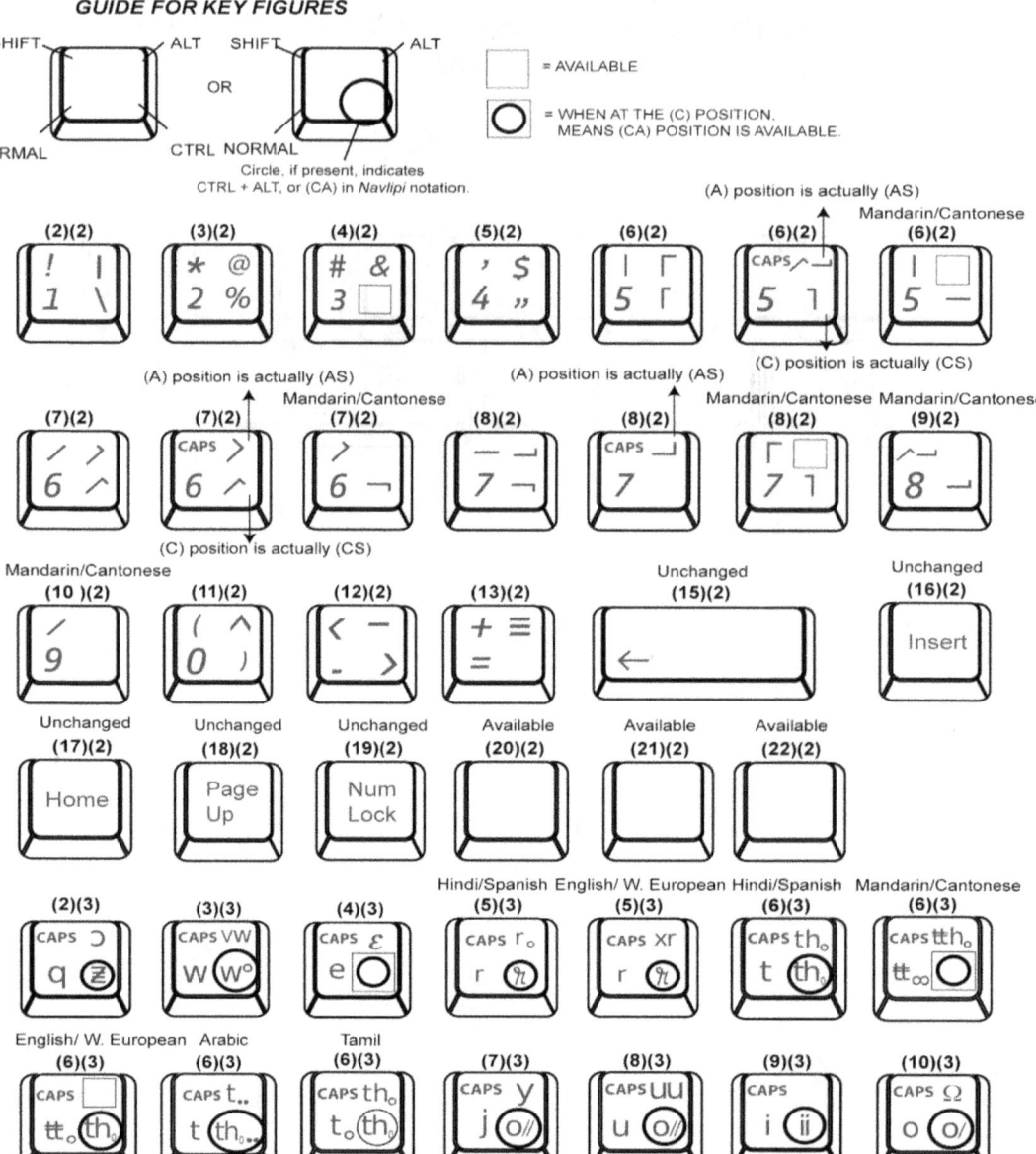

PART 1: THE NAVLIPI SUMMARY TABLES

INDIVIDUAL KEYS (continued)

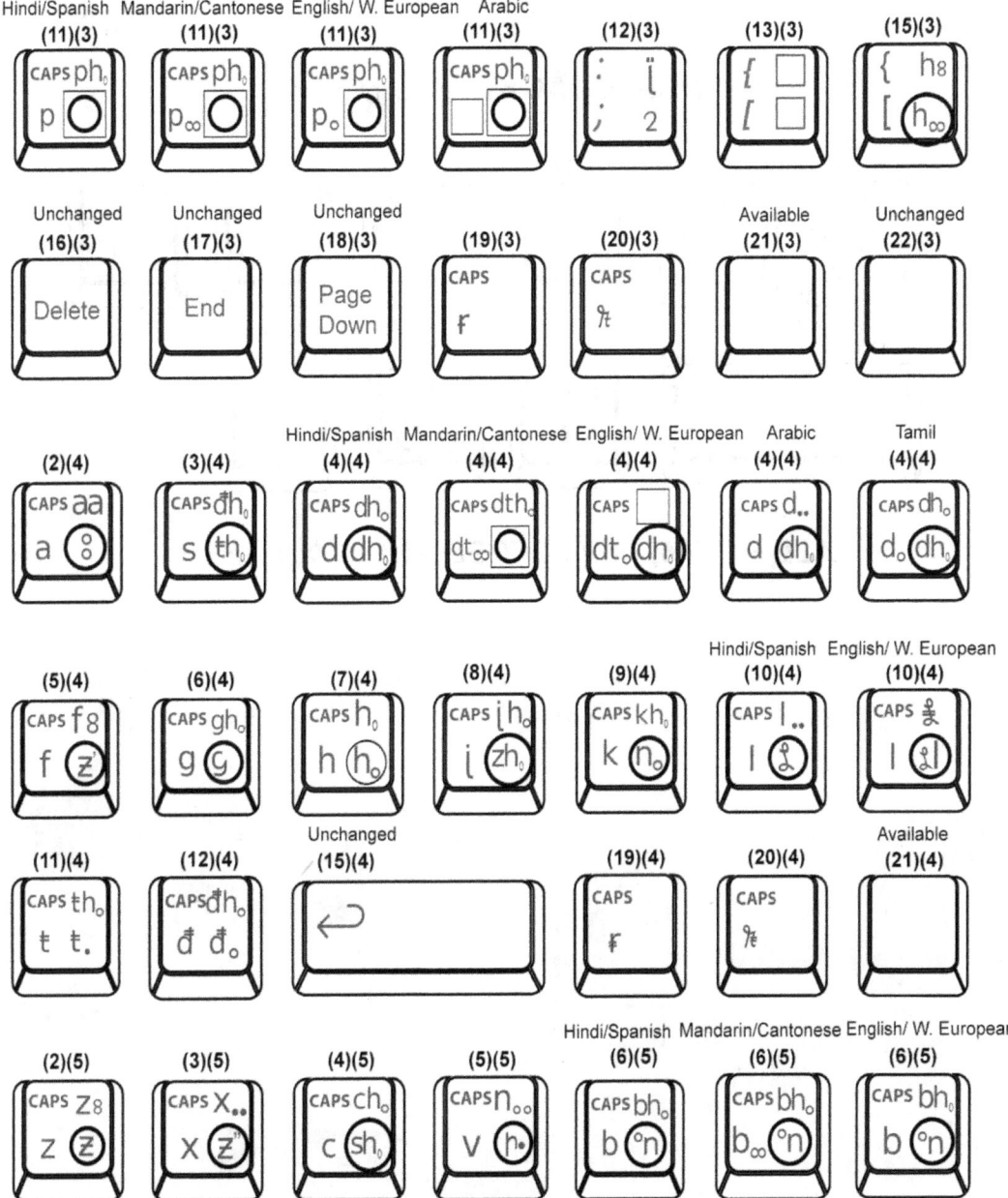

PART 1: THE NAVLIPI SUMMARY TABLES

84

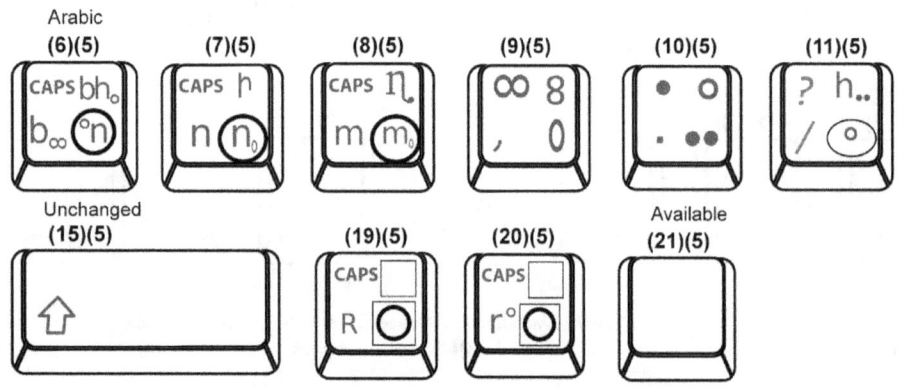

ALL ROW 6, (m)(6), FREE AND AVAILABLE

PART 1: THE NAVLIPI SUMMARY TABLES

11.6 LIST OF KEY CHANGES REFLECTING MAJOR REASSIGNMENTS

(For convenience in reference, keys are addressed in (m)(n)(X) key notation described earlier.)

Serial #	Old Key	Old Key #	New Key #	New Key Representation (*Blank = Place Available*)	Comments
1.	c (*lower case*)	(4)(5)(N)	(2)(3)(A) [ALT+q]	(2)(3) [CAPS, q, key image]	
2.	C (*upper case*)	(4)(5)(S)	(2)(3)(AS) [ALT+SHIFT+q]		
3.	< >	(9)(5)(S) (10)(5)(S)	(12)(2)(S) (12)(2)(C)	(12)(2) [< —, _ >]	< and > moved from comma, period (full-stop) keys to this new key
4.	\ |	(15)(3)(N) (15)(3)(S)	(2)(2)(C) (2)(2)(A)	(2)(2) [!, \, 1, \\]	
5.	] }	(13)(3)(N) (13)(3)(S)	(15)(3)(N) (15)(3)(S)	(15)(3) [},]]	(15)(3)(C, A) are still available (free)
6.	[{	(12)(3)(N) (12)(3)(S)	(13)(3)(N) (13)(3)(S)	(13)(3) [{, []]	(13)(3)(C, A) are still available (free)

PART 1: THE NAVLIPI SUMMARY TABLES

(11.6: List of key changes reflecting major reassignments, cont.)

Serial #	Old Key	Old Key #	New Key #	New Key Representation (*Blank = Place Available*)	Comments
7.	; :	(11)(4)(N) (11)(4)(S)	(12)(3)(N) (12)(3)(S)	(12)(3) key showing : ¨ ; 2	For the new glyphs (12)(3)(C, A) shown, see under Section **16.2.8** below
8.	' (apostrophe) " (quote mark)	(12)(4)(N) (12)(4)(S)	(5)(2)(N) (5)(2)(S)	(5)(2) key showing ' $ 4 "	(12)(4) is now fully available (free)
9.	ALL NUM LOCK NUMBER KEYS, When NUM LOCK is *not* on	(19-22)(2-6)(X)	(19-22)(2-6)(X)		*When NUM LOCK is not on, these keys will be used to render various, very rare phonemic condensates, as discussed later in this chapter. When NUM LOCK is on, they will simply render numbers.*

PART 1: THE NAVLIPI SUMMARY TABLES

11.7 CHANGED NUMBER KEYS, AS TO BE USED IN NAVLIPI

- *The keys for numbers 5 to 9 are shown with their SHIFT, ALT and CTRL places blank, since the characters for the SHIFT setting of these keys in the QWERTY keyboard.*
- *That is to say the characters %, ^, &, * and (, have been moved to other locations in the Navlipi keyboard.*
- *These free places are then to be used for Tones (see further below). Note that the keys (15 to 22)(2), <u>i.e. all the Row # 2 keys in columns 15 through 22, remain unchanged</u>.*

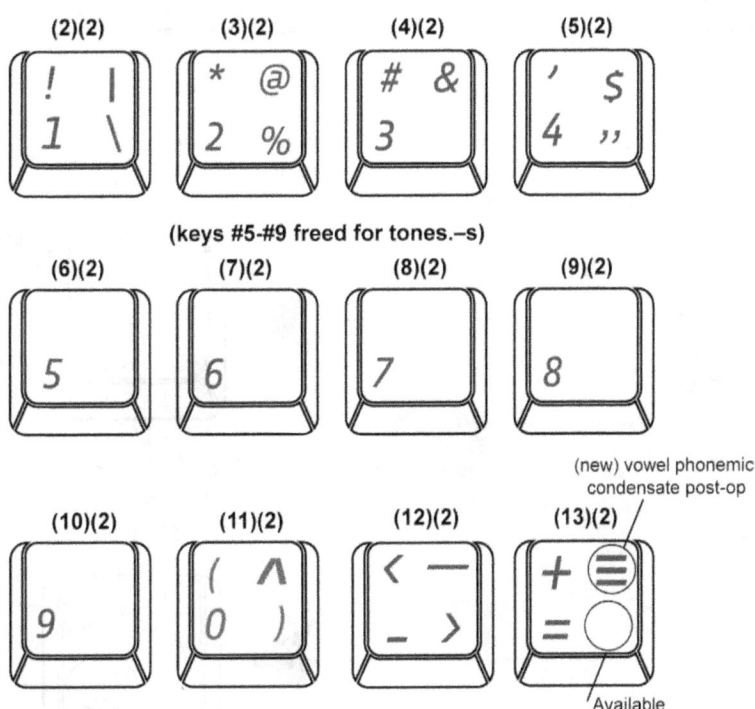

PART 1: THE NAVLIPI SUMMARY TABLES

11.8 LIST OF KEY CHANGES: KEYS WITH HIGH FREQUENCY OF USE AND SOME MAJOR POST-OPS

(Once again, for convenience in reference, the keys are referenced in the (m)(n)(X) key notation described earlier.)

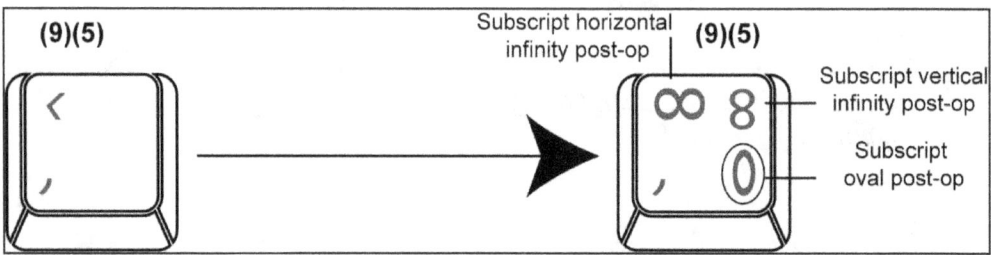

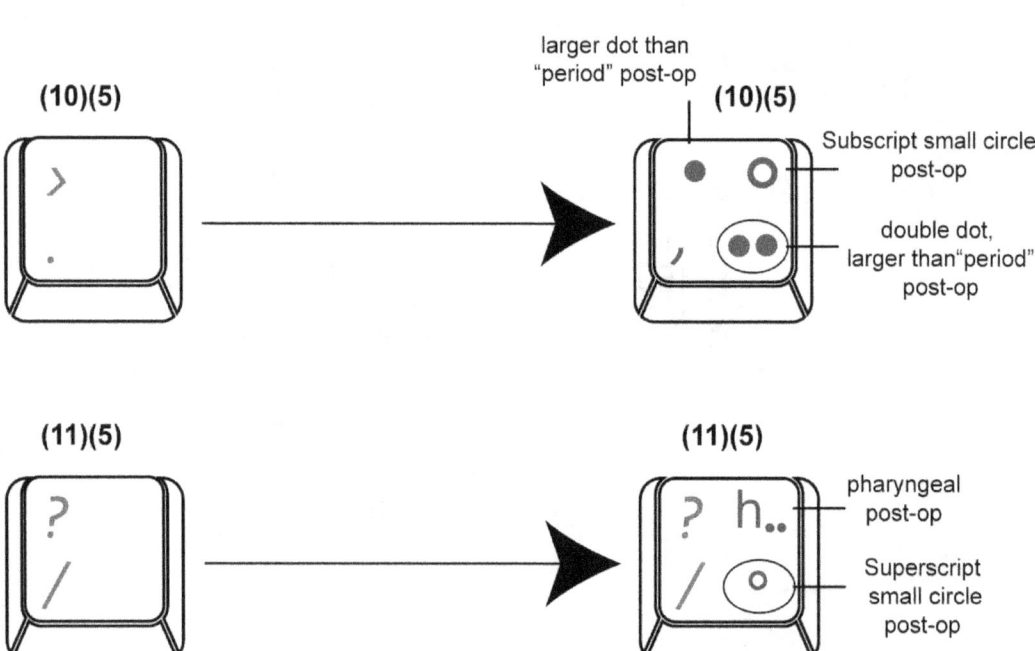

PART 1: THE NAVLIPI SUMMARY TABLES

(List of key changes: High frequency use, major post-op keys, cont.)

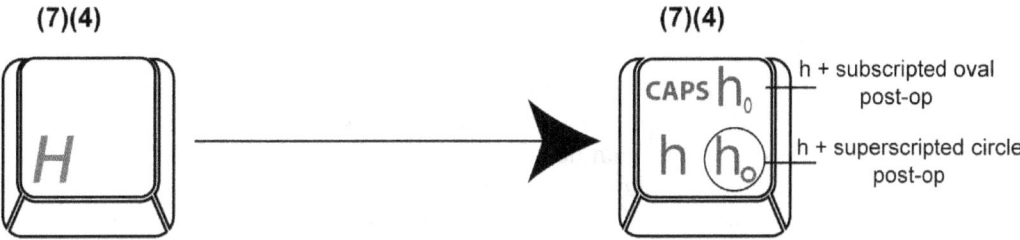

11.9 CENTRAL ("R") KEY AND CENTRAL GLYPHS, INCLUDING PHONEMIC CONDENSATES

- *Navlipi* uses *two (2) major language-specific variants* of the central ("r") key, as shown below.
- Other language-specific *Navlipi* keyboards may use either of the above keyboard variants.

For the ***Hindi/Spanish/Russian/Indonesian keyboard***, we have the representation at right. Here, **(5)(3)(N)** is the most common alveolar tap/flap/semivowel phonemic condensate; **(5)(3)(A)** is the alveolar semivowel; and finally, **(5)(3)(CA)** is the retroflex semivowel. The latter is used in American English, and also Tamil, Mandarin/Cantonese. It may be redundant in this, Hindi/Spanish... keyboard, except for use in Sanskrit.

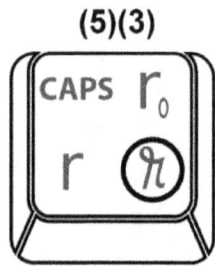

For the ***English/French/German/West European languages keyboard*** (i.e. for West European languages), we have the representation at right Here: **(5)(3)(N)** is the alveolar semivowel only; **(5)(3)(A)** is the phonemic condensate (note that if one needs to use this in other keyboards, e.g. the Hindi/Spanish.. keyboard, then one can simply render it by typing **x** and **r** in sequence; and finally, **(5)(3)(CA)** is the retroflex semivowel, used in American English, also Tamil.

PART 1: THE NAVLIPI SUMMARY TABLES

(11.9, Central ("R") keys, cont.)

Rarely used central glyphs may be summarized as follows:

- The unique Tamil retroflex central with a jaw-forward position in articulation, phonemically distinct from the same central in jaw-normal position and discussed at some length in several other chapters of this book, presents a unique situation. In *Navlipi,* this is rendered as the glyph r_o, i.e. a *script-r* with a subscripted little circle. Since its use is expected to be only for Tamil and thus somewhat rare, rather than assigning a separate key for it, *Navlipi* will simply transcribe this as the serial combination of the two keystrokes, i.e. **(5)(3)(CA) (r)** followed by **(10)(5)(A)** (₀).

- Several ***phonemic condensates*** of central or central plus some other articulation, which are expected to be rarely used, are assigned by *Navlipi* to keys that are commensurate with their rare use. These do not appear in the Table above. Summarizing these:

    - The *alveolar (r+l) (i.e. central + lateral) phonemic condensate*, transcribed as ɼ in *Navlipi*, will use the key **(19)(3)(N)**, i.e. the *Numeric-7* key used with NUM LOCK off.
    - The *retroflex (r+l) (i.e., central + lateral) phonemic condensate*, transcribed as ɼ (script-r with single overstrike) in *Navlipi*, will use the key **(20)(3)(N)**, i.e. the *Numeric-8* key used with NUM LOCK off.
    - The *alveolar (r+l+n) (i.e. central + lateral + nasal) phonemic condensate*, transcribed as ɼ in *Navlipi*, will be use the key **(19)(4)(N)**, i.e. the *Numeric-4* key used with NUM LOCK off.
    - The *retroflex (r+l+n) (i.e. central + lateral + nasal) phonemic condensate*, transcribed as ɼ (script-r with double overstrike) in *Navlipi*, will use the key **(20)(4)(N)**, i.e. the *Numeric-5* key used

PART 1: THE NAVLIPI SUMMARY TABLES

92

with NUM LOCK off.
- The *alveolar (flap + trill + semivowel) central phonemic condensate*, transcribed as **r°** in *Navlipi*, will use the key **(20)(5)(N)**, i.e. the *Numeric-2* key used with NUM LOCK off.
- The "*generic R*" *phonemic condensate*, transcribed as **R** in *Navlipi*, will use the key **(19)(5)(N)**, i.e. the *Numeric-1* key used with NUM LOCK off.

These **rare central glyphs** may then be summarized in the following representations:

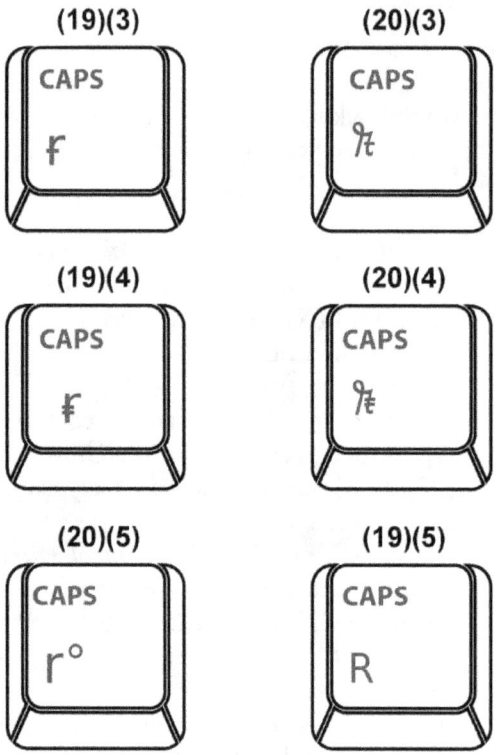

PART 1: THE NAVLIPI SUMMARY TABLES

11.10 MAJOR LATERAL ("L") KEY

- **There is only one major lateral ("L") key.**
- **Other lateral phones are incorporated into phonemic condensates, most of which are in common with central ("R") phones and have been dealt with earlier.**
- ***Navlipi* uses only *two (2) language-specific variants* of the major lateral key. These are represented below.**

For the ***Hindi/Spanish//Indonesian*...** etc. keyboard, we have the key at right. This will also be used for the ***Arabic***, ***Mandarin/Cantonese*** and ***Tamil*** keyboards.

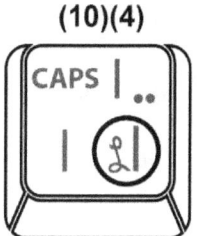
(10)(4)

For the ***English/French/German/West-European languages*...** keyboard, we have:

(10)(4)

PART 1: THE NAVLIPI SUMMARY TABLES

11.11 MAJOR VELAR KEYS LANGUAGE-SPECIFIC IN NAVLIPI

- The velar keys in *Navlipi* are *language-specific*.
- They are also the *Navlipi* keys with one of the largest language-specific diversities.
- The reason the velar keys have such large diversity is because, for many language groups, even very small phonemic distinctions in the velar articulation require the use of a separate key.

The *Navlipi* language-specificities for the *velar* keys are:

(1) The *Hindi/Spanish/Russian/Indonesian.....* group.
(2) The *Chinese languages* group, including all major Chinese languages such as *Cantonese, Fujienese* and *Mandarin*.
(3) The *English/French/German/West-European languages....* group.
(4) The *Arabic* group. This would include Hebrew and Amharic.
(5) The *Tamil* group, including all five major Dravidian languages (Tamil, Telugu, Kannadaa, Malayaalam and Tulu). Each of the above is represented separately below.

Hindi/Spanish/Russian/Indonesian..... group: If we accommodate the aspirated stops, [kh_o] and [gh_o], then we can use a single velar key type for all the languages in this group. The resultant keys are shown below:

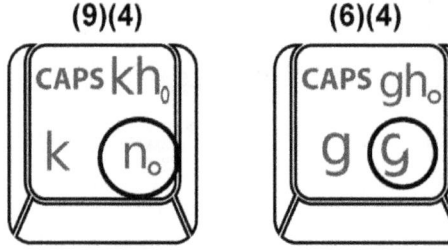

PART 1: THE NAVLIPI SUMMARY TABLES

Chinese languages **group**: The only difference with the *Hindi/...* group is that in place of **(9)(4)(N)**, which is **k** in the *Hindi/...* group, we use the phonemic condensate for unvoiced and voiced velar stop, ([k]+[g]), as applicable to the Chinese languages; these usually articulate this as [g], i.e. **g**$_\square$. The **(6)(4)** key, i.e. the **g** key, would then not be used in the Chinese languages. We nevertheless leave it as it is for the Hindi/... languages.

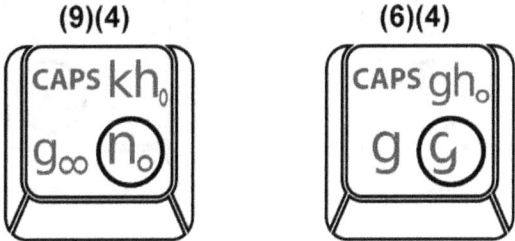

English/French/German/West-European languages....: For both the unvoiced and voiced keys, the **(A)** position, i.e. **(9)(4)(A)** and **(6)(4)(A)**, representing the aspirated stops **kh$_o$** and **gh$_o$**, , would not be used. Nevertheless, we leave them intact; perhaps they may be used in cross-language passages, e.g. an English passage having many Indian names! For the unvoiced key, at the **(N)** position, i.e. **(9)(4)(N)**, the **k** is replaced by **k$_o$**, indicating the (unaspirated + aspirated) phonemic condensate. For the voiced key, the **(N)** position, i.e. **(6)(4)(N)**, retains the pure phone, **g**. This is shown in the figures below.

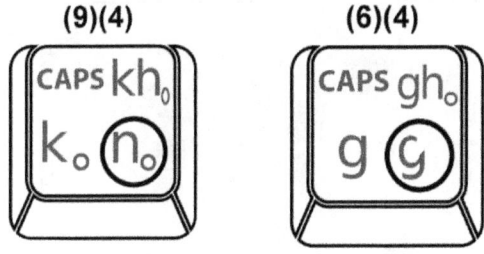

PART 1: THE NAVLIPI SUMMARY TABLES

96

Arabic **group:** The only difference with the *Hindi/..etc..* group is that for **(9)(4)(A)**, we use **k..**, for the uvular stop. Similarly, for **(6)(4)(A)**, we use **g..** .

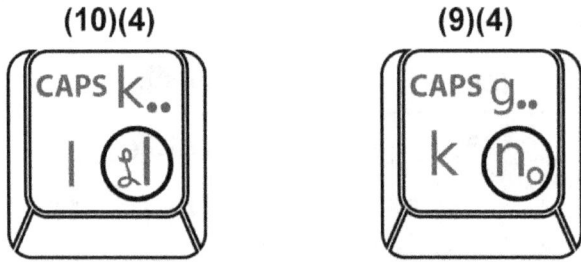

Common velar keys for ALL keyboards: For the velar *unvoiced* and *voiced* fricatives, the keys **(3)(5)** and **(6)(4)**, respectively, are common to *all* language-specific keyboards in *Navlipi*. They are shown below.

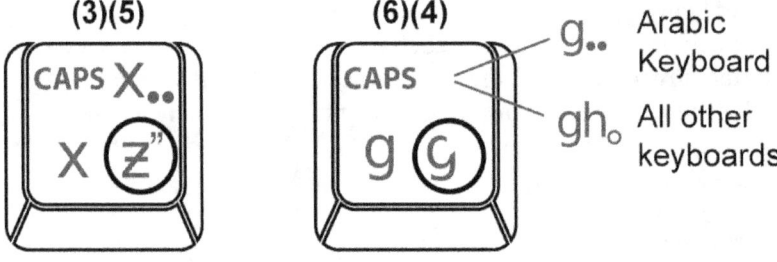

PART 1: THE NAVLIPI SUMMARY TABLES

97

11.12 MAJOR PALATAL AND SIBILANT KEYS

- For these, *Navlipi* is able to use common keys for *all* language groups.
- Thus, these keys are *not* language-specific. They are represented in summary below.

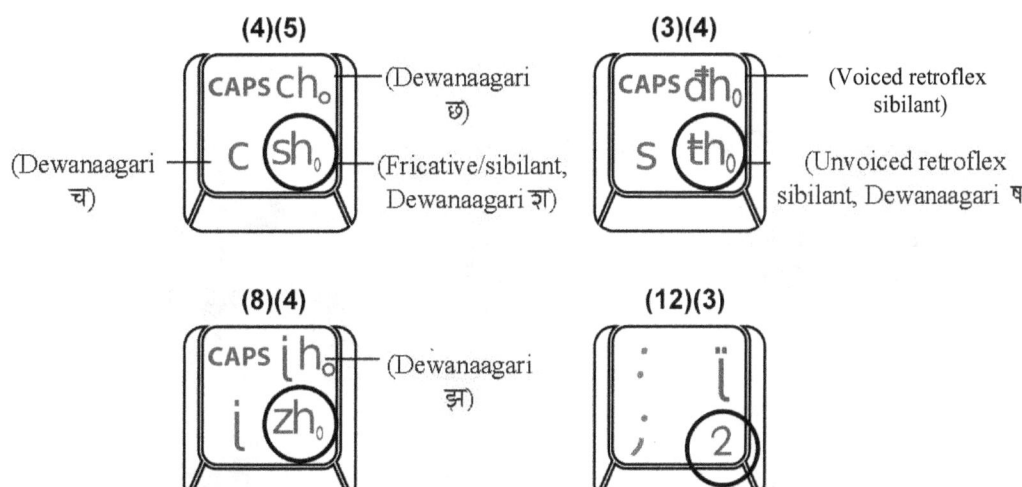

PART 1: THE NAVLIPI SUMMARY TABLES

11.13 MAJOR DENTAL, ALVEOLAR AND RETROFLEX PLOSIVE ("T-D") KEYS

- Much more extensively than even the central ("r") keys described earlier, these keys are *highly language-specific.*
- Accordingly, they are grouped by the language keyboard they are specific to in the representations below.

A. (6)(3) KEY
(Unvoiced; current QWERTY "t" key)

LANGUAGE-SPECIFIC KEYBOARD **KEY**

Hindi/Spanish/Russian/Indonesian....
(Dental, except (CA) position):

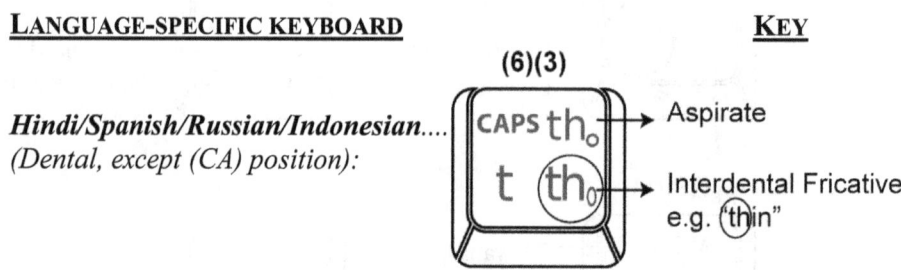

Mandarin/Cantonese
(Alveolar):

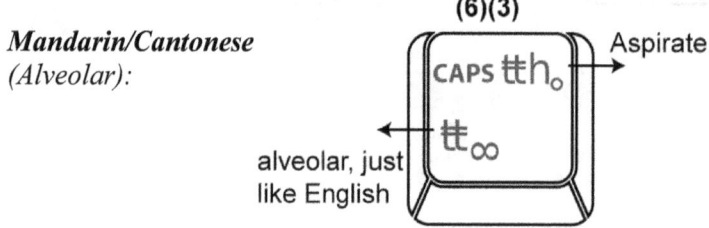

PART 1: THE NAVLIPI SUMMARY TABLES

(11.13, Major dental, alveolar, retroflex plosive ("T-D") keys, cont.)

LANGUAGE-SPECIFIC KEYBOARD   **KEY**

English/ W. European languages...
(Alveolar, except (CA) position):

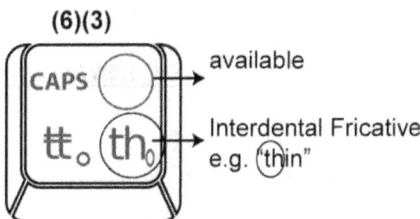

Arabic:

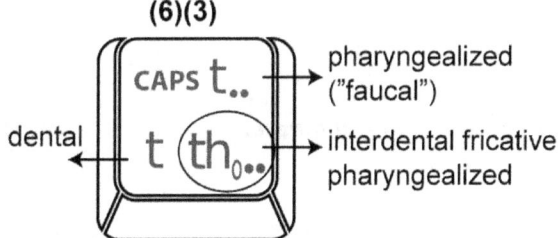

Tamil
(Dental, except (CA) position):

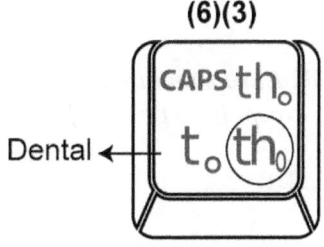

PART 1: THE NAVLIPI SUMMARY TABLES

(11.13: Major dental, alveolar and retroflex plosive ("T-D") keys, cont.)

B. (4)(4) KEY
(Voiced, current QWERTY "d" key)

LANGUAGE-SPECIFIC KEYBOARD   **KEY**

Hindi/Spanish/Russian/Indonesian....
(Dental, except (CA) position):

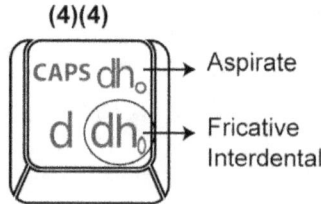

Mandarin and *Cantonese*:
(Alveolar):

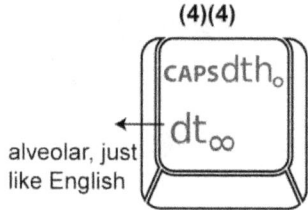

English/ W. European languages...
(Alveolar, except (CA) position):

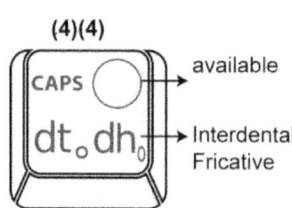

PART 1: THE NAVLIPI SUMMARY TABLES

(11.13: Major dental, alveolar and retroflex plosive ("T-D") keys, cont.)

LANGUAGE-SPECIFIC KEYBOARD   **KEY**

Arabic
(Dental, except (CA) position):

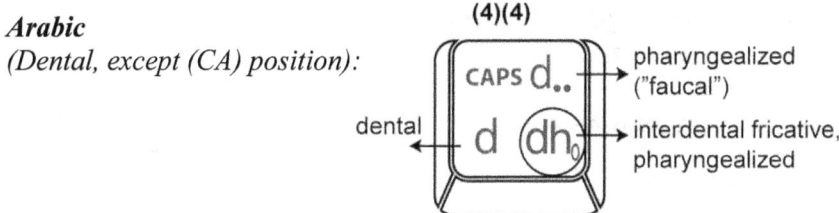

Tamil
(Dental, except (CA) position):

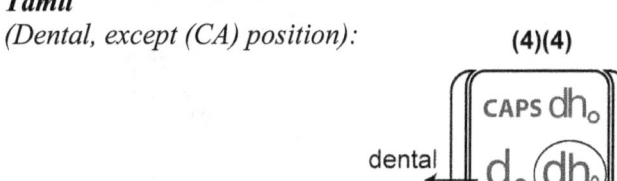

PART 1: THE NAVLIPI SUMMARY TABLES

(11.13: Major dental, alveolar and retroflex plosive ("T-D") keys, cont.)

C. (11)(4), (12)(4) KEYS, FOR RETROFLEX NON-VOWELS
(Current QWERTY (; :) and (' ") keys)

LANGUAGE-SPECIFIC KEYBOARD	**KEY**
Hindi/Spanish/Russian/Indonesian.... *(Retroflex):*	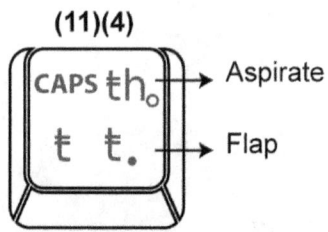
	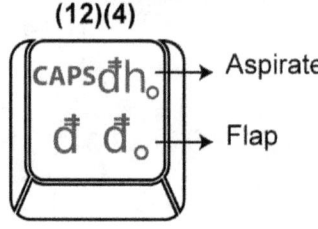

PART 1: THE NAVLIPI SUMMARY TABLES

11.14 SUMMARY OF THE BILABIAL (11)(3) (P) AND (6)(5), (B) KEYS FOR MAJOR LANGUAGE-SPECIFIC KEYBOARDS

- *NOTE*: There would be several other, language-specific keyboards, not shown here for space reasons, e.g. for the *Min-Chinese* languages such as Fujienese/Hokka, for the *Tamil/South Indian* languages, etc.

LANGUAGE-SPECIFIC KEYBOARD   **KEY**

Hindi/Spanish...
Also used for:
    -Russian/East-European-languages
    -Swahili:

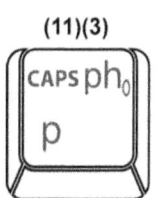

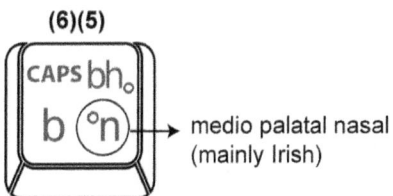

English/French/German/-
West-European-languages:

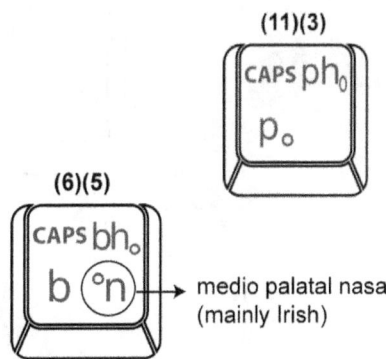

PART 1: THE NAVLIPI SUMMARY TABLES

104

(11.14: Major bilabial keys, cont.)

LANGUAGE-SPECIFIC KEYBOARD   **KEY**

Mandarin/Cantonese:

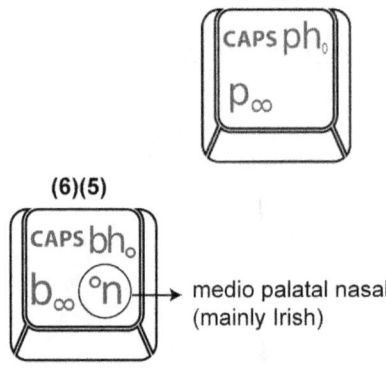

Arabic:

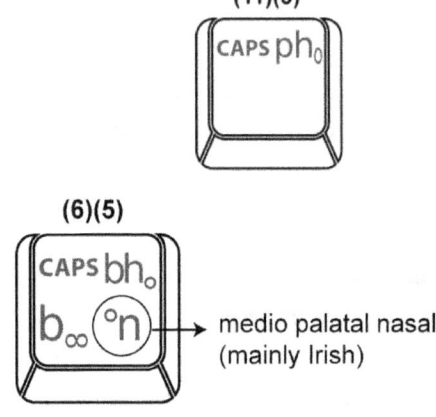

PART 1: THE NAVLIPI SUMMARY TABLES

11.15 MAJOR NASAL ("M-N") KEYS

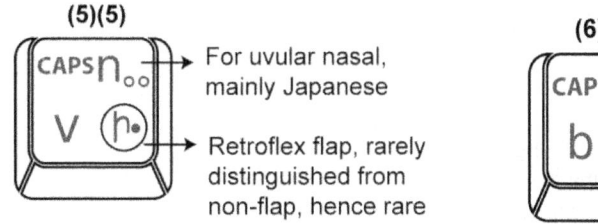

- For uvular nasal, mainly Japanese
- Retroflex flap, rarely distinguished from non-flap, hence rare

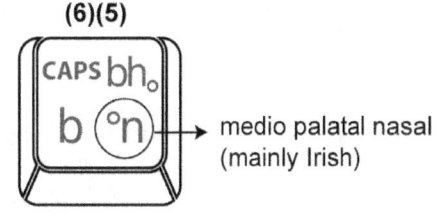

- medio palatal nasal (mainly Irish)

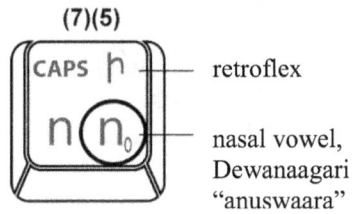

- retroflex
- nasal vowel, Dewanaagari "anuswaara"

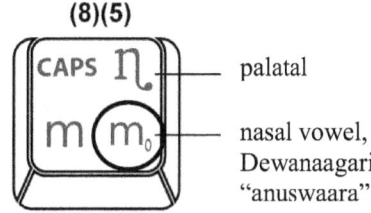

- palatal
- nasal vowel, Dewanaagari "anuswaara"

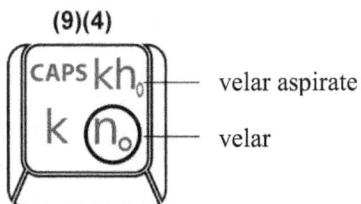

- velar aspirate
- velar

PART 1: THE NAVLIPI SUMMARY TABLES

11.16 MAJOR *STANDARD*-SEMIVOWEL KEYS

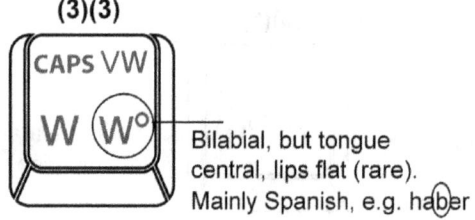

Bilabial, but tongue central, lips flat (rare). Mainly Spanish, e.g. haber

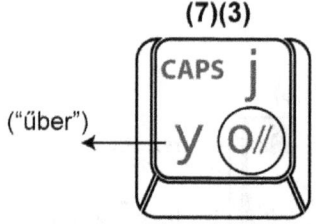

("über")

PART 1: THE NAVLIPI SUMMARY TABLES

11.17 MAJOR *VOWEL* KEYS

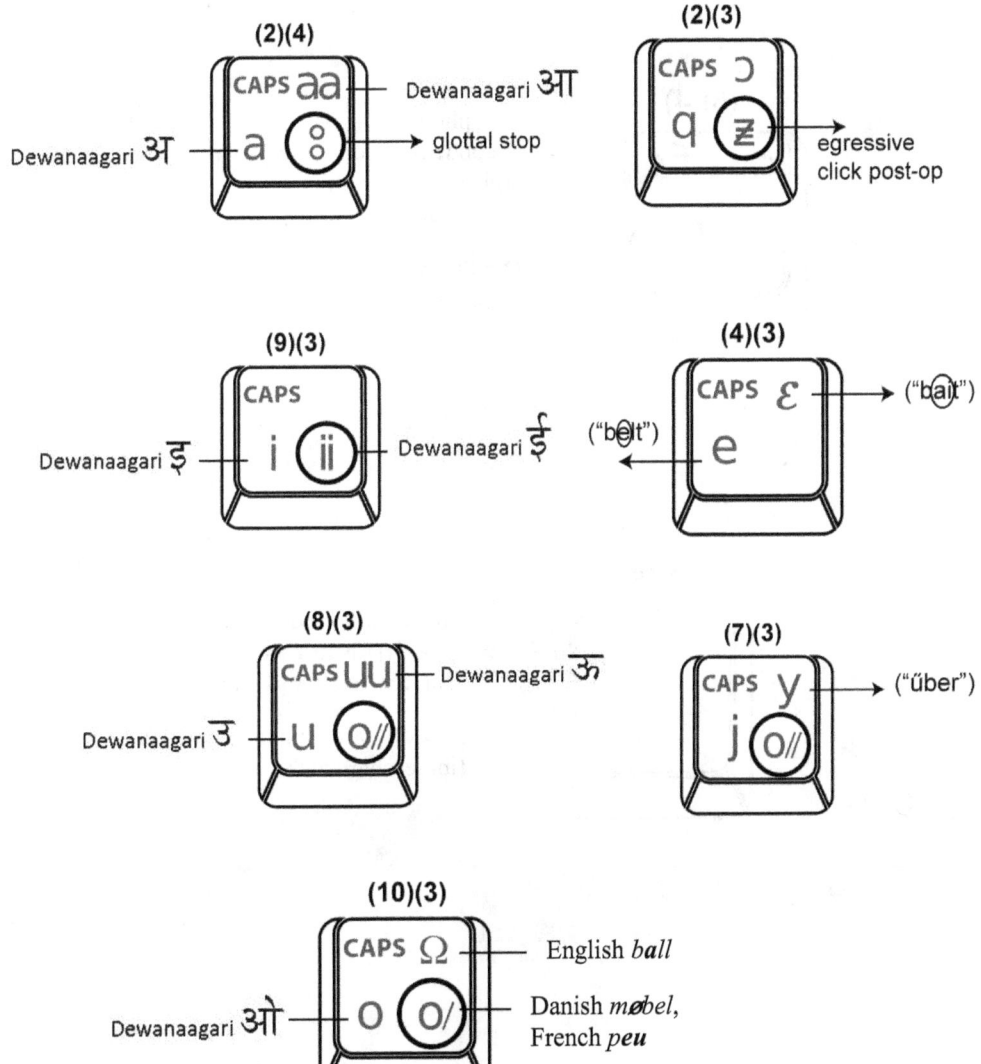

PART 1: THE NAVLIPI SUMMARY TABLES

11.18 SPECIAL *NON-VOWEL* KEYS

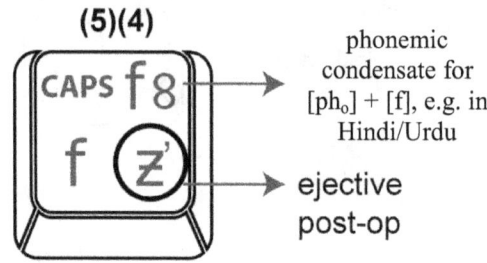

(5)(4) — phonemic condensate for $[ph_o] + [f]$, e.g. in Hindi/Urdu; ejective post-op

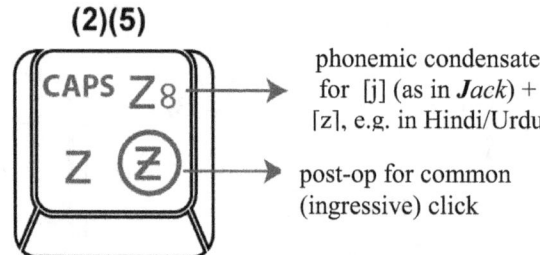

(2)(5) — phonemic condensate for [j] (as in *Jack*) + [z], e.g. in Hindi/Urdu; post-op for common (ingressive) click

PART 1: THE NAVLIPI SUMMARY TABLES

11.19 KEYS FOR VERY RARE POST-OPS

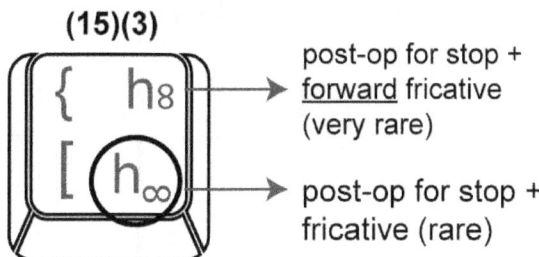

PART 1: THE NAVLIPI SUMMARY TABLES

11.20 TONE KEYS

GENERIC:

Number Key	Navlipi notation	Shift (S)	Ctrl (C)	Alt (A)	Alt + Shift (AS)	Ctrl + Shift (CS)
5	(6)(2)	―	˪	˪	˅	˥ (rare)
6	(7)(2)	╱	˄	˄	˄	˄
7	(8)(2)	―	˥ (rare)	˩	˩	
8	(9)(2)			Use these for combination, unique tones, etc., language specific.		
9	(10)(2)					

PART 1: THE NAVLIPI SUMMARY TABLES

(11.20, Tone Keys, cont.)

MANDARIN/CANTONESE:

Number Key	Navlipi notation	Shift (S)	Ctrl (C)
5	(6)(2)	˧ (*M, C*, 1st tone)	ˉ (*C*, 3rd tone)
6	(7)(2)	˅ (*M*, 2nd tone)	˥ (*C*, 4th tone)
7	(8)(2)	˦ (*M*, 4th tone)	˩ (*C*, 5th tone)
8	(9)(2)	˯ (*M*, 3rd tone)	˥ (*C*, 6th tone) *
9	(10)(2)	ˊ (*C*, 2nd tone)	

* This is treated as low to mid.

M- Mandarin
C- Cantonese

PART 1: THE NAVLIPI SUMMARY TABLES

112

(11.20, Tone Keys, cont.)

YORUBA/IGBO:

Number Key	Navlipi notation	Shift (S) Yoruba	Shift (S) Igbo	Alt (A) Yoruba	Alt + Shift (AS) Yoruba
5	(6)(2)	| (1st tone)	| (1st tone)	⌐ (5th tone)	
6	(7)(2)	/ (2nd tone)	/ or rarely ⌐ (3rd tone)		
7	(8)(2)	− (3rd tone)	− (2nd tone)		¬ (4th tone)

PART 1: THE NAVLIPI SUMMARY TABLES

(11.20, Tone Keys, cont.)

CASHINAHUA (A PERUVIAN LANGUAGE):

Number Key	Navlipi notation	Shift (S)
5	(6)(2)	| (1st tone)
7	(8)(2)	— (2nd tone)

SWEDISH:

Number Key	Navlipi notation	Shift (S)	Alt (A)
5	(6)(2)		⌈ (1st tone)
7	(8)(2)	— (2nd tone)	

PART 1: THE NAVLIPI SUMMARY TABLES

(11.20, Tone Keys, cont.)

INDO-EUROPEAN PITCH ACCENTS (E.G. FOR ANCIENT SANSKRIT, GREEK AND LATIN):

Number Key	Navlipi notation	Shift (S)
5	(6)(2)	| (Uddaata, acute)
6	(7)(2)	∕ (Swarita-1, circumflex-neutral)
7	(8)(2)	— (Anuddaata, grave)
8	(9)(2)	⌐∕ (Swarita-2, circumflex-active)

STRESS (ICTUS) ACCENTS (E.G. AS USED IN SPANISH):

Number Key	Navlipi notation	Shift (S)
5	(6)(2)	| (only 1 stress accent)

11.21 INVENTORY OF LEFTOVER, UNUSED (AVAILABLE) KEYS, REFERENCED BY NAVLIPI KEY NOTATION

- **(5)(5)(C)** (CTRL + V); **(5)(5)(CA)** (CTRL+ALT+V).

- **(4)(3)(A)** (ALT + E).

- **(6)(3)(A)** (ALT + T) and **(4)(4)(A)** (ALT + D) *in the English/West-European language keyboard only.*

- **(11)(5)(A)** (ALT + " /? ") .

- **(13)(2)(C)** (CTRL + " =+ ") .

- **(9)(2)(A)** (ALT + 8) and **(9)(2)(C)** (CTRL + 8) .

- **(10)(2)(A)** (ALT + 9) and **(10)(2)(C)** (CTRL + 9) .

- **(21)(3)(X), (21)(4)(X), (21)(5)(X)** i.e. the **3, 6** and **9** number keys on the NUM LOCK section of the keyboard, in all positions (ALT, CTRL, SHIFT and normal).

- **(20)(2)(X), (21)(2)(X), (22)(2)(X)** i.e. the rightmost three keys (**/, *** and **-**) on the top row of NUM LOCK section of the keyboard, in all positions (ALT, CTRL, SHIFT and normal).

- All FUNCTION keys, **(3 to 18)(1)(X)** in generic *Navlipi* notation, except **(7)(1)(X)**. A total of 15 keys. These may be used in word processors or other programs for other functions. However, if they are free, they could, technically, be used by *Navlipi*.

PART 1: THE NAVLIPI SUMMARY TABLES

12. TRANSCRIPTIONS OF THE FIVE (5) MOST WIDELY SPOKEN LANGUAGES IN THE WORLD (IN 2005) IN NAVLIPI, LISTED IN ORDER OF DECREASING NUMBER OF SPEAKERS

12.1 NOTES ON THE TRANSCRIPTIONS

- *Rather than following the IPA custom of translating an identical story (e.g. the "man with coat in the wind" used in the IPA Handbook) into various languages and then having that transcribed, it is planned to use, wherever possible, passages uniquely applicable to the particular language.*
- *Nearly all passages are no more than one short paragraph.*
- *All passages have been actually spoken and recorded by (usually native) speakers of the language. These audio recordings will eventually be posted on the Navlipi website.*

The language transcriptions herein contain the following parts:

(1) The orthography in the *original script* of the language (e.g. Dewanaagari script for Hindi/Urdu or the Arabic script for Arabic). In the case of multiple scripts being used for a single language, the most widely used script is used. Thus, for Hindi/Urdu, the Dewanaagari (rather than the Arabic-based Urdu) script is used, and if we were to transcribe Serbo-Croat, the Cyrillic script would be used rather than the Roman.

(2) Orthography in a *"simplified Roman" script*. Admittedly crude, but will give a rough idea of the sound of the passage for the reader otherwise unfamiliar with the language in question.

(3) The actual <u>Navlipi</u> *orthography*.

(4) *English translation* of the passage.

PART 1: THE NAVLIPI SUMMARY TABLES

12.2 *MANDARIN* TRANSCRIPTION PASSAGE

TRANSCRIPTION OF MANDARIN PASSAGE INTO NAVLIPI

Lines in the transcription give:

(1) The Chinese script.
(2) The Roman transcription according to the official Chinese government method.
(3) Rough, word-for-word translation, into English.
(4) The Navlipi PRINT transcription.
(5) The Navlipi CURSIVE transcription.
(In the latter two, the alternative transcription for nasalizations is given in square brackets.)

NOTE: *For clarity, the Navlipi post-ops for the TONES are highlighted in dotted circles with an arrow pointer for cursive.*

Tones:

1st *tone*: Level, high, Chinese government Roman transcription (ˉ). *Navlipi* print transcription: |

2nd *tone*: Rising, mid to high, Chinese government Roman transcription (ˊ). *Navlipi* print transcription:

╱

3rd *tone*: Falling (mid-to-low) + rising (low-to-mid), Chinese government Roman transcription (ˇ). *Navlipi* print transcription:

⌒⌐

4th *tone*: Falling, high-to-low, Chinese government Roman transcription (ˋ). *Navlipi* print transcription:

⌐

English translation of passage:

Who is he? Is he your friend? Yes, he is my friend. His name is Xie Wen. He teaches at Beijing University. Don't you know him? I have heard of him. He is from Beijing, isn't he?

PART 1: THE NAVLIPI SUMMARY TABLES

(Mandarin transcription, cont.)

(1) 他 是 谁？
(2) Tā shì shuí?
(3) He is who?

(4) Th₀aal sh₀qſ sh₀wii↗?

(5)  *[handwritten Navlipi script]* ?

(1) 他 是 你 朋友 吗？
(2) Tā shì nǐ péngyou ma?
(3) He is your friend?

(4) Th₀aal sh₀qſ nii↗⌐ ph₀q↗n₀gjou

(5)  *[handwritten Navlipi script]*

PART 1: THE NAVLIPI SUMMARY TABLES

(Mandarin transcription, cont.)

(1) 是，他 是 我 朋友。
(2) Shì, tā shì wǒ péngyou.
(3) Yes, he is my friend.

(4) Sh₀qɼ, th₀aaI　　Sh₀qɼ　　wo↗–,　ph₀q↗n₀gjou.

(5)  *[handwritten Navlipi script]*

(1) 他　叫 谢文，在
(2) Tā　jiào Xiè Wén, zài
(3) He (is) called Xie Wen, at

(4) Th₀aaI　ȷiaaoɼ　Fh₀iɛɼ　We↗n,zaaiɼ

(5)  *[handwritten Navlipi script]*

PART 1: THE NAVLIPI SUMMARY TABLES

(Mandarin transcription, cont.)

(1) 北京 大学 教书。
(2) Běijīng Dàxué jiāoshū.
(3) Peking University teaches.

(4) B∞εi⌃—⌊iln₀g D∞aatth₀wε⌐ ⌊iaao'sh₀u'.

(5) [handwritten Navlipi script]

(1) 你 不 认识 他 吗?
(2) Nǐ bú rènshi tā ma?
(3) You not know him?

(4) Nii⌃— B∞u⌐ ɾqᴦnsh₀i th₀aa',maa?

(5) [handwritten Navlipi script]

PART 1: THE NAVLIPI SUMMARY TABLES

12.3 *HINDI/URDU* TRANSCRIPTION PASSAGE

TRANSCRIPTION OF HINDI/URDU PASSAGE INTO NAVLIPI

Note to reader unfamiliar with these languages:

- *Hindi and Urdu are essentially the same language. The base, everyday vocabulary is identical. The higher vocabulary is preferentially derived from Sanskrit roots in Hind and from Arabic or Faarsi roots in Urdu.*
- *Common street "Hindi", e.g. as spoken today in the streets of Delhi, has many, many words of Arabic and Faarsi origin, and, conversely, common street "Urdu", e.g. as spoken today in the streets of Karachi, has many words of Sanskrit origin.*
- *Thus, in the street in India or Pakistan where these languages are spoken, both word origins are, generally, equally well understood, and there is really no distinction between Hindi and Urdu, unless one is reading high-level poetry. This is in spite of some efforts in the 1990's in Pakistan to "cleanse" Urdu of Sanskrit-based words.*
- *Thus, e.g., samay (Hindi, Sanskrit origin) and waqt (Urdu, Arabic origin), for "time", or samaachaar (Hindi, Sanskrit origin) and khabar (Urdu, Arabic origin) for "news", are equally well understood in the street in India. This situation might thus be somewhat compared to German, where, e.g., the Germanic-origin auskunft and the Latin-origin information have similar though not identical meanings.)*
- *For the written language only, an important difference is that Hindi is written in Dewanaagari script and Urdu is written in an adapted, Arabic-based script. This may be compared to Serbo-Croat, which may be written in both the Cyrillic and Roman alphabets.*

PART 1: THE NAVLIPI SUMMARY TABLES

122

Lines in the transcription give:

(1) The Dewanaagari script.
(2) The "rough" Roman transcription, in italics.
(3) The Navlipi PRINT transcription.
(4) The Navlipi CURSIVE transcription.
(In the latter two, the alternative transcription for nasalizations is given in square brackets.)

English translation of passage:

One beautiful day, a man and a woman (couple, husband-wife) went out for a walk with their two beautiful children. The sun was shining, filling the day with light. The kids were weaving circles around their parents. The whole family sat down under the shade of a big banyaan tree. In their pleasure, the parents went to sleep. Who knows what dreams they had? The kids continued playing.

PART 1: THE NAVLIPI SUMMARY TABLES

(Hindi transcription, start):

(1) एक सुन्दर दिन, एक आदमी और औरत
(2) Ek sundar din, ek aadmii aur aurat

(3) Eεk sundar din, εεk aadmii Ωr Ωrat

(4) *Eεk sundar din, εεk aadmii Ωr Ωrat*

(1) (मिया बिबी, वधुवरे),
(2) (miyaa biibii, wadhuware),

(3) (mijaa biibii, vwadh₀u vwarε),

(4) *(mijaa biibii, vwadhuwarε),*

(1) अपने दो सुन्दर बच्चों के साथ, घूमने निकले।
(2) apne do sundar bachchon ke saath, ghuumne nikle.

(3) apnε do sundar baɔɔo~ [baɔɔon₀] kε saath₀, gh₀uumnε niklε.

(4) *apnε do sundar baɔɔõ [baɔɔoy] kε saath, ghuumnε niklε.*

PART 1: THE NAVLIPI SUMMARY TABLES

(Hindi transcription, cont.)

(1) सूरज चमक रहा था,
(2) Suuraj chamak rahaa thaa,

(3) Suuraj camak rahaa th₀aa,

(4) *Suuraj camak rahaa thaa,*

(1) दिन को भरपूर उजाला देते ।
(2) din ko bharpurr ujaalaa dete.

(3) din ko bh₀arpuur uɟaalaa dɛtɛ.

(4) *din ko bharpuur ujaalaa dete.*

(1) बच्चे माबाप के फेरे ले रहे थे ।
(2) Bachche maabaap ke phere le rahe the.

(3) Baccɛ maabaap kɛ ph₈ɛrɛ lɛ rahɛ th₀ɛ.

(4) *Baccɛ maabaap kɛ ph₈ɛrɛ lɛ rahɛ thɛ.*

PART 1: THE NAVLIPI SUMMARY TABLES

(Hindi transcription, cont.)

(1) सब परिवार एक बन्यान पेड़

(2) *Sab pariwaar ek banyaan ped*

(3) Sab   parivwaar   ɛk banjaan   pɛɗ.

(4) *Sab parivwaar ɛk banjaan pɛɗ*

(1) कि बड़ि छाये में बैठे ।

(2) *ki badi chhaaye mein baithe.*

(3) ki baɗ.i   ch₀aajɛ   mɛ~ [mɛn₀]   beeth₀ɛ

(4) *ki baɗi chaajɛ mɛ̃ [mɛn] beethɛ*

(1) आनन्द में आदमी और

(2) *Aanand mein aadmii aur*

(3) Aanand   mɛ~ [mɛn₀]   aadmii   Ωr

(4) *Aanand mɛ̃ [mɛn] aadmii Ωr*

PART 1: THE NAVLIPI SUMMARY TABLES

(Hindi transcription, cont.)

(1) उसकी बीबी सो गए ।
(2) *uskii biibii so gae.*
(3) uskii   biibii so   gaɛ.
(4) *uskii biibii so gaɛ.*

(1) पता नहिं क्या सपने पाये ।
(2) *Pataa nahin   kyaa sapne paaye.*
(3) pataa   nahi~[nahin₀]   kjaa   sapnɛ   paajɛ.
(4) *Pataa nahĩ [nahin₀] kjaa sapnɛ paajɛ.*

(1) बच्चे खेलते रहे ।
(2) *Bachche khelte rahe.*
(3) Baccɛ   kh₀ɛltɛ   rahɛ.
(4) *Baccɛ khɛltɛ rahɛ.*

PART 1: THE NAVLIPI SUMMARY TABLES

12.4 *ENGLISH* TRANSCRIPTION PASSAGE

TRANSCRIPTION OF ENGLISH PASSAGE (AMERICAN ENGLISH PRONUNCIATION) INTO NAVLIPI

Lines in transcription give:

(1) The English.
(2) The Navlipi PRINT transcription.
(3) The Navlipi CURSIVE transcription.
(In the latter two, the alternative transcription for nasalizations is given in square brackets.)

(1) A man and a woman go out

(2)   Q   mɔɔn   ɔndt   q   wumqn   gou   aautt$_o$

(3) 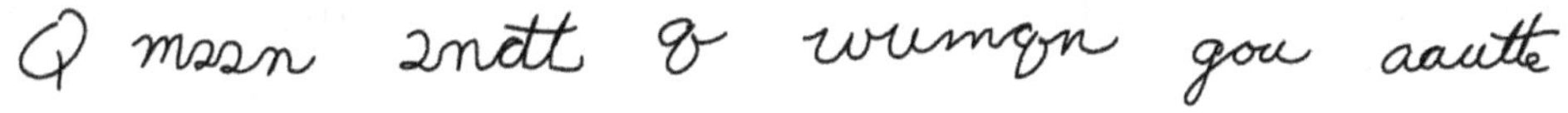 *[cursive]*

(1) for a walk with their

(2)   fΩr   q   wΩk   widh$_o$ dh$_o$εqʔ

(3) *[cursive]*

(1) two beautiful children.

(2)   tt$_o$uu   bjuutt$_o$iful   cildtʔqn.

(3)  *[cursive]*

PART 1: THE NAVLIPI SUMMARY TABLES

(American English transcription, cont.)

(1) It is a sunny day.

(2)   Itt$_o$ iz   q   sani   dtɛi.

(3) *Itte iz q sani dtɛi.*

(1) They sit down on the grass

(2)   Dh$_o$ɛi   sitt$_o$ dtaaun   Ωn   dh$_o$q   grɔɔs

(3) *Dhɛi sitte dtaaun Ωn dhq grɔɔs*

(1) below a shady tree.

(2)   bi$_o$ou   q   sh$_o$ɛdtii   tt$_o$rii.

(3) *bilou q shɛdtii ttɛrii.*

PART 1: THE NAVLIPI SUMMARY TABLES

(American English transcription, cont.)

(1) The children play nearby.

(2) Dhq   cildtʱqn   plɛi   njqʱbaaɛ.

(3) *Dhq cildtʱqn plɛi njqʱbaaɛ.*

(1) After some time,

(2) ɔftt₀qʱ   sam   tt₀aaim,

(3) *ɔfttəqʱ sam ttəaaim,*

(1) they head home.

(2) dh₀ɛi   hedt   houm.

(3) *dh₀ɛi hedt houm.*

PART 1: THE NAVLIPI SUMMARY TABLES

12.5 *SPANISH* TRANSCRIPTION PASSAGE

TRANSCRIPTION OF SPANISH PASSAGE INTO NAVLIPI

Lines in the transcription give:

(1) The Spanish.
(2) The Navlipi PRINT transcription.
(3) The Navlipi CURSIVE transcription.
(*In the latter two, the alternative transcription for nasalizations is given in square brackets.*)

English translation of passage:

Another earthquake sufficiently strong to generate a small tsunami with a height of two meters occurred last week below Indonesia. The quake was 6.9 on the Richter scale. The inhabitants of the coastal areas were told to move temporarily to higher locations.

(1) Un otro terremoto suficientemente

(2) Uun   otro   terrɛmoto   suuficientɛmentɛ

(3)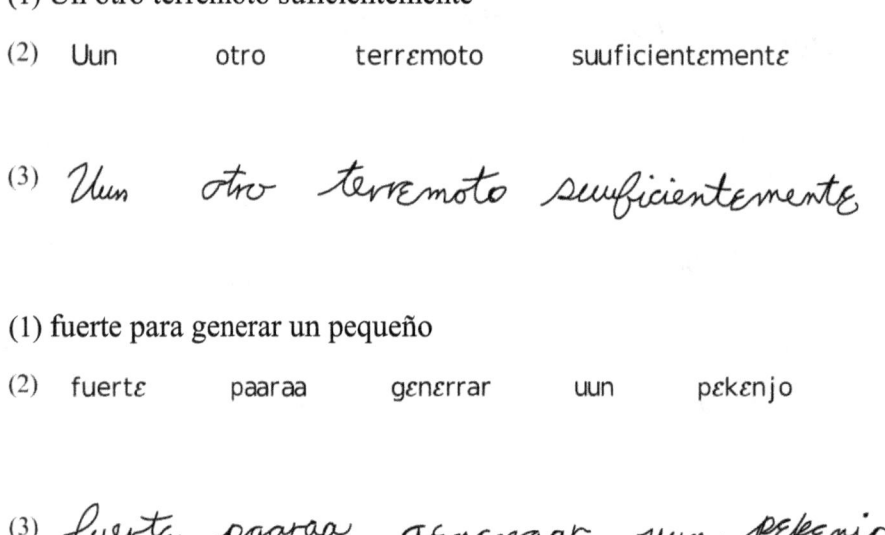

(1) fuerte para generar un pequeño

(2) fuertɛ   paaraa   genɛrrar   uun   pɛkɛnjo

(3)

(Spanish transcription, cont.)

(1) tsunami con una ola de dos metros

(2) tsuunaami kon uunaa olaa dɛ dos metros

(3) *tsuunaamii kon uunaa olaa dɛ dos metros*

(1) ocurrido la semana pasada dejó

(2) okurriido laa sɛmaanaa paasaadaa dɛhó

(3) *okurriido laa sɛmaanaa paasaadaa dɛhó*

(1) a Indonesia. El sismo estaba de 6,9 grados

(2) aa Indoniisiaa. el siismo estaabaa dɛ 6,9 graados

(3) *aa Indoniisiaa. El siismo estaabaa dɛ 6,9 graados*

(1) en la escala de Richter. Se les recomendó

(2) en laa eskaalaa dɛ rixtqr. Sɛ les rrɛkomɛndó

(3) *en laa eskaalaa dɛ rixtqr. Sɛ les rrɛkomɛndó*

PART 1: THE NAVLIPI SUMMARY TABLES

(Spanish transcription, cont.)

(1) a los habitantes de las áreas costeras

(2) a los haabitaantɛs dɛ laas áarrɛaas kosteerraas

(3) *a los haabitaantɛs dɛ laas áarrɛaas kosteerraas*

(1) que se movieran por un tiempo

(2) kɛ sɛ moviɛrraan por uun tiempo

(3) *kɛ sɛ moviɛrraan por uun tiempo*

(1) a suelo más alto.

(2) aa suelo maás aalto.

(3) *aa suelo maás aalto.*

PART 1: THE NAVLIPI SUMMARY TABLES

12.6 *ARABIC* TRANSCRIPTION PASSAGE

ARABIC (SYRIAN PRONUNCIATION)

Notes:

The original Arabic is given first. Next, in order, are the rough Roman transcription, the *Navlipi* PRINT transcription and the *Navlipi* CURSIVE transcription. (In the latter two, the alternative transcription for nasalizations, where applicable, is given in square brackets.)

Approximate English of the Passage:

A man and a woman go out for a walk with their two beautiful children, a girl and a boy, whom they love very much. It is a sunny day. They sit down on the grass below a shady tree. The children play nearby at the bank of a stream. The boy yells. He is hurt. His sister runs to their parents to tell them. She is worried. The parents decide it is time to go home. They gather their belongings, get the children, and head home.

PART 1: THE NAVLIPI SUMMARY TABLES

(Arabic transcription, cont.)

Original Arabic:

إستيقظ السا بُ الطويل القامةِ فجْأةً وكأنّهُ يُكملُ آخرَ ما تبقى من حُلمٍ مُزعِج. ألقى نظرةً مِنَ الشُبّاكِ كانَ يوماً جميلاً. الشَمسُ كانتْ ساطعةً وبالرَغمِ مِن تجاورِها الأُفقِ ما زالَتْ تغلُوها مَسحةٌ وتُنقلِبُهُ اللَونِ آثارَ الشُروقِ. تَثاءَبَ وتَمَطّطَ ثمّ فتَحَ النافذةَ فجْأةً زفْرَةَ العَصافيرِ وكأنّها مَدينةٌ.

كالمُعتادِ في كلّ صَباح أخَذَ وعاءَ ماءٍ فارغ لِمَلئهِ مِنَ المضَخّةِ في القَريَةِ المُجاوِرةِ وغادرَ المَنزلَ مُعْطَشاً طَوَى البَيْنَ تمنّى مُلاقاةَ جديدَتِهِ الحَديدَةَ التي الّتي بها هُناكَ بالأُمسِ سيكونُ يوماً جميلاً لو قَدِمَتْ.

PART 1: THE NAVLIPI SUMMARY TABLES

(Arabic transcription, cont.)

Rough Roman, Navlipi PRINT and Navlipi CURSIVE Transcriptions:

Estaeyaqata eshaabu attawilu alqamati

Ɔstɔaak..at̪a   esh₀aabu   at..aawilu   alk..amati

faejaeʻaeten wo kaannau yukmelu

Fɔjɔ8ɔten   wo   kaannaau   jukmelu

aʼ-kherae maetaebaeqae men holmen mozeshe~.

åɛ   axɛyc   mɔtɔbɔk..ɔ   men   holmen   mozesh₀e~
[mozesh₀en₀]

Alqae nalhraten miinaa aeʼshoubeki.

Alk..ɔ   nalh₀raten   miinaa   ɔɔ8   sh₀uubeki.

PART 1: THE NAVLIPI SUMMARY TABLES

(Arabic transcription, cont.)

O kaanaa yaaoume~ jaemilaen.

O   kaanaa   jaaoumɛ~ [mɛn₀]   ɟemilɔn.

Ashaemsu kaenet saetaataan waa berraaghme

A sh₀ɔmsu   kɔnet   sɔt   aaˤ   taan   waa   beraaɠmɛ

mean taajaawezehae aloufouq mmmae zaelet

mɛaan   taaɟaawɛzɛzhɔ   aloufouk..   m₀m₀mɔzɔɔlet

taa~luhaa maashaatun burtukaliiaatu

taa~ [taan₀]   lu haa   maas   haatun   burtukaliiaatu

allaawne aalhaafaaraa shuruq.

allaaw   nɛ   aalh₀aafaavaa   sh₀uruk..

PART 1: THE NAVLIPI SUMMARY TABLES

(Arabic transcription, cont.)

Taethaeaabae wae taemaataataa.

Te th₀ɔɔ aa bɔɔ cw tɔ maataataa

Thuma faetaehae aelnaefelhata, faja'at zoqzoqaetu.

th₀uma fet ɔɔhɔɔ ɔlnɔ fɛth₀ata, faja⁸at zok..zok..ɔtu

al'assaefiire waa. Kae'anna-haa thaay-fuu~.

al⁸assɔfiirɛ   waa.   kɔ⁸annahaath₀aai   [fuu~].
                                              [fuun₀].

Kalmoaataede fi kolli saabaehii~ aakhaa thae

kalmoaatɔdɛ   fi   kolli   saabɔɔhe   aaxaa   th₀ɔ

PART 1: THE NAVLIPI SUMMARY TABLES

(Arabic transcription, cont.)

weaeae maein faereghiin limalehe

wɛ   ɔ̃ɛ̃ɔ   mɔ̃in   fɔrɛgiin   limalɛhɛ

miim almiitaekhate fii alkaryate

miim   almiitcxatɛ   fii   alkarjate

al mujaaweraatea wa waatea ghadaaraa almaenziilae

al   muʝaa   wɛ   yaatɛa   wa   gadaaraa   al   mɔnziilɔ

'muuta'aeteashen liibulughi al biaeri.

ʕmuutaʕtaʕɔtɛashₒen   liibulugi   albiɔri

PART 1: THE NAVLIPI SUMMARY TABLES

(Arabic transcription, cont.)

Ta-mnae mulaeqaatea sadiikaetiihe

Ta manɔ   mulɔk..ɔtεa   sadiikεtiihε al

Ta manɔ mulɔkɔtεa   sadiikεtuhεal

aljaediidaetii. Allaatii

al jɔdiidɔtii.   Allaatii

jɔdiidɔtii. Allaatii

Iltaeqae biinaehae hunaekae billaemsi.

iltɔk..ɔ   biinɔhɔ   hunɔkɔ   billɔmsi.

iltɔkɔ biinɔhɔ   hunɔkɔ billɔmɔi.

Sa-ya-kunu yaau-maen jaamii laen lou qaedii mat.

Sa   jakunu   jaaumɔn   jaamiilɔn   lou   k..ɔdiimat.

Sa jakunu   jaaumɔn   jaamiilɔn   lou kɔdiimat.

PART 1: THE NAVLIPI SUMMARY TABLES

140

13. TRANSCRIPTIONS OF SELECTED OTHER LANGUAGES IN NAVLIPI

13.1 FRENCH

(1) Un homme et sa femme partent aller se promener,

(2)   Qn   o//m   ε   saa   faam   paaxrtt   aalε   sq   pxrΩmqnε,

(3)  *[handwritten: Qn ǿm ε saa faam paaxrtt aalε sq pxrlmqnε,]*

(1) avec leurs deux beaux enfants.

(2)   aavek   lo/xr   dtq   boz   Ω~fΩ~[Ωn₀fΩn₀] .

(3)  *[handwritten: aavek lǿxr dtq boz Ω~fΩ~ [Ωnfϕn].]*

(1) Le soleil brille, remplissant le jour

(2)   Lq   solεi   bxriij, xrΩ~mpliisΩ~   lq   zh₀uuxr
                         [xrΩn₀mpliisΩn₀]

(3) 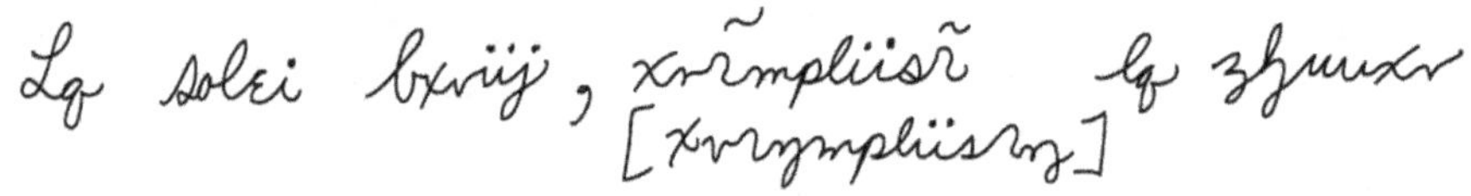 *[handwritten: Lq solεi bxriij, xrΩ~mpliisΩ~ lq zh₀uuxr [xrΩn₀mpliisΩn₀]]*

PART 1: THE NAVLIPI SUMMARY TABLES

141

(French transcription, cont.)

(1) avec son eclat. En jouant, les enfants font

(2) aavek sΩn εklaa. Ω~   zh̬uuΩ~,   lεz   Ω~fΩ~   fΩ~
              [Ωn̬]   [zh̬uuΩn̬],   [Ωn̬fΩn̬]   [fΩn̬]

(3) *aavek sΩn Eklaa. Ω̃   zh̬uũ , lez Ω̃fΩ̃ fΩ̃*
                    [Ωŋ] [zh̬uuŋ]   [ΩŋfΩŋ][fΩŋ]

(1) des cercles autour de ses parents. La famille

(2) dtε seexrklq   ottuuxr dtq sε   paaxrΩ~.   Laa   faamiij
                                           [paaxrΩn̬]

(3) *dtε seexrklq ottuuxr dtq sε paaxrΩ̃. Laa faamiij*
                                   [paaxrŋ].

(1) s'arret au-dessous d'un grand arbre

(2) s'aaxrett o-dtqsuu dt'q~   gxrΩ~   aaxrbxrq
                             [d'qn̬]   [gxrΩn̬]

(3) *s'aaxrett o-dtqsuu dt'q̃   gxrΩ̃ aaxrbxrq*
                        [d'qŋ] [gxrŋ]

(French transcription, cont.)

(1) donnant une grande ombre.

(2) dtΩ~nΩ~ uunq gxrΩ~dt Ω~bxrq.
[dtΩn̥nΩn̥] [gxrΩn̥dt] [Ωn̥bxrq].

(3)
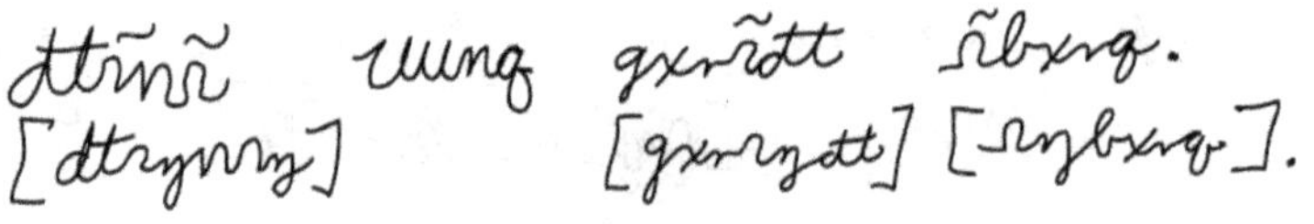

(1) Dans l'ambience, le sommeil engloute les parents.

(2) dtΩ~ l'Ω~biΩ~s, lq somεij Ω~gluutt lε paaxrΩ~
[dtΩn̥] [l'Ωn̥biΩn̥s] [Ωn̥gluutt] [paaxrΩn̥]

(3)
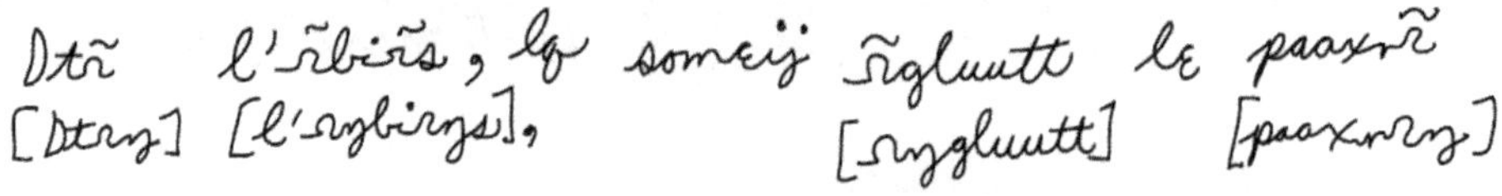

(1) Qui sache quel sort de reves ils ont?

(2) Kii saash̥ kel sΩxr dtq xrev iilz Ω~
[Ω~]

(3)
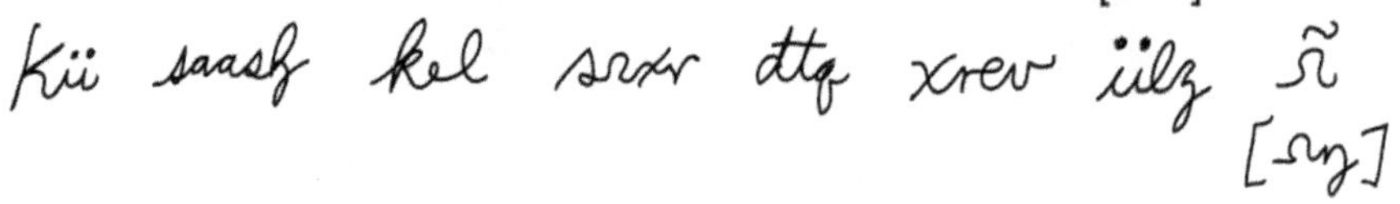

13.2 GERMAN

Original German, Followed by Navlipi (PRINT), Navlipi (CURSIVE); (Hochdeutsch (Radio deutsche Welle) Pronunciation)

Die meisten Menschen sind so subjektiv, dass im

Dtii   maaistt$_o$en   Mensh$_o$n   zintt$_o$ zo   subjek$_o$tt$_o$iiv,   dtaas   im

Grunde nichts Interesse für sie hat als ganz allein

Gxrundtq   ni2h$_o$tt$_o$s   Intt$_o$qxrεsq   fyr   zii   haatt$_o$ aalz   gaantt$_o$s   aallaain

sie selbst. Daher kommt es, dass sie bei allem,

zii   zelbstt$_o$.   Dtaahεqr   k$_o$omtt$_o$ es,,   dtaas   zii   baai   aalem,

PART 1: THE NAVLIPI SUMMARY TABLES

(German transcription, cont.)

was gesagt wird, sogleich an sich denken

vaas gezaagtt$_o$ viiqdt, zoglaai2h$_o$ aan zi2h$_o$ dtenk$_o$n

und jede zufällige, noch so entfernte Beziehung auf irgend etwas

untt$_o$ jedta tt$_o$sufeeliga, nox.. zo entt$_o$fexrntt$_o$
Bett$_o$siihun$_o$g aauf iiqgntt$_o$ ett$_o$vaas

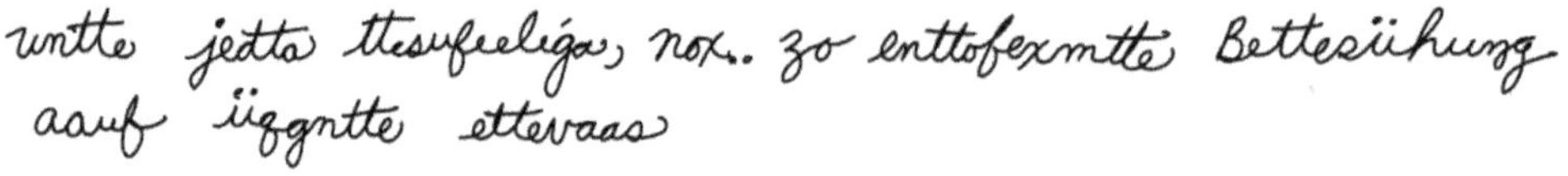

ihnen Persönliches ihre ganze Aufmerksamkeit

iinqn P$_o$εqzo/nlish$_o$qs iixrq gaantt$_o$sq Aaufmεqxrkzaamk$_o$aaitt$_o$

(German transcription, cont.)

an sich reißt und in Besitz nimmt; so dass

aan zi$_0$h$_0$ xraaisstt$_0$ untt$_0$ in Bezitt$_0$s nimtt$_0$; zo dt$_0$aas

sie für den objektiven Gegenstand der Rede

zii fyxr dten objek$_0$tt$_0$iivn Gεgnsh$_0$tt$_0$aandt dtεqxr Xrεdta

keine Fassungskraft übrig behalten;

k$_0$aaina Faasun$_0$gzk$_0$xraaftt$_0$ ybxrig bεhaaltt$_0$n;

wie auch, dass keine Gründe etwas bei ihnen

vii aaux, daas k$_0$aaina Gxrynda ett$_0$vaas baai iinqn

PART 1: THE NAVLIPI SUMMARY TABLES

(German transcription, cont.)

gelten, sobald ihr Interesse oder ihre

geltt$_o$n,   zobaaldt   iixr   Intt$_o$qxresq   odta   iixra

geltten, zobaaldt iixr Inttegxresq odta iixra

Eitelkeit denselben entgegensteht.

Aaitt$_o$lk$_o$aitt$_o$ dtenzelbn   entt$_o$gɛgnsh$_o$tt$_o$ɛtt$_o$.

Aaittelkoaitte dtenzelbn enttegegnshtteette.

PART 1: THE NAVLIPI SUMMARY TABLES

13.3 MARAATHI (MARATHI)

Lines in the transcription give:

(1) The Dewanaagari script.
(2) The "rough" Roman transcription, in italics.
(3) The Navlipi PRINT transcription.
(4) The Navlipi CURSIVE transcription.
(In the latter two, the alternative transcription for nasalizations is given in square brackets.)

(Transcription starts overleaf.)

PART 1: THE NAVLIPI SUMMARY TABLES

(Maraathi transcription, start):

(1) एक शान्त दिवस, मुम्बई महानगरी मध्ये

(2) ek shaanta diwas, mumbai mahaanagari madhe

(3) Ek sh₀aanta diwas, Mumbai mahaanagarii madh₀ɛ

(4) Ek shaanta diwas, Mumbai mahaanogarii madhɛ

(1) एक सम्मेलनात, प्रत्येक जण त्या

(2) ek sammelanaat, pratyek jan tyaa

(3) Ek sammɛlanaat, pratjɛk ȷaʰ tjaa

(4) Ek sammɛlanaat, pratjɛk ȷaʰ tjaa

(1) क्षणाची वाट पाहत होता, जेव्हां

(2) kshanaachii waat paahat hotaa, jewhaan

(3) kshȧhaacii waat paahat hotaa, ɩɛwh₀aa~[ɩɛwh₀aan₀]

(4) kshȧpaacii waat paahat hotaa, ȷɛwɓaã [ȷɛwɓaanȷ]

PART 1: THE NAVLIPI SUMMARY TABLES

(Maraathi transcription, cont.)

(1) विदेष मंत्रि एक घोषणा कर्णार होता.

(2) widesh mantri ek ghoshanaa karnaar hotaa.

(3) widɛsh₀ mantri ɛk gh₀osh₀ahaa karʰaar hotaa.

(4) *widesh mantri ek ghoshahaa karhaar hotaa.*

(1) प्रत्येकाची उत्सुकता ताणली गेली होती

(2) pratyekaachii utsuktaa taanlii geli hoti

(3) pratjɛkaaci utsuktaa taaʰlii gɛlii hotii.

(4) *pratjɛkaacii utsuktaa taaplii gɛlii hotii.*

(1) कि विदेष मंत्रि आपल्या उप-मंत्रि

(2) ki widesh mantri aaplyaa upa-mantri

(3) ki widɛsh₀ mantri aapljaa upa-mantri

(4) *ki widesh mantri aapljaa upa-mantri*

PART 1: THE NAVLIPI SUMMARY TABLES

(Maraathi transcription, cont.)

(1) स्याठी कोणाला पसंती देणार?

(2) syaathi konaalaa pasantii denaar?

(3) sjaath₀i koɦaalaa pasanti dɛɦaar?

(4) *sjaathi koɦaalaa pasanti dɛɦaar?*

(1) याबाबत एकमेकांमध्ये अटकळ

(2) yaabaabat ekamekaanmadhe atakal

(3) jaabaabat ɛkamɛkaa~madh₀ɛ atakaɭ₀
    [ɛkamɛkaan‚madh₀ɛ]

(4) *jaabaabat ɛkamɛkaã madhɛ atakaɭɛ*
    [*ɛkamɛkaanmadhɛ*]

(1) बांधली जात होती.

(2) baandhlii jaat hoti.

(3) baandh₀lii ɟaat hotii.

(4) *baandhlii ɟaat hotii.*

(Maraathi transcription, cont.)

(1) अखेर विदेष मंत्रिनी आश्चर्यवत

(2) akher widesh mantrinii aashcharyawat

(3) akh₀ɛr widɛsh₀ mantrinii aash₀carjawat

(4) *akhɛr widɛsh mantrinii aashcarjawat*

(1) बाबासाहेब रानाडे याला पसंती दिली.

(2) babaasaaheb raanaade yaalaa pasantii dilii.

(3) Baabaasaahɛb ɾaanaaɖɛ jaalaa pasantii dilii.

(4) *Baabasaahɛb ɾaanaaɖɛ jaalaa pasantii dilii.*

13.4 MAAGYAAR (MAGYAR, HUNGARIAN)

TRANSCRIPTION KEY:

Hungarian	*NAVLIPI*, PRINT	*NAVLIPI*, CURSIVE
a	aa	*aa*
à	aae, ɔ (when initial)	*ee*, 2 (when initial)
è	je	*je*
ì	ji	*ji*
ö	o/	*ø*
ő	o/o/, ju (rarely)	*øø*, *ju* (rarely)
ò	oo o/	*oo*, *ø*
ü	y	*y*
ű	yy	*yy*
ù	ju	*ju*
cs	2	*2*
css	2h₀	*2h*
gy	ï	*ï*
s	sh₀	*sh*
sz	s, sz (s + z, occasionally)	*s, sz* (occasionally)

PART 1: THE NAVLIPI SUMMARY TABLES

(Hungarian transcription, start)

Original Hungarian, Followed by Navlipi (PRINT), Navlipi (CURSIVE)

A magas, fiatal fèrfi hirtelen felèbredt,

Aa maagaash₀ fiaattaal fjerfi hiiqrttelen feljebredt,

kiugrott az àgyböl, mintha egy zavaros

kiugrott aaz aaiĵbool, mintth₀aa eĵ zaavaarosh₀

alom utolsò rèszeit fejezte volna be.

aaεlom utolsh₀o/ rjeszεitt fejeztte volnaa be.

PART 1: THE NAVLIPI SUMMARY TABLES

(Hungarian, transcription, cont.)

Kinèzett az ablakon. Gyönyörű nap volt.

kinjezett   aaz   aablaakon.   ḱo/ɳjo/ryy   naap   voltt.

A nap fènyesen sütött, mèg mindig kissè

Aaf   naap   fjeɳjesen   sh$_0$ytto/tt,   mjeg   mindtig   kissje

narancssàrgàn kora hajnali ragyogàsàban,

naaraan2h$_0$eergeen   koraa   haajnaali   raaïogeesh$_0$eebaan,

bàr màr magasan a horizont felett. Àsìtott,

beer   meer   maagaasaan   aa   horizontt   felett.   Ɔsh$_0$ittott

PART 1: THE NAVLIPI SUMMARY TABLES

(Hungarian, transcription, cont.)

nyùjtòzkodott ès kinyitotta az ablakot. A madarak

ɳ‚jujttoozkodtott jesh₀ kiɳ‚jitt₀ttaa   aaz aablaakoott. Aa maadtaaraak

*njujttoozkootlott jesh kinjittöttaa aaz aablaakoott. Aa maadtaa-
                                                             raak*

èneke ùgy àradt be, mint egy meghìvott vendèg.

jeneke juï eeraadt be, mintt eï megjvot vendtjeg.

jeneke jüj eeraadt be, mintt ej megjivott vendtjeg.

Megragadta a vizes kancsòt, amibe a falusi kùt

Megraagaadtaa   aa   vizesh₀   kaan2oott, aamiibe   aa faalush₀ikjutt

Megraagaadtaa aa vizesh kaan2ovtt, aamiibe aa faalushikjutt

melletti csapbòl kellett vizet tölteni, a reggel elsö

meletti   2aapbool   kelett   vizett   tto/ltten, aa regel elsh₀o/o/

meletti 2aapbool kelett vizett ttöltteni, aa regel elshöö

PART 1: THE NAVLIPI SUMMARY TABLES

(Hungarian, transcription, cont.)

szertartàsakent, ès kiment az ajtòn, alig vàrva, hogy elèrje

szerttaartteesh₀aakentt,   jes kimentt aaz aajttoon, aalig veervaa
hoj̈ eljerje

a kutat. Remèlte, hogy ott talàlkozik tegnapi

aa kuttaatt. ſemjeltte, hoj̈ ott ttaaleelkozik ttegnaapi

baràtjàval, hàtha ott lesz. Szèp nap lenne.

baareettjeevaal,   heeth₀aa ott les. Sjep naap lennɛ.

PART 1: THE NAVLIPI SUMMARY TABLES

13.5 VIETNAMESE

NOTES ON THE TRANSCRIPTION:

- Vietnamese, a language with complex tones is used ***primarily to demonstrate the great facility of NAVLIPI with transcription of tones***.
- For clarity, therefore, only the tones of the original Vietnamese transcription are transcribed in NAVLIPI.
- Also for clarity, in the cursive NAVLIPI transcription, the tones are ***highlighted with small arrows***.

PART 1: THE NAVLIPI SUMMARY TABLES

(Vietnamese transcription, cont.):

TRANSCRIPTION KEY:

Vietnamese tone (post-op), *(Illustrated with a)*	**NAVLIPI (post-op), PRINT**	**NAVLIPI CURSIVE**
1) ạ (*dot below*) → short, falling, Mid-to-low.	∧	
2) Á (*acute accent*) → rising, Mid-to-high.	⟩	
3) À, â (*grave or circumflex accent*) → Falling, low-to-lower	⌐	
4) Ã (*tilde*) → nasal, falling, high-to-mid, Plus rising, mid-to-high	⌈⟩	(⌈ +)
5) A' (*hook or quotation mark*), falling, Mid-to-low, rising, Low-to-mid	∧⌐	(+)
6) A *(no diacritic)* or ā *(bar above)* → Mid, level, elongated	╱	

PART 1: THE NAVLIPI SUMMARY TABLES

(Vietnamese transcription, cont.):

<u>**O**RIGINAL **V**IETNAMESE SCRIPT**, PRINT**</u>

Một người đàn ông cao lớn đột nhiên tỉnh dậy và nhảy ra khỏi giường như thể anh ta vừa trải qua một giải mợ khủng khiếp. Anh nhìn ra bên ngoài của số. Thời tiết thật là đẹp. Mặt trời đang tỏa ánh nắng, vẫn là ánh nắng mẫu da cam của buổi sang sớm mặc dù đến lúc này đã lên cao tận đường chân trời. Anh ngáp một cái, vươn vai rồi sau đó mở của số.

PART 1: THE NAVLIPI SUMMARY TABLES

(Vietnamese transcription, cont.):

NAVLIPI, PRINT

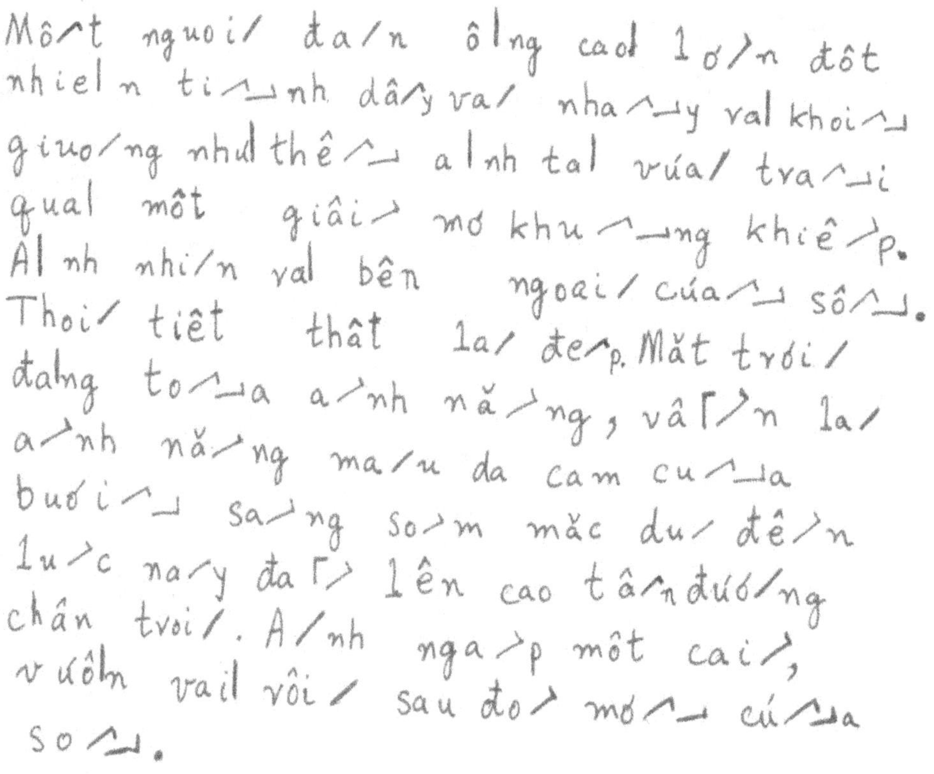

[Handwritten Vietnamese text in Navlipi script:]

Một người đàn ông cao lớn đốt nhiên tính dây và nhảy và khỏi giường như thế anh ta vừa trải qua một giấc mơ khủng khiếp. Anh nhìn và bên ngoài của sổ. Thời tiết thật là đẹp. Mặt trời đang toả ánh nắng, vẫn là ánh nắng màu da cam của buổi sáng sớm mặc dù đến lúc này đã lên cao tận đường chân trời. Anh ngáp một cái, vươn vai rồi sau đó mở cửa sổ.

(Vietnamese transcription, cont.):

NAVLIPI, CURSIVE

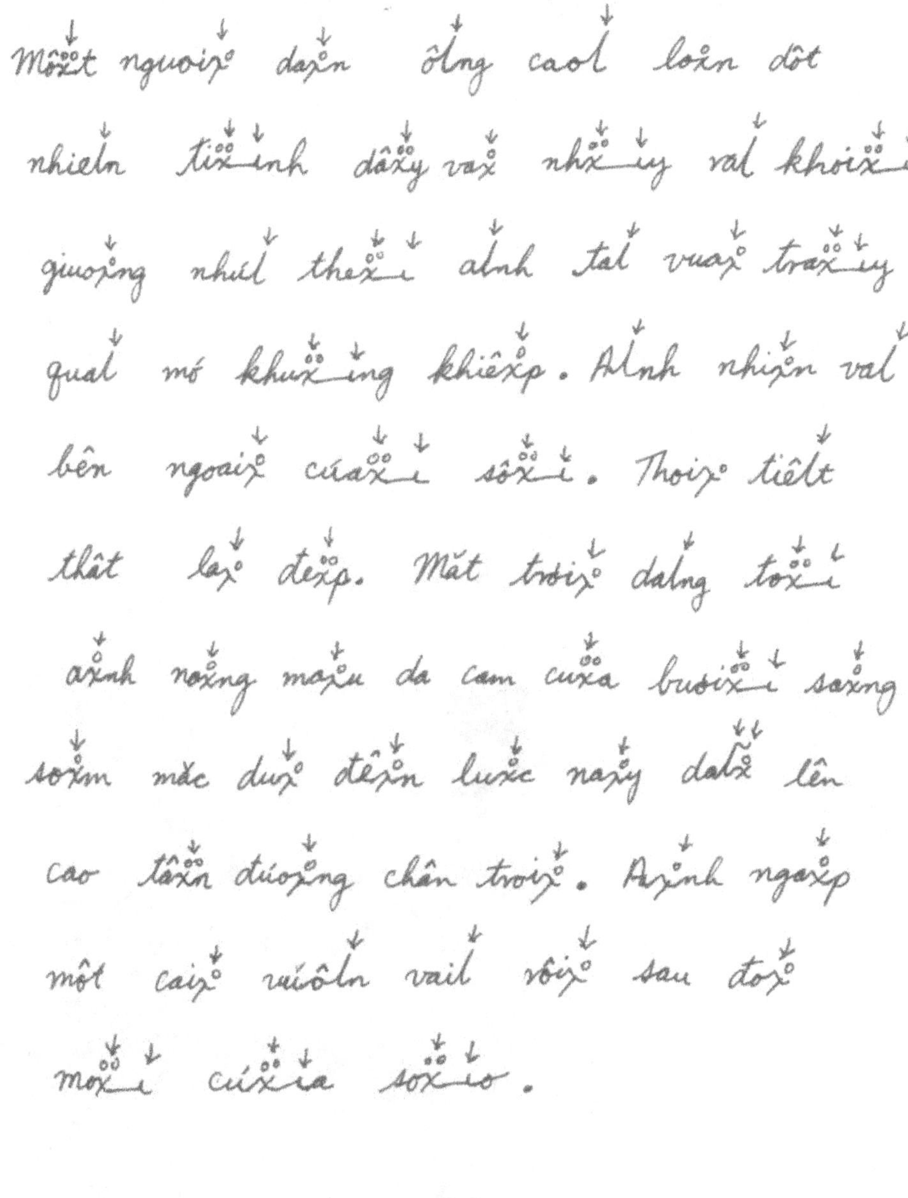

PART 1: THE NAVLIPI SUMMARY TABLES

--- END OF PART 1, NAVLIPI SUMMARY TABLES ---

PART 2:

INTRODUCTION

PART 2: INTRODUCTION

164

CHAPTER 1.
NEED FOR A NEW SCRIPT AND "PHONEMIC IDIOSYNCRASY"

TABLE OF CONTENTS

1.1 NEED FOR A NEW SCRIPT 166

1.2 AUDIENCE ADDRESSED 167

1.3 "PHONEMIC IDIOSYNCRASY" 169

    1.3.1 THE SIGNIFICANCE OF "PHONEMIC IDIOSYNCRASY" 169
    1.3.2 TWO VIEWS OF PHONEMIC IDIOSYNCRASY 171
    1.3.3 THE HEART OF THE PROBLEM CREATED BY PHONEMIC IDIOSYNCRASY: *HOW DOES ONE ACCOMMODATE AND TRANSCRIBE PHONEMIC IDIOSYNCRASY IN A NEW SCRIPT?* 173
    1.3.4 HOW NAVLIPI TRANSCRIBES PHONEMIC IDIOSYNCRASY; *PHONEMIC CONDENSATES* 174

PART 2: INTRODUCTION

1.1 NEED FOR A NEW SCRIPT

As noted in the **PREFACE AND OBJECTIVES OF THIS BOOK**, this book emanated from a direly felt need for a universal orthography (script) capable not only of representing, systematically and scientifically, every phone and tone found in the world's major languages, (really a minimum requirement for any universal orthography!). But also, perhaps equally importantly, of addressing what was felt to be an even more important and urgent issue: The ***phonemic idiosyncrasies*** of the world's languages. The term *phonemic idiosyncrasy* has been defined in the **PREFACE AND OBJECTIVES OF THIS BOOK** and is defined again further below, in this chapter.

This book thoroughly addresses the problem of phonemic idiosyncrasy across language families, for the first time ever, to the best of published knowledge.

1.2 AUDIENCE ADDRESSED

Navlipi is humbly addressed not just to situations ripe for its use, one of the most important of which is a *common script for India* that bridges the "Aaryan/Dravidian" (North/South) divide. This divide (see **PREFACE**) is a prime example of the problems associated with transcription in the same script of phonemic idiosyncrasy between languages. Rather, *Navlipi* also humbly seeks to address itself *to existing Romanized transcriptions* which are still not entirely adequate. Examples of these include, but are not limited to, Swaahili, Vietnamese, Indonesian/Malaysian (the main Bahasa), Turkish, and the Romanized Mandarin (*pinyin*), which was vigorously promoted by the Chinese government many years ago. And finally, *Navlipi* also seeks *potential new markets*, such as the Turkic languages of the new Central Asian republics, which were originally transcribed in Arabic script, then in Cyrillic under the Soviet Union, and now are seeking a Romanization based on the Turkish.

With respect to China, it is well recognized that modern China has adapted its ancient ideographic script well to the 21st century. For instance, even Windows and Mac OS are used in china today entirely in Chinese characters. One might then say that there appears to be absolutely no need for the Roman script in everyday life, except when interfacing with non-Chinese. There is also a certain degree of unity that this common ideographic script provides for the Chinese languages.

Nevertheless, many of today's Chinese in the science and literature fields express a desire for a more easily learned and palatable, "Romanized" script, saying that ideographic Chinese is a handicap in intellectual discourse. In earlier times, it was also considered a handicap to universal literacy, since basic literacy required the learning of at least 2,000 characters, and "educated" literacy at least 20,000 characters.

Thus, in a sense, India and China, the two most populous countries in the world today (2005), and, potentially, economic powers of tomorrow, represent the two largest potential markets for *Navlipi*. Apart from these, there is of course also the hope that, if a truly capable universal script catches on, it could eventually replace the Cyrillic, the Arabic, the Hebrew, the Chinese, etc. scripts; it could also be used where the Roman script does somewhat poorly, e.g. for the Slavic languages that use it (Czech, Slovak, Serbo-Croat (further divided, after the new, politically-instigated divisions, into Croatian, Bosnian etc.), Polish etc.). On the other hand, this author fully appreciates that attempting to replace existing ways of doing things (here, scripts), is a daunting task, and may be unsuccessful. In this context, replacement of an existing script would make the problems

PART 2: INTRODUCTION

168

encountered with present (2006) attempts at replacing Windows with Linux pale by comparison!

Scope of the work: The author also humbly notes that a single-author work such as this can only be a first basis, a guide for future work. As such therefore, it was his intention only to provide a *maargadarshan* (a Maraathi, Hindi and Sanskrit word somewhat poorly translated as "direction for the way ahead") in devising a new, universal script. The work would thus, hopefully, be refined further by others. A single-person work perhaps cannot, ultimately, compete with the work of a team of savants in the field.

1.3 "PHONEMIC IDIOSYNCRASY"

1.3.1 THE SIGNIFICANCE OF "PHONEMIC IDIOSYNCRASY"

Phonemic idiosyncrasy can be defined as *the existence of very different sets (usually, pairs) of phones as allophones of the same phoneme in one language, whereas the same phones exist as distinct phonemes in another language*. Phonemic idiosyncrasy is best illustrated by citing some examples from a few of the world's languages:

(1)   The bilabial stop [p] and its aspirated counterpart, [ph], are allophones of the same phoneme, /p/, in English, whereas they are distinct phonemes in Hindi/Urdu. This is one of the best examples of phonemic idiosyncrasy, in our very own English language: In the American, British or Australian pronunciations, unaspirated/aspirated phone pairs, e.g. [p]/[ph], or [t]/[th], are usually members of the same phoneme. For example, in *put* or *pain*, the plosive is aspirated, i.e. [ph], whereas in *spy* or *spam* the plosive is unaspirated, i.e. [p], yet both these plosives are allophones of the same English phoneme, /p/. (Pointedly, in most Indian or Irish articulations of English, the aspirated plosives are usually absent!)

(2)   The [v]/[w] and [f]/ph] (semivowel/fricative) phone pairs of Hindi/Urdu are freely interchanged and have the same phonemic value, although they are quite obviously very different phones: The [v] and [f] are labiodental fricatives, whilst the [w] is a bilabial semivowel and the [ph] is an aspirated bilabial stop. Thus, in Hindi/Urdu, one can equally well say *phal* or *fal* for "fruit"; or *vijay* or *wijay* for "victory". This sort of free interchange of these phone pairs, e.g. the [ph]/[f], is found not only in North Indian languages, but also in some Greek dialects; indeed, in Greek, it represents a phonetic shift, from an original, exclusive [ph] in Classical Greek, to an interchangeable [ph]/[f] in medieval and later Greek (and exclusive [f] for Greek-derived words in modern European languages, e.g. *phone*).

(3)   The unvoiced and voiced bilabial stops, [p] and [b] are allophones of the same phoneme in many Chinese languages, whereas they are of course different phonemes in most Indo-European languages. Indeed, in many Chinese languages, there is no phonemic distinction between the unvoiced and voiced versions of

PART 2: INTRODUCTION

170

important plosives: Besides the [p]/[b] pair, this extends to other unvoiced/voiced plosive pairs, e.g. [k]/[g], [t]/[d]. In Mandarin pronunciation, for instance, it is said that the [p] phone does not exist. The non-Chinese speaker is told that the older (pre-1972) transliterations *Teng Hsiao Ping* and *Peijing* are more correctly rendered *Deng (or Dang) Xiao Bing* and *Beijing*. Nevertheless, the former pronunciations, occasionally freely interchanged with the latter by native Mandarin speakers, do not change the meaning of the words.

(4) In a very similar vein, in the most common renditions of Arabic, [p] is said not to exist, and native Arabic speakers may mispronounce English *pay* as *bay*. However, substituting [p] for [b] in most Arabic dialects does not change the meaning of the word, and it may still be well understood. As another unvoiced/voiced phone pair example from Arabic, the [g] officially does not exist, but [k] and [g] are freely interchanged in many Arabic dialects. And interestingly, the Arabic proper name *Kamal* may be pronounced *Kemel* or *Gemel* or *Gamel* without any change in meaning, a something unrelated to regional accent!

(5) As another example, in a Dravidian South Indian language such as Tamil, there is no phonemic distinction between aspirated and unaspirated plosives, e.g. [t] and [th] (or [p] and [ph]). Many of speakers Dravidian South Indian languages, including speakers of Kannadaa and Telaguu, where the unaspirated/aspirated distinction is officially taught in the script, have trouble distinguishing unaspirated from aspirated phones, or pronouncing aspirated phones such as [bh]. This also leads to curious South Indian renditions of North Indian words (where such a phonemic distinction is strong): Thus, e.g. *Lalitaa* is rendered *Lalithaa*. The [t] and [th] may represent the same phoneme in Tamil, but they are nevertheless used differently and distinctly and, in contrast to the Mandarin and Arabic examples cited above, usually *not* freely interchanged. Indeed, the official linguistic position is that, for Tamil, the phone [th] does not exist, but this position is belied by the random substitution of [th] in place of [t] in everyday Tamil speech.

(6) As another example, in Japanese, the alveolar lateral, [l], is said not to exist, and native Japanese speakers render this as the palato-alveolar flap, [r]. However, the [l] is never rendered into any phone other than [r] in Japanese, and the [r] and [l] may be considered to represent the same phoneme.

Chapter 1: Need for a New Script and "Phonemic Idiosyncrasy"

(7) As yet another example of peculiar allophones found in some languages similar to the [ph]/[f] of Hindi/Urdu in (ii) above, we can cite [x], [r] and [rrr], three radically different phones of modern French and German, which are part of the same phoneme. The first of these is an uvular or sometimes velar fricative, the famous French/German "uvular r", whilst the second is an alveolar tap or semivowel and the third is an alveolar trill, the famous "rolled r" [rrr].

(8) Although in most of the above examples of phonemic idiosyncrasy, the artitions of the phones are similar or identical, e.g. bilabial for [p]/[b], in two of the examples ((2) and (7)), *the artitions are radically different*.

1.3.2 TWO VIEWS OF PHONEMIC IDIOSYNCRASY

As this book has noted earlier, there are ***two*** *potentially very different views of phonemic idiosyncrasy*:

1) That phonemic idiosyncrasy *is indeed a unique phenomenon*, as exemplified by the many allophonic examples cited above: the prominent [p]/[ph] allophones of English vs. their clear phonemic distinction in Hindi/Urdu; the prominent [v]/[w] and [f][ph] allophones of Hindi/Urdu vs. their phonemic distinction in nearly all other world languages; the [x]/[r] allophones of modern French and German. While the first (English) example is only somewhat odd, the latter two (Hindi/Urdu, French/German) examples are truly idiosyncratic!

2) That there is in fact no such thing: What appears to be phonemic idiosyncrasy is simply the total absence of certain phones in certain languages. This may at first glance appear to apply to some languages: For example, the [p] of the [p]/[b] pair can be said to be simply absent in standard Arabic or Mandarin, the [l] of the [l]/[r] pair can be said to be simply absent in Japanese, and the aspirated stops such as [ph] and [th] can be said to be simply absent in Tamil. However, the English, Hindi/Urdu and French/German examples in (i) above clearly refute this view.

This book will seek to clearly show that the first view, i.e. that phonemic idiosyncrasy *is* indeed a unique phenomenon, is the correct one. This is done by referring to the examples cited in the previous Section, and other examples as appropriate. And by showing that, where one phone is supposedly absent in a certain language, it is invariably

PART 2: INTRODUCTION

mistaken *only* for its allophonic counterpart from another language and no other phone. Indeed, one of the first arguments in support of the first view has already been presented above: The English ([p]/[ph]), Hindi/Urdu ([v]/[w], [f]/[ph]) and French/German ([x]/[r]) examples above.

Let us look again at some of the examples cited above, and how they shed light on the problem of phonemic idiosyncrasy:

(1) In everyday Mandarin (common speech, Putonghua) and Arabic speech, there are instances when [p] is articulated for [b], randomly and freely, yet both phones are understood as the same phoneme. But any other phone besides [p], even one identical in artition such as [m] (let alone an entirely unrelated phone such as [t]), is *never* mistaken for [p]. At the same time, we must still acknowledge that most Arabic or Mandarin speakers will articulate the [p] phone very rarely, so at times it may appear that [p] "does not exist" in these languages. (In the nomenclature from an earlier chapter, the [p] is a *galatophone* of the parent phone [b].)

(2) Similarly, in Tamil, individual speakers may articulate [t] as [th], e.g. *tatta* ("a hit") as *thatta*. Neither articulation will change the meaning of the word and both will be well understood. However, if the word is articulated as *datta*, it will not be understood at all, even though [d] is identical in artition (dental) as [t], and thus a closely related phone. Once again, however, we must still acknowledge that most Tamil speakers will use *tatta,* and the rare *thatta* may be heard only in certain caste segments of the population. (In the nomenclature from an earlier chapter, the [th] is a *galatophone* of the parent phone [t].)

(3) In English /p/, we have a much clearer example of two allophones, [p] and [ph], e.g. in the examples cited above, *spy* ([p]) and *put* ([ph]). Here however, there is no question that one phone does not exist in the language. Both exist and are articulated in almost equal proportion.

(4) Where two allophones have quite different artitions, e.g. the [f] and [ph] of Hindi/Urdu and Greek discussed briefly above, it becomes very clear that these are genuine allophones, since both phones definitely exist in these languages, as freely interchangeable allophones.

(5) A Japanese speaker may mistake the alveolar lateral, [l], for the alveolar central flap [r], in pronunciations of foreign (e.g. English) words. Thus *fly* may be

Chapter 1: Need for a New Script and "Phonemic Idiosyncrasy"

173

pronounced *fry*. The official position is that the phone [l] does not exist in Japanese. However, *no other phone will ever be confused by a Japanese speaker with [r] except [l],* even one in the same tongue artition (alveolar) as [l] and [r]. Thus, e.g., the alveolar aspirated plosive, [th], or the alveolar *fricatized* central flap [rh] would never be confused for [r], i.e. *f[th]y* or *f[rh]y*, if these words existed in any language, would never be confused with and pronounced *fry* by a Japanese speaker. This indicates that the phones [l] and [r] are uniquely related in Japanese, even though the [l] is officially said to not exist in Japanese. And this relationship is allophonic, substantiating the first view above.

We must also recognize that phonemic idiosyncrasy is not simply an issue of variation in pronunciation, i.e. *accent* (e.g. American vs. British English, or lower-caste vs. upper-caste Tamil): For example, the two different diphthongs of Australian vs. American pronunciation of *Day* in *Good Day!* are genuinely different phonemes in Australian and American English, and well recognized as such. (This example was presented in an earlier chapter as well in the discussion of phonemes.)

1.3.3 THE HEART OF THE PROBLEM CREATED BY PHONEMIC IDIOSYNCRASY: *HOW DOES ONE ACCOMMODATE AND TRANSCRIBE PHONEMIC IDIOSYNCRASY IN A NEW SCRIPT?*

Regardless of which of the above views of phonemic idiosyncrasy one subscribes to (and it has been clearly expressed that this book subscribes to the first view), **transcription of phonemic idiosyncrasy in a way understandable across different languages** is clearly a serious problem that needs to be addressed.

To appreciate some examples of such problems in transcription, let us briefly look at the following situations:

- An English speaker, when reading Hindi/Urdu in any universal script, *must* be able to immediately recognize that the phone [v] can also be pronounced as a [w].
- Similarly, a Hindi/Urdu speaker should be immediately comprehend, when reading English in the *same* script, that [p] and [ph] have the same value in English.

PART 2: INTRODUCTION

174

- An English speaker, when reading Arabic in the *same* script, should be immediately able to understand that [p] and [b] are not separate phonemes in Arabic, and, furthermore, that such bilabial sounds are usually but not always pronounced as [b].
- English or Hindi/Urdu speakers, when reading Mandarin in the *same* script should be able to immediately appreciate that [p] and [b] are many times freely interchanged and have the same value.

The problem for an orthography with respect to phonemic idiosyncrasy then becomes this: ***To find a <u>single</u>, universal system of transcription (i.e., a script) that, clearly shows the phonemic distinctions present in a language to the speaker of a different language***. For instance, the phonemic distinction between the [p] and [b] phones in English must be clear to the Arabic speaker reading English in the universal script. At the same time, it should be equally clear to the English speaker reading Arabic in the same script that, in Arabic, [p] and [b] are components of the same phoneme, but this phoneme is usually (but not always!) pronounced [b]. Similarly, the North Indian must understand from the universal script that it makes no difference when speaking Tamil whether one says *tatta* or *thatta* ("a hit").

1.3.4 HOW *NAVLIPI* TRANSCRIBES PHONEMIC IDIOSYNCRASY; *PHONEMIC CONDENSATES*

When artitions of allophones are similar or identical, e.g. the bilabial [p] and [ph] in the above examples, the orthography may be straightforward. For example, *Navlipi* uses the [$_o$] (subscripted circle *post-op*), to represent the combined *(aspirated + unaspirated)* phoneme. This is very amenable to cursive writing as well as keyboarding, yet distinct and recognizable. This post-op then gives us three sets of glyphs for the components of the English phoneme /**p**/:

- **[p]** (unaspirated *phone*);
- **[ph$_o$]** (aspirated *phone*); (h_o is the *Navlipi* post-op for aspiration)
- **p$_o$** (aspirated/unaspirated *combined phoneme* but generally pronounced [p]);

Navlipi calls **[p$_o$]** a ***PHONEMIC CONDENSATE***. That is to say, the [p] and [ph] phones are said to be condensed into one *entity*, i.e.:

Chapter 1: Need for a New Script and "Phonemic Idiosyncrasy"

$$\mathbf{p_o} = [p] + [ph] \quad \text{(in transcription of English)}$$

$$....(1.1)$$

In *Navlipi* transcription, only the $\mathbf{p_o}$ would be used for English, i.e. all letters *p* would be written as p_o. Thus, when writing English, we would write *spy* and *put* as sp_oy and p_out.

In a similar manner, *Navlipi* tackles the transcription of another phonemic idiosyncrasy, the [p]/[b] allophonic idiosyncrasy, as follows: It uses a subscripted "little double circle" or "two little circles" (or "infinity symbol") postop [∞] to universally represent the unvoiced/ voiced (surd/sonant) phonemic condensate. Thus $\mathbf{b_\infty}$ represents the [p]/[b] phoneme when it is usually (but not always) articulated as [b], e.g. in Arabic. And, similarly, $\mathbf{p_\infty}$ represents the same phoneme when it is usually (but not always) articulated as [p], e.g. in Fujienese, a Chinese language spoken in Fujien Province in coastal southern China. This postop is easily rendered in cursive as two little circles, as illustrated in the main *NAVLIPI* **SUMMARY TABLES** (**PART 1** in this book).

In equation fashion then:

$$[p] + [b] = \mathbf{p_\infty} \quad \textit{(in transcription of most Chinese languages)}$$

$$[p] + [b] = \mathbf{b_\infty} \quad \textit{(in transcription of Standard Arabic)}$$

$$....(1.2, 1.3)$$

Advantages of a script that addresses phonemic idiosyncrasy: Now let us look at the tremendous advantage ensuing from a universal script that addresses phonemic idiosyncrasy from the following brief examples:

- When a Hindi/Urdu reader sees [p_o] in our new universal script (say when reading English), he/she will instantly recognize it as different from Hindi/Urdu [ph] or [p]. If well enough versed in the language he/she is reading, he/she will also know how to pronounce it correctly (pronouncing the phones in *spy* and *put* as [p] and [ph] respectively in our English example).
- Similarly, an English speaker reading Arabic in our universal script would easily

Chapter 1: Need for a New Script and "Phonemic Idiosyncrasy"

recognize b_∞ for what it stands for, and realize that it is distinct from the [b] of English, even though it is articulated exactly like the [b] of English.

- And once again, an English speaker reading Putonghua (Mandarin common speech) in our universal script would easily recognize p_∞ for what it stands for, and realize that it is distinct from the [p] of English, even though they are articulated exactly like the [p] of English.

More complex phonemic condensates: Thus far, the above examples of transcription of phonemic idiosyncrasy have been fairly straightforward to tackle, by arriving at two new *phonemic condensates*. They were straightforward because the artitions of the phones involved were close: E.g., the [p]/[ph] and [p]/[b] pairs are all bilabial. The problem of transcription of phonemic idiosyncrasy becomes more difficult *when the artitions of allophones are radically different*, e.g. the French/German "uvular r" [x] and semivowel [r] and "rolled r" [rrr], or the Hindi/Urdu or Greek [ph]/[f] or the Hindi/Urdu [v]/[w]. What does one do then? As will be seen in this book, **Navlipi** addresses this difficult problem in a remarkably simple, yet clear and succinct way. For example, the [x]/[r] and [v]/[w] issues are addressed simply by arriving at new phonemic condensates expressed as *digraphs*: ***xr*** and ***vw*** respectively. In equation form:

$$[v] + [w] = \mathbf{vw} \quad \quad ....(1.4)$$

$$[x] + [r] + [rr] = \mathbf{xr} \quad \quad ....(1.5)$$

CHAPTER 2.
OBJECTIVES SET FORTH FOR A NEW SCRIPT, HOW *NAVLIPI* MEETS THESE OBJECTIVES, AND ARGUMENTS *AGAINST* A NEW, UNIVERSAL SCRIPT

TABLE OF CONTENTS

2.1 OBJECTIVES SET FORTH IN THIS BOOK FOR A UNIVERSAL ORTHOGRAPHY AND HOW *NAVLIPI* MEETS THESE OBJECTIVES 179

2.1.1 TEN (10) REQUIREMENTS FOR A UNIVERSAL ORTHOGRAPHY 179
2.1.2 UNIVERSALITY AND COMPLETENESS (REQUIREMENT #1) 180
2.1.3 RECOGNIZABILITY, DISTINCTIVENESS, SIMPLICITY AND INTUITIVE NATURE (REQUIREMENT #S 2, 3, 4) 180
2.1.4 HIGH AMENABILITY TO CURSIVE WRITING (REQUIREMENT #5) AND THE GAMBLE IN ASSUMING CONTINUED USE OF HANDWRITING BY HUMANS IN THE FUTURE.. 181
2.1.5 EASE AND RAPIDITY OF TRANSCRIPTION FROM THREE POINTS OF VIEW: CURSIVE, PRINT AND KEYBOARD (REQUIREMENT #5, CONT.) 183
2.1.6 SYSTEMATIC, SCIENTIFIC CLASSIFICATION, AND ACCURACY (REQUIREMENT #6) 185
2.1.7 DISCRETIZATION (REQUIREMENT #7) 188
2.1.8 PRACTICAL PHONEMICS RATHER THAN PHONICS (REQUIREMENT #8) 189
2.1.9 VOICE-RECOGNITION COMPATIBILITY AND A VOICE-RECOGNITION SOFTWARE PACKAGE (REQUIREMENT # 9) 189
2.1.10 ABILITY TO ACCOMMODATE THE PHONEMIC IDIOSYNCRASIES OF ALL THE WORLD'S LANGUAGES (REQUIREMENT # 10)... 189

PART 2: INTRODUCTION
178

2.2 ARGUMENTS *AGAINST* A NEW, UNIVERSAL, PHONIC OR PHONEMIC ORTHOGRAPHY (SCRIPT).. 190

Chapter 2: Objectives Set Forth for a New Script, How Navlipi Meets These Objectives, and Arguments Against a New, Universal Script

2.1 OBJECTIVES SET FORTH IN THIS BOOK FOR A UNIVERSAL ORTHOGRAPHY AND HOW *NAVLIPI* MEETS THESE OBJECTIVES

2.1.1 TEN (10) REQUIREMENTS FOR A UNIVERSAL ORTHOGRAPHY

This book set for itself the following *major requirements set for a universal orthography*:

Table 2-1: Major *requirements* set for a universal orthography.

1. *UNIVERSALITY AND COMPLETENESS.*
2. *RECOGNIZABILITY.*
3. ***Distinctiveness****:* Distinguishability of one glyph (letter) of the script from another, especially those representing related phones
4. *SIMPLICITY AND INTUITIVE NATURE.* Simplicity is also reflected in *ease of learning.*
5. *EASE AND RAPIDITY OF TRANSCRIPTION FROM THREE POINTS OF VIEW: KEYBOARD, CURSIVE, AND PRINT. High amenability to cursive writing.*
6. *SYSTEMATIC, SCIENTIFIC CLASSIFICATION AND ACCURACY.*
7. *DISCRETIZATION.*
8. *PRACTICAL PHONEMICS RATHER THAN PHONICS.* A fundamentally *phonemic* system. Thus, e.g., while some scripts can be used to transcribe the different pronunciations of two individuals speaking the same language, that was not the objective set forth in this book
9. *VOICE-RECOGNITION COMPATIBILITY and a voice-recognition software package*
10. *THE ABILITY TO ACCOMMODATE THE PHONEMIC IDIOSYNCRASIES OF ALL THE WORLD'S MAJOR LANGUAGES*: This is of course the most important requirement of all, in the view of this author and this book.

Each of the above requirements is now briefly defined and described in turn, below.

PART 2: INTRODUCTION

2.1.2 UNIVERSALITY AND COMPLETENESS (REQUIREMENT #1)

Universality and the associated property, ***completeness,*** imply being able *to represent, systematically and scientifically, every single phone and tone found in the world's major languages*, really a minimum requirement for any universal orthography.

2.1.3 RECOGNIZABILITY, DISTINCTIVENESS, SIMPLICITY AND INTUITIVE NATURE (REQUIREMENT #S 2, 3, 4)

Recognizability necessarily means the use of the Roman "alphabet" (script) as a basis, since historical happenstance has rendered this particular orthography ubiquitous in all corners of the world. Thus, for instance, a highly scientific and easily keyboarded orthography based purely on geometric shapes, as presented as an exercise in a later chapter, would be useless in terms of recognizability. The property of ***distinctiveness***, is closely related to recognizability. It implies that two glyphs, especially those representing similar phones, should be easily distinguishable.

Lack of recognizability, and distinctiveness are two major deficiencies of the "alphabet" of the **International Phonetic Association** based in London, England (referred to throughout this book as ***the IPA***) [SCr-2 to SCr-4]: In the IPA, many glyphs appear to be straight from outer space. And many very similar glyphs, are highly confusing, even to the expert. Examples among these are the various inverted and rotated *e*'s and *a*'s, the inverted/rotated/hooked, etc. variants of *r* and *R* used to represent the various alveolar trills and flaps or uvular *"r's"*, and the variants of *n* with inward/outward hooks, etc. used for the various nasals. They are also, incidentally, very difficult to transcribe cursively and to keyboard. (A detailed discussion of the IPA and its drawbacks is given in the chapter on Prior Art, later in this book.)

Navlipi makes use of the Roman alphabet with very few new letters/symbols, by, among other techniques, using redundant letters in orthographically very recognizable fashion. It also uses *intuitive renditions*. Thus, e.g.: the redundant *"c"* (redundant vs. *"k"*) is used as a vowel, from its "iconic, intuitive" resemblance to *"e"*, and to an open mouth. So also the redundant *"q"*, from its similar iconic, intuitive resemblance to *"a"*. The various cursive and print renditions of *"r"* in the Roman-script are used differently and in easily recognizable fashion to denote various, differing centrals (r-sounds). Rare fricatizations

Chapter 2: Objectives Set Forth for a New Script, How Navlipi Meets These Objectives, and Arguments Against a New, Universal Script

of plosives are rendered with a *fricatization post-op* (again derived from *"h"*), obviating the need for a new symbol.

Simplicity and Intuitive Nature are also properties associated with *recognizability*: In regard to *simplicity*, the sheer, unmanageable number of IPA glyphs and diacritics is mind-boggling. This leads to associated problems, such as slow keyboarding. *Intuitive nature* can be expressed in many ways. In orthography, for instance, it can be expressed by using [aa] and [a] for the open and open-mid jaw positions of the central vowel, as already used in modern Finnish. In keyboarding, it can be expressed by using (Ctrl+h) and (Alt+h) to keyboard the aspirate-postop [h$_o$] and fricative-postop [h$_0$], or (Ctrl+n), (Alt+n) and (Ctrl-Shift+n) to keyboard various nasal stops. (These are just examples of possibilities of keyboarding, and not necessary those followed by *Navlipi*.)

Other examples of "intuitive" selections include the duplication of vowel letters to indicate vowel lengthening, e.g. short [i], [u] vs. long [ii], [uu]. This is a very simple method already used, e.g., in modern Finnish. It may be compared to the keyboard-unfriendly and difficult-to-recognize long-vowel post-op used by the IPA. Similarly, trills are simply and intuitively rendered by repetition of the flap symbol, e.g. [rr] is the trilled version of [r].

2.1.4 HIGH AMENABILITY TO CURSIVE WRITING (REQUIREMENT #5) AND THE GAMBLE IN ASSUMING CONTINUED USE OF HANDWRITING BY HUMANS IN THE FUTURE

High Amenability to Cursive Writing necessarily means that we are taking a very important *gamble*: That, say, a hundred years from now, ***writing by hand will still remain one of the main methods of language transcription***.

This assumes that such technologies as voice recognition, which are already very far along and in good use as of the date of this writing (2006), will exist side by side with, *but will not replace*, old-fashioned, manual transcription.

Unfortunately, even at the time of this writing, in the first decade of the 21st century, many are already pronouncing the demise of cursive writing, and even all writing [SCr-72]. Furthermore, a futuristic, direct-brain-wave-to-electronic-medium transcription may

PART 2: INTRODUCTION

eventually render all orthography superfluous (although the present author feels that this still is some centuries away). Some ground work has already been done for this as of this writing (2006): For example, Cyberkinetics Neurotechnology Systems reported a chip implanted in the brain of paralyzed people with the help of which they are able to move a cursor on a screen by *thinking* in a certain way. John Donoghue of Brown University, Providence, RI, USA demonstrated [SCr-73, SCr-74] the placement of a tiny, 100-electrode array in the primary motor cortex of a paralyzed, 25-year-old man. The electrical impulses from this were collected and sent to signal processors, enabling a sophisticated algorithm to actually translate the man's thoughts of moving his arm and hand. The man could, within one day, move the computer cursor, play video games, open emails, operate a TV remote control, draw, and move a prosthetic hand, all using just his thoughts! Thus, if one is able to control cursors etc. simply by using one's thoughts today (2006), then, by extension, such methods could, in the very near future, be used for a direct thought-to-writing system, without the intervention of handwriting or voice communication. Indeed, S. Wolf of the University of Virginia, Charlottesville, VA, USA has proposed that advances in this technology will allow humans to communicate with machines *as well as each other* (i.e. without voice or visual signals) by 2026 [LN-105].

In spite of these developments, however, this author puts some confidence in his gamble that cursive writing may not disappear, by noting that print newspapers, forever forecast for extinction, still coexist well with e-versions today. And we know that we already live in a world where our children have little use for longhand and are atrocious at spelling (and, concomitantly, grammar), because their school assignments are almost completely done on a computer with a spell/grammar-checker. Nevertheless, they still use cursive writing (or its modern version, used by children today, which more resembles printing in lower case rather than truly joined cursive writing).

Additionally, and more importantly, it is noted that this book also thoroughly treats keyboard transcription and voice-recognition-transcription, with separate chapters or sections devoted thereto, and thus our gamble is somewhat hedged!

Amenability to cursive writing (or event print) necessarily implies some elements of an earlier-cited property, i.e. *recognizability*, since the cursive letters must be easily distinguishable from each other, and, preferably, relatable to a common script such as the Roman. It also implies that the cursive writing flow is logical and easy, and that ***the pen (or other writing instrument) is lifted as little as possible from the paper (or tablet)***. This means dealing with such things as diacritics as little as possible.

Chapter 2: Objectives Set Forth for a New Script, How Navlipi Meets These Objectives, and Arguments <u>Against</u> a New, Universal Script

Lack of amenability to cursive writing, and the resulting very slow transcription, is one of the major deficiencies of, for instance, the Indian scripts, which are otherwise highly scientifically designed and very phonetic. It is also a deficiency of the older Chinese characters, and by extension, of the Japanese and Haangul scripts. And again, it is also a deficiency in the latest versions of the IPA, which, in contrast to prior versions, do not even treat cursive writing seriously. Interestingly, a cursive script, the *Modi* script, was devised hundreds of years ago for Maraathii (a major language of western India). One of its primary emphases was no lifting of the pen from the paper *between words* [SCr-75]. It however suffered from lack of recognizability or easy correlation with *Dewanaagari*, the common script for Maraathii. In a similar vein, the Pitman and other systems of shorthand transcription, discussed at length in a separate chapter in this book, are highly amenable to cursive writing but again suffer from lack of recognizability.

2.1.5 EASE AND RAPIDITY OF TRANSCRIPTION FROM THREE POINTS OF VIEW: CURSIVE, PRINT AND KEYBOARD (REQUIREMENT #5, CONT.)

Many features of *Navlipi* yield this property. For example, *Navlipi* makes very substantial use of *postpositional operators* (*"**postops**"* or *"**post-ops**"* for short, briefly presented above). Among these are the subscripted circle discussed above (e.g. in [p] vs. [p_o]), and a subscripted oval. The subscripted circle is rendered in cursive as a "following-little-e". The subscripted oval is rendered in cursive as a "small leg". These are shown in the Table below.

The post-ops shown below are far easier to write than diacritics over or above the letter, or combination letters, as, for instance, the IPA might use. For example, using their prior work as basis, one might conjecture that the IPA might render ([p] + [ph]) as [p-ph].

PART 2: INTRODUCTION

Table 2-2: Examples of *post-ops* (post-positional operators) used by *Navlipi*.

post-op for	*description*	*print*	*cursive*
(aspirated + unaspirated) phonemic condensate	Subscripted "little circle"	[$_o$], e.g. [p$_o$]	*e p$_o$*
aspirate	Letter "h" with subscripted "little circle"	h$_o$	*h$_o$*
fricative	Letter "h" with subscripted oval	h$_0$	*h$_0$*

The use of postops also facilitates keyboarding, because it means that, rather than entirely new symbols (and entirely new keys) being required for new letters, just a few postops (in our count in *Navlipi*, just **ten distinct post-ops**, of which five are very rare), combined with existing letters, suffice to accommodate a huge number of new letters. Thus, just a few additional keys assigned to these postops take the place of a slew of new keys that may be required if entirely new letters were used. And in actual practice, due to the use of *language-specific keyboards* by *Navlipi*, even these post-op keys are not required in most cases.

Keyboard selections in *Navlipi* are very logical, with almost no disruption of the American QWERTY scheme, yet minimal addition of new keys (see separate chapter on keyboarding).

Navlipi also uses a set of very distinct, easy to write, print and keyboard postops for *tones* as well. This makes tones much easier to recognize and render in print, cursive and keyboard. Furthermore, the *Navlipi* tone postops are also extremely easy and quick to render in cursive, yet also remain very distinctive in cursive. This is in contrast to the diacritics and confusing accents used in many other transcriptions of tones, including that of the IPA. Indeed, in this author's opinion, the IPA's rendition of tones is so difficult

Chapter 2: Objectives Set Forth for a New Script, How Navlipi Meets These Objectives, and Arguments Against a New, Universal Script

that many have termed reading these "decipherment" rather than reading!

2.1.6 SYSTEMATIC, SCIENTIFIC CLASSIFICATION, AND ACCURACY (REQUIREMENT #6)

Systematic, scientific classification is unfortunately a feature lacking in the IPA, perhaps due to its ad-hoc, "build-as-you-go-along" origins. Thus, to this day, the IPA Chart unfortunately remains a rather disorganized presentation lacking meaningful form.

In this respect and in contrast, *Navlipi* uses as a starting point the highly scientific and systematic phonological classification and arrangement of the ancient Indian scripts. Thus, there is an inherent scientific and systematic base in *Navlipi*. As discussed in much more detail elsewhere in this book, this phonological classification is, today, highly inadequate and incomplete, even for transcription of the Indian languages for which it is used. Nevertheless, it remains the best starting point, even today. The Indian phonological classification and scripts are discussed in detail in a later, separate chapter in this book. As shown therein, the Indian classification system for nonvowels presents itself as a two-dimensional matrix, and bases itself, in extremely logical sequence, on the articulation or contact position (*sparsha*) of the articulating organs, starting with the back of the speech apparatus. It uses just five positions: *velar (kanthya), palatal (taalavya), retroflex and retroflex/alveolar (muurdhanya), dental (dantya)* and *bilabial (oshthya)*, for the vertical, "y-axis" of the matrix. It then further breaks these down into *unvoiced* vs. *voiced, aspirated* vs. *unaspirated, nasal, semivowel* and *fricative*, giving five positions for the horizontal, "x-axis", and thus yielding a 5 X 7 matrix.

For the sole purpose of providing a "flavor" of *Navlipi*, we show how *Navlipi* expands the Indian classification. *Navlipi* takes the basic Indian classification and expands it to **15** artitions, which constitute the "**y-axis**" of the *Navlipi* phonological classification for *non-vowels*. Similarly, *Navlipi* takes the five "x-axis" classes of the Indian classification, i.e. the phonochromaticity (*unvoiced/unaspirated, unvoiced/aspirated, voiced/unaspirated, voiced/aspirated, nasal*) and expands them into **35**. These comprise the "**x-axis**" of the *non-vowel* segment of the *Navlipi* phonological classification. These are shown in the Tables below.

Table 2-3: *THE 15 ARTITIONS (ARTICULATION POSITIONS) OF NAVLIPI*

1. *Glottal*
2. *Pharyngeal*
3. *Uvular*
4. *Velar*
5. *Retroflex*
6. *Medio-Palatal*
7. *Palatal*
8. *Alveolar*
9. *Apico/Medio-Dental*
10. *Standard Dental*
11. *Pharyngealized Dental*
12. *Interdental*
13. *Infralabio-Supradental*
14. *Supralabio-Infradental*
15. *Bilabial*

Chapter 2: Objectives Set Forth for a New Script, How Navlipi Meets These Objectives, and Arguments <u>Against</u> a New, Universal Script

Table 2-4:   *THE 35 PHONOCHROMES OF NAVLIPI*

1. *Unvoiced/unaspirated*
2. *Unvoiced/aspirated*
3. *Voiced/unaspirated*
4. *Voiced/aspirated*
5. *Nasal*
6. *Fricative/unvoiced*
7. *Fricative/voiced*
8. *Flap/unaspirated*
9. *Flap/aspirated*
10. *Flap/nasal*
11. *Flap/fricatized*
12. *Trill/normal*
13. *Trill/fricatized*
14. *Click, ingressive, central, single, unvoiced*
15. *Click, ingressive, central, single, voiced*
16. *Click, ingressive, central, single, nasal*
17. *Click, ingressive, central, trill*
18. *Click, ingressive, lateral, single, unvoiced*
19. *Click, ingressive, lateral, single, voiced*
20. *Click, ingressive, lateral, single, nasal*
21. *Click, ingressive, lateral, trill*
22. *Click, egressive, central*
23. *Click, egressive, lateral*
24. *Ejective, unvoiced*
25. *Ejective, fricative*
26. *Implosive, unvoiced*
27. *Implosive, voiced*
28. *Semivowel, simple*
29. *Semivowel, pharyngeal*
30. *Semivowel, central*
31. *Semivowel, lateral, unaspirated*
32. *Semivowel, lateral, aspirated*
33. *Semivowel, lateral, fricatized*
34. *Semivowel, lateral, palatalized*
35. *Semivowel, lateral, pharyngealized*

PART 2: INTRODUCTION

Regarding *completeness* and *accuracy*, it will be seen from **PART 1,** the **Navlipi Summary Tables,** at the beginning of this book that there are certain phones which the IPA and most other orthographies simply do not address. And there are representations, such as the "rhoticity" used by the IPA, where the present author feels an error has been made in classification by the IPA (as discussed in the chapter on Prior Art).

2.1.7 DISCRETIZATION (REQUIREMENT #7)

Human phonology, as exemplified by tongue-articulation/contact or jaw positions, embodies nearly *continuous* variables. For example, between the dental and the palatal artitions, one can essentially vary the tongue contact position continuously, starting from the dental and slowly inching up to the palatal. Indeed, tongue contact positions are actually continuously variable, and do not have the discrete values such as "alveolar" or "dental" that phoneticians like to assign. Jaw positions are similarly nearly continuous, although most phoneticians discretize these into four (open, open-mid, close-mid, close). And again, lip positions are actually continuous between the discretized three (rounded, stretched, flat). Some *discretization* of this continuity is absolutely necessary to keep any phonological classification within limits.

As one specific example of the need for discretization, we may note that, between the dental and palatal tongue artitions, there may be as many as *12* different positions found in the world's languages. Further reduction of these 12 positions is thus absolutely necessary. *Navlipi* discretizes these into just five: Four which comprise *dental, alveolo-dental, alveolo-palatal,* and *palatal,* with *tongue-apex (apico)* contact; and a fifth *alveolo-palatal* position with *tongue-apico/medio* contact (to accommodate the most common *s*-sound).

Without discretization, it is evident that the non-vowel phonological matrix of *Navlipi* briefly shown in the previous Section, which is at an already large **15 X 33 elements**, would be unmanageable, perhaps 25 X 50 elements or larger!

Chapter 2: Objectives Set Forth for a New Script, How Navlipi Meets These Objectives, and Arguments <u>Against</u> a New, Universal Script

2.1.8 PRACTICAL PHONEMICS RATHER THAN PHONICS (REQUIREMENT #8)

It is important to note that, in spite of its very thorough and scientific treatment of **phones**, *Navlipi remains fundamentally a* **phonemic** *system*. Thus, while the IPA can be used to accurately transcribe the differences in pronunciation of two individuals speaking the same language, that was not the intention in the formulation of Navlipi. Navlipi's objective was different: *To phonemically accommodate the world's languages*.

2.1.9 VOICE-RECOGNITION COMPATIBILITY AND A VOICE-RECOGNITION SOFTWARE PACKAGE (REQUIREMENT # 9)

Following publication of the print version of this book, it was the author's intention to produce a voice-recognition package for an American English version of *Navlipi*, and possibly to offer it as a freely downloadable package on the Internet. This would serve as a beginning.

2.1.10 ABILITY TO ACCOMMODATE THE PHONEMIC IDIOSYNCRASIES OF ALL THE WORLD'S LANGUAGES (REQUIREMENT # 10)

This, final property of *Navlipi*, which has been demonstrated with some examples above and will further crystallize in the sequel in this book, is its strongest and most unique property. As mentioned many times elsewhere in this book, *to the best of our knowledge as of this writing (2005)*, **no other world script addresses phonemic idiosyncrasy; no other world script conveys information on phonemic idiosyncrasy of a language to its reader.**

PART 2: INTRODUCTION

2.2 ARGUMENTS *AGAINST* A NEW, UNIVERSAL, PHONIC OR PHONEMIC ORTHOGRAPHY (SCRIPT)

Although there are many arguments *for* a universal phonetic and phonemic orthography, most of which are expounded in this book, there are, in fairness, a few not entirely weak arguments *against* one. We cite here several examples of arguments *against* a universal orthography, especially one to replace the ubiquitous, all-pervasive Roman script:

(1) *Historic baggage and word origins:*

A phonetic orthography will remove the *historic baggage carried by transcriptions* of such languages as modern French and English. Thus, one would have greater difficulty in guessing, from their modern pronunciations, that French *monts* ("mountains") and Spanish or Italian *montes* are related, or that English *light, fight, night* are close cognates of German *licht, fecht, nacht*. One would also have great trouble, e.g., in tracing French words to their Latin origins, since in many cases the modern French pronunciations have no resemblance to their modern French orthography (or the Old French pronunciation), and thence to the Latin origins.

(2) *Homophones*:

Homophones with different spellings, e.g. English *cite, sight* and *site*, would now have to be distinguished purely from context in reading.

(3) *Mental exercise:*

A more abstract, argument relates to the concept of *"mental exercise"*: When reading a highly *un-phonetic* transcription such as English or Dutch, there is a lot of intellectual exercise involved in remembering the different pronunciations of the same spellings, which some believe sharpens the intellect.

(4) *"If it ain't broke, don't fix it":*

One of the perhaps most important arguments *against* a new orthography is of course the most mundane one: *"Why do it at all, when everything's working*

Chapter 2: Objectives Set Forth for a New Script, How Navlipi Meets These Objectives, and Arguments Against a New, Universal Script

fine today?", or the street-wise *"If it ain't broke, don't fix it."* In answer to this, this author might reply "It isn't really working all that fine today. Besides, we can't communicate between languages, except those written in Roman script. And it's very hard to learn another's language when you have to learn a new script too. Just try learning Russian or Arabic. For an even worse situation, look at India with its at least ten different scripts for more than 15 languages. These throw up a huge obstacle when one Indian tries to learn another Indian's language. (This actually helps the propagation of English in India, but that is another story.) We thus modify our street-wise saying to *"It ain't quite broke, but it ain't all that fixed either, and it still doesn't work in many places."*

(5) *Difficulty in changing set habits:*

Another argument, related to the previous one, that militates against attempting a new, universal script is the sheer difficulty of dislodging an established script, whether it be Roman in Europe, Dewanaagari in India, or the Chinese ideography in China. The problems encountered by Linux in dislodging Microsoft Windows (as an operating system for PC's), a subject of current relevance at the time of this writing (2005-6), would appear to pale by comparison. This book thus seeks to accomplish what would appear to be a gargantuan, *perhaps impossible* task, and this author acknowledges that it may not succeed. On the other hand, we note that the Linux/Windows analogy may not be accurate, for *Navlipi* is similar to and based upon the Roman script which it humbly seeks to dislodge, whereas the Unix-based Linux is definitely not based on Microsoft Windows and differs substantially from it. As a means of slow introduction of *Navlipi* in a country such as India, it could perhaps be taught alongside the local script, but not replace it: Kids would learn, along with their standard *"ka kha ga"*, the *Navlipi* equivalents. Books may initially be printed in both scripts. As one such example, one could propose that the great ancient works in Sanskrit can be brought out in such dual-script representation as a means of promoting *Navlipi*.

PART 2: INTRODUCTION

CHAPTER 3.
OTHER PRIOR ART

TABLE OF CONTENTS

3.1 WHAT IS COVERED IN THIS CHAPTER: *NEW* SCRIPTS SPECIFICALLY ATTEMPTING SYSTEMATIC, SCIENTIFIC, PHONIC OR PHONEMIC CLASSIFICATION 195

3.2 ASIAN CONTRIBUTIONS 198

    3.2.1 HAANGUL (HANGUL) 198
    3.2.2 OTHER ASIAN CONTRIBUTIONS: THE VARIOUS MODI'S, JAPANESE, PAHAWH, VARANG KSHITI AND OTHERS 201
    3.2.3 THE INDIAN SCRIPTS 204
        3.2.3.1 SCIENTIFIC AND SYSTEMATIC CLASSIFICATION OF THE INDIAN SCRIPTS AND USE OF THIS AS BASIS FOR EXPANSION 204
        3.2.3.2 THE ORIGINAL INDIAN CLASSIFICATION, IN SUMMARY 208
        3.2.3.3 THE VOWELS 210
        3.2.3.4 JAW, LIP AND TONGUE POSITIONS AS INDEPENDENT VARIABLES IN THE INDIAN CLASSIFICATION 215
        3.2.3.5 PROBABLE ORIGINAL SIGNIFICANCE OF SOME ELEMENTS OF THE INDIAN VOWEL CLASSIFICATION: THE WISARGA AS GLOTTAL STOP AND THE DIPHTHONGS AS PURE VOWELS 216
        3.2.3.6 THE NON-VOWELS: ARTITION AND PHONOCHROMATICITY AS THE TWO INDEPENDENT VARIABLES 218
        3.2.3.7 ACCURACY OF THE ANCIENT CLASSIFICATION, DESPITE LACK OF MODERN SCIENTIFIC INSTRUMENTATION 220
        3.2.3.8 INADEQUACIES OF THE ANCIENT CLASSIFICATION EVEN FOR TODAY'S INDIAN LANGUAGES 220

3.3 EARLY EUROPEAN CONTRIBUTIONS: FROM HART TO MULCASTER 225

PART 2: INTRODUCTION

3.4 RECENT EUROPEAN AND NORTH AMERICAN CONTRIBUTIONS...... 229

3.4.1 "Shorthands" and the Seminal Phonological Classification of Pitman 229
3.4.2 The Alphabets/Scripts of Pitman, Ellis, Graham, Watt, Lepsius, Bell, Sweet, Jespersen, Janvrin, Story, Johnston, Owen, Pike, and Others......... 233

3.5 NATIVE NORTH-AMERICAN AND AFRICAN CONTRIBUTIONS 260

3.5.1 Scripts for Native American Languages of North America: Cherokee, Cree, Inuktitut, Others 260
3.5.2 New Scripts for African Languages: Vai, N'ko 262

3.6 OTHER RECENT CONTRIBUTIONS 264

3.6.1 Assorted Other Attempts at New Scripts: Unifon, Shavian, Columbian, Abulhab, Fraser, Pollard 264
3.6.2 Assorted Other Attempts at New Scripts, cont.: Tolkien, LeGuin, Bloquerst, Wilbur, Arthur, Greenaway, Others 269

3.7 THE IPA (ALPHABET OF THE INTERNATIONAL PHONETIC ASSOCIATION) AND SERIOUS DEFICIENCIES THEREOF 270

3.8 *AMERICANIST* PHONETIC NOTATION (SCRIPT) 279

3.9 BRIEF SYNOPSIS OF DEFICIENCIES OF ALL ALPHABETS/SCRIPTS CITED ABOVE 283

Chapter 3: Other Prior Art

3.1 WHAT IS COVERED IN THIS CHAPTER: *NEW* SCRIPTS SPECIFICALLY ATTEMPTING SYSTEMATIC, SCIENTIFIC, PHONIC OR PHONEMIC CLASSIFICATION

It is expressly noted at the outset that this chapter focuses on and *limits* itself to the following:

> ### *DEFINITION OF THE ONLY SCRIPTS COVERED IN THIS CHAPTER*
>
> **(1)** *NEW* scripts ("alphabets") that have *specifically been attempts at a **scientific and/or systematic phonic or phonemic classification**.* (By "new" we imply anything within the last 1500 years or so!)
>
> **(2)** *Of these,* in turn, *scripts that are either **entirely new creations or involve substantial new innovation**,* rather than those that are simply derived from or based on older phonic/phonemic classifications.

SCRIPTS PRECLUDED BY THE FIRST PART OF DEFINITION: The *first* part of the above, dual, definition precludes most ancient scripts, for example those listed below:

- The very first ideographic scripts, including, e.g.:
    - The older **Egyptian hieroglyphic.**
    - The old **Chinese**.
- Well known ancient scripts such as **Cuneiform** (for languages ranging from Sumerian to Persian).
- **Demotic Egyptian**.
- **Linear B**.
- All the **Semitic** scripts.
- The ancient **Mayan** scripts.
- **Classical Greek** and **Roman** scripts.

PART 2: INTRODUCTION

This is because *none of them were based on a scientific or systematic classification of phones*, nor, indeed, much semblance of organization. Needless to say, tomes are available in the literature on these ancient scripts. Indeed, the only ancient scripts not excluded by our definition are the Indian.

The first part of the dual definition also precludes relatively more *modern* inventions: One example of these is the script used for the present-day **Georgian** language, which, according to several accounts [SCr-76, SCr-77], is thought to have been derived from the Greek script with Persian influence in the year 412 B.C., by Georgian followers of the Persian god Mithra (Indian Mitra). (The oldest written examples date from a Georgian Orthodox church in Jerusalem dating from about 430 C.E.)

The first part of the definition also precludes such very recent inventions as the script for the **Cherokee**, **Lakota** *(Sioux)* and many other Native North American languages [SCr-62 to SCr-64], although it does *not* preclude some, like the **Inuktikut** [SCr-78 to SCr-80]. Many of these scripts are precluded because none have a systematic or scientific organization. We nevertheless discuss them briefly in this chapter, if only because they represent good faith (although unsuccessful) attempts at arriving at a systematic, scientific script *ab initio*, i.e. from first principles.

And parenthetically, we also note that mere *typographic reform*, e.g. that carried out by Jan **Tschichold** of Leipzig for German in the 1920's [SCr-81], is also not covered in this chapter.

SCRIPTS PRECLUDED BY THE SECOND PART OF THE DEFINITION: The *second* part of the above dual definition precludes such scripts as:

- The **Tibetan**.
- The **South East Asian** (**Khmer, Thai, Burmese**, etc.).
- The Mongolian **Phagspa**, and others, since these were derived from Indian scripts based on **Braahmi**.

Those among the above scripts that are relevant to the discussion, such as *Phagspa*, are discussed very briefly in this chapter.

In fact, of the Asian scripts, only **Haangul** is left as satisfying both parts of the above dual definition.

YET UNDECIPHERED ANCIENT SCRIPTS: For completeness, we must mention the fact that several ancient scripts that are as yet undeciphered *could, conceivably, have contained some element of a scientific or systematic phonological classification*. Among these are the ***Olmec***, as represented by just a few glyphs found on a monument in La Venta, Mexico and in the "Cascajal Block" in the Veracruz area of Mexico [SCr-38], and the ***Harappan***, found on Indus Valley seals and dating from about 3300 to 2500 B.C. (the earliest Harappan writing, discovered recently by Harvard University's Harappan project, has been dated at about 3350 B.C.E. [HIi-6 to HIi-8, LAi-13 to LAi-23]). There is general agreement by varied scholars that the Harappan script was most likely logophonetic [LAi-13 to LAi-18]. However, such intriguing, telltale features as the use of ligatures, which has survived through to the modern Indian script, and the grouping of variations of particular glyphs, provide some indication of a possible phonetic organization as well. If such phonetic organization is true, then it is possible that the Harappan script may have been a precursor to Braahmi and its phonological classification, as discussed in more detail elsewhere in this book.

PART 2: INTRODUCTION

3.2 ASIAN CONTRIBUTIONS

3.2.1 HAANGUL (HANGUL)

The Korean Haangul (Hangul) was briefly presented earlier in this book, and is discussed at greater length here.

Origins: Haangul (Hangul) [SCr-46 to SCr-53] remains *one of the truly innovative and scientific scripts* developed in recent (post 1000 C.E.) times, some would say *the* most scientific.

Haangul's provenance, as ascribed by Koreans, is from King Sejong of the Choson dynasty. He is said to have devised it himself [SCr-47 to SCr-51], with the secret assistance of family members schooled in Buddhist scholarship. The main document, *Hunmin Jeongeum*, was published in the year 1446 C.E., either on 9 October (according to South Koreans) or 15 January (according to North Koreans).

Haangul is known to have been based, in part, on the Mongolian ***Phagspa*** script, in which script an extensive collection of books existed in King Sejong's library [SCr-53, SCr-54]. Phagspa itself was derived from the Tibetan script, which in turn is of course based on Braahmi.

Thus, in a very indirect way, Haangul may be said to be ultimately based on Braahmi. Now Phagspa strictly falls within the purview of the exclusion of the first part of our dual definition above. However, it does have relevance to the origins of Haangul. Phagspa was named after its eponymous inventor. It is said to have been derived from the Tibetan script in the year 1368, during the Yuan dynasty in China [SCr-53, SCr-54]. Being derived ultimately from the Indian phonological classification, Phagspa included, for instance, variants of the unvoiced/voiced/nasal and aspirated/unaspirated differentiations and the classification based on oral articulation position for non-vowels, which are all characteristic of Indian phonology. Some scholars have even identified which specific letters within Haangul originated in Phagspa [SCr-53].

Thus, we may say that the ultimate basis of the *classification system* (but certainly not the actual glyphs) that Haangul used may have been brought to Korea along with Buddhist teachings. We must also qualify this immediately by noting that Haangul extended the scientific classification and presentation much beyond anything imagined by the ancient Indian phoneticians.

This Buddhist provenance alluded to above needs some greater elaboration. The Southeast Asian scripts, such as Thai or Khmer or Indonesian or Burmese, were brought by either Hindu or Buddhist cultural streams entering these regions. In this respect, the Buddhist (i.e. religious) influence is of particular significance. All the Buddhist *suutra:* (scriptures) were in Sanskrit, and, for an understanding of the Sanskrit language one needed, of course, to know the Sanskrit "alphabet" (script), with the systematic and scientific phonetic classification inherent in it. And to know the Sanskrit script was of course to know and understand phonological classification. Thus, ultimately, to study the Buddhist *suutra:* one had to learn the Indian phonological classification! Furthermore, the Japanese acknowledge (and the discussion of the Japanese script further below confirms) that the vowel order and part of the nonvowel order of the Japanese script is taken from Buddhist teachings [SCr-55, LAs-59]. Thus Buddhist provenance for neighboring Korea's script is also plausible.

Hints that Haangul was indeed based on the Indian phonological classification are somewhat evident in the "alphabetical" order of the phones listed. For example, the "consonants" are ordered thus: [g]/[k], [n], [d]/[t], [r]/[l], [m], [b]/[p]..., [ch]/[j], [chh]/[jhh], etc. The resemblance to the Indian *warga* (articulation positions, i.e. artitions) is rather strong. And the Haangul displays telltale use of *maatra's* (non-initial-vowel markers) for some of its vowel modifications (e.g. lengthening). And we of course know that *maatra's* originated thousands of years earlier, in India.

Features: ***Haangul*** *represents several* ***major advances*** *and several* ***startling, innovative features*** :

- Haangul represents, *a major step forward, beyond the Indian phonological classification,* in the critical aspect of a having a **scientific notation**, which we shall call, here, **denotation** for reference purposes.
- Haangul in fact uses *a specific symbol or notation for a specific phonic property*, such as voicing, aspiration, fricatization, etc.. This is of course missing in all Indian scripts.
- Furthermore, the specific symbol chosen is ***iconic***. For example, the symbol for velar phones is a half-rectangle that represents the back of the tongue touching the velum!
- Such a scientific and iconic presentation represents, to some extent, the "dream" of every phoneticist!

PART 2: INTRODUCTION

These features, a *highly scientific notation* and, further, a specific, iconic *denotation* for a specific phonic property, are seen in the illustrative examples below:

> **Fig. 3-1**: Some representative glyphs from the ***Haangul*** (Hangul) script together with a description their significance. After references [SCr-46 to SCr-54]

- As an example, the **jamo** ㅌ is composed of three strokes, each one meaningful.
    - The top stroke indicates it is a plosive, like ㄱ g, ㄷ d, ㅈ j.
    - The middle stroke indicates that it is aspirated, like ㅎ h, ㅊ ch;
    - And the curved bottom stroke indicates that it is dental/aveolar like ㄴ n, ㄷ d.

- **Glottal** consonants, their basic shape: ㅇ is an outline of the throat.

- **Velar** consonants, these have the basic shape: ㄱ which is a side view of the back of the tongue raised toward the velum (soft palate).

- **Bilabial** consonants, e.g. ㅁ m [m], ㅂ b [p], ㅍ p [ph], have the basic shape ㅁ. This represents the outline of the lips in contact with each other, and is used for all bilabials. The top of ㅂ represents the plosive character of the b. The top stroke of ㅍ is for the aspiration.

Some drawbacks of Haangul: On the negative side, Haangul does have some drawbacks. In the modern context, Haangul suffers from some problems of *recognizability*. Unfortunately, this today necessarily implies some affiliation with or resemblance to the Roman script! However, Haangul is not recognizable even with respect to Chinese or Japanese glyphs, thus narrowly limiting itself to the Korean peninsula. Haangul also has some issues with regard to rapid manual cursive writing, since the pen must be lifted from the paper frequently. Cursive forms of Haangul also have legibility problems for all other than the writer; these problems are greater than for other scripts.

On a somewhat facetious note here, this author notes that, with the "creative imagination" of some scholars such as Bühler [LAi-78, LAi-79] (discussed in an earlier chapter), displayed so well when it comes to Semitic vs. Indian scripts, one could well imagine *all* the Haangul letters coming from Braahmi letters! Indeed, it may be contended that, were one to apply the same methods applied by Bühler for the derivation of Braahmi from Semitic alphabets, one would have a much *stronger* case for the derivation of Haangul from Braahmi than Bühler did for his derivation! For example, the bilabial non-vowels of Haangul, e.g. [ba], [ma], are nearly identical to the corresponding Braahmi letters. Other evidence however strongly establishes that Haangul glyphs were *not* derived from Braahmi, and we will certainly not make a Bühler-type argument here!

3.2.2 OTHER ASIAN CONTRIBUTIONS: THE *VARIOUS MODI'S, JAPANESE, PAHAWH, VARANG KSHITI* AND OTHERS

The various Modi's: There have been several other attempts at improvement of prior systematic or scientific phonological classification within the last two millennia. Many of these have been on the Indian subcontinent, and all of these in turn have of course been based on the already well established principles of the ancient Indian phonological classification.

Of these contributions on the Indian subcontinent, we shall mention only one that is of particular note. This was developed in medieval times in western India and given the appellation ***Modi***, or "curved", i.e. cursive, script. There were various *Modi's* and they were primarily applied to medieval and, later, modern Maraathi and Gujaraati. Among the various *Modi* variants for Maraathi, a variant invented by one Hemadripant, the prime minister in the Yaadavaa court, around 1260 C.E., ended up being the most widely used [SCr-75].

Japanese: The Japanese script [SCr-55, LAs-59, SCr-1], a syllabary, represents a highly organized and strictly phonological system that is able to accommodate its target language, Japanese, very well. It uses some borrowed Chinese characters (*Kanji*), and different spellings (*Hiragana* vs. *Katagana (Katakana)*) depending on context and foreign origin. It is phonemic, in the sense that there is a nearly one-to-one correspondence between glyphs and phonemically distinct syllables found in the language. The syllabary has the distinct advantage that the language that it represents contains a limited number of syllables, just 66.

Although its glyphs are clearly of indigenous origin, it displays, in its "alphabetic" order (identical for *Hiragana* and *Katagana*), clear traces of an origin in the Indian

PART 2: INTRODUCTION

phonological classification [SCr-55]: **(1)** The vowels have the same order as the Indian classification. **(2)** The nonvowel plosives have the same order as the Indian classification (*ka, cha, t~a, ta, pa*) with some accommodation made for Japanese phonology (e.g. *sa* substituted for *cha*) and the voiced and unvoiced plosives have separate series. **(3)** The semivowels follow the Indian classification exactly (*ya, ra, la, wa*) except for the deletion of the *la*, which of course does not exist in Japanese. Thus, somewhat as for Haangul, the Japanese script's phonological foundations appear to have been in Budhhist literature, and thus ultimately, in Braahmi. However, its glyphs and refinements are very clearly Japanese.

The primary deficiency of the Japanese script is its narrow applicability, to only one language, Japanese; that is to say, it is *incomplete*.

Pahawh: The *Pahawh* script is said to have been created for *Hmong* as recently as the 1950's, by a Hmong farmer, Shong Lue Yang, said to have been illiterate [SCr-67, SCr-1]. It is very scientific, in the sense of associating one type of glyph with one vowel, and one type of diacritic with one of the eight tones of Hmong. One representation of this script is given in the Figure below. Its limitation to Hmong only, i.e. its *incompleteness*, is evident from this.

Sorang Sampeng, Ol Ciki and **Varang Kshiti**: Other scripts in this category deserve mention only in passing, for purpose of documentation only, since most do not meet our dual definitions above.

Among these are scripts for the Austro-Asiatic languages of India: The *Sorang Sampeng* script for *Sora* and *Ol Ciki* for *Santhali* [SCr-1]. The *Varang Kshiti* script used for *Ho*, a dialect of Santhali, is extremely unique, in that it is a sort of surviving, adapted Braahmi! Many of its glyphs are the original Braahmi forms. It is as if time held still in the isolated regions inhabited by the Santhals while scripts in the rest of India changed from Braahmi to its modern descendants [SCr-1].

Chapter 3: Other Prior Art

Fig. 3-2: A representation of the *Pahawh* script invented for Hmong. Reproduced with permission from Refs. [SCr-1, SCr-67].

HMONG

—´ high level	—. low glottalized	—̬ low rising	—ˆ high falling	—ˆ mid rising	— mid level	—` low level	—.. falling breathy
keeb	keem	keed	keej	keev	kee	kees	keeg
kib	kim	kid	kij	kiv	ki	kis	kig
kaub	kaum	kaud	kauj	kauv	kau	kaus	kaug
kub	kum	kud	kuj	kuv	ku	kus	kug
keb	kem	ked	kej	kev	ke	kes	keg
kaib	kaim	kaid	kaij	kaiv	kai	kais	kaig

PART 2: INTRODUCTION

3.2.3 THE INDIAN SCRIPTS

3.2.3.1 Scientific and Systematic Classification of the Indian Scripts and Use of This as Basis for Expansion

The ancient Indian phonological classification provides **an extremely scientific, systematic, remarkably well-organized, and elegant basis from which to further develop a more complex phonological classification.**

Together with Korean Haangul and the Pitman shorthand, the Indian scripts, including the ancient ones as well as the modern ones in use today, remain one of the most scientific and systematically organized of any orthography to date. All Indian scripts used today (12 major ones, several minor ones), excepting the Arabic-based scripts used for Urdu and Sindhi, are descended from a script denoted as **Braahmi** [LAi-60 to LAi-64, LAi-36]. This was widely used *for the Indian vernacular languages (Praakrts)* in the middle of the 1st millennium B.C.E.. The variant used by Emperor Asoka (Ashoka) on his edicts is known as Asokan (Ashokan) Braahmi. Braahmi inscriptions have been found as far afield as Sri Lanka (500 B.C.E.), Bengal and Gandhaara (present-day Kandahar in Afghanistan, 350 B.C.E.).

Among modern descendants, the most well known is *Naagari,* "urban", also known as *Dewanaagari (Devanagari)*, "refined urban". This is used today in minor variations for Hindi, Maraathi, Nepaali and Sanskrit. In addition to the present-day Indian scripts, the original Indian phonological classification gave rise to many other scripts in Southeast Asia and elsewhere [LAi-65 to LAi-73], including, e.g., Thai, Khmer (Cambodian), Indonesian (Indonesian Malay, Balinese, etc., replaced at Indonesian independence by the Roman script), Tibetan, and Burmese (Myanmari). For example, Thai and Khmer are descended from a script whose closest modern Indian descendants are the scripts used for Kannadaa (Kannada) and Telaguu (Telugu).

Along with the Korean Haangul [SCr-46 to SCr-53] and the Pittman shorthand (and later, other shorthands) [SCr-56 to SCr-61], the Indian scripts are also the first attempts at an *ab initio*, systematic, scientific phonic classification. They can, for example, be contrasted with the "alphabet" of the IPA, which, as noted in many earlier parts of this book, is a somewhat disorganized, ad-hoc expansion from the already disorganized, ad-hoc Roman "alphabet" on which it is based, although it might be presented in a phonologically clear tabular form in the IPA Charts.

Chapter 3: Other Prior Art

205

A common misconception, especially among scholars of non-Indian origin, is *that Braahmi was a script widely used for Sanskrit*. As many references in the ancient Indian literature establish [LAi-10, LAi-60 to LAi-64], however, *Braahmi was not generally used for Sanskrit, for which it was considered inadequate and for which a now-lost script was thought to be used*. Braahmi itself is thought to descend from an earlier, now-lost script.

Indeed, **the precise scripts used in ancient India are almost immaterial, since it is the phonological classification used, which is referred to in the earliest Vedic writings, that is of greater importance**: This tabular (matrix) formulation or template of the ancient Indian phoneticians could really be filled in with any "alphabetical" letters, even Roman letters!

In the specific context of **Navlipi**, we may now briefly present and discuss the *non-vowel* portion of the modern *Dewanaagari* script, shown in the **Tables** below.

PART 2: INTRODUCTION

Table 3-1: *Non-vowel* (*wyanjana, vyanjana*) portion of the ancient Indian phonological classification, including semivowels and fricatives, as represented in the *Dewanaagari* script. The Table includes a column for the corresponding vowels, inserted in highlight before the semivowels, to show their relation with the nonvowels in terms of artition. (*Ashokan Braahmi script is also shown, for reference.*)

Legend:
R= ROMAN EQUIVALENT
D= DEWANAAGARI
B= BRAAHMI

ARTI-TION (*y-axis*) ↓	PHONOCHROMATICITY (*x-axis*) ⇒											
	PLOSIVES											
	Unaspirated (Unvoiced)			Aspirated (Unvoiced)			Unaspirated (Voiced)			Aspirated (Voiced)		
	R	D	B	R	D	B	R	D	B	R	D	B
GLOT-TAL												
VELAR	[ka]	क	+ (DEMO)	[kha]	ख	↑	[ga]	ग	∧	[gha]	घ	⊔
PALA-TAL	[cha]	च	d	[chha]	छ	ф	[ja]	ज	ε	[jha]	झ	⊢
RETRO-FLEX	[.ta]	ट	(	[.tha]	ठ	O	[.da]	ड	┌	[.dha]	ढ	6
DEN-TAL	[ta]	त	ʎ	[tha]	थ	⊙ (DEMO)	[da]	द	♭	[dha]	ध	D
BILA-BIAL	[pa]	प	Ử	[pha]	फ	⊾	[ba]	ब	□	[bha]	भ	⊓

(Table 3-1, cont.)

Legend:

R= ROMAN EQUIVALENT
D= DEWANAAGARI
B= BRAAHMI

ARTI-TION (y-axis) ↓	PHONOCHROMATICITY (x-axis) ⇒											
	NASALS			SEMI-VOWELS			FRICATIVES			(CORRESPONDING VOWELS)		
	R	D	B	R	D	B	R	D	B	R	D	B
GLOTTAL							[ha]	ह	↳	[a]	अ	H
VELAR	[ⁿna]	ङ	[									
PALATAL	[ña]	ञ	ђ	[ya]	य	↓	[sha]	श	⋀	[i]	इ	∵
RETRO-FLEX	[.na]	ण	I	[ra]	र	ʃ	[retroflex-sha]	ष	ᴄ	[r]	ऋ	ʃ
DENTAL	[na]	न	⊥	[la]	ल	⌄	[sa]	स	⌄	[l]	ॡ	⌄
BILABIAL	[ma]	म	8	[wa]	व	♂				[u]	उ	L

PART 2: INTRODUCTION

3.2.3.2 The Original Indian Classification, in Summary

Table 3-1 above has summarized the *non-vowel* portion of the Indian classification. **Table 3-2** below summarizes the *vowel* portion of the classification.

> **Table 3-2:** The *vowel* (*swara*) portion of the ancient Indian phonological classification, as represented in the *Dewanaagari* script. (The *non-vowels* were presented in the previous **Table**.) Note that the vowels shown are used only as initial or stand-alone. "Interconsonantal" vowels, i.e. those between non-vowels, are expressed only as *maatraa*'s. (*Ashokan Braahmi script is again shown for reference as well*.)

ARTITION ↓	FUNDAMENTAL VOWELS			DERIVATIVE VOWELS		
	Roman equi-valent	Dewa-naagari	Braahmi	Roman equivalent	Dewa-naagari	Braahmi
Glottal		ः	ः			
Velar	[a]	अ	H	[aa]	आ	HÇ
Palatal	[i]	इ	∴	[e, aae]	ए, ऐ	▷, ▷
Bilabial	[u]	उ	L	[o, aau]	ओ, औ	L, = *(latter diacritic only)*
Retroflex	[r] *(vocalic)*	ऋ	ƭ			
Dental	[l] *(vocalic)*	ऌ	ᒎ			
Nasal	[~]	ँ	ं			

Chapter 3: Other Prior Art

It is important to note that the classification, as embodied in **Tables 3-1, 3-2** above, was originally applied to the Sanskrit language from *time immemorial*. Our phrase *time immemorial* has a particular significance: The earliest known Sanskrit writings, in the *RgWeda (RgVeda, Rig Veda)* , already included exegesis, i.e. analysis (including the *padapaatha, vyaakhyaa* or *bhaashya* or *tiikaa* and other elements [LAi-6 to LAi-8, LAi-80, LAi-81]), as an integral part of their text. That exegesis in turn discussed phonology in some detail, and pre-assumed a knowledge of the already well-established Sanskrit grammatical rules. And again, the *first* chapter in the teaching of any Sanskrit grammar was phonology. And, in turn, the first chapter in teaching phonology was the "alphabet" as embodied in the Tables above!

It is also important to note that **Table 3-2** (the vowels) followed by **Table 3-1** (the nonvowels) is the "alphabetical" order in which all the Indian scripts (not just Dewanaagari) are taught even today. Thus, learning them automatically constitutes a lesson in phonological classification as well.

The above **Tables** illustrate the basis of the Indian phonological classification, and *how it is a template that can form the basis of any phonological classification*. In fact, as this author has noted earlier in this book, *Navlipi* is simply an expansion of this classification to accommodate phones found in all other world languages (although the expansion is admittedly considerable), and of course to accommodate phonemic idiosyncrasy.

Let us take a quick look at the classification, as embodied in the above **Table.** It is basically a (5 X 7) two-dimensional matrix. (In the Table, we actually show a (5 X 8) matrix to reference the fundamental vowels to the Table, as routinely done by Indian phoneticians.)

Along the 1st, *x*-dimension of this matrix, we have the *warna (varna)*, which we can equate to our term ***phonochromaticity***, i.e. the "color of the phone". This is broken down into seven sub-categories:

- *Unvoiced/unaspirated;*
- *Unvoiced/aspirated;*
- *voiced/unaspirated;*
- *voiced/aspirated;*
- *nasal*;
- *semivowel;*
- *fricative.*

PART 2: INTRODUCTION

Along the 2nd, *y*-dimension, we have the *warga (varga)* i.e. the **artition**. This is taken, quite logically, starting from the back of the mouth and progressing towards the front, in five classes:

- *Velar;*
- *Palatal;*
- *Retroflex;*
- *Dental;*
- *Bilabial.*

3.2.3.3 The Vowels

The *vowels* follow a highly scientific definition, which we gave (and discussed at some length) in an earlier chapter, namely: *Vowels are phones for which there is no impediment to the breath during articulation.* All phones which do not comply with this definition are then automatically classified as *nonvowels*.

The vowels in **Table 3-2** (above) start with the *fundamental* vowels:

Table 3-3: (*Excerpted from Table 3-2 above:*) The *fundamental* vowels.

FUNDAMENTAL VOWELS

EQ.	VOWEL	EXAMPLE	DEWANAAGARI EQUIVALENT
1.	*[a] (velar or flat)*	English *but*	अ
2.	*[i] (palatal)*	English *hit*	इ
3.	*[u] (bilabial)*	Spanish *tu*	उ
4.	*vocalic-[r] (central)*	American English *maker*	ऋ
5.	*vocalic-[l] (lateral)*	American English *able*	ऌ

These in turn are said to lead to the ***derivative*** vowels through the application of very simple, mathematical, vowel equations, which also form part of the **Sandhi** rules used in Sanskrit grammar:

> **Table 3-4**: (*Excerpted from Table 3-2 above:*) The *derivative* vowels, also giving equations showing their derivation from fundamental vowels.

DERIVATIVE VOWELS

EQ. #	VOWEL	EXAMPLE	DEWANAAGARI EQUIVALENT
6.	*[a] + [a] = [aa]*	English *father*	आ
7.	*[i] + [i] = [ii]* (*i.e. long [i]*)	English *beet*	ई
8.	*[u] + [u] = [uu]* (*i.e. long [u]*)	English *boot*	ऊ
9.	*vocalic-[r] + vocalic-[r] = [rr]* (*i.e., long vocalic-[r]*)	American English *purr*	ॠ
10.	*[a] + [i] = [e]*	Spanish *me, que*	ए
11.	*[a] + [u] = [o]*	Spanish *lo*	ओ

Combination of the vowel [aa], itself a derivative of [a], yields two further derivative vowels as follows (today, these are articulated as diphthongs, see discussion further below):

PART 2: INTRODUCTION

Table 3-5: (*Excerpted from Table 3-2 above:*) The *derivative* vowels, cont., again also giving equations showing their derivation from fundamental vowels.

DERIVATIVE VOWELS, CONT.

EQ. #	VOWEL	EXAMPLE	DEWANAAGARI EQUIVALENT
12.	[aa] + [i] = [ae] (as in *Jack*); (today rendered as diphthong, [aae] or [aai], see discussion below.)	originally, English *Jack*; today, English *lie*	ऐ
13.	[aa] + [u] = [aw] (as in *draw*); (today rendered as diphthong, [aau], see discussion below.)	originally, English *draw*; today, English *house*	औ

Finally, two other parameters relating to vowels, though not vowels themselves, are taught as part of the regular "alphabetical" order of the vowels. They are the final two elements in the vowel series:

Table 3-6: Nasalization and glottalization.

NASALIZATION AND GLOTTALIZATION:

EQ. #	VOWEL	EXAMPLE	DEWANAAGARI EQUIVALENT
14.	*[a~]* **(nasalization, anuswaara)**	French, *pont*	ṁ
15.	*[a:]* **(glottalization, wisarga (visarga)) *(today articulated as a light, "voiceless" aspiration)***	English Cockney, *lo' o' money* (lot of money)	ः

Some discussion of the above presentation of the fundamental vowels and their derivatives is now pertinent. Firstly, the scientific thoroughness, yet simplicity, of the entire classification is evident. For example, we know from modern analyses of formant frequencies that the three fundamental vowels, [a], [i], [u], *are in fact truly fundamental* (see **Fig. 3-3** below). These fundamental vowels are in turn used to derive almost all the other vowels.

Secondly, the scientific accuracy of the Sandhi equations that lead to derivative vowels is astounding: For example, taking Eq. 5, we see that when we try to articulate the [a], (i.e. tongue-flat, lips-flat, jaw close-mid) with the characteristics of [i], (i.e. tongue-forward,

PART 2: INTRODUCTION

214

lips-stretched), we immediately arrive at [e]. Therefore, [a] + [i] = [e] (Eq. 10). In a similar fashion, when we try to articulate [a] with the characteristics of [u], (i.e. tongue-back, lips-rounded), we immediately get [o], i.e. [a] + [u] = [o] (Eq. 11). We can do this more rigorously with formant frequency analysis, but do not need to. In a similar fashion, if we "add" two close-mid jaw positions, [a] and [a], we figuratively get an open-mid or open jaw position, i.e. [a] + [a] = [aa] (Eq. 6). (It is worth noting that the "derivative vowels" in (12.) and (13.) have today in Indian usage degenerated into diphthongs, as embodied in the equations. This is discussed in more detail in a subsequent section below.)

Fig. 3-3: Formant frequencies of the fundamental vowels, [**a**], [**i**] and [**u**], showing how truly "fundamental" they are: Nearly all other vowels lie within the solid line figure shown.

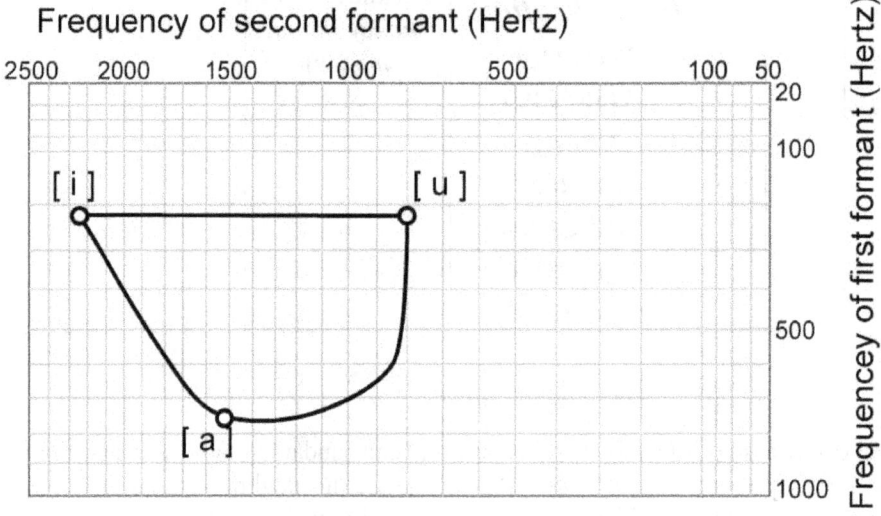

3.2.3.4 Jaw, Lip and Tongue Positions as Independent Variables in the Indian Classification

Another important feature of the Indian vowel classification should now be apparent from the above: It clearly gives us *three **independent variables*** upon which to base a classification, as shown in **Table 3-7**.

> **Table 3-7**: The *three independent variables* used in the ancient Indian phonological classification of vowels.

---

1. Jaw position: *Three* positions are recognized, *(1) close ("ardha-viraama"), (2) mid ("guna"), (3) open ("vrddhi")*. As is well known, of course, the IPA splits *mid* further into *open-mid* and *close-mid*, yielding four total positions in the IPA. And neither the Indian nor the IPA classification considers horizontal movements of the jaw, e.g. jaw-forward, jaw-retracted (as does *Navlipi*)).

2. Tongue position: *Five* are recognized, of which two correspond to vocalic-r (*retroflex*, "*muurdhanya*") and vocalic-l (*dental*, "*dantya*"). The other three positions are *velar, palatal* and *bilabial*, corresponding respectively to the Indian terms *kanthya, taalawya, oshthya*.

3. Lip position: Three are recognized: *stretched ("taalawya"), flat ("kanthya")* and *rounded ("oshthya")*. (The Indian terms are the same ones used for tongue contact position, as in 2). (It may be noted that the IPA's vowel chart recognizes only two lip positions, *rounded* and *not-rounded*.)

We can thus already start to see the utility of presenting the Indian classification as a sort of "primer" phonological classification, upon which to build a more complex one.

PART 2: INTRODUCTION

3.2.3.5 Probable Original Significance of Some Elements of the Indian Vowel Classification: The Wisarga as Glottal Stop and the Diphthongs as Pure Vowels

There is strong evidence that two aspects of the Indian *vowel* classification presented above, as used today, are different from what they were originally:

- The *wisarga (visarga)* (Eq. 15 above- *this and other equation #s hereinafter refer to those in **Tables 3-3 to 3-6** above*) was quite probably, originally, the *glottal stop* [LAi-3]. It is today articulated as a light, "voiceless" aspiration, i.e. a voiceless glottal fricative, *[voiceless-h]* [LAi-5].

- The derivative vowels represented by Eqs. 12, 13 were quite probably, originally, *true derivative vowels*. Today, they are articulated as diphthongs, as noted in the equations.

Glottalization vs. aspiration, the wisarga (visarga) (Eq. 15 above): Today, the *wisarga* is pronounced, in Sanskrit and all other Indian languages, as a type of light *aspiration*. Some phonologists and textbooks even call this a "voiceless" aspiration, or a "voiceless glottal fricative" [LAi-5], in contradistinction to the generally voiced articulation of the glottal fricative [h]. However, there is strong evidence that this phone was in fact originally a **glottal stop** [LAi-3, LAi-6, LAi-11, LAi-12]. We cite some of this evidence here briefly:

- The ancient texts [LAi-3, LAi-6, LAi-7, LAi-11, LAi-12] differentiate the glottal fricative [h] from the *wisarga* as do modern texts [LAi-5], but do not refer to it as a fricative, but rather, hint that it is a stop.

- It occurs whenever a terminal -*s* is elided in Sanskrit. The cognacy of this feature with the terminal-s of other old Indo-European languages is immediately apparent. We can most especially cite Classical Greek letter *sigma*, where non-terminal σ and terminal ς are clearly different glyphs (letters), although in original, upper-case-only inscriptions, both are rendered as Σ. We can also cite Latin, where, terminal-*s* becomes -*o* before voiced stops, exactly as in Sanskrit, e.g. *Marius* becomes *Mario*. These citations strongly indicate that the *wisarga (visarga)* was a glottal stop. This terminal-*s* relation is too large a subject to discuss here, but should be apparent to anyone with even a passing knowledge of Sanskrit, Classical Greek and Latin.

- The glottal fricative [h] is described by the ancient Indian phoneticians

[LAi-3, LAi-6, LAi-7, LAi-11, LAi-12] as a "voiced aspiration" whereas the *wisarga* is described as an "unvoiced, post-vocalic aspiration preceded by closure (*sparsha*)". The closest approximation to an "unvoiced aspiration preceded by closure" in ordinary articulation is really the glottal stop. Indeed, one cannot envision what else this description could describe.

- With such a thorough phonological treatment as their "alphabet" obviously represents, it is extremely unlikely that the ancient Indian phonologists would have omitted such an important phone as the glottal stop. Additionally, they would have been unlikely to have had two separate letters (glyphs) for a single phone, the glottal fricative ([h]), alone.

- The glottal stop thesis is corroborated by a quick analysis of the way in which glottal stops develop via elision in modern accents such as the Cockney of English. Cockney has a frequent desire to elide terminal unvoiced stops, including plosives such as [t] and fricatives such as [s]. Whenever such elision occurs, the elided stop is *invariably substituted by a glottal stop*. Thus the standard English *lot of fun* becomes Cockney *lo: o fun*, where the *[:]* is the glottal stop.

Diphthongs vs. pure derivative vowels (Eqs. 12, 13 above): In a discussion analogous to that in the previous section, the products shown on the right hand side in Eqs. 12 above are, today, denoted and pronounced as *diphthongs*, [aai], [aau]. However, there are strong indications that *they were originally pure vowels*, respectively the *a* and *ou* of English *Jack* and *bought*: Once again, we cite here briefly some of the evidence for this:

- The ancient Indian classification puts them in the same class as the derivative vowels of Eqs. 10, 11, i.e. [e], [o]. It is very unlikely that the ancient Indian phonologists, who came up with such an accurate scientific classification, would mistake diphthongs for vowels.

- If we apply Eq. 12 to [aa] in the same way as done in Eq. 10 to [a], i.e. if we apply the characteristics of [i] (lips-stretched, tongue-forward) to [aa], i.e. we immediately get the pure vowels of English *Jack* and *bought*, not any diphthongs. Similarly, if we apply Eq. 13 exactly as done in Eq. 11, we get the result seen in Eq. 13.

- Remnants of this original, true pronunciation can still be found in

PART 2: INTRODUCTION

218

modern Hindi, Baanglaa (Bengali) and other Indian languages: For example, a Hindi word such as *Mai* (मैं , "me, I") is still pronounced with a pure vowel, of the value of the *a* in English *Jack*, rather than the diphthong [aae]. In fact, this frequently leads to confusion by South Indians who have learned Hindi only by the book, and expect to hear native Hindi speakers pronounce *Mai* with the diphthong (as *Maae*), but are surprised to hear instead the pure vowel! Similarly, all Hindi words containing the supposed diphthong [aau] are actually pronounced with the pure vowel having the value of the *a* in English *ball*, rather than as the diphthong, as in *Kaun?* ("who?"). Similarly, in Baanglaa *aekta chalo* ("(let's) go alone"), the *ae* is pronounced as a pure vowel rather than a diphthong. And there is every indication that these pure-vowel pronunciations existed in the immediate predecessor languages as well, Sauraseni and Maagadhi for Hindi and Baanglaa, respectively.

3.2.3.6 The Non-Vowels: Artition and Phonochromaticity as the Two Independent Variables

The elegance and simplicity of the Indian phonological classification of non-vowels is apparent in the Non-Vowel table in Table 1 above. It can be noted firstly that the classification is basically a *two-dimensional matrix*, incorporating *just* **two independent variables**. These two independent variables are sufficient to describe the entire classification:

> **(1)** *Artition* along the *x-dimension* (the rows)
> **(2)** *Phonochromaticity* along the y-dimension (the columns).
>
> *(Both these terms were defined in an earlier chapter.)*

…(3.1)

Chapter 3: Other Prior Art

The ***artitions***, starting from the back of the speech apparatus and going towards the front, are:

> ***(Back of speech apparatus)***
> *Velar (Kanthya)*
> → *Palatal (Taalavya)*
> → *Retroflex (Muurdhanya)*
> → *Dental (Dantya)*
> → *Bilabial (Oshthya)*
> ***(Front of speech apparatus)***

...(3.2)

The artitions are of course highly incomplete by modern standards, For example, they omit the *uvular*, and intermediate positions such as *alveolar*. However, they were remarkably complete for the languages they addressed, those of India at the time.

Similarly, the simplicity yet thoroughness of the phonochromatic classification is also apparent: We start with the simplest of the plosives, the unaspirated, unvoiced ones (*ka, cha, ta,* etc.). We then add aspiration, voicing and nasalization in order. Finally, we have the semivowels and the fricatives, each with their own column. We thus have the following ***phonochromaticities*** in the Indian classification:

> *Unvoiced, Unaspirated (Karkasha, Alpapraana)*
> → *Unvoiced, Aspirated (Karkasha, Mahaapraana)*
> → *Voiced, Unaspirated (Mrdu, Alpapraana)*
> → *Voiced, Aspirated (Mrdu, Mahaapraana)*
> → *Nasal (Anunaasika)*
> → *Semivowel (Anta:stha)*
> → *Fricative (Uushman)*

...(3.3)

PART 2: INTRODUCTION

What is more, *all* phones, including nonvowels, and, through the intermediacy of the semivowels, the corresponding vowels as well, are tied into a *single matrix*, a *single* phonological presentation, as in the Non-vowel representation in **Table 3-1**. For this purpose, the artition is used as the fundamental linking mechanism.

The semivowels are derived from the parent vowels through the simple addition of [a], which again forms part of the rules of *Sandhi* thus:

Semivowels as derived from vowels:

> 1. [i] + [a] = [**ja**] (or [i] + [u] = [**ju**], etc.)
> 2. [u] + [a] = [**wa**] (or [u] + [i] = [**wi**], etc.)
> 3. [vocalic-r] + [a] = [**ra**] (or [r] + [u] = [**ru**], etc.)
> 4. [vocalic-l] + [a] = [**la**] (or [l] + [u] = [**lu**], etc.)

...(3.4)

3.2.3.7 Accuracy of the Ancient Classification, Despite Lack of Modern Scientific Instrumentation

It is important to take into perspective the high accuracy and extremely scientific, systematic methodology of classification that is apparent from the Indian classification. *The ancient Indian phoneticians did not have the instrumentation we have at our disposal today*, such as the audio instrumentation that generates phonic or audio "spectrograms" (sonograms, sound frequency vs. amplitude graphs) and soft-X-ray photography of tongue contact positions and pharynx movement used by modern linguists. Yet they had no problem in figuring out the artitions, the voicing/devoicing, the aspiration, fricatization, etc.

3.2.3.8 Inadequacies of the Ancient Classification Even for Today's Indian Languages

Wonderful as it was for its time and the languages it applied to then, the ancient Indian classification of course had gross inadequacies. Let us itemize just *some* of the deficiencies *even for Indian languages of today*. For the moment, we do not even

Chapter 3: Other Prior Art

221

consider non-Indian languages:

- It does not address even *common fricatives* such as the infralabio-supradental [f] and [v]. These are found, e.g., in many words borrowed in Hindi, Maraathi and other Indian languages from Faarsi. They are also found in Hindi from phonemic interchange (equivalence), e.g. between [f] and [ph].

- It does not address the voiced form of the sibilants [s] and [sh], i.e. [z] and [zh].

- It does not consider the alveolar plosives, e.g. the [t] of English *today*.

- It does not consider the heavily retroflexed, so-called "Dravidian" laterals and centrals (which we temporarily denote as [l~] (Tamil ழ), [r~] (Maraathi), as in Tamil *pal~am* ("fruit"), Maraathi *kar~la* ("understood").

- It does not consider later additions to Indian languages from Arabic and Faarsi, such as the uvular and the unvoiced velar fricative ([k..] and [x] respectively), and their voiced counterparts.

Many of the new phones in the above bulleted list, not addressed in the original Indian classification, have in fact been adapted into modern Indian scripts in a completely ad-hoc manner (memories of the IPA!). This has been done primarily by the addition of diacritics such as dots-underneath: For example, in the letters ([f]), ([z]) and ([k.], uvular), as shown in the **Table** below.

PART 2: INTRODUCTION

Table 3-8: Selected Adaptations of Dewanaagari Glyphs (Letters) for "foreign" phones. (Only six are given for simplicity).

Phone (*Roman equivalent*)	Adapted Dewanaagari rendition in Hindi, Maraathi, etc.	Parent Dewanaagari [*Roman equivalent in brackets*]
[f]	फ़	फ [pha]
[z]	ज़	ज [ja]
[k.] (*uvular stop*)	क़	क [ka]
[x] (*velar unvoiced fricative*)	ख़	ख [kha]
[g.] (*uvular voiced stop*)	ग़	ग [ga]
[d..] (*retroflex voiced flap*)	ड़	ड [d.a]

The Indian classification of course also does not even consider more truly "foreign" sounds widely prevalent in non-Indian languages, such as the interdental fricatives (of English *thought, though*). Indeed, for this reason, many Indians will pronounce the initial phones in these English words as the aspirated plosive [th] rather than as true fricatives!

Another great deficiency of the Indian scripts has been their poor adaptability to *cursive writing*. The speed of writing is extremely slow (though not as slow as written Chinese) and the writing instrument has to be lifted from the tablet or paper much too often. There have, from time to time, been innovations, such as the ***Modi*** (literally, "curved" or

Chapter 3: Other Prior Art

"bent") script, a variation of Dewanaagari used for Maraathi in medieval times [SCr-75]. Overall, however, these innovations have failed to address deficiencies in cursive writing.

From even a cursory glance at the above Tables, *a method for its expansion to accommodate the non-vowel phones of all the languages of the world is very clearly seen*:

METHODS FOR EXPANDING THE ANCIENT INDIAN PHONOLOGICAL CLASSIFICATION TO OUR (MODERN) NEEDS

1) Expand the x-axis (representing the ***phonochromaticity*-** the "color" of the phone) to include other categories and sub-categories, e.g. *voiced vs. unvoiced fricatives*, *clicks*, etc.

2) Similarly, expand the y-axis (representing the ***artition***) to include other artitions not covered, e.g. *pharyngeal* and *glottal* (before the *velar*), *alveolar* (before the *dental*), and *labio-dental* (after the *bilabial*), etc.

...(**3.5**)

Thus, the ancient Indian phonological classification, as exemplified by its non-vowel portion in the Tables above, forms a superb basis for developing any further, more extensive phonological classification, just as we said at the outset of this section. It is an elementary, yet firm and wonderful jumping off point for us.

There are several other features of the Indian classification which we may mention for the record and in passing only, since they do not have a direct bearing on *Navlipi*:

- It was the world's first script which attempted a one-to-one correspondence between the glyph (letter or symbol) and phoneme, although admittedly, this was valid only for the Sanskrit language of the time. That is to say, it had the unique property of *one phoneme = one phone = one glyph (symbol or letter)*.

PART 2: INTRODUCTION

- The classification appears to have been *deliberately designed*, apparently by a person or group of persons who sat down and carefully considered the phones (sounds) to be classified, and how best to classify them. Again, it is noted that this is similar to the deliberate design of the Korean Hangul script several millennia later, and is, e.g., in contrast to the "alphabet" of the International Phonetic Association (IPA), which developed in a purely ad-hoc, add-as-you-go-along, fashion from the Roman script. Although the person(s) who designed the Indian scripts did not have the benefit of modern instrumentation, e.g. for X-ray images of artitions or comparative frequency audiograms for voiced vs. unvoiced sounds, their classification nevertheless appears to have been extremely accurate and scientific.

Chapter 3: Other Prior Art

225

3.3 EARLY EUROPEAN CONTRIBUTIONS: FROM HART TO MULCASTER

Most of the European (and North American) contributions have been in the extremely recent past, within the last 400 years [SCr-82]. Among these, we briefly discuss some of the earlier ones in this section.

Some of the early European work was carried out in the 18th, 19th and 20th centuries. Driving forces for orthographic reform were the desire to increase literacy in Europe, and the realization that the transcription of languages such as English or Dutch completely confounded the notion of phonetic scripts. In this respect, Spanish was found to be "more phonetic"; yet it was acknowledged that no European language had even the one-to-one correspondence of symbol/phoneme possessed by the Indian scripts, the Korean Haangul, and, to a limited extent, the Japanese syllabary.

In the English language, one of the first to attempt a systematic phonetic transcription, in such areas as pairing of "surd/sonant" (unvoiced/voiced) stops, was one ***John Hart*** (d. ca. 1574 C.E.) [SCr-83, SCr-84]. He authored a volume entitled, simply, *Orthography* (also called *Orthology*) [SCr-83, SCr-84]. Needless to say, his treatments were deficient and incomplete by standards we know today, although advanced for the Europe of the time. For example, one of Hart's glaring errors was not to recognize the true nature of voicing vs. devoicing evidenced in his statement that the [sh] sibilant sound in English had no voiced counterpart, although it did even in the English of the time (e.g. in *plea**s**ure*). Also in England, ***Robert Robinson*** [SCr-85], working around the time of Shakespeare, was one of the first modern Europeans to classify sounds according to the place of articulation in the oral apparatus, much like the ancient Indian classification. Robinson classification for vowels is shown in the Figure below. As the figure shows, Robinson's was also one of the first examples of attempts to make use of the Roman alphabet by *inverting, turning, angling* and otherwise manipulating Roman letters, which is in full flower in the modern IPA alphabet.

The Englishman ***John Wilkins*** (d. 1672 C.E.) [SCr-86] attempted to organize both vowels and non-vowels in a single classification, seen in the Figure below. The terminology he used for unvoiced/voiced was "mute/sonorous". A comparison of this chart with the standard ancient Indian classification shows that it is incomplete, but nevertheless better than other, prior European work. Importantly, however, there is no attempt to arrive at new letters, i.e. a new script. Wilkins uses the Roman script with

PART 2: INTRODUCTION

variations of capitalization, twist and digraphs with the letter *h* which are difficult to distinguish. To his credit, though, he uses almost no diacritics. Wilkins' graphical depiction of the phones that he was able to classify is shown in the **Figure** further below.

It is worth noting that many European works in phonology before 1800 contained serious *errors* due, apparently, to a lack of a full, scientific understanding of the phones of human speech. Authors such as **Richard Mulcaster** [SCr-87]*,* **Charles Butler** [SCr-88]*,* **William Holder** [SCr-89] and **Thomas Smith** [SCr-90] working in English, or **Meigret** [SCr-91] working in French, come to mind in this category. For example, Butler characterized the sibilant [sh] sound as an "aspirate"!

In view of such errors, and the sobering fact that some of the 16th and 17th century European work had been anticipated or already carried out in antiquity, it is, in this author's opinion, somewhat surprising that modern Western scholars still accord wide respect to these authors (see, e.g., [SCr-82]). This is much like the adoration given by Europeans to Copernicus in astronomy, even though he simply rediscovered something (the Earth's rotation around the Sun and around itself) already discovered by ancient Greeks such as Eratosthenes, not to mention ancient Indian and Chinese scientists predating Eratosthenes by hundreds of years and perhaps millennia [HIh-2]!

Chapter 3: Other Prior Art

Fig. 3-4: Examples of the orthographies of *John **Hart**, Robert **Robinson*** and *John **Wilkins***. After references [SCr-82 to SCr-86], reproduced with permission.

John Hart's Orthography.

oh mein oun-lam, hou ar iu lam? O mein oun man, mei mar ran ru8-8 in mei hil on a uaul, an le mi in a mei-ēr. her mi, wuil iu hiel mei hil?

"Oh, mine own lamb, how are you lame? Oh mine own man, my mare ran rushin' my heel on a wall, and lay me in a mire.
Hear me, will you heal my heel.

Robinson's Scale of Vowels

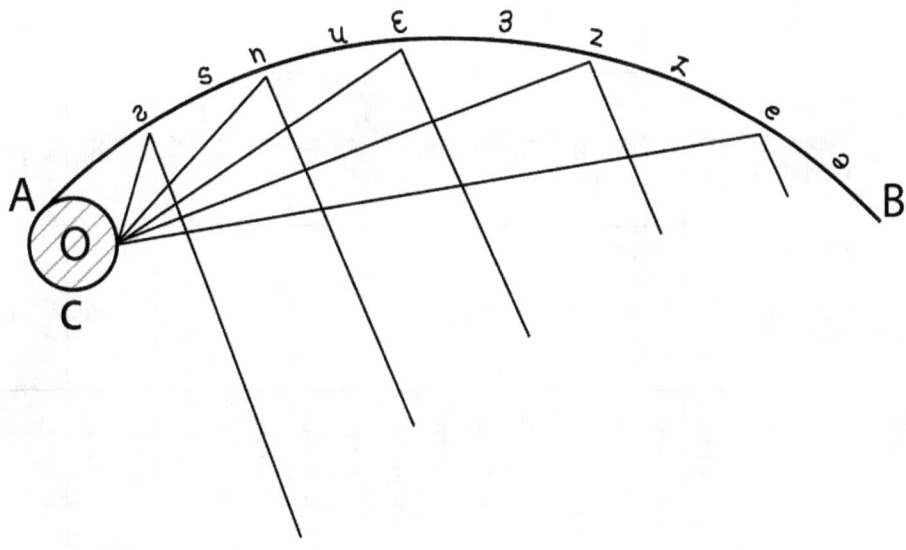

(Fig. 3-4, cont.)

WILKINS SOUND CHART

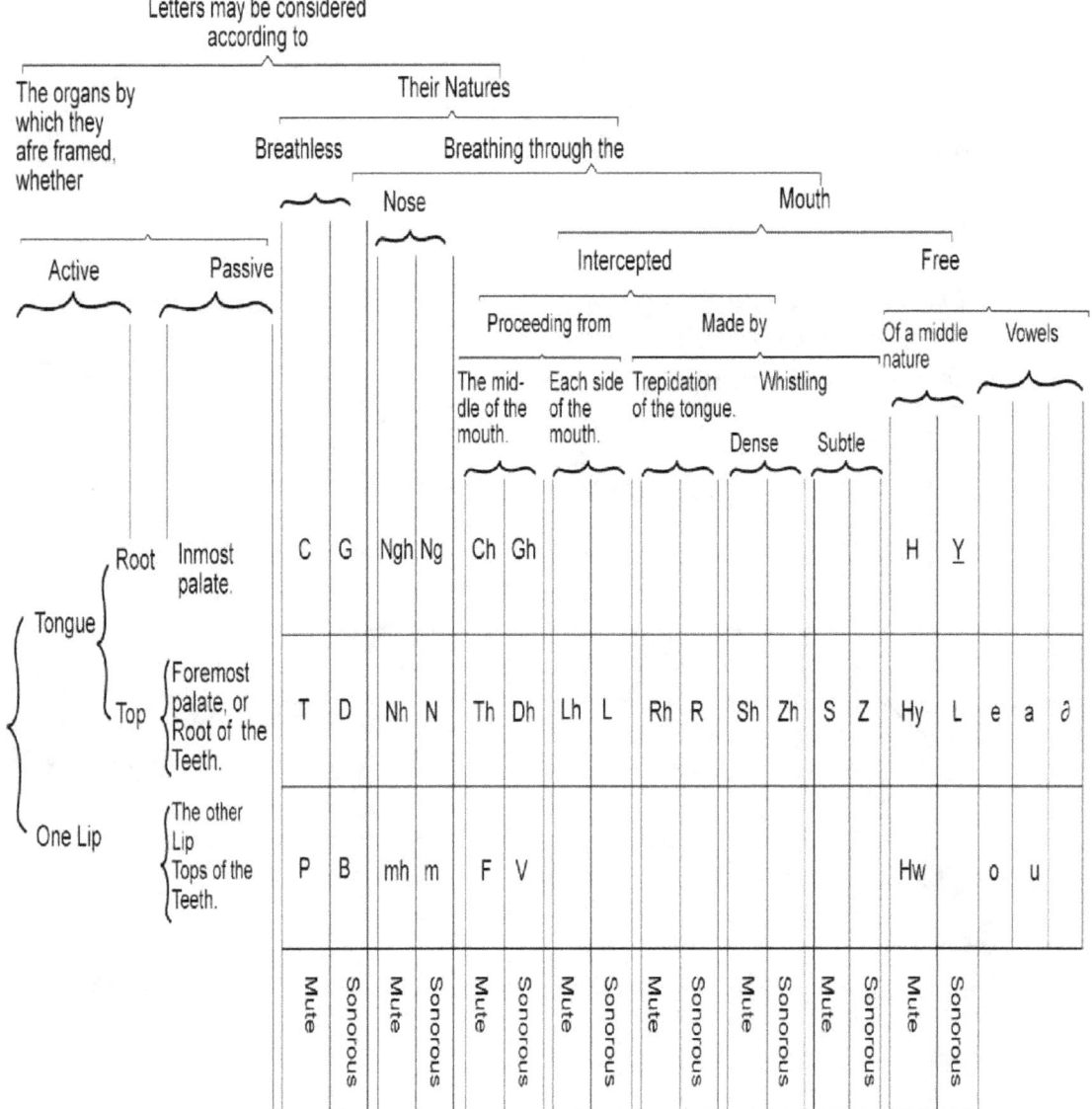

Chapter 3: Other Prior Art

3.4 RECENT EUROPEAN AND NORTH AMERICAN CONTRIBUTIONS

3.4.1 "SHORTHANDS" AND THE SEMINAL PHONOLOGICAL CLASSIFICATION OF PITMAN

Shorthands, i.e. methods of transcription capable of keeping pace with human speech, were known since antiquity. In *Yaaska*'s *Nirukta*, an ancient Indian work on etymology said to predate Paanini, there are references to shorthand [LAi-12]. The Roman *Marcus Tullius Tiro* is said by a slightly later author, *Aulus Gellius*, to have invented a shorthand for Latin called the Tiromian system and comprised of 4,000 glyphs, in 63 B.C.E. which was used to record speeches of Roman senators and was taught in Roman schools [SCr-92]. Variants of the *Modi* script, the medieval western Indian script alluded to above, were basically shorthands.

In the English language, shorthands were invented by various authors, e.g. *Timothy Bright* (1588 A.D.), *John Willis* (1602 A.D.), *Thomas Shelton/Samuel Pepys* (1626 A.D.), *William Mason* (1672 A.D.) and *Samuel Taylor* (1786 A.D.) [SCr-82]. A widely used German shorthand was invented by *Franz Gabelsberger* in 1834 C.E. [SCr-93]. However, none of these attempted to base their work on a phonological or scientific or even systematic classification. Nearly all were merely expedient attempts at a shorthand notation usually based on the extant script used for the language (Roman for the English language, Dewanaagari for Modi, etc.). Only with the advent of the seminal work of *Sir Isaac Pitman* [SCr-56 to SCr-58] was there true innovation in the form of a shorthand transcription method based on a true phonological classification.

Pitman published his system of shorthand in 1837. The remarkable ingenuity of the system, and its highly systematic and scientific classification, can be seen from even the truncated depiction in the Figure below.

Pitman's was the West's first truly *scientific* and *systematic* phonological classification and transcription. In Pitman's system, firstly, the stops or "consonants" as he denominated them, are classified from the back to the front of the oral apparatus, as in the ancient Indian system, i.e. velar, palatal, alveolar and bilabial. This is unremarkable. However, quite ingeniously (and very scientifically) then, Pitman used a straight line to represent each of these points of articulation, and then used the *direction* of the line to differentiate between them, as seen in the first graphic in the Figure below: Thus, a flat

PART 2: INTRODUCTION

line represented the velars, a line with a 45° angle the palatals, a 90° angle the alveolars, and a 135° angle the bilabials. Voiced (sonant) stops were then further differentiated from un-voiced (surd) stops, again very ingeniously, by simply making the line used in writing the former much thicker. Then yet further, fricatives within or close to a given point of articulation were denoted by curving the line, as seen in the line below the stops in the Figure below ([f] below [p], etc.).

The depiction of vowels by Pitman was also highly scientific and similarly ingenious. For example (see the Figure below), the vowels represented in the English words *all, whole* and *food*, i.e. lips rounded and jaw in the open, mid and closed positions, were represented by a short bar whose position (high, mid, low) approximated the jaw position. A thick bar further denoted a long vowel, a thin bar a short vowel.

In spite of being an astoundingly systematic and logical orthography, however, the incompleteness of Pitman's system is already visible in the representation of the Figure below: The vowels are severely limited to English, and even here to the Received Pronunciation (RP) of England or to Bostonian American English. "Consonants" are likewise limited to English, with, e.g., no distinction between alveolar and dental. And labiodentals such as [f] and [v] and classed with bilabials such as [p, b].

One of the limitations of Pitman's shorthand was that it still could not keep up with speech, especially rapid speech, and Pitman himself published nine (9) modifications of his system from 1837 through 1857 [SCr-57].

Andrew Graham [SCr-58] modified and refined Pitman's system for American English in 1886, and it is Graham's system that is actually depicted in the above Figure.

Other workers, such as the Irishman ***John Gregg***, and later, ***J. Evans*** published shorthands for English and other languages [SCr-59 to SCr-61]. Gregg's system [SCr-59, SCr-60] came to be adopted widely in America. As the above Figure shows, however, Gregg's system is, at least in this author's opinion, not nearly as scientific, systematic or ingenious as Pitman's. For example, the "consonant" progression from velar to bilabial is not systematic in angularity as in Pitman (flat, 45°, 90°, etc.), but rather, arbitrary. Yet the fact that it is based on Pitman's principles is clearly evident: For example, the voiced counterpart of an unvoiced "consonant" is made by using a longer stroke (rather than a thicker line, as in Pitman). Gregg's shorthand was nevertheless more practical, and was able to keep up with normal human speech.

Chapter 3: Other Prior Art

Fig. 3-5: A selection of features of *Pitman*'s remarkable shorthand system, first published in 1837, as refined further by *Graham* in 1886 (see discussion in the text). After [SCr-56 to SCr-58], reproduced with permission.

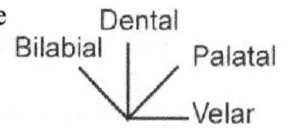

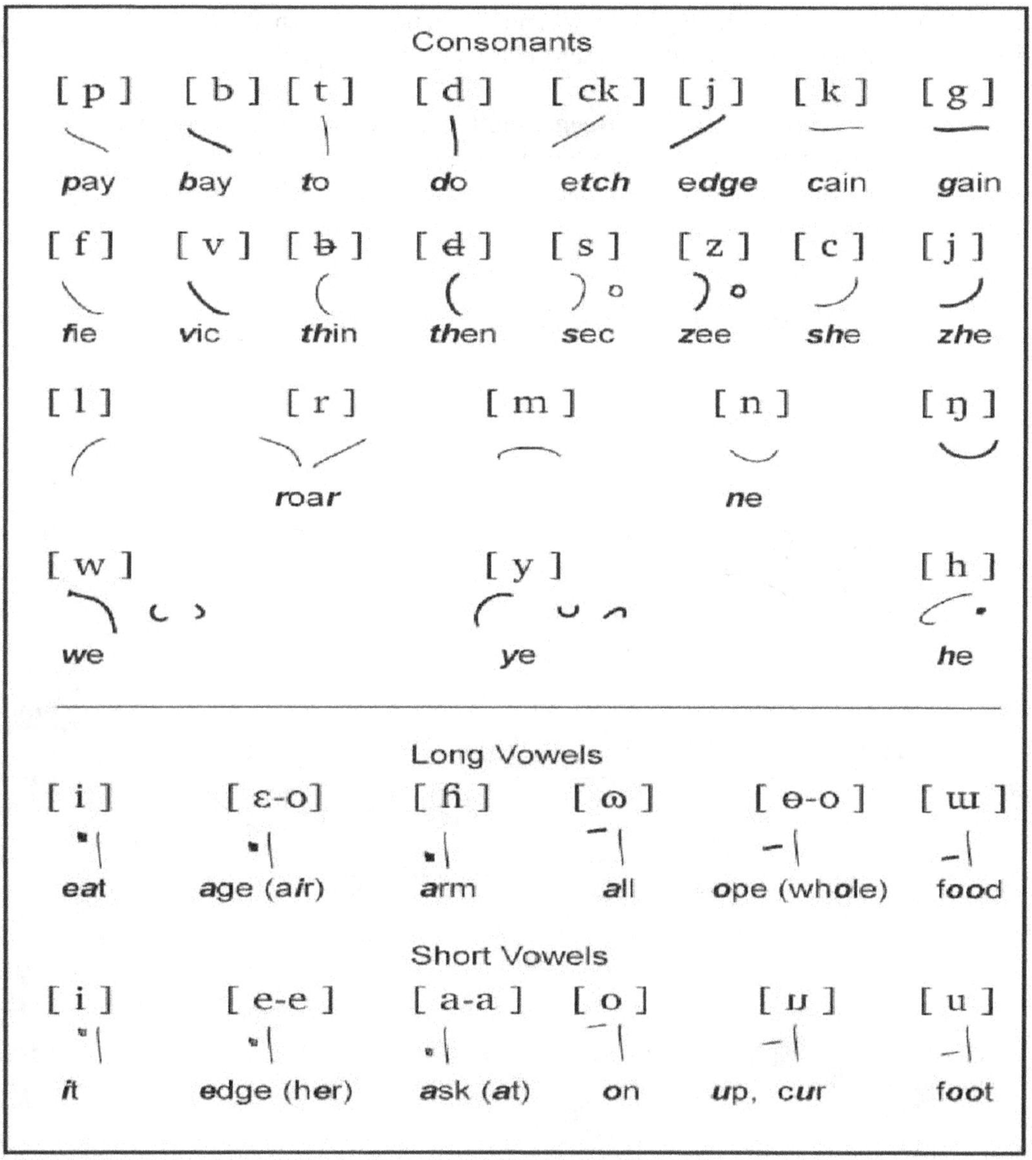

			Consonants				
[p]	[b]	[t]	[d]	[ck]	[j]	[k]	[g]
╲	╲	╲	╲	╱	╱	—	—
pay	bay	to	do	etch	edge	cain	gain
[f]	[v]	[ꞛ]	[ꝺ]	[s]	[z]	[c]	[j]
╲	╲	(	(	) ○	) ○	⌣	⌣
fie	vic	thin	then	sec	zee	she	zhe
[l]		[r]		[m]		[n]	[ŋ]
(		╲╱		⌢		⌣	⌣
		roar				ne	
[w]				[y]			[h]
╲ ⸦ ⸧				(ᴗ ᴧ			⸦ •
we				ye			he

		Long Vowels				
[i]	[ɛ-o]	[ɦ]	[ω]	[ɵ-o]	[ɯ]	
▪|	▪|	▪|	⁻|	⁻|	⁻|	
eat	age (a*i*r)	arm	all	ope (whole)	food	

		Short Vowels				
[i]	[e-e]	[a-a]	[o]	[ʊ]	[u]	
▫|	▫|	▫|	⁻|	⁻|	⁻|	
*i*t	edge (her)	ask (at)	on	up, cur	foot	

PART 2: INTRODUCTION

232

Although remarkable for the time, the phonological classification represented in the Pitman, Gregg and other shorthands was nevertheless quite deficient. There was, for instance, no distinction between trilled, flap and retroflex sounds in the centrals ([r]'s). Indeed, in their very first publications, there was no treatment of flaps vs. trills. Points of articulation were very rough, e.g. there was no distinction between alveolar and dental, between labiodental and bilabial, between velar and uvular or pharyngeal.

> **Fig. 3-6**: A selection from *Gregg's* shorthand system. A comparison with *Pitman's* shows, in this author's opinion, that it is not nearly as scientific, systematic or ingenious as Pitman's. After references [SCr-56 to SCr-61], reproduced with permission.

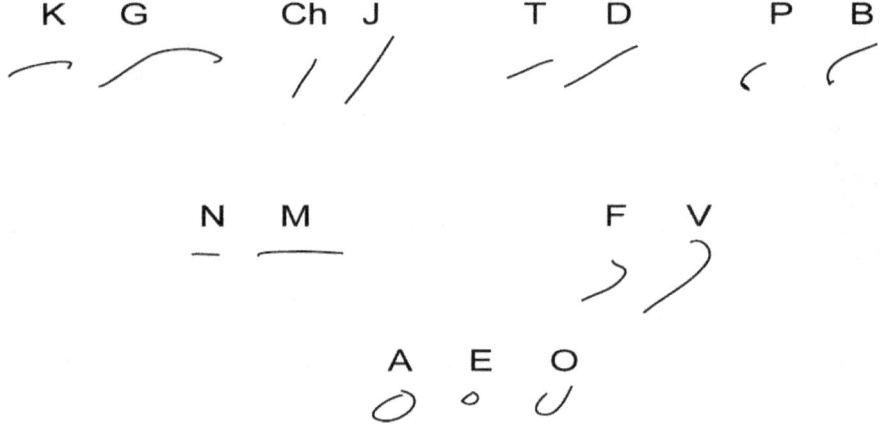

Chapter 3: Other Prior Art

233

While we are on the subject of shorthand, we must also mention shorthand transcription **machines.** These were used in courts before the advent of audio recording. They were very different from typewriters (for those among readers who still know what *they* are in this 21st century!) in that they allowed all keys to be depressed simultaneously, and rendered a shorthand that kept pace with the most rapid human speech. Their underlying principles were however ultimately the same as those first published by Pitman, and so they are not discussed further here.

3.4.2 THE *ALPHABETS/SCRIPTS* OF *PITMAN, ELLIS, GRAHAM, WATT, LEPSIUS, BELL, SWEET, JESPERSEN, JANVRIN, STORY, JOHNSTON, OWEN, PIKE*, AND OTHERS

Due to the large number of authors covered in this section, we attempt to roughly proceed in *chronological order*, except where the importance of a particular work or other need takes precedence.

It is also noteworthy that, approximately contemporaneous with the first publications of Pitman and Ellis, London hosted, in 1854, the so-called *Alphabetic Conferences*, under the chairmanship of the German Chevalier Bunsen [SCr-82]. These were held in an effort to arrive at a new, universal alphabet that could, at a minimum, accommodate all the European languages. These conferences surprisingly concluded in exasperation, with a declaration that "…it would be useless and impossible to attempt to find for each possible variety of sound a different graphic sign."!

Pitman and Ellis: Following the publication of his shorthand, **Pitman** also developed two "alphabets" [SCr-56, SCr-57], one in collaboration with Alexander **Ellis** (1848-1850 C.E.., given the appellation **Phonotype**), and one independently (1876 A.D.) [SCr-94, SCr-95]. These two alphabets are shown in the **Figure** below.

Several features are evident in them. Firstly, they attempt to use Roman letters as far as possible. Secondly, where new letters are required, many that are chosen are quite logical, e.g. the capital-sigma and its inverted version for the de-voiced and voiced sibilants [sh], [zh]. In this respect, these letters are far more recognizable than those of the IPA.

Ellis [SCr-94, SCr-95] also independently published several other alphabets later, which

PART 2: INTRODUCTION

he denoted **Glossic, Nomic** and **Palaeotype**. These are of importance for historical completeness only. Their poor quality and deficiencies are evident in two transcriptions we can cite here, in the Figure below.

>**Fig. 3-7**:   Transcriptions of English and German phrases in ***Ellis*'s *Nomic*** and ***Glossic***. After references [SCr-94, SCr-95], reproduced with permission.

>>**English:** *That is, customary English spelling, so called from the Greek...*
>>**Nomic**:   *dhat iz, kustemeri Ingglish speling, soa kauld from dhi Greek.....*

>>**German:** *Wer reitet so spät durch Nacht und Wind?*
>>**Glossic**: *V'air r'aay'tet zoa shpae't duor'ky'h Năakht uond V'ěent?*

Many deficiencies are evident in the above alphabets, from both a scientific (phonological) and a practical point of view. To cite just a few:

>**(1)** There is no systematic classification in the presentation, i.e. in the alphabetical order (as there is for instance in the ancient Indian "alphabets").
>**(2)** The alphabets are grossly incomplete, even when it comes to neighboring European languages such as French and German (vowels such as [ü] and [ø] are not covered), let alone languages such as Mandarin or Xo! Bushman (tones and clicks etc. are not covered).
>**(3)** There is no distinction between trilled, flap and retroflex sounds, e.g. in the central [r] sounds.   Indeed there is no coverage of flaps.
>**(4)** Many lower-case and capital letters can be confused with each other. In Pitman's later   alphabet, single glyphs (letters) are assigned to diphthongs.
>**(5)** And as a general observation, the Pitman-Ellis and Pitman alphabets are simply quite   unremarkable, being as they are just minor refinements of the Roman alphabet applicable narrowly to English. (In contrast, Pitman's shorthand is a pathbreaking seminal contribution!)

Fig. 3-8: *Pitman's* 1876 **alphabet** (*below*) and the *Graham* **alphabet** (*overleaf*), a sequel to his shorthand. Note that these are distinct from the Pitman *shorthands*. After references [SCr-56 to SCr-58, SCr-82, SCr-94, SCr-95], reproduced with permission.

CONSONANTS.

Explodents.

P	p.....rope.....pce	L	l....fall........el
B	b.....robe....bee	R	r....rare......ar
T	t .....fate......tee		
D	d ....fade.....dee		
Ꞓ	ɡ ....etch...chay		
J	j .....edge.....jay		
K	k ...leek.....kay		
G	g ....league..gay		

Liquids.

L   l....fall........el
R   r....rare......ar

Coalescents.

W   w....wet.....way
Y   y....yet......yay

Aspirate.

H   h...hay...aitch

VOWELS.
Lingual.

A   a......am, far..at
Ḁ   ɑ.....alms....ah
E   e......ell, fern..et
Ɛ   ɛ..... ale, air..eh
I   i...... ill........it
Ŧ   i......eel, fear..ee

Continuants.

F   f.....safe.......ef
V   v....save......vee
Ƀ   ꝥ....breath.. ith
Đ   d...breathe..thee
S   s....hiss......ess
Z   z....his......zee
Σ   ʃ.....vicious...ish
Ӡ   ʒ.....vision..zhee

Labial.

O   o..... on, or...ot
Ꝏ   ɔ......all..... aw
ɤ   ʌ......up, cur..ut
Ơ   o......ope, ore..oh
U   u......full....ŏŏt
Ꮜ   u...food, poor..ōō

Nasals.

M   m...seem ...em
N   n...seen.......en
Ŋ   ŋ...sing......ing

DIPHTHONGS: ei,   ou,   iu,   ai,   oi.
  as heard in   by,   now,   new,   ay (yes),   boy.

PART 2: INTRODUCTION

(Fig. 3-8, cont.)

GRAHAM ALPHABET

Long Vowels

ι	ȷ	1	eat, fear
Ɛ	ɛ	2	ale (air)
A	ß	3	arm
Ω	ω	4	all, form
Ơ	ơ	5	ope (whole)
Ⱳ	ⱳ	6	food

Short Vowels

I	i	it
E	e	ell (her)
Λ	a	ask (at)
O	o	not, on
Ʊ	ʋ	7 up, cur
U	υ	foot, full

Consonants

Ʒ	ʓ	8	then
Ⱨ	ɵ	9	thin
ɲ	ŋ	10	sing
C	c		ocean, shall
J	j		vision, zh.

and in their usual sense

b, d, f, g, h, k
be, do, foe, go, he, key

l, m, n, p, r, s
let, me, no, up, roar, so

t, v, w, y, z —
tc, vie, we, ye, zeal, —

Diphthongs

Double Letters	Single Letters		
ai	Ħ ȷ̇	11	aisle, find
oi	θ ө	12	oil, boy
ou	ð ȣ	13	out, now
iu	ɯ ꭎ	14	new, mute
dj	Ɗ ɟ	15	ed-ge, join
tc	Ɛ ç	16	et-ch, chin

Optional Letters

Ɛ̄	ə	17	air, where
Ā	a	18	at, an
Ē	e	19	her, bird
Ō	o	20	whole
Q	q		or hw=wh in when; thus, "qen" or "Hwen"

Chapter 3: Other Prior Art

237

Graham: In addition to his refinement of Pitman's shorthand, as discussed in the previous section, Andrew ***Graham*** also published an alphabet [SCr-58]. He gave the appellations *Phonotypy* and *Phonography* to, respectively, the print and cursive versions of this alphabet. His alphabet is shown in summary in the Figure below. Graham's alphabet is of course incomplete, usable primarily with English. It also contains some errors and omissions: For example, the vowels in English ***air*** and ***ale***, or ***up*** and ***cur***, are given the same glyph (letter) (see the Figure). Diphthongs are represented by single glyphs.

Watt: Brigham ***Young***, one of the founders of the Mormon sect of Christianity, commissioned one George D. ***Watt*** to come up with a new alphabet. Mr. Watt based his new alphabet, first introduced in 1854, on the phonological classification inherent in Pittman shorthand. As a result, the 39-letter alphabet addressed mainly to English (Figure below), showed a good degree of phonetic organization and systematicity. The alphabet was designated as the ***Deseret Alphabet***, after the University of Deseret, as the University of Utah in Salt Lake City was initially known [SCr-96]. Its narrow application to English only precluded its completeness and wider applicability.

Lepsius: In 1860, C.R. ***Lepsius*** published his *Standard Alphabet* [SCr-68, SCr-69] (2nd edition published in English in 1863), shown in summary form in the Figure below. As evident in the Figure, it appeared to be more complete than the Pitman-Ellis or Graham alphabets, at least as far as Indo-European languages were concerned. For example, Lepsius covered vocalic-[r] and vocalic-[l], recognizing them as such, i.e. as true vowels, perhaps due to his knowledge of Sanskrit. Interestingly also, Lepsius even covered "Faucal" (uvular or pharyngeal) sounds, which were rare in Europe (excepting for the French-German "uvular-r") but prominent in Arabic, Hebrew, and other Afro-Asiatic languages.

Two of the drawbacks of Lepsius' alphabet were the extensive use of diacritics, and the use of many symbols that were unrecognizable to people used to the Roman script (e.g. a variant of the Greek gamma for the guttural (velar) voiced fricative). In the present author's opinion, Lepsius's alphabet was probably one of the better ones to emanate from Europe.

PART 2: INTRODUCTION

238

Fig. 3-9: The alphabet devised by **Watt** for Mormon use, based on Pitman's classification and known as the *Deseret* alphabet. After references [SCr-96], reproduced with permission.

```
            DESERET ALPHABET.                    3

              𐐆 𐐔𐐇𐐝𐐀𐐡𐐇𐐓  𐐈𐐢𐐙𐐀𐐒𐐇𐐓.

         Long Sounds.              Letter.  Name.        Sound.
  Letter.  Name.      Sound.        𐐑 .... p
   𐐀 .... e ... as in .... eat.    𐐒 .... b
   𐐁 .... a      "      ate.       𐐓 .... t
   𐐂 .... ah     "      art.       𐐔 .... d
   𐐃 .... aw     "      aught.     𐐕 .... che as in cheese.
   𐐄 .... o      "      oat.       𐐖 .... g
   𐐅 .... oo     "      ooze.      𐐗 .... k
        Short Sounds of the above. 𐐘 .... ga...as in...gate.
   𐐆 ..... as in ...... it.        𐐙 .... f
   𐐇      "           et.          𐐚 .... v
   𐐈      "           at.          𐐛 .... eth..as in .thigh.
   𐐉      "           ot.          𐐜 .... the    "       thy
   𐐊      "           ut.          𐐝 .... s
   𐐋      "           book.        𐐞 .... z
        Double Sounds.              𐐟 .... esh..as in..flesh.
   𐐌 .... i .... as in ... ice.    𐐠 .... zhe    "    vision.
   𐐍 .... ow     "      owl.       𐐡 .... ur     "    burn.
   𐐎 .... ye                       𐐢 ..... l
   𐐏 .... woo                      𐐣 ..... m
   𐐐 .... h                        𐐤 ..... n
                                    𐐥 .... eng.as in.length.
```

Chapter 3: Other Prior Art

239

Fig. 3-10: Nonvowel portion of *Lepsius' Standard Alphabet* (1863), in summary form. After references [SCr-68, SCr-69], reproduced with permission.

LEPSIUS 1863

The Consonants of the General Alphabet

	Plosives			Fricatives			Semivowels	
	Unvoiced	Voiced	Nasal	Unvoiced	Voiced	Nasal		
I. Uvular	ʾ	ʿ		ħ	h			
II. Velar	k	q, g	ṅ	χ	γ		ṙ	
III. Palatal	ḱ	ǵ	ṅ	χ́,š,ś	γ́,z̃,ź y			ł
IV. Retroflex	ṭ	ḍ	ṇ	ṣ̌	ẓ̃		ṛ	ḷ
V. Pharyngealized (Velar)		ḏ(ṯ)		ș	z̃, ḏ			
VI. Dental	t	d	n	s,ϑ	z, ð		r	l
VII. Bilabial	p	b	m	f	v	w		

PART 2: INTRODUCTION

240

Bell: Alexander Melville **Bell**, father of Alexander Graham Bell, the inventor of the telephone, published a tome entitled *Visible Speech: The Science of Universal Alphabetics; on Self-Interpreting Physiological Letters for the Writing of All Languages in One Alphabet* in 1867 [SCr-97].

This script was very different from any prior European work, or for that matter any other, work, with the possible exception perhaps of Haangul. The similarity with Haangul is the attempt to graphically represent in some way the *physical* status of the speech apparatus in the articulation of a phone.

The Figure below gives some representations of Bell's system. The graphical nature of the system can be seen by viewing just the first ten "Radicals" as he called them. #1 is a large circle, depicting an open throat, #2 is an oval depicting a contracted throat, #4 appears to be a picture of the vocal chords vibrating together, and so forth.

The somewhat confused and inexact nature of Bell's phonological classification is however apparent even in the very first "Radicals". For example, #6, "Part of the Mouth contracted" and #7, "Part of the Mouth divided", both of which are lumped together as being "The Stems of all Consonants" is rather confused and, from modern phonological analysis, outright wrong.

Chapter 3: Other Prior Art

Fig. 3-11: Some representations of Alexander Melville **Bell**'s *Visible Speech*. (He was the father of Alexander Graham Bell, inventor of the telephone.) After references [SCr-97].

LETTER-VALUE OF THE PRINCIPAL VOWEL SYMBOLS.

1	I	ſ	1	T	ſ
laogh (Ga.)	first (Am.) I|[bI] (Russ.)	il (F.) I| eel (E.) Iʎ fille (F.)	-tion* ⎱ (E.) -tious ⎰	-shire (E.) -es (pl.) (E.)	ill (E.) ſ\?new (Am.)
]	ι	ɩ	]	ι	ɩ
up (E.)]ɤ urn (E.)	que (F.) ιʎ zeit (Ge.) ιʃ un (F.)	et (F.) ɩ| day (Sc.) ɩʎ day (E.)	ask (E.) mann (Ge.)]ʎ high (E.)]\? how (E.)	a [article] (E.) -al ⎱ -ance ⎰ (E.) ιʎ day (Cock.)	ill (Sc.) -ment ⎱ -ness ⎰ (E.) ɩɤ air (E.)
J	I	ɩ	J	I	ɩ
up (Sc.) J\?out (Sc.)	sir (Prov.)	ell (E.) [I ell (Sc.) [ʃ vin (F.)	man (Sc.) J|psalm (E) Jɤ are (E.) Jʎkaiser (Ge.) J\?haus (Ge.)	Iɤ err (E.) up (Cock.)	man (E.) ɩ|papa (Ir.) ɩI eye (Sc.) ɩ\? now (Cock.) ɩɤ our (Cock.)
ǂ	ɨ	ꬹ	ǂ	ɨ	f
book (Sc.) ǂ|pool (E.) ◯ǂ| ū (E.)	u (Sw.)	uber[|](Ge)	to, good (E.) ǂɤ poor (E.)	-ure (E.) ɨ\? do (Am.)	boot (noun) (Sc.)
ɟ	ʇ	ɛ	ɟ	ʇ	ɛ
home[|](Sc) ɟ\?home (E.)	homme (F.) ʇʃ on (F.)	une (F.)	-ough (E.) chaud (F.) ɟɤ ore (E.)	stone (Am.) note (Sc.)	jeu (F.) boot (v. imp behooved) (Sc.)
ɟ	ɨ	ꬹ	ɟ	ɨ	ꬹ
all [|] (E.) ɟɤ war (E.)	sir (Ir.) ɨʎ I (Ir.) ɨʃ en (F.)	beurre [|] (F.)	on (E.) ɟɤ or (E.) ɟʎ boy (E.)	ask (Cock.) not (Ir.)	I'll (Sc.) ꬹI out (Cock.)

* Syllables preceded by a hyphen are unaccented terminations.

(Fig. 3-11, cont.)

EXPLANATORY TABLE OF SYMBOLS FOR VOWEL CONFIGURATIONS.

Explanation.

Primary. Wide. (1)

1. ⟩ ⟩   Back of tongue(2) high and retracted.
2. ⟩ ⟩   "   retracted at a middle elevation.
3. J J   "   low and retracted.

4. Ɩ Ɩ   Back and front(3) of tongue high.
5. ɩ ɩ   "   "   at a middle elevation.
6. I I   "   "   low.

7. ſ ſ   Front of tongue(4) high and advanced.
8. ɾ ɾ   "   advanced at a middle elevation.
9. ɩ ɩ   "   low and advanced.

10. ⟩̵ ⟩̵   No. 1, rounded, (lip aperture narrow.)
11. ⟩̵ ⟩̵   " 2,   "   ("   mid.   )
12. J̵ J̵   " 3,   "   ("   broad.)

13. Ɩ̵ Ɩ̵   " 4,   "   ("   narrow.)
14. ɩ̵ ɩ̵   " 5,   "   ("   mid.   )
15. I̵ I̵   " 6,   "   ("   broad.)

16. ſ̵ ſ̵   " 7,   "   ("   narrow.)
17. ɾ̵ ɾ̵   " 8,   "   ("   mid.   )
18. ɩ̵ ɩ̵   " 9,   "   ("   broad.)

Chapter 3: Other Prior Art

243

(Fig. 3-11, cont.)

Consonants

	Modifying Breath	Modifying Voice	
1.	0	θ	Throat-passage contracted
2.	C	e	Back of of tongue contracting mouth-passage
3.	ꜫ	ꜫ	Back of of tongue dividing mouth-passage
4.	ꝏ	ꝏ	Back of of tongue closing mouth-passage
5.	ꝏ	ꝏ	Back of of tongue closing mouth-passage with nasal emission
6.	⌒	⌒	Front of of tongue contracting mouth-passage
7.	ɷ	ɷ	Front of of tongue dividing mouth-passage
8.	⌒	⌒	Front of of tongue closing mouth-passage
9.	⌒	⌒	Front of of tongue closing mouth-passage with nasal emission
10.	○	○	Point of of tongue contracting mouth-passage
11.	ω	ω	Point of of tongue dividing mouth-passage
12.	○	○	Point of of tongue closing mouth-passage
13.	○	○	Point of of tongue closing mouth-passage with nasal emission
14.	○	ə	Lips contracting mouth-passage
15.	З	З	Lips dividing mouth-passage
16.	D	D	Lips closing mouth-passage
17.	⊃	⊃	Lips closing mouth-passage with nasal emission
18.	ꝏ	ꝏ	Back position (c) modified by partial effect of ↻
19.	ꝏ	ꝏ	Front position (⌒) modified by partial effect of ↺
20.	ꝏ	ꝏ	Point position (○) modified by partial effect of ○
21.	ꝏ	ꝏ	Lip position (○) modified by partial effect of ○
22.	ꝏ	ꝏ	Divided emission with the organs in the position ꝏ
23.	ꝏ	ꝏ	Divided emission with the organs in the position ꝏ
24.	ꝏ	ꝏ	Divided emission with the organs in the position ꝏ
25.	ꝏ	ꝏ	Divided emission with the organs in the position ꝏ

Glides or Transitional Semivowels

1.	ꝏ	Partial effect of	θ	with vowel quality predominating
2.	ꝏ	Partial effect of	e	with vowel quality predominating
3.	ꝏ	Partial effect of	ꝏ	with vowel quality predominating
4.	ꝏ	Partial effect of	⌒	with vowel quality predominating
5.	ꝏ	Partial effect of	⌒ ○ ○	with vowel quality predominating
6.	ꝏ	Partial effect of	ω	with vowel quality predominating
7.	ꝏ	Partial effect of	ω ○ ○	with vowel quality predominating
8.	ꝏ	Partial effect of	ə	with vowel quality predominating
9.	ꝏ	Partial effect of	ꝏ	with vowel quality predominating

Modifiers

} Inner position	} Applicable to any of	c Inverted	} Applicable to point
{ Outer position	ʃ the consonants	ɔ Protruded	ʃ the consonants

PART 2: INTRODUCTION

(Fig. 3-11, cont.)

O he (E.)	Ο (Vowel whisp.)	θ variety of defective r		Χ bü'er for butter (west of Scot.)	
C nach (Ge.) pech (Sc.)	Ϲ auch (Ge.) sough (Sc.)	Ɛ hiss of waterfowl.	Ɛ	ɑ c, k, q, (E.) ɑ} kind (E.)	ɢ sink* (E.)
ᴐ ich (Ge.)	ᴐ s, c, (E.) ᴐ}ciudad(Sp)	ꟼ variety of defective s	ᵜ thin (E.)	ᴅ variety of t	ᴅ variety of n*
ʊ theatre (F.) -rh (W.)	ʊ show (E.) chaud (F.)	ω temple (F.) felt* (E.)	ω ll (W.) hl (Z.)	ʊ tie (E.)	ʊ tent* (E.)
ɔ variety of f or wh	ɔ why (E.)	3 fie (E.)	3 gutturalized variety of f	ᴅ pie (E.)	ᴅ lamp* (E.) mhm! (Sc.)
ɛ tage (Ge.) ɛ} zeige(Ge.) ɛ} burred r	ɛ var'y of g (Ge.) and of defective r (E.)	ɛ laogh (Ga.) barred l (Po.)	ɛ labialized variety of Gaelic l	ɘ go (E.) ɘ} guide (E.)	ɘ sing (E.)
ʘ yes (E.)	ᴓ zeal (E.) ᴓ}d, final (Sp.)	ᴔ llano (Sp.) gli (It.)	ᴔ then (E.)	ᴔ Magyar (Hu.)	ᴔ Boulogne (F.)
ω race (E.) ω} r (Sc. Sp. &c.)	ω pleasure (E.) jour (F.)	ω lie (E.)	ω dhl (Z.)	ʊ die (E.)	ʊ sin (E.)
ɜ weg (Ge.) b, (Sp.)	ɜ way (E.)	ɜ vie (E.)	ɜ gutturalized variety of v	ɵ buy (E.)	ɵ seem (E.)

(Fig. 3-11, cont.)

RADICAL SYMBOLS

1. ○ The throat open [Aspirate]
2. ◊ The throat contracted [Whisper]
3. Χ The throat closed [Glottal [Catch]
4. Ι The throat sounding [voice] ⎫
5. Ι̵ The throat sounding and the lips 'rounded' ⎬ The stems of all vowels.
6. C Part of the mouth contracted ⎫
7. Ɛ Part of the mouth divided ⎬ The stems of all consonants.
8. (The nasal valve open [Soft palate]
9. • Vowel definer ⎫
10. ∩ Wide vowel definer ⎬ Joined to 4 and 5.
11. | Shutter. Joined to 6.
12. ⚭ Mixer. Joined to 6 and 7.
13. ⟨ Consonant definer
14. V Force director
15. > Breath director
16. ᴄ Tounge director
17. · Stopper
18. ‖ Divider
19. ⸗ Vibrator
20. ✝ Holder, or long
21. ‹ Abrupt
22. › Hiatus
23. ○ Link
24. ˈ Accent

PART 2: INTRODUCTION

(Fig. 3-11, concluded)

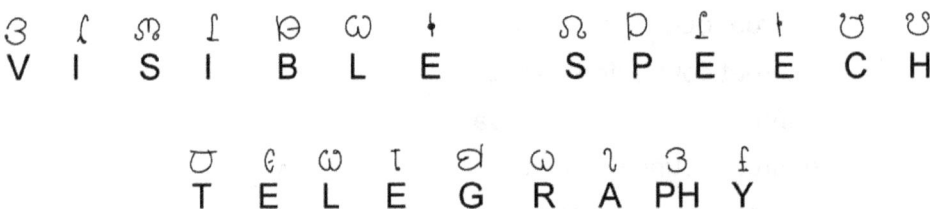

Some of the other deficiencies of Bell's "Visible Speech" were: **(1)** Its complete unrecognizability not only vis-á-vis any extant script, but also graphically (although Bell intended that the reader would be able to guess that such and such a letter indicated the throat closed and the vocal chords vibrating, etc.!). **(2)** Its great complexity. In this regard, it may be noted that it took approximately five times the effort to master Bell's system as it did to Pitman's or Gregg's shorthand, which are themselves considered difficult to master by many highly educated people even today. **(3)** Other deficiencies are seen in the table shown in the above Figure that represents the actual "alphabetical order" used by Bell. There is little semblance of organization, systematization or classification, and the contrast with the ancient Indian or Pitman's "alphabetical order" is stark.

Sweet: Henry **Sweet** published in 1890 an alphabet he called **Romic** (i.e. a variation on the Roman script) [SCr-98]. He claimed this alphabet would address the deficiencies of the Pitman-Ellis alphabets [SCr-94]. Sweet [SCr-98] is primarily responsible for introducing, to the Western orthographic world, various glyphs (letters) that are unrecognizable in relation to Roman script, such as the triangle, and others which are turned, inverted or rotated Roman letters and thus extremely confusing. All these were, unfortunately, subsequently embraced by the IPA. Sweet's alphabet is shown in the Figure below.

Chapter 3: Other Prior Art

247

Fig. 3-12: *Sweet*'s **Romic** alphabet and the English sentence "*The written and printed representation of the sounds of language.*" rendered in what Sweet designated as its "Narrow" and "Broad" transcriptions. After reference [SCr-98], reproduced with permission.

1. Conventional spelling: "The written and printed representation of the sounds of the language."
2. "Broad" <u>Romic</u>: [— ðə ritnʌn printid:reprəzən teiʃənəvðə saund(d)zəv læŋgwidʒ].
3. "Narrow" <u>Romic</u>: [— dhʌ rit ɪ nʌn printe'dr·eprʌzʌn teishʌn-ʌvdhʌ sœhʌw ɪ nzʌv lœq ɪ gwe'dzh].[77]

Jespersen, Janvrin: Working in the late 19th century, Otto ***Jespersen*** proposed a transcription system he denoted as the ***Analphabetic System*** [SCr-99].

Jespersen first assigned the first six Greek letters, alpha (α) through zeta (ζ), to, respectively, the lips, tonge-tip, upper surface of the tongue, (soft palate + uvula, no differentiation there), (larynx and vocal chords, again no distinction) and, finally, respiratory organs. More confusingly then, he assigned the *Roman* letters from *a* through *l* to the points of articulation in *just the upper part only* of the oral cavity, e.g. *a* for supra-labial, *b* for labial...*k* for uvular and *l* for pharyngeal (but with little consideration of the point of contact and position of the tongue!). Numbers or Roman letters or symbols were then used in conjunction with the Greek letters to indicate the size and shape of the organs represented by the Greek letters! Thus, the transcription of human speech in Jespersen's system resembled a musical score, i.e. left-to-right as well as up-and-down, but with Greek letters, numbers and exponents! An example of a word transcribed in Jespersen's system is shown in the Figure.

In this author's humble opinion, it is not easily understood why any of Jespersen's contemporaries gave serious consideration to this system, except perhaps for the high respect Jespersen's other work in linguistics was held. It was, in this author's opinion, so complex, so unrecognizable and so utterly convoluted,. In fact, Jespersen appeared to succeed in making what should have been an extremely simple problem (witness Pitman's work and the work of the ancient Indian phonologists) into an extremely complex representation on paper! And this, without really adding any further phonological information into the transcription.

Fig. 3-13: An example of the German word *Baden* transcribed in ***Jespersen's*** *Analphabetic* system. After reference [SCr-99], reproduced with permission.

Jespersen's An Alphabetic System

	B	A	.	D	N
α	0^b	8^h	..	(6)	..
β	,,	..	..	0te	..
γ	,,	1^j	..	,,	..
δ	0	..	..	..	2
ε	1	..	..	..	..
ζ		4			1

Thus, *Baden* ⟹ $\beta 0^{te} \delta 0 \varepsilon 1$

Unfortunately, later workers such as **F. Janvrin** [SCr-100] attempted to emulate Jespersen in constructing analphabetic systems in which transcriptions resembled mathematical equations. To use the cliché that they made a mountain out of a molehill would, in this author's opinion, be an understatement. **B. Emsley**'s later work [SCr-101] was in part based on that of Jespersen and Janvrin.

Story: Alphabets such as that published in 1906 by the American Charles A. ***Story*** in his work entitled *The Fonetic Primer* [SCr-102] are worth mentioning in passing, if only because they show how misguided some well-meaning efforts can be when the underlying principles of phonological classification are not understood by their authors.

Story made such notable phonological pronouncements in his work as:

Chapter 3: Other Prior Art

> "It is impossible for any human being to spell a word of one syllable with less than one letter, and that one letter must be a vowel or compound vowel. This is the smallest and lowest limit. It is impossible for any human being to pronounce a word of one syllable containing more than seven sounds. [Thus,] One sound is the smallest and lowest limit [and seven sounds are] the largest and highest limit. ....No human being can, in any word of one syllable, sound more than three consonants before the vowel." [SCr-102].

It is unclear on what basis Story came upon these conclusions! His alphabet is depicted in the **Figure** below, again for completeness only.

Johnston: Harry ***Johnston*** published, in 1913, a book entitled *Phonetic Spelling: A proposed Universal Alphabet for the rendering of English, French, German and all other forms of Speech* [SCr-103].

His book contained lengthy denunciations of virtually all the world's known scripts at that time, and had such pronouncements as:

> "...the clicks of Bushman...are half-brutish speech-sounds, vestiges of pre-human speech, resembling the vocal utterances of baboons and apes...... ...objections will be raised by our fellow-subjects of non-European race, more especially in Asia, who... will try to keep alive the barbarous palaeography of their own land.." [SCr-103].

We are unlikely to find such phrases in books today in the early 21st century. But, despite the title of his book, the script he developed (the **Figure** below gives a summary) was far from universally applicable. As is seen, Johnston employs diacritics liberally, and there are many borrowings from the Greek alphabet. He tries to maintain a roughly Roman alphabetical order, while accommodating some Arabic and other Semitic phones. There is no attempt to accommodate the aspirate/non-aspirate phonemic dichotomy of North Indian languages.

To his credit, however, Johnston was one of the first European workers to recognize the critical need for the concept of *discretization* of phones discussed elsewhere in this book. In addition, his representation of the clicks of the South African languages was rather ingenious, as the comparison with the Lepsius/Bleek and official South African

PART 2: INTRODUCTION

Government representations shown in the Figure below reveals.

Fig. 3-14: Representative excerpts from the alphabet of Charles A. ***Story***. After reference [SCr-102], reproduced with permission.

First Vowel	=	O
Fourth Vowel	=	ᴃ
Eighth Vowel	=	ɑ
Ninth Vowel	=	Θ
Fourteenth Vowel	=	ᵿ
Forty-Third Vowel	=	C

C c — ice, isle, , tie, die, my, high, buy, rye, lie, tine, rhyme.

ɷ ɷ — oil, toy, boy, oy, soil, void, noise, boil, foil, coin, quoit.

ᴔ ᴔ — buoyed, buoys, buoyant, buoy.

ɷ ɷ — out, owl, ounce, down, town, noun, house, mouse, found.

ɯ ɯ — wew, dew, pew, hue, view, cue, glue, news, through.

ŋ n nu — This is the half-consonant, or half nasal. The half-vowel placed after it suggest its name. This letter shows that the vowel standing before it is sounded "nasally," as in the French bon ton, mon, sou, pain and maison.

ŋ ŋ ŋε — for ng in in sing, song, ring, sung, hang, lung, tongue.

Y y yε — yet, yes, yell, yoke, you, young, use, youth, yatcht.

W w wε — we, way, will, win, wou, woe, wean, oue, wine.

H h hε — The Perfect Aspirate; hot, hop, hip, hoe, how, hum, home, he, hew, high.

H h̠ h̠ε — The Smooth Guttural Aspirate; easily, learned from the German ich, noch, bach, recht, licht, lachen.

Chapter 3: Other Prior Art

Fig. 3-15: Excerpts from *Johnston*'s alphabet. After reference [SCr-103], reproduced with permission.

NAMES IN OLD ENGLISH SPELLING; AND ARBITRARY ORDER OF ALPHABET

(Ah)	A	(Eng)	Ñ
(Ŭt)	ɑ	(Aw)	Ō or ⊙
(Ăt)	Æ	(Oh)	Ω
(Bee)	B	(Uȋ)	Ɵ
(Chee)	C	(The surd vowel)	3
(Dee)	D	(Pee)	P
(Dādd)	Ḋ	(Koo)	Q
(Dhee)	ɑ̃	(Ar)	R
(Ay)	E	(Ess)	S
(French Uȋ)	Ɛ	(Shay)	Ş
(Ef)	F	(Tee)	T
(Gay)	G	(Ttā)	Ṫ
(Ghain)	Γ	(Thee)	ƀ
(Ha)	H	(Oo)	U
(Arab Ha)	Hʻ	(Üpsilon)	Ü
(Ee)	I	(Vee)	V
(Guttural Ee)	Ψ	(Way)	W
(Jay)	J	(Ekh)	X
(Kay)	K	(Yay)	Y
(El)	L	(Zed)	Z
(Polish El)	Ł	(Zzā)	Ż
(Em)	M	(Zhay)	Ƶ
(En)	N		

PART 2: INTRODUCTION

Fig. 3-16: Comparison of ***Johnston***'s representation of the clicks of the South African languages with those of ***Lepsius/Bleek*** and the official one of the South African Government. After references [SCr-103, SCr-68 to SCr-71], reproduced with permission.

PHONETIC SPELLING

VOWELS.

Ō ō or Θ ϴ, O o, Ө ө (or Ø ø, or Ö ö); Ɛ ɛ; з ɜ; Ω ω; Ɑ ɑ, A a, Æ æ; E e, Ē ē; I i, Ī ī, Ψ ψ; Ü ü, U u.

MARKS, ACCENTS, HALF-CONSONANTS, ETC.

' apostrophe or *spiritus lenis*.
; hiatus or *hamza*.
' light aspirate breathing.
ʕ the Arabic áin (ع) or faucal contraction of utterance.
~ nasalization.
ˈ palatalization.
ͽ vocalization or indeterminate vowel.
´ acute accent or raised tone.
` grave accent or low tone.
ˇ, ˊ, –ˊ other tones met with in Chinese, Burmese, and Siamese, etc.
^ the extreme stress accent.
¯ stress mark.
˘ unstress mark.

C = Dental Click; Ɔ = Alveolar Click; Ç = Palatal Click; Ɒ = Lateral Click. Proportionately reduced forms—ç, ƅ, etc.—in "lower case" letters. Also rendered by Ċ, Q̇ċ, Q̇, and Ẋ.

Chapter 3: Other Prior Art

253

Owen: Robert L. **Owen**, a U.S. Senator from Oklahoma, managed to have the U.S. Government Printing Office publish his *The Global Alphabet* in 1944 [SCr-104], at taxpayers' expense. This "alphabet" was however more like a shorthand, and used many of Pitman's principles. It is depicted in the **Figure** below. Among many its limitations are its total unrecognizability and its limited capacity (e.g. only 15 vowels).

Pike: In 1947, Kenneth **Pike**, working at the University of Michigan, published a 255-page tome entitled *Phonemics: A technique for Reducing Language to Writing* [SCr-105, SCr-106]. Pike apparently set out with the larger and nobler objective of coining a universal *phonemic* alphabet, but then appeared to give up towards the latter part of his work. He classified vowels as *vocoids* and nonvowels, including "consonants", as *non-vocoids*.

The non-vocoid and vocoid segments of his alphabet are shown in the Figure below. To his credit, his was one of the more comprehensive classifications to emerge from the West. For example, in his non-vocoid table, he includes pharyngeal, glottal and retroflex classes of phones, which are mostly absent in European languages but widely found elsewhere. Unfortunately, in his vocoid table, he does not include vocalic-[r, l], and his vocoid (vowel) table is otherwise deficient, even for European languages. He does, however, consider elsewhere in his work such modifications of his vocoids as utterance with the tongue in a retroflex position.

Pike also developed a complex symbology to account for specific properties of phones, such as egressive lung air vs. ingressive pharynx air; these are also shown in the Figure below. Although certainly very thorough, his symbology used the typography available at the time of his publication (1947), and thus suffered from problems of poor recognizability and extreme complexity. Nevertheless, his system is far easier to transcribe and comprehend than that, e.g., of Jespersen. The thoroughness of his analysis can be seen in *the many degrees of lip rounding* that he considered in the utterance of vocoids, as seen in the Figure below. The five degrees of lip rounding he considers are even more than those considered in this book; due to the necessity of *discretization* as discussed elsewhere in this book, we limit ours to three. The Figure below gives the transcriptions of some English words in Pike's alphabet.

In the bulk of his work, Pike first gives a methodology for phonemic analysis of *any* language from first principles. He then shows how his alphabet can be used for phonemic representation of any hypothetical language. He however does make some rather simplistic statements, e.g. "A practical orthography should be phonemic. There should be

PART 2: INTRODUCTION

a one-to-one correspondence between each phoneme and [its] symbolization...". Of course, all phoneticists recognize this! The problem is to arrive at such a phonemic orthography that is applicable to *all* the world's languages. This problem is rather difficult and our book attempts to solve it.

Fig. 3-17: Excerpts from ***Owen's*** alphabet. After reference [SCr-104], reproduced with permission.

Owen - Vowels

| at | ate | far | all | it | biae | met | me | her | got | go | for | rut | lute | due | out | near | now |

Owen - Consonants

bun pun dun tun fun vun gun kun hun jun lun run mun nun sun

wun yun zun chin shin thin sing why

Owen - Examples of words in the global alphabet

mat   met   sip   back   deck   make   rat   c at

Chapter 3: Other Prior Art

255

Further along in his book (specifically, on p. 223 [SCr-105]), Pike finally appears to give up! He notes:

> "After reading the bewildering variety of alternatives presented in the preceding pages, one may well ask why it should not be possible to propose a single alphabet which would be used ...for all languages...There are several reasons why such a uniform alphabet is....at the present stage of knowledge, impossible." [SCr-105].

He then proceeds to assign different symbols to particular phonemes in different languages. For example, the /x/ phoneme (the velar unvoiced fricative and its variants) is to be expressed, in Pike's system, as the phones [j] in Latin American Spanish, [x] in Arabic, and [h] in European languages! He then also starts to employ complicated letters, e.g. $[d^z]$ and $[d^{z^\wedge}]$ for certain European affricates, the complex superscripts rendering transcription tedious.

Fig. 3-18 (*overleaf*): Excerpts from ***Pike's*** alphabet. Parts of the *"**non-vocoid**"* (non-vowel, ***Top***) and *"**vocoid**"* (vowel, ***Middle***) segments are shown. At ***Bottom*** is a summary of symbology used by Pike. After references [SCr-105, SCr-106], reproduced with permission.

PART 2: INTRODUCTION

General Type of Nonvocoid		Bilabial	Labio-Dental	Inter-Dental	Point of Articulation							
					Alveolar	Retro-flex	Alveo-Palatal	Retro-flex	Palatal	Velar	Back Velar	Uvular	Phar-yngeal	Glottal
Stops													
One-segment Unaspirated	vl.	p		t̪	t	ṭ			ḱ	k	ḵ (q)		ʔ
	vd.	b		d̪	d	ḍ			ǵ	g	g̱ (G)		
Two-segment													
Aspirated	vl.	pʰ (pʻ)¹			tʰ (tʻ)					kʰ(kʻ)			
	vd.	bʱ (bʻ)²			dʱ (dʻ)					gʱ(gʻ)			
Affricated	vl.	pᵽ		tθ	ts (ŝ)					kx			
	vd.	bƀ		dð	dz (ẑ)					gɣ			
Laterally released	vl.				tɫ (ƛ)								
	vd.				dl (λ)								
Fricatives Central													
Flat	vl.	ɸ	f	θ	θ̠	θ̣			x́	x	x̱	x̱	ħ
	vd.	β	v	ð	ð̠	ð̣			γ́	γ	γ̱	ʁ	ʕ [For ħ, h, and ɦ, see footnotes, p. 5]
Grooved	vl.	s̱+ ²			s	ṣ	š						
	vd.	ẕ+			z	ẓ	ž						
Lateral	vl.				ɬ+								
	vd.				ɮ+								
Frictionless Nasal	vl.	m̥ (M)			n̥ (N)	ṇ̥	ɲ̥ (Ñ)			ŋ̥ (N)			
	vd.	m			n	ṇ	ɲ			ŋ			
Lateral	vl.				l̥ (L)		l̥ʸ						
	vd.				l		lʸ						
Vibrants Flapped	vl.	ⱱ̥			ɾ̥	ɽ̥							
	vd.	ⱱ			ɾ	ɽ							
Trilled	vl.	ʙ̥			r̥	ṛ̥						ʀ̥	
	vd.	ʙ			r	ṛ						ʀ	

(Fig. 3-18, cont.)

Pike- Vocoids

		Front	Central	Back
High	Close	i	ɨ	ï
	Open	ɪ		ɪ̈
Mid	Close	e	ə	
	Open	ɛ	ʌ	
Low	Close	æ		
	Open	a	ɑ	

Pike- Typical Symbology

Fronting: C̣ , V˂

Backing: C. , V˃

Raising: V^

Lowering: Vˇ

Ingressive lung air: C←

Egressive pharynx air: C˚

Ingressive pharynx air: Oꜝ

Egressive mouth air: C˃

Ingressive mouth air: C˂

PART 2: INTRODUCTION

258

Fig. 3-19: Degrees of lip rounding considered by *Pike* in the utterance of "vocoids" (vowels). After references [SCr-105, SCr-106], reproduced with permission.

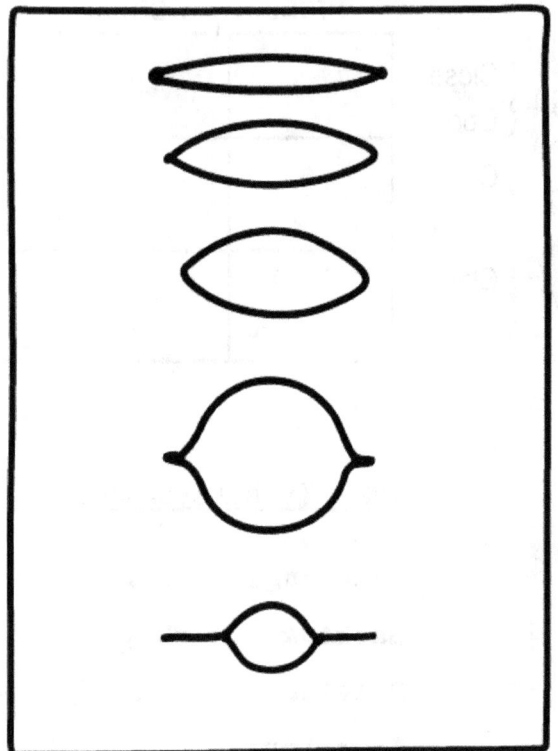

Chapter 3: Other Prior Art

259

Fig. 3-20: Some English words transcribed in *Pike's* alphabet, shown in square brackets; these specifically use Pike's "non-vocoids". After references [SCr-105, SCr-106] reproduced with permission.

Nonsyllable Consonants:

[p]	['pɔl]	pall
[t]	['tek]	take
[k]	['kærəktr̩]	character
[č]	['čenǰ]	change
[f]	['fon]	phone
[θ]	['θɪŋk]	think
[s]	['so]	sew
[š]	['šɪp]	ship

[b]	['æbət]	abbot
[d]	['du]	do
[g]	['gud]	good
[ǰ]	['ǰorǰ]	George
[r]	['ren]	rain
[ð]	[ðə]	the
[z]	[æz]	as
[ž]	['vɪžn̩]	vision

3.5 NATIVE NORTH-AMERICAN AND AFRICAN CONTRIBUTIONS

3.5.1 SCRIPTS FOR NATIVE AMERICAN LANGUAGES OF NORTH AMERICA: *CHEROKEE, CREE, INUKTITUT*, OTHERS

As noted earlier in this chapter, many scripts devised for Native American languages do not meet our dual definition above. For example, a script such as the **Cherokee** [SCr-62 to SCr-64], which was specifically invented, *ab initio*, for the Cherokee language (a Native American language of a people originally inhabiting regions of the states of North Carolina and Tennessee in the U.S.), is disqualified because it does not attempt a systematic, scientific phonological classification.

Nevertheless, these scripts are worthy of mention simply because they were good-faith attempts at arriving at a script based on scientific and phonological basis, and *ab initio*. Yet another of these scripts is the **Cree** script, devised originally for the *Algonquian* languages *Cree* and *Ojibwe (Ojibwa)* [SCr-1]. The Cree script is unique in the sense that it uses geometrical symbols. In that respect, it is based on the same principles as the geometric script we arrive at when we undertake exercises in inventing new scripts in a later chapter of this book. Cree is disqualified by our dual definition for the same reasons as Cherokee.

A script based on the Cree but devised specifically for the **Inuit** (formerly "Eskimo") languages and denoted generally as **Inuktitut** (literally, "like the Inuit") has a much better claim at scientific and systematic classification [SCr-78 to SCr-80]. It *does* meet our dual definition above. This script was finalized by the Inuit Cultural Institute. It is presented in the Figure below. What is noteworthy is the attempt at iconic or intuitive design of the glyphs. For example, compare the [vi] row ([vi] through [v]). The Inuktitut script nevertheless has the standard deficiencies that we have encountered with most of the scripts we have discussed thus far: *Lack of recognizability, incompleteness, lack of systematic organization* (the phones are arranged in no particular order from a phonological point of view), *difficulty in manual and keyboard transcription*, etc.

Chapter 3: Other Prior Art

261

Fig. 3-21: The *Inuktitut* script, used for *Inuit* languages. From publications of the Language Commission of the Inuit Cultural Institute and other references [SCr-78 to SCr-80], reproduced with permission.

△	△̇	i	▷	▷̇	u	◁	◁̇	a	"	h
∧	∧̇	pi	>	>̇	pu	<	<̇	pa	<	p
∩	∩̇	ti	⊃	⊃̇	tu	⊂	⊂̇	ta	ᒼ	t
ᑭ	ᑭ̇	ki	ᑯ	ᑯ̇	ku	ᑲ	ᑲ̇	ka	ᑉ	k
ᒋ	ᒋ̇	gi	ᒍ	ᒍ̇	gu	ᒐ	ᒐ̇	ga	ᶹ	g
ᒥ	ᒥ̇	mi	ᒧ	ᒧ̇	mu	ᒪ	ᒪ̇	ma	ᒻ	m
σ	σ̇	ni	⊙	⊙̇	nu	ᓇ	ᓇ̇	na	ᓐ	n
ᔨ	ᔨ̇	si	ᔪ	ᔪ̇	su	ᔅ	ᔅ̇	sa	ᔅ	s
ᓕ	ᓕ̇	li	ᓗ	ᓗ̇	lu	ᓚ	ᓚ̇	la	ᓪ	l
ᐱ	ᐱ̇	ji	ᐳ	ᐳ̇	ju	ᐸ	ᐸ̇	ja	ᑦ	j
ᕕ	ᕕ̇	vi	ᕗ	ᕗ̇	vu	ᕙ	ᕙ̇	va	ᕝ	v
ᕆ	ᕆ̇	ri	ᕈ	ᕈ̇	ru	ᕋ	ᕋ̇	ra	ᕐ	r
ᕿ	ᕿ̇	qi	ᖁ	ᖁ̇	qu	ᖃ	ᖃ̇	qa	ᖅ	q
ᙱ	ᙱ̇	ngi	ᙳ	ᙳ̇	ngu	ᙰ	ᙰ̇	nga	ᖕ	ng
ᙱ̈	ᙱ̈̇	nngi	ᙳ̈	ᙳ̈̇	nngu	ᙰ̈	ᙰ̈̇	nnga	ᖖ	nng
ƛi	ƛi̇	ɬi	ƛu	ƛu̇	ɬu	ƛa	ƛȧ	ɬa	ᐦ	ɬ

PART 2: INTRODUCTION

Among other North American scripts, a variation of the Cree script was adapted as a syllabary for *Chippewa* [SCr-1], and a good faith attempt at inventing a scientific, phonological script for Inuit by *Uyaqoq* in Alaska in the 1900's degenerated into a unique, "ideographic syllabary" [SCr-1, SCr-78].

3.5.2 NEW SCRIPTS FOR AFRICAN LANGUAGES: *VAI, N'KO*

A unique script, now called *Vai* was said to have been invented by M.D. **Bukele**, a Liberian, in the mid-1800's. [SCr-107 to SCr-109]. It was invented *ab initio*, with many glyphs being geometric symbols. It is said to be a syllabary. It is organized systematically although not in any phonological order, except as applicable to the *Vai* and other West African languages that it primarily addresses. Interestingly, although it addresses tonal languages, the script has no way of transcribing tone. A representation is shown in the **Figure** below.

A scientifically organized script, called *N'ko*, was created in the 1950's for West African languages by S. **Kante**, a Guinean. [SCr-1, SCr-107]. The script has just 25 major glyphs. Diacritics above or below vowels indicate nasalization, length and tone. The script has narrow applicability to the West African languages centered around Guinea, such as *Mandekan*. It is mentioned here for completeness only.

Fig. 3-22 (*overleaf*): Excerpts from the *Vai* script invented by *Bukele*. Reproduced with permission from References [SCr-1, SCr-107 to SCr-109].

Translit.[a]	Value	e	i	a	o	u	ɔ (ọ)	ɛ (ẹ)
p	[p]							
b	[b]							
ɓ	[ɓ]							
mɓ	[mɓ]							
kp	[kp]							
mgb	[mgb]							
gb	[gb]							
f	[f]							
v	[v]							
t	[t]							
d	[d]							
l	[l]							
ḍ	[ɗ]							
nḍ	[nɗ]							
s	[s]							
z	[z]							
c	[c]							
j	[ɟ]							
nj	[nɟ]							
y	[j]							
k	[k]							
ṅg	[ŋg]							
g	[g]							
h	[h]							
w	[w]							
−								

PART 2: INTRODUCTION

3.6 OTHER RECENT CONTRIBUTIONS

3.6.1 ASSORTED OTHER ATTEMPTS AT NEW SCRIPTS: *UNIFON, SHAVIAN, COLUMBIAN, ABULHAB, FRASER, POLLARD*

Many of the other attempts at new scripts/alphabets are mentioned here for reasons of historical completeness only.

In the early 1950's, John R. *Malone* developed an alphabet denoted as *Unifon* [SCr-110], as a commercial venture for the Bendix Corporation, directed at teletype avionics communications. Its lack of any particular merit (at least in this author's humble opinion) can be seen in the transcription in the Figure below:

Fig. 3-23: Sample transcription in *Unifon* (of Malone). After reference [SCr-110], reproduced with permission.

English:
Our father, who art in heaven, hallowed be thy name. Thy kingdom come, thy will be done, on earth as it is in heaven.

Unifon:

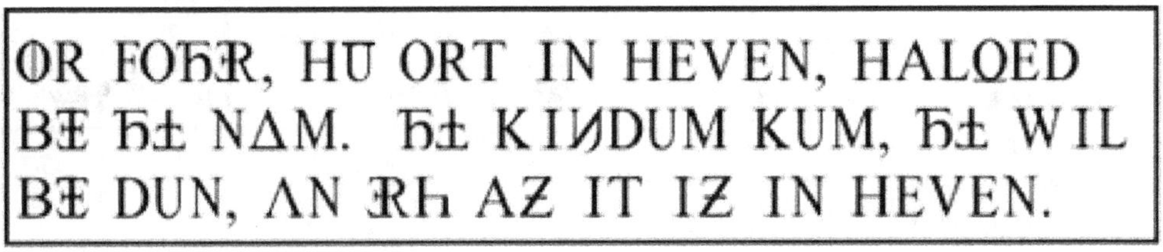

```
OR FO�историR, HU ORT IN HEVEN, HALOED
BE Ƕ± NΔM.  Ƕ± KIɅDUM KUM, Ƕ± WIL
BE DUN, ΛN ᴚh AZ IT IZ IN HEVEN.
```

The estate of George Bernard *Shaw*, the English/Irish playwright, held a competition after his death for the invention of a new alphabet, with one of the requirements being complete lack of resemblance to the Roman alphabet. The competition was won by one Ronald *Kingsley*, and the result was what is known as the *Shavian* or *Shaw Alphabet* [SCr-111]. This alphabet is shown in the Figure below. As seen therein, it suffers from lack of recognizability and completeness, and poor applicability beyond English.

Chapter 3: Other Prior Art

Fig. 3-24: Kingsley's *Shavian* or *Shaw* Alphabet, commissioned by George Bernard Shaw, the English/Irish playwright. After reference [SCr-111], reproduced with permission.

Tall and deep letters:

Shavian letter	𐑐	𐑚	𐑑	𐑛	𐑒	𐑜	𐑓	𐑝	𐑔	𐑕
Unicode text										
Pronunciation (may vary, see below)	/p/	/b/	/t/	/d/	/k/	/g/	/f/	/v/	/θ/	/ð/
Name/example	peep	bib	tot	dead	kick	gag	fee	vow	thigh	they

Shavian letter	𐑖	𐑗	𐑘	𐑙	𐑚	𐑛	𐑜	𐑝	𐑞	𐑟
Unicode text										
Pronunciation	/s/	/z/	/ʃ/	/ʒ/	/tʃ/	/dʒ/	/j/	/w/	/ŋ/	/h/
Name/example	so	zoo	sure	measure	church	judge	yea	woe	hung	ha-ha

Short letters:

Shavian letter	𐑦	𐑩	𐑥	𐑯	𐑤	𐑰	𐑧	𐑱	𐑨	𐑲
Unicode text										
Pronunciation	/ɪ/	/ʊ/	/m/	/n/	/l/	/i:/	/ɛ/	/eɪ/	/æ/	/aɪ/
Name/example	loll	roar	mime	nun	if	eat	egg	age	ash	ice

Shavian letter	𐑼	𐑳	𐑪	𐑴	𐑫	𐑵	𐑬	𐑶	𐑭	𐑷
Unicode text										
Pronunciation	/ə/	/ʌ/	/ɒ/	/oʊ/	/ʊ/	/u:/	/aʊ/	/ɔɪ/	/ɑ:/	/ɔ:/
Name/example	ado	up	on	oak	wool	ooze	out	oil	ah	awe

Ligatures:

Shavian letter	𐑸	𐑹	𐑺	𐑻	𐑼	𐑽	𐑾	𐑿
Unicode text								
Pronunciation	/ɑɚ/	/ɔɚ/	/ɛɚ/	/ɝ/	/ɚ/	/ɪɚ/	/ɪə/	/ju:/
Name/example	are	or	air	err	array	ear	Ian	yew

PART 2: INTRODUCTION

266

In 1798, James *Ewing* published what he denoted as the *Columbian alphabet* [SCr-112] In this, he attempted to arrive at a phonemic alphabet for English, where one letter (or symbol or digraph) represented one phoneme of English. Adaptations of Roman letters were used. The limitation to British English of the time only is evident.

It is to be noted that attempts at the invention of new scripts, and orthographic reform in general, continue in the *21st century*. For example, a refined Arabic script was recently (2004) published, and indeed, patented by Saad D. *Abulhab* [SCr-113]. And of course reform of the present difficult state of keyboarding for the world's languages continues, through *Unicode 4.1* and its successors, and other projects.

A missionary working in China and other parts of Asia, J.O. *Fraser,* invented a unique script in the 1910's [SCr-114]. This used the Indian phonological classification and uniquely Indian features such as *maatra's,* but employed Roman letters in upper case, many in inverted or turned form. Tones were represented by punctuation marks or combinations thereof. The script is summarized in the Figure below. Its limitations in terms of *recognizability, incompleteness, ease of transcription* and other parameters we have defined is evident.

Another missionary working in China, S. *Pollard*, invented a script for the western variety of *Hmong* [SCr-115]. This was somewhat unique in the sense that it used some Roman letters, some symbols such as a triangle, and some invented glyphs such as an inverted upper case "L". It also used the *maatra* concept: Vowels were represented by diacritics, with the position of the diacritic determining the tone as well. A representation of this script is given in the Figure below. Its limitations in terms of *recognizability, incompleteness, ease of transcription* and other parameters we have defined is evident.

Chapter 3: Other Prior Art

Fig. 3-25: The *Fraser* script in summary. Reproduced with permission from References [SCr-1, SCr-114].

P	[p]	T	[t]	F	[ts]	C	[c]	K	[k]		
ᑯ	[pʰ]	⊥	[tʰ]	ꟻ	[tsʰ]	Ɔ	[cʰ]	ꓘ	[kʰ]		
B	[b]	D	[d]	Z	[dz]	J	[ɟ]	G	[g]	Ꙅ	[ɦ]ᵃ
ſ	[f]	S	[s]			X	[ʃ]	H	[x]	V	[h]
W	[v]	ꓤ	[z]			R	[ʒ]	ᙠ	[ɣ]		
M	[m]	N	[n]					Λ	[ŋ]		
		L	[l]								
W	[ʋ]					Y	[j]				
		I	[i]	∩	[ü]	⅂	[ɯ]	U	[u]		
		E	[e]	Ǝ	[ø]	ꓷ	[ə]	O	[ʊ]		
		Ɐ	[æ]			A	[ɑ]				
.	high tone	,	mid rising	.,	mid tone	..	mid tense	:	low tone	;	low tense
'	nasal-ization	_	[a̰]	-.	comma	=	period	-	in names	?	ques-tion

PART 2: INTRODUCTION

Fig. 3-26: The *Pollard* script in summary. Reproduced with permission from References [SCr-1, SCr-115].

⌐	[p]	T	[t]	Δ	[tl]	Ɩ	[ṭ]	⊐	[k]	J	[q]	Y	[ʔ, Ø]			
⌐'	[pʰ]	T'	[tʰ]	Δ'	[tlʰ]	Ɩ'	[ṭʰ]	⊐'	[kʰ]	J'	[qʰ]					
		†	[ts]			⊏	[tʂ, tɕ]									
		†'	[tsʰ]			⊏'	[tʂʰ, tɕʰ]									
Γ	[f]	S	[s]	Ɫ	[ɬ]	J	[ʂ, ɕ]	ʃ	[χ]			⏋	[h]			
V	[v]	3	[z]	L	[l]	R	[ʐ]	ǀ	[ɣ]							
ɔ	[m̥]	Ƈ	[n̥]					Ƙ	[ŋ̊]							
)	[m]	(	[n]					Ƈ	[ŋ]	[ɯ (< ŋ)]						
U	[w]					Λ	[z̞, y]									

⋂	[i]	⋅	[y]	⋅	[ɯ]	ᵘ	[u]
⋅	[ɪ]	⋅	[ʏ]	⋅	[ə]		
⋅	[e]	⋅	[œj]	⁻	[a]	º	[o]
⋅	[ei]	=	[ie]	⋅	[ai]	⋅⋅	[au]

3.6.2 ASSORTED OTHER ATTEMPTS AT NEW SCRIPTS, CONT.: TOLKIEN, LEGUIN, BLOQUERST, WILBUR, ARTHUR, GREENAWAY, OTHERS

Interestingly, J.R.R. **Tolkien**, the author of *The Hobbit, Lord of the Rings* and other related fantasies, invented a script for his denizens of Middle Earth, which he called **Tengwar**. This script, invented around 1931 but published in 1965, is scientific and systematic in organization, though somewhat modeled on Pitman's shorthand [SCr-116]. Thus, e.g., in this script plosives are represented by a descending vertical, fricatives by an ascending vertical, somewhat analogous to Pitman's shorthand. The script's limitations to the languages of the denizens of Middle Earth is evident. A similar script, also invented for a work of fiction, was arrived at in the mid 1980's by U.K. **LeGuin**.

As can be imagined, there have been many other attempts by all manner of authors to attempt to arrive at "new alphabets" which would solve problems encountered with existing scripts. We shall mention here only a few, as a matter of reference only. None of these are very different from the ones cited above, and none, in this author's opinion, offers any feature different, more significant, or more innovative than the features of the scripts already cited above. The reader may access the references for further information on these. In this category we have the *"Novel abécédaire"* published by A.J. **Bloquerst** [SCr-117], the *"grammatical alphabet"* of Josiah **Wilbur** [SCr-118], and **Greenaway** [SCr-120], and a multiple-author alphabet directed at children, known as *Arthur's Alphabet* [SCr-119].

Among other attempts at new scripts that are worthy of mention, if only for completeness, are the "phonetic alphabet" of Raymond **Weeks** [SCr-121], the alphabet of William Makepeace **Thackeray** [SCr-122], the works of **Emsley** [SCr-101], the work of **Sapir**, **Swadesh** and coworkers [SCr-123], and the work of **Roudet** [SCr-124]. Some of the newer works, such as that of ***Abulhab*** [SCr-113], have attempted to establish Unicode [SCr-125] transcriptions as well. These did not meet many or most of the requirements and objectives of a new world script, as set forth in an earlier chapter.

PART 2: INTRODUCTION

3.7 THE IPA (ALPHABET OF THE INTERNATIONAL PHONETIC ASSOCIATION) AND SERIOUS DEFICIENCIES THEREOF

We refer here and throughout this book to the alphabet of the International Phonetic Association (IPA) simply as the "*IPA*" [SCr-2 to SCr-4]. Since tomes are available on this in the literature, we do not discuss it further except to note its *deficiencies* within the context of the present book. For this purpose, we may briefly recollect the criteria we have set for ourselves in this book for the *ten* desirable characteristics of a universal script (as first identified in the PREFACE, *universality and completeness, recognizability, distinctiveness, simplicity and intuitive nature, ease and rapidity of keyboard/-cursive/print transcription, systematic scientific classification and accuracy, discretization, practical phonemics, voice recognition capability and, finally, ability to accommodate the phonemic idiosyncrasies of all the world's languages*). *Some*, though by no means all, of the IPA's deficiencies can be summarized as follows:

1) *Unrecognizability*: Many glyphs (letters, symbols) are difficult for the layman, even one who has grown up with the Roman or Greek scripts (alphabets), to recognize. Some glyphs appear to be straight from outer space! Examples of some unrecognizable IPA glyphs are given in the **Figure** below

2) *Confusing nature* of many of the letters, a property related to the unrecognizability. Many very similar glyphs, are difficult to differentiate, and are highly confusing, even to the expert. Examples among these are the various inverted and rotated *e*'s and *a*'s, the inverted/rotated/hooked, etc. variants of *r* and *R* used to represent the various alveolar trills and flaps or uvular *"r's"*, and the variants of *n* with inward/outward hooks, etc. used for the various nasals. They are also, incidentally, very *difficult to transcribe cursively* and to keyboard. Examples of IPA glyphs that are confusing even for the layman for whom the Roman script is native are given in the **Figure** below.

3) *Poor amenability to cursive writing*, as the **Figure** below shows.

Chapter 3: Other Prior Art

271

Fig. 3-27: Examples of *unrecognizable* (***Top***) and *confusing* (***Bottom***) *IPA* glyphs. ***Overleaf*** are shown *cursive* forms of some of the IPA glyphs. Reproduced with permission from the IPA Handbook [SCr-3]. (Copyright 2005, all rights reserved by the IPA).

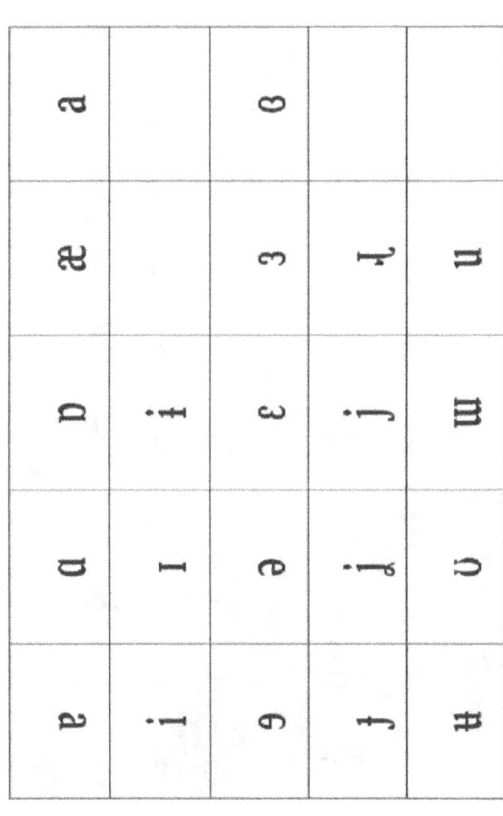

PART 2: INTRODUCTION

(Fig. 3-27, cont.)

CURSIVE FORMS

Chapter 3: Other Prior Art

4) ***Too many diacritics***, leading to *difficult manual transcription, even when not written in cursive*. Manual transcription implies pen/pencil on paper. Difficulty also implies slowness. The diacritics are further compounded by *too many differentiating symbols, exponents*, etc. These features of the IPA are seen in the summary of IPA diacritics presented in the **Figure** below.

5) ***Poor keyboarding***, made even more difficult by the large number of diacritics, exponents, etc. used, and the sheer number of independent glyphs (letters). Anyone having tried transcribing a passage in the IPA using all manner of software (including embedded fonts in word processors) will readily attest to this!

6) ***Lack of systematic organization, lack of pedagogical sense and inapplicability for everyday use:*** The IPA, in its various presentations (e.g. in the IPA summary chart at the beginning of its Handbook), actually ends up using, for its "consonants", the ancient Indian system of classification: Grouping the "consonants" based on points of articulation, starting from the back (pharyngeal/-uvular/-velar) to the front (bilabial) of the oral apparatus, and then further differentiated as plosive, nasal, fricative, etc.. However, the alphabetic order retained is still that of the Roman alphabet. As a result, it is not clear from the IPA Summary Table ("IPA Chart") what is the exact order of the letters, and how the alphabet would be learned, e.g., by schoolchildren. Does it, for example, start with [p], the very first letter at the top left of the IPA chart, and end with [inverted-a] [ɒ], the last vowel shown in the chart? The assumption of course is that it is *not* meant for schoolchildren, only for highly educated phoneticists and linguists!

7) ***Incompleteness:*** *the IPA treatment of vowels does not even consider horizontal jaw position, and only two lip positions* (rounded and not rounded) are considered, these being shoehorned in to the IPA vowel charts.

Fig. 3-28: The "DIACRITICS" and "TONES AND WORD ACCENTS" portions of the *IPA* chart. Reproduced with permission from the IPA Handbook [SCr-3]. (Copyright 2005, all rights reserved by the IPA).

DIACRITICS

˳	Voiceless	n̥ d̥	̈	Breathy voiced	b̤ a̤	̪	Dental	t̪ d̪
ˬ	Voiced	s̬ t̬	̃	Creaky voiced	b̰ a̰	̺	Apical	t̺ d̺
ʰ	Aspirated	tʰ dʰ	̼	Linguolabial	t̼ d̼	̻	Laminal	t̻ d̻
̹	More rounded	ɔ̹	ʷ	Labialized	tʷ dʷ	̃	Nasalized	ẽ
̜	Less rounded	ɔ̜	ʲ	Palatalized	tʲ dʲ	ⁿ	Nasal release	dⁿ
̟	Advanced	u̟	ˠ	Velarized	tˠ dˠ	ˡ	Lateral release	dˡ
̠	Retracted	e̠	ˤ	Pharyngealized	tˤ dˤ	̚	No audible release	d̚
̈	Centralized	ë	̴	Velarized or pharyngealized	ɫ			
̽	Mid-centralized	ẽ	̝	Raised	e̝	(ɹ̝ = voiced alveolar fricative)		
̩	Syllabic	n̩	̞	Lowered	e̞	(β̞ = voiced bilabial approximant)		
̯	Non-syllabic	e̯	̘	Advanced Tongue Root	e̘			
˞	Rhoticity	ɚ a˞	̙	Retracted Tongue Root	e̙			

(Fig. 3-28, cont.)

Fig. 3-29: One of the latest additions to the IPA, in 2005, the labiodental flap (for African languages. After reference [SCr-4], reproduced with permission.

Avurungu

PART 2: INTRODUCTION

8) ***Ad-hoc, "build-as-you-go" and Eurocentric nature***: These properties are transparent in the IPA, in its very nature, and in its origins in the ad-hoc Roman script. They are also evident in the way it has attempted to adapt to new languages with modifications of the same Roman letters. This has ultimately made the alphabet even more confusing and unwieldy. For example, some of the latest (2005) additions, for African languages, include new glyphs [SCr-4], as shown in the Figure below. This ad-hoc, build-as-you-go characteristic is due to the origins of the IPA in 19th-century Europe. An alphabet that started with a small modification of the Roman alphabet to accommodate English, French and German and then tried to gradually accommodate all the world's languages, cannot equal, in its qualities, an alphabet or script designed *ab initio*, from first principles at the outset, with a knowledge of the world's languages.

9) ***Emphasis on "narrow transcription" rather than practical phonemics for everyday use***. The IPA, in its "narrow transcription" version, is excellent for distinguishing the different pronunciation of individual speakers of the same dialect of the same language. This is no doubt a very useful property to have. However, it is of little use for practical, everyday phonemics and phonemic transcription.

10) ***Outright errors and erroneous classification***: As just *some* examples of these:

   (a) The IPA designates the phones [s] and [z] as alveolar fricatives, which is entirely incorrect. The alveolar artition is made with the tip of the tongue touching the region of the alveolar ridge, whereas the [s] and [z] phones of virtually all major languages are articulated with the apico/medio portion, i.e. a bit back from the tip, of the tongue touching the alveolar ridge (or further up, closer to the dental area). The alveolar fricatives per se are quite different sounds from the [s] and [z]. The reader can verify this himself/herself, by first articulating the alveolar stop [t], as in the English *t* of *sty*, and then retaining that same artition and articulating a fricative. What ensues is something quite different from an [s]. The [s] and [z] are in fact *apico/medio-dental* fricatives, which is how *Navlipi* classifies them. That is to say, the contact is made with the apico/medio portion of the tongue, and the tip of the tongue itself is closer to the upper teeth than the alveolar ridge.

   (b) The IPA does not treat of vocalic-[r] and vocalic-[l] at all, even though these phones are well established in languages from Sanskrit to Serbo-Croat. These phones *were* treated of by prominent modern phoneticists such as Lepsius [SCr-68 to SCr-70], not to mention the ancient Indian phoneticists [LN-31 to LN-33, LAi-3, LAi-6, LAi-11, LAi-12]. Instead of recognizing these phones to accommodate vocalic-[r], the IPA comes up with a unique term, *rhoticity*, which is somewhat nebulously defined as an "[r]-flavor to a vowel"!

(c) The IPA then further confuses non-vocalic and vocalic phones by not recognizing a bilabial semivowel [w], but, rather, only a labiodental "approximant" ("approximant", roughly, is the IPA term for a semivowel). Since this yields problems with the distinction of lateral and central vowels, it then distinguishes some of the lateral vowels as "lateral approximants"!

(d) In the treatment of both Hindi and Sindhi in its main and most popular publication, the *Handbook of the International Phonetic Association* [SCr-3], the *palatal stops*, of which there are four in nearly all North Indian languages (unvoiced/voiced, unaspirated/aspirated combinations), are treated as *affricates*. The reasons for this are not hard to find, and lie, unfortunately, in the still Eurocentric view of the IPA: Since Western European languages do not phonemically differentiate between aspirated and unaspirated stops, Western Europeans always pronounced these Indian palatal stops with aspiration, as a result of which they always came out as affricates, exactly like the identical affricates in their own languages. However, Indians articulate these clearly as *stops*, *not* affricates, and the highly adept ancient Indian phoneticists recognized them as stops (*sparsha*), not a combination of stops and fricatives (*uushman*). Strangely, though, the IPA *does* recognize palatal stops elsewhere, e.g. in its treatment of Irish in the very same IPA Handbook! Thus, in a sense it contradicts itself! Now anyone who has heard an Irishman's and an Indian's pronunciation of the palatal unvoiced stop (IPA designation [c]) will acknowledge that they are identical. One may thus speculate that the early classification of the Indian palatal stops as affricates, and not true stops, emanated from audio (spectrographic) analysis of the Indian sounds uttered into a microphone by *a non-Irish European* sometime in the 19th or 20th centuries!

(e) Another example of erroneous classification is the (incomplete) IPA treatment of vowels. For, as noted above, the IPA does not even consider the horizontal jaw position, and considers only two lip positions (rounded

PART 2: INTRODUCTION

and not rounded), these being shoehorned in to the IPA vowel charts. In contrast, even Pike [SCr-105, SCr-106] recognized many different lip and jaw positions, and *Navlipi* treats of two horizontal jaw positions and three lip positions. *Navlipi* does not consider any more lip and jaw positions for reasons of discretization and practicality.

11) ***Sheer number of glyphs (172)***: The IPA's individually distinct glyphs number *172*. One reason for this is the absence of use of such glyph-saving devices as *post-ops* or other indicators of phonological class, as used by *Navlipi*.

12) ***Finally, the most important deficiency of all: INABILITY TO ACCOUNT FOR THE PHONEMIC IDIOSYNCRASIES OF THE WORLD'S LANGUAGES***: This is perhaps the IPA's most important deficiency, although, admittedly, it is also a deficiency of *all* scripts prior to *Navlipi*. This deficiency is reflected in the following examples:

- **(a)** The IPA is unable to indicate to the native English speaker reading Hindi in the IPA that the unaspirated [p] and aspirated [ph] have distinct phonemic values in Hindi, whereas they have the same values in English.
- **(b)** Similarly, an English speaker reading Mandarin would not be able to tell that [p] and [b] have the same value in Mandarin, or that [r] and [l] have the same value in Japanese.
- **(c)** Conversely, the Arabic speaker reading English in the IPA for the very first time could not guess that the [b], the only bilabial that he/she is familiar with, has an unvoiced counterpart, [p], that has a different value than the [b].
- **(d)** As another example, the IPA is unable to convey, through its orthography alone, that in Hindi, the phones [w] (bilabial semivowel) and [v] (labiodental voiced fricative) constitute part of the same phoneme and are freely interchanged.
- **(e)** In a similar vein, the IPA cannot convey that, in Parisian French and "proper" German (Hochdeutsch), the phones [x] (velar unvoiced fricative), [r] [alveolar flap] and [rr] (alveolar trill) constitute part of the same phoneme and are frequently interchanged.

Chapter 3: Other Prior Art

3.8 *AMERICANIST* PHONETIC NOTATION (SCRIPT)

Somewhat analogous to the script of the IPA, but predating it, is a "phonetic notation" or script known as the ***Americanist*** (also called *American Phonetic Alphabet, **APA***) [SCr-127 to SCr-132]. This may in some ways be thought of as an American counterpart of the IPA script.

The Americanist script appears to have originated in initial work by Powell in 1880 for specific application to Native American ("American Indian") languages [SCr-127]. It appears then to have been expanded upon by Boas in 1911 [SCr-128] and finally published in its first, complete form in 1916 by the American Anthropological Society [SCr-129]. It was then further modified by Bloomfield and Bolling, and Herzog et al. [SCr-130, SCr-131]. It was widely used by American linguists in the first half of the 20th century, especially to transcribe Native American languages. The Americanist scripts attempts to be more "practical" than the IPA script, in that it seeks to use existing glyphs (letters) of the Roman and Greek alphabets. Unfortunately, the Americanist script also uses diacritics much more heavily, making transcription using a standard keyboard more cumbersome.

The Americanist script is reproduced in nearly complete form in **Fig. 3-29** below [SCr-132]. Even a quick glance at this figure shows that the description of this script in the preceding paragraphs is accurate. Additionally, let us take a moment to quickly recollect the criteria we have set forth for ourselves in this book for the *ten* desirable characteristics of a universal script (as first identified in the PREFACE: *(1) Universality and completeness; (2) recognizability; (3) distinctiveness; (4) simplicity and intuitive nature; (5) ease and rapidity of keyboard/-cursive/print transcription; (6) systematic scientific classification and accuracy; (7) discretization; (8) practical phonemics; (9) voice recognition capability; (10)* and, finally, *ability to accommodate the phonemic idiosyncrasies of all the world's languages*). We can quickly appreciate the deficiencies of the Americanist script in respect of these 10 criteria and characteristics: Our 2nd, 3rd, 4th, 5th, 7th, 8th, 9th and 10th characteristics are in large part lacking.

PART 2: INTRODUCTION

Fig. 3-30: The *Americanist* script in partial representation. (Reproduced with permission from refs. [SCr-132].)

Vowels and "Glides"

		Front		Central		Back	
		spread	rounded	spread	rounded	spread	rounded
	glide	y	ẅ			ÿ	w
High	tense	i	ü	ɨ	ʉ	ï	u
	lax	ɪ	Ü			ï̈	U
Mid	tense	e	ö	ə		ë	o
	lax	ɛ	ö̀	ʌ		ɛ̈	ɔ
Low		æ		a		ɑ	ɒ

Chapter 3: Other Prior Art

(Fig. 3-30, cont.)
"Consonants"

			Bilabial	Labio-dental	Dental	Alveolar	Retroflex	Alveo-palatal	Palatal (pre-velar)	Velar	Uvular (post-velar)	Pharyngeal (faucal)	Laryngeal
Stop (oral)	plain	voiceless	p		t̪	t	ṭ	t̠	k̟	k	q		
		voiced	b		d̪	d	ḍ	d̠	ĝ	g	ġ		
	glottalized	voiceless (ejective)	ṗ		t̪'	t'	ṭ'	t̠'	k̟'		q̇		ʔ
		voiced (imploded)	ḅ			ḋ				ġ	g̈		
Affricate	central	voiceless		pf	tθ	c	č̣	č	kˣ		qˣ		
		voiced		bv	dð	ʒ	ǯ	ǯ	gʸ		ġʸ		
		glottalized			tθ	ċ		č̇					
	lateral	voiceless				ƛ							
		voiced				λ							
		glottalized				ƛ'							
Fricative	central	voiceless	φ	f	θ / s̩	s	ṣ	š	x̠	x	x̣	ḥ	h
		voiced	β	v	ð / z̩	z	ẓ	ž	ŷ	γ	γ̇	ʕ	
		glottalized			ṡ								
	lateral	voiceless			ɬ								
		glottalized			ɬ'								
Nasal		voiceless	M	Ṃ		N		Ñ		Ṇ			
		voiced	m	ɱ	n̪	n	ṇ	ñ	n̂	ŋ	ŋ̇		
		glottalized	ṁ		ṅ					ŋ̇	ŋ̈		
Liquid	rhotic	plain				r	ṛ				R		
		glottalized				ṙ							
	lateral	plain			l̪	l	ḷ		l̂	L			
		glottalized				l'							
	glide	plain	w						y				
		glottalized	w'						y'				

(Fig. 3-30, cont.)

Alternate Glyphs for "Consonants"

- j = ʒ
- ǰ = ž
- ƭ = ɫ
- ɸ = φ

- G = ġ
- X = ẋ
- ʸ = ˷   (e.g., kʸ = k̰)

"Rhotics" (r-sounds)

Rhotics	Dental	Alveolar	Retroflex	Uvular
Tap		r		
Flap		D		
Trill		r̃		
Fricative (spirant)		ř		
Frictionless spirant				

Chapter 3: Other Prior Art

3.9 BRIEF SYNOPSIS OF DEFICIENCIES OF ALL ALPHABETS/SCRIPTS CITED ABOVE

The deficiencies of the above alphabets/scripts (and that of the Indian scripts discussed at length in an earlier chapter) have been dealt with at some length in their respective discussions above. In particular, those of the IPA alphabet have been delineated in detail in the previous section. Here, we briefly summarize these deficiencies.

Nearly all of the scripts of the prior art suffer from a *lack of systematic organization or classification based on phonological principles*. Even in the few that possess this (e.g. that of Pike) [SCr-105, SCr-106], the "alphabetical order" from a pedagogical point of view is not immediately apparent. There are some notable exceptions, e.g. Pitman's shorthand [SCr-56 to SCr-58] and Haangul [SCr-46 to SCr-52]; these *do* possess a good, systematic organization based on phonological principles.

However, these then suffer from other deficiencies. For example, Pitman's shorthand is applicable mainly to European languages, and Haangul mainly to Korean; they are both inapplicable, say, to Mandarin common speech (*Putonghua*) or !Xo Bushman. Pitman's is also not meant for lay readership. The Indian scripts, although possessing a remarkable, systematic organization and classification, are grossly incomplete and thus inadequate, even for the Indian languages of today that they purportedly address.

In addition to *incompleteness*, almost all the above scripts suffer from *lack of recognizability*. Recognizability does not necessarily imply a relation to the Roman script. It simply implies some manner of graphical or iconic recognition, as, e.g., attempted by Haangul (with some success) and the Bell script (without success). As noted earlier in this chapter, some scripts, such as that of the IPA, contain many letters "straight from outer space", as it were and are thus most unrecognizable. Indeed, in scripts such as the Shavian (Shaw) or Watt or even Bell [SCr-96, SCr-97, SCr-110, SCr-111, SCr-9], *all* letters appear to be from outer space! And none of these scripts make up by having some sort of iconic or graphic recognition for their "outer-space" letters. Recognizability also implies lack of similarity, and thus absence of confusion. The many turned, inverted and rotated *a*'s, *e*'s and *u*'s of the IPA are the antithesis of this. Those scripts that start with the Roman and thus should have a good measure of recognizability, end up importing so many foreign, strange or otherwise unrecognizable glyphs that these end up being a good portion of the script. The Lepsius, Johnston and Pike scripts [SCr-68, SCr-69, SCr-103, SCr-105, SCr-106] fall in this category.

PART 2: INTRODUCTION

By *incompleteness*, we also refer to incompleteness of the phonological classification. That is to say, if a script does not include all phones of all classes found in all the world's languages it is incomplete. The result of this is that such a script is frequently inapplicable to all except the few languages that it directly addresses. Pike's and the IPA's scripts come closest to completeness. However, while addressing completeness, these scripts end up with too many glyphs (letters) that then become difficult to transcribe, remember and distinguish.

Many of the scripts use diacritics, exponents, super/sub-scripts, etc.. These make them not only *difficult to transcribe* (both typographically and manually, with manually these days implying both cursive writing and manual "printing"), but also *difficult to render on a keyboard*. Ultimately, thus, they are also then difficult to learn, distinguish and recognize. Indeed, one can say without hesitation that, from the above scripts, *not a single script* that is reasonably complete, i.e. is able to address most of the world's languages, is also convenient to keyboard. And in most scripts, diacritics or qualifying symbols, when used, are not iconic or obvious; the $[n_\square]$ of the IPA is a good example. A few scripts, such as Jespersen's or Bell's, are simply impossible to use by the lay public.

Nearly all the scripts also have difficulty in dealing with *clicks and tones*. Those scripts that *do* accommodate clicks and tones, such as those of the IPA and Johnston, render them in a very difficult manner, rather than in a natural, iconic manner, as they should be rendered. For example, the tone renderings of the IPA (Figure in previous section) are extremely difficult to master and transcribe. Even expert phoneticists and linguists end up constantly referring to the "Tones and Word Accents" portion of the IPA Chart like a dictionary to "decipher" tones in an IPA transcription. In this respect then, *trans*cription ends up more like an exercise in *en*cryption. Yet, it must be remembered that we are not trying to create a cipher for "encryption" of a language, but rather, simply, a universal script! And due to their diacritic nature, they are very difficult to accommodate in a keyboard or printing loop.

And, most important of all, *none* of the above scripts/alphabets deals with the singular problem that this book ventures forth to address: That of the **accommodation of the phonemic idiosyncrasies of all the world's languages** *(including tonemic idiosyncrasies)*, as briefly described in point # 10) in the previous Section, and also embodied in the subtitle of this book.

It will be seen from the sequel that *none of the above deficiencies are found in **Navlipi***.

That is to say, ***Navlipi*** *addresses, with reasonable success in this author's view,* **all** *of the above deficiencies*!

PART 2: INTRODUCTION

286

PART 3:

PRESENTATION AND DISCUSSION OF *NAVLIPI*

PART 3: PRESENTATION AND DISCUSSION OF NAVLIPI

288

CHAPTER 4.
THE FULL PHONIC CLASSIFICATION OF *NAVLIPI*: THE "SHELL" MATRICES (TEMPLATES)

TABLE OF CONTENTS

4.1 THE CONCEPT OF AN EMPTY "SHELL" MATRIX (TEMPLATE)........... 291

4.2 THE SIX (6) NAVLIPI VOWEL VARIABLES AND THE 5-DIMENSIONAL VOWEL CLASSIFICATION MATRIX... 294

4.3 REDUCTION OF THE 5-DIMENSIONAL VOWEL CLASSIFICATION MATRIX TO THREE (3) DIMENSIONS, ALONG WITH A 4TH VARIABLE FOR VOWEL DURATION, FOR PRACTICAL PURPOSES................................. 303

4.4 SEMI-VOWELS AND THEIR RELATION TO PARENT VOWELS............. 305

4.5 THE TWO-DIMENSIONAL, (35 X 15), NON-VOWEL MATRIX................... 310

    4.5.1 TWO PHONOLOGICAL VARIABLES, 15 ARTITIONS, 35 PHONOCHROMES............ 310
    4.5.2 BRIEF DISCUSSION OF THE *UNUSUAL ARTITIONS* 313
    4.5.3 BRIEF DISCUSSION OF THE *UNUSUAL PHONOCHROMES*..................................... 315

4.6 TONES ("MUSICAL" OR "PITCH" ACCENTS) 317

4.7 MATRIX NOTATION AND USE OF MATRIX ELEMENT NUMBERS WHEN REFERENCING THE NAVLIPI TABLES... 318

PART 3: PRESENTATION AND DISCUSSION OF NAVLIPI

4.8 OUR RESULT: COMPLETE, EMPTY PHONIC CLASSIFICATION "SHELL" MATRICES (TEMPLATES), FOR SUBSEQUENT FILLING-IN WITH A NEW SCRIPT'S GLYPHS (LETTERS, SYMBOLS).. 320

4.9 ALPHABETICAL ORDER, PEDAGOGY, AND SUBSETS OF THE NAVLIPI SUMMARY TABLES 321

Chapter 4: The Full Phonic Classification of Navlipi: The "Shell" Matrices (Templates)

4.1 THE CONCEPT OF AN EMPTY "SHELL" MATRIX (TEMPLATE)

It is pertinent to start this chapter by introducing the concept of a *shell matrix* or *template*. This concept is based on the following premise:

> ***When trying to devise a new script, it is easier to complete one's phonological classification first, leaving the actual selection of the glyphs (letters, symbols) for the script until later.***

....(4.1)

This results in a *"shell"* or empty matrix, i.e. a template, comprising only the phonological classification, with suitable word examples. There are no actual glyphs, or "letters of the alphabet" yet. This template can then be conveniently filled in later with the actual choices for the glyphs (letters) of the script. The easiest way to visualize an empty, shell matrix or template is simply to view the *NAVLIPI SUMMARY TABLES (PART 1 of this book) with the contents of the cells of the tables empty,* i.e. with just the headings.

We can further briefly illustrate shell matrices or templates with a few short examples. In the example in **Table 4-1** below, the columns, corresponding to *phonochromaticity* (the "color" of the phone, such as voicing, aspiration and nasalization, as defined in a previous chapter) are assigned the x-axis, whilst the rows, corresponding to the *artition* (velar, bilabial, etc.), are assigned the y-axis.

We can then use a *two-number matrix notation*, borrowed with slight modification from mathematics, to represent the individual cells in our 2-dimensional matrix. Thus, (2-2) represents the unvoiced, aspirated, palatal stop, etc.. (The hyphen is used to allow for cases where our matrix may be large and numbers larger than 9 need to be represented, e.g. (2-12)).

In our empty matrix then, we can cite word examples to illustrate the phone. However, we do not, as yet, assign any glyphs (letters or symbols) to the phones. This then allows

PART 3: PRESENTATION AND DISCUSSION OF NAVLIPI

us to chose these letters very carefully after we have an overview of our full matrix. Thus, we have just a "shell" or empty matrix.

The extension of the principles embodied in the above *non-vowel* Table to an empty *vowel* matrix is straightforward, although we would use a three-dimensional matrix in the case of vowels, as done in *Navlipi*.

The vowel example will also show us another important observation: That we may find that some elements, i.e. phones, of our shell matrix *do not in fact have any application in any of the world's languages*. That is to say, there are simply no phones extant in the world's major languages that correspond to them. Thus, for the *Navlipi* vowel matrix elements **2(1)(n)**, (see *NAVLIPI SUMMARY TABLES*) i.e. lip-position= flat ($x = 2$), tongue-articulation-position= medio-palatal ($y=1$) and jaw position= any of four possible [*close* ($z=1$), *close-mid* ($z=2$), *open-mid* ($z=3$) and open ($z=4$)], phones simply do not exist in any major world language!

Another important feature worthy of note in our above treatment is the fact that we have substantially ***discretized*** all our variables. For example, in the case of the shell matrix of **Table 4-1** (below), we note that there are other artitions, e.g. the alveolar position between the retroflex and the dental, or the infralabio-supradental position just before the bilabial position. And in the vowel matrices, there are many intermediate positions between *"lips-fully-rounded"* and *"lips-fully-stretched"* positions, whereas we list only one, the *"flat"* position. And there are also of course many, many gradations of opening of the jaw, whereas we list only four.

Discretization is absolutely essential if we are to keep any phonological classification, and the resulting script, at a manageable level. At the same time, it must be noted that discretization cannot be carried out in a blanket fashion, without any guiding principle. Rather it must be carried out in consideration of *practical phonemics and phonetics as applied to major modern world languages*. For example, if we find that an intermediate tongue position between retroflex and palatal is used only in an obscure Papuan language, then we should omit it.

Chapter 4: The Full Phonic Classification of Navlipi: The "Shell" Matrices (Templates)

Table 4-1: Illustration of the concept of *shell matrices* or *templates*. Here, for clarity, we illustrate with, first, a (3 X 4) matrix, having just three phonochromaticities and four artitions from the non-vowel segment of *Navlipi*. The matrix elements (cells) are *left empty*, with only matrix element #s and word examples given. They are to be filled in later once the glyphs (letters) for them are chosen. As shown, within the cells, a question mark (***glyph ?***) is put, for illustrative purposes only, where the actual glyphs would be placed, once they have been selected. *Different sets of glyphs can be used to arrive at different scripts using the same shell matrix.*

PHONOCHROMATICITY VS. ARTITION, 3X4 TABLE, WITH EXAMPLE WORDS IN ENGLISH

Phonochromaticity (x-axis) →

Artition (y-axis) ↓

	Unvoiced, Unaspirated	Voiced, Unaspirated	Nasal
Velar	glyph ? English *sky*	glyph ? English *go*	glyph ? English *king*
Palatal	glyph ? Spanish *chico*	glyph ? English *gender*	glyph ? English *inch*
Alveolar	glyph ? English *stop*	glyph ? English *do*	glyph ? English *not*
Bilabial	glyph ? English *spy*	glyph ? English *but*	glyph ? English *me*

4.2 THE SIX (6) NAVLIPI VOWEL VARIABLES AND THE 5-DIMENSIONAL VOWEL CLASSIFICATION MATRIX

Having now seen the significance of a "shell" matrix or template and how to construct one, we can now go about the task of actually constructing the *vowel* shell-matrix of *Navlipi*. In a chapter in the second, companion volume of the *NAVLIPI* series, in the discussion of phonological classification as applied to vowels, the variables involved with respect to vowels were presented. We can summarize these briefly here again. It is to be noted that these variables *inherently incorporate discretization*, as discussed in the previous section. There are **six (6)** *independent* vocalic (vowel) variables in *Navlipi*, as given in **Table 4-2** below.

> **Table 4-2 (*cont. overleaf*)**: THE *SIX (6)* INDEPENDENT VARIABLES OF THE NAVLIPI *VOWEL* CLASSIFICATION. (The terms *apico-, medio-* etc. in the compounds under the Description column refer to the portion of the tongue making the contact. Thus "medio-palatal" means that the medial part of the tongue, rather than the apex, is making the contact with the palate.)

1. LIP POSITION (*X*-axis)		
(Discretized to three (3) in all)		
$x=$	DESCRIPTION	EXAMPLE
1	*Stretched*	As in English *beet*
2	*Flat*	As in English *but*
3	*Rounded*	As in English *boot*

Chapter 4: The Full Phonic Classification of Navlipi: The "Shell" Matrices (Templates)

(Table 4-2, cont.)

2. TONGUE OR OTHER ARTICULATION POSITION (ARTITION, *y*-axis) *(Discretized to 14 in all)*			
y=	**Description**	**IPA Nomenclature**	**Example**
1	*Medio-Palatal*	"front" and "front-central"	As in English *beet*
2	*Flat*	"central" and "central-back"	As in English *but*
3	*Retracted*	"back"	As in English *boot*
4	*Apico-Retroflex, Central (r-sound)*	- - -	As in American *maker*
5	*Apico-Retroflex, Lateral (l-sound)*	- - -	
6	*Apico-Palatal, Central (r-sound)*	- - -	Very rare
7	*Apico-Palatal, Lateral (l-sound)*	- - -	Vocalic counterpart of Polish, Serbo-Croat and Portuguese *l*-phone (e.g. Serbo-Croat *lj*eti)
8	*Apico-Alveolo-Dental, Central (most common r-sound)*	- - -	English *purr*, Hindi/Maraathi/Sanskrit *rshi*
9	*Apico-Alveolo-Dental, Lateral (most common l-sound)*	- - -	English and American English *able*
10	*Interdental, Lateral (r-sound)*	- - -	Exists in no major language

PART 3: PRESENTATION AND DISCUSSION OF NAVLIPI

	(Table 4-2, cont.)	[2. TONGUE... POSITION, cont.]	
y=	Description	IPA Nomenclature	Example
11	Apico-Supradental, Lateral (l-sound)	- - -	
12	Nasal, Bilabial (m-sound, no tongue contact)	- - -	Phonemically distinct in many African languages. Example: Name *Mbeki* (South African President)
13	Nasal, (n-sound, tongue contact any of following: dental, alveolar, palatal, retroflex, velar)	- - -	Phonemically distinct in many African languages. Example: Name *Nkomo*
14	Nasal, (uvular, but no tongue contact)	- - -	

3. JAW POSITION, VERTICAL (Z-axis), (Discretized to just four (4) in all)			
z=	Description	IPA Nomenclature	Example
1	*Close*	Close	English *hit*
2	*Close-Mid*	Close-Mid	English *hate* (first part of diphthong only)
3	*Open-Mid*	Open-Mid	English *belt*
4	*Open*	Open	English *hat*

(Table 4-2, cont.)

4. JAW POSITION, HORIZONTAL (*U*-axis),		
(Discretized to just three (3) in all)		
u=	Description	IPA Nomen-clature	Example
1	*Forward*	---	Vocalic portion of central (*r*-sound) in Tamil word *pazham*, "fruit"
2	*Mid*	---	Vocalic portion of lateral (*l*-sound) in Tamil word *pal.am*, "hole"
3	*Retracted*	---	

5. TONGUE FIRMNESS,	
(*V*-axis),		
(Discretized to just two (2))		
v=	Description	IPA Nomenclature
1	*Normal*	---
2	*Firmly Pressed*	---

6. VOWEL DURATION (LENGTH),		
(Discretized to just three (3) in all)		
Length	IPA Nomenclature	Example
Short	*Short*	English *wit*
Long	*Medial*	English *weed*
Extra-Long	*Long*	English *wheeeee*

Before discussing the above tables, in the paragraphs below, we briefly note that the *total number of vowels possible* based on even the above, discretized, variables is very large, as seen in the box below. Quite obviously, not all are intelligibly articulated. And, certainly, not all are used in the world's languages.

> **Total number of vowels possible based on the six (6) independent variables in the tables above:**
>
> *(3 X 14 X 4 X 3 X 2 X 3) = 3024 total possible vowels!*

......(4.2)

Compensation: Also before discussing the above Tables, we briefly dwell on another important concept, what modern phoneticists dub *"compensation"*.

This concept is best illustrated by citing an example: The English word *beet* is normally thought of as being pronounced with the lips *stretched* and tongue forward (the reader may try it to confirm that this is true). However, this word can also be pronounced, though less accurately, with the lips *flat* or *rounded* rather than stretched, through this process of "compensation". The reader is urged to try this as well. Indeed, as the reader may verify, virtually any *vocalic* (vowel) sound can be articulated with lip, tongue and even jaw positions that are radically different from the standard articulation and thus the standard classification for that sound. As another example, the English exclamation *Oh!* is, in standard articulation, pronounced with the lips rounded, the tongue slightly back and the jaw in open-mid or fully open position. However, this sound can also be articulated with the lips flat or even stretched (in which case the jaw would have to close slightly), the tongue central, and the jaw close-mid or even close (teeth clenched). Once again, the reader can try these variations for verification. In all these cases, the brilliant human brain of the hearer can easily recognize that these "compensated" articulations are somewhat strange, not normal, but nevertheless still understand them as *Oh!*. We say "brilliant human brain" because the same is not the case, e..g., for voice-recognition software, which would be quite fooled by these different articulations! (Once again, the reader may try this with any commercial voice-recognition program.)

In the context of such *compensation*, then, it is important to note that, *in this book, we confine our discussions to "normal" rather than "compensated" (or perhaps more*

Chapter 4: The Full Phonic Classification of Navlipi: The "Shell" Matrices (Templates)

accurately) "contorted" speech. **Navlipi** *does* **not** *treat of such "compensation" at all.*

This brief discussion of *compensation* also tells us that what we consider as independent variables (tongue, lip and jaw position) can in fact frequently become interdependent: If one is forced to use an unusual articulation position of, say the lips, then one automatically compensates by also using an unusual position for the tongue or jaw, so that the final utterance is as close as possible to what is intended to be articulated.

We now briefly discuss each of the individual sub-tables in **Table 4-2** in turn in the paragraphs below.

Lip position: The variable of *lip position* (x) is self explanatory. It is noted again that the three positions listed, *stretched, flat* and *rounded*, are discretizations of what is essentially a continuous variable. This discretization to just three positions however fits most if not all of the world's major languages. In this respect, we note that the IPA considers only two (2) lip positions, "rounded" and "not-rounded", and even these are incorporated very perfunctorily into the IPA's vowel diagrams.

Tongue position: The designations of *tongue position* in the second sub-table refer to the tongue contact positions. Thus, e.g., for $y=1$, *"Medio-Palatal" refers to the medial (mid) portion of the tongue contacting the palate*, as in the long [ii] of English *beet*. It is felt that this is a much more accurate description than that used by the IPA ("front" and "front-central"). Similarly, "Apico-Retroflex, Central" ($y=4$) refers to the apex (tip) of the tongue retroflexed (curled back) and the avenue for breath egress at the center of the tongue; thus, a typical retroflexed *r*-sound as in the American *maker*. Row 7 in the table ($y=7$), "Apico-Palatal, Lateral" then obviously refers to the apex of the tongue touching the palate, and the breath being let out through the sides of the tongue. For $y=8$, the designation "Apico-Alveolo-Dental" refers to the fact that the most common *r*-sound in nearly all the world's major languages is uttered variously as the apico-alveolar and apico-dental phone, both these phones having the same phonemic value. (As an aside, we note that the IPA does not consider this distinction.) Thus, for practical phonemic purposes, we have combined these phones into a single cell. The first nasal sound ($y=12$) is uttered with the tongue loose in the oral cavity. In contrast, the second ($y=13$) is uttered with the tongue contacting any of the positions listed; this gives this sound a different flavor than that of $y=12$. Once again, the combination of dental through velar contact position for this cell is for practical phonemic purposes. The last cell ($y=14$), nasal with uvular articulation, is a very different sound from the previous two, as the reader can see by trying it. Thus, for purposes of thoroughness, it is given a separate cell.

PART 3: PRESENTATION AND DISCUSSION OF NAVLIPI

Artition: The combination of the *y* variable (*artition*) with other variables, such as the *x* variable (*lip position*), is easily visualized. For example, in the American pronunciation of the *l*-sound in *able*, the lips are in the flat position. However, this phone can also be uttered with the lips in the rounded or stretched positions. These produce a different phone, but one which is really not phonemically distinguished, but just liable to misinterpretation as incorrect or slurred speech.

Similarly, the vocalic-*r* in the Hindi-/Maraathi-/Sanskrit word *rshi*, meaning "sage" or "seer", is also normally pronounced with the lips flat. It can also however be pronounced with the lips rounded or stretched. Indeed, in Maraathi, this sound is usually uttered with the lips rounded, whereas it is uttered with the lips flat in Sanskrit; both phones however have the same phonemic value. Thus, we note that the *y* and *x* (and the other) variables are truly independent variables, for they can be combined independently to produced different phones. However, i n practical phonemic application to most of the world's languages, the unusual combinations are not used.

Jaw vertical-position: The third sub-table representing *jaw vertical-position* is also quite self-explanatory. In addition to the extreme positions, *open* and *close*, we have two intermediate positions, *close-mid* and *open-mid*, to conform to general Western phonetic treatments. Again here, it is noted that jaw vertical-position is very much a continuous variable, and must be discretized to at most three or four positions. Otherwise, phonic classification would be a nightmare! It is noted that the ancient Indian phonological classification treated of just three (3) positions, designated *ardha-wiraama* (for *close*), *guna* (for *mid*) and *wrddhi* (for *open*); these terms were then used as addends and subtrahends in the near-mathematical manipulations of Sanskrit phonetics for purposes as varied as Sandhi and generation of verbal stems from verbal roots.

Jaw horizontal-position: The fourth sub-table, representing *jaw horizontal-position*, requires more elaboration, since it only applies to languages that may not be familiar to the general reader.

Firstly, it should be apparent to the reader that, in addition to the vertical opening and closing of the jaw, it can also be *slid forward and back*, i.e., in a *horizontal* position. Combination of even the four (4) discretized jaw-vertical positions and a three (3) discretized positions (forward, normal, back) for the jaw-horizontal position yields (4 X 3) = 12 potential jaw positions! Again, however, very few of these variations carry any phonemic, and thus linguistic, significance in any of the world's languages. This allows us to perform further discretization, by considering only languages where the jaw-

Chapter 4: The Full Phonic Classification of Navlipi: The "Shell" Matrices (Templates)

301

forward position *is* phonemically significant. As we learn in the next paragraph, and much to our relief, there are only two (2) jaw-horizontal positions of phonemic significance in any major language, the *forward* and the *normal* positions.

The best known example of the application of the jaw horizontal-position that can be cited is **Tamil**, where the jaw-forward and the jaw-normal positions are phonemically distinct. In Tamil, we have an standard *alveolo-dental* lateral (*l-sound*), similar to the English [*l*]. This is seen in the word *paalam* (பாலம்), "bridge". We also have the standard *retroflex* lateral, seen in the word *pal.l.am* (பள்ளம்), "hole", where we have transcribed the phone as *l.l.* . For this phone, the jaw is held in the normal horizontal position, i.e. neither forward horizontally nor retracted horizontally. Finally, we have in Tamil a *retroflex* lateral, similar to our *l.l.*, but articulated with the *jaw forward*. This is seen in the word in the vocalic portion of the phone highlighted in the word usually transcribed in Roman script as *pazham* (பழம்), "fruit", where we have used the standard Roman transliteration used for this phone in most Tamil documents today (2005), *zh*. This is actually close to the standard American English *central* (*r*-sound), as in American English *maker* but with the important distinction that the *jaw is thrust fully forward* in a *horizontal* direction. If one were to utter this word without thrusting the jaw forward, when the phone would degenerate to a regular American *r*, it would change the meaning of the word and it would not be understood. Thus, the jaw-forward and jaw-normal positions are, in Tamil, phonemically distinct.

As an aside, we note that *the IPA does not treat of jaw-horizontal position at all*.

Tongue firmness position: The fifth sub-table, representing the variable of *tongue firmness position*, also requires some elaboration.

This variable is introduced primarily for reasons of thoroughness and completeness of our phonological treatment. It has practical, phonemic application in very few of the world's major languages. To illustrate with an example, the vowels in English *weed* or American *able* can be pronounced in the "normal" fashion, with the tongue making light contact at the appropriate position (medio-palatal in the first word, apico-alveolar in the second). The same words can also however be uttered with the tongue making heavy or strong contact, changing the sound significantly. The reader can try this. Such heavy vs. light tongue contact or firmness has a phonemic distinction in some very uncommon languages in the world, and thus we need not dwell on it further.

Vowel duration: The final sub-table, representing *vowel duration*, is also self-explanatory. In most of the world's major languages, there are only two vowel durations that are phonemically distinct: short and long. However, even in languages where it does not have a phonemically distinct value, the third vowel duration, extra-long, does have use. In the English example given in the Table, we have the short and long [i] and [ii], as in *wit* and *weed*. We also however have the extra-long [iii] as in *wheeeee,* an exclamatory sound we utter when going for rides, etc. This does on occasion have some phonemic value (for example, if we pronounced the word as *whee* with a standard "long" [ii], it may not be completely understood as the exclamatory sound). However, it is not a distinct phoneme recognized in English phonemics. There are however languages where at least three vowel lengths have distinct phonemic value, e.g. the Mixe (Mixteco) languages found in Oaxaca state in Mexico [LAs-70]. Some linguists like to apply the term **chroneme** to a phonemically distinct vowel length, but we will not use this term.

Chapter 4: The Full Phonic Classification of Navlipi: The "Shell" Matrices (Templates)

4.3 REDUCTION OF THE 5-DIMENSIONAL VOWEL CLASSIFICATION MATRIX TO THREE (3) DIMENSIONS, ALONG WITH A 4th VARIABLE FOR VOWEL DURATION, FOR PRACTICAL PURPOSES

As is evident, the above *5-dimensional* vowel matrix and the sixth variable of vowel duration must needs be reduced to something more manageable, especially considering that some of its variables, such as tongue firmness, are rarely if at all used in any of the world's languages. Moreover, graphical representation of this 5-d matrix would be somewhat difficult in a layman's book such as this, without resorting to mathematical matrix representations. (Those young readers who find the combination "must needs" in the first sentence of this paragraph odd are referred to the older English literature!)

As a first step in this *reduction* then, we can, for our purposes, dispense with *tongue firmness*, since it finds extremely rare application.

As a second step, we note that jaw horizontal-position is also fairly rare, found mainly in Dravidian languages such as Tamil (per the examples cited above). Furthermore, for practical phonemic purposes there are only two positions, *jaw-forward* and *jaw-normal*, as found in Tamil. We can thus attempt to incorporate this variable into the *z-axis* description (the jaw vertical-position variable), thus avoiding the need for a 4-d matrix. We do this by keeping the $z=1$ to 4 descriptions as we already have in the third sub-table above, but then introducing additional values of z, $z=(-1)$ and $z=(-2)$, respectively representing *jaw-forward* and *jaw-retracted*. For the *l*-sound in the Tamil word *pazham*, "fruit", we would then have jaw-forward, i.e. $z=(-1)$. This value of this variable, i.e. $z=(-1)$, would almost be its only major use.

Incorporating these two changes, we are then able *to reduce our 5-d matrix to arrive at a 3-dimensional vowel matrix* representing all the variables in **Table 4-2** except for vowel duration. Vowel duration is then incorporated into the matrix by bifurcating each matrix element (cell) into sub-cells for short and long vowels. (We treat only two vowel lengths, short and long.) These steps, and the resultant 3-d vowel matrix, are of course presented in the *NAVLIPI SUMMARY TABLES*, at the beginning of this book.

It can be seen from these that even a reduced, 3-d, matrix is a bit cumbersome to depict graphically, especially if one would like to also include word examples. Thus, it is easier to represent the matrix as "slices" of the y-dimension. We then have enough space to give word examples as well. That is of course what is done in the *NAVLIPI SUMMARY TABLES*.

Chapter 4: The Full Phonic Classification of Navlipi: The "Shell" Matrices (Templates)

4.4 SEMI-VOWELS AND THEIR RELATION TO PARENT VOWELS

It is noted that *semi-vowels* are of course *non-vowels*. They are treated in this sub-section, separately from the treatment of non-vowels below, for convenience only. For the academically particular reader, we note that the IPA generally refers to semi-vowels as "*approximants*".

An earlier chapter described how semi-vowels can be derived from parent vowels. *Navlipi* stays with the concept that semi-vowels are merely derivatives of vowels, obtained from the vowels through the addition of a following *fundamental* vowel (such as [a], [i] or [u]). This is of course the same treatment used in the ancient Indian phonological classification, where the addition of an *unjoined guna* to a vowel yielded a semivowel.

Among the sub-tables in **Table 4-2** above, the one most directly applicable to this derivation is the second one, for the y variable. The derivation of common semi-vowels from their parent vowels using this sub-table is given below in **Table 4-3**.

Table 4-3 (*cont. overleaf*): Semi-vowels, as derived from their parent vowels, based on the *y-axis* sub-table in **Table 4-2** above.

		SEMI-VOWELS AND THEIR PARENT VOWELS				
	$y=$	PARENT VOWEL DESCRIPTION	PARENT VOWEL IPA NOMENCLATURE	EXAMPLE OF PARENT VOWEL	SEMI-VOWEL	EXAMPLE OF SEMI-VOWEL
	1	*Medio-Palatal*	"front" and "front-central"	As in English *beet*	[j]	English *yes*
	2	*Flat*	"central" and "central-back"	As in English *but*	--	--
	3	*Retracted*	"back"	As in English *boot*	[w]	English *wit*

	(Table 4-3, Semi-Vowels and Parent Vowels, cont.)				
y=	PARENT VOWEL DESCRIPTION	PARENT VOWEL IPA NOMENCLATURE	EXAMPLE OF PARENT VOWEL	SEMI-VOWEL	EXAMPLE OF SEMI-VOWEL
4	Apico-Retroflex, Central (r-sound)	---	As in American English *maker*	[r]	American *right*
5	Apico-Retroflex, Lateral (l-sound)	---		Here shown as [*l.*]	*l*-sound in Tamil *pal.am* ("hole")
6	Apico-Palatal, Central (r-sound)	---	Very rare	---	---
7	Apico-Palatal, Lateral (l-sound)	---	Vocalic counterpart of Polish, Serbo-Croat and Portuguese *l*-phone (e.g. Serbo-Croat *lj*eti)		Serbo-Croat *lj*eti, Portuguese *pilha*

y=	(Table 4-3, Semi-Vowels and Parent Vowels, cont.)				
	PARENT VOWEL DESCRIPTION	PARENT VOWEL IPA NOMENCLATURE	EXAMPLE OF PARENT VOWEL	SEMI-VOWEL	EXAMPLE OF SEMI-VOWEL
8	Apico-Alveolo-Dental, Central (*most common r-sound*)	---	English *purr*, Hindi/Maraathi-/Sanskrit *rshi*	[r]	Rare (in most major languages, degenerates into the flap or trill)
9	Apico-Alveolo-Dental, Lateral (*most common l-sound*)	---	English and American English *able*	[l]	English *let*
10	Interdental, Lateral (*r-sound*)	---	Exists in no major language	---	---
11	Apico-Supradental, Lateral (*l-sound*)	---	Rare	Here [lll]	Rare, found in some Arabic dialects, Turkish (*lllaalllaa*, "servant") and Irish (*Galll*, "foreigner")

	(Table 4-3, Semi-Vowels and Parent Vowels, cont.)				
y=	**PARENT VOWEL DESCRIPTION**	**PARENT VOWEL IPA NOMENCLATURE**	**EXAMPLE OF PARENT VOWEL**	**SEMI-VOWEL**	**EXAMPLE OF SEMI-VOWEL**
12	*Nasal, Bilabial (m-sound, no tongue contact)*	---	Phonemically distinct in many African languages. Example: Name **M***beki* (South African President)	---	Semi-vowel counterparts do not exist for these vowels
13	*Nasal, (n-sound, with tongue contact being any of the following: dental, alveolar, palatal, retroflex, velar)*	---	Phonemically distinct in many African languages. Example: Name **N***komo*	---	Semi-vowel counterparts do not exist for these vowels
14	*Nasal, (uvular, but no tongue contact)*	---	---	---	Semi-vowel counterparts do not exist for these vowels

Chapter 4: The Full Phonic Classification of Navlipi: The "Shell" Matrices (Templates)

It can be seen from the above **Table** that, apart from the common semi-vowels such as [j], [w], [r] and [l], very few semi-vowels in the table are actually found in the major languages of the world. Thus, from the *practical phonemics* point of view, a prominent feature of *NAVLIPI*, we may ignore many of these.

It is also important to note that, in the above **Table**, some of the *other* vocalic variables described in the previous section, such as jaw vertical-position (the z variable), have *not* been applied in the derivation of the semi-vowels from their parent vowels. This is so for an important reason: In practical phonemic application, the other variables are rarely of relevance to semi-vowels. For example, in the articulation of the semi-vowel [w] in the English *wit* or *weed*, one always commences with the jaw in the mid position (somewhere in between close-mid and open-mid). If one were to try to articulate these words commencing with the jaw in the fully *open* position, pronunciation would be difficult (the reader may try it). Yet it would still not alter the meaning of the word. That is, it would not be phonemically significant. Thus, we need not consider more than one jaw position in the articulation of [w]. The situation is similar if we tried to articulate these words commencing with the lips in the stretched position first (i.e. using the x variable).

It is precisely for this reason, i.e. that these other variables (x, z, u, v) do **not** produce phonemically significant variations in the semi-vowel, that we use the y variable, i.e. "tongue or other articulation position", as the *only* variable of relevance when deriving semi-vowels from vowels.

Finally, we need to discuss an important point regarding the *fricatization of vowels*, particularly laterals and centrals. *Navlipi* takes the position that **when vocalic laterals and centrals are fricatized, they automatically become non-vowels**. Fortunately, we rarely encounter fricatized vowels in any major world language. What we do encounter are fricatized *semi-vowels*. Examples are the Czech central [ř] or the Welsh lateral [ll].

PART 3: PRESENTATION AND DISCUSSION OF NAVLIPI

4.5 THE TWO-DIMENSIONAL, (35 X 15), NON-VOWEL MATRIX

4.5.1 TWO PHONOLOGICAL VARIABLES, 15 ARTITIONS, 35 PHONOCHROMES

We note at the outset that our discussion of non-vowels in this section treats *semi-vowels* only briefly, since these have already been treated separately above.

Fortunately, our treatment of non-vowels is made rather simple, as compared to the treatment of the vowels above, due to the fact that we have to *deal only with a 2-dimensional* matrix. This is because there are *only two (2) variables* that we must consider. This 2-d matrix really boils down to a simple table. The non-vowel phonological classification of *Navlipi* was discussed at some length in an earlier chapter, to which reference is made. The *only* two variables we must consider are given below:

THE TWO (2) PHONOLOGICAL VARIABLES FOR NON-VOWELS IN *NAVLIPI*

(1) ARTITION: We identify a total of **15 artitions**. These start at the back of the speech apparatus and progress towards the front, exactly as in the ancient Indian classification, which however had just five artitions. The artitions thus constitute the *rows* (***y-axis***) of our 2-d matrix or table. This *y*-axis thus corresponds exactly to the *y*-axis of the vowels: Both represent "tongue or other articulation position".

(2) PHONOCHROMATICITY, the "color" of the phone: We identify a total of **35 basic phonochromes**, including those for semivowels. To refresh the reader's memory again, *phonochromaticity* denotes such properties such as aspiration, voicing, fricatization, flapping, clicking, etc.. This is once again based upon the simpler, ancient Indian classification, which had just seven phonochromes, the variables along its column axis (unaspirated surd, unaspirated sonant, aspirated surd, aspirated sonant, nasal, semi-vowel, fricative). These constitute the columns (***x-axis***) of our 2-d matrix or table. Semi-vowels are technically also phonochromes, since they also technically denote a variation of the "color" of the phone articulated for a particular artition. E.g., the [b] is a variation of the bilabial artition (with the property of voicing), but so is the [w] (has property of semi-vowel articulation). ....(4.3)

Chapter 4: The Full Phonic Classification of Navlipi: The "Shell" Matrices (Templates)

The *15 artitions* of *Navlipi*, corresponding to the *y-axis* of the *Navlipi* 2-d non-vowel matrix, are, from the back to the front of the speech apparatus:

THE 15 ARTITIONS OF *NAVLIPI* FOR NON-VOWELS

(1) *Glottal*
(2) *Pharyngeal*
(3) *Uvular*
(4) *Velar*
(5) *Retroflex*
(6) *Medio-Palatal*
(7) *Palatal*
(8) *Alveolar*
(9) *Apico/Medio-Dental*
(10) *Standard Dental*
(11) *Pharyngealized Dental*
(12) *Interdental*
(13) *Infralabio-Supradental*
(14) *Supralabio-Infradental*
(15) *Bilabial*

….(4.4)

PART 3: PRESENTATION AND DISCUSSION OF NAVLIPI

The **35 phonochromes** of *Navlipi* i.e. its *phonochromaticity* variables, corresponding to the ***x-axis*** of the *Navlipi* 2-d non-vowel matrix, are:

THE 35 PHONOCHROMES OF *NAVLIPI* FOR NON-VOWELS

- (1) *Unvoiced/unaspirated*
- (2) *Unvoiced/aspirated*
- (3) *Voiced/unaspirated*
- (4) *Voiced/aspirated*
- (5) *Nasal*
- (6) *Fricative/unvoiced*
- (7) *Fricative/voiced*
- (8) *Flap/unaspirated*
- (9) *Flap/aspirated*
- (10) *Flap/nasal*
- (11) *Flap/fricatized*
- (12) *Trill/normal*
- (13) *Trill/fricatized*
- (14) *Click, ingressive, central, single, unvoiced*
- (15) *Click, ingressive, central, single, voiced*
- (16) *Click, ingressive, central, single, nasal*
- (17) *Click, ingressive, central, trill*
- (18) *Click, ingressive, lateral, single, unvoiced*
- (19) *Click, ingressive, lateral, single, voiced*
- (20) *Click, ingressive, lateral, single, nasal*
- (21) *Click, ingressive, lateral, trill*
- (22) *Click, egressive, central*
- (23) *Click, egressive, lateral*
- (24) *Ejective, unvoiced*
- (25) *Ejective, fricative*
- (26) *Implosive, unvoiced*
- (27) *Implosive, voiced*
- (28) *Semivowel, simple*
- (29) *Semivowel, pharyngeal*
- (30) *Semivowel, central*

Chapter 4: The Full Phonic Classification of Navlipi: The "Shell" Matrices (Templates)

> **(The 35 Phonochromes of Navlipi for Non-Vowels, cont.)**
>
> (31) *Semivowel, lateral, unaspirated*
> (32) *Semivowel, lateral, aspirated*
> (33) *Semivowel, lateral, fricatized*
> (34) *Semivowel, lateral, palatalized*
> (35) *Semivowel, lateral, pharyngealized*
>
> ....(4.5)

This 2-d non-vowel classification *shell matrix* is then relatively easy to construct from the above *15 X 35* variables. It is embodied in the *NAVLIPI* SUMMARY TABLES given at the beginning of the book, complete with word-examples. The reader needs only to empty the Tables shown therein of the *Navlipi* glyphs (letters).

4.5.2 BRIEF DISCUSSION OF THE UNUSUAL ARTITIONS

Now that we have presented the full set of *Navlipi* non-vowels, it is pertinent to briefly discuss those among this set that are not self-evident or completely clear, i.e. the *unusual artitions*.

The *velar* artition is of course an extremely common artition, found in almost all languages. Further back from this artition's position, we have three positions, the *uvular*, *pharyngeal* and *glottal*. The glottal position is common in most languages only for the glottal fricative ([*h*]). The pharyngeal position is rare. We do however have pharyngeal fricatives that are phonemically distinct from the glottal fricative in languages such as Arabic and Hebrew.

The ***uvular*** position is common in Afro-Asiatic languages. For example, Arabic phonemically distinguishes the velar and uvular unvoiced stops, [k] and ["faucal"-k] (IPA rendition [q]). In the form of the fricative, it is also common in some European languages as well, for example German, which retains an uvular rather than a velar fricative.

PART 3: PRESENTATION AND DISCUSSION OF NAVLIPI

The ***retroflex artition*** is common only in Indian languages, although it may have a wide variety of possible origins (i.e., Indo-European, Dravidian, Austro-Asiatic) which are newly disputed.

The common wisdom is that this artition is supposedly of Dravidian origin or due to "Dravidian influence". However, there is no evidence for this other than the circumstantial evidence that it happens to occur mostly in Indian languages, and the Dravidian language family is presumably one of the older language families of India; Indians consider it older than the Indo-European languages.

There is however some substantial evidence that the retroflex artition may in fact truly be an original Indo-European artition. This evidence is seen, for instance, in the phonemic distinction of retroflex vs. other phones in "primordially" Indo-European words. Some of these words were cited in the earlier chapter on the Indian phonological classification, under the discussion of the *"shredder effect"* with respect to Sanskrit, and may be cited briefly here as well. These words include, for instance, the Sanskrit verbal root *mrsh* (*retroflex* [sh]), "to forgive, pardon" (whence English *mercy*, Spanish *merced*, French *merci*, etc.); now this is in phonemic opposition to the verbal root *mrsh* (*palatal* [sh]), "to touch, rub; to deliberate". And the Sanskrit verbal root *mush* (retroflex [sh]), "to steal" (whence English *mouse* etc., i.e. "the stealthy one"), in phonemic opposition to the separate Sanskrit verb *mus* which means "to cleave, divide, break into pieces". It is very difficult to contend that the Indo-European roots *mrsh* ("to forgive") and *mush* ("to steal"), both with retroflex-[sh], are of Dravidian origin. There is, thus, *absolutely no reason to preclude the retroflex artitions being a native component of the parent Indo-European language.* Thus, while the [retroflex-t] of the Indian languages is not found in any other Indo-European languages, the proximate [alveolar-t] is certainly found as abundantly as the presumably original [dental-t], especially in Europe. However, the alveolar-[t] is never phonemically opposed to the [dental-t] in *any* Indo-European language.

In *Navlipi*, we distinguish two palatal positions, ***medio-palatal*** and ***"standard" palatal***, which we can also term *apico-palatal*. This terminology is identical to that we used in describing vowel artitions earlier in this chapter: Apico-palatal implies that the apex of the tongue contacts the upper palate, e.g. in the Indian or Irish pronunciation of the English word *cheat*, or the Hindi word *chup* ("quiet") or Spanish word *chica*. On the other hand, *medio-palatal* implies contact with the palate of the portion of the tongue further back from the apex, closer to the medial portion, as in the German *ich* (the same contact position as in the French *agneau*). This medio-palatal position is phonemically

Chapter 4: The Full Phonic Classification of Navlipi: The "Shell" Matrices (Templates)

distinguished from the "standard" palatal position in languages such as Turkish, Irish and Serbo-Croat.

Navlipi also lists several dental positions: ***medio-dental***, ***"standard" dental*** and ***pharyngealized dental***. The additional positions of ***interdental, infralabio-supradental*** and ***supralabio-infradental*** are considered separately from these. The first two denotations, *medio-dental* and *standard-dental*, are used primarily to distinguish two types of phones that are important in virtually all languages: The dental phones, e.g. [t], and the common *s*-sound (e.g. in English *sit*), which is frequently labeled as a dental fricative (even in the ancient Indian classification), but is in reality quite a different phone. In the [dental-t], the *apex* of the tongue contacts the supra-dental ridge; it is thus truly a *dental* (we say *"standard" dental*) phone. In contrast, the [s] has three features that distinguish it from the [dental-t]: (1) the portion of the tongue making the contact is further behind, towards the *medial* section of the tongue, hence our terminology *medio-palatal*; (2) the *jaw* is much more closed than in the articulation of the [th], once again pointing out the importance of the interplay of a myriad of variables in the articulation of phones; (3) and the sides of the tongue make a pressing contact with the teeth. The *pharyngealized dental* is an entirely different beast from these two. It represents the articulation of a normal dental phone but with pharyngeal air. It is phonemically distinct from the "standard" dental in such languages as Arabic.

Navlipi also posits several other positions that are related to the dental, and mean exactly what their names imply: ***inter-dental***, meaning the tongue is placed between the teeth rather than at the dental ridge during articulation; ***infralabio-supradental***, which implies contact of the lower lips with the upper teeth and which most phonetics texts simply refer to as labio-dental, and ***supralabio-infradental***, which implies contact of the lower teeth with the upper lips, and is extremely rare.

4.5.3 BRIEF DISCUSSION OF THE UNUSUAL PHONOCHROMES

A perusal of the list of 35 phonochromes shows the principle of *discretization* well at work: For example, while the number of variations on *clicks* seems large, it is clear from the list that many more types could be included. The few that are included are done so for completeness.

Thus, e.g., when one makes a lateral, dental click, like the "giddyap" sound one may use

PART 3: PRESENTATION AND DISCUSSION OF NAVLIPI

when trying to egg a horse on, one can articulate this as a single phone as well as in the form of a continuous phone; hence the need to include both "single" and "trilled" clicks of this category.

The other, unusual or rare phones listed, e.g. the implosives, are best understood through the word examples cited for them in the main *NAVLIPI* SUMMARY TABLES in PART 1.

The *flaps* listed are also obviously a greatly reduced number from those possible, after discretization. For example, it is not necessary to list separate unvoiced and voiced flaps, since in almost all languages where they are used, flaps are voiced.

Chapter 4: The Full Phonic Classification of Navlipi: The "Shell" Matrices (Templates)

4.6 TONES ("MUSICAL" OR "PITCH" ACCENTS)

In *Navlipi, tones are represented as **post-ops**,* thus *dispensing completely with unwieldy diacritics.*

The *Navlipi* post-ops used are highly intuitive. Most importantly, the cursive rendition is extremely elegant and simple. So too is their keyboard rendition (see Keyboarding chapter).

For the purposes of this chapter, however, we do not wish to present the *Navlipi* orthography for tones, which is seen in the main *NAVLIPI* SUMMARY TABLES in PART 1. We merely wish to present the nature of the tonal classification. This yields a "shell" matrix for tones.

The *Navlipi* tonal classification is based on several variables. Firstly it is based on the **point of origin** of the tone, e.g. high or low. This point of origin is discretized into just three (3), **high**, **mid** and **low**.

Once we fix the starting point for the tone, we then have three things that can happen to it: It can *stay **level**, **rise*** or ***fall***. Furthermore, the rise or fall can be of **small magnitude** (e.g. a rise from low to mid) or **large magnitude** (e.g. a rise from low to high).

Using this very basic classification method, we arrive at the tonal classification shown in the *NAVLIPI SUMMARY TABLES* at the beginning of this book. Again, the "shell matrix" can be constructed from the tone tables therein by simply emptying the cells, leaving only the headers for the columns and rows.

It is noted once again that, from the point of view of discretization and practical phonemics (or in this case, tonemics), *NAVLIPI* considers only a limited number of values for each variable. Thus, we do not, e.g., consider more than three values, high, mid and low, for the point of origin.

PART 3: PRESENTATION AND DISCUSSION OF NAVLIPI

4.7 MATRIX NOTATION AND USE OF MATRIX ELEMENT NUMBERS WHEN REFERENCING THE NAVLIPI TABLES

Much like mathematicians assign elements of a matrix specific numbers to refer to them, for example the element corresponding to $x=3, y=4, z=7$ in a 3-d matrix would be assigned the number *(347)*, we can use **matrix element numbers** to identify matrix elements. These elements can be from our incomplete, *shell matrix* (template), or in the completed *Navlipi* **Summary Tables** at the beginning of this book. In the present chapter we refer constantly to these *Navlipi* Summary Tables without actually reproducing them. This is obviously done to spare redundant duplication. The reader is kindly requested to refer to these Tables whenever appropriate. It is then convenient *to use the matrix element numbers to refer to individual phones*.

Thus, for example, the glyph (letter) [i] (of English *hit*) is **[1(1)(1)]** ($x = 1, y = 1, z = 1$ for this glyph, in the reduced, 3-dimensional vowel classification matrix). Similarly, for non-vowels, the glyph [p], the bilabial, unvoiced, unaspirated stop, is **[1-15]** ($x = 1$ and $y = 15$ for this glyph, in the 2-dimensional non-vowel classification matrix). This notation is slightly modified from conventional mathematical and physical notation (e.g. that indicating crystallographic spacegroups) to accommodate our needs, and thus deserves brief clarification with regard to nomenclature and conventions; this is effected in **(4.6)** below:

Chapter 4: The Full Phonic Classification of Navlipi: The "Shell" Matrices (Templates)

1. For all matrix notation referenced in text, we use **bold lettering**, and **square brackets**. We also use *dash (hyphen) separators* for the non-vowels only.

2. Thus, for **vowels** we have the notation **[x(y)(z)]** (e.g. [1(2)(-1)]) and for **non-vowels**, we have the notation **[x-y]** (e.g. [3-4]).

3. The parentheses are used for the y and z values of the vowels because these may exceed 9 (for y) or be negative numbers (for z). This notation is easier for the layman to understand than that used conventionally in mathematics (e.g., a bar over the number to indicate a negative number). For non-vowel matrices, we do not have negative numbers, so we don't need the parenthetical notation.

4. We can also then use this matrix notation to refer to *an entire series of phones*. Thus, e.g., for vowels, the notation **[1(1)(z)]** would refer to the phones **[1(1)(1)]**, **[1(1)(2)]**, **[1(1)(3)]** and **[1(1)(4)]**, i.e. the series of phones represented by the highlighted letters in English *hit, bait, belt* and *hat*. Similarly, in the case of non-vowels, **[x-15]** refers to the *entire* series of bilabial sounds (including voiced and unvoiced sounds, fricatives etc. etc.), whilst **[1-y]** refers to the *entire* series of unaspirated, unvoiced stops, etc.

5. Finally, we note one other element of our nomenclature: The regular-brackets notation, {}, is used specifically to enclose a ***Navlipi*** glyph (letter), thus differentiating it from a phone, **([ ])**, or phoneme, **(/ /)**.

....(4.6)

4.8 OUR RESULT: COMPLETE, EMPTY PHONIC CLASSIFICATION "SHELL" MATRICES (TEMPLATES), FOR SUBSEQUENT FILLING-IN WITH A NEW SCRIPT'S GLYPHS (LETTERS, SYMBOLS)

The result of our work in this chapter is a set of *empty*, phonic classification "shell" matrices, i.e. templates, for vowels, semi-vowels and non-vowels. These are embodied in the Figures and Tables above, and, more completely, in the *NAVLIPI SUMMARY TABLES* at the beginning of this book, *if we empty these tables of their elements* (i.e. the glyphs therein), leaving only their column and row headings.

We now thus have the task of *finding appropriate glyphs (letters or symbols) to fill these matrices*. This would then give us our new script or "alphabet". Our glyphs must be chosen keeping in mind the objectives set forth for a new, universal script in an earlier chapter, such as universality, recognizability, distinctiveness, intuitive nature, high amenability to cursive writing, etc.

4.9 ALPHABETICAL ORDER, PEDAGOGY, AND SUBSETS OF THE NAVLIPI SUMMARY TABLES

Before ending this chapter, we must make one other observation about our newly generated shell matrices. This relates to their "***alphabetical order***".

> *The alphabetical order in which the Navlipi script will be taught will be exactly as presented in the shell matrices (developed above and represented in the NAVLIPI SUMMARY TABLES at the beginning of this book).*
>
> .....(4.7)

For persons familiar with the Indian scripts, this will come naturally, for it will follow closely the alphabetical order that the Indian scripts are taught in, i.e. [*a, aa, i, ii, u, uu*] etc. for vowels, and [*ka, kha, ga, gha*...] etc. for non-vowels.

More particularly with respect to the *Navlipi* script and its "alphabetical order", however, it is noted that **the script can be taught to any degree of detail desired**.

For example, it is most likely that the rarer phonochromes, e.g. those starting with #14) (*"click, ingressive, central, single"*) and ending with #23) (*"implosive, voiced"*) will never be taught for most languages. As another example, the entire series of phonochromes from #14) through #19), which deal only with clicks, would apply almost exclusively to South African and South-West African languages, and could be dispensed with elsewhere. Thus, e.g., in Indo-European languages, only the first ten or so phonochromes need be taught.

The pedagogical "alphabetical order" will thus differ for different languages.

The alphabetical order of the *full Navlipi script* is given in **PART 1** of this book, which gives each actual glyph but also references each glyph by matrix element number.

What we are trying to say then is that ***Navlipi** in actual application for most of the world's languages will be considerably less daunting* than the impression conveyed by the shell matrices above and the *NAVLIPI SUMMARY TABLES* at the beginning of this book. But at the same time, *Navlipi* will remain far more complete than any other script created to date.

PART 3: PRESENTATION AND DISCUSSION OF NAVLIPI

CHAPTER 5.
PRELUDE TO *NAVLIPI*:
EXERCISES IN PHONIC CLASSIFICATION, OR "LET'S TRY TO MAKE A NEW SCRIPT".
(FILLING IN THE TEMPLATES PRODUCED IN THE PREVIOUS CHAPTER)

TABLE OF CONTENTS

5.1 INTRODUCTION AND PRINCIPLES 324

5.2 A SCRIPT BASED ON GEOMETRIC SYMBOLS WHICH IS HIGHLY SCIENTIFIC BUT UTTERLY USELESS 325

5.3 A SCRIPT BASED ENTIRELY ON POST-OPS 328

5.4 A VERY BASIC ("*SIMPLE VERSION*") SCRIPT BASED ON DEWANAAGARI WHICH IS ALSO HIGHLY SCIENTIFIC BUT SUFFERS FROM RECOGNIZABILITY AND OTHER PROBLEMS 333

5.5 A MORE REFINED ("*COMPLEX VERSION*") SCRIPT BASED ON DEWANAAGARI WHICH STILL SUFFERS FROM RECOGNIZABILITY AND OTHER PROBLEMS 341

5.6 A SCRIPT BASED ON PITMAN-GRAHAM SHORTHAND-TYPE TRANSCRIPTION 345

5.7 *SHALL WE GIVE UP?!* LESSONS LEARNED 350

PART 3: PRESENTATION AND DISCUSSION OF NAVLIPI

5.1 INTRODUCTION AND PRINCIPLES

In the last chapter, we arrived at an extremely complete, and highly systematic, classification of phones found in all the world's languages. We constructed several matrices embodying this classification. However, ***we left the choice of the actual glyphs (letters or symbols) for the phones themselves, the "letters of our alphabet" as it were, for later***. This, we noted, would allow us to carefully select of our glyphs. *We now proceed to do precisely this in this chapter.*

We start, as an exercise, by first attempting to do this in different ways. As we shall see, while these efforts do not yield good, or in some cases, even usable scripts, they are a very useful exercise in learning about the pitfalls to be encountered in devising a new script!

Thus, as we shall see, although these are extremely useful and instructive exercises, *they all yield scripts that are seriously deficient in one or more aspects.*

The types of example scripts to be tested are outlined in the box below. The actual exercises are elaborated in the rest of this chapter.

TYPES OF SCRIPTS WE SHALL ATTEMPT TO ARRIVE AT IN OUR EXERCISES IN THIS CHAPTER

1. A *GEOMETRIC* script.
2. A script based entirely on *POST-OPS*.
3. A simple *("SIMPLE VERSION")* adaptation of the *DEWANAAGARI* script.
4. A *more refined ("COMPLEX VERSION")* adaptation of the *DEWANAAGARI* script.
5. An adaptation of the *PITMAN SHORTHAND*.

We now look at each of the above five scripts in turn in the Sections below.

Chapter 5: Prelude to Navlipi: Exercises in Phonic Classification, or "Let's Try to Make a New Script" (Filling in the Templates Produced in the Previous Chapter)

5.2 A SCRIPT BASED ON GEOMETRIC SYMBOLS WHICH IS HIGHLY SCIENTIFIC BUT UTTERLY USELESS

Fig. 5-1 shows a script based entirely on geometric symbols, as the glyphs ("letters") of the script. For brevity, and as this is only an exercise, only one form of the letters is shown rather than the standard four (i.e. small and caps, cursive and print).

As can be seen, the script's organization is self-explanatory. Also for brevity, only a limited portion of the non-vowel classification is presented, and no vowels are covered. The script as presented in the Figure is nevertheless sufficient to illustrate the principles involved.

As is evident, the script is highly scientific, but as is evident even on a cursory glance and as is discussed below, it is *utterly useless*.

> **Fig. 5-1 (*overleaf*):** A script based entirely on *geometric symbols* which is *highly scientific*, but *utterly useless*. For brevity only a limited portion of the non-vowel classification is presented. The *unvoiced plosive* constitutes the **base** glyph. All other glyphs are then derived from it, *with changes as indicated*. Compound phones, such as the velarized bilabials of some Baantu (Bantu) languages [(kp) (gb) etc], can then be formed as *conjuncts*, as shown.

PART 3: PRESENTATION AND DISCUSSION OF NAVLIPI

Chapter 5: Prelude to Navlipi: Exercises in Phonic Classification, or "Let's Try to Make a New Script" (Filling in the Templates Produced in the Previous Chapter)

Advantages (a Few) and Drawbacks (Many) of Our New Script: We can evaluate our new script by comparing it against the objectives we set forth for a new, universal script. These were enumerated briefly in the **PREFACE**, and in more detail in an earlier chapter. To identify the good features of our new, geometric script first, we note that it is *highly scientific* and also *very distinctive* (the glyphs or "letters" are easily distinguished from each other).

However, when we start enumerating the bad features of our new script, we quickly see that these are overwhelming.

To start with, it has no *recognizability* or *universality*. Those geometric "letters" would be so much robotic machine language to the layman! There is certainly no universality, for the "letters" relate to no known world script, be it the Roman, Dewanaagari, Arabic, Chinese, Haangul or Cyrillic. We also see that our script is poor in *ease of transcription* from all three points of view: *cursive, print* and *keyboard*. Cursive writing of such a script would be as or more difficult than Chinese; the length of time taken to write an equivalent sentence in our new geometric script would probably be much longer than in Chinese. Devising a font for keyboarding, using any of the font-generation programs available today, would also be difficult. Some of the other objectives we identified for a universal script earlier in this book, such as *simplicity* and *intuitiveness*, are also lacking in our geometric script.

Thus, we must unfortunately reject our geometric script on many grounds.

PART 3: PRESENTATION AND DISCUSSION OF NAVLIPI

5.3 A SCRIPT BASED ENTIRELY ON POST-OPS

We next consider a script based entirely on post-ops, as shown partially in **Fig. 5-2** below. In this figure, again for brevity and as this is only an exercise, only one form of the letters, small print, is shown, and only two artitions, the velar and alveolo-dental (combining the alveolar and dental), are shown. The extension to other artitions, e.g. glottal, palatal, etc., would be obvious. And we do not cover vowels at all.

In our limited post-op based script, then, we first start with the **unvoiced, unaspirated stop** of each artition, designating this **as the base (**or **parent) phone**. Thus, e.g., the [k] is the base phone for the velar series of artitions, the [p] is the base phone for the bilabial series of artitions, etc. Furthermore, for purposes of reference, the base phone is identified by its name; thus **k** is identified by "velar".

We then designate the following *post-ops* for our new script:

1) For *aspirate*: [h_o] (the letter *h* with subscript ($_o$), thus emulating the use of the letter *h* in Roman script transcriptions of aspirates (e.g. [ph]), yet distinguishing it from the letter *h* itself, i.e. from the glottal fricative. The script form of this letter is extremely easy to render, with the ($_o$) as a short loop on the foot of the letter, although, strictly speaking, we are not discussing script forms here. (In fact, *Navlipi* uses precisely this post-op for aspirate, but that is not relevant to our discussion here.)

2) For *voiced*, [∞] (the infinity sign, or figure-8 placed horizontally, *not* subscripted).

3) For *nasal*, [n_o] (the letter *n* with subscript ($_o$). Again, the script form of this letter is extremely easy to render, with the ($_o$) as a short loop on the foot of the letter, although, strictly speaking, we are not discussing script forms here.

4) For *fricative*: [$h_|$] (the letter *h* with subscript ($_|$) (a bar), again taking into consideration the intuitive correspondence of the letter *h* in Roman script with "rough breath" or some sort of fricatization, yet distinguishing it from the letter *h* itself. Once again, the script form of this letter is also extremely easy to render, with the ($_|$) as a *long* loop on the foot of the letter, although, strictly speaking, we are not discussing script forms here.

5) For *flap*, [f̶] (the letter *f* with strikeout, i.e. a "crossing" of the letter

Chapter 5: Prelude to Navlipi: Exercises in Phonic Classification, or "Let's Try to Make a New Script" (Filling in the Templates Produced in the Previous Chapter)

similar to crossing of a *t*).

6)   For *trill*, [r̄r̄] (the double letter *rr* with a bar on top)

7)   For *click, ingressive, central, single*, [z̶] (the letter *z* with strikeout, i.e. a "crossing" of the letter similar to crossing of a *t*). The strikeout of course distinguishes it from the regular letter *z* (the medio-dental, voiced fricative).

8)   For *click, ingressive, central, trill*, [z̶z̶] (a mere re-duplication of the previous click, i.e. the letter *z* with strikeout, i.e. a "crossing" of the letter similar to crossing of a *t*).

9)   For *click, egressive, central, single*, [z̶$_o$] (the letter *z* with strikeout and with a subscript ($_o$)).

10)   For *semi-vowel, central*, [r]. That is to say, the Roman letter *r* now becomes a general representative of *all* central semi-vowels. Thus, the retroflex central semivowel, the American *r*, is represented by the letter for the retroflex base phone (say [*t*~] plus this post-op, i.e. [*t*~*r*]. The alveolar central semi-vowel, the "common" *r*, is represented as [#*r*], using our representation of [#] as the alveolar base phone.

11)   In a nearly identical fashion, for *semi-vowel, lateral*, [l]. That is to say, the Roman letter *l* now becomes a general representative of all lateral semi-vowels. Thus, the dental lateral semivowel, the "common" *l*, is represented as just [*tl*], where the [*t*] is of course the base dental phone and the [*l*] is the post-op designating a lateral semi-vowel.

12)   For *implosive*, [z"], i.e. the letter *z* (*no* strikeout) and a quotation mark.

13)   For *ejective*, [z'], i.e. the letter *z* (*no* strikeout) and an apostrophe.

Thus, the application of our post-op-based script is fairly straightforward: The unvoiced, unaspirated plosive (stop) for each artition (e.g. ***k*** for velar or ***t*** for dental) is taken as the base. All other phonochromaticities are then generated simply by appending a post-op. Thus, e.g., the voiced, unaspirated, velar plosive (the [g] sound) is generated from the base (***k***) simply by appending the post-op for voicing, the subscripted infinity sign, [$_\infty$], yielding ***k***$_\infty$

In use of our post-op script, we need to lay down a rule that, the fairly rare cases where we need to use *multiple post-ops, the first post-op operates first, the second post-op operates second*, etc.

Thus, e.g., in [**k**$_\infty$**h**$_o$], where we have the base, velar phone [k], the post-op for voicing,

PART 3: PRESENTATION AND DISCUSSION OF NAVLIPI
330

[∞], and the post-op for aspiration, [h$_o$], the first post-op operates *first*. This yields, first, the voiced velar stop, i.e. the [g]-sound. The second post-op operates *next*, yielding an aspiration of this, i.e. the [gh]-sound. Thus, *[gh] in our post-op-based script is written as [k$_∞$h$_o$]*. In this particular case, of course, the order of operation of the post-ops makes no difference. I.e., we could just as easily have written [**k h$_{o∞}$**] with the same result. However, there *would* be cases where the order of operation of the post-op *does* make a difference.

We can now present our much-abbreviated new script based entirely on post-ops, in the **Figure** below:

> **Fig. 5-2 (*overleaf*) :** **A script based entirely on *post-ops*.** For brevity, and as this is only an exercise, *only two artitions (velar and alveolo-dental) are shown*. Also, only one form of the letters (small print), is shown, rather than the standard four (small and caps, cursive and print), and some phonochromaticities are not shown. The extension to other artitions and phonochromes would however be obvious. For purposes of reference, the base phone is identified by its name; thus ***k*** is identified by "velar". (Where appropriate, the Dewanaagari is also given, for convenience.) As seen, the unvoiced, unaspirated plosive (stop) for each artition (here, ***k*** and ***t***) is taken as the base. All other phonochromaticities are then generated simply by appending a post-op. Thus, e.g., the voiced, unaspirated, velar plosive (the [g] sound) is generated from the base (***k***) simply by appending the post-op for voicing, the subscripted infinity sign, [∞], yielding ***k*$_∞$**.

Chapter 5: Prelude to Navlipi: Exercises in Phonic Classification, or "Let's Try to Make a New Script" (Filling in the Templates Produced in the Previous Chapter)

D = Dewanaagari, where applicable	PARENT PHONE			
	VELAR	D	ALVEOLO-DENTAL	D
PLOSIVE UNVOICED, UNASPIRATED	k	क	t	त
PLOSIVE UNVOICED, ASPIRATED	kh_o	ख	th_o	थ
PLOSIVE VOICED, UNASPIRATED	k_∞	ग	t_∞	ढ
PLOSIVE VOICED, ASPIRATED	$k_\infty h_o$	घ	$t_\infty h_o$	ज
NASAL	kn_o	ङ	tn_o	ङ॒
FRICATIVE UNVOICED	kh_1	ख़	th_1	ग़
FRICATIVE VOICED	$k_\infty h_1$	ग़	$t_\infty h_1$	ज़
FLAP UNASPIRATED			tf	
FLAP ASPIRATED			tfh_o	
FLAP FRICATIZED			tfh_1	
TRILL NORMAL			trr^-	
TRILL FRICATIZED			$trr^- h_1$	
CLICK INGRESSIVE, CENTRAL, SINGLE	kz		tz	
CLICK INGRESSIVE, CENTRAL, CONTINOUS (TRILL)	kzz		tzz	
CLICK INGRESSIVE, LATERAL, SINGLE				
CLICK INGRESSIVE, LATERAL, CONTINOUS (TRILL)				
EJECTIVE UN VOICED, PLOSIVE	kz'		tz'	
IMPLOSIVE UNVOICED	kz''		tz''	
SEMIVOWEL CENTRAL			tr	
SEMIVOWEL LATERAL				

PART 3: PRESENTATION AND DISCUSSION OF NAVLIPI

Advantages (a Few) and Drawbacks (Many) of Our New Script: Referring once again to the objectives we set forth for a new, universal script in the **Preface**, and in more detail in an earlier chapter, we can evaluate this new, post-op-based, script as well.

In terms of good features, our new script is *highly scientific* and also *moderately distinctive* (the glyphs, i.e., "letters", are fairly distinguished from each other, due to the very distinct character of the post-ops). It also possesses *universality* and *intuitive nature*: the letters are based on the Roman, and the post-ops, e.g. those for aspirate and fricative, are quite intuitive. It would also be fairly easy to render in *cursive writing*, as the examples for the aspirate and fricative post-ops cited above show.

This new script however again possesses many more disadvantageous features. To start with, it has poor *recognizability*. The superimposition of so many post-ops would be taxing for the mind during normal reading. It also lacks *simplicity*: it is extremely cumbersome to write, whether in print, cursive or on the keyboard. This is due to the fact that each phone, except the base phone, is represented by at least two glyphs (letters, i.e., a digraph), and sometimes three; occasionally, it is even four. *Keyboarding* would be somewhat simplified, in the sense that there would be less letters required, but it would also be much slower and more cumbersome, because so many keystrokes would be required (with each phone being one to four keystrokes), perhaps double or triple the number of the regular Roman script.

Chapter 5: Prelude to Navlipi: Exercises in Phonic Classification, or "Let's Try to Make a New Script" (Filling in the Templates Produced in the Previous Chapter)

5.4 A VERY BASIC ("*SIMPLE VERSION*") SCRIPT BASED ON DEWANAAGARI WHICH IS ALSO HIGHLY SCIENTIFIC BUT SUFFERS FROM RECOGNIZABILITY AND OTHER PROBLEMS

As our third, and fourth, (see next section) exercises, we turn now to *Dewanaagari*.

One reason we have picked *Dewanaagari* is because one of the main "markets" targeted by *Navlipi* is the Indian subcontinent. It would therefore be inappropriate to not give consideration to one of the Indian scripts, and certainly the most prominent Indian script (*Dewanaagari*), as the basis for a potential new script. Such a script would, at least in the Indian context, be more recognizable than a Roman-based one. Such consideration may also placate, to some extent, those few strong Indian nationalists who may rage against any "foreign" (Roman) based script!

However, as the exercise here will show, the Indian scripts are unusable as the basis for a new, universal script for a very wide variety of reasons.

Once again, for brevity and since this is only an exercise, we cover a limited number of non-vowels.

We note at the outset that we directly use, with minimal or no changes, the adaptations already in place in the modern Dewanaagari script, e.g. as used in Hindi and Maraathi, for phones that were not in the original, ancient Indian phonological classification. Some, though by no means all, of these are of non-Indian origin. The short Table below shows some of these phones.

PART 3: PRESENTATION AND DISCUSSION OF NAVLIPI

Table 5-1 (*cont. overleaf*): *Adaptations already in place in the modern Dewanaagari script*, e.g. as used in Hindi and Maraathi, for phones that were not in the original, ancient Indian phonological classification, for reference. These are used directly, with minimal or no changes, in the *"Simple Version"* of our new, Dewanaagari-based universal script.

PHONE	ORIGINAL DEWANAAGARI PHONE	ADAPTATION	IN...	COMMENTS
[fricative-*g*] (voiced velar fricative, primarily of Arabic borrowing, e.g. Hindi *g*aban, (ग़बन , "funds or treasure eaten up")	ग	ग़	Hindi	
[flap-*retroflex-d*], voiced, unaspirated retroflex flap, e.g. Hindi *badaa*, (बड़ा, "big"); the phone is presumed to be of Dravidian provenance.	ड	ड़	Hindi	The "dot-below" is in effect an operator (but *not* a post-op, but rather an *under*-op!). *Navlipi* adopts this with minimal modification (see text).
[flap-*retroflex- -dh*] voiced, aspirated retroflex flap, e.g. Hindi *padhnaa*, (पढ़ना , "to study"); the phone is presumed to be of Dravidian provenance.	ढ	ढ़	Hindi	The "dot-below" is in effect an operator (but *not* a post-op!). *Navlipi* adopts this with minimal modification (see text).
[z] (English *z*oo), Hindi *z*indagi, (ज़िन्दगी , "life")	ज	ज़	Hindi	

Chapter 5: Prelude to Navlipi: Exercises in Phonic Classification, or "Let's Try to Make a New Script" (Filling in the Templates Produced in the Previous Chapter)

(Table 5-1, cont.)				
PHONE	ORIGINAL DEWANAAGARI PHONE	ADAPTATION	IN...	COMMENTS
[f] (English *fat*), Hindi *fikar* (फ़िकर, "care, worry")	फ	फ़	Hindi	
[v] (English *view*), Hindi *varshaa* (वर्षा, "rain")	व	व (i.e. unchanged)	Hindi	Original phone was semi-vowel. Used in modern Hindi for both semi-vowel and its forward-fricative, i.e. the voiced fricative (spirant) [v]. *Navlipi* treats this as a phonemic condensate, designated *vw*.
Vowel of English *hat*	ए	ऍ	Maraathi	
Vowel of English *awkward*	आ	ऑ	Maraathi	

In addition to the above adaptations, we also use several other features of Dewanaagari without change, for example, the *anuswaara* (nasalization) and the *wisarga* (glottal stop).

It is also worth noting that Dewanaagari, and all Indian scripts in general, *already use the concept of operators*, although these *are not post-ops.* (They're actually *under*-ops and *over*-ops!) It would be hard to define a "post-op" in the context of ligature-based scripts such as the Indian scripts. For example, the various *maatraa*'s are of course operators, as are such elements as the *anuswaara* (nasalization).

Thus, the concept of operators is already available to us in Dewanaagari and we do not need to create it. We *do* however introduce additional operators, as detailed in **Table 5-2**

PART 3: PRESENTATION AND DISCUSSION OF NAVLIPI
336

below.

Fig. 5-3, further below, shows our new, universal script based on *Dewanaagari*, formulated on the basis of the above principles.

Table 5-2 (*overleaf*): New operators introduced in ***our new, Dewanaagari-based script, Simple Version***. The Examples use randomly selected original letters (glyphs) of Dewanaagari.

Chapter 5: Prelude to Navlipi: Exercises in Phonic Classification, or "Let's Try to Make a New Script" (Filling in the Templates Produced in the Previous Chapter)

OPERATOR	SIGNIFI-CANCE	EXAMPLE	COMMENTS
Two dots below the glyph (letter)	flap	ड → ड़	Adaptation of (change from) the single-dot-below-letter already in use in modern Dewanaagari (see previous **Table**).
Reduplication or triplication	trill	र → ररर	
Two curved bars above the glyph	click, ingressive, central, single	त → तँ	The curved bars resemble the single curved bar sometimes used in addition to the *anuswaara* for indicating nasalization in modern Hindi
Two curved bars plus cross above the glyph	click, ingressive, lateral, single	त → तँ	The curved bars resemble the single curved bar sometimes used in addition to the *anuswaara* for indicating nasalization in modern Hindi; slight variation on previous operator
Two curved bars plus a dot above the glyph	click, egressive, central, single	त → तँ	The curved bars resemble the single curved bar sometimes used in addition to the *anuswaara* for indicating nasalization in modern Hindi; slight variation on previous two operators
Two curved bars plus cross plus a dot above the glyph	click, egressive, lateral, single	त → तँ	The curved bars resemble the single curved bar sometimes used in addition to the *anuswaara* for indicating nasalization in modern Hindi; slight variation on previous operators
Single tilde above glyph	ejective	त → त̃	Very rare
Double tilde above glyph	implosive	त → त̃	Very rare
Two short, slanted bars to right of glyph, slanting down	Semi-vowel, central	त → त	
Two short, slanted bars at left or bottom of glyph, slanting up	Semi-vowel, lateral	त → त	

PART 3: PRESENTATION AND DISCUSSION OF NAVLIPI

(Table 5-2, cont.)

The *awagraha*	The *Schwa* or close, central, *a*-vowel, of English *fath**e**r*	ऽ, E.g. with क → कऽ	The *awagraha*, a redundant letter, is co-opted from standard Dewanaagari
Two dots above the glyph	Voicing (Sonant)	त → तˮ	Clearly distinguished from *anuswaara*. Also will be rarely used.

Fig. 5-3 (*overleaf*): **A NEW, UNIVERSAL SCRIPT BASED ON THE CURRENT (ORIGINAL) *DEWANAAGARI*,** using the new operators and other principles described in the Table above. ***Simple Version***. It may be noted that the first five rows (in bold box) are identical to the current (original) *Dewanaagari*. (For simplicity, only non-vowels, and not all artitions or phonochromes, are shown. The extension to other Dewanaagari phones is self-explanatory and identical. N/A= Not Applicable or Rare.)

Chapter 5: Prelude to Navlipi: Exercises in Phonic Classification, or "Let's Try to Make a New Script" (Filling in the Templates Produced in the Previous Chapter)

ARTITION → PHONOCHROMATICITY ↓	Velar	Palatal	Retroflex	Dental	Bilabial
PARENT PHONE: Plosive, Unvoiced, Unaspirated	क	च	ट	त	प
Plosive, Unvoiced, Aspirated	ख	छ	ठ	थ	फ
Plosive, Voiced, Unaspirated	ग	ज	ड	द	ब
Plosive, Voiced, Aspirated	घ	झ	ढ	ध	भ
Nasal	ङ	ञ	ण	न	म
Fricative, Unvoiced	ख़	श	ष	स**, थ##	प़
Fricative, Voiced	ग़	झ़	ष̈	ज़**	ब़
Flap, Unaspirated	N/A	N/A	ड̤	त̤**, र̤##	N/A
Flap, Aspirated	N/A	N/A	ढ̤	थ̤	N/A
Flap, Nasal	N/A	N/A	ण̤	न̤	N/A
Trill, Normal	N/A	N/A	N/A	ररर	N/A
Click, Ingressive, Central, Single	N/A	च̆	ट̆	त̆	प̆
Click, Ingressive, Lateral, Single	N/A	च̰	ट̰	त̰	प̰
Ejective, Unvoiced, Plosive	N/A	च̃	ट̃	त̃	प̃
Implosive, Unvoiced	N/A	च̂	ट̂	त̂	प̂
Semivowel, Central	N/A	य	र	त̥	व
Semivowel, Lateral	N/A	N/A	ऌ	ल	N/A

Notations: ** Medio-dental only; ## interdental.

PART 3: PRESENTATION AND DISCUSSION OF NAVLIPI

Advantages (a Few) and Drawbacks (Many) of Our New Script: Referring once again to the objectives we set forth for a new, universal script in the **PREFACE**, and in more detail in an earlier chapter, we can evaluate this new, *Dewanaagari*-based, script as well.

Now *Dewanaagari* is already very cumbersome to write in handwriting (there is really no "cursive", except if one were to go to a different script such as *Modi*), and fairly cumbersome to keyboard. Our adaptation as embodied in **Fig. 5-3** in fact makes this problem much *worse*. The various, new operators become additional, burdensome diacritics. Thus, lack of *ease of transcription* becomes a serious problem.

One also finds that, with all the new operators, some of which look similar, lack of *recognizability and distinctiveness*, never problems in the original *Dewanaagari*, now become problems. Yet, to avoid introducing new operators, one would have to come up with new glyphs, and this would in its own right create problems with transcription.

Slowness of transcription, again already a problem in standard *Dewanaagari*, is even worse in our new script.

And of course, one does not have *universality*, since, outside the Indian subcontinent, *Dewanaagari* is virtually unknown, and even within the Indian subcontinent, there would be a problem. For example, even those used to similar, Braahmi-based sister scripts such as Gujarati or Gurmukhi or Bengali, would have serious problems in recognizing and adapting to this new script. And for those outside the Indian subcontinent and unfamiliar with Indian scripts, our new script would be no different from something brought straight from another galaxy!

Chapter 5: Prelude to Navlipi: Exercises in Phonic Classification, or "Let's Try to Make a New Script" (Filling in the Templates Produced in the Previous Chapter)

5.5 A MORE REFINED ("*COMPLEX VERSION*") SCRIPT BASED ON DEWANAAGARI WHICH STILL SUFFERS FROM RECOGNIZABILITY AND OTHER PROBLEMS

We now proceed to the exercise of devising a script based on the ***Dewanaagari*** that is ***more complex and refined*** than the one we have presented in the previous section. This is shown in summary form in the **Figure** below. Again, since this is only a feasibility exercise, we limit ourselves to equivalents for letters of the original Dewanaagari script as used with Sanskrit, and nothing more. Thus, not only are phones from other languages, such as the spirant [th] in English *thin*, not included, but recent borrowings into Hindi, e.g. the phone [f], which is written in Hindi with a dot under the phone for [ph], are also not included. Also, no attempt is made to accommodate phones not represented in Dewanaagari, except for two (the vowels of German *Hütte* and Danish *møbel*).

Several "rules" and points are to be observed with regard to this new script:

> **1.** Although the final product (script) is more refined, it is nevertheless still a "quick and dirty" effort. We are simply seeking to demonstrate feasibility of the exercise, rather than to arrive at an elegant-looking, aesthetically pleasing, artistically refined script or font.
>
> **2.** *The script's letters are devised to be as close to the original Dewanaagari letters as possible*. Nevertheless, key refinements are made. The Table in **Fig. 5-4** below shows the transition from the original Dewanaagari letter used to arrive at the new letter. For example, to add vowels to the non-vowels to make syllables, *maatra*'s as in the Dewanaagari are not used. Rather, a Roman-type "alphabetic" system is used, i.e. the letters for the vowels are appended to the letters for the non-vowels. However, in some cases, a dual system of transcription is maintained. Thus, the addition of the vowel [aa] to a non-vowel (e.g. to [k]) can be done by adding the vowel on its own, or by adding the single-bar *maatra* that is used in Dewanaagari. In the new script, the bar is just an easily rendered "cursive bar", as seen in the figure below. For an augmented *maatra* then, a loop is added to the cursive bar. This applies to [uu] vs. [u], etc. In overall appearance, the script has some

PART 3: PRESENTATION AND DISCUSSION OF NAVLIPI

resemblance to Dewanaagari, some resemblance to the Roman script (but no concordance with the latter of phones, e.g. the letter for [p] resembles a Roman lower case "q", but obviously the two sounds have no affinity). In a few places, the script even resembles Arabic!

3. When writing with hand on ruled paper, this new script can be written, as is the Roman, i.e. with the letters of the script resting "on the ruled line" at the bottom. However, it can also equally well be written with the letters of the script hooked onto the ruled line which would then be at the top. In fact, this would be the preferred method of writing. In this, second method, then, the script would have the appearance of Dewanaagari, with the line at the top appearing much like the top bar of Dewanaagari.

4. The print form of the script's letters are simply a formalized version of the cursive letters.

5. This is much like in many present-day Indian scripts, e.g. Tamil, Kannada, etc.

6. The punctuation used is the same as the Roman, much like modern Maraathi today.

7. All nasals are denoted by a "dot-above" (*anuswaara*). This "dot-above" is, furthermore, used in *post-op* fashion (i.e. placed after the letter it is designating, to facilitate keyboarding rather than above the letter as is present-day Dewanaagari. This also means that we need not always come up with a new letter for the nasal, but can simply use the "dot-above" post-op on the parent phone of the *warga*. For example, the [ta] for the [ta]-*warga*, plus the dot-above post-op, is used to represent the [na].

8. Where glyphs have two parts and may thus confuse the reader, a top bar is used over the two to indicate conjunction (i.e. that the two are a single glyph).

Chapter 5: Prelude to Navlipi: Exercises in Phonic Classification, or "Let's Try to Make a New Script" (Filling in the Templates Produced in the Previous Chapter)

Fig. 5-4 (*cont. overleaf*): *A MORE REFINED ("COMPLEX VERSION") SCRIPT BASED ON THE DEWANAAGARI* (but still "quick and dirty"). The second column in the Table shows the transformation/-transition used to arrive at the new glyph (letter) from the original Dewanaagari glyph (letter).

ORIGINAL DEWANAAGARI GLYPH (LETTER) (Approximate Roman Equivalent Also Shown in Square Brackets)	TRANSFORMATION	NEW GLYPH (CURSIVE)	NEW GLYPH (PRINT)	EXAMPLE OF CURSIVE USE (for vowels, shown with [k])	COMMENTS
1. क [ka]	क → ch	ch	ch	k, ch	(1)
2. अ [a]	अ → ʒ	ʒ	ʒ	ka,	(2)
3. आ [aa]	आ → ʒ|	ʒ| or ʒʒ	ʒ|, ʒʒ	kaa,	(3)
4. इ [i]	इ → → ı	ı	ı	ki,	(4)
5. ई [ii]	इ + ˊ → ı̇	ı̇ or ıı	ı̇	kii,	(5)
6. उ [u]	उ → ʒ	ʒ	3	ku,	(6)
7. ऊ [uu]	ऊ → ʒ → ʒ	ʒ or ʒʒ	ʒ, ʒʒ	kuu,	(7)
8. ए [e]	ए → ⟨ → h	h	⟨	ke,	(8)
9. ऐ [ai]	ऐ → ⟨ˋ → ⟨	h	⟨	kai,	(9)
10. ओ [o]	ओ → ʒl	ʒl	ʒl	ko,	(10)
11. औ [au]	औ → ʒle	ʒle	ʒle	kau,	(11)
12. अं [a~]	अ + ˙ → ʒ˙	ʒ˙	ʒ˙	ka~, kan,	
13. अः [a:, aha]	अ + ः → ʒ:	ʒ:	ʒ:	ka:, kaha,	

PART 3: PRESENTATION AND DISCUSSION OF NAVLIPI

(Fig. 5-4, cont.)

ORIGINAL DEWANAAGARI GLYPH (LETTER) (Approximate Roman Equivalent Also Shown in Square Brackets)	TRANSFORMATION	NEW GLYPH (CURSIVE)	NEW GLYPH (PRINT)	EXAMPLE OF CURSIVE USE	COMMENTS
1. क [ka]	क → ch	ch	ch	kik,	(1)
14. ख [kha]	ख → ≥ → ≥	≥	≥	khik,	(14)
15. ग [ga]	ग → ↓ → ∂	∂	∂	gik,	
16. घ [gha]	घ → ṁ →			ghik,	(16)
17. ङ [nga]	ङ → ṡ· → ḣ·	ḣ·	ḣ·	king,	(17)

Chapter 5: Prelude to Navlipi: Exercises in Phonic Classification, or "Let's Try to Make a New Script" (Filling in the Templates Produced in the Previous Chapter)

5.6 A SCRIPT BASED ON PITMAN-GRAHAM SHORTHAND-TYPE TRANSCRIPTION

As yet another, and final, exercise, we attempt a new script based on Pitman's path-breaking and highly scientific shorthand notation, originally developed for English, and adapted subsequently by Graham.

Once again, for brevity and since this is only an exercise, we cover only a limited number of non-vowels, and only the simplest of vowels. The vowels are illustrated in examples with just one base phone, the velar, unvoiced stop ([k]), i.e. [ka], [kaa], [ki], [kii], [ku], [kuu] etc.).

The following principles are *used directly from the Pitman-Graham shorthand without change*:

1) *Thin line = unvoiced:*
2) *Thick line = voiced.*
3) *Various angles to represent different artitions.*
4) *Curved line to indicate fricative.*
5) *Different vowels added to a non-vowel (to make a syllable) by placing vowel symbols, such as a dot or bar, at different position along the non-vowel line.*

We however now use the following *additional* principles in our new, Pitman-type script:

(6) Various *angles* to represent *different **artitions***, as in Pitman, but the angles differ from those chosen by Pitman et al. This is done to accommodate the much large number of artitions in our phonic classification as compared to Pitman's.

(7) *Hook* at *beginning* of stroke to indicate **aspiration**. E.g.:
unaspirated —> aspirated

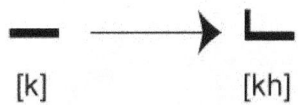

[k]   [kh]

PART 3: PRESENTATION AND DISCUSSION OF NAVLIPI

(8) Notation for vowels differs a bit from that of Pitman et al.

(9) *Hook* at *end* of stroke to indicate ***flap***. E.g.:
   plosive   —> *flap*

[t]   flap-[r]

(10) Small *bar* below stroke for ***trill***. E.g.
   plosive   —> *trill*

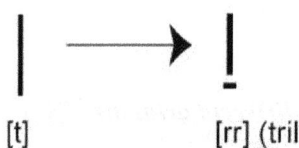

[t]   [rr] (trill)

(11) An *eye-hook* for ***semi-vowel, central***. E.g.
   plosive   —> *central semivowel*

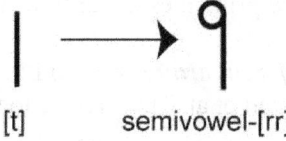

[t]   semivowel-[rr]

(12) An *eye-hook plus bar* for ***semi-vowel, lateral***. E.g.
   plosive   —> *lateral semivowel*

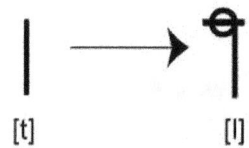

[t]   [l]

Chapter 5: Prelude to Navlipi: Exercises in Phonic Classification, or "Let's Try to Make a New Script" (Filling in the Templates Produced in the Previous Chapter)

(13) A *double-eye-hook* for **click, ingressive, central**. E.g.
  plosive   –> click, ingressive, central

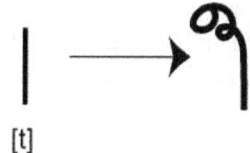
  [t]

(14) A *double-eye-hook plus bar* for **click, ingressive, lateral**. E.g.
  plosive   –> click, ingressive, lateral

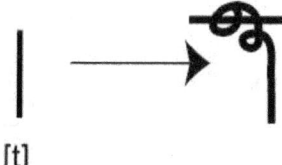
  [t]

(15) A *tilde* anywhere above syllable for **nasal**.

(16) *Curve inwards* only with stroke, for **fricative**. This is similar to Pitman's notation, except that the curve is restricted to always being inwards only. Examples:
  plosive   –> fricative

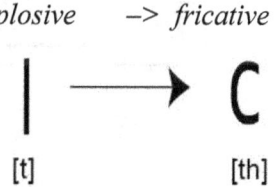
  [t]   [th]

Other points to be noted with respect to our new Pitman-type script are that *we do not treat of egressive or trilled clicks at all*, and *we present only two phones from the glottal artition*: the glottal stop and the glottal fricative ([*h*]). Our new script is presented below.

PART 3: PRESENTATION AND DISCUSSION OF NAVLIPI

Fig. 5-5: A *NEW SCRIPT BASED ON PRINCIPLES SIMILAR TO PITMAN-GRAHAM-SHORTHAND*, and using the other principles as enumerated above. (For added clarity, the new script has been illustrated with both Dewanaagari and Roman transcriptions. The Dewanaagari is illustrated with *ka*.)

Vowel Illustrations in क
(Also Illustration of Nasal)

कऽ	——	[k]
क	—•—	[ka]
का	—°—	[kaa]
कि	•—	[ki]
की	°—	[kii]
कु	•—	[ku]
कू	°—	[kuu]
कृ	—⊖—	[kr]
कॢ	—φ—	[kl]

के	⌐	[ke]
कै	⌐	[kae]
को	⊥	[ko]
कौ	⊥	[kau]
कं	∼	[kã]
कः	⁰₀	[ka:]

Chapter 5: Prelude to Navlipi: Exercises in Phonic Classification, or "Let's Try to Make a New Script" (Filling in the Templates Produced in the Previous Chapter)

Advantages (a Few) and Drawbacks (Many) of Our New Script: Referring once again to the objectives we set forth for a new, universal script in the **Preface**, and in more detail in an earlier chapter, we can evaluate our new, Pitman-based script.

We note firstly that it possesses many of the same drawbacks that Pitman shorthand does: While the script is very rapidly and excellently transcribed in *cursive* - that is in fact what the Pitman shorthands were invented for - it is *very poorly transcribed in print*, and *difficult to keyboard* using a standard keyboard such as the QWERTY keyboard (we omit from our present discussion court-based mechanical transcription machines of yore).

The script also of course suffers from *recognizability* and *distinctiveness* problems, since, to the layman, all shorthands look like undecipherable scribblings! And it is also of course difficult to master (our *simplicity, ease of learning* criteria), except for the experienced stenographer; and not as easily learned by children as Roman/other "alphabets".

We also note that the script as presented in the above Figure is *incomplete*. If one were to present such Pitman-type letters for the full *Navlipi* phonic classification, some of the other advantageous properties of our Pitman-type script, such as ease of cursive transcription, may also be somewhat diminished.

Conversely, the script also possesses some of the *advantages* of the Pitman-type shorthands, e.g. the above-discussed ease of cursive writing, and a highly scientific basis (e.g. thick and thin lines for voiced and unvoiced phones). For the experienced stenographer, there is also a substantial *intuitive nature*, e.g. the above-described thick vs. thin lines; however, the layman may not feel the same way.

Other Tools Available in Pitman-Type Transcriptions: We note in conclusion that there is indeed one other important tool available to us in devising a Pitman-type transcription which we have *not* utilized in our exercise above at all: *Variable line position,* that is to say, position above or below the written line, e.g. on a ruled paper. This could add another method of distinction between the "letters" or our new "alphabet". This would certainly reduce the number of orthographic techniques we have used above. In this regard however, it is noteworthy that Pitman and other shorthand innovators never proposed such a method for an important reason: When shorthand is transcribed, it is difficult to follow line position, and will slow it down very considerably. That is indeed why the shorthand writing pads of yore were mostly unruled. Such a line-based shorthand script can probably be left to a future exercise. We have made our point in our present exercise!

5.7 *SHALL WE GIVE UP?!* LESSONS LEARNED

The *drawbacks* of our new scripts have been clearly enunciated under their respective discussions above.

Many of the drawbacks are common to all the scripts. For example, all the scripts excepting the post-op-based script, suffer from problems of *universality* and *recognizability*. We can gather by now that this necessarily implies a Roman-based script or something close to it. Only one, the Pitman-based script, offers ease of transcription, and that too only for cursive writing. None offer ease of keyboarding using the QWERTY or other standard keyboards. And while none suffer extremely serious problems of *distinguishability*, they don't show particularly good properties in this regard either.

We can also gather, from our exercises above, that some of the properties to look for in any new script we devise should include the **efficient use of redundant letters and post-ops,** the **avoidance of diacritics** due to their cumbersome character, and the *need for iconic and logical feel* of any new letters that we come up with. This is a positive outcome of our exercises.

As will be seen in the next chapter (and as is seen in the *Navlipi* SUMMARY TABLES presented in **PART 1**), ***Navlipi addresses all the above drawbacks, and produces a script vastly superior to those arrived at from all our exercises above.***

CHAPTER 6.
SUMMARY OF ALL POST-OPS USED IN *NAVLIPI*

TABLE OF CONTENTS

6.1 THE POST-OPS (POST-POSITIONAL OPERATORS) OF *NAVLIPI* 353

6.2 THE FIRST THREE POST-OPS: PO-1 (*ASPIRATE/NON-ASPIRATE PHONEMIC CONDENSATE*), PO-2 (*LENGTH OF VOWELS*), PO-3 (*LENGTH OF TONEMES*) 355

6.3 PO-4 (*ASPIRATION*), PO-5 (*FRICATIZATION*) 357

6.4 PO-6 ((*VOICED + UNVOICED*) PHONEMIC CONDENSATE) AND PO-7 (*GENERAL VOICING*) 358

6.5 PO-8 (*NASALIZATION OF VOWELS*) AND PO-9 (*NASAL + NON-NASAL*) PHONEMIC CONDENSATE) 360

6.6 PO-10 (*FLAP*) 361

6.7 PO-11 (*UVULARIZATION, SHARED WITH PHARYNGEALIZATION*) 362

6.8 PO-12 (*STOP + FRICATIVE*) PHONEMIC CONDENSATE) 364

6.9 PO-13 (*STOP + FORWARD FRICATIVE*) PHONEMIC CONDENSATE) 365

6.10 PO-14 (*INGRESSIVE CLICK*) AND PO-15 (*EGRESSIVE CLICK*) 367

6.11 PO-16 (*EJECTIVE*) AND PO-17 (*IMPLOSIVE*) 368

6.12 PO-18 (*STOP + SEMIVOWEL*) PHONEMIC CONDENSATE) 369

PART 3: PRESENTATION AND DISCUSSION OF NAVLIPI

6.13 PO-19, THE IMPORTANT PHONEMIC CONDENSATE DENOTING A "MOBILE, GENERIC" VOWEL 371

6.14 PO-20, COMBINATION OF PHONES.. 372

6.15 PO-21, "SILENT" NON-VOWEL 373

6.16 PO-22 AND FURTHER (TONES, TONEMES, ICTUS ACCENTS).............. 374

Chapter 6: Summary of All Post-Ops Used in Navlipi

6.1 THE POST-OPS (POST-POSITIONAL OPERATORS) OF *NAVLIPI*

The reader is referred to the full *post-op* segment of the ***NAVLIPI* SUMMARY TABLES** (**PART 1** of this book) for reference in the discussions in this chapter. This gives the full list of *Navlipi* post-ops for quick reference.

As already discussed at some length in various earlier chapters and the Preface, one of the unique and key features of *Navlipi* is its wide use of a limited number of *post-ops*, i.e. post-positional operators. Among the many key advantages of this feature is the drastic reduction in the number of new letters required (as discussed in more detail in the next chapter). As an example, instead of coming up with a new letter for an aspirated, unvoiced, bilabial stop [ph], as already exists, e.g. in the Indian scripts (e.g. in फ Dewanaagari) and in Classical Greek (ϕ), we can simply take the corresponding unaspirated phone, [p], and add a post-op for aspiration, [h_o], i.e. h with a subscripted circle, getting [ph_o].

As we will show in the sequel, the number of post-ops needed thus is surprisingly few. And if we make the post-ops intuitive yet distinct, we have achieved success.

Thus the [h_o] is intuitive (because the letter [h] represents an aspiration and is already used to transcribe aspirated phones in much of the phonetics literature), yet it is distinct from the letter [h]. And we note that *Navlipi* uses post-ops for this purpose, *not* diacritics. The drawbacks of diacritics are well known and have been discussed at length in earlier chapters. *In contradistinction, post-ops blend seamlessly with cursive writing and keyboarding as well*, as the sequel will show.

Just as we have given a numerical reference notation (specifically, the matrix element number) for vowel and non-vowel phones in the overall *Navlipi* phonic classification in an earlier chapter, we find it convenient to give an ***alphanumeric reference notation*** for *post-ops* as well.

Thus, **"PO-1"** quite obviously means post-op number 1. The post-ops are ordered in decreasing order of importance and expected frequency of use (two characteristics which may go hand in hand in many cases).

Finally, as noted in an earlier chapter, there is an additional notation we use: The regular-

PART 3: PRESENTATION AND DISCUSSION OF NAVLIPI
354

brackets notation, { }, is used specifically to enclose a *Navlipi* letter, thus differentiating it from a phone, ([ ]), or phoneme, (/ /).

Chapter 6: Summary of All Post-Ops Used in Navlipi

6.2 THE FIRST THREE POST-OPS: PO-1 (ASPIRATE/NON-ASPIRATE PHONEMIC CONDENSATE), PO-2 (LENGTH OF VOWELS), PO-3 (LENGTH OF TONEMES)

The *"subscripted little circle"* character chosen for the first three post-ops is convenient from a number of points of view, e.g. clear distinguishability and recognizability, and ease of cursive and keyboard transcription. This "little circle" post-op is easily and quickly rendered in *cursive*, as seen in the post-op segment of the *Navlipi* SUMMARY TABLES, as a simple "little *e*", i.e. a subscripted cursive *e*, added to the *Navlipi* letter that it operates on (the operand).

PO-1, designates this "little circle" character when it is used to denote the *non-aspirate/aspirate phonemic condensate*. Thus, e.g., $\{p_o\}$ indicates both the phone [p] and its aspirated counterpart, [ph], i.e.:

$$\{p_o\} = [p] + [ph]$$

...(6.1)

It would be used, e.g., to represent the /p/ phoneme of English, which as we know is sometimes articulated as [p] and at other times as [ph]. Thus, a non-English reader, especially one from North India in whose language these phones are distinct phonemes, would immediately be alerted as to the nature of the innocuous *"p"* of English.

It is important to note that *this post-op is to be used invariably with the non-aspirate member of the non-aspirate/aspirate pair*. That is to say, we will always use $\{p_o\}$ to designate ([p] + [ph]), never $\{ph_o\}$.

PO-2, designates this same "little circle" character when it is used to denote *long vowels*. The reader may immediately ask the question "didn't we already use this "little circle" for something else just now and won't it be confusing?" There is however no possibility of confusion with **PO-1** because **PO-1** is always used with non-vowels, whereas **PO-2** is always used only with vowels.

In addition, it is important to note that *PO-2 will be an extremely rarely used post-op*, for the simple reason that length of vowels in *Navlipi* is indicated by simple reduplication of

PART 3: PRESENTATION AND DISCUSSION OF NAVLIPI

the vowel. Thus, e.g., the long counterpart of [i] is {ii} in *Navlipi*, not {i_o}. On the rare occasions when we have three vowel lengths (short, medium, long), we would use {i}, {ii} and {iii} in *Navlipi*. In fact, **PO-2** is to be used with vowels only in *two cases*: To indicate the long counterparts of the [a] and [aa] vowels (of English *but* and *father* respectively). Thus, only when there is a further, vowel-length distinction in these vowels, would they be represented by **PO-2**.

For example, the short, long and extra-long renditions of the vowel of English *but* would be indicated in *Navlipi* with {**a**}, {**a_o**} and {**a_{oo}**}, respectively. Similarly, the short, long and extra-long renditions of the vowel of English *father* would be indicated in *Navlipi* with {**aa**}{**aa_o**}{**aa_{oo}**}. These six (6) glyphs constitute the entirety of when **PO-2** is used in *Navlipi*.

PO-3, designates, in a manner very similar to that for **PO-2**, this same "little circle" character when it is used *to differentiate the length of tones*. Once again, there is no possibility of confusion of this post-op, **PO-3,** with either **PO-1** or **PO-2**, because each of these applies to different speech entities (respectively, tones, non-vowels and vowels). And once again, this will be an extremely rare post-op, in fact even rarer than **PO-2**. An example of its use would be to differentiate short and long renditions of the tones, found e.g. in Cantonese.

Chapter 6: Summary of All Post-Ops Used in Navlipi

6.3 PO-4 (*ASPIRATION*), PO-5 (*FRICATIZATION*)

PO-4 has been discussed, as an example of a prototypical post-op, earlier in this chapter and in several earlier chapters of this book. As noted therein, this post-op, {h_o}, i.e. *h* with the subscripted little circle, is intuitive, since the letter [h] represents an aspiration and is already used to transcribe aspirated phones, as in [ph]. Yet, h_o is distinct from [h].

PO-4 is rendered very quickly and easily in *cursive*, as the post-op segment of the *NAVLIPI* SUMMARY TABLES show: The foot of the letter *h* is simply looped (*on* the writing line, not below it).

Even though it is quick and easy, this cursive rendering is still very distinct (e.g. from the letter *h* itself), easily recognizable, and difficult to confuse with anything else.

PO-5: In the layman's perception, fricatization has some intuitive similarity with aspiration, both being "roughing" sounds of sorts. It is thus logical to devise a post-op for fricatization that has some similarity to that for aspiration. That is exactly what **PO-5**, the post-op for fricatization, {h_0}, does: It is an *h* with a *subscripted oval*. Its use will be infrequent: It is set aside particularly for cases where glyphs (letters) may not exist for a fricative, e.g. for the *r* of Czech *Dvořak*. Where glyphs already exist, e.g. for the fricatives [z] or [f] or [x] (velar fricative), of course, it would not be used. Sibilants are also fricatives. Thus, in the rare cases where a separate letter is not available for the sibilant, e.g. for the phone ((6-6 medio-palatal, unvoiced fricative), this post-op would be used.

In *cursive*, the subscripted oval of **PO-5** is easily rendered as the same loop at the foot of the letter *h* as for **PO-4**, but with the clear distinction that it is much *longer* and goes *below* the writing line, as shown in the *NAVLIPI SUMMARY TABLES*. In this fashion, it is clearly distinct and recognizable from **PO-4**.

6.4 PO-6 ((*VOICED* + *UNVOICED*) PHONEMIC CONDENSATE) AND PO-7 (*GENERAL VOICING*)

PO-6: This post-op, representing the *combination of unvoiced and voiced as a phonemic condensate*, deserves separate discussion due to its importance.

This post-op would be used in languages such as the Beijing "common speech" (Putonghua) version of Mandarin, where many unvoiced/voiced pairs (e.g. [p]/[b] or [k]/[g]), have the same phonemic value, and may sometimes be freely interchanged.

The symbol that *Navlipi* chooses for this important post-op is the *"infinity"* or *"horizontal figure-8"* symbol, but *subscripted*, i.e. $\{_\infty\}$. With the letter p, for example, this would appear as $\{p_\infty\}$.

There are several reasons for the choice of this post-op. One of them, its high distinguishability and recognizability, is quite evident. Less evident reasons include ease of rendering in *cursive*: This subscripted symbol can easily be rendered as a "subscripted double-*e*", e.g. as seen in the post-op segment of the *NAVLIPI* SUMMARY TABLES.

An important point to note in the application of this post-op is that *it is always to be used with the most common rendering of the phoneme in the language in question*. This is done to inform the foreign reader reading these languages about the actual articulation of this phoneme.

Thus, e.g. for standard Mandarin, the [p]/[b] phoneme is usually articulated as the phone [b], so the phonemic condensate would be represented as $\{b_\infty\}$, *not* $\{p_\infty\}$. In contrast, for Cantonese, this phoneme is usually articulated as [p], so in Cantonese, it would always be rendered as $\{p_\infty\}$, *never* as $\{b_\infty\}$, i.e. the exact opposite of Mandarin!

PO-7, *"general voicing"*, is a variant of **PO-6**, which would be used very, very rarely. The reason it would be so rare is that almost all voiced (sonant) phones have or would have separate glyphs (letters) assigned to them. This is true not only for *Navlipi*, but for virtually every world script or "alphabet", including the Roman. Thus, for the bilabial plosives, we have separate letters assigned in the Roman script for the unvoiced ([p]) and the voiced ([b]), so we don't need to use a voicing/post-op operating on the [p] to

Chapter 6: Summary of All Post-Ops Used in Navlipi

359

designate [b].

As will be seen later in this book, PO-7 finds use in *Navlipi only for the case of* **clicks**: Specifically, it is used to transcribe the rare cases *where unvoiced and voiced clicks are phonemically distinct*, e.g. the dental lateral clicks of !Xo Bushman, a South African language.

Because it is so rare, **PO-7** would be rendered in *cursive* as the actual "infinity" or "horizontal figure-8" symbol, suitably *super*scripted: Thus, **PO-7** uses the same symbol used for **PO-6**, i.e. the *"infinity"* or *"horizontal figure-8"* symbol, except that it is *superscripted*, rather than *subscripted*, i.e. $\{^{\infty}\}$, not $\{_{\infty}\}$.

Thus, the unvoiced and voiced versions of the dental lateral click of !Xo Bushman would be represented in *Navlipi* as {l𝗓} and {l𝗓$_{\infty}$} respectively ({𝗓} being the post-op for clicks, as described later in this chapter).

PART 3: PRESENTATION AND DISCUSSION OF NAVLIPI

6.5 PO-8 (*NASALIZATION OF VOWELS*) AND PO-9 (*NASAL + NON-NASAL*) PHONEMIC CONDENSATE)

PO-8, the *nasalization* post-op, is perhaps one of the simplest of the *Navlipi* post-ops. It performs the function of the *tilde* ([~]) diacritic used in the IPA alphabet to indicate nasalization, generally of vowels, or the *anuswaara* diacritic of Dewanaagari, transcribed as a "dot above" (*bindam* in Dewanaagari) the vowel being nasalized.

The glyphs (letters) allotted to this post-op by *Navlipi* are the following *three*, shown in the small-caps, print rendering:

> 1. $\{n_0\}$;
> 2. $\{m_0\}$;
> 3. $\{\sim\}$.
>
> ....(6.2 to 6.4)

These three glyphs are, respectively, the *letter n with a subscripted oval*, the *letter m with a subscripted oval,* and the *tilde*. Thus, for this post-op, we have, uniquely, *three* letters that may be used.

The letters *n* and *m* are chosen because both are used to represent nasals, the *m* not being infrequent (witness the French *Comte* (Count) or the oftentimes transcription of Sanskrit as *Samskrta*, etc.). More importantly, these two different nasal phones, the bilabial (m_0) and the non-bilabial (n_0), *are* phonemically distinct in many languages, e.g. several African Baantu languages. The Baantu example is exemplified by the proper last names *Mbeki* (the President of South Africa in 2007) and *Nkomo* (a leader of the freedom struggle in Zimbabwe in the last century).

For *cursive* rendering, the subscripted oval of this post-op is rendered in a manner identical to that for **PO-5**, the fricatization post-op: The foot of the letters *n* or *m* is looped, *below* the writing line, as seen in the post-op segment of the *NAVLIPI* SUMMARY TABLES. The *tilde* is rendered exactly as it is in the IPA, i.e. as a diacritic over the phone being nasalized. The tilde is retained to reflect its common usage to represent nasals in the phonetic literature of European languages that has spilled over from its use in the IPA alphabet. Its use in *Navlipi* will be very infrequent.

6.6 PO-10 (*FLAP*)

This post-op is especially important for all Indian languages, which possess a surfeit of flaps. It is also one of the simplest in *Navlipi*.

In *print* form, this post-op is rendered simply as a *following dot*. In print form, the dot is *thicker* than a *period* (American) or *full-stop* (British).

It is easily distinguished from the period (full-stop), not only by its thickness, but also by the fact that the period is unlikely to be found in the middle of a word, and is very likely to be followed by a space. As examples: Hindi/Urdu *kad.ak* (here, "tough, brittle") which uses the flap {*d.*}, cannot be confused with anything else, and certainly not with two words separated by a period (full-stop). In a similar manner, multiple periods (full-stops), sometimes used to denote continuation or other nuances (e.g., "....and so on.....") are also very unlikely to be confused with this post-op.

In *cursive* form, this post-op is rendered as a *"dot under"* the glyph that it operates on. This then is nearly *identical to the modern Hindi adaptation of the Dewanaagari script for rendition of flaps* (cf., e.g. the retroflex, voiced, unaspirated stop, ड, and its flap counterpart, ड़). We also note that many flaps may have their own glyph, and so do not need this post-op: For example, for the alveolar flap, the "common *r*" of many languages, one does not need to write the corresponding alveolar stop followed by post-op **PO-10**, i.e. one does not need to write {**t.**}, since we already have available, for this phone, the {**r**}.

PART 3: PRESENTATION AND DISCUSSION OF NAVLIPI

6.7 PO-11 (*UVULARIZATION, SHARED WITH PHARYNGEALIZATION*)

PO-11 is transcribed in its *print* version simply as *two dots* (i.e. two periods or full-stops). These *two* dots are of course easily distinguished from the single dot of the flap post-op (**PO-10**). Nonetheless, as for **PO-10**, these dots are also a bit thicker, in print form, than a period (full-stop).

The reader may venture the question, "What if a uvular phone also needs simultaneously to be a flap, then how would the double dots of **PO-11** be added to the single dot of **PO-10**?"

The answer to this is very simple: A thorough analysis of nearly all the world's languages reveals that a uvular flap, on the very rare occasions that it is found, almost always degenerates into a uvular fricative, and is phonemically indistinct from the latter. There is thus never a need to transcribe an uvular flap!

In its *cursive* version **PO-11** (cf. **Table 1**) is transcribed as two dots *over* the glyph operated on. This avoids any potential confusion with **PO-10** when one of the two dots may be missed by people with poor handwriting.

A very important and unique feature of **PO-11** is that *the glyph operated on is always that for the corresponding **velar** phone*. Thus, e.g., the *uvular*, unvoiced, unaspirated stop, transcribed as **{k..}** in *Navlipi*, is obtained by adding two dots to the corresponding *velar* stop, {k}; similarly, the uvular unvoiced fricative, {x..} is obtained by adding two dots to the corresponding velar fricative, {x}, etc. etc.

The uvular post-op application of **PO-11** is *shared* with its application as a post-op for *pharyngealization*. This is possible without conflict because, again in practical phonemic application in nearly all the world's languages, there is only *one* case of a pharyngeal *and* an uvular phone having the same phonochromaticity. A look at the *NAVLIPI* SUMMARY TABLES shows the phones (x-2), i.e. the pharyngeal phones, are phonemically distinct from the uvular phones *only* for the unvoiced fricative (x= 6). For this phonochrome, i.e. unvoiced fricative (x= 6), all artitions neighboring the pharyngeal are found. These phones, with their *Navlipi* transcriptions in brackets, are, respectively: *glottal* {h}, as in the common [h] phone of most languages; *pharyngeal* {h..}, phonemically distinct from the glottal and the velar fricatives in some languages, e.g.

Chapter 6: Summary of All Post-Ops Used in Navlipi

standard Arabic and Hebrew; *uvular* {x..}, as in the German *doch*; and *velar* {x}, as commonly found in many languages.

It is seen that the confusion of the pharyngeal transcription with the velar is avoided by using different operands for the post-ops. Thus, we have the velar phone {x} which when operated on by **PO-11** yields the uvular phone {**x..**}, and the glottal phone {h} which with **PO-11** yields the pharyngeal phone {**h..**}. For all other phonochromes, the pharyngeal phones exist, for all practical phonemic purposes, in almost no world language. Thus, the use of the same post-op for the pharyngeal and uvular artitions presents no problems for these.

6.8 PO-12 (*STOP* + *FRICATIVE*) PHONEMIC CONDENSATE)

This post-op is represented in *print* as the letter *h* followed by a *subscripted infinity sign (horizontal figure-8)*, i.e. {h_∞}. The subscripted infinity sign alone has been encountered earlier, for the post-op for the (voiced + unvoiced) phonemic condensate, **PO-6**.

In *cursive*, this post-op is rendered as the letter *h* followed by two "little *e*'s", as seen in the post-op segment of the *NAVLIPI* SUMMARY TABLES. This is of course identical to the cursive rendition for **PO-6**.

The uses of this post-op would be rare: The stop and forward fricative are phonemically identical in very few languages. A prominent example is Peruvian Arabella, in which the velar unvoiced, unaspirated stop ({k} in *Navlipi*) and its corresponding fricative ({*x*} in *Navlipi*) are the same phoneme. This then would be rendered {kh_∞} in *Navlipi*, i.e. {kh_∞} = {k} + {*x*}.

6.9 PO-13 (*STOP + FORWARD FRICATIVE*) PHONEMIC CONDENSATE)

Surprisingly, as the examples below will show, this phonemic condensate, **PO-13**, is more common than the previous one (**PO-12**).

And more importantly, it is even found represented in and has a unique significance for certain standard phonetic shifts.

In *print*, this is transcribed as the letter *h* followed by a subscripted *vertical infinity sign* or a *figure-8*. The subscripted figure-8 is rendered easily in keyboarding via a *subscripted number-8*: as {h_8}. As the separate chapter dealing with keyboarding later in this book describes, in actual practice the unique, language-specific keyboarding of *Navlipi* would have such post-ops "built in".

In *cursive*, the rendition of **PO-14** is extremely easy, as the post-op segment of the *NAVLIPI* SUMMARY TABLES shows. This post-op is also one of the most distinct and recognizable of *Navlipi*.

One common example of the use of this phonemic condensate is Hindi/Urdu. Here, for example, the phones [*j*], the palatal, voiced stop, (Dewanaagari ज , as in Hindi *jaan-na* (जानना), "to know"), and [z], its forward fricative, the alveolo-dental voiced fricative (Dewanaagari ज़), are sometimes freely interchanged without phonemic effect (e.g. *jaraa* and *zaraa*, "a little bit", have the same meaning, as do *sabzi* and *sabji*, "vegetables", of Faarsi borrowing (Faarsi *sabz* = "green"). (We have italicized the *j* here to distinguish it from the palatal semivowel (jod).

Also, and perhaps more importantly, in Hindi/Urdu, the phones [ph], the aspirated, unvoiced bilabial stop (Dewanaagari फ) and [f], its forward fricative, the infralabio-supradental unvoiced fricative (Dewanaagari फ़) are freely interchanged (e.g. *phal* and *fal*, both meaning "fruit" in Hindi). As the above Hindi/Urdu examples show, the parent phone (the stop) may be aspirated or unaspirated.

Another example is seen in medieval Greek, which shows the transition (i.e. phonetic shift) from the [ph] to the [f] in such words as ***phono***.

Yet another example is seen in Gothic, where the transition (phonetic shift) from [p] to

[f], reflected in such modern Germanic-language words as *father*, is still seen frozen in such modern German words as *pferd* ("horse"). In these medieval languages (medieval German and Greek), the [ph] and [f] phones were freely interchanged, as they are in modern Hindi today, until the transition from [ph] to [f] was complete.

In actual application of this phonemic condensate, the "parent" phone, i.e. the stop, is used with the vertical-infinity marker with this post-op. Thus, e.g., in Hindi/Urdu, the [f]/[ph] phoneme would be rendered in *Navlipi* as {**ph$_8$**} (and not as f$_8$). Similarly, the [j]/[z] phoneme of Hindi/Urdu is rendered in *Navlipi* as {***inverted-j$_8$***}, i.e. $\int_8$, that is to say, the glyph for the non-vowel **3-7**, $\int$, (an inverted *j*), followed by a *subscripted* "vertical infinity sign" or "number 8".

However, as a note to an important exception, the [v]/[w] phoneme of Hindi is rendered in *Navlipi* as a *digraph*, {**vw**}. That is to say, **PO-13** is not used in this case.

6.10 PO-14 (*INGRESSIVE CLICK*) AND PO-15 (*EGRESSIVE CLICK*)

PO-14 is an important although extremely simple post-op.

In *print*, it is simply the letter *z* with a bar across it. It is effected in most word current processors by the "overstrike" or "strikeout" feature i.e. {z̶}, the way many Europeans write their *z*'s (i.e. with a little strikeout). The strikeout feature ensures distinction from the standard letter *z*, eliminating any confusion.

In *cursive*, it is the letter *z* written in the manner of the print letter, i.e. without the loop below the writing line typical of the cursive letter (see the post-op segment of the *NAVLIPI* SUMMARY TABLES).

In practical use, this post-op operates on the phone that is closest to the click sound in question. Thus, e.g., for the *lateral ingressive click* (the "horse" or "giddyap" sound of cowboys or horsemen), we simply operate on the alveolar lateral, the "common *l*", [l], we thus get {lz̶} for this click. Once again, the strikeout feature ensures distinction from the standard letter *z*: Thus the English word *ills* would be rendered {ilz} in *Navlipi*, and could not be confused with the combination ([i] + lateral click), i.e. {ilz̶}.

As another example of the use of this post-op, the *ingressive dental click* (the "tsk tsk" sound) would simply be rendered {tz̶} in *Navlipi*.

To generate the extremely rare *egressive* clicks, Navlipi simply adds the "*double dot*" post op to the {z̶}, yielding **PO-15**, {z̶..}.

Print rendering of this post-op is then similar to **PO-14**. *Cursive* rendering is done by putting the double dots above the overstrike-*z* letter, as shown in the post-op segment of the *NAVLIPI* SUMMARY TABLES. We treat of egressive clicks for completeness only.

6.11 PO-16 (*EJECTIVE*) AND PO-17 (*IMPLOSIVE*)

Quite evidently, these post-ops will be extremely rare, as ejectives and implosives are found in very few major languages.

To generate these two post-ops, we again revert to the strikeout-z character, {z̶}. For **PO-16**, we simply follow it with an *apostrophe*, getting {z̶'} in the *print* rendition. In *cursive* rendition, we transcribe the strikeout-*z* letter in a manner identical to that for **PO-14, PO-15** above, but add the apostrophe *above* this letter (rather than following it), as seen in the post-op segment of the *NAVLIPI* SUMMARY TABLES.

For **PO-17**, we use *two apostrophes*, i.e. the English-language *quotation marks*, {"}, getting {z̶"} in the *print* rendition. Again for the *cursive* rendition, we add the double apostrophe *above* this letter (rather than following it), as seen in the post-op segment of the *NAVLIPI* SUMMARY TABLES.

For both these post-ops, the operand is the relevant phone. Thus, e.g. a velar ejective would be **{kz̶'}** in *Navlipi*, since the relevant phone is the velar stop [k]. Similarly, a velar voiced implosive stop would be **{gz̶"}** in *Navlipi*, since [g] is the relevant phone.

Chapter 6: Summary of All Post-Ops Used in Navlipi

369

6.12 PO-18 (*STOP* + *SEMIVOWEL*) PHONEMIC CONDENSATE)

This post-op applies to such pairs as *([b] + [w])* or *([j] + [y] (jod))*.

It is rendered using the *subscripted figure-8*, i.e. {$_8$}. The operand is the relevant *stop* (*not* the semivowel). Thus, the ([b] + [w]) phonemic condensate would be transcribed as {b_8} in *Navlipi*. *Print* and *cursive* versions are self-evident, as seen in the post-op segment of the *NAVLIPI* SUMMARY TABLES.

There is an important distinction to remember in application of this phonemic condensate, which in effect makes its use very rare: It does ***not*** apply to *corruptions* or *differing accents* within a language. Such corruptions may occasionally interchange a stop and its corresponding semivowel, but the stop and semivowel still remain distinct phonemes.

The most prominent example of this is the interchange of the palatal semivowel (as in English *yes*) with the palatal voiced, unaspirated stop (as in Hindi *jaa*, "go"), as occurs in Spanish or Hindi/Urdu. Thus, in the various Spanish renditions of the word *yo* ("I"), the official Madrid rendition is with the semivowel, as written, but corruptions and accents may include [*jo*], i.e. with the palatal stop (or sometimes, an affricate [*djo*]). However, the [j] and [y] still remain distinct phonemes in Spanish.

Similarly, in Hindi/Urdu, the river name *Yamuna* has become corrupted to *Jamuna* and the two are sometimes interchanged. However, the fact that the [*y*] and the [*j*] are two different phonemes in Hindi/Urdu is apparent from the fact that we cannot substitute *yaan-naa* for *jaan-naa* (जानना "to know") without being unintelligible! Similarly, if we said *yaa* in Hindi, it would certainly not be understood as *jaa* ("go").

PO-18 then does ***not*** apply to these variations, since in both Hindi/Urdu and Spanish, the palatal stop or affricate and its corresponding semivowel are distinct phonemes.

In other modern languages, this phonemic condensate represents a transition, i.e. a phonetic shift, from the semivowel to the stop, or vice versa. Thus, in modern Baanglaa (Bengali), the [w] of Sanskrit has invariably become [b] (e.g. Sanskrit *wimal* has become Bengali *bimal*), but in medieval Bengali, both these phones were freely interchanged. Conversely, in the Russian, the [b] has become [v] through the intermediate [w], but the medieval Russian freely interchanged the two, still reflected in the modern Cyrillic letter (B).

As the previous two paragraphs demonstrate, the actual use of this phonemic condensate would be *very rare*. An analogous use, the articulation of the *alveolar and dental central sounds* (*r*-sounds) in both semivowel and flap form as part of the same phoneme, is treated separately, in the chapter on phonemic condensates.

Chapter 6: Summary of All Post-Ops Used in Navlipi

6.13 PO-19, THE IMPORTANT PHONEMIC CONDENSATE DENOTING A "MOBILE, GENERIC" VOWEL

As the experienced linguist knows, there are some major languages in the world in which the articulation of a vowel is not really that important!

One such example that comes to mind immediately is the many extraordinary colloquial dialects of modern Arabic. Here, there is frequently no phonemic distinction, for example, between the phones [i] and [u]! Indeed, as is well known, the original Semitic scripts were written with only the non-vowels transcribed prominently, leaving it to the reader to interpret the vowels in between as he/she pleased.

Another example is the many Chinese languages. Thus, in the Mandarin common speech of Beijing (*Putonghua*), it frequently (but not always!) does not make any difference, i.e. it has no phonemic significance, whether one says *Deng* rather than *Dang*!

As can be appreciated, to accommodate such phenomenal phonemic idiosyncrasy within a phonemic condensate becomes a major task!

Navlipi tackles this task by coming up with a *post-op* for this phonemic condensate. Moreover, the post-op is a very simple, easily recognizable, yet very distinct symbol, *viz.*, the *"equals"* sign.

This sign is distinct and recognizable because, in transcription, it would appear right in the middle of words, directly following vowels, for example {*Da=ng*} in a crude transcription of the Mandarin word cited above. There would thus be *no possibility of confusion with an actual "equals" sign*, or anything else for that matter.

The *print* version of this is of course straightforward, as above. Also, no additional key is needed in keyboarding: The "equals" sign suffices.

The *cursive* version is also very straightforward, as seen in the post-op segment of the *NAVLIPI* SUMMARY TABLES. Basically, just three horizontal "squiggles", somewhat resembling a Greek capital sigma. This is very recognizable and distinct, yet nearly impossible to confuse with anything else.

PART 3: PRESENTATION AND DISCUSSION OF NAVLIPI

6.14 PO-20, COMBINATION OF PHONES

There are some languages, only a few of them widely spoken, which combine multiple articulation points. Several West African Baantu languages fall in this category, for example Igbo and Miina (a language from the vicinity of Togo).

As one example in these languages, the phones [k] and [p] are distinguished from a *velarized* bilabial which we can express for the moment as *[kp]*. In order to avoid, and to ensure distinction from, confusion with simple, successive articulation of [k] and [p], one must arrive at some method of transcription to accommodate these multiply articulated phones. The IPA of course uses a curved bar, e.g. [k͡p].

Navlipi will use a simple *bar-above* (-) for such a combination of phones.

In print, unlike the IPA symbol, the *Navlipi* bar-above will be written as a *post-op*, e.g. [kp^-]. In cursive, it will be written directly above the phones it acts on, and its use will thus be much like "crossing a t".

Chapter 6: Summary of All Post-Ops Used in Navlipi

6.15 PO-21, "SILENT" NON-VOWEL

There is a unique phone heard in languages such as Malay (Bahasa Malaysia) that is not really a phone at all, but rather, for want of a better way to describe it, a *"non-phone"*!

This is heard, for instance, in the colloquial pronunciation of the Malay (Bahasa Malaysia) word *tidak* ("no"). In the colloquial pronunciation, the terminal [k] is not really pronounced. Rather, one *starts* to pronounce it, i.e. puts the vocal apparatus in the correct artition (velar), but then abruptly stops! This has a unique sound and a unique effect. It is *quite different* from having no phone there at all, or from a glottal stop, or, of course, from actually articulating the terminal [k]. Thus, again for want of a better term, we can characterize this as a *silent non-vowel*.

We render this unique phone in *Navlipi* through the use of a post-op that is a set of closed, empty parentheses, i.e. *[()]*. In cursive, this would be rendered simply by circling the relevant glyph, a very easy cursive motion.

6.16 PO-22 AND FURTHER (TONES, TONEMES, ICTUS ACCENTS)

These are dealt with in a separate chapter, quod vide.

Chapter 7: Presenting the Full, Phonic Navlipi Script, Including a Discussion of Reasons for Selection of its Glyphs (Letters)

CHAPTER 7.
PRESENTING THE FULL, PHONIC *NAVLIPI* SCRIPT, INCLUDING A DISCUSSION OF REASONS FOR SELECTION OF ITS GLYPHS (LETTERS)

TABLE OF CONTENTS

7.1 PRELIMINARY NOTES 377

    7.1.1 THE "FULL PHONIC" (NON-PHONEMIC) NAVLIPI... 377
    7.1.2 REDUNDANT AND RE-USED/BORROWED GLYPHS (LETTERS) 377
    AND REASONS FOR SELECTING THEM... 377
    7.1.3 NEW GLYPHS (LETTERS) AND THE MINIMAL NEED FOR THEM IN NAVLIPI: JUST ONE BORROWED GLYPH, ONE NEW GLYPH AND THREE TRANSFORMED GLYPH IN NAVLIPI (TOTAL FIVE) 380
    7.1.4 DISCRETIZATION AND PHONEMIC IRRELEVANCE... 382

7.2 THE EMPTY TEMPLATE ("SHELL" MATRIX) AND THE NAVLIPI SUMMARY TABLES 384

    7.2.1 THE TEMPLATE ("SHELL" MATRIX) AND ITS FILLING WITH NAVLIPI GLYPHS (LETTERS).. 384
    7.2.2 NOTATION USED FOR NAVLIPI LETTERS THROUGHOUT THIS BOOK 384
    7.2.3 THE VOWEL SEGMENT OF THE NAVLIPI SUMMARY TABLES 385
    7.2.4 THE NON-VOWEL SEGMENT OF THE NAVLIPI SUMMARY TABLES 386

7.3 THE VOWEL MATRIX AND SELECTION OF NAVLIPI GLYPHS (LETTERS) FOR IT 387

7.4 THE TWO-DIMENSIONAL (35 X 15) NON-VOWEL MATRIX AND SELECTION OF GLYPHS (LETTERS) FOR IT 390

PART 3: PRESENTATION AND DISCUSSION OF NAVLIPI

376

7.5 POST-OPS (POSTPOSITIONAL OPERATORS) 393

7.6 PHONEMIC CONDENSATES USED AND REASONING 393

7.7 BILABIAL AND MEDIO-PALATAL SEMIVOWELS AND PHONEMIC CONDENSATES THEREOF 394

7.8 CENTRALS (R-SOUNDS) AND SELECTION OF LETTERS FOR THESE . 395

7.9 LATERALS (L-SOUNDS) AND SELECTION OF LETTERS FOR THESE . 396

7.10 TONES ("MUSICAL" OR "PITCH" ACCENTS) 397

7.11 TRANSCRIPTION OF UNUSUAL PHONES 397

Chapter 7: Presenting the Full, Phonic Navlipi Script, Including a Discussion of Reasons for Selection of its Glyphs (Letters)

7.1 PRELIMINARY NOTES

7.1.1 THE "FULL PHONIC" (NON-PHONEMIC) *NAVLIPI*

As a first note, *it is strongly recommended to the reader to refer to the **NAVLIPI SUMMARY TABLES (PART 1**, at the beginning of this book) while reading this chapter*. Much of the discussion in this chapter makes constant reference to part or all of these tables, without, for obvious reasons of redundancy, reproducing them within this chapter. It is also noted that the *matrix element numbers* and matrix notation used to refer to the matrix elements of the shell matrix (covered in an earlier chapter) will be used extensively in this chapter.

The title of this chapter has the words *"... **FULL, PHONIC** NAVLIPI SCRIPT ...."*, and we must at the outset clarify what these words mean. "Full, phonic" simply indicates *non-phonemic*. That is to say, in this chapter, *we simply present a filling in of the templates, the empty, "shell" phonic classification matrices (templates) we arrived at in an earlier chapter, with the specific glyphs (letters) we select for **Navlipi***. (We defer the treatment of phonemic condensates to a later chapter.)

7.1.2 REDUNDANT AND RE-USED/BORROWED GLYPHS (LETTERS) AND REASONS FOR SELECTING THEM

Before plunging into a presentation of the *Navlipi* script and reasons for selection of its glyphs (letters), we digress here briefly to denote some of the letters of the Roman script that *Navlipi* finds *redundant*, and thus available for use elsewhere within *Navlipi*.

1. The letters *c* and *q* of the Roman script are, self-evidently, redundant. The original Latin use of *c* was of course the sound of [k], i.e. a velar, unvoiced stop ("hard *c*" in quaint modern English jargon!). Some languages, e.g. modern Italian, use the reduplicated letter to represent a palatal unvoiced phone (though the IPA frequently classifies this as an affricate). Other languages, e.g. English, occasionally use *c* for [s]. The original Latin pronunciation of *q* in the digraph *qu* was probably that of a velar fricative ([x]), thus distinguished from the velar stop *c*, i.e. [k], which is why Latin had two separate ways of transcribing these sounds, i.e. two separate letters. This would make the Latin cognate with related

Indo-European velar fricatives such as those of the Germanic languages where it was most commonly found. Thus, the Latin interrogative pronouns (*quo, quis, quid* etc., would originally have been pronounced with a velar fricative, i.e. *xwo, xwis, xwid*; they would in this way have been cognate with Anglo-Saxon *hwo, hwaet* (English *who, what*, most likely pronounced with the velar fricatives, i.e. *xwo, xwaet* etc.) etc. Although redundant, these two letters, **c** and **q**, are nevertheless highly recognizable, and thus ideal for being put to use elsewhere in *Navlipi*.

2. Similarly, the cursive capital (uppercase) form of the letter *e*, i.e. [ϵ], is also a highly recognizable and redundant letter easily put to use elsewhere.

3. These three letters *(c, q, ϵ)* are the most prominent examples of redundant letters of the Roman script being put to use elsewhere in *Navlipi*.

4. Another letter of the *modern* Roman script that turns out to be redundant, yet very useful, is the letter *y*, (very aptly called "y-greque" in French and "y-greco" in Spanish). As it turns out, in *Navlipi* we can simply revert this letter to its original use, i.e. as the Greek "ypsilon", with the sound of the German *über*, French *pu*, and the corresponding Cyrillic letter, etc.. This then is our *Navlipi* phone (31(1)) (i.e., lip position = rounded, tongue position = medio-palatal, jaw position = close).

5. For the "jod" ("yod") sound of English *yes*, we retain the letter *j*, i.e. [j].

Chapter 7: Presenting the Full, Phonic Navlipi Script, Including a Discussion of Reasons for Selection of its Glyphs (Letters)

Table 7-1:

SUMMARY OF REDUNDANT GLYPHS (LETTERS) OF THE ROMAN SCRIPT, USED AS IS BY NAVLIPI

GLYPH (LETTER)	*Use in Navlipi*	COMMENTS
c	"Ch" sound as in Hindi *chandra*, English *chin*.	Used, with slight modification, in Italian; also in 19th century Western transcriptions of Sanskrit and Indian languages.
q	"Schwa", as in American English *about*	Intuitive, resembles *a*
ϵ	Initial vowel of diphthong in English *they*	Intuitive
y	German *über*	Original significance of Greek letter "ypsilon"

PART 3: PRESENTATION AND DISCUSSION OF NAVLIPI

7.1.3 NEW GLYPHS (LETTERS) AND THE MINIMAL NEED FOR THEM IN *NAVLIPI*: JUST ONE BORROWED GLYPH, ONE NEW GLYPH AND THREE TRANSFORMED GLYPH IN *NAVLIPI* (TOTAL FIVE)

In devising any new script, one of the biggest problems and burdens is to find new glyphs (letters) that are distinct, yet easily recognizable, and also easily transcribed, via print, cursive *and* keyboard.

In the 19th century, many workers attempting a new "alphabet" raided the Greek alphabet for this purpose. Others went to completely unrecognizable symbols, such as Bell with his "Visible Speech" letters (glyphs) supposedly resembling the speech apparatus but, for all intents and purposes for the layman, symbols from another planet. And we are of course all familiar with the result of the IPA's attempt at new letters: Simply taking existing letters and turning them in various ways - upside down, right-to-left, etc., producing another series of very confusing, mutually-indistinguishable letters.

Happily for *Navlipi*, we can say that *we need very few new glyphs, due to Navlipi's unique and wide use of a limited number of post-ops*. Thus, for example, instead of coming up with a new glyph for an aspirated, unvoiced, bilabial stop (as already exists, e.g. in the Indian scripts and in Classical Greek), we can simply take the corresponding unaspirated phone, [p], and add a post-op for aspiration, [h$_o$], getting [ph$_o$].

The number of post-ops needed thus is surprisingly few. And if we make the post-ops intuitive, yet distinct, we have achieved success. Thus the [h$_o$] is intuitive because the letter [h] represents an aspiration and is already used to transcribe aspirated phones, yet [h$_o$] is distinct from the letter [h]. And we note that *Navlipi* uses post-ops for this purpose, *not* diacritics. The drawbacks of diacritics are well known and have been discussed at length in earlier chapters. In contradistinction, post-ops blend seamlessly with cursive writing and keyboarding as well, as the sequel will show.

There are very few cases of *Navlipi* actually *borrowing* glyphs, or of using entirely *new* glyphs (i.e., not just existing Roman letters modified in a minor way) or even of it using *transformed* glyphs. These are however worth a brief mention here.

NEW GLYPHS (LETTERS): *Navlipi* uses **only one** entirely new glyph:

Chapter 7: Presenting the Full, Phonic Navlipi Script, Including a Discussion of Reasons for Selection of its Glyphs (Letters)

- For non-vowel phone 2 **(1-6)**, the *medio*-palatal, unaspirated, unvoiced stop,

TRANSFORMED GLYPHS (LETTERS): *Navlipi* uses ***just three*** transformed letters:

(1) A variant of the Roman *c*, namely a right-to-left inversion of this "*c"*, for the tongue-front-central, lips-stretched, jaw-open-position vowel, as in English *Jack.* denoted #1(1)(4) in *Navlipi* matrix notation: *Navlipi* phone ᴐ.

(2) A variant of the Roman *j* for the standard-palatal, unaspirated, *voiced* stop, phone i̤ (3-7) (the *medio*-palatal, voiced, unaspirated stop, phone i̤ (3-6), is just a derivative of i̤ (3-7).

(3) And, lastly, a variant of the Roman *g* for the velar, voiced fricative, phone ɡ (7-4) (the *uvular*, voiced fricative, phone ɡ•• (7-3), is simply derived from ɡ (7-4) through the addition of the uvular post-op, the two double dots).

BORROWED GLYPHS (LETTERS): *Navlipi* uses ***only one*** borrowed glyph:

- For the *Navlipi* phone Ω [3(3)(4)] (i.e. the sound *ou* in English *bought* or *aw* in English *awful*), *Navlipi* borrows the capital (upper case) Greek *omega*, [Ω]. (See Summary Tables).

Apart from just the ***five glyphs*** identified above, *all other new phones are accommodated in Navlipi through post-ops.*

PART 3: PRESENTATION AND DISCUSSION OF NAVLIPI

Table 7-2:

NEW, TRANSFORMED AND BORROWED GLYPHS (LETTERS) USED BY NAVLIPI

NEW GLYPHS

GLYPHS (LETTERS)	SIGNIFICANCE
2, [(1-6)]	medio-palatal, unaspirated, unvoiced stop

TRANSFORMED GLYPHS

GLYPHS (LETTERS)	SIGNIFICANCE
ɔ, [(1-7)]	tongue-front-central, lips-stretched, jaw-open-position vowel, as in English *Jack*
ʟ, [(3-7)]	standard-palatal, unaspirated, voiced stop
ɠ, [(7-4)]	velar, voiced fricative

BORROWED GLYPHS

GLYPHS (LETTERS)	SIGNIFICANCE
Ω *(Greek Omega)* [3(3)(4)]	Vowel of English *caught*

7.1.4 DISCRETIZATION AND PHONEMIC IRRELEVANCE

A final, editorial comment is necessary before plunging into a presentation of the *Navlipi* glyphs (letters). This relates to *discretization* and *phonemic irrelevance*.

As the *Navlipi* letters are presented in the sequel, the reader will clearly note a unique feature: *There are many phones* (i.e., many "cells" in the phonic classification templates (shell matrices) produced in an earlier chapter) *which are simply skipped over*. That is to say, **Navlipi simply does not assign any glyphs (letters) to them**. This is done for the two obvious reasons of **discretization** and **phonemic irrelevance**.

Chapter 7: Presenting the Full, Phonic Navlipi Script, Including a Discussion of Reasons for Selection of its Glyphs (Letters)

Turning first to the property of *phonemic irrelevance*, we take, as an example, the series of vowel phones corresponding to $y=1$ (i.e., tongue position = medio-palatal). We note here that we *do* use all the positions corresponding to $x=1$ (i.e., lip position = stretched). That is to say, we *have* assigned glyphs for all the phones corresponding to $x=1$ (lip position = stretched), $y=1$ (tongue position = medio-palatal) and $z = 1, 2, 3, 4$ (jaw position = close, close-mid, open-mid and open, respectively). Thus, all the phones (11(1)), (11(2)), (11(3)), (11(4)), corresponding respectively to the English sounds *hit, bait, belt* and *hat*, have been assigned glyphs by *Navlipi*.

However, if we now go to $x=2$, (i.e. lip position = flat), we note that *Navlipi* has assigned *no* glyphs to these phones at all! The reasons for this are obvious: These sounds are *phonemically indistinct* and thus *irrelevant* in nearly all the world's languages (by this author's count, in 95% of the world's languages by number of speakers). That is to say, if one pronounces the [i] of English *hit* with the lips flat rather than stretched, it has no phonemic significance in English; the phone is phonemically still the same, i.e. it has the same linguistic value. The reader will see that this is in fact the case for nearly *all* the world's languages. Thus, assigning a glyph to the phones (21(1)) or (21(2)), perhaps for completeness, is simply a waste. *Navlipi* thus does not bother with it.

Turning now to the property of *discretization*, we can also see in the above series of phones, i.e. (11(1)), (11(2)), (11(3)), (11(4)), English *hit, bait, belt* and *hat*, that we could, theoretically, have sounds in between the values of jaw position that these phones represent (close, close-mid, open-mid, open). We could, e.g., make two further distinctions, *very-close-mid* and *close-mid*. Once again, we defer to *phonemic relevance* when addressing such issues: The distinction between very-close-mid and close-mid, i.e. a sound intermediate between English *hit* and *bait,* is phonemically irrelevant in nearly all the world's languages. Thus, we need to *discretize* our jaw positions to just these four (close, close-mid, open-mid, open), and no more. We do not consider such intermediate positions as *very close-mid, extra-open*, etc.

7.2 THE EMPTY TEMPLATE ("SHELL" MATRIX) AND THE *NAVLIPI* SUMMARY TABLES

7.2.1 THE TEMPLATE ("SHELL" MATRIX) AND ITS FILLING WITH *NAVLIPI* GLYPHS (LETTERS)

At the end of an earlier chapter, we arrived at finalized *vowel and non-vowel classification matrices*, in their "empty" or "*shell*" (template) form. These were of course unfilled with the *Navlipi* glyphs (letters), symbols, or any other glyphs. Selection of the *Navlipi* glyphs to be used to fill in these matrices yields the full *Navlipi* script. The result of this exercise, i.e. the full *Navlipi* script, of course appears in the *NAVLIPI* SUMMARY TABLES, found at the beginning of this book (in **PART 1**). The reader is referred to these now for the discussions in the rest of this chapter.

We now proceed to discuss these *Navlipi* letters, i.e. we proceed to a discussion of our **Navlipi** *script*, and the reasons that particular glyphs have been selected.

7.2.2 NOTATION USED FOR *NAVLIPI* LETTERS THROUGHOUT THIS BOOK

As already noted in an earlier chapter, throughout this book we cite *phones in general* between *square brackets*, e.g. [p] for the unaspirated, unvoiced, bilabial stop. And per standard linguistic notation, *slashes* are used to encase *phonemes*, e.g. /p/ for the English phoneme representing the phones [p] and [ph]. **To recapitulate here again, for *Navlipi* phones, we use *regular brackets*.** Thus, e.g., the *Navlipi* phone for the unaspirated, unvoiced, bilabial stop will be represented as {p}.

Additionally, where we wish to distinguish **words** in *Navlipi* transcription from transcription in any other script, we will again use the ***encasement in regular brackets***. Thus, e.g., the English word *hit* would be written in *Navlipi* as {hitt} (the phone (1-8), i.e. the alveolar, unvoiced, unaspirated stop which is the "English *t*", is transcribed as {tt} in *Navlipi*).

Lastly, we address phones by the ***matrix element numbers***, e.g. phone (1-8) discussed in the previous paragraph.

Chapter 7: Presenting the Full, Phonic Navlipi Script, Including a Discussion of Reasons for Selection of its Glyphs (Letters)

It is very important for the reader to note the above notation, as it is used throughout this book.

7.2.3 THE VOWEL SEGMENT OF THE *NAVLIPI* SUMMARY TABLES

In the ***vowel*** segments of the ***Navlipi*** **Summary Tables**, the *matrix element* (i.e. block or cell) for each phone contains the following elements:

1. ***Capital*** (***upper-case***) and ***lower-case, print*** and ***cursive*** versions of the *Navlipi* glyph, for the ***short vowel*** as well as the ***long vowel***. Thus a total of eight (8) forms are presented in each cell.
2. With regard to vowel length, ***the length of vowels is in nearly all cases expressed simply via reduplication of the short vowel***. For example, [ii] (as in English *heat*) is the long English vowel corresponding to the short vowel [i] (as in English *hit*). In the rare cases of languages with more than two, phonemically distinct, vowel lengths, the reduplication is simply extended. Thus, [i], [ii] and [iii] would then become short, long and extra long vowels respectively. The *only* exception to this method of expressing long and short vowels is the case of the vowels **(2(2)(3))** and **(2(2)(4))**, i.e. **[a] and [aa]**; This was discussed at some lenth in an earlier chapter.
3. Where relevant, an inset showing *how* the glyph is rendered in ***cursive***, with direction arrows, etc.
4. The corresponding ***IPA letters*** (glyphs) for this phone. In some cases, several IPA letters are given; this is when the *Navlipi* phone has been broadened to encompass several phones which are phonemically equivalent in most languages. This is done from the point of view of the *discretization* and *phonemic irrelevance* arguments propounded earlier in this chapter.
5. The corresponding ***Dewanaagari*** glyph, where relevant.
6. The mathematical representation of the matrix element, i.e. the ***matrix element number***, as discussed in earlier chapters. This is, for example, (11(1)) for the [i] vowel. This is placed in the top left corner of the cell.
7. ***Word examples***. A first attempt is made to find examples from English and one Indian language, generally Hindi/Urdu. This is in consideration of the primary audience that this book addresses. Then, where appropriate, and especially where there are no relevant word examples from these languages, examples are found from other languages. Thus, example words for retroflex

vowels and for the phone (31(1)) (the lips-rounded, tongue-medio-palatal, jaws-close vowel), would be, respectively, from Tamil and German/French, since these phones of course do not exist in English or Hindi/Urdu. Example words can be from languages as diverse as Danish, Mandarin and Igbo.

8. Explanatory *footnotes*, where appropriate.

7.2.4 THE NON-VOWEL SEGMENT OF THE *NAVLIPI* SUMMARY TABLES

In a similar fashion, in the ***non-vowel*** segments of the *Navlipi* **Summary Tables**, the matrix element (i.e. block or cell) for each phone contains the following elements:

1. *Capital* (***upper-case***) and ***lower-case, print*** and ***cursive*** versions of the *Navlipi* glyph. Thus a total of four (4) from each cell.
2. Where relevant, an inset showing *how* the glyph is rendered in ***cursive***, with direction arrows, etc.
3. The corresponding ***IPA letters*** (glyphs) for this phone. In some cases, several IPA letters are given; this is when the *Navlipi* phone has been broadened to encompass several phones which are phonemically equivalent in most languages. This is done from the point of view of the discretization and phonemic irrelevance arguments propounded earlier in this book.
4. The corresponding ***Dewanaagari*** glyph, where relevant.
5. The mathematical representation of the matrix element, i.e. the ***matrix element number***, as discussed earlier in this chapter. This is, for example, (1-15) for the phone [p]. This is placed in the top left corner of the cell.
6. ***Word examples***. A first attempt is made to find examples from English and one Indian language, generally Hindi/Urdu. This is in consideration of the primary audience that this book addresses. Then, where appropriate, and especially where there are no relevant word examples from these languages, examples are found from other languages. Thus, example words for uvular stops and for retroflex semivowels, would be, respectively, from Arabic and Tamil, since these phones of course do not exist in English or Hindi/Urdu, etc. Again, example words can be from languages as diverse as Danish, Mandarin and Igbo.
7. Explanatory *footnotes*, where appropriate.

Chapter 7: Presenting the Full, Phonic Navlipi Script, Including a Discussion of Reasons for Selection of its Glyphs (Letters)

7.3 THE VOWEL MATRIX AND SELECTION OF NAVLIPI GLYPHS (LETTERS) FOR IT

It is noted at the outset that, in all our discussions of the *Navlipi* glyphs in this and subsequent sections of this chapter, *only the unusual or remarkable glyphs are discussed*. Glyphs that are self-explanatory, e.g. *Navlipi* {i}, {ii}, {e}, {ee} (of English *hit, heat, belt,* and *fair* respectively), are not discussed. (In these four examples, the long vowel is simply the reduplicated short vowel.)

We also note that, for reference, *we may occasionally use the matrix element of the phone under discussion*, e.g. (11(1)) for {i}. We may further refer to *groups of phones* by *generic matrix notation* as described in an earlier chapter. For example, the group *(x2(z))*, i.e. $x=$ any of the three lip positions (flat, rounded, stretched), $y=2$, and $z=$ any of the four jaw positions (from closed to fully open), would represent the phones {q} (22(1)), {a} (22(3)), {aa} (22(4)) etc.. Finally, of course, the discussion assumes constant referral to the *NAVLIPI* SUMMARY TABLES.

We now turn to a discussion of the *vowel segment* of the *Navlipi* script.

We start our discussion with the remarkable glyphs in the group of phones *(x(1)(z))*, i.e. $x=$ any of the three lip positions (flat, rounded, stretched), $y=1$, and $z=$ any of the four jaw positions (from closed to fully open). The {i}, {ii}, {e}, {ee} cited in the previous paragraph belong to this group but are not remarkable, so are not discussed further.

Two redundant glyphs from the Roman script, {ɛ} and {c}, are used to represent, respectively, the vowels of English *hate* and *hat*. Glyphs (3(1)(1)), {y}, is just the original Greek *Ypsilon* finding its original function. The two *new* glyphs are (3(1)(2)) and (3(1)(3)), of French *peu* and *peur* respectively, are simply the glyph *o* with a single and double slash through it, respectively. (3(1)(2)) then is actually identical to the Danish [ø].

The reasons for the choice of the phones (2(2)(1) ({c}) and (1(1)(4) ({q}) have already been given in an earlier section above.

Turning now to the group *(x(3)(z))*, the only remarkable glyph here is (3(3)(4)). Here we use the Greek omega, [Ω], to represent this vowel (of English *caught*). Only the capital (upper case) form of this Greek letter is used, for both upper and lower case representations, which are distinguished only by size.

PART 3: PRESENTATION AND DISCUSSION OF NAVLIPI

Turning now to the group *(x(4)(z))*, the remarkable phone here is only (2(4)(-1)), { ꝛ₀}. This represents the vocalic segment of the central, *jaw-forward* semivowel of Tamil *{pa ꝛ ₀am}*, "fruit". The common use of this glyph would be mainly in its semivowel form, where it would be followed by a fundamental vowel such as {a}, {i} or {u}, exactly as in the above Tamil word. The choice of a script-*r* with a subscripted "little circle" distinguishes this sufficiently from other centrals (*r*-sounds), yet is distinctly recognizable.

In the group *(x(5)(z))*, the only phone assigned a glyph is the retroflex lateral (*l*-sound), the vocalic component of the lateral found in Indian languages as varied as Tamil and Panjaabi. A capital script-*L* is used for this for both upper and lower case, thus making it sufficiently distinct from the "ordinary" (most common) alveolar-lateral.

Turning now to the group *(x(7)(z))*, the single glyph assigned by *Navlipi* in this entire group is for the phone (2(7)(2)).

We need to explain why in this entire group, with potentially 12 elements, only one element, (2(7)(2)) has been assigned a glyph by *Navlipi*. Now it is evident from an examination of this $y=7$ position that none of the other 11 phones of this group are found in any major or even minor language of the world. This then is an example of the *practical phonemics* aspect of *Navlipi* at work in screening out unneeded or unnecessary phones.

glyph (2(7)(2)) in the group *(x(7)(z))* is basically a capital (upper case) script *L* with a crossbar through it. It is used to represent the vocalic portion of the palatalized laterals as in Portuguese *pilha* ("battery") or Croatian *ljeti* (locative case of "summer"). Once again, the common use of this glyph would be mainly in its semivowel form, where it would be followed by a fundamental vowel such as {a}, {i} or {u}, exactly as in the above Croatian and Portuguese words.

In the group *(x(8)(z))*, the only phone assigned a glyph is also the most common "*r*-sound", the vocalic component of the alveolo-dental semivowel. The glyph assigned to it by *Navlipi* is distinct yet recognizable.

In the entire set from $y=9$ to $y=11$, the only remarkable phone is (2(11)(2)). This is the vocalic component of the *apico-supradental* lateral semivowel. This phone is distinct

Chapter 7: Presenting the Full, Phonic Navlipi Script, Including a Discussion of Reasons for Selection of its Glyphs (Letters)

from the standard "*l*", which is an *apico-alveolar* lateral, i.e. the apex of the tongue touches the alveolar ridge. Although in most languages, the *apico-supradental* and *apico-alveolar* central *l*-sounds are not phonemically distinct, they *are* distinct in certain Arabic dialects. Hence the inclusion of this phone for assignment of a *Navlipi* letter, simply for completeness.

The last phones assigned glyph by *Navlipi* are the nasal phones (2(12)(2) and (2(13)(2)), respectively the bilabial and non-bilabial nasal sounds. As a discussion in an earlier chapter has shown, these are typically represented in such words as French *Comte* and Sanskrit *Samskrta* (the phonetically correct rendition of *Sanskrit*) and the African proper names *Mbeki* and *Nkomo*. *Navlipi* simply uses the Roman letters *m* and *n* for these with a subscripted "*o*" {$_o$} and reduplication.

PART 3: PRESENTATION AND DISCUSSION OF NAVLIPI

7.4 THE TWO-DIMENSIONAL (35 X 15) NON-VOWEL MATRIX AND SELECTION OF GLYPHS (LETTERS) FOR IT

We now turn to a discussion of the *nonvowel segment* of the *Navlipi* script. Once again, we note that *only the unusual or remarkable glyphs are discussed*, and that, wherever possible, we will refer to the *Navlipi* phones by their matrix element numbers, e.g. **[1-4]** for [k], the unvoiced, unaspirated velar stop. And of course, again, the discussion constantly refers to the *NAVLIPI* SUMMARY TABLES.

We start our discussion with phone (1-1), the unaspirated glottal stop. A heavy colon is used as the letter representing this phone, taken from the *wisarga* (*visarga*) the glottal stop of Dewanaagari. The cursive rendering of this is extremely simple, as seen in the *NAVLIPI* SUMMARY TABLES: It is simply rendered as a *figure-8*. Although the phone (1-2), i.e. the aspirated glottal stop, is extremely rare, if required, it can be transcribed simply as phone (1-1) together with the post-op for aspiration, [h_o].

The series of uvular phones, *(x-3)*, are simply expressed by using the post-op for uvular/-pharyngeal applied to the velar phones. Thus, the uvular, unvoiced, unaspirated stop, is [k..].

The four retroflex phones (1-5), (2-5), (3-5) and (4-5) are expressed using a double-cross through the corresponding dental phones, as seen in the *NAVLIPI* SUMMARY TABLES.

The phone (1-7), the unvoiced, unaspirated palatal stop, is transcribed as a "backward *c*"; in cursive, it is given a small loop for distinction and ease of writing. This is one of the "new" glyphs of *Navlipi*. Its medio-palatal counterpart, (1-6), is written somewhat like the number "2", but with double loops in the cursive rendering. The phone (3-7), the *voiced*, unaspirated palatal stop (non-affricate rendition of English *jet*) is a new letter (as discussed above). It is simply an inverted letter *j*. In *Navlipi*, it will be rendered *with* the dotting, just as in the letter *i*. The inversion gives it a very distinct and recognizable character.

The alveolar stops (1-8), (2-8), (3-8) and (4-8) are slight modifications of the original dental glyphs of the Roman script. Thus, the unvoiced alveolar plosive [t] is written [#]. Cursive renderings are again extremely simple, merely involving an "extra-crossing" of the *t*. The voiced alveolar stop, (3-8), is transcribed [dt], thus resembling the spelling

Chapter 7: Presenting the Full, Phonic Navlipi Script, Including a Discussion of Reasons for Selection of its Glyphs (Letters)

391

already used in many German words for this phone.

The phones (1-11) and (1-13), the pharyngealized dentals, are used primarily to accommodate languages such as Arabic, where these phones are common and phonemically distinct.

The nasal phones, *(5-y)*, deserve separate discussion. (5-3), the uvular nasal found most prominently in Japanese, is expressed simply by using the uvular/-pharyngeal post-op with the dental nasal, [n]. The velar nasal (5-4) (of English *king*), is simply expressed by adding the subscripted-little-circle identifier. This again is easily rendered in cursive as a small loop, as shown.

The retroflex nasal, (5-5), found most prominently in Indian languages, looks, in print, like an *n* but with the first-leg lengthened. In cursive, it has the appearance of a cursive "open *p*"; anyone who learned cursive writing in Europe more than 50 years ago will be familiar with this. The medio-palatal nasal, (5-6), has an identifying initial loop. It would be of rare use (in Irish and Croatian, most prominently). The palatal nasal, (5-7), has a lengthened second-leg, and the appearance of the Greek *eta (η)*.

Importantly, *Navlipi does not distinguish the nasal phones (5-8), (5-9) and (5-10) (alveolar, medio-dental and dental), but rather assigns them just one glyph, {n}*. The reasons for this are obvious: These three phones are phonemically distinct in almost no world language. Once again, the *practical phonemics* aspect of *Navlipi* orthography is in action here!

Turning now to the fricatives *(6-y)* and *(7-y)* and the flaps *(8-y),* we see first that the pharyngeal, unvoiced fricative (6-1) of Hebrew and Arabic is rendered easily as the uvular/-pharyngeal post-op applied to the letter *h*. In a similar fashion, the uvular fricatives (6-3) and (7-3) are rendered by applying the same post-op to the corresponding velar fricatives ((6-4) and (7-4)). The velar fricative ((6-4) is just *{x}* in *Navlipi*, in accordance with its common use in many Roman transcriptions and of course its original value in the Greek alphabet. The velar fricative(7-4)) is one of the three transformed *Navlipi* glyphs. It is derived from the *g*. The open end makes it very distinct (there is no confusion with *g, q, j* or any other letters) and yet very easy to render in cursive.

The retroflex fricatives (7-4) and (7-5) are rendered by using the *fricative* postop ($\{h_0\}$) on the corresponding, parent retroflex phones. The fricatives (6-6),(6-8), (7-6), and (7-8) are rendered simply by appending this post-op to the corresponding parent phones.

PART 3: PRESENTATION AND DISCUSSION OF NAVLIPI

The very common fricatives (6-7) and (7-7) *are given special treatment*, to allow for greater recognizability and greater conformity to extant usage: Although these also use the fricative post-op, ($\{h_0\}$), this post-op is applied not to the parent phones ((1-7) and (2-7)), but rather to the glyphs *s* and *z*. This brings them in line with current usage: The **sh**, e.g. of English *shoot* and the **zh**, e.g. in the English transcription of Russian *zhurnal*. This is thus a case of *Navlipi* bending its orthographic rules somewhat in the interests of recognizability and adaptation to current usage!

The fricative flap (9-8) is rare, being prominent only in Czech, and thus its transcription as the fricative post-op applied to the flap *r* is justified. Similarly, the bilabial fricatives (6-15) and (7-15) are rare, found in Hausa, some Indonesian languages (e.g. Tukang Besi), and in dialectical pronunciations in such languages as Spanish and even English (in some pronunciations of **ph**ooey!).

The entire series of *click, ejective* and *implosive* phones, *(12-y)* through *(21-y)*, are very rare in the world's major languages. Thus, their rendition purely through the use of post-ops, as done in *Navlipi*, is justified. These use their respective, assigned post-ops (*click-ingressive, click-egressive, ejective, implosive*), and so need not be discussed further.

Chapter 7: Presenting the Full, Phonic Navlipi Script, Including a Discussion of Reasons for Selection of its Glyphs (Letters)

7.5 POST-OPS (POSTPOSITIONAL OPERATORS)

These are discussed in a separate chapter, quod vide.

7.6 PHONEMIC CONDENSATES USED AND REASONING

These are discussed in a separate chapter, q.v..

7.7 BILABIAL AND MEDIO-PALATAL SEMIVOWELS AND PHONEMIC CONDENSATES THEREOF

Of note among these are the bilabial semivowel articulated with the tongue in the central position and lips flat, in contrast to the tongue-back, lips-rounded articulation of the standard [w]. This is designated *{w°}* in *Navlipi*: the cursive rendition is facile and easily recognizable, with a simple loop. This semivowel phone is found, e.g., in some pronunciations of Spanish *haber*.

The bilabial semivowel articulated with a pharyngeal emphasis, is phonemically distinct in Hebrew. It can and somewhat crudely be described as a "vomit-like sound" (for want of a better way to describe it, apologies for any offense!) to someone who has not heard it. It is easily rendered in *Navlipi* by using the pharyngeal post-op on the [w], yielding *{w..}*.

The table of semivowels in *Navlipi* also includes some phonemic condensates, (e.g. *[vw]*, used to represent the voiced infralabio-supradental spirant (fricative) + bilabial semivowel of Hindi).

Another phonemic condensate is the (uvular-fricative + trilled-*r* + flap-*r* + semivowel-*r*) found in French and German. This is, very logically and conveniently, assigned the digraph *{xr}*.

Chapter 7: Presenting the Full, Phonic Navlipi Script, Including a Discussion of Reasons for Selection of its Glyphs (Letters)

7.8 CENTRALS (R-SOUNDS) AND SELECTION OF LETTERS FOR THESE

The centrals covered here comprise the complete range of central phones, including semi-vowel, flap, trill, etc.

The semivowels among these are also related in the *NAVLIPI* SUMMARY TABLES to their corresponding *parent vowels*, as also to the nonvowels. It may also be noted that the selection of letters closely parallels the selection of the letters for the parent vowels, as was discussed in earlier chapters.

The *Navlipi* glyphs for the main central (*r*-sound) semivowels make a distinction between the *retroflex* phones, as in the American and some Indian *r*-sounds, and the standard *alveolar* phones found in most languages. A distinction is also made between the *flap* and the semivowel. The *trill* is rendered simply as a reduplicated flap. What this thus ends up doing is yielding the standard letter *r*, i.e. *{r}* in *Navlipi*, to represent ***a phonemic condensate that combines the alveolar semivowel, tap/flap and trill***. If a further distinction is required for the alveolar semivowel only, the letter *{r$_o$}* is used. The retroflex semivowel then remains distinct, using the script-*r*, *{ ꓤ }*.

PART 3: PRESENTATION AND DISCUSSION OF NAVLIPI

7.9 LATERALS (L-SOUNDS) AND SELECTION OF LETTERS FOR THESE

These again include the complete range of lateral phones, including semi-vowel, flap, trill, etc, and their fricatized versions. The semivowels among these are also related in the table to their corresponding *parent vowels*, as also to the nonvowels. It may also be noted that the selection of glyphs closely parallels the selection of the letters for the parent vowels, as discussed in earlier chapters, to which reference is made.

The only glyphs that are exceptional and do not parallel the parent vowels in the case of these lateral phones are the click sounds, e.g. the various lateral clicks (e.g. *{lʒ}*). All these use their assigned post-ops, and so are self-explanatory and need not be further discussed. The *aspirated* alveolar central, i.e. the aspirated version of the common, alveolar *l*-sound, is found in some renditions of Panjaabi and Sindhi as a phonemically distinct entity. It is easily enough expressed as in the *NAVLIPI* SUMMARY TABLES, i.e. using the aspiration post-op ($\{h_0\}$). The *fricatized* alveolar central, i.e. the fricatized version of the common, alveolar *l*-sound, is found in Welsh (the famous Welsh "double-l" which non Welsh speakers sometimes render as an [f], as in *Floyd* vs. *LLoyd*) Again, it is easily enough rendered as $\{lh_0\}$. Thus, in *Navlipi,* one would render the Welsh name *Lloyd* as $\{Lh_0\Omega id\}$, and would not need to write it as the approximate *Floyd*!

Chapter 7: Presenting the Full, Phonic Navlipi Script, Including a Discussion of Reasons for Selection of its Glyphs (Letters)

7.10 TONES ("MUSICAL" OR "PITCH" ACCENTS)

These are discussed in a separate chapter, q.v..

7.11 TRANSCRIPTION OF UNUSUAL PHONES

Due to the immense richness of human language, as expressed through the great variety of phonemic distinctions even within the same language family or sub-family, one frequently encounters peculiar phones which are phonemically distinct and which test the limits of the capabilities of the phonetic classifier as well as the orthographer. It is important to discuss these.

Such phones usually have *combinations* of distinct artitions or phonochromaticities, such as labial *and* velar (two distinct and, usually, separately occurring, artitions), or flap *and* fricative (two distinct phonochromaticities).

One such example is the fricatized central alveolar flap (*r*-sound) of Czech, as in the proper name *Dvořak*. This is not found in even neighboring, cognate languages of the same sub-family, such as Polish. And it is phonemically distinct, in Czech, from the standard central alveolar flap, i.e. the standard [r]. Another example is the pharyngealized nonvowels of Arabic (*{t..}* etc.), discussed in an earlier chapter, which are again phonemically distinct, in Arabic, from [t] etc..

These Czech and Arabic examples are from what we call "major" languages (even though Czech has a relatively small number of speakers). They are thus accommodated by *Navlipi* through the assignment of distinct glyphs for them. *Navlipi* can thus not ignore them. There are many examples of such odd phones from other world languages, such as Amharic or Igbo. Some of these other examples are:

1) *Amharic,* **labialized nonvowels**: These are represented in IPA orthography as [f^w], [b^w], [m^w] etc. That is to say, in Amharic, the phone [b] uttered as one would in English and the same phone uttered with the lips rounded during or just after its utterance have two different phonemic values.

2) *Hausa,* **palatalized and labialized non-vowels**: Here, we have velar

stops, [k] and [g], that can be uttered in two different, phonemically distinct ways: palatalized and labialized, expressed in IPA orthography as [kʲ], [gʲ], [kʷ] and [gʷ].

3) *Igbo, **labialized velar stops***: Here, we have the labialized velar stops as in Hausa, [kʷ], [gʷ] in IPA orthography, plus what are denoted as "labial-velar" stops, denoted in IPA orthography as [k͡p], [g͡b]. In certain other West and Central African languages, one also finds "labialized" velar-labial phones, [k͡p͡w], [g͡b͡w].

4) *Igbo, **pharyngealized vowels***: Here, we also have a peculiar phonemic distinction among vowels themselves. The "standard" vowels [i], [e], [u] and [o] have phonemically distinct, *pharyngealized* counterparts, in which the pharynx is expanded during utterance. The IPA uses the term "**ATR**" (Advanced Tongue Root) to distinguish these vowels, because the pharynx can be expanded by simply advancing the tongue root forward. The IPA then distinguishes such vowels with the notations *[+ATR]* and *[-ATR]* to signify presence or absence of ATR, i.e. pharyngeal expansion. (Transcriptions using these IPA notations would be a nightmare, but that is another story!)

5) *Irish, **velarized and palatalized nonvowels***: Here, we have, ostensibly, "standard", "velarized" and "palatalized" articulations of nonvowels that are all phonemically distinct.

6) *Tukang Besi* (an Indonesian language), ***pre-nasalized stops***: Here, we have what are denoted as "pre-nasalized" velar, dental and bilabial plosives. That is to say, the utterance of the plosive is preceded by a nasal vowel, and this makes the nasalized plosive phonemically distinct from its non-nasalized counterpart. Thus, [*n*-k] is phonemically distinct from [k] (where *n* crudely denotes the nasalization).

The above six examples of unusual or odd phones appear at first to create some difficulty for the orthographer. However, on closer examination of the actual pronunciations involved, it is seen that their phonetic component analysis is really quite simple, and hence their orthography is quite straightforward!

Turning to the above examples in sequence then,

Chapter 7: Presenting the Full, Phonic Navlipi Script, Including a Discussion of Reasons for Selection of its Glyphs (Letters)

399

(i) In *Amharic*, the labialized nonvowels [fʷ], [bʷ], [mʷ] etc. are in fact seen to be the initial phone and the bilabial semivowel uttered in extremely close succession. Thus, they can just as easily be orthographed, in *Navlipi*, as digraphs *{fw, bw, mw}*, etc. For practical, phonemic purposes, this would be well understood in Amharic.

(ii) In a similar fashion, in *Hausa*, the velar stops [kʲ], [gʲ], [kʷ] and [gʷ] can easily be orthographed, in *Navlipi*, as digraphs *{kj, gj, kw, gw}*, etc.

(iii) The labialized velar stops of *Igbo*, [kʷ], [gʷ], can similarly be orthographed, in *Navlipi*, as *{kj, gj}* etc.

(iv) The "labial-velar" stops of *Igbo* and related languages, [k͡p], [g͡b], are true *multiple-artitions*. *Navlipi* uses a special *post-op* for them, **PO-20**, the "bar-above". In print, this is written as a post-op, e.g. *[kp⁻]* and *[gb⁻]*. In cursive, the post-op is written as a true bar-above, placed above the phones it acts on, be they just two, as [k] + [p], or multiple. The cursive bar-above is rendered much like "crossing a t".

(v) The *pharyngealized* counterparts of the vowels [i], [e], [u] and [o] of *Igbo* can be very simply expressed, in *Navlipi*, using the *uvular/-pharyngeal post-op* of *Navlipi*, i.e. *{i..}, {e..}, {u..}* and *{o..}*. This does away with the cumbersome [+ATR]/[-ATR] notation of the IPA!

(vi) The "palatalized" articulations of nonvowels in *Irish* can similarly be orthographed, in *Navlipi*, as digraphs, with *j* used as a post-op, as in *{lj}* for the palatalized alveolar lateral. The so-called "velarized" articulations of Irish, e.g. the velarized alveolar lateral, are seen, on closer examination, to actually be phones of a slightly different artition. For example, the "velarized" alveolar lateral is in fact seen to be a slightly retroflexed alveolar lateral. It may thus be expressed, in *Navlipi*, as a digraph of the alveolar lateral and the retroflex lateral, i.e. {ℓℓ} Alternatively, these phones may be orthographed using the *Navlipi* post-op **PO-20**, to join the two component phones. Thus, the velarized alveolar lateral would be written as [l] + [k] + PO-20 = *{lk⁻ }*.

(vii) The "pre-nasalized" plosives of *Tukang Besi*, can simply be orthographed, in *Navlipi*, as the *Navlipi* nasal vowel followed by the plosive. For example, the pre-nasalized-[k] can simply be orthographed as **{n₀k}**.

PART 3: PRESENTATION AND DISCUSSION OF NAVLIPI

400

In a similar fashion, other unusual or odd phones in even less well known languages can similarly be broken down into components and then orthographed as digraphs, or occasionally, with post-ops, thus obviates the need for arriving at distinct glyphs (letters) for them in *Navlipi*.

Chapter 8: Tones, Tonemes and Ictus (Stress) Accents

CHAPTER 8.
TONES, TONEMES AND ICTUS (STRESS) ACCENTS

TABLE OF CONTENTS

8.1 EXTANT SYSTEMS FOR TRANSCRIPTION OF TONES AND THE NEED FOR A NEW SYSTEM **402**

8.2 VARIATION OF TONES FOUND IN LANGUAGES TODAY **408**

    8.2.1 TONAL LANGUAGES AND ILLUSTRATIONS WITH MANDARIN, CANTONESE, YORUBA, CASHINAHUA, NAMA 408
    8.2.2 "SEMI-TONAL" LANGUAGES AND ILLUSTRATIONS WITH SWEDISH, VEDIC SANSKRIT, HOMERIC GREEK 412
    8.2.3 LANGUAGES WITH ICTUS (STRESS) ACCENTS AND ILLUSTRATIONS WITH ENGLISH, SPANISH, EUROPEAN NAMES 417

8.3 THE TRANSCRIPTION OF TONES IN *NAVLIPI*: USE OF FOUR *ATTRIBUTES* OF TONES **420**

    8.3.1 ATTRIBUTES OF TONES IN NAVLIPI 420
    8.3.2 DESCRIPTION OF THE TONE TRANSCRIPTION SYSTEM OF NAVLIPI
    423

8.4 EXAMPLES OF TRANSCRIPTIONS OF A VARIETY OF TONAL LANGUAGES IN *NAVLIPI* **426**

PART 3: PRESENTATION AND DISCUSSION OF NAVLIPI

8.1 EXTANT SYSTEMS FOR TRANSCRIPTION OF TONES AND THE NEED FOR A NEW SYSTEM

To get our bearings, it is useful to first quickly look at typical transcription systems for tones *available and used today* (2005). Some of these, for well-known tone languages, are given in **Table 8-1**.

> **Table 8-1**: Selected, representative systems for transcribing *tones* in the *Roman script*, extant today (2005). The drawbacks of these systems are apparent: *Overwhelming presence of diacritics*, and *difficulty and slowness in cursive writing and keyboarding*.
>
> **1) *IPA (International Phonetic Association, London)*:** **Tone Transcription System and Exemplary Illustration with Cantonese** (Reproduced with permission from *The IPA Handbook* [SCr-3], Copyright 2005, International Phonetic Association.)

TONES AND WORD ACCENTS

LEVEL			CONTOUR		
ế or	˥	Extra high	ě or	∧	Rising
é	˦	High	ê	∨	Falling
ē	˧	Mid	ẽ̄	↗	High rising
è	˨	Low	ẽ̀	↗	Low rising
ȅ	˩	Extra low	ẽ	↑	Rising-falling
↓		Downstep	↗		Global rise
↑		Upstep	↘		Global fall

Chapter 8: Tones, Tonemes and Ictus (Stress) Accents
403

(Table 8-1, cont.)

IPA, Cantonese sample

Original Transcription

　　有一次，北風同太陽喺度拗緊邊個叻啲。佢哋啱啱睇到有個人行過，哩個人着住件大褸。佢哋就話嘞，邊個可以整到哩個人除咗件褸呢，就算邊個叻啲嘞。於是，北風就搏命咁吹。點知，佢越吹得犀利，嗰個人就越係嚟實件褸。最後，北風冇晒符，唯有放棄。跟住，太陽出嚟晒咗一陣，嗰個人就即刻除咗件褸嘞。於是，北風唯有認輸啦。

Tones from IPA

[˥, ˧, ˧˩, ˩, ˨˥, ˨˧] (= high; mid; low-mid; low-mid to low, falling; low-mid to high, rising; low-mid to mid, rising) are long tones; [˧˩] is relatively shorter.

IPA Transcription

jeu˨ jet˥ tsʰi˧ | pek˥ fuŋ˥ tʰuŋ˨ tʰai˧ jœn˨ hei˨˥ tou˧ au˧ ken˨˥ pin˥ kɔ˧ lɛk˥ ti˥ ‖ kʰøy˨ tei˧ am˥ am˥ tʰei˨˥ tou˨˥ jeu˨ kɔ˧ jen˨˥ haŋ˨ kʷɔ˧ | li˥ kɔ˧ jen˨ tsœk˧ tsy˧ kin˧ tai˧ leu˨ ‖ kʰøy˨ tei˧ tseu˨ wa˨ lak˧ | pin˨˥ kɔ˧ hɔ˧ ji˨ tsɪŋ˨ tou˧ li˥ kɔ˧ jen˨˥ tsʰøy˨ tsɔ˨ kin˧ leu˨ lɛ˨ | tseu˨ syn˧ pin˥ kɔ˧ lɛk˥ ti˥ lak˧ ‖ jy˥ si˨ | pek˥ fuŋ˥ tseu˨ pɔk˧ meŋ˨ kem˧ tsʰøy˥ ‖ tim˨˥ tsi˥ | kʰøy˨ jyt˧ tsʰøy˥ tɐk˥ sei˥ lei˨ | kɔ˥ kɔ˧ jen˨˥ tseu˨ jyt˧ hei˧ la˨˥ set˧ kin˧ leu˨ ‖ tsøy˧ heu˨ | pek˥ fuŋ˥ mou˨ sai˧ fu˨ | wei˨ jeu˨ fɔŋ˧ hei˧ ‖ ken˨ tsy˧ | tʰai˧ jœn˨ tsʰet˥ lei˨ sai˧ tsɔ˥ jet˥ tsen˨ | kɔ˥ kɔ˧ jen˨˥ tseu˨ tsɪk˥ hak˥ tsʰøy˥ tsɔ˥ kin˧ leu˨ lak˧ ‖ jy˥ si˨ | pek˥ fuŋ˥ wei˨ jeu˨ jɪŋ˨ sy˥ la˥ ‖

PART 3: PRESENTATION AND DISCUSSION OF NAVLIPI

(Table 8-1, cont.)

    2) *__Official Chinese Government Roman Transcription of Mandarin__*:
[SCr-29-a], showing diacritic accents used.
Reproduced from Reference [SCr-29-b].

长城 是 两 千 多 年 以前 开始
Chángchéng shì liǎng qiān duō nián yǐqián kāishǐ

修建 的。到了 秦朝 （公元 前 二二一—
xiūjiàn de. Dàole Qíncháo (gōngyuán qián èrèryī-

二〇七年），又 用了 十几 年 的 时间，
èrlíngqī nián), yòu yòngle shíjǐ nián de shíjiān,

把 原来 一 段 一 段 的 城墙 连接起来。
bǎ yuánlái yí duàn yí duàn de chéngqiáng liánjiēqǐlai.

以后，长城 又 进行过 很 多 次 修整。
Yǐhòu, Chángchéng yòu jìnxíngguo hěn duō cì xiūzhěng.

现在 我们 看到 的 长城 虽然 经过
Xiànzài wǒmen kàndào de Chángchéng suīrán jīngguò

两 千 多 年 的 风 吹 雨 打，但是
liǎng qiān duō nián de fēng chuī yǔ dǎ, dànshì

大 部分 还 很 完整，根基 也 很 牢固。
dà bùfen hái hěn wánzhěng, gēnjī yě hěn láogù.

Chapter 8: Tones, Tonemes and Ictus (Stress) Accents

405

(Table 8-1, cont.)

3) *Vietnamese*:
(Reproduced from the *Transcriptions* section of **PART 1 (*NAVLIPI SUMMARY TABLES*.)**

Một người đàn ông cao lớn đột nhiên tỉnh dậy và nhảy ra khỏi giường như thể anh ta vừa trải qua một giấc mơ khủng khiếp. Anh nhìn ra bên ngoài cửa sổ. Thời tiết thật là đẹp. Mặt trời đang tỏa ánh nắng, vẫn là ánh nắng màu da cam của buổi sáng sớm mặc dù đến lúc này đã lên cao tận đường chân trời. Anh ngáp một cái, vươn vai rồi sau đó mở cửa sổ.

PART 3: PRESENTATION AND DISCUSSION OF NAVLIPI

(Table 8-1, cont.)

4) **_Standard Roman transcription of Igbo_**:
(Reproduced with permission from *The IPA Handbook* [SCr-3], Copyright 2005, International Phonetic Association.)

IPA Transcription

ikuku ụ́gụ̄ɹụ̄ na á↓ŋwụ́ naaɹụ́ɹ̣́tá ụ́↓kà óɲé ↓ká íbe já íké mgbe ɦá ɦụ̄ɹụ̄ ótu óɲé ídʒe ka ó ji uwé ụ́gụ̄ɹụ̄ já náabı̣́á. ɦá kwekọ̄ɹ̣itaɹa na óɲé ↓buɹu ụ́zọ̄ méé ka óɲé ídʒe áɦụ̄ jípụ̄ uwé ↓ja ka á ga éwe dị̣ ka oɲé ka íbe já íké. ikuku ụ́gụ̄ɹụ̄ wéé malíté féé, féé, féé, otu íké ↓já ɦa; ma ka ọ̣ na efé ka óɲé ídʒe áɦụ̄ na edʒídésí ↓úwé ↓já ↓íké na aɦụ̄ ↓já. já fékatá ɦápụ̄. mgbe áɦụ̄ a↓ŋwụ́ wéé tʃápụ̄tá, tʃásí↓ké méé ka ebe níí↓lé kpoɹo ọ̣́↓kụ̄ ná↓átufuɣi óge oɲé ídʒe áɦụ̄ jipụ̄ɹụ̄ uwé ↓já ŋké a meɹe ikuku ụ́gụ̄ɹụ̄ kweɹe na a↓ŋwụ̄ ka já íké.

Original Transcription

Ìkùkù úgừrừ nà Ánwū̧ nà-arúṛ̣́tá úkà ónyé kā ībè yá íké m̀gbè há hừrừ ótù ónyé íjè kà ó yì ùwé úgừrừ yá nà-àbị̣́á. Há kwèkọ̀ṛ̣itàrà nà ónyé būrū úzọ̀ méé kà ónyé íjè áhừ yípừ ùwé yā kà á gà-éwè dị̣̀kà ónyé ka íbè yá íké. Ìkùkù úgừrừ wéé màlíté féé, féé, òtù íké yā hà; mà kà ọ̣ nà-èfé kà ónyé íjè áhừ nà-èjídési ūwē yā īkē nà àhú yā. Yá fékàtá hápừ. M̀gbè áhừ Ánwū̧ wéé chápừtá, chásíkē, méé kà ébé níílē kpòró ọ̣́kū̧; ná-ātừfūghì ógè ónyé íjè áhừ yìpừrừ ùwé yā. Ǹké à mèrè ìkùkù úgừrừ kwèrè nà Ánwū̧ kà yá íké.

Chapter 8: Tones, Tonemes and Ictus (Stress) Accents

Some features immediately apparent from even a cursory glance at the above transcriptions are the overwhelming presence of what appear to be ***diacritics*** ("accent marks"); these are present even in the IPA transcriptions.

The variation of IPA transcription that uses post-ops (used in the first, Cantonese example) is more convenient to transcribe due to its post-op form. It is nevertheless still extremely difficult and confusing to read due to the substantial similarity in its symbols. Its tone symbols are difficult to differentiate in quick reading. In fact, one needs to "decipher" rather than "read" a passage that uses this transcription!

Additionally, *all* the above transcriptions are also ***very difficult and slow to render in cursive***. As anyone who writes the modern Roman-based Vietnamese script, or the Igbo transcription, both shown above, will acknowledge, the "accent marks" (diacritics) that one has to constantly place slow the cursive writing down excruciatingly. They also make the writing very cluttered. The cursive rendering of the IPA post-op transcription of tones is not immediately apparent, or has at least not been widely disseminated by the IPA. And again, the IPA transcriptions have post-ops (or diacritics) that are rather difficult to distinguish.

Lastly, for all these transcription systems for tones, including that of the IPA, ***keyboarding is very difficult***.

Thus, in summary, *transcription methods for tones available today have numerous, very serious drawbacks relating to such features as the overwhelming presence of diacritics, and difficulty and slowness in cursive writing and keyboarding.*

PART 3: PRESENTATION AND DISCUSSION OF NAVLIPI

8.2 VARIATION OF TONES FOUND IN LANGUAGES TODAY

8.2.1 TONAL LANGUAGES AND ILLUSTRATIONS WITH MANDARIN, CANTONESE, YORUBA, CASHINAHUA, NAMA

To get an idea of the variety of tone systems found in tonal languages today that a new script such as *Navlipi* must address, and the common threads (if any) that run through them, it is best to look at some typical tonal languages. These are listed in the several Figures and Tables below.

Fig. 8-1: O'Connor's graphical representation of the four tones of Mandarin. After reference [PHo-1], reproduced with permission.

Chapter 8: Tones, Tonemes and Ictus (Stress) Accents

Table 8-2: Typical *tonal* languages and their tone systems. The *Navlipi PRINT transcription* is also shown.

1) MANDARIN, Beijing:

TONE # AND DESCRIPTION	TYPICAL WORD EXAMPLE ("MEANING")	NAVLIPI TRANSCRIPTION
1. high, level	*yi* ("one")	*yi*⌐
1. high, level	*ma?* (interrogative particle at end of sentence)	*ma*⌐ ?
2. rising, mid → high	*shi* ("ten")	*shi*⟩
2. rising, mid → high	*ma* ("hemp")	*ma*⟩
3. falling (mid → low), rising, (low → mid)	*hao* ("good")	*hao*⌒⟩
4. falling, high → low	*yi* ("hundred million")	*yi*⌐̣
4. falling, high → low	*ma* ("scold")	*ma*⌐̣

(Table 8-2, cont.)

2) CANTONESE:

Cantonese is said to have nine (9) rather than six (6) tones. To obtain the additional three, the first three tones above are further partitioned into whether the syllables are long ("fermata") or short ("staccato") [PHo-17-a]. However, it is recognized that this new short/long partition represents the same tonemes, and so the distinction is not generally used. Thus, we show only six (6) tones here.

TONE # AND DESCRIPTION	TYPICAL WORD EXAMPLE ("MEANING")	NAVLIPI TRANSCRIPTION
1. level, high	*si* ("silk")	*si*|
2. level, mid	*si* ("to try")	*si*/
3. level, low-mid	*si* ("matter")	*si*__
4. falling, low-mid → low	*si* ("time")	*si*¬
5. rising, low-mod → high	*si* ("history")	*si*⌐|
6. rising, low-mod → mid	*si* ("city")	*si*⌐⌐

4) YORUBA:

TONE # AND DESCRIPTION	TYPICAL WORD EXAMPLE ("MEANING")	NAVLIPI TRANSCRIPTION
1. level, high	*ba* ("to meet")	*ba*|
2. level, mid	*ba* ("to hide")	*ba*/
3. level, low	*ba* ("to perch")	*ba*__
4. rising, low → high	*yi* ("this")	*yi*⌐|
5. falling, high → low	*na* ("the")	*na*¬

(Table 8-2, cont.)

5) CASHINAHUA (a Peruvian language):

TONE # AND DESCRIPTION	TYPICAL WORD EXAMPLE ("MEANING")	NAVLIPI TRANSCRIPTION
1. level, high	*mawaxuki* ("he died")	*ma|wa|xu|ki|*
2. level, low	*mawaxuki* ("he imitated something")	*ma__ wa__ xu__ ki__*

6) NAMA:

A "click" language and the major language of the Khoisan ("click") language family found in South Africa, Namibia, Botswana, and proximate areas, also known formerly as *Hottentot*. It is of the same family as, e.g. !Xo Bushman). Nama has three tones, (represented, e.g., with *a*, as *á, ā, à*, which may occur on vowels and nasal stops. The mid tone is not written.. After references [PHo-17-a,b,c]. Example passage taken from ref. [PHo-17-b]

TONE AND DESCRIPTION	TYPICAL WORD EXAMPLE ("MEANING")	NAVLIPI TRANSCRIPTION
1. rising, low-mid → high, e.g. *á*	*Tsií ma tsès hòásàp ge ||iba kèrè `óa-|xií tàn|aose.* **	*Tsií┘ ma tsè¬s hò┘ á┘ sà┘ p ge ||iba kè¬rè¬ `ó¬ a-|xií┘ tà┘ n|aose***
2. level, mid, e.g. *ā*, but usually not written	("And every day he would return the victor.")	
3. falling, high → low-mid, e.g. *à*		

**(\|\| , ` *represent clicks*)

PART 3: PRESENTATION AND DISCUSSION OF NAVLIPI

8.2.2 "SEMI-TONAL" LANGUAGES AND ILLUSTRATIONS WITH SWEDISH, VEDIC SANSKRIT, HOMERIC GREEK

The reader may immediately note the word "*semi-tonal*" in the title of this subsection, to be contrasted with the word "*tonal*" of the previous section. We clarify and differentiate these two terms as follows (a subject dealt with in an earlier chapter as well):

- *True TONAL* languages can be differentiated by the characteristic that even *monosyllabic words* can be distinguished in meaning solely by tone, and that tones are **determinative** of meaning. By this characteristic, for example, Mandarin is a true tonal languages, whereas Swedish is not, as elaborated further in the discussion below.

- **SEMI-TONAL** languages can be differentiated from true tonal languages by the characteristic that *monosyllabic words* are **not** differentiable solely by tone. Furthermore, in many semi-tonal languages, the tone is highly **significant** but frequently not *determinative*. The previously cited Swedish, and the ancient Indo-European languages, which had three tones (*uddaata, anuddaata, swarita*, i.e. acute, grave, circumflex), would fall into the semi-tonal category according to this definition. Thus, in Swedish, the two (2) tones can be used to distinguish meaning between identical multi-syllabic words: For example, *anden*, with both syllables having a falling tone means "soul", whereas when it has a falling tone in the first syllable and a low, level tone in the second, it means "duck" [PHo-1]. However, monosyllabic words in Swedish *have no determinative tone characteristics*.

The above distinction of **tonal** vs. **semi-tonal** languages may appear instinctive to many readers, since almost anyone will feel the clear, intrinsic difference between Mandarin (*tonal*) and Swedish (*semi-tonal*).

On the other hand, the distinction between the stress-accent-based English and the semi-tonal Swedish is not as clear. It shows up in odd ways, e.g. when a native Swedish speaker new to English speaks English in a "sing-song", two-tone manner.

Table 8-3 cites, by way of example, some *semi-tonal* languages and the tones found in them. The reader may note that the ancient Indo-European languages are also listed therein.

Chapter 8: Tones, Tonemes and Ictus (Stress) Accents

We all of course know well that the acute, grave and circumflex accents that we find in modern French or even late Latin are just moribund survivors of the original, Indo-European tone (pitch) accents, having lost their significance. Remnants still survive in modern Italian and Maraathi. That these represent a *semi-tonal* rather than a true *tonal* character is elaborated in the discussion further below. A true appreciation of the semi-tonal character of the ancient Indo-European languages would be apparent to anyone who has heard the tonal *recitativo* of Vedic hymns recited by priests in any Hindu temple today.

PART 3: PRESENTATION AND DISCUSSION OF NAVLIPI

Table 8-3: Examples of tone systems in some *SEMI-TONAL* languages.

a) SWEDISH

1) *Bi-syllabic "first tone"*, also called *"first accent"*: (*fall, high to low + fall, high to low*), but frequently has the appearance of (*fall, high to low + high, level*) due to the sometimes barely audible high to low transition in the second syllable.
2) *Bi-syllabic "second tone"*, also called *"second accent"*: (*fall, high to low + level, low*)

TONE (ACCENT) # AND DESCRIPTION	TYPICAL WORD EXAMPLE ("MEANING")	*NAVLIPI* TRANSCRIPTION
1. (1) fall, high → low; (2) fall, high → low; but frequently having the appearance (1) fall, high → low; (2) level, high.	*anden* ("soul")	*an⌈den⌈*
2. fall, high → low; level, low.	*anden* ("duck")	*an⌈den__*
1. (1) fall, high → low; (2) fall, high → low; but frequently having the appearance (1) fall, high → low; (2) level, high.	*buren* ("cage")	*bu⌈ren⌈*
2. (1) fall, high → low; (2) level, low.	*buren* ("carried")	*bu⌈ren__*
1. (1) fall, high → low; (2) fall, high → low; but frequently having the appearance (1) fall, high → low; (2) level, high.	*tanken* ("tank")	*tan⌈ken⌈*
2. (1) fall, high → low; (2) level, low.	*tanken* ("thought")	*tan⌈ken__*
1. (1) fall, high → low; (2) fall, high → low; but frequently having the appearance (1) fall, high → low; (2) level, high.	*komma* ("come")	*kom⌈ma⌈*
2. (1) fall, high → low; (2) level, low.	*komma* ("comma")	*kom⌈ma__*

Chapter 8: Tones, Tonemes and Ictus (Stress) Accents

(Table 8-3, cont.)

b) VEDIC SANSKRIT

Accents:
(1) Uddaata, (acute); equivalent to level, high.
(2) Anuddaata, (grave); equivalent to level, low.
(3) Swarita, (circumflex); combination of acute and grave, generally not indicated in any transcription.

ACCENT AND DESCRIPTION	TYPICAL WORD EXAMPLE ("MEANING")	*NAVLIPI* TRANSCRIPTION
1. *Uddaata (acute)* (Roman transcription- here as apostrophe, ')	*A_gnim ii'l.e* (अ_ग्निमी'ळे "I praise Agnis (god of fire)") (*RV* I.1.1)	A_lgnim i*l*.e
2. *Anuddaata, (grave)* (Roman transcription- here as underscore, _)		
3. *Swarita (circumflex)* (Roman transcription- not transcribed)	*Tubhyede_te ba'hulaa* (तुभ्येदे_ते ब'हुला , "Only to you, many....") (*RV* I.54.9)	*Tubhyede_ te ba_hulaa*

PART 3: PRESENTATION AND DISCUSSION OF NAVLIPI

(Table 8-3, cont.)

c) HOMERIC GREEK

Accents:
Acute; equivalent to level, high.
Grave); equivalent to level, low.
Circumflex; combination of acute and grave; not indicated in our transcription.

ACCENT AND DESCRIPTION	TYPICAL WORD EXAMPLE ("MEANING")	NAVLIPI TRANSCRIPTION
1. *Acute* (Roman transcription here as apostrophe, ')	aagatho's (αγαθός, "good")	aagath$_o$ols
1. *Acute* (Roman transcription here as apostrophe, ')	en' skinaa'is (ἔν σκιναῖς ,"in tents")	en skinadis
2. *Grave* (Roman transcription here as underscore, _)	skinaa_i (σκιναὶ , "tents")	skinaa__i
3. *Circumflex* (Roman transcription- not transcribed)	syllables in example words above having no diacritics	

In the semi-tonal languages, such as the old Indo-European languages, e.g. Vedic Sanskrit and Homeric Greek in the examples above, the tone (pitch) accent is highly *significant*, but not necessarily *determinative* of the meaning.

Thus, e.g., one must, in Vedic Sanskrit, say the phrase shown in the example above with the accentuation as noted. If one utters this phrase in a different accentuation, it will be considered very wrong, but will not necessarily be misunderstood.

As a weaker example of such a significant" but not "determinative" accent, we can cite the modern Italian *Non' fu'ma_re* ("No Smoking" or "Don't Smoke" in an entreaty rather than a command sense, with again the apostrophe used to indicate the acute or high-pitched accent). If articulated as *Non_ fu_ma're'* (underscore again indicating grave or low-pitched accent), it would be considered rather odd by the native Italian speaker, but nevertheless still understood. Thus, again, here, the pitch accent is significant, but not necessarily determinative of the meaning, as it would be in, say, Mandarin.

8.2.3 LANGUAGES WITH ICTUS (STRESS) ACCENTS AND ILLUSTRATIONS WITH ENGLISH, SPANISH, EUROPEAN NAMES

Nearly *all* non-tonal languages have some form of a *stress* accent, not only to describe proper modes of speech, but also to distinguish words with identical syllables. In older linguistics literature, the stress accent is also called the *ictus* accent, after terminology found in prosody and poetry.

We can first orient ourselves by looking at *stress* accents that differentiate words in our very own English and in Spanish, as given in **Table 8-4** below.

Several features are immediately apparent from **Table 8-4**.

Firstly, the *stress accents also appear to mirror pitch* accents in many cases and, less often, the duration of a syllable. That is to say, a stressed syllable in English is usually also of acute (high) pitch, and frequently of longer duration as well. However, this accent identification is not absolute, especially in languages other than English. For example, in the pronunciation of the name *Anton* in German, the stress which is on the first syllable, can be rendered with the first syllable having a high (acute) pitch *(An'ton)* as well as a low (grave) pitch *(An_ton)*, although both these have long duration.

Secondly, the accent differentiation also sometimes leads to a change in the phoneme used, so that the words contrasted are no longer identical and so no longer solely distinguished by accent. For example, in the English example [contest' (verb) / con'test (noun)], the vowel of first syllable in the *verb* is close to the Schwa of English *concur*, whereas in the *noun* it is the vowel of British English *John*. Thus, in this example, we are no longer really strictly comparing two identical words distinguished only by stress or tone accent. However, in the example [pervert' (verb) / per'vert (noun)], there is no change of phoneme, so we are in fact comparing two words solely distinguished by stress accent. Another feature apparent from the Spanish words is that stress accent is important (i.e., it must be put in the right place), but there may not necessarily be two words distinguished solely by stress accent.

Table 8-4: *Ictus (stress)* accents differentiating words in English and Spanish. *(For our purposes here, accents are shown with a post-op apostrophe)*

a) ENGLISH

Verb/noun or adjective/noun differentiation: (In some of these examples, there is also a small change in the accented phone due to the needs of euphony, but this does not detract from out argument.)

[Again, the apostrophe (') is used to indicate acute (high-pitched) accent.]

    contest' (accent on last syllable, verb) / *con'test* (accent on first syllable, noun)
    object' (verb) / *ob'ject*; (noun)
    pervert' (verb) / *per'vert*; (noun)
    contrast' (verb) /*con'trast* (noun)
    content' *(adjective)* /con'tent *(noun)*
    incite' (verb) / *in'sight* (noun)
    below' (adjective)/ *bill'ow* (verb)

(The last two are examples of co-incidental words, with different spelling, but nevertheless accurate. Also, *contest, object, contrast* and *content* also involve a change of initial vowel in articulation of the pairs shown in common pronunciations; however, they are still good illustrations of the principle.)

b) SPANISH

[Again, the apostrophe (') is used to indicate acute (high-pitched) accent.]

    sa'bado ("Saturday")
    pla'tano ("plantain, banana")
    pito'n ("beginning of animal horn; nozzle, spout")

(Table 8-4, cont.)

c) GENERAL- NAMES, COMMON WORDS, ETC. FROM VARIOUS LANGUAGES

Name *Anton* (Anthony)
[Again, the apostrophe (') is used to indicate acute (high-pitched) accent.]

    Anton' (in Russia, Bulgaria, etc.)
    An'ton (in Germany, Austria, etc.)

The third feature addresses the question of why we are discussing stress accents at all in a chapter dealing with tones, and is perhaps the most important feature! We can see why by realizing from the above discussion that a notation for stress accent is highly useful in pronunciation of words in a language one does not know.

Thus, Navlipi must deal with stress accents because a notation for stress accents for non-tonal languages is still pretty much a requirement for any new script.

PART 3: PRESENTATION AND DISCUSSION OF NAVLIPI

8.3 THE TRANSCRIPTION OF TONES IN *NAVLIPI*: USE OF FOUR *ATTRIBUTES* OF TONES

8.3.1 ATTRIBUTES OF TONES IN NAVLIPI

Table 8-2 above is representative enough of the world's tonal languages that it gives a good idea of the variety of tones and tone systems found, and the *common threads* running through them. (It also, incidentally, shows the *Navlipi* and standard Roman transcriptions comparatively.) We can briefly outline these *common threads*, i.e. **ATTRIBUTES**, in the **Table** below.

> **Table 8-5**: *ATTRIBUTES* of tones, as used in *Navlipi*.
>
> 1. **POINT OF ORIGIN**: Firstly, without exception, *all the languages' tones can be represented accurately with just **four (4) points of origin***:
>   - *high,*
>   - *mid,*
>   - *low,*
>   - and a fourth, **"low-mid"**, intermediate between the mid and the low.
>
>   Thus, the point of origin is the first attribute.
>
> 2. **DIRECTION**: If we then start with this *"point of origin"* reference for the tones, they can all further be described as either
>   - *level,*
>   - *rising*
>   - or *falling*.
>
>   This gives us a second attribute.
>
> 3. **EXTENT OF DIRECTION**: For the rising and falling tones, we have a third attribute in the *extent of the rise/fall*. For example, in Cantonese, we have the 6th tone, (rising, low-mid → mid), with a smaller rise, contrasted with the 5th tone, (rising, low-mid → high), with a larger rise.

(Table 8-5, cont.)

4. **_COMBINATION, WHERE APPLICABLE_**: When tones have a *combination* rise/fall or fall/rise, they can invariably be expressed *simply as a combination of individual rising and falling tones*. For example, the 3rd Mandarin tone, as in the word [hao], "good", (falling, rising, mid → low → mid), can simply be expressed as a combination of two tones, (falling mid → low, and rising low → mid). Thus, the fourth attribute is the combination of tones, which can be addressed by simply breaking up the combination into its individual components.

We thus see that, although there may more attributes that tones may possess, they are sufficiently well described by these *four (4) attributes of tones.* These four attributes are exactly what *Navlipi* uses to characterize tones, as seen further below. These attributes are restated in the **Table** below for convenience:

Table 8-6: **FOUR ATTRIBUTES OF TONES USED BY *NAVLIPI***

---

(1) ***POINT OF ORIGIN:***
   Four (4) points are sufficient for representing nearly all languages: *High, mid, low-mid and low.*

(2) ***DIRECTION: Level, Rising or Falling Character:***

(3) ***EXTENT (i.e., of Rise or Fall):***
   If rising or falling, extent of rise or fall: We can conveniently assign just two values for this:
   Small and *large.*

(4) ***COMBINATION, of individual Rising or Falling tones:***
   If having *rising and falling tones*, then can be expressed simply as *combination of individual rising or falling tones separately present in the language already.*

PART 3: PRESENTATION AND DISCUSSION OF NAVLIPI

With the above discussion as basis, we are now in a position to look at *Navlipi*'s system for transcription of tones.

Now in looking again at the 1st attribute, ***point of origin***, in relation to the tone language examples summarized in **Table 2** above, we see further that ***the number of points of origin can be further reduced to just three (3)***, with the *low-mid* and *low* combined into one. This is because *in no language are there more than three levels in the point of origin of tones*. For example, in Cantonese, while the 4th and 6th tones are, respectively, (low-mid to low), (low-mid to mid), there are still only three points of origin: (high), (mid), (low-mid). The same is true of languages with a multitude of tones such as Somali, Yoruba and even Hagu (with eight (8) tones): All of these have no more than three points of origin, which are in most cases described simply as (high), (mid), (low). Thus, our reduction of the points of origin from four to three is quite justified.

Looking now at the third attribute, ***extent of rise***, which applies to rising and falling tones, we see again, based on a perusal of all major tone languages, that ***just two (2) values, small and large, for the extent of rise/fall attribute are sufficient*** to cover all major tone languages of the world. In fact, in a majority of the tone languages, just one value is sufficient to describe the extent of rise or fall. Only in a few languages does one find more than one value. An example of more than one value is, again, Cantonese: The 5th tone is (rising, low-mid to high), whereas the 6th tone is (rising, low-mid to mid).

Chapter 8: Tones, Tonemes and Ictus (Stress) Accents

We briefly summarize the two *reductions/simplifications* we have enunciated above in the **Table** below.

Table 8-7: REDUCTIONS/SIMPLIFICATIONS EFFECTED FOR TONES IN *NAVLIPI*

- ***Points of origin of tones are reduced to just three (3)***:
  - high
  - mid
  - low and low-mid

- ***Extent of rise in rising or falling tones is reduced to just two (2)***:
  - Small
  - Large

8.3.2 DESCRIPTION OF THE TONE TRANSCRIPTION SYSTEM OF *NAVLIPI*

Based on these further simplifications then, *Navlipi* is able to arrive at a simple yet comprehensive, and easily distinguishable system of transcription of tones. This system still *remains very easy to transcribe, via print, cursive and keyboard*.

This system has been summarized in the extensive discussion above. It is also represented in the *NAVLIPI SUMMARY TABLES* at the beginning of this book. These *TABLES* USE THE hypothetical, monosyllabic word, **[paad]** (its vowel to be pronounced like the [*a*] in English *father*), as an example for the tone and accent representations.

As is seen from these *TABLES*, as the ***first basis*** *of its orthography of tones*, Navlipi uses ***post-ops***. Thus, cumbersome diacritics ("accent marks"), and their accompanying problems (slowing down of cursive transcription, difficulty in recognition or distinction, cluttered appearance), are dispensed with.

PART 3: PRESENTATION AND DISCUSSION OF NAVLIPI

As the ***second basis*** *of its orthography*, *Navlipi* **uses the level tones as the foundation for orthography of all other tones**. The level tones (low, mid and high) are represented very intuitively, in degree of vertical character, by, respectively: **(1)** A horizontal bar; **(2)** a 45° slanted bar identical to a French acute accent; and **(3)** a vertical bar.

Rising and falling character are then represented by *small hooks* at the end of this (horizontal, slanted or vertical) bar: A rising hook (facing counter-clockwise) represents a rising tone, a falling hook (facing clockwise) a falling tone.

The ***extent of rise or fall*** (remember, per the simplifications above, we have to represent only *two* degrees, large and small) can then be represented in a straightforward manner by the *length* of the hook, as seen in the *TABLES*.

In ***cursive*** rendition the *Navlipi* orthography of tones is even simpler, as seen in the *TABLES*. The vertical bar of the (high, level) tone is rendered just like an uncrossed *t*, perhaps slightly taller. The hooks to indicate rising and falling tones originating at the high level are then easily rendered, much like crossing a *t*, except that the cross is made towards the left side of the *t* (rising tone) or right side of the *t* (falling tone). And once again, the extent of the rise or fall is simply represented by the length of this hook or cross, remembering again that we are required to represent only two lengths, short and long, for small and large rise/fall.

This author has run repeated ***recognizability*** tests, contrasting this cursive rendering with the regular letter *t*, using three undergraduate students at a major university in New Jersey, USA, in 2006, and found a 97% recognizability rate (results to be reported elsewhere).

For the cursive rendering of the (mid, level) tone, we use a post-op that comprises the letter *x* with a dot on top. The bar is again very easy to render, much like the dotting of an *i*. At the same time, it very clearly distinguishes this post-op from the regular letter *x*. To indicate a falling or rising tone originating at this, mid- level, i.e. (falling, mid to low or to low-mid) or (rising, mid to high), the cross of the x can be rendered with a long "foot" (falling tone) or "head" (rising tone), as seen in the *TABLES*.

The *TABLES* also show *alternate renderings* for the tones originating at the *mid* level, for both print and cursive renderings. The alternate for print, the ***letter x*** modified with various dots or hooks, as seen in the *TABLES,* is simply taken from the cursive rendering.

Chapter 8: Tones, Tonemes and Ictus (Stress) Accents

This author came up with these alternate renderings first, but then found them somewhat confusing and less easily recognized than the "standard" ones shown in the *TABLES*.

For the cursive rendering of the tones originating at the *low* level, what is used is simply a direct cursive analog of the print version, i.e. the horizontal bar. There is one small difference, however, as seen in the *TABLES*: In cursive, the hooks indicating rising or falling tone are placed at close to the end but not the very end of the horizontal bar, whereas in the print version, they are placed of course at the very end of the bar.

As seen from tones represented in the *TABLES* and the discussion above, the *recognizability* and *intuitive nature* of the *Navlipi* tonal orthography set it apart, in this author's opinion, from the IPA or other tonal transcriptions. However, what most clearly distinguishes the *Navlipi* transcription, and, again in this author's opinion, gives it an overwhelming advantage over other transcriptions, is the ease, simplicity and recognizability of the *cursive* rendering.

PART 3: PRESENTATION AND DISCUSSION OF NAVLIPI

8.4 EXAMPLES OF TRANSCRIPTIONS OF A VARIETY OF TONAL LANGUAGES IN *NAVLIPI*

Transcriptions in *Navlipi* of full passages in several tonal languages are given in **PART 1 (*NAVLIPI* SUMMARY TABLES)** and also discussed in a separate chapter later in this book devoted exclusively to language transcriptions. These languages include, e.g., Mandarin, the world's most widely spoken language as of 2005, and Vietnamese.

CHAPTER 9.
PHONEMIC CONDENSATION AND CLASSES OF PHONEMIC CONDENSATES USED IN *NAVLIPI*

TABLE OF CONTENTS

9.1 SIGNIFICANCE AND PRINCIPLES OF PHONEMIC CONDENSATION 429

9.2 SUMMARY TABLE OF PHONEMIC CONDENSATES 429

9.3 ASPIRATE/NON-ASPIRATE PHONEMIC CONDENSATE, PCON-1, = PO-1 429

9.4 (UNVOICED + VOICED) PHONEMIC CONDENSATE, PCON-2, = PO-6 429

9.5 (STOP + FRICATIVE) PHONEMIC CONDENSATE, PCON-3, =PO-12 430

9.6 (STOP + FORWARD FRICATIVE) PHONEMIC CONDENSATE, PCON-4, =PO-13 .. 430

9.7 (STOP + SEMIVOWEL) PHONEMIC CONDENSATE, PCON-5, =PO-18 430

9.8 (SEMIVOWEL + FORWARD FRICATIVE) PHONEMIC CONDENSATE, PCON-6, DIGRAPH 430

9.9 (STOP + FLAP) PHONEMIC CONDENSATE, PCON-7, DIGRAPH 431

9.10 THE IMPORTANT PHONEMIC CONDENSATE FOR (FLAP + TRILL + SEMIVOWEL) IN APICO-ALVEOLO-DENTAL, CENTRAL ARTITION (THE "COMMON R" PHONEME), PCON-8 432

9.11 THE RARE PHONEMIC CONDENSATE FOR (RETROFLEX) ARTITION, (FLAP + TRILL + SEMIVOWEL) PHONOCHROME, PCON-9 433

9.12 ([X] - [R]) COMBINATION: PHONEMIC CONDENSATE COMBINING PCON-8 (FOR THE COMMON /R/-PHONEME) WITH THE UVULAR FRICATIVE, PCON-10, REPRESENTED AS A DIGRAPH 433

PART 3: PRESENTATION AND DISCUSSION OF NAVLIPI

9.13 ALVEOLAR-R-L COMBINATION, PCON-11: PHONEMIC CONDENSATE COMBINING PCON-8 WITH THE (APICO-ALVEOLO-DENTAL LATERAL) ARTITION (L-SOUND).. 434

9.14 RETROFLEX-R-L COMBINATION: PHONEMIC CONDENSATE COMBINING RETROFLEX CENTRAL SEMIVOWEL (R-SOUND) WITH RETROFLEX LATERAL SEMIVOWEL (L-SOUND), PCON-12... 435

9.15 ALVEOLAR-R-L-N COMBINATION, PCON-13: PHONEMIC CONDENSATE COMBINING PCON-8 WITH THE (APICO-ALVEOLO-DENTAL LATERAL) ARTITION (L-SOUND), AND THE (APICO-ALVEOLO-DENTAL NASAL STOP) (N-SOUND)................. 435

9.16 RETROFLEX-R-L-N COMBINATION: PHONEMIC CONDENSATE COMBINING RETROFLEX CENTRAL SEMIVOWEL (R-SOUND) WITH RETROFLEX LATERAL SEMIVOWEL (L-SOUND) AND THE RETROFLEX NASAL STOP (N-SOUND), PCON-14 436

9.17 SIGNIFICANCE OF R-L-N EQUIVALENCES, EMBODIED IN PCON #S 11, 12, 13 AND 14, TO PHONETIC SHIFTS AND HISTORICAL LANGUAGE DEVELOPMENT 436

9.18 THE IMPORTANT PHONEMIC CONDENSATE DENOTING A "MOBILE, GENERIC" VOWEL, PCON-15, =PO-19... 438

9.19 THE RARE (NASAL + NON-NASAL) PHONEMIC CONDENSATE, PCON-16, =PO-9 438

9.20 PCON-17: THE "UNIVERSAL R", TO BE RARELY USED....................................... 438

Chapter 9: Phonemic Condensation and Classes of Phonemic Condensates Used in Navlipi

9.1 SIGNIFICANCE AND PRINCIPLES OF *PHONEMIC CONDENSATION*

The significance and principles of phonemic condensation and the need for it have been discussed at length in several earlier chapters, to which reference is made.

In this chapter, we use the abbreviations of earlier chapters:

- *PO-nn* signifies *Post-op #nn*, e.g. PO-1.
- *PCON-nn* similarly signifies *Phonemic Condensate #nn*, e.g. PCON-1.

9.2 SUMMARY TABLE OF PHONEMIC CONDENSATES

A Summary Table of phonemic condensates appears in the *NAVLIPI* SUMMARY TABLES, in **PART 1** of this book. The reader is referred to this for all discussions in the present chapter.

We now discuss each phonemic condensate in turn.

9.3 ASPIRATE/NON-ASPIRATE PHONEMIC CONDENSATE, PCON-1, = PO-1

This phonemic condensate has been dealt with at some length in the chapter dealing with post-ops), to which reference is made. It uses a post-op, **PO-1**.

9.4 (UNVOICED + VOICED) PHONEMIC CONDENSATE, PCON-2, = PO-6

This phonemic condensate has been dealt with at some length in a later chapter, to which reference is made. It uses a post-op, **PO-6**.

PART 3: PRESENTATION AND DISCUSSION OF NAVLIPI

9.5 (STOP + FRICATIVE) PHONEMIC CONDENSATE, PCON-3, =PO-12

This phonemic condensate has been dealt with at some length in a later chapter, to which reference is made. It uses a post-op, **PO-**16.

9.6 (STOP + FORWARD FRICATIVE) PHONEMIC CONDENSATE, PCON-4, =PO-13

This phonemic condensate has been dealt with at some length in a later chapter, to which reference is made. It uses a post-op, **PO-14**.

9.7 (STOP + SEMIVOWEL) PHONEMIC CONDENSATE, PCON-5, =PO-18

This phonemic condensate has been dealt with at some length in a later chapter, to which reference is made. It uses a post-op, **PO-19**.

9.8 (SEMIVOWEL + FORWARD FRICATIVE) PHONEMIC CONDENSATE, PCON-6, DIGRAPH

This phonemic condensate is represented very simply as a *digraph of its component phones*.

For example, the very commonly found phonemic condensate which is a combination of the phones [w] (the semivowel) and [v] (its forward fricative), can be represented simply as {vw} in *Navlipi*. This condensate is common in Hindi/Urdu, where [v] and [w] have the same phonemic value and are freely interchanged without effect. This condensate has been discussed at length in several earlier chapters.

Chapter 9: Phonemic Condensation and Classes of Phonemic Condensates Used in Navlipi

9.9 (STOP + FLAP) PHONEMIC CONDENSATE, PCON-7, DIGRAPH

This phonemic condensate is also represented very simply as a ***digraph*** *of its component phones*.

For example, the phonemic condensate comprising the alveolar, unvoiced stop (rendered as {tt} in *Navlipi*) and its corresponding flap, the "common *r*", are rendered in *Navlipi* simply as {ttr}.

This condensate is rather rare. It is found, e.g., in American English, in the pronunciation of *hitter*, where the highlighted phone can be pronounced either as the alveolar, unvoiced stop or its corresponding flap, which is more common, without any phonemic significance, i.e. without changing the meaning or nuance of the word. The alveolar flap is basically equivalent to the alveolar central, i.e. the common *r*-sound, [r]. Thus, as noted above, this phonemic condensate is rendered in *Navlipi* as {ttr}.

This condensate is also found in Indian languages, where, e.g. the retroflex voiced, unaspirated stop (ड in Dewanaagari, rendered as {d} in *Navlipi*) and its corresponding flap (ड़ in Dewanaagari, rendered as {d.} in in *Navlipi*) are freely interchanged, also without any phonemic significance.

The interchange from the stop to the flap, in both American English and Indian languages, occurs especially in rapid speech. The mode of articulation in slow or accurate speech however is the stop, not the flap.

It is important to note here however that *this phonemic condensate is to be rarely used in Navlipi. This stems from the need for practicality*, a foundation of the "practical phonemics" aspect of *Navlipi*.

Thus, the very two examples from American English and Indian languages cited in the previous paragraph will *not* use this phonemic condensate, for *practical* reasons. Rather, *Navlipi* will use the parent stops, rendered in *Navlipi* as {tt} and {d} respectively in these examples. Again, this is the mode of articulation in slow or accurate speech.

Thus, we have cited this phonemic condensate here for purposes of completeness only.

PART 3: PRESENTATION AND DISCUSSION OF NAVLIPI

9.10 THE IMPORTANT PHONEMIC CONDENSATE FOR (FLAP + TRILL + SEMIVOWEL) IN APICO-ALVEOLO-DENTAL, CENTRAL ARTITION (THE "COMMON r" PHONEME), PCON-8

This very important phonemic condensate represents the "common *r-sound*" phoneme in the vast majority of the world's languages.

As is well known and as the reader will by now appreciate, in nearly all languages, this phoneme can be articulated as a ***flap/tap***, as a ***trill*** (most common) or occasionally as a ***semi-vowel***, without affecting its phonemic value. These three articulations nevertheless represent very different phones. (In some languages, e.g. French (Parisian pronunciation) and standard (Hochdeutsch) German, a fourth articulation, the velar/uvular fricative, is added to this phoneme; this is dealt with further below).

The reader may notice that we have indicated an *apico-alveolo-dental* artition. The *apico*- portion of this of course indicates that the apex of the tongue is what is making the contact. The alveolar and dental artitions are combined in the term *alveolo-dental* for an important reason: *The common r-sound is articulated in most of the world's languages interchangeably between the alveolar and dental positions, again without phonemic effect*, i.e. as part of the same phoneme. Thus, in consideration of the importance that *Navlipi* places on *practical phonemics*, we combine these two very distinct artitions for the purposes of this phonemic condensate.

To retain recognizability for this phonemic condensate, one must necessarily use some variation of the Roman letter *r* for it. And we simply use the "standing r", exactly as it appears in most lower-case print, as opposed to the cursive or script r (*𝓇*).

Thus, this phonemic condensate encompasses the common articulations of the /r/- phoneme of most languages, i.e. *flap/tap*, *trill* and *semi-vowel*. This is yet another example of *Navlipi*'s "practical phonemics" in action!

Chapter 9: Phonemic Condensation and Classes of Phonemic Condensates Used in Navlipi

9.11 THE RARE PHONEMIC CONDENSATE FOR (RETROFLEX) ARTITION, (FLAP + TRILL + SEMIVOWEL) PHONOCHROME, PCON-9

For the sake of completeness, we must include a phonemic condensate corresponding to **PCON-8** (the common /r/-phoneme) for the *retroflex* artition.

Although we designate this as **PCON-9**, since it is so rare and has no phonemic significance in any known world language, *Navlipi* does not bother to come up with a separate letter for it. (The retroflex semivowel, as in the common American pronunciation of the letter *r*, has its own glyph.)

9.12 ([x] - [r]) COMBINATION: PHONEMIC CONDENSATE COMBINING PCON-8 (FOR THE COMMON /r/-PHONEME) WITH THE UVULAR FRICATIVE, PCON-10, REPRESENTED AS A DIGRAPH

As noted in Section **9.10** above, in addition to the three widely used phonochromes for the alveolo-dental /r/-phoneme (*flap/tap, trill, semivowel*), a fourth one, the *velar/uvular fricative*, is used in such languages as French (Parisian pronunciation) and German (standard pronunciation Hachdeutsch). This is the Parision "uvular r". Evidently, this phone has an artition that is radically different from the alveolo-dental, which as students of French know, is a relatively recent development.

To represent the addition of this phone to the letter for the /r/-phoneme that *Navlipi* has already come up with in Section **9.10**, i.e. **PCON-8**, it is easiest to *simply add the letter for the phone to PCON-8* and create a digraph, **{xr}**, which we designate **PCON-10**.

PCON-10 is very distinct: There is almost no possibility of its confusion with a separate, individual articulation of its two components, $\{x\} + \{r^o\}$, since these two elements almost never occur together in the relevant languages (e.g. French, German). On the extremely rare occasions that they might occur together, whether they represent the condensate **PCON-10** or its individual components can easily be picked out from the context in the reading of the relevant words.

PART 3: PRESENTATION AND DISCUSSION OF NAVLIPI

9.13 ALVEOLAR-*r-l* COMBINATION, PCON-11: PHONEMIC CONDENSATE COMBINING PCON-8 WITH THE (APICO-ALVEOLO-DENTAL *LATERAL*) ARTITION (*l*-SOUND)

This phonemic condensate finds use notably in Japanese, as well as some southern Chinese and South-East Asian languages. It is what Westerners erroneously perceive as the "*r-l* confusion" of native speakers of Japanese and some Chinese languages.

For this phonemic condensate, we are unable to use a digraph such as {*lr*}, for the obvious reason that {l} and {r}, *do* occur together in many languages, and so the possibility of confusion is large. We instead revert to the "overstrike" or "strikeout", which in *print* is rendered {ɍ}. In *cursive*, this is easily rendered as a bar placed in the middle of the stem of the letter *r*, much like crossing a *t*.

As the discussions on phonemic condensates in earlier parts of this book have dealt with in some detail, in all the languages to which this phonemic condensate applies, it is a case of a genuine phonemic condensate, not just an absence of one or the other of its component phones.

Thus, in Japanese, the official position is that the *l*-sounds simply do not exist. Yet, *l*-sounds of other languages are invariably confounded in Japanese *only* with the /*r*/-phoneme and with no other phone or phoneme. And some Japanese speakers, especially those having knowledge of other languages, freely interchange *r*- and *l*- sounds. We defined such a phenomenon as a ***galatophone*** elsewhere, i.e. the [*r*] is a galatophone for the [*l*] in Japanese.

The use of this phonemic condensate in Japanese differs from its use in southern Chinese and South-East Asian languages. In Japanese, the primary articulation is that of an ***r***-sound, whereas in the other languages in question, the primary articulation is that of an ***l***-sound.

As the above examples illustrate, the "*r-l-n* confusion" at the same artition is not unique to Japanese, but rather, is a common confusion. It appears to indicate that, at some stage in many languages, *r*- and *l*- and *n*– sounds at the same artition (usually alveolar or dental) *represented the same phoneme*. This subject is discussed in more detail in another chapter. Thus, phonemic condensates such as **PCON-11** have some historical significance as well.

9.14 RETROFLEX-*r*-*l* COMBINATION: PHONEMIC CONDENSATE COMBINING RETROFLEX CENTRAL SEMIVOWEL (*r*-SOUND) WITH RETROFLEX LATERAL SEMIVOWEL (*l*-SOUND), PCON-12

This direct analogue of **PCON-11** is treated for completeness. It also combines the *r*- and *l*- sounds, but in the *retroflex* rather than the alveolo-dental artition.

This phonemic condensate is actually found to a limited extent in some accents of Tamil and Maraathi.

The *print* and *cursive* renditions of the phonemic condensate are straightforward, as seen in the *Navlipi* SUMMARY TABLES. For the cursive rendition, again, the bar would be effectuated much like crossing a *t*.

9.15 ALVEOLAR-*r*-*l*-*n* COMBINATION, PCON-13: PHONEMIC CONDENSATE COMBINING PCON-8 WITH THE (APICO-ALVEOLO-DENTAL LATERAL) ARTITION (*l*-SOUND), AND THE (APICO-ALVEOLO-DENTAL NASAL STOP) (*n*-SOUND)

This phonemic condensate, combining the alveolo-dental *r*-, *l*- and *n*- sounds, would find very rare use. It is again included in *Navlipi* primarily for reasons of completeness. Its *print* and *cursive* versions are shown in the *NAVLIPI* SUMMARY TABLES. As seen, these transcriptions are analogous to those for **PCON-8**, except that an additional "bar" is introduced. In cursive, this bar would again be written just like crossing a *t*.

9.16 RETROFLEX-*r-l-n* COMBINATION: PHONEMIC CONDENSATE COMBINING RETROFLEX CENTRAL SEMIVOWEL (*r*-SOUND) WITH RETROFLEX LATERAL SEMIVOWEL (*l*-SOUND) AND THE RETROFLEX NASAL STOP (*n*-SOUND), PCON-14

This direct analogue of **PCON-13** and **PCON-12** is again treated for completeness only. Its application would be very rare. It combines the *r-*, *l-* and *n-* sounds, but in the *retroflex* rather than the alveolo-dental artition.

The *print* and *cursive* renditions of the phonemic condensate are straightforward, as seen in the *NAVLIPI* SUMMARY TABLES. For the cursive rendition, again, the bars would be effectuated much like crossing a *t*.

9.17 SIGNIFICANCE OF *r-l-n* EQUIVALENCES, EMBODIED IN PCON #S 11, 12, 13 AND 14, TO PHONETIC SHIFTS AND HISTORICAL LANGUAGE DEVELOPMENT

The phonemic condensate **PCON-11** and **PCON-13** also have important significance in *phonetic shifts* between languages within a language family and even within a single language. Such shifts are found even in the Indo-European languages and also in common, everyday corruptions in pronunciation of one language by speakers of another. There is an abundance of cognate words in which centrals (*r*-sounds) are replaced by corresponding laterals (*l*-sounds) of the same artition. Sometimes, these words exist in the same language (e.g. the Sanskrit examples below). We cite here just a few examples, in the **Table** below:

Chapter 9: Phonemic Condensation and Classes of Phonemic Condensates Used in Navlipi

Table 9-1: *EXAMPLES ILLUSTRATING THE QUITE COMMON NATURE OF THE [r-l-n] PHONETIC SHIFTS AND EQUIVALENCES, WITHIN MANY WORLD LANGUAGES AND LANGUAGE FAMILIES*

- *Spanish/Portuguese*: Spanish *playa*, Portuguese *praia*, "beach".

- *English/French:* Title/titre.

- *Sanskrit*: *Ruchi, luchi* (both with connotations of "light", cognate with Latin *luce* etc.); *roma, loma*, "hair".

- *Sanskrit/German*: Sanskrit verbal root *wr* "to choose", German *wahlen*, "to select, choose"

- *Sansrkit/Classical-Greek/Latin*: Sanskrit root *suur*, Latin/Greek *sol,* "sun".

- *Sanskrit/Other I-E Languages*: Sanskrit *wrk*, other I-E *wlk* and variants thereof, "wolf".

- *Modern Hindi/English*: Hindi corruptions of borrowed English words: *Angrezi, Angrez* for *"English", "Englishman"*. *Lambar* for "*number*", *limlet* for lemonade.

- *Cantonese*: Pronunciations of the proper name *Lai*, articulated both as *Rai* and *Lai*.

- *Hindi/Maraathi*: Maraathi *limba*, "lemon", probably of Portuguese borrowing, becomes Hindi *nimbu*.

9.18 THE IMPORTANT PHONEMIC CONDENSATE DENOTING A "MOBILE, GENERIC" VOWEL, PCON-15, =PO-19

This phonemic condensate has been dealt with at some length in a later chapter, to which reference is made. It uses a post-op, **PO-19**.

9.19 THE RARE (NASAL + NON-NASAL) PHONEMIC CONDENSATE, PCON-16, =PO-9

This phonemic condensate has been dealt with at some length in a later chapter, to which reference is made. It uses a post-op, **PO-9**.

9.20 PCON-17: THE "UNIVERSAL R", TO BE RARELY USED

This phonemic condensate, to be rarely used in *Navlipi*, is devised purely to be able to accommodate a so-called "universal R", in case there are people who do not wish to be bothered with the various distinctions of *r*-sounds made in this chapter! Its glyph is simply the upper-case Roman R, i.e. ***R***.

CHAPTER 10.
NAVLIPI KEYBOARDING USING THE *QWERTY, AZERTY* OR OTHER COMMON KEYBOARDS

TABLE OF CONTENTS

10.1 IMPORTANT FEATURES OF *NAVLIPI* KEYBOARDING.......................... 441

10.1.1 KEYBOARD WILL BE LANGUAGE SPECIFIC (FOR BROAD GROUPS OF LANGUAGES), REDUCING NUMBER OF KEYS NEEDED 441
    10.1.1.1 LANGUAGE-SPECIFIC KEYBOARDS FOR BROAD GROUPS OF LANGUAGES *441*
    10.1.1.2 ILLUSTRATION OF LANGUAGE-SPECIFICITY *442*
    10.1.1.3 LANGUAGE-SPECIFIC KEYBOARDS DRASTICALLY REDUCE NUMBER OF GLYPHS, AND HENCE KEYS *443*
    10.1.1.4 REASONING BEHIND LANGUAGE GROUPINGS FOR SOME OF THE LANGUAGE-SPECIFIC KEYBOARDS... *443*
10.1.2 NUMERICAL NOTATION (MATRIX NOTATION) USED FOR KEYBOARD KEYS IN NAVLIPI, AND FOUR PART KEY NOTATION ON EACH KEY (FOR NORMAL, SHIFT, CONTROL AND ALTERNATE POSITIONS), ILLUSTRATED HERE FOR THE QWERTY KEYBOARD 445
    10.1.2.1 NAVLIPI'S MATRIX NOTATION FOR THE KEYBOARD AND KEY NOTATION FOR INDIVIDUAL KEYS.. *445*
    10.1.2.2 EXAMPLES *449*
    10.1.2.3 FOUR-PART NOTATION AND MARKINGS FOR EACH KEY *450*
10.1.3 CONCERNS WITH THE [CTRL], [ALT] AND OTHER KEYS IN RELATION TO UNIX (LINUX), WINDOWS®, OTHER OPERATING SYSTEMS, MOST WORD PROCESSORS, AND OTHER PROGRAMS 450
10.1.4 ONLY MAJOR PHYSICAL CHANGES IN OTHERWISE NEARLY UNDISTURBED QWERTY, AZERTY, OR OTHER COMMON KEYBOARD: MUCH SMALLER SPACE BAR, MUCH LARGER ALT BARS, AND NON-NUMERIC PART OF NUMERIC (NUM LOCK) KEYS CHANGED 452

PART 3: PRESENTATION AND DISCUSSION OF NAVLIPI

10.1.5 TWO OPTIONS FOR IMPLEMENTATION OF NAVLIPI ON THE KEYBOARD, AND REGISTRATION OF NAVLIPI WITH UNICODE 454

10.2 LIST OF KEYS WITH MAJOR CHANGES 455

10.2.1 MAJOR REASSIGNMENTS 455
10.2.2 MAIN (I.E. NOT NUM LOCK) NUMBER KEYS (ALSO USED FOR TONES, SEE LATER) 457
10.2.3 MAJOR POST-OP KEYS AND KEYS WITH HIGH FREQUENCY OF USE AND KEYS 458
10.2.4 CENTRAL ("R") KEY AND CENTRAL GLYPHS, INCLUDING PHONEMIC CONDENSATES 459
10.2.5 MAJOR LATERAL ("L") KEY 462
10.2.6 MAJOR VELAR KEYS 463
10.2.7 MAJOR PALATAL AND SIBILANT KEYS 466
10.2.8 MAJOR RETROFLEX, ALVEOLAR AND DENTAL PLOSIVE ("T-D") KEYS 467
10.2.9 MAJOR BILABIAL KEYS 473
10.2.10 MAJOR NASAL ("M-N") KEYS 477
10.2.11 MAJOR STANDARD-SEMIVOWEL KEYS 478
10.2.12 MAJOR VOWEL KEYS 479
10.2.13 SPECIAL NON-VOWEL KEYS 480
10.2.14 POST-OP KEYS FOR CLICKS, IMPLOSIVES AND EJECTIVES, THE "MODIFIED-Z" KEYS 481
10.2.15 KEYS FOR VERY RARE POST-OPS 481
10.2.16 TONE KEYS (SEE ALSO NUMBER KEYS, ABOVE) 482

10.3 INVENTORY OF LEFTOVER, UNUSED/AVAILABLE KEYS (FOR POTENTIAL FUTURE USE) 490

10.4 FURTHER NOTES ON PRACTICAL USE OF THE *NAVLIPI* KEYBOARD(S) 491

10.5 THE KEYBOARD PRESENTATION IN PART 1 (*NAVLIPI SUMMARY TABLES*) 492

Chapter 10: Navlipi Keyboarding Using the QWERTY, AZERTY or Other Common Keyboards

10.1 IMPORTANT FEATURES OF *NAVLIPI* KEYBOARDING

10.1.1 KEYBOARD WILL BE *LANGUAGE SPECIFIC* (FOR BROAD GROUPS OF LANGUAGES), REDUCING NUMBER OF KEYS NEEDED

10.1.1.1 Language-Specific Keyboards for Broad Groups of Languages

The *Navlipi* keyboard is **language-specific**, for broad *groups* of languages.

These groups encompass languages which have similar phonologies. For reasons that will become clearer in the sequel, *some* of these groups might be, for example:

- Hindi(/Urdu)/-Spanish/-Indonesian.
- English/French/German/Other-European-Languages.
- Arabic.
- Yoruba/Igbo.
- Mandarin/Cantonese.
- South-African (incorporating the *click*-phones).

This **language-specificity** very significantly *reduces the number of separate and distinct keys required*. Additionally, it is important to note that *Navlipi* keyboarding is **platform-independent.**

As a by-product, language-specificity also reduces the need to use separate keys for common post-ops, although these are still provided.

The language-specific keyboards would function much like *main fonts* and *subset fonts* function in common word processors such as Microsoft Word or Corel Word Perfect. Thus, e.g., in Microsoft Word, one has the Arial font and its subsets, Narrow, Black and Unicode. If one selects more specialized fonts, e.g. through the Insert>Symbols option, one has access, e.g., to Times New Roman font and many "sub-fonts" thereunder, e.g. In the Navlipi keyboards, one would similarly have, e.g., the English/French/German keyboard with a subset for American English; one would not need other subsets, since the

PART 3: PRESENTATION AND DISCUSSION OF NAVLIPI

442

phonologies of English, French and German are very similar, and the phonologies unique to French and German, e.g. the phonemic condensate corresponding to (uvular fricative + rolled-central) ([x] + [r]), could remain on the keyboard, simply not being used in English.

10.1.1.2 Illustration of Language-Specificity

As an illustration of how the *language-specificity* works, we can cite the following brief *examples*:

- The **p** key in the Hindi/Spanish... keyboard would print as **p**. However, in the English/-French/-German/-etc. keyboard, it would print as **p$_o$**, indicating that it is a phonemic condensate of the unaspirated and aspirated stops (i.e., [p] + [ph$_o$]).

- In the Arabic keyboard, this same **p** key would print as **b$_\infty$**, indicating that it is now a phonemic condensate of the voiced and unvoiced stops, but with preferred articulation as [b]. Alternatively, this key may not be used at all in Arabic, reflecting the true absence of the [p] phone in standard Arabic (but not in some Arabic dialects). And of course, the **b** key would also print in the Arabic keyboard as **b$_\infty$**.

- In Cantonese, this **[p]** key would print as **p$_\infty$**, once again indicating that it is now a phonemic condensate of the voiced and unvoiced stops, but now with preferred articulation as [p].

- The **[ALT+k]** key in the Hindi/Spanish... keyboard would print as the velar unvoiced aspirated stop, **kh$_o$**. However, in the Arabic keyboard, it would print as the uvular unvoiced stop, **k.**, the Arabic "*qaaf*". (Indeed, the ALT key would be used in the case of plosives in the Hindi/Spanish... keyboard to represent *all* aspirated sounds; e.g. ALT+d, ALT+b, ALT+t etc. would represent, respectively, the *Navlipi* **dh$_o$, bh$_o$, th$_o$**, etc..)

- The **[r]** key would print in the Hindi/Spanish keyboard as **r**, indicating the alveolar flap/-tap/trill of Hindi and Spanish. However, in the English/-etc. keyboard, this same key would print as **r$_0$**, indicating the alveolar semivowel. In the American *subset* of the English/-etc. keyboard, this would print as ɻ, indicating the retroflex semivowel of American pronunciation.

Chapter 10: Navlipi Keyboarding Using the QWERTY, AZERTY or Other Common Keyboards

10.1.1.3 Language-specific Keyboards Drastically Reduce Number of Glyphs, and Hence Keys

Language-specific keyboard subsets also serve another important purpose, in that they also cut down drastically on the number of *glyphs* required, in addition to the number of *keys*. Thus, for instance, the many click phones will be rarely be used in any subset except the South-African. Hence, it is not necessary to incorporate these into the main keyboard, just to have them available in the South-African subset keyboard.

10.1.1.4 Reasoning Behind Language Groupings for Some of the Language-Specific Keyboards

Hindi(/Urdu)/Spanish/Malay... etc. keyboard: This is distinguished by having true *dental* stops (**[t]**, **[d]**) as opposed to *alveolar* stops, and a general preference for the *flap or trilled form of the central phone* (the "r-sound") rather than its semivowel form. To accommodate the Hindi/North-Indian component, this keyboard has a strong presence of aspirated phones, which are usually represented as (ALT+key) (e.g. $[ph_o]$ = (ALT+P)). This keyboard can be used for a wide variety of languages, for example Swaahili, because Arabic borrowings in the Swaahili have lost their uvular components.

English/French/German/-OtherWest-European-languages keyboard: This is distinguished by having *alveolar* stops as opposed to dental stops, a general preference for the *semivowel form of the central phone* ("r-sound") rather than the flap or trilled form, and, most importantly *absence of phonemic distinction between aspirated and unaspirated unvoiced phones* such as [p] and [t]. Thus, in this keyboard, the common unvoiced plosives are represented as aspirate/non-aspirate phonemic condensates; e.g. the unvoiced bilabial stop is $[p_o]$.

Tamil-South-Indian keyboard: This is applicable to South Indian languages other than Tamil (Kannadaa, Malayaalam, Telaguu (Telugu), Toda, Sinhala) as well, in their standard pronunciation, although the orthography of these non-Tamil languages would appear to indicate otherwise. It is distinguished by *absence of phonemic distinction of aspirated/-unaspirated stops* and *use of several retroflex phones not found in other languages*.

Arabic keyboard: This is distinguished by *strong presence of uvular phones* (stops as well as fricatives) and *absence of voiced or unvoiced counterparts of certain phones* (e.g. bilabial, velar). The "pharyngealized" ("faucal") phones are universally represented by

PART 3: PRESENTATION AND DISCUSSION OF NAVLIPI

444

the (ALT+*key*) in this keyboard.

Mandarin/Cantonese keyboard: This is distinguished by *absence of phonemic distinction between voiced and unvoiced forms of some common phones* (e.g. [p], [b]) and, more importantly, just by the *four* distinct *tones* of Mandarin and *six* distinct *tones* of standard Cantonese. Both Mandarin and Cantonese are accommodated. Thus, e.g., the **b** key prints as **b$_\infty$**, accommodating Mandarin's [p] and [b] phones which form a phonemic condensate usually articulated as [b], and is expected to use primarily by Mandarin. On the other hand, the **p** key prints as **p$_\infty$**, accommodating the same phones in Cantonese which form a phonemic condensate usually articulated as [p]; it in turn is expected to be use primarily by Cantonese. Some aspirate and non-aspirate phones (e.g. the alveolar stops) are also distinguished, as in North Indian languages, since they are phonemically distinct in Mandarin and Cantonese. It is noted that the **t** and **d** keys print as alveolar stops, as in the *English/West-European* languages keyboard, but with the important distinction that they print as *(unvoiced+voiced) phonemic condensates*, having the post-op for this phonemic condensate, i.e. the subscripted infinity sign [$_\infty$].

Other Chinese languages keyboards: These are not presented in this book for space reasons, but the extension from the Mandarin/Cantonese keyboard is straightforward. One may expect the ***Chinese-Min keyboard*** to be a major one, accommodating important Min languages such as Fujienese/Hokka.

Yoruba/Igbo/-Other-West-African-Languages keyboard: This is distinguished by accommodation of the *several tones of West Yoruba* (again represented by the **(2)(n)S** keys, and, more importantly, *representation of the <u>velarized</u> stops*, e.g. the ([k] + [p]) etc. (See discussion elsewhere in this book.)

Turkish/Irish/Japanese keyboard: This is distinguished by presence of sounds that are phonemically distinguished uniquely in these languages, e.g. the *uvular nasal* (Japanese), by the opposition between dental and palatal laterals ("l-sounds") (Turkish) and by the opposition between dental and alveolar laterals (Irish).

South-African Languages keyboard: This is distinguished by *presence of all the <u>click</u> phones*. Use expected to be less wide than other language keyboards.

Chapter 10: Navlipi Keyboarding Using the QWERTY, AZERTY or Other Common Keyboards

445

10.1.2 NUMERICAL NOTATION (MATRIX NOTATION) USED FOR KEYBOARD KEYS IN NAVLIPI, AND FOUR PART KEY NOTATION ON EACH KEY (FOR NORMAL, SHIFT, CONTROL AND ALTERNATE POSITIONS), ILLUSTRATED HERE FOR THE QWERTY KEYBOARD

10.1.2.1 Navlipi's Matrix Notation for the Keyboard and Key Notation for Individual Keys

For facility in addressing the keyboard, *Navlipi* uses a very simple *numerical matrix notation* for the keyboard. This is illustrated, for the *QWERTY* keyboard, in **Fig. 10-1** below. For convenience, we confine our discussion to the English *QWERTY* keyboard. Extension to other common keyboards, e.g. the French *AZERTY* keyboard, is straightforward.

> **Fig. 10-1 (*overleaf*)**: *Numerical notation* used by the *Navlipi* keyboard. The notation is *(x,y)*, with x= *columns* and y= *rows*. Thus, e.g., the notation for the current QWERTY *s* key is (3,4), and the notation for the *r* key is (5,3). (This Figure also appears in **PART 1** under the full discussion of *Navlipi* keyboarding.)

PART 3: PRESENTATION AND DISCUSSION OF NAVLIPI

446

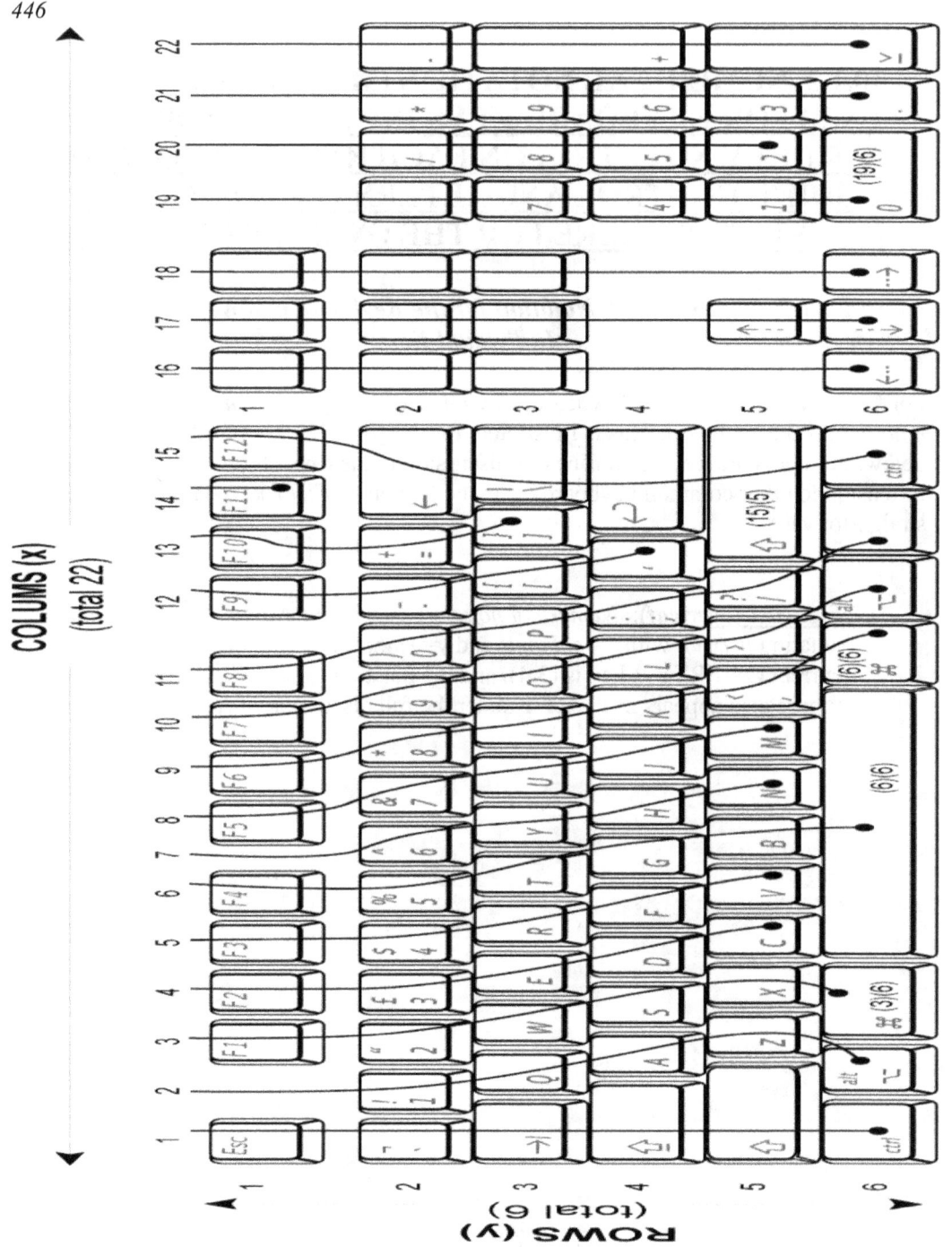

Chapter 10: Navlipi Keyboarding Using the QWERTY, AZERTY or Other Common Keyboards

As **Fig. 10-1** shows, in *Navlipi*, the keyboard, here the QWERTY keyboard, is represented as a 2-dimensional matrix, very similar to the 2-d matrix used for the Vowel and Non-Vowel Tables. The *columns* represent the *x-axis* and the *rows* the *y-axis*. Thus, e.g., the notation for the current QWERTY *s* key is (3,4), and the notation for the *r* key is (5,3).

Further to the numerical notation shown in **Fig. 10-1**, each key will have *four (4) representations* on it, for the *Normal, Shift, Control* and *Alternate* positions. This is shown in **Fig. 10-2**.

Fig. 10-2: Schematic illustration of the *four (4) representations* used by *NAVLIPI* for each key, for the *Normal, Shift, Control* and *Alternate* positions. In the illustration, the current QWERTY *$-4* key is used as an example.

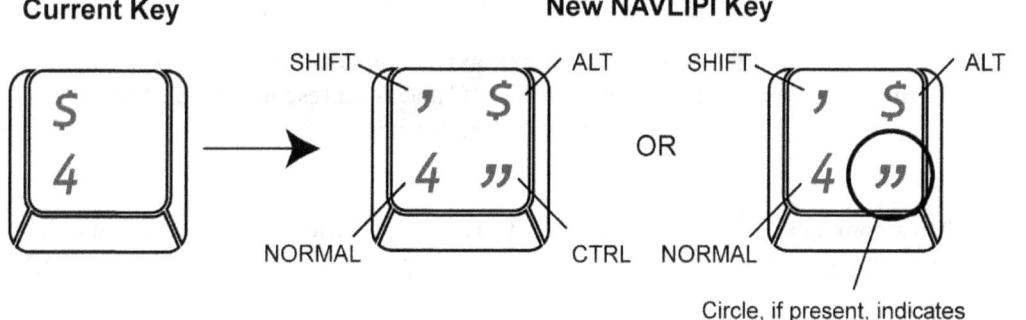

PART 3: PRESENTATION AND DISCUSSION OF NAVLIPI

The above *matrix notation* and *4-part keys* can be combined in a useful ***key notation***, used conveniently to refer to *Navlipi* keyboard keys. This is shown schematically in **Fig. 10-3**.

Fig. 10-3: Combination of the *matrix notation* and *4-part keys*, to arrive at the ***key notation***, used conveniently to refer to *Navlipi* keyboard keys.

KEY NOTATION
USED FOR REPRESENTATION OF KEYS ON THE NAVLIPI KEYBOARD

$(m)(n)(N,S,C,A)$
(*generically referenced as **$(m)(n)(X)$***)

where ***m*** is the column number (x-axis, a total of 22), ***n*** is the row number (y-axis, a total of 6) and N, S, C and A represent *Normal, Shift, Control* and *Alternate*.

When a combination of functions, e.g. CTRL+ALT, is required, then the notation is simply changed accordingly, e.g. as **(C+A)** or simply, and *more preferably*, as **(CA)**

For the American **QWERTY** keyboard, we then have:

22 columns (m) and 6 rows (n) in all

Chapter 10: Navlipi Keyboarding Using the QWERTY, AZERTY or Other Common Keyboards

10.1.2.2 Examples

Taking the key illustrated in the previous Figure as an example (the old [**$/4**] key, changed to the new key [**'/4/$/"**]), we have:

- The key number, *(m)(n) = (5)(2)* (see **Fig. 10**-1).
- Going further, the notation for each of the four glyphs on this key is:
    - *4 = (5)(2)(N)*
    - *' = (5)(2)(S)*
    - *$ = (5)(2)(A)*
    - *" = (5)(2)(C)*

....(10.1)

Citing other examples:

- **(5)(3)(A)** represents [**ALT+R**].
- **(5)(3)(SC)** represents [**SHIFT+CTRL+R**].
- **(11)(3)(C)** represents the (Ctrl+P) key.
- **(11)(3)(CA)** represents the (Ctrl+Alt+P) key.
- For *more general notation*, **(m)(2)** represents all the *Row-2* keys (~, 1, 2, 3....etc.) whilst **(8)(n)** represents all the *Column-8* keys, (i.e. F5, 7, U, J, M).
- In a similar vein, **(11)(4)** alone represents the "**P**" key in general, i.e. *all* its functions (Normal, Shift, Ctrl, Alt).
- Once again in a similar vein, **(2-11)(2)** represents *all* the number keys *only* (1, 2, 3.....0).
- When we wish to refer to several keys together, we may use a ***combined notation***. Thus, e.g., **(2,3,4)(2)** refers to three keys, the number keys for the numbers **1, 2** and **3**, whilst **(5)(3,4,5)** refers to the keys **R, F** and **V**.

...(10.2)

PART 3: PRESENTATION AND DISCUSSION OF NAVLIPI

10.1.2.3 Four-Part Notation and Markings for Each Key

We are at present used to keyboards with just one marking (e.g. the **"P"** key described above) on the key, or at most two (e.g. the *?* / key, with (**?**) being upper case, i.e. (Shift + the key).

However, in *Navlipi,* since *each* key has *four* possible renderings --- *Normal* (no Shift, Ctrl or Alt pressed), *Shift, Ctrl* and *Alt* --- each key should properly have *four* markings on it.

10.1.3 CONCERNS WITH THE [CTRL], [ALT] AND OTHER KEYS IN RELATION TO UNIX (LINUX), WINDOWS®, OTHER OPERATING SYSTEMS, MOST WORD PROCESSORS, AND OTHER PROGRAMS

Software engineers will immediately recognize that *reassignment* of keyboard keys at will is not an easy or straightforward task.

In particular, there are problems with assignment of [CTRL], [ALT] and other keys, especially with Unix-based systems and popular word processors. The following keys are *some* examples of these, representative and by no means exhaustive:

- [CTRL+C]: Used for copy functions in Windows as well as many word processors. More seriously and problematically, used for "Abort" functions in many older UNIX based systems.
- [CTRL+A]: Select-all function.
- [CTRL+V]: Used for copy functions in Windows as well as many word processors.
- [CTRL+P]: Print function.
- [CTRL+S]: Save function.
- [CTRL+X]: Cut function.
- [CTRL+B]: Bold function.
- [CTRL+I]: Italicize function.
- [CTRL+U]: Underline function.
- [ALT+I]: Insert function.
- [ALT+O]: Open function.

Navlipi provides the following solution to the above conundrum:

- ***All the original combination keys, such as those in the list above, will retain their original significance.*** Thus, e.g., [CTRL+C] would continue to mean "Copy" on Windows-based systems. We may summarize this, by noting that all the following keys will retain their original significance. Once again, the list includes the *most commonly used keystrokes*, but is *by no means exhaustive*:

> - [CTRL+(A,C,V,P,S,X,B,I,U,J,R,L,E,F,G,O,+,-,<,>] *all retain their original significance in Navlipi.*
> - [ALT+(I,O,F,P,B)] *all retain their original significance in Navlipi.*

- ***Where a key combination is required by NAVLIPI which conflicts with the any of those above, NAVLIPI will use a corresponding <u>multiple</u> combination.*** For example, if *Navlipi* were to require the use of [**CTRL+C**] for any reason, it would instead use [**CTRL+ALT+C**]. The combination keys are indicated on the physical key with a circumscribed circle, as illustrated for the (") in the **(5)(2)** key in **Fig. 10-2** above.

...(10.3)

10.1.4 ONLY MAJOR PHYSICAL CHANGES IN OTHERWISE NEARLY UNDISTURBED QWERTY, AZERTY, OR OTHER COMMON KEYBOARD: MUCH SMALLER SPACE BAR, MUCH LARGER ALT BARS, AND NON-NUMERIC PART OF NUMERIC (NUM LOCK) KEYS CHANGED

The discussion in this section relates to the *more complex option* for *Navlipi* keyboard implementation discussed in the previous section. The changes listed in the title of this section can be briefly described as follows:

Table 10-1: Summary of *physical* keyboard changes for the "more complex" keyboard option of *Navlipi*, for the QWERTY keyboard.

PHYSICAL* KEYBOARD CHANGES IN THE QWERTY KEYBOARD FOR THE "MORE COMPLEX" KEYBOARD OPTION OF *NAVLIPI

♦ Left and right ALT keys made *much larger* so that the *forefingers* can easily and naturally access them.

♦ SPACEBAR made correspondingly smaller to accommodate the larger ALT keys. Spacebar would be accessible only via *thumbs*. [*For "ergonomic" keyboards (keyboards that are larger and have a curved surface to prevent carpal tunnel syndrome), this ALT and SPACEBAR placing can be modified slightly in the following way: The ALT keys can be placed slightly above although still to the right of the spacebar, in the intervening blank space created by the bifurcation of the keyboard.*]

♦ The *non-numeric* ("lower case") keys of the NUMERIC part of the keyboard (i.e. those in effect when there is no Numeric Lock on) are deleted and replaced by other keys, as discussed later in this chapter.

Chapter 10: Navlipi Keyboarding Using the QWERTY, AZERTY or Other Common Keyboards

The new keyboard layout incorporating the first two bullets in **Table 10-1** above is shown in the Figure below.

Fig. 10-4:   *NAVLIPI* Keyboard layout, for the American QWERTY keyboard, showing *changes* to the ALT keys and Spacebar enumerated above. (Only the regular (non-"ergonomic") keyboard is shown for simplicity.)

PART 3: PRESENTATION AND DISCUSSION OF NAVLIPI

10.1.5 TWO OPTIONS FOR IMPLEMENTATION OF *NAVLIPI* ON THE KEYBOARD, AND REGISTRATION OF *NAVLIPI* WITH UNICODE

Two options are then available in respect of the general discussion above for implementation of *Navlipi* on the keyboard:

(1) The *simpler option* is to generate a (*.ttf*) font file, which can be incorporated into word processors as an additional font. Although this is relatively straightforward from the software point of view, it is rather cumbersome for keyboarding. For the keyboarder must then either go constantly to the "fonts" menu and change fonts, or, worse, in some word processors go to the Insert/Symbols menu, then input every glyph via mouse clicks from a pop-up menu (as in older versions of Microsoft Word®); alternatively, the user must have a key handy for the equivalence of every QWERTY key (or AZERTY in French, etc. etc.), or worse, memorize this key.

(2) The *more complex option* is to write software that completely reassigns the keyboard *only when in the word processing program* and then blends seamlessly into whatever operating system is being used. This author feels that, even this is the more complex option, it is preferred, since, once implemented, it will make *Navlipi* keyboarding extremely facile.

The simpler option, i.e., the (*.ttf*) font, will already be available as freeware via an Internet download. The (*.ttf*) font will be available in several subsets: The full *Navlipi* as well as the language-specific subsets, as briefly described in the first section in this chapter.

It is also noted that the availability of *Navlipi* subsets in (*.ttf*) does not preclude the availability of several "font types", such as Arial or Times New Roman. These would be available as sub-subsets within each subset of *Navlipi*.

The more complex option will be sold separately. *It is this, more complex option that is described in subsequent parts of this chapter.*

Finally, it is noted that each *Navlipi* glyph will be registered with Unicode and a Unicode code assigned to it.

Chapter 10: Navlipi Keyboarding Using the QWERTY, AZERTY or Other Common Keyboards

10.2 LIST OF KEYS WITH MAJOR CHANGES

10.2.1 MAJOR REASSIGNMENTS

These are listed in **Table 10-2** below. The reassignment of the NUM LOCK number keys when NUM LOCK is not on is particularly worthy of note.

Table 10-2 *(cont. overleaf)*: *List of key changes reflecting major reassignments.* For convenience in reference, the keys are addressed in the **(m)(n)(X)** *key notation* described earlier in this chapter (see **Fig. 10-3**). (The reader may reference **Fig. 10-3** to identify the original QWERTY keys.)

Ser. #	OLD KEY	OLD KEY #	NEW KEY #	NEW KEY REPRESENTATION (BLANK = PLACE AVAILABLE)	COMMENTS
1.	c (lower case)	(4)(5)(N)	(2)(3)(A) [ALT+q]	(2)(3) CAPS q	
2.	C (upper case)	(4)(5)(S)	(2)(3)(AS) [ALT+SHIFT+q]		
3.	< >	(9)(5)(S) (10)(5)(S)	(12)(2)(S) (12)(2)(C)	(12)(2) < — _ >	< and > moved from comma, period (full-stop) keys to this new key
4.	\ |	(15)(3)(N) (15)(3)(S)	(2)(2)(C) (2)(2)(A)	(2)(2) ! 1 \	

PART 3: PRESENTATION AND DISCUSSION OF NAVLIPI

456

Ser. #	OLD KEY	OLD KEY #	NEW KEY #	NEW KEY REPRESENTATION (*BLANK = PLACE AVAILABLE*)	COMMENTS
5.	] }	(13)(3)(N) (13)(3)(S)	(15)(3)(N) (15)(3)(S)	(15)(3) } □] □	(15)(3)(C, A) are still available (free)
6.	[{	(12)(3)(N) (12)(3)(S)	(13)(3)(N) (13)(3)(S)	(13)(3) { □ [□	(13)(3)(C, A) are still available (free)
7.	; :	(11)(4)(N) (11)(4)(S)	(12)(3)(N) (12)(3)(S)	(12)(3) : ï ; 2	For new glyphs (12)(3)(C, A) shown, see under Section **10.2.8** below
8.	' *(apostrophe)* " *(quote mark)*	(12)(4)(N) (12)(4)(S)	(5)(2)(N) (5)(2)(S)	(5)(2) ' $ 4 "	(12)(4) is now fully available (free)
9.	###	(19-22)(2-6)(X)	(19-22)(2-6)(X)		***

<u>ALL</u> NUM LOCK NUMBER KEYS, *When NUM LOCK is <u>not</u> on*

*** *When NUM LOCK is not on, these keys will be used to render various, very rare phonemic condensates, as discussed later in this chapter. When NUM LOCK is on, they will simply render numbers.*

Chapter 10: Navlipi Keyboarding Using the QWERTY, AZERTY or Other Common Keyboards

10.2.2 MAIN (I.E. NOT NUM LOCK) NUMBER KEYS (ALSO USED FOR TONES, SEE LATER)

These are shown in the **Table** below. It is important to note that the keys for numbers **5** to **9** are shown in this Table with their SHIFT, ALT and CTRL places blank, since the characters for the SHIFT setting of these keys in the QWERTY keyboard, i.e. %, ^, &, * and (, have been moved to other locations in the *Navlipi* keyboard. These free places are then to be used for *Tones*, addressed in Section **10.2.12** below.

Table 10-3: Changed *number* keys, as to be used in *Navlipi*. The keys for numbers **5** to **9** are shown with their SHIFT, ALT and CTRL places blank, since the characters for the SHIFT setting of these keys in the QWERTY keyboard, that is to say the characters %, ^, &, * and (, have been moved to other locations in the *Navlipi* keyboard. These free places are then to be used for *Tones* (see Section **10.2.12** below).

Note that the keys **(15 to 22)(2)**,
i.e. all the Row # 2 keys in columns 15 through 22, remain unchanged.

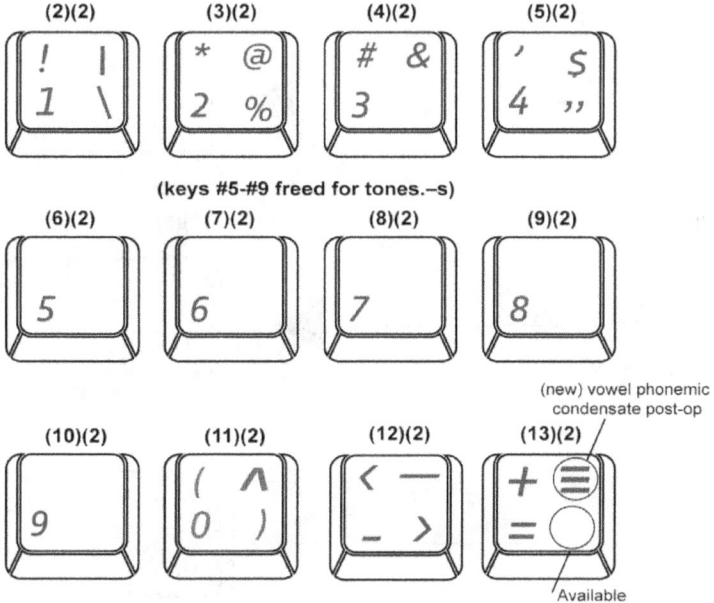

PART 3: PRESENTATION AND DISCUSSION OF NAVLIPI

458

10.2.3 MAJOR POST-OP KEYS AND KEYS WITH HIGH FREQUENCY OF USE AND KEYS

These are shown in the Table below.

Table 10-4: : List of key changes reflecting keys with high frequency of use and some major post-ops. Once again, for convenience in reference, the keys are addressed in the **(m)(n)(X)** *key notation* described earlier in this chapter. (The reader may reference **Fig. 10-3** to identify the original QWERTY keys.)

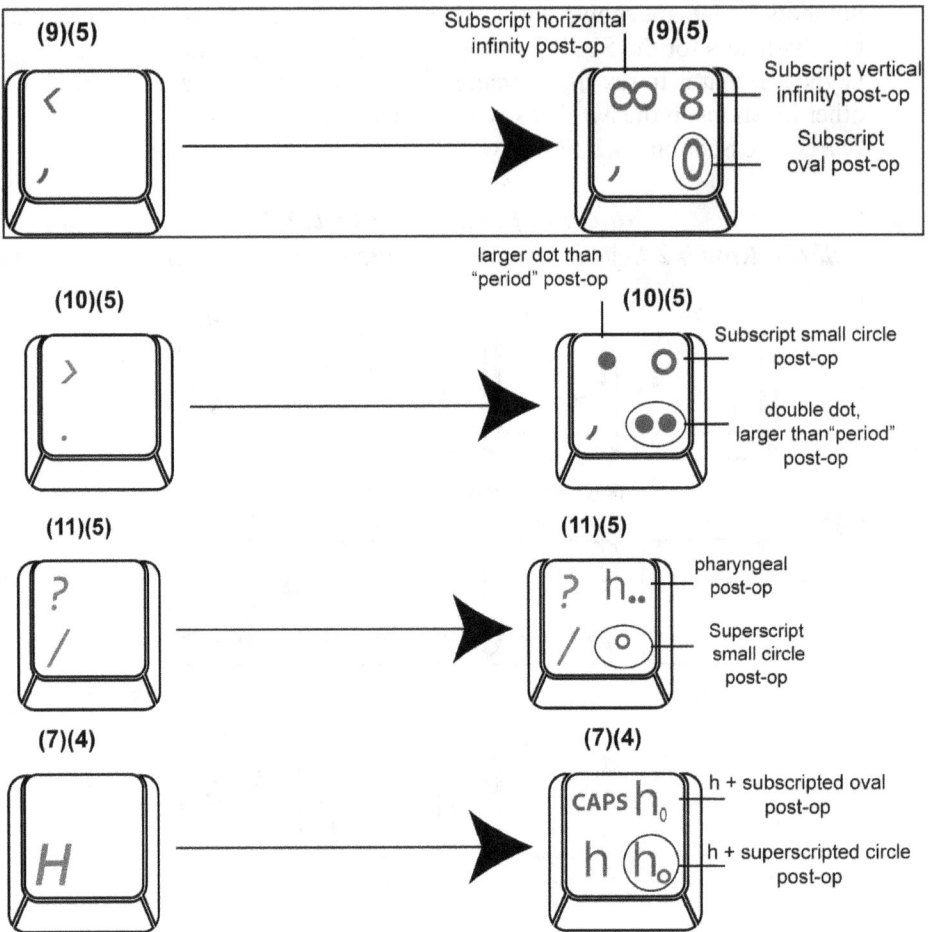

Chapter 10: Navlipi Keyboarding Using the QWERTY, AZERTY or Other Common Keyboards

10.2.4 CENTRAL ("R") KEY AND CENTRAL GLYPHS, INCLUDING PHONEMIC CONDENSATES

Navlipi uses *two (2) **major** language-specific variants* of the central ("R") key:

For the ***Hindi/Spanish/Russian/Indonesian keyboard***, we have the following representation. Here: **(5)(3)(N)** is the most common alveolar tap/flap/semivowel phonemic condensate; **(5)(3)(A)** is the alveolar semivowel; and finally, **(5)(3)(CA)** is the retroflex semivowel. The latter is used in American English, and also Tamil, Mandarin/Cantonese. It may be redundant in this, Hindi/Spanish... keyboard, except for use in Sanskrit.

...(10.4a)

For the ***English/French/German/West European languages keyboard*** (i.e. for West European languages), we have the following representation. Here: **(5)(3)(N)** is the alveolar semivowel only; **(5)(3)(A)** is the phonemic condensate (note that if one needs to use this in other keyboards, e.g. the Hindi/Spanish.. keyboard, then one can simply render it by typing **x** and **r** in sequence; and finally, **(5)(3)(CA)** is the retroflex semivowel, used in American English, also Tamil.

...(10.4b)

PART 3: PRESENTATION AND DISCUSSION OF NAVLIPI

Rarely used central glyphs may be summarized as follows:

- The unique Tamil retroflex central with a jaw-forward position in articulation, phonemically distinct from the same central in jaw-normal position and discussed at some length in several earlier chapters of this book, presents a unique situation. In *Navlipi,* this is rendered as the glyph

    ♪₀, i.e. a *script-r* with a subscripted little circle. Since its use is expected to be only for Tamil and thus somewhat rare, rather than assigning a separate key for it, *Navlipi* will simply transcribe this as the serial combination of the two keystrokes, i.e. **(5)(3)(CA) (♪)** followed by **(10)(5)(A) (₀)** .

- Several *phonemic condensates* of central or central plus some other articulation, which are expected to be rarely used, are assigned by *Navlipi* to keys that are commensurate with their rare use. These do not appear in the Table above. Summarizing these:
    - The *alveolar (r+l) (i.e. central + lateral) phonemic condensate*, transcribed as ⱳ in *Navlipi*, will use the key **(19)(3)(N)**, i.e. the *Numeric-7* key used with NUM LOCK off.
    - The *retroflex (r+l) (i.e., central + lateral) phonemic condensate*, transcribed as ♣ (script-r with single overstrike) in *Navlipi*, will use the key **(20)(3)(N)**, i.e. the *Numeric-8* key used with NUM LOCK off.
    - The *alveolar (r+l+n) (i.e. central + lateral + nasal) phonemic condensate*, transcribed as ⱳ in *Navlipi*, will be use the key **(19)(4)(N)**, i.e. the *Numeric-4* key used with NUM LOCK off.
    - The *retroflex (r+l+n) (i.e. central + lateral + nasal) phonemic condensate*, transcribed as ♣ (script-r with double overstrike) in *Navlipi*, will use the key **(20)(4)(N)**, i.e. the *Numeric-5* key used with NUM LOCK off.
    - The *alveolar (flap + trill + semivowel) central phonemic condensate*, transcribed as r^o in *Navlipi*, will use the key **(20)(5)(N)**, i.e. the *Numeric-2* key used with NUM LOCK off.
    - The "*generic R*" *phonemic condensate*, transcribed as **R** in *Navlipi*, will use the key **(19)(5)(N)**, i.e. the *Numeric-1* key used with NUM LOCK off.

Chapter 10: Navlipi Keyboarding Using the QWERTY, AZERTY or Other Common Keyboards

The ***rare central glyphs*** may then be summarized in the following representations:

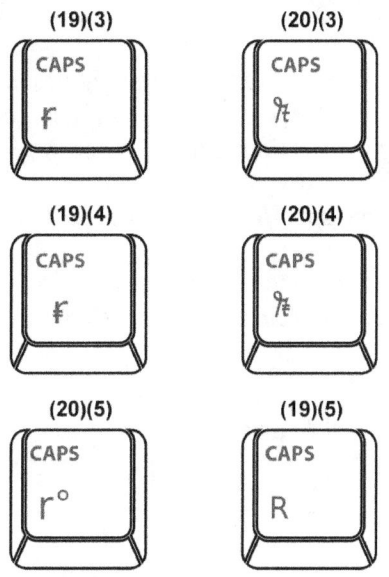

....(10.5)

PART 3: PRESENTATION AND DISCUSSION OF NAVLIPI

10.2.5 MAJOR LATERAL ("L") KEY

There is only one major lateral ("L") key. Other lateral phones are incorporated into phonemic condensates, most of which are in common with central ("R") phones and have been dealt with in the preceding sub-section in this chapter.

Navlipi uses only *two (2) language-specific variants* of the major lateral key:

For the ***Hindi/Spanish//Indonesian...*** etc. keyboard, we have the key below. This will also be used for the ***Arabic***, ***Mandarin/Cantonese*** and ***Tamil*** keyboards.

...(10.6)

For the ***English/French/German/West-European languages...*** keyboard, we have:

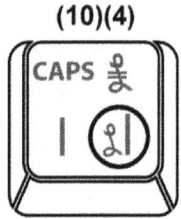

....(10.7)

As for central keys, there are several important features of note with regard to the lateral keys:

- As for the central keys, it is important to note that, per the extensive treatment of the close relationship between *pure vowels* and the *semivowels* at many

Chapter 10: Navlipi Keyboarding Using the QWERTY, AZERTY or Other Common Keyboards

points earlier in this book, glyphs for laterals are used in *Navlipi* for both the vowel and the semivowel. The vowel and semivowel are then distinguished contextually and via their following glyphs. For example, in American English *light,* the highlighted glyph (letter) is an alveolar lateral *semivowel,* distinguished contextually as well as by the fact that it is followed by a vowel. However, in American English *able,* the highlighted glyphs represent a *pure vowel*, distinguished contextually as well as by the fact that no pure vowel follows them.

- Since the **(10)(4)(C)** position, i.e. [CTRL+L], presents a conflict, e.g. with the left-justify function of many word processors, we do not use this in *Navlipi*. Rather, we use **(10)(4)(CA)**, i.e. [CTRL+ALT+L].

10.2.6 MAJOR VELAR KEYS

The velar keys in *Navlipi* are ***language-specific***. They are also the *Navlipi* keys with one of the largest language-specific diversities.

The reason the velar keys have such large diversity is because, for many language groups, even very small phonemic distinctions in the velar articulation require the use of a separate key.

For example, the *Hindi/Spanish//Indonesian...* group uses the ALT position of the **(9)(4)** key (the **k** key) to render the aspirated stop, **kh$_o$** in *Navlipi*. However, this rendition cannot be used for the *Tamil* keyboard: Tamil for the most part has *no* velar aspirated stop, [kh$_o$]; nevertheless, there are still just a very few words in Tamil, such as *kokkhara* ("crowing of a cock"), which *do* articulate an aspirated stop! That is to say, in Tamil, as in English the velar unvoiced stop is actually a phonemic condensate, combining aspirated and unaspirated.

Similarly, most of the Chinese languages *do* have an aspirated/unaspirated phonemic distinction for this stop, so technically, one might be able to use the Hindi/Spanish/etc... keyboard for the Chinese languages. However, in these Chinese languages, the unvoiced and voiced stops, i.e. [k] and [g], form a phonemic condensate, so alas, we cannot use the Hindi/Spanish/etc.. [k] key for the Chinese languages! However, we do, in the Mandarin/Cantonese keyboard, retain the aspirated phones just as they are in the Hindi/... keyboard, i.e. at the (A) (ALT) position. Once again, we might technically be able to use

PART 3: PRESENTATION AND DISCUSSION OF NAVLIPI

464

the Chinese language keyboard for Arabic, since Arabic also has a ([k]+[g]) phonemic condensate. Alas, Arabic also has the uvular stop, [q] in current Roman transliteration, which we must needs accommodate!

The *Navlipi* language-specificities for the ***velar*** keys are:

(1) The ***Hindi/Spanish/Russian/Indonesian.....*** group.
(2) The ***Chinese languages*** group, including all major Chinese languages such as Cantonese, Fujienese and *Mandarin*.
(3) The ***English/French/German/West-European languages....*** group.
(4) The ***Arabic*** group. This would include Hebrew and Amharic.
(5) The ***Tamil*** group, including all five major Dravidian languages (Tamil, Telugu, Kannadaa, Malayaalam and Tulu).

We can now discuss each of the above groups in turn.

Hindi/Spanish/Russian/Indonesian..... group: If we accommodate the aspirated stops, [kh_o] and [gh_o], then we can use a single velar key type for all the languages in this group. The resultant keys are shown below:

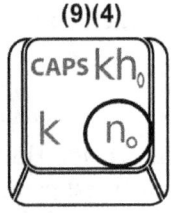 

...(10.8)

Chapter 10: Navlipi Keyboarding Using the QWERTY, AZERTY or Other Common Keyboards

Chinese languages **group**: The only difference with the *Hindi/...* group is that in place of **(9)(4)(N)**, which is **k** in the *Hindi/...* group, we use the phonemic condensate for unvoiced and voiced velar stop, ([k]+[g]), as applicable to the Chinese languages; these usually articulate this as [g], i.e. g_∞ . The **(6)(4)** key, i.e. the **g** key, would then not be used in the Chinese languages. We nevertheless leave it as it is for the Hindi/... languages.

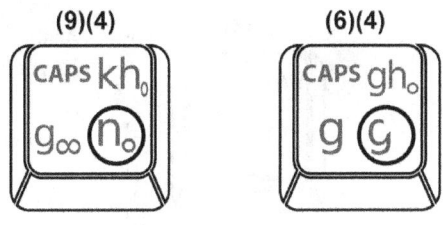

...(10.9)

English/French/German/West-European languages....: For both the unvoiced and voiced keys, the **(A)** position, i.e. **(9)(4)(A)** and **(6)(4)(A),** representing the aspirated stops kh_o and gh_o, , would not be used. Nevertheless, we leave them intact; perhaps they may be used in cross-language passages, e.g. an English passage having many Indian names! For the unvoiced key, at the **(N)** position, i.e. **(9)(4)(N)**, the **k** is replaced by k_o, indicating the (unaspirated + aspirated) phonemic condensate. For the voiced key, the **(N)** position, i.e. **(6)(4)(N),** retains the pure phone, **g**. This is shown in the figures below.

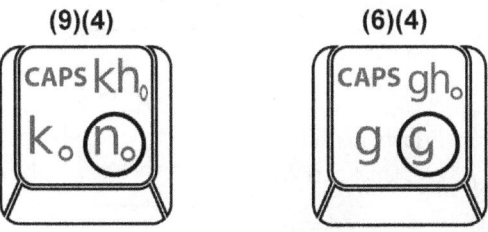

...(10.10)

Arabic **group:** The only difference with the *Hindi/..etc..* group is that for **(9)(4)(A)**, we use **k..**, for the uvular stop. Similarly, for **(6)(4)(A),** we use **g..** .

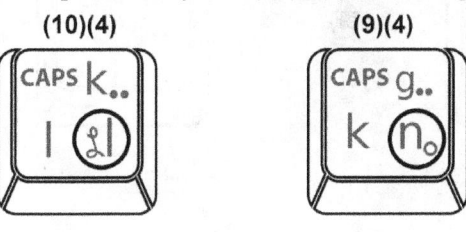

...(10.11)

PART 3: PRESENTATION AND DISCUSSION OF NAVLIPI

Common velar keys for ALL keyboards: For the velar *unvoiced* and *voiced* fricatives, the keys **(3)(5)** and **(6)(4)**, respectively, are common to *all* language-specific keyboards in *Navlipi*. They are shown below.

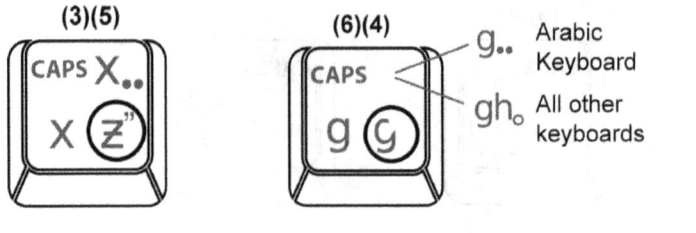

....(10.12)

10.2.7 MAJOR PALATAL AND SIBILANT KEYS

For these, *Navlipi* is able to use common keys for all language groups. Thus, these keys are ***not*** language-specific. They are summarized below.

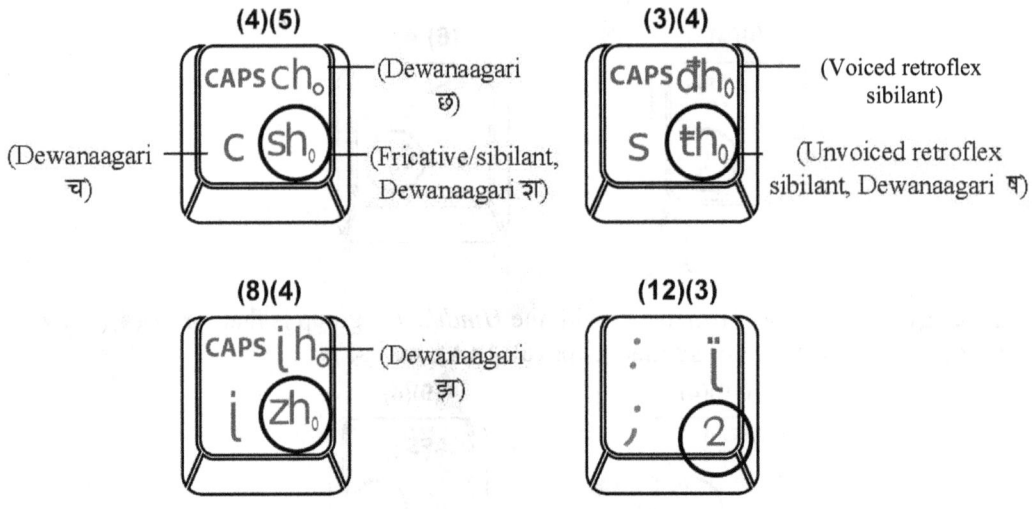

....(10.13)

Several points are of note with regard to *Navlipi*'s palatal and sibilant keys:

- For the *medio-palatal unvoiced sibilant*, as in German (Hochdeutsch pronunciation) *ich*, the *Navlipi* transcription is $\overset{..}{2}$. Rather than assign this a separate key or key position, since it is so rare (except in German!), we use two keystrokes for this: the keystroke for the medio-palatal plosive, **C (12)(3)(CA)**, and that for the fricative post-op, **h₀, (7)(4)(A)**. The same applies for the *medio-palatal voiced sibilant*: It is rendered as a combination of the voiced plosive **(12)(3)(A)** and the fricative post-op, **h₀, (7)(4)(A)**, i.e. as $\overset{..}{t}h_0$

- The *medio-palatal plosive*, $2h_0$ finds wide use in diverse languages, e.g. Turkish, Irish and Serbo-Croat (Croatian). Thus, *Navlipi* provides it with its own key.

- The reader may wonder why the old QWERTY **j** key, **(N)** position, is assigned to the palatal voiced plosive, (Hindi/Dewanaagari ज , the English "*j*" sound), rather than its original Roman significance as still used in German and other European languages, i.e. *ya* (Hindi/Dewanaagari य . We have a simple answer for this: The keyboard is an American invention of the late 19th century, and its original use reflected the English *j* (as in English *joke*) phone rather than the *y* phone!

10.2.8 MAJOR RETROFLEX, ALVEOLAR AND DENTAL PLOSIVE ("T-D") KEYS

Like the central ("r") keys described in the previous section, but much more extensively, these keys are ***highly language-specific.*** Accordingly, these are grouped by the language keyboard they are specific to, as listed in the **Table** below.

PART 3: PRESENTATION AND DISCUSSION OF NAVLIPI

Table 10-5: Major *dental*, *alveolar* and *retroflex* plosive ("T-D") keys, grouped by language-specificity.

A. (6)(3) KEY
(Unvoiced; current QWERTY "t" key)

LANGUAGE-SPECIFIC KEYBOARD   **KEY**

Hindi/Spanish/Russian/Indonesian....
(Dental, except (CA) position):

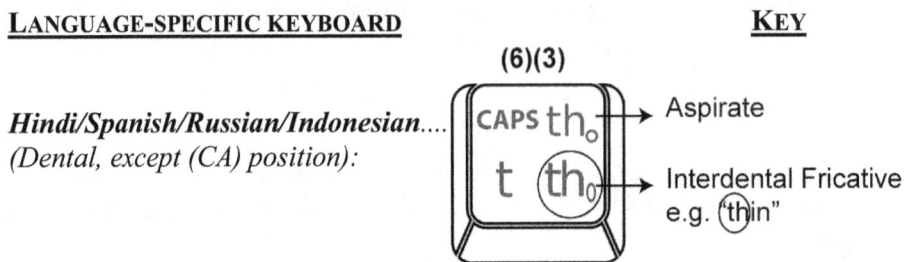

Mandarin/Cantonese
(Alveolar):

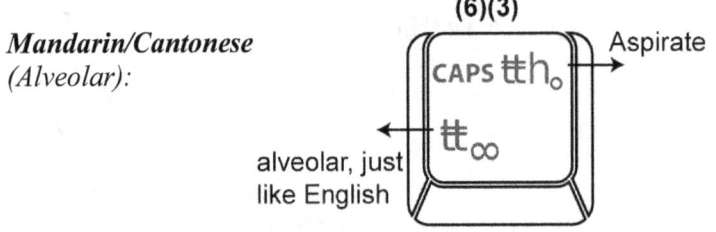

Chapter 10: Navlipi Keyboarding Using the QWERTY, AZERTY or Other Common Keyboards

(11.13, Major dental, alveolar, retroflex plosive ("T-D") keys, cont.)

LANGUAGE-SPECIFIC KEYBOARD   **KEY**

English/ W. European languages...
(Alveolar, except (CA) position):

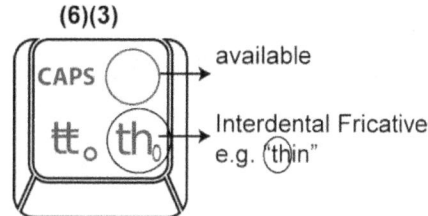

Arabic:

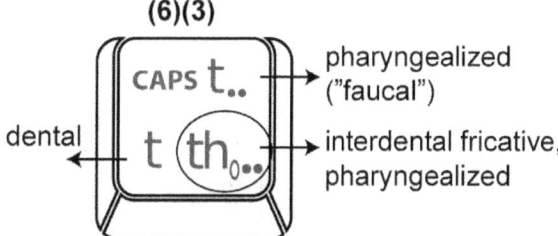

Tamil
(Dental, except (CA) position):

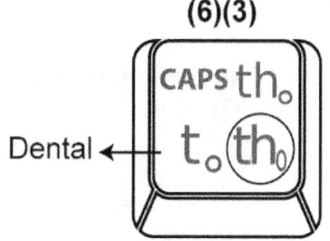

PART 3: PRESENTATION AND DISCUSSION OF NAVLIPI

(11.13: Major dental, alveolar and retroflex plosive ("T-D") keys, cont.)

B. (4)(4) KEY
(Voiced, current QWERTY "d" key)

LANGUAGE-SPECIFIC KEYBOARD   **KEY**

Hindi/Spanish/Russian/Indonesian....
(Dental, except (CA) position):

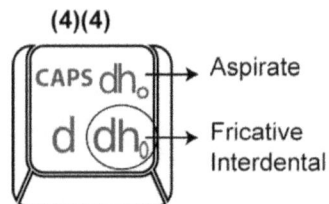

Mandarin and *Cantonese*:
(Alveolar):

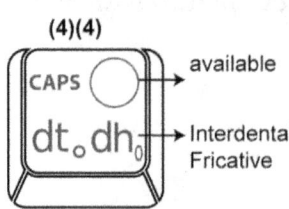

English/ W. European languages...
(Alveolar, except (CA) position):

Chapter 10: Navlipi Keyboarding Using the QWERTY, AZERTY or Other Common Keyboards

471

(11.13: Major dental, alveolar and retroflex plosive ("T-D") keys, cont.)

LANGUAGE-SPECIFIC KEYBOARD   **KEY**

Arabic
(Dental, except (CA) position):

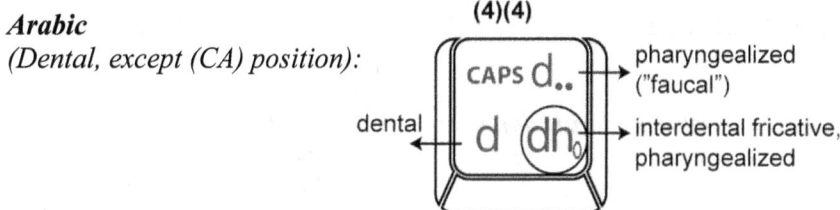

Tamil
(Dental, except (CA) position):

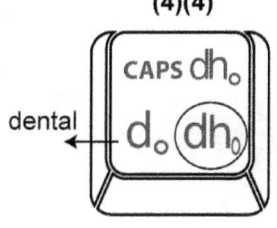

PART 3: PRESENTATION AND DISCUSSION OF NAVLIPI

472

(11.13: Major dental, alveolar and retroflex plosive ("T-D") keys, cont.)

C. (11)(4), (12)(4) KEYS, FOR RETROFLEX NON-VOWELS
(Current QWERTY (; :) and (' ") keys)

LANGUAGE-SPECIFIC KEYBOARD   **KEY**

Hindi/Spanish/Russian/Indonesian....
(Retroflex):

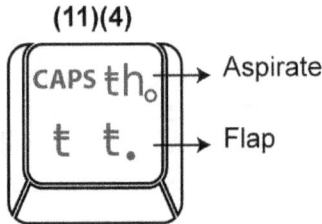

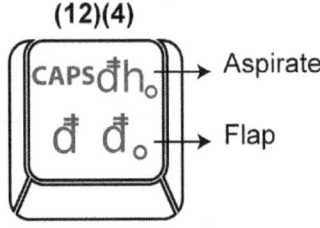

Chapter 10: Navlipi Keyboarding Using the QWERTY, AZERTY or Other Common Keyboards

10.2.9 MAJOR BILABIAL KEYS

The major *non*-nasal bilabial keys are just two:

- **(11)(3)**, the current QWERTY **p** key, and
- **(6)(5)**, the current QWERTY **b** key.

In *Navlipi*, these are *highly* language-specific; indeed, *they are among the most language-specific keys in Navlipi*. This is seen in the discussion below.

For these two keys, *all* the language-specific keyboards use the **S**, **N**, **A** and **C+A** positions only. The **C** position, i.e. CTRL, is not used, since (CTRL+P) and (CTRL+B) conflict with other operating system and/or word processor functions, as discussed at some length in an earlier section.

Further, in *all* the keyboards, the **S** position, i.e. the CAPS position, alone (for **N**) or in combination with any of the other positions, prints as the *capital* or *upper-case* glyph. The remaining positions then become highly language-specific, as discussed below.

In the *Hindi/Spanish....* keyboard, the **N** position will print as **p** (i.e., the unaspirated, unvoiced bilabial stop). The **A** position will print as ph_o (i.e., the aspirated, unvoiced bilabial stop). The **C** position is blank. The **(6)(5), b** key would be analogous to the **(11)(3), p** key, i.e. with the aspirated plosive at the **A** position, etc. This version of the two keys would also be used for the *Russian/East-European-languages* and the *Swahili* keyboards.

In the *English/ West-European-languages* keyboard, the **N** position of the **(11)(3) p** key will print as p_o, indicating that it is a phonemic condensate of the unaspirated and aspirated plosives. The **A** position will still print as ph_o (i.e., the aspirated, unvoiced bilabial stop), as in the *Hindi/Spanish...* keyboard. This is merely to accommodate multilingual or name-based passages, i.e. where Hindi/Urdu words or Indian names may appear in otherwise British or American or Australian English passages. This would avoid the minor inconvenience of having to toggle between language keyboards when typing names! The **(6)(5), b** key in this keyboard would differ from the **(11)(3) p** key in that the **N** position would print as **b** only, reflecting the fact that in this group of languages the **b** and bh_o do *not* form a phonemic condensate. The **A** position would again print as bh_o.

PART 3: PRESENTATION AND DISCUSSION OF NAVLIPI

474

In the *Arabic* keyboard, the **N** position of the **(11)(3) p** key will print as **b$_\infty$**, indicating that the [p] and [b] phones in these languages form a phonemic condensate usually pronounced as a [b], unaspirated. The **(6)(5), b** key in this keyboard would also print as **b$_\infty$**. The **A** position in both keys would not be used.

In the *Mandarin/Cantonese* keyboard, the **N** position of the **(11)(3) p** key will print as **p$_\infty$**, whereas the **N** position of the **(6)(5), b** key would print as **b$_\infty$**. The common usage for the bilabial unaspirated plosive, both unvoiced and voiced, would then differ for Cantonese and Mandarin: In Cantonese, one would use , **p$_\infty$**, to indicate that the common articulation is [p], whereas in Mandarin, one would use **b$_\infty$**, to indicate that the common articulation is [b]. For the *Arabic* keyboard, the **N** position of the **(11)(3) (p)** key would be blank. The **p** and **b** keys can then be summarized as given below.

Chapter 10: Navlipi Keyboarding Using the QWERTY, AZERTY or Other Common Keyboards

Table 10-6: Summary of the ***bilabial* (11)(3) (p)** and **(6)(5), (b)** keys for *major* language-specific keyboards. There would be several other, language-specific keyboards, not shown here for space reasons, e.g. for the *Min-Chinese* languages such as Fujienese/Hokka, for the *Tamil/South Indian* languages, etc.

LANGUAGE-SPECIFIC KEYBOARD   **KEY**

Hindi/Spanish...
Also used for:
  -Russian/East-European-languages
  -Swahili:

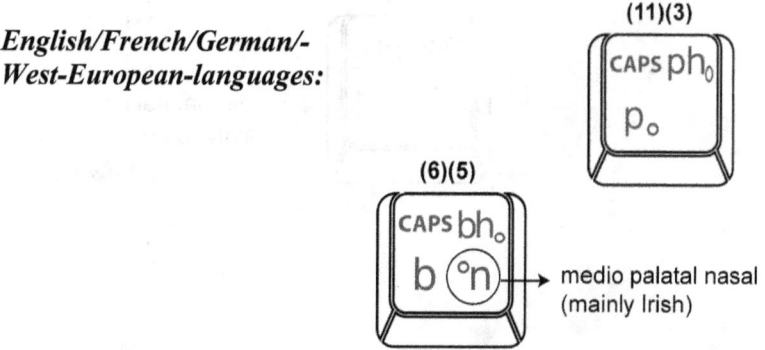

English/French/German/-
West-European-languages:

PART 3: PRESENTATION AND DISCUSSION OF NAVLIPI

476

(Major bilabial keys, cont.)

LANGUAGE-SPECIFIC KEYBOARD　　　　　　　　　　**KEY**

Mandarin/Cantonese:

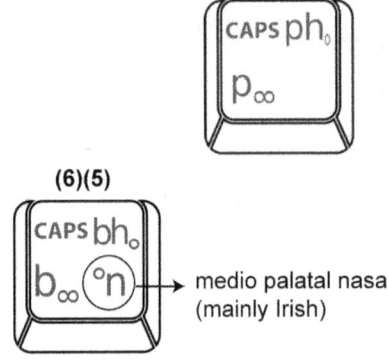

Arabic:

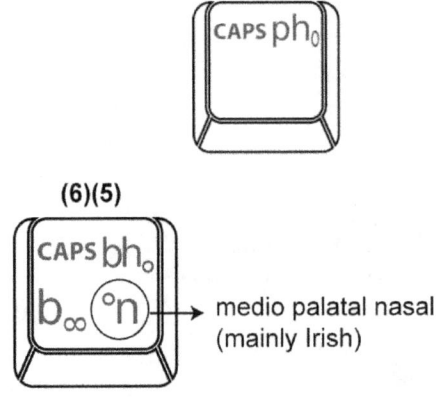

Chapter 10: Navlipi Keyboarding Using the QWERTY, AZERTY or Other Common Keyboards

10.2.10 MAJOR NASAL ("M-N") KEYS

Navlipi uses a single set of keys for the nasals that are common to ***all** the language-specific keyboards*. That is to say, ***there is no language-specificity in the case of nasals in the Navlipi keyboard***.

Another feature of the *Navlipi* nasal keys is that the **CTRL setting is not used**, but rather, is *replaced entirely by the CTRL+ALT setting*. That is to say, there are no **(C)** keys, just **(CA)** keys. This is to avoid conflict with the common CTRL functions for these keys, e.g. CTRL+N, CTRL+V, CTRL+B, found in many operating systems and word processors.

The *Navlipi* nasal keys are as follows:

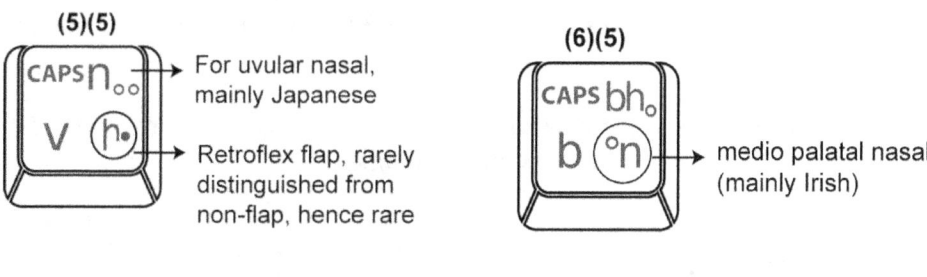

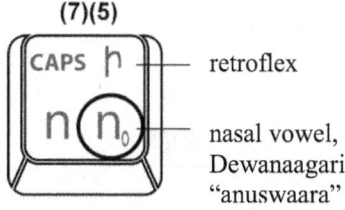

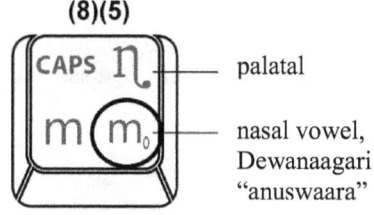

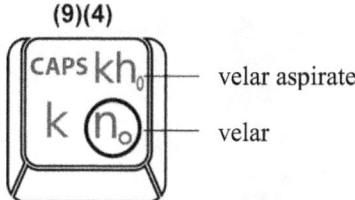

PART 3: PRESENTATION AND DISCUSSION OF NAVLIPI

478

....(10.14)

It may be noted from the above that the *Navlipi* nasal keys are the following:

- **(5,6,7,8)(5)** (four keys)
- and **(9)(4)**
- Giving a total of *five* keys.

All these keys are next to each other. Thus, *Navlipi* is able to keep all the nasal keys proximate.

10.2.11 MAJOR STANDARD-SEMIVOWEL KEYS

Standard semivowel designates those semivowels that are *not* centrals ("r"-sounds) or laterals ("l"-sounds).

The *Navlipi* keys for these semivowels are common to all language group keyboards, i.e. **the Navlipi standard-semivowel keys are *not* language-specific**. They are listed below.

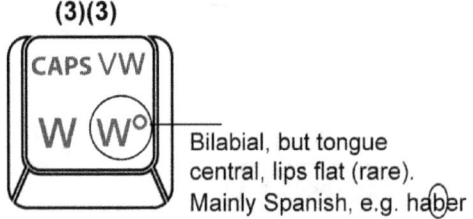

Bilabial, but tongue central, lips flat (rare). Mainly Spanish, e.g. haber

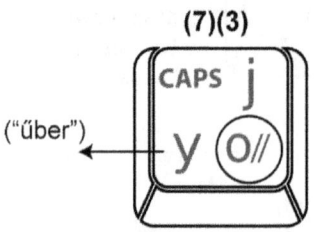

("über")

....(10.15)

Chapter 10: Navlipi Keyboarding Using the QWERTY, AZERTY or Other Common Keyboards

10.2.12 MAJOR VOWEL KEYS

The *Navlipi* keys for the major vowels are common to *all* language group keyboards, i.e. *the Navlipi vowel keys are **not** language-specific*. They are listed below.

Table 10-7: Major *Navlipi* vowel keys, in summary. These keys are *not language-specific* and thus to be used as shown for *all* the language-specific keyboards.

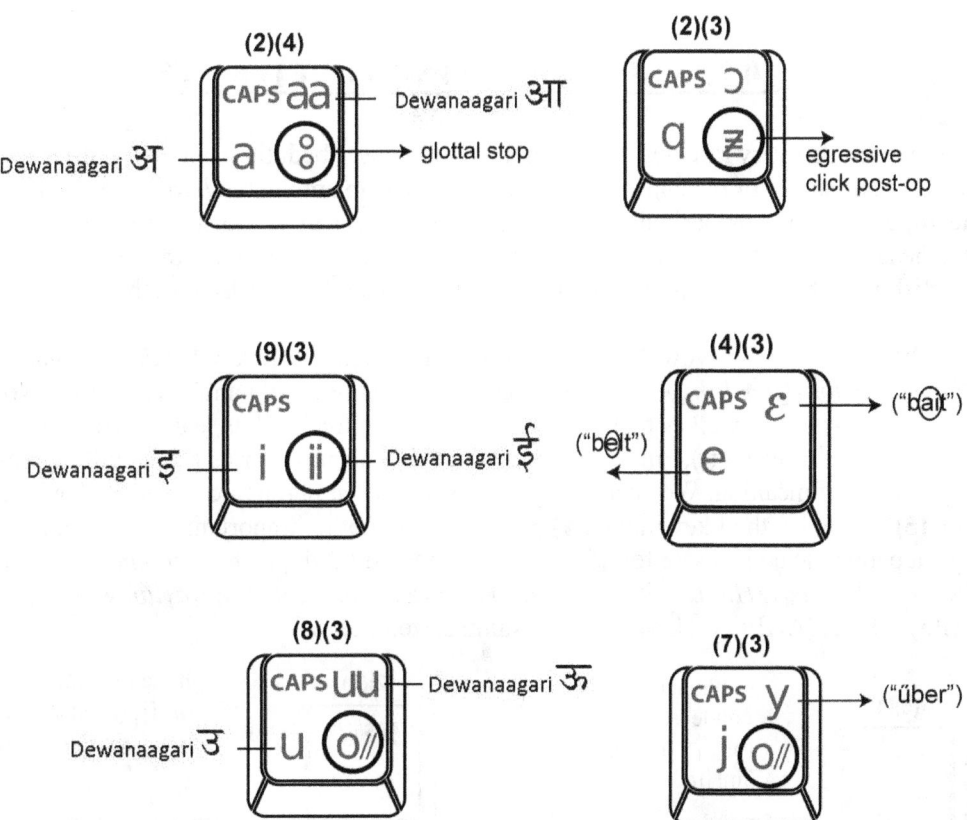

PART 3: PRESENTATION AND DISCUSSION OF NAVLIPI

(Table 10-7, cont.)

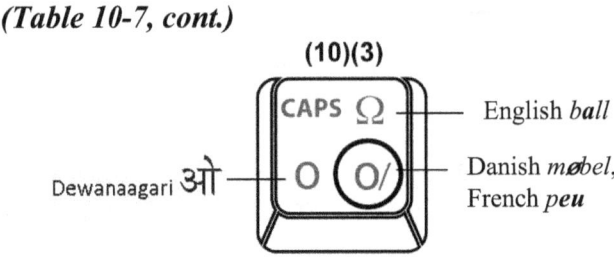

10.2.13 SPECIAL NON-VOWEL KEYS

In the event that very rare non-vowels need to be transcribed, they may be transcribed with the assistance of the appropriate post-ops. As an example, the *bilabial fricative*, heard, e.g., in the rapid articulation of English *phooey!*, can be transcribed simply as **p** + **h₀**, the latter (**h** with subscripted oval) being the post-op for fricative. In the English/French.... keyboard, this will necessarily transcribe as $p_o h_0$, but that is no matter.

Another important non-vowel key is worthy of note. This is the key for *the phonemic condensate for ([f] + [ph₀])*, used very frequently in Hindi/Urdu and several other North Indian languages, as well as many dialects of modern Greek. Thus, e.g., in Hindi/Urdu, the word for "fruit" (फल), may be articulated either as $ph_o al$ or as *fal*, at will, without any change of meaning. We accommodate this important phonemic condensate with the key **(5)(4)(A)**, i.e. the **f** key in the **(A)** position. Yet another important non-vowel key, also a phonemic condensate found commonly in Hindi/Urdu, is the *combination of ([j] (as in Jack) + [z]) (Hindi* ज , ज़ *)*. This is accommodated in *Navlipi* with the key **(2)(5)(A)**, i.e. (ALT+z). These keys are summarized below.

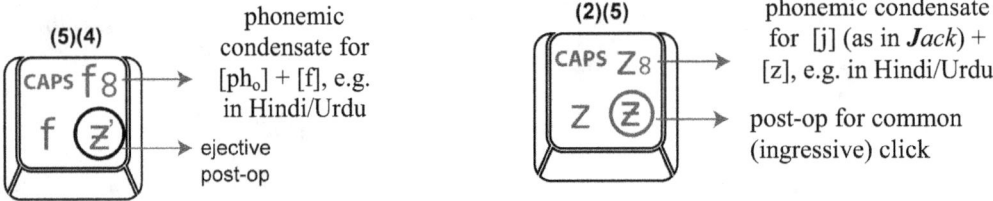

....(10.16)

Chapter 10: Navlipi Keyboarding Using the QWERTY, AZERTY or Other Common Keyboards

10.2.14 POST-OP KEYS FOR CLICKS, IMPLOSIVES AND EJECTIVES, THE "MODIFIED-Z" KEYS

For egressive and ingressive clicks, implosives and ejectives, all fairly rare, *Navlipi* uses modifications of the letter (glyph) z, as *post-ops*. Many of these "modified-z" post-op keys have been covered and graphically illustrated in the previous Section, above. We cover two additional ones here:

- The glyph for the *ingressive* (i.e. more common) *click* post-op, ⱬ, has the key **(2)(5)(CA)**, i.e. the **z** key with (CTRL+ALT).
- The glyph for the implosive post-op, ⱬ″ has the key **(3)(5)(CA)** i.e. the **x** key with (CTRL+ALT).
- The glyph for the egressive click post-op, ⱬ, has the key **(2)(3)(CA)** i.e. the **q** key with (CTRL+ALT).

10.2.15 KEYS FOR VERY RARE POST-OPS

Two other post-op keys, expected to be used very rarely, are noted here.

The first is for the post-op for (*stop + forward-fricative*), denoted by the glyph h_8. The second is for the post-op for the (*stop + fricative*), denoted by the glyph h_∞. These are summarized in the key graphic below.

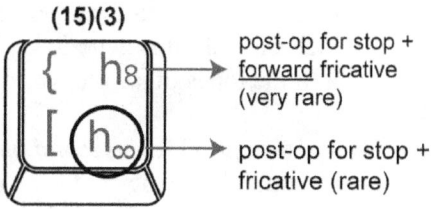

....(10.17)

PART 3: PRESENTATION AND DISCUSSION OF NAVLIPI

10.2.16 TONE KEYS (SEE ALSO NUMBER KEYS, ABOVE)

For **tones**, more specifically **tone post-ops**, *Navlipi* uses the **number keys 5 to 9**. These are the "standard" or "regular" number keys, i.e. the ones at the top of the main keyboard, rather than the ones off to the side in the NUM LOCK section of the keyboard.

These keys have been freed up, except for the number itself (used in the **(N)** position), in the key reassignments noted earlier in this chapter. They are thus readily available to us, in this very convenient position on the main keyboard, for the use of tone post-ops. Tones are a feature of importance in languages spoken by a vast number of people, from Mandarin, Cantonese and Vietnamese, to many West African languages.

Navlipi adopts the following approach with respect to the *language-specificity* of the tones:

- It uses a ***generic*** or ***default*** *keyboard* which is ***not*** language-specific and has the following features:
    - This generic keyboard incorporates the complete complement of *Navlipi* tone post-ops (see PART 1 of this book). It can thus be used to represent *all* tones found in *all* the major tone languages of the world, such as Mandarin, Cantonese, Vietnamese and Yoruba.
    - This generic keyboard uses *only* the number keys **5, 6** and **7**, leaving **8** and **9** for more specialized use in language-specific keyboards, if necessary.
    - Since it *does* incorporate the complete complement of *Navlipi* tone post-ops, it can also be used for other tone languages.
    - Indeed, in and of itself, this generic keyboard suffices for the description of the tones of *all* the world's tone languages.

- Nevertheless, *Navlipi* also provides a ***second option*** of the use of *language-specific keyboards*, should this be desired:
    - For example, a comprehensive, language-specific keyboard specific to the Chinese languages is used, as illustrated further below, which incorporates tones of Mandarin, Cantonese and other Chinese languages in place of the generic or default keyboard.
    - Another, similar, language-specific keyboard may be specific to the West African languages together.
    - Vietnamese would probably also be served well with its own language-

Chapter 10: Navlipi Keyboarding Using the QWERTY, AZERTY or Other Common Keyboards

specific keyboard with separate tone post-ops.

This ***tone post-op*** implementation of *Navlipi* is illustrated in the Tables below, for the following:

- The ***generic keyboard.***
- The ***Mandarin-Cantonese keyboard.***
- The ***generic keyboard***, *as usable for the following languages:*
  - *Yoruba* and *Igbo.*
  - *Cashinahua* (a Peruvian language).
  - *Swedish*.
  - ***Indo-European pitch (musical) accents.***
  - *Standard **stress (ictus) accents,*** as used, e.g., in Spanish.

For the Chinese languages, it is felt that ***Mandarin*** and ***Cantonese*** are well suited to be grouped into a single keyboard. However, other Chinese languages are best suited to be grouped into their own keyboards. For example, the ***Min*** Chinese languages, e.g. various *Fujienese* dialects, generally possess seven (7) tones; however, these tones are alterable by the peculiar property of tone Sandhi unique to these languages. It is thus best to assign them a separate keyboard.

PART 3: PRESENTATION AND DISCUSSION OF NAVLIPI

Table 10-8: Implementation of *TONE POST-OPS* in the *Navlipi* **keyboards**: Note on key notation used.

> ### NOTE ON KEY NOTATION USED TO ADDRESS THE NUMBER KEYS IN THE SEVERAL TABLES ON TONES AND TONE POST-OPS BELOW:
>
> We use *two* notations. We use the standard *Navlipi* notation, described in detail above, inserted in square brackets. We also use a shorthand notation, for convenient and quick reference.
>
> Thus, for example, the key selection **ALT + 5** (i.e. the number **5** key with the ALT key depressed) is written in the standard *Navlipi* notation as:
> **(6)(2)(A)**.
>
> It is also more convenient to refer to this key selection as **(#5)(A)**, since this allows the reader to identify the key without having to look up the key in the *Navlipi* key charts

Chapter 10: Navlipi Keyboarding Using the QWERTY, AZERTY or Other Common Keyboards

485

Table 10-9: Implementation of *TONE POST-OPS* in the various, different *Navlipi keyboards*, as identified.

GENERIC:

Number Key	Navlipi notation	Shift (S)	Ctrl (C)	Alt (A)	Alt + Shift (AS)	Ctrl + Shift (CS)
5	(6)(2)	‾	⌐	⌐	⌐̌	‾ (rare)
6	(7)(2)	/	ˇ	∧	∧	ˇ
7	(8)(2)	–	⌐ (rare)	⌐	⌐	
8	(9)(2)				Use these for combination, unique tones, etc., language specific.	
9	(10)(2)					

PART 3: PRESENTATION AND DISCUSSION OF NAVLIPI

(Tone Keys, cont.)

MANDARIN/CANTONESE:

Number Key	Navlipi notation	Shift (S)	Ctrl (C)
5	(6)(2)	ˉ (M, C, 1st tone)	ˇ (C, 3rd tone)
6	(7)(2)	ˋ (M, 2nd tone)	˩ (C, 4th tone)
7	(8)(2)	˩ (M, 4th tone)	˥ (C, 5th tone)
8	(9)(2)	ˬ (M, 3rd tone)	˥ (C, 6th tone) *
9	(10)(2)	ˊ (C, 2nd tone)	

* This is treated as low to mid.

M- Mandarin
C- Cantonese

Chapter 10: Navlipi Keyboarding Using the QWERTY, AZERTY or Other Common Keyboards

(Tone Keys, cont.)

YORUBA/IGBO:

Number Key	Navlipi notation	Shift (S) Yoruba	Shift (S) Igbo	Alt (A) Yoruba	Alt + Shift (AS) Yoruba
5	(6)(2)	ǀ (1st tone)	ǀ (1st tone)		Yoruba
6	(7)(2)	/ (2nd tone)	/ or rarely ⌈ (3rd tone)	⌈ (5th tone)	
7	(8)(2)	− (3rd tone)	− (2nd tone)		⌐ (4th tone)

PART 3: PRESENTATION AND DISCUSSION OF NAVLIPI

(Tone Keys, cont.)

CASHINAHUA (A PERUVIAN LANGUAGE):

Number Key	Navlipi notation	Shift (S)
5	(6)(2)	│ (1st tone)
7	(8)(2)	— (2nd tone)

SWEDISH:

Number Key	Navlipi notation	Shift (S)	Alt (A)
5	(6)(2)		Γ (1st tone)
7	(8)(2)	— (2nd tone)	

Chapter 10: Navlipi Keyboarding Using the QWERTY, AZERTY or Other Common Keyboards

(Tone Keys, cont.)

INDO-EUROPEAN PITCH ACCENTS (E.G. FOR ANCIENT SANSKRIT, GREEK AND LATIN):

Number Key	Navlipi notation	Shift (S)
5	(6)(2)	│ (Uddaata, acute)
6	(7)(2)	╱ (Swarita-1, circumflex-neutral)
7	(8)(2)	─ (Anuddaata, grave)
8	(9)(2)	─╱ (Swarita-2, circumflex-active)

STRESS (ICTUS) ACCENTS (E.G. AS USED IN SPANISH):

Number Key	Navlipi notation	Shift (S)
5	(6)(2)	│ (only 1 stress accent)

10.3 INVENTORY OF LEFTOVER, UNUSED/AVAILABLE KEYS (FOR POTENTIAL FUTURE USE)

Subsequent to the treatment above, the following keys are still available in *Navlipi*, for potential future use:

- **(5)(5)(C)** (CTRL + V); **(5)(5)(CA)** (CTRL+ALT+V).
- **(4)(3)(A)** (ALT + E).
- **(6)(3)(A)** (ALT + T) and **(4)(4)(A)** (ALT + D) *in the English/West-European language keyboard only.*
- **(11)(5)(A)** (ALT + " /? ") .
- **(13)(2)(C)** (CTRL + " =+ ") .
- **(9)(2)(A)** (ALT + 8) and **(9)(2)(C)** (CTRL + 8) .
- **(10)(2)(A)** (ALT + 9) and **(10)(2)(C)** (CTRL + 9) .
- **(21)(3)(X), (21)(4)(X), (21)(5)(X)** i.e. the **3, 6** and **9** number keys on the NUM LOCK section of the keyboard, in all positions (ALT, CTRL, SHIFT and normal)
- **(20)(2)(X), (21)(2)(X), (22)(2)(X)** i.e. the rightmost three keys (/, * and -) on the top row of NUM LOCK section of the keyboard, in all positions (ALT, CTRL, SHIFT and normal)
- All FUNCTION keys, **(3 to 18)(1)(X)** in generic *Navlipi* notation, except **(7)(1)(X)**. A total of 15 keys. These may be used in word processors or other programs for other functions. However, if they are free, they could, technically, be used by *Navlipi*.

...(10.18)

10.4 FURTHER NOTES ON PRACTICAL USE OF THE *NAVLIPI* KEYBOARD(S)

It is noted that *Navlipi* has many post-ops, for example the [$_o$] (subscripted little-circle), the [h_o] (**h** + subscripted little-circle, to indicate aspiration) and the [h_0] (**h** + subscripted oval, to indicate fricatization).

While all these post-ops have their own key on the *Navlipi* keyboards, **these individual post-op keys may find use very rarely or not at all**. The reason is quite obvious: *They are incorporated into individual glyphs in the Navlipi language-specific keyboards*, with individual, distinct keys. For example, for **ph$_o$**, the aspirated, unvoiced bilabial stop (plosive), one could, theoretically, use two keystrokes to render this glyph: **p** + **h$_o$**. However, in the relevant *Navlipi* language-specific keyboard, for *Hindi/Spanish....*, **ph$_o$** is simply rendered as **ALT** + **p**; thus, there is no need to use the key for the post-op, **h$_o$**.

As another example, in Mandarin, one need not keystroke **b** + $_\infty$ for the bilabial (unvoiced + voiced) phonemic condensate, **b$_\infty$**, since merely pressing the **b** will render this glyph in the *Mandarin/Cantonese....* language-specific keyboard. Thus, again, one has no use for the key for the [$_\infty$] post-op.

It is also noted that other means of differentiation of keys were considered for generating additional glyphs in the *Navlipi* keyboards. One example of these was the use of ***duration of the keystroke*** to differentiate glyphs, especially, e.g., for short and long vowels, which would be very intuitive. The duration of the keystroke is already used in most keyboard software, in generating multiple characters (e.g., when one depresses the **r** key continuously, one gets **rrrrrrrr**, etc.); thus, so modification of keyboard software would have been straightforward. However, such esoteric methods of differentiation for generating additional glyphs were ultimately shot down for two important reasons: **(1)** It was found that, with the unique keyboarding methodology used by *Navlipi*, there were already more than enough keys to accommodate *all* the *Navlipi* glyphs and post-ops for *all* the world's language. Thus there was found to be no need. **(2)** Since there was no need, it was best to keep the keyboarding simple by leaving out such esoteric methods of differentiation as duration of the keystroke or amount of pressure used in pressing a key.

10.5 THE KEYBOARD PRESENTATION IN PART 1 (*NAVLIPI SUMMARY TABLES*)

It is noted that the Keyboard presentation in **PART 1** of this book is essentially a paraphrased version of this chapter.

More importantly however, **PART 1** lists each and every key of the *Navlipi* keyboards individually, under the heading ***individual keys,*** something which the present chapter does not do. This list includes multiple versions where there are different keys for different language-specific keyboards. In that respect then, it contains significantly more detail than this chapter.

PART 4:

GLOSSARY, LITERATURE CITED, INDEX, ABOUT THE AUTHOR

PART 4: GLOSSARY, LITERATURE CITED, INDEX, ABOUT THE AUTHOR

GLOSSARY

OF PHONOLOGICAL, LINGUISTIC AND RELATED TERMS

N.B.: The definitions herein are abbreviated. For a fuller definition, see the sections in the main text of the book. It is also noted that these definitions do <u>not</u> include grammatical terms, terms relating to the form of language, and any other terms not having a direct phonological connotation.

THE FOLLOWING WORDS (a total of 104) ARE DEFINED IN THIS GLOSSARY.
(THE DEFINITIONS FOLLOW THIS LIST OF WORDS.)

abjad
abugida
affricate
allophone
alveolar
angramaya
apico- (examples apico-alveolar)
approximant
artition
aspirate, aspirated, aspiration
avaigyaanic
bilabial
central
click (egressive, ingressive)
close
close-mid
closure

PART 4: GLOSSARY, LITERATURE CITED, INDEX, ABOUT THE AUTHOR

completeness
de-voiced
dental
determinatives
digraph
egressive
ejective
empiricity
epiglottal
featural
flap
forward-fricative
fricative
galatophone
geminate
glottal
glyph
guttural
ictus
ideographic
idiosyncrasy, phonemic, see *phonemic idiosyncrasy*
implosive
infralabio-supradental
ingressive
lateral
liaison
logographic
logophonetic
logosyllabic
maatraic
morpheme
morphographic
medio- (example medio-palatal)
medio-palatal
multigraph
nasal
nonvowel
open

open-mid
orthography
palatal
pharyngeal
phone
phoneme
phonemic condensate
phonemic idiosyncrasy
phonemo-idiosyncratic
phonochromaticity
phonographic
phono-indicative
pictographic
plosive
post-op
pre-op
quasi-phonetic (vs. phonetic)
Rebus (principle)
retroflex
rhoticity
sandhi
semivowel
shibilant
sibilant
sonant
spirant
stop
supralabio-infradental
surd
syllabary
syllabic
tap
tone
toneme
trill
unaspirated
uniphonemographic
uniphonographic

PART 4: GLOSSARY, LITERATURE CITED, INDEX, ABOUT THE AUTHOR

498

unvoiced
uvular
vaigyaanic
velar
voiced
voiceless
vowel
vowel, derivative
vowel, cardinal
vowel, fundamental
vowel, primary

DEFINITIONS OF THE WORDS IN THE ABOVE LIST START HERE:

abjad: A script wherein each glyph represents a single non-vowel. Vowels are either "filled in" by the reader or indicated by diacritics or other markers. Modern Arabic and Hebrew scripts are *abjad's*.

abugida: A script wherein non-vowels and vowels are represented by single glyphs. The addition of a vowel to a non-vowel is further indicated by *maatra's*, i.e. markers or indicators of some sort. All Indian-type or Indian-base scripts, starting from Braahmi, including modern South-East Asian scripts. are *abugida's*. There are some newly invented abugida's as well.

affricate: A combination phone that is composed of a stop followed by a fricative of the same artition. Example: *[t]* (phone) + *[s]* (fricative = *[ts]* (affricate).

allophone: A phone that is one of the two or more phones belonging to a single phoneme. Usually denoted by square brackets (as opposed to slashes, //, for phonemes). Examples: [p] and [ph] are allophones of the English phoneme /p/; [v] and [w] are allophones of the Hindi phoneme /vw/.

alveolar: Relating to the alveolar ridge, the ridge between the upper teeth and the palate in the roof of the mouth. Usually denoting the articulation position (artition) corresponding to this, when the apex of the tongue makes contact with the alveolar ridge.

angramaya: Having a language structure like English, i.e. base language from one language family or sub-family, higher vocabulary from other language families of sub-families. Examples: English, with base language Germanic (sub-family of the Indo-European family), higher vocabulary Romance (Italic) and Greek; Hindi, with base language Indo-European, higher vocabulary from Sanskrit (Indo-European) as well as Arabic (Afro-Asiatic), Faarsi (Indo-European), Turkish (Altaic), etc; Indonesian and Thaai, with base language Austronesian (Indonesian) and Daic (Thaai), higher vocabulary Indo-European (Sanskrit). [From Sanskrit, "English-like".]

apico- Relating to the apex of the tongue, as in *apico-alveolar*, denoting the artition corresponding to the apex of the tongue contacting the alveolar ridge.

approximant: The IPA term used to denote a semi-vowel.

artition: Short for *articulation position*.

aspirate, aspirated, aspiration: Additional expression of the breath, during articulation of a phone.

avaigyaanic: Not *vaigyaanic* (see *vaigyaanic*)

bilabial: Of both lips. As in the articulation of [p].

central: "r"-sound. The breath is expelled or taken in along the *central* portion of the

tongue. This can be visualized by holding the tongue in the "r"-articulation position and breathing out and in heavily. The central portion of the tongue will cool with the breath.
click (egressive, ingressive)
close: Jaw closed. Usually referring to articulation of vowels.
close-mid: Jaw partially closed. Usually referring to articulation of vowels.
closure: Closing of the points of articulation. For example, prior to articulation of [p], *closure* of the lips occurs.
completeness: A characteristic of a script representing how completely it is able to address all phones found in all of the world's languages.
de-voiced: See *unvoiced*.
dental: Of the teeth. Usually relating to articulating position. Further bifurcated into *supradental* (upper teeth) and *infradental* (lower teeth). The [t] is a (supra)dental artition.
determinatives: See under *Rebus principle*.
digraph: Having two letters, as in *gh*.
egressive: Relating to expulsion of the breath.
ejective: Articulation of a phone through egress of the breath but with the vocal chords firmly closed as in a glottal stop. Crudely put, "talking with the throat closed". Opposite, in a sense, of an *implosive,* where the breath is taken in rather than let out. Can include fricatives such as [s] and [f] as well. Present and phonemically distinguished in languages such as Georgian and Zulu.
empiricity: Whether there is an ad-hoc, "adapt-as-you-go" nature to way the script represents a language, and whether there are certain empirical rules that must be learned along the way.
epiglottal: See *glottal*.
featural: A characteristic of a script wherein each glyph has markers or indicators indicating the properties of the phone, such as voicing, phonochromaticity and artition. Haangul (Korean) is the prototypical example of a *featural* script.
flap: Light and quick or ("flapping", "tapping"), rather than full closure, of the articulation position. A typical flap is the common "r-sound" of Spanish or Hindi when it is not trilled. Usually synonymous with *tap*.
forward-fricative: The fricative at one articulation position in front of a phone, called the *parent* phone of the forward-fricative. Thus, the forward-fricative of [t] is [s], of [p] is [f], of [k] is [sh]. Usually retains the voicing characteristics of the parent. Thus, the forward-fricative of [p] is [f], but of [b] is [v]; similarly the forward fricative of [k] is [sh], but of [g] is [zh].
fricative: A phone characterized by a partial impediment of the breath and usually by a hissing or frictional sound, as in the phones [s], [sh], [f], [v], etc.
galatophone: A phone that does not exist or is seldom used in a particular language but

GLOSSARY

which is invariably mistaken for another, usually closely related phone that exists in the language. Thus, e.g., [p] does not exist or is rarely used in most dialects of Arabic. When it is articulated, it is invariably articulated as [b]. Thus, [p] is a galatophone of [b] in Arabic. Similarly, [r] is a galatophone of [l] in Japanese. Each galatophone must always be associated with a parent phone. We then say that the galatophone *"is a galatophone for the parent phone"*. Thus, e.g., in Arabic, "[p] is a galatophone for the parent phone [b]", and in Japanese, "[l] is a galatophone for the parent phone [r]", etc. Galatophones almost always have the same phonemic value as the parent phone. Thus, when an Arabic speaker mistakenly substitutes [p] for [b] in a word, it will not change the meaning of the word, although some Arabic speakers may in fact occasionally pronounce [b] as [p]. Similarly, when a Japanese speaker substitutes [l] for [r] in a word, it will not change the meaning of the word. In a sense, galatophones are *"nonexistent allophones"*. [From Hindi *galti* ("error", of Arabic origin) + *phone*]

geminate: A twin or double phone, almost always non-vowel, usually expressed by a dual letter. Phonemically distinguished in many languages from the corresponding single phone. Thus, e.g., Hindi *pakaa* ("cooked, ripe") vs. *pakkaa* ("sure, certain, permanent, firm, pucca"), where the [kk] is a geminate.

glottal: Of the glottis. Usually relating to articulation position obtained by closure of the glottis, as in the *glottal stop*.

glyph: A character, letter or symbol of a script.

guttural: See *velar*.

IPA: International Phonetic Association. Also used to refer to the alphabet of the association, as in "the letter *a* of the IPA".

ictus: In phonology, relating to stress, "accent", usually used to distinguish a stress accent from a tonal or musical accent.

ideographic: A characteristic of a script wherein each glyph in the script represents a word, an object or an idea. Roughly synonymous with *pictographic*.

idiosyncrasy, phonemic, see *phonemic idiosyncrasy*

implosive: Articulation of a phone through ingress of the breath but with the vocal chords firmly closed as in a glottal stop. Crudely put, "talking with the throat closed". Opposite, in a sense, of an *ejective,* where the breath is let out rather than taken in. Can include fricatives such as [s] and [f] as well. Present and phonemically distinguished in languages such as Georgian and Zulu.

infralabio-supradental: An artition corresponding to contact of the lower lip with the upper teeth, as in [f].

ingressive: Involving intake of the breath.

lateral: "l"-sound. The breath is expelled or taken in along the *lateral* (side) portion of the tongue, usually along the left or right side but not both. This can be visualized by holding the tongue in the "r"-articulation position and breathing out and in heavily. The lateral portion of the tongue will cool with the breath.

liaison: In French, pertaining to euphonic combination of adjacent phones (Sandhi), usually through introduction of additional phones. As in $y + a + il?$ ---> *ya't-il?* ("Is there?").

logographic: A characteristic of a script wherein each glyph represents one word (Cl. Greek *logos*, "word").

logophonetic: A characteristic of a script wherein it is partially *logographic* and partially phonetic.

logosyllabic: A characteristic of a script wherein it is partially *logographic* and partially syllabic.

medio- Relating to the medial portion of the tongue, as in *medio-alveolar*, which denotes the artition corresponding to the middle of the tongue contacting the alveolo-dental position, as in the fricative [s]. This is distinguished from the *apico-dental* fricative [th] (of English *think*).

maatraic: A characteristic of a script of the Indian type, i.e., one that uses *maatraa's* (markers or indicators) for vowels and ligature (close joining together) of adjacent phones, where applicable. All Indian and South-East Asian scripts (except the ancient Nomic Vietnamese and the modern Roman-based ones such as modern Vietnamese and Indonesian/Malay) are *maatraic* scripts.

medio-palatal: Artition having medial portion of tongue contacting the palate. As in the German *ich*, French *agneau*. Distinguished from the *apico-palatal* (also called just *palatal*), as in *Jack*.

morpheme: The Webster's dictionary defines this as "any word or part of a word, as an affix or combining form, that conveys meaning, cannot be further divided into smaller elements conveying meaning, and usually occurs in various contexts with relatively stable meaning." Morphemes can be *free* or *bound*, and example of the latter being the *-ness* in English *happiness*.

morphographic: A characteristic of a script wherein each glyph represents one morpheme.

multigraph: Multiple letters used to represent a phone, as in *ggh*. Rare. Cf. *digraph* (but not *monograph*!)

nasal: In phonology, pertaining to passage (usually egress) of the breath through the nasal passage.

nonvowel: Any phone in which the breath is impeded partially or completely. Thus [p], [w], and [w] are all nonvowels.

open: Jaw open. Usually referring to articulation of vowels.

open-mid: Jaw partially open. Usually referring to articulation of vowels.

orthography: System of writing or transcription, particularly relating to expression of language.
palatal: Of the palate, usually denoting the artition.
pharyngeal: Of the pharynx. Can denote the artition, but also the mechanism of breath egress or ingress, i.e. related to pharynx air.
phone: Any sound. [From Greek noun φονε, (*phone*), "sound, voice", Sanskrit verb *bhan*, "to speak, to sound".]
phoneme: A phone or set of phones with linguistic value. A phone or set of phones, the replacement of which will change the meaning of a word. Specific to individual languages. In modern Western linguistic practice, denoted by slashes, //. Thus, the phones [r] and [l] of English *root* and *loot* are different phonemes, denoted /r/ and /l/, because substitution of one by the other changes the meaning of a word (from *root* to *loot*). Similarly, the phones [p] and [ph] are different phonemes, /p/ and /ph/, in Hindi, because substitution of one by the other changes the meaning of a word, as in *pal* ("a moment, an instant") vs. *phal* ("fruit"), whereas they are not different phonemes, but rather allophones of the same phoneme, /p/, in English, since articulation of English *put* with or without aspiration does not change the meaning of the word.
phonemic condensate: The result of a combination of different phones to produce a single phoneme. For example, the aspirated and unaspirated stops (plosives) can be combined to yield a single, *aspirated/unaspirated phonemic condensate*, applicable, e.g., in English and Tamil, which do not phonemically distinguish unaspirated from aspirated phones. A sort of opposite to an *allophone,* in the sense that an allophone is a result of breaking up of a phoneme into its phones, whereas a phonemic condensate is the result of combining phones to represent a phoneme in a particular language. Like the phoneme, it is very language-specific. Thus, [p] and [b] can be condensed in many Chinese languages into a single phonemic condensate, but they of course cannot in any Indo-European language. In *Navlipi*, represented sometimes by a *post-op*, and sometimes by digraphs or multigraphs.
phonemic idiosyncrasy: For a definition that does justice, see **PREFACE** and an earlier chapter. **phonemo-idiosyncratic**: A characteristic of a script wherein it addresses phonemic idiosyncrasies found across the world's languages.
phonochromaticity: "Color of the phone", encompassing such phone properties as voicing, aspiration, nasalization, fricatization, clicking, taps, trilling, implosive/ejective articulation, etc.
phonographic: A characteristic of a script wherein it is based on "*phonographs*", i.e. a script in which each *glyph* ("letter", "symbol") represents a *separate phone,* and one strives to assign to each *phone* a separate *glyph.*
phono-indicative: A characteristic of a script wherein each glyph indicates the

characteristics or properties of the phone. An example is Haangul.
pictographic: See *ideographic*.
plosive: Phone, prior to the articulation of which full closure of some part of the articulation apparatus is achieved, followed by an explosion of the breath when the phone is articulated. Thus, [p] (closure of the lips), [t] (closure at the apico-alveolar artition), and [k] (closure at the velum) are plosives.
post-op: Post-positional operator, placed *after* the phone on which it operates. As in the *Navlipi* phone *{kh$_o$}* in which *h$_o$* is the post-op for aspiration, operating on the phone [k]. An "opposite" or *pre-op*.
pre-op: Pre-positional operator, placed *before* the phone on which it operates. An "opposite" or *post-op*. *Navlipi* does not use pre-ops.
quasi-phonetic (vs. phonetic): Whether the script has a truly phonetic (i.e., phonological) nature or only a partial (i.e., *quasi-phonetic*) one. There are degrees of quasi-phoneticity, with some scripts as used for certain languages being more or less phonetic than others.
Rebus (principle): A principle of orthography best illustrated by examples: Thus, to write English *treat* we could use a symbol we've come up with for *tree*, say a picture of a tree, and add a mnemonic dot at the end to indicate the final *t* of *treat*. Or to write *God*, we could use some symbol we've already come up with for *got*, with perhaps a little halo marker for the deity. This principle was developed universally in *all* orthographies that were originally ideographic. The little distinguishing markers, such as the halo to turn *got* into *God*, are called *determinatives***.**
retroflex: Artition position with the apex of the tongue curled back and touching the palate, as in many Indian plosives.
rhoticity: Term used by the IPA to denote vocalic central phones ("r"-sounds which are vowels).
Sandhi: Term borrowed from Sanskrit grammarians denoting the *euphonic* ("good sounding", *su-bhan*) joining together of two adjacent phones, usually accompanied by a phonological reduction or change of some sort. Denoted sometimes by other terms, e.g. *liaison* in French (as in *a + il = a t'il*, done for euphony). This melding together of adjacent phones occurs naturally in most languages. Thus, in English, we have the following examples of Sandhi: *want + to = wanna; give (let) + me = gimme (lemme); got (did)+ you = gotcha (didja),* etc. etc.. Sanskrit Sandhi originated in similar, natural, common usage but then degenerated into rigid grammatical rules that *had* to be followed *every time, without fail*; this would be the equivalent of being told, in English, that *got + you* could *never* be pronounced as *got you*, but *always* had to be changed into *gotcha!* A few Sanskrit Sandhi rules are given elsewhere in this book. [(Sanskrit "union").]
semivowel: A nonvowel derived directly from a vowel, usually by addition of a

GLOSSARY

505

fundamental vowel ([a], [i], [u]). Semivowels are never plosives. Examples: [w], [j], from parent vowels [u], [I].

shibilant: A term similar to *sibilant*, denoting a fricative of the [sh], i.e. palatal, variety, e.g. [sh] and [zh]. A subset of sibilants.

sibilant: A fricative with an *"s-sound"*, e.g. [s], [z]. Also includes shibilants.

sonant: See *voiced*.

spirant: See *fricative*.

stop: See *plosive*.

supralabio-infradental: An artition corresponding to contact of the upper lip with the lower teeth.

surd: See *unvoiced*.

syllabary: A script in which one glyph represents one syllable.

syllabic: A *syllabic* script is a *syllabary*, i.e. one in which one glyph represents one syllable.

tap: Nearly synonymous with *flap*, q.v..

tone: The pitch or musical accent or musical value for a phone. Relevant not only to tone languages such as Mandarin or Yoruba, but also "semi-tonal" languages such as Vedic Sanskrit and the oldest Greek and Latin, where the "acute, grave, circumflex" accents were originally musical. One may have high, mid and low tones, but also combinations. One may have rising, following and steady tones.

toneme: A tone with a linguistic value. The tone::toneme relation is analogous to the phone::phoneme relation. (See *phoneme*.) As an example, one may have a high/steady and a high/falling tone in a language, two obviously distinct tones, but they may have the same linguistic value, and thus belong to the same toneme.

trill: Repeated phone, usually but not always relating to a flap. E.g., [rrr] is the trilled version of the flap-[r]. The term trill may also apply to phones other than flaps: For example, the lateral, "giddyap" click, denoted {lƶ} in *Navlipi*, can be trilled, producing a continuous sound.

unaspirated: Without additional breath, usually in reference to articulation of phones.

uniphonemographic: A characteristic of a script wherein one glyph represents one and only one phoneme in the language that the script addresses, and vice versa.

uniphonographic: A characteristic of a script wherein one glyph represents one and only one phone, and vice versa.

unvoiced: Vocal chords do not vibrate, e.g. in [p]. Can be easily visualized by holding two fingers lightly on the vocal chords (Adam's apple in males) and articulating [p] (unvoiced) then [b] (voiced). **uvular:** Artition relating to the uvula.

vaigyaanic: A characteristic of a script wherein it possesses a scientific and systematic phonological organization and presentation in full force.

velar: Artition relating to the velum, e.g. in the phones [k], [g]. Also called *guttural*.
voiced: Vocal chords vibrate, e.g. in [b]. Can be easily visualized by holding two fingers lightly on the vocal chords (Adam's apple in males) and articulating [p] (unvoiced) then [b] (voiced). One will feel the vocal chords vibrate.
voiceless: See *unvoiced*.
vowel: A phone for which there is no impediment to the breath during utterance.
vowel, derivative: Any vowel derived from the fundamental vowels such as [a], [i], [u], [vocalic-alveolar-r], [vocalic-alveolar-l].
vowel, cardinal: One of the eight or so vowels designated by Western phonological practice, and also by the IPA, as of fundamental nature, and used to anchor "vowel diagrams".
vowel, fundamental: A vowel having an anchoring *formant frequency* and from which all other non-fundamental vowels can be derived. Some examples are [a], [i], [u], [vocalic-alveolar-r], [vocalic-alveolar-l].
vowel, primary: See *vowel, fundamental*.

LITERATURE CITED

INCLUDING 624 REFERENCES, CITED IN ORDER OF THEIR APPEARANCE IN THE TEXT, BUT WITH ADDITIONAL GROUPING AND SUB-GROUPING TO FACILITATE EASY REFERENCE

THE BIBLIOGRAPHY LISTED HEREIN COMPRISES OVER 600 REFERENCES. A VAST MAJORITY OF THESE ARE IN ENGLISH, BUT THERE ARE A FEW CITATIONS IN OTHER EUROPEAN LANGUAGES, AND THERE ARE OF COURSE CITATIONS TO CLASSICAL WORKS IN THE FIELD IN THEIR ORIGINAL LANGUAGES, E.G. CLASSICAL GREEK AND SANSKRIT.

IT IS ALSO TO BE NOTED THAT THIS BIBLIOGRAPHY ENCOMPASSES *ALL THREE* VOLUMES OF THE *NAVLIPI* SERIES. THUS, IT MAY APPEAR TO THE READER TO HAVE REFERENCES NOT CITED IN ONE OR THE OTHER OF THE VOLUMES THAT HE/SHE IS READING- THIS MUST BE BORNE IN MIND.

EDITORIAL NOTE ON METHOD OF LITERATURE CITATION USED

It may be noted that the literature citations in this book are referenced in a somewhat unique, even quixotic, way, specifically adapted to this work. (Needless to say, this is done to make the literature cited easier to peruse by the reader.)

Firstly, they are represented with *square brackets* and with sequential numbers, e.g. "[3]", as used in the physical sciences literature, rather than alphabetically and by year, e.g. "Sapir, E., 1955a", as used in the linguistics or biological sciences literature. The author feels that this method is more concise and less disruptive of the flow of discussion in any passage.

Secondly and more unusually, reference citations are *grouped by category* and then numbered sequentially therein and further sub-grouped, all for the sake of easier reference. The categories used are represented by three letters, the first two of which are caps. For example, we have the categories *GLi, PHo* and *SLa*, respectively representing Linguistics-General, Phonology and relating to Specific Languages (such as Yoruba or Faarsi). Thus, the citations are given as "[GLi-3]" or "[SLa-(4-6)]", etc. Due to this method of numbering, reference citations may turn out *not* to be in order sometimes. For example, a passage an initial chapter may cite references [GLi-1] and [GLi-2] first, but then suddenly jump to reference [PHo-29]. This is certainly very much against the convention even in the physical sciences. However, once again, the author feels that the grouping of references by category makes referring to them (and looking them up, if necessary), much, much more convenient for the reader.

Thirdly, within each category, references are further sub-grouped and given a descriptive title that is highlighted (underlined, italicised and bolded) above the group. Some examples of such descriptive titles are "Origins of language", "Sign language (including Nicaraguan Sign Language, Arabic Sign Language)" and "Relating to mathematical and genetics aspects of language".

As an aside, it may be noted that either an original (in the case of books) or a (single) photocopy or pdf (in the case of journal articles and out-of-copyright works) of *each and every reference* cited is actually in the possession of the author, and it has been thoroughly perused for relevance. Thus, it goes without saying that *only the minimal, relevant literature is cited*, since otherwise the number of references may have run into unworkable thousands.

LITERATURE CITED IS LISTED UNDER EACH OF THE FOLLOWING CATEGORIES IN ORDER AND NUMBERED SEQUENTIALLY WITHIN EACH CATEGORY

LN
(General linguistics, seminal or more significant references)

PHo
(Phonetics)

SCr
(Relating to scripts in general and to other scripts. Also, other scripts not technically part of Prior Art competing with Navlipi. e.g. Maya script. Also orthography.)

LAs
(Relating to specific languages, e.g. to Yoruba or Faarsi, etc., except Indian languages)

LAi
(Relating to Indian languages)

HIh
(Relating to general human history, including migrations, except Indian history)

HIi
(Relating to Indian history)

IEu
(Relating to Indo-European languages, history, migration, etc.)

GDn
(Relating to genetics, DNA, etc.)

LN
(General linguistics, seminal or more significant references)

Widely consulted references:
LN-1. Aronoff, M.; Rees-Miller, J., *Handbook of Linguistics, The,* Blackwell Publishing, Cambridge, MA (USA), (2006).

LN-2. Grimes, B. F. (Ed.), *Ethnologue: Languages of the World, 13th edn.,* Summer Institute of Linguistics, Dallas (USA), (1996).

General linguistics, including primers:
LN-3. **(a)** Moseley, C. (Co-Editor), *Atlas of the World's Languages* Routledge Publishers, Oxford, U.K. and New York, USA, (1994). **(b)** Asher, R. E.; Simpson, J. M. Y, (Eds.), *Encyclopedia of Language and Linguistics,* Pergamon, Oxford (England) **8,** 4101-9, (1994)

LN-4. Woodard, R.D., *The Atlas of Languages: The Origin and Development of Languages throughout the World,* Quarto, London (England); Facts on File, New York (USA), 162-209, (1996).

LN-5. Schmitt, N. (Ed.), *An introduction to applied linguistics,* Arnold, London (England); Oxford University Press, New York (USA), (2002).

LN-6. Frawley, W.J., *International Encyclopedia of Linguistics: 4-Volume Set,* Oxford University Press, New York, NY (USA), (1 May 2003).

LN-7. Fromkin, V.A., (Ed.), with contributions by: Curtiss, S.; Hayes, B.P.; Hyams, N.; Keating, P.A.; Koopman, H.; Munro, P., Sportiche, D.; Stabler, E.P.; Steriade, D.; Stowell, T.; Szabolsci, *Linguistics, An Introduction to Linguistic Theory,* Blackwell Publishing, Cambridge, MA (USA), (2000), (ISBN: 0-205-42118-0).

LN-8. Crystal, D., *A Dictionary of Linguistics and Phonetics, 5th edition* Blackwell Publishing Ltd, Malden, MA (USA), (2003).

LN-9 Newmeyer, F., *Linguistics: The Cambridge Survey,* Cambridge University Press, Cambridge (England), (1989).

LN-10 Fremantle, A., *A primer of linguistics,* St. Martin's Press, New York (USA), (1974).

LN-11 (a) Radford, A., *Linguistics: an introduction,* Cambridge University Press, Cambridge (England), (1999), (ISBN: 0631226648). **(b)** Gleason, H.A., *An Introduction to Descriptive Linguistics,* Holt, Rinehart and Winston, New York (1961) (ISBN 0030104653 / 9780030104657 / 0-03-010465-3)

LN-12 Akmajian, A., *Linguistics, an introduction to language and communication, 3rd edition,* M.I.T Press, Cambridge, MA (USA), (1990).

PART 4: GLOSSARY, LITERATURE CITED, INDEX, ABOUT THE AUTHOR

LN-13 O'Grady, W., *Contemporary linguistics: an introduction,* St. Martin's Press, New York (USA), (1989).
LN-14 Newmeyer, F., *Generative Linguistics: A Historical Perspective,* Routledge Press, London, (England), (1997).
LN-15 Todd, L., *An introduction to linguistics,* Longman, Burnt Mill, Harlow, Essex (England); York Press, Beirut (Lebanon), (1987).
LN-16 Matthews, P. H., *Linguistics: a very short introduction,* Oxford University Press, Oxford, (England), (2003).
LN-17 Hudson, G., *Essential Introductory Linguistics,* Blackwell Publishing Ltd, Malden, MA (USA), (2000).
LN-18 Hockett, C.F., *Course in Modern Linguistics,* Macmillan, New York, NY (USA), (1958).
LN-19 Martinet, A. (Ed.), *Elements de Linguistique Generale,* Armand Colin, Paris (France), (1960).
LN-20 Palmer, L.R., *An Introduction to Modern Linguistics,* Macmillan, New York, NY (USA), (1936).
LN-21 Potter, S., *Modern Linguistics,* Bonn University Press, Deutsch (Germany), (1957).
LN-22 Saussure, F. de, *Course in General Linguistics,* Peter Owen, London (England), (1959).
LN-23 Sturtevant, E.H., *An Introduction to Linguistic Science,* Yale University Press, London (England), (1947).
LN-24 Whorf, B.L., *Language, Thought and Reality,* Wiley and M.I.T. Press, Cambridge, MA (USA), (1956).
LN-25 Carroll, J.B., *Study of Language,* Blackwell Publishing, Cambridge, MA (USA), (1953).
LN-26 Hockett, C.F., *Refurbishing Our Foundations: Elementary Linguistics from an Advanced Point of View,* John Benjamins Publishing Co., Philadelphia, PA (USA), (1987).
LN-27 Hockett, C.F.;Greenberg, J. (Eds.), *Universals of Language,* MIT Press, Cambridge, MA (USA), (1963).
LN-28 Jespersen, O., *Language: Its Nature, Development and Origin,* Allen and Unwin, New South Wales (Australia), (1954).
LN-29 Jespersen, O., *Mankind, Nation and Individual,* Allen and Unwin, New South Wales (Australia), (1946).
LN-30 Lord, R., *Comparative Linguistics [Teach Yourself Books],* David McKay Company, Inc., New York, NY (USA), (1971).

Paanini (Panini):

LN-31 Salus, P., *Panini to Postal: a bibliography in the history of linguistics,* Linguistic Research, Edmonton, Alberta (Canada), (1971).

LN-32 Panditraj, M.M.; Shastri, G.; Pande, G.D. (Eds.), *Astadhyayi of Panini, [The Chaukhamba Surbharati Granthamala],* Chaukhambha Sanskrit Prathishthan, Varanasi (India), (2007).

LN-33 Dahiya, Y., *Panini as a Linguist: Ideas and Patterns,* Eastern Book Linkers, Delhi (India), (1995).

Prominent authors in linguistics (e.g. Sapir, Bloomfield, Chomsky):

LN-34 Sapir, E.; Mandelbaum, D.G. (Eds.), *Selected Writings of Edward Sapir in Language, Culture and Personality,* University of California Press, Berkeley, CA (USA), (1949).

LN-35 Sapir, E.; Mandelbaum, D.G. (Eds.), *Culture, Language and Personality, Selected Essays,* University of California Press, Berkley & Lost Angeles, CA, (USA), (1956, rev. ed. 1960).

LN-36 Sapir, E., *Language, An Introduction to the Study of Speech,* Harcourt, Brace & World, Inc., NY (USA), (1949).

LN-37 (a) Bloomfield, L., *An Introduction to the Study of Language,* Kessinger Publishing, LLC., Kila, MT (USA), (1914). **(b)** Bloomfield, L., *Language,* Henry Holt & Company, NY (USA), & London (England), (1933 & 1935).

LN-38 Bolinger, D.L.M.: For a complete bibliography of Prof. Bolinger's works, see the excellent and complete compilation at: http://www.cinestatic.com/bolinger.htm

LN-39 Chomsky, N., *Reflections on Language,* Pantheon, New York (USA), (1975).

LN-40 Chomsky, N., "Linguistics and cognitive science: problems and mysteries", Kasher, A. (Ed).,*The Chomskyan Turn,* Blackwell, Oxford (England), 26-53, (1991).

LN-41 Chomsky, N., *Knowledge of Language: Its Nature, Origin and Use,* Praeger, New York (USA), (1986).

Origins of language:

LN-42 Pinker, S., *The Language Instinct: How the Mind Creates Language (P.S.),* Harper Perennial Modern Classics, New York, NY (USA), (3rd edition, 2007).

LN-43 (a) Liebermann, P., *Biology and Evolution of Language,* Harvard University Press, Cambridge, MA (USA), (1984). **(b)** Bickerton, D., *Roots of Language,* Karoma, Ann Arbor, MI (USA), (1981).

LN-44 Ruhlen, M., *The Origin of Language: Tracing the Evolution of the Mother Tongue,* Wiley, New York (USA), (1994).

PART 4: GLOSSARY, LITERATURE CITED, INDEX, ABOUT THE AUTHOR

LN-45 Chandrasekhar, P., State University of New York at Buffalo, meeting of French Language Group, Amherst Campus, (September 1982).
LN-46 Eakin Emily, K.C, "The First Word, The Search for the Origins of Language", *The New Yorker,* (12 August 2007).
LN-47 Newmeyer, F., *Grammatical Theory: Its Limits and Its Possibilities,* University of Chicago Press, Chicago, IL (USA), (1983).
LN-48 Newmeyer, F., *Language Form and Language Function,* M.I.T Press, Cambridge, MA (USA), (2000).
LN-49 Hirsh-Pasek, K.; Golinkoff, R., *The Origins of Grammar: Evidence from Early Language Comprehension,* M.I.T Press, Cambridge, MA (USA), (1996).
LN-50 Trubetzkoy, N.; Liberman, A. (Ed.), *Studies in General Linguistics and Language Structure,* Duke University Press, Durham, NC (USA) and London (England), (2001).
LN-51 Hauser, M.D.; Chomsky, N.; Fitch, W.T., "The Faculty of Language: What Is It, Who Has It, and How Did It Evolve?", *Science,* **298**, 1569-1579, (2002).
LN-52 Seydel, C., "Ancient Roots for an African language?", *Science,* **13:6**, (22 October 2001).
LN-53 Keller, R., *On Language Change: The Invisible Hand in Language,* Routledge, London (England), (1994).
LN-54 Jackendoff, R., *Foundations of Language: Brain, Meaning, Grammar, Evolution,* Oxford University Press, New York (USA), (2002).
LN-55 Wade, N., "Early Voices: The Leap to Language", *New York Times Science Times,* F1, (15 July 2003).

Sign language (including Nicaraguan Sign Language, Arabic Sign Language):
LN-56 Senghas, A.; Kita, S.; Ozyurek, A., "Children Creating Core Properties of Language: Evidence from an Emerging Sign Language in Nicaragua", *Science* **305: 5691**,1779-1782, (17 September 2004).
LN-57 Senghas, A., The development of Nicaraguan Sign Language via the language acquisition process, MacLaughlin, D.; McEwen, S., (Eds.), *Proceedings of the 19th Annual Boston University Conference on Language Development,* Cascadilla Press, Somerville, MA (USA), (1995).
LN-58 Sandler, W.; Meir, I.; Padden, C.; Aronoff, M., "The emergence of grammar: Systematic structure in a new language", *Proceedings of the National Academy of Science USA (PNAS),* **102**, 2661-2665, (15 February 2005).
LN-59 "The evolution of language: Gestures of Intent", *The Economist*, 99, (5 May 2007).

LN-60 Pollick, A.; Waal-Frans, B.M. de, "Ape gestures and language evolution", *Proceedings of the National Academy of Science USA (PNAS)*, **104,** 8184-8189, (8 May 2007).

LN-61 Gardner, R. A.; Gardner, B. T.; Cantfort, T. E. (Eds.), *Teaching Sign Language to Chimpanzees,* State University of New York Press, Albany, NY (USA), (1989).

LN-62 Peperkamp, S.; Mehler, J., "Signed and spoken language: a unique underlying system?" *Language and Speech,* Kingston Press Services, Middlesex (England), 42, 333-46, (1999).

LN-63 Padden, C. A., *Interaction of Morphology and Syntax in American Sign Language,* Garland, New York (USA), (1988).

LN-64 Wilbur, R. B., *American Sign Language: Linguistic and Applied Dimensions,* Little Brown, Boston, MA (USA), (1987).

LN-65 Corballis, M.C., *From Hand to Mouth: The Origins of Language,* Princeton University Press, Princeton, NJ (USA), (2002).

LN-66 Fox, M., *Talking Hands [What Sign Language Reveals About the Mind],* Simon Schuster, New York, NY (USA), (2007), (ISBN: 0-15-648233-9).

LN-67 "The talking cure", *The Economist Technology Quarterly,* (12 March 2005).

LN-68 Newport, E.; Meier, R., The Acquisition of American Sign Language, Slobin, D. (Ed.), *The Crosslinguistic Study of Language Acquisition, The Data*, Erlbaum, Hillsdale, NJ (USA), **1,** (1985).

LN-69 Humphries, T., Padden, C., O'Rourke, T. J., *A Basic Course in American Sign Language, 2nd edn.,* T.J. Publishers, Silver Spring, MD (USA), (1994).

LN- 70 Brentari, D., in: Sign language phonology, Goldsmith, J. (Ed.), *The Handbook of Phonological Theory,* Blackwell, Cambridge, MA (USA), 615-39, (1995).

LAs-71. Corina, D.; Sandler, W., "Phonological structure in sign language", *Phonology* **10:2,** 165-208, (1993).

LN-72 Bowerman, M., "The origins of children's spatial semantic categories: Cognitive vs. linguistic determinants", in: Gumperz, J. J.; Levinson, S.C., (Eds.), *Rethinking Linguistic Relativity,* Cambridge University Press, Cambridge (England), (1991).

Primers and general references containing significant errors:

LN-73 Ohio State University Dept. of Linguistics. Tserdanelis, G.; Wong, W.Y.P. (Eds), *Language Files, Materials for an Introduction to Language & Linguistics (Ninth Ed.),* Ohio State University Press, Columbus, OH (USA), (2004), (ISBN 10: 0-631-19711-7).

LN-74 See pp. 53ff. and pp. 415ff. in Reference LN-73.

PART 4: GLOSSARY, LITERATURE CITED, INDEX, ABOUT THE AUTHOR

LN-75 Crystal, D., *Linguistics [Second Ed.]*, Penguin Group, New York, NY (USA), 415ff, (1985).

LN-76 Parker, F., Riley, K., *Linguistics for Non-Linguistics, A Primer with Exercises*, Pearson Publishing, NY (USA), (2005).

Relating to mathematical and genetic aspects of language, including analysis thereof:

LN-77 (a) Gray, R.; Atkinson, Q.D., "Language-tree divergence times support the Anatolian theory of Indo-European origin", *Nature* **426**, 435-439, (27 November 2003). **(b)** Atkinson, Q.D., "Phonemic Diversity Supports a Serial Founder Effect Model of Language Expansion from Africa. (Analysis of word sounds suggests that language originated once, in central and southern Africa.)", *Science* **332**, 346-349 (15 April 2011).

LN-78 Fodor, I., "The Rate of Linguistic Change: Limits of the Application of Mathematical Methods in Linguistics", *Janua Linguarum, Series Minor* **43**, Mouton, The Hague, (1965).

Historical and extinct languages:

LN-79 Friedrich, J., *Extinct Languages*, Dorset Press, New York, NY, (USA), (1989).

LN-80 (a) Moseley, C., (Editor-in-chief), *UNESCO Atlas of the World's Languages in Danger* (UNESCO Press, 3rd Edition, Paris, 2010- includes online interactive version). **(b)** Moseley, C. (Editor), *Encyclopedia of the World's Endangered Languages*, Routledge Publishers, Oxford, U.K. and New York, USA, (2007). **(c)** Harrison, D., *When Languages Die: The Extinction of the World's Languages and the Erosion of Human Knowledge*, Oxford University Press, New York, NY (USA), (2008).

LN-81 Hitt, J., "Say No More: On a remote island in Patagonia, the last six speakers of Kawesqar struggle to find the right words. What gets lost when a language dies?", *New York Times Magazine*, 52-58 and 100, (29 February 2004).

LN-82 For additional material on languages of the world and extinct languages, see Chapter 2 in Reference LN-1.

Historical and language origins, cont., significant references:

LN-83 Diamond, J.; Bellwood, P., "Farmers and Their Languages: The First Expansions", *Science*, **300**, 597, (2003).

LITERATURE CITED

517

Relating to most common and most unchanging words in languages:
LN-84 Pagel, M.; Atkinson, Q.; Meade, A., "Frequency of word-use predicts rates of lexical evolution throughout Indo-European history", *Nature* **449**, 717-720, (11 October 2007).

Historical and extinct languages, cont.:
LN-85 Joseph, B. D.; Janda, R. D. (Eds.), *Handbook of Historical Linguistics,* Blackwell, Oxford (England), (2000).
LN-86 Jones, C, (Ed.), *Historical Linguistics: Problems and Perspectives,* Longman, New York (USA), 237-78, (1993).
LN-87 Koerner, E. F. K.; Asher, R. E. (Eds.), *Concise History of the Language Sciences: From Sumerians to the Cognitivists,* Pergamon, Oxford (England), (1995).

Morphology, grammar, intonation, etc.:
LN-88 Vajda, E., "Distinguishing referential from grammatical function in morphological typology", *Linguistic Diversity and Language Theories*, University of Colorado, Boulder, CO (USA), (2005).
LN-89 (a) Spencer, A.; Zwicky, A., (Eds.), *Handbook of Morphology,* Blackwell, Oxford (England), (1999). **(b)** Spencer, A., *Morphological Theory,* Blackwell, Oxford (England) and Cambridge, MA (USA), (1991).
LN-90 Hirst, D.; Di Cristo, A., *Intonation Systems. A Survey of Twenty Languages* , Cambridge University Press, London and Cambridge, England (1998).
LN-91 Aronoff, M., *Word Formation in Generative Grammar*, M.I.T. Press, Cambridge, MA (USA), (1976).
LN-92 Fodor, J.A.; Katz, J. (Eds.), *The Structure of Language: Readings in the Philosophy of Language*, Prentice-Hall, Englewood Cliffs, NJ (USA), (1964).
LN-93 Gleason, H.A., *Workbook in Descriptive Linguistics*, Holt, Rinehard and Winston, New York (USA), (1955).
LN-94 Hamp, E.P.; Househoulder, F.W.; Austerlitz, R. (Eds.), *Readings in Linguistics II*, University of Chicago Press, Chicago, IL (USA), (1966).

Acquisition of language by children, young adults and adults, and language learning:
LN-95 Gee, J. P. "First Language Acquisition as a guide for theories of learning and pedagogy", *Linguistics and Education* **6**, 331-54, (1994).
LN-96 Eimas, P., Speech perception in early infancy, Cohen, L. B.; Salapatek, P. (Eds.), *Infant Perception: From Sensation to Cognition,* Academic Press, New York (USA), (1975).

LN-97 Eimas, P., The perception and representation of speech by infants, In Morgan, J.; Demuth, K. (Eds.), *Signal to Syntax: Bootstrapping from Speech to Grammar in Early Acquisition,* Lawrence Erlbaum, Mahwah, NJ (USA), 25-39, (1996).

LN-98 Miesel, J. M.; Hyltenstam, K.; Obler, L. K., (Eds.), "Early differentiation of languages in bilingual children", *Bilingualism across the Lifespan,* Cambridge University Press, Cambridge (England), 13-40, (1990).

LN-99 Clark, E., "What's in a word? On a child's acquisition of semantics in his first language", In Moore, T. E. (Ed.), *Cognitive Development and the Acquisition of Language,* Academic Press, New York (USA), (1973).

LN-100 Ingram, D., "Phonological rules in young children", *Journal of Child Language* **1,** 49-64, (1979).

LN-101 Oller, D., The emergence of speech sounds in infancy, Yeni-Komshiam, G.; Kavanagh, J.; Ferguson, C. (Eds.), *Child Phonology,* Academic Press, New York (USA), (1980).

LN-102 Gnanadesikan, A., *Markedness and Faithfulness Constraints in Child Phonology,* University of Massachusetts, Cambridge, MA (USA), (1995).

LN-103 Ingram, D., "Phonological rules in young children", *Journal of Child Language* **1,** 49-64, (1979).

LN-104 Menn, L., "Development of articulatory, phonetic, and phonological capabilities", In Butterworth, B. (Ed.), *Language Production* **Vol. 2,** 3-50, Academic Press, London (England), (1983).

LN-105 *The Economist,* Technology Quarterly, (2 December 2006), p. 20.

LN-106 (a) Pinker, S., *Language Learnability and Language Development,* Harvard University Press, Cambridge, MA (USA), (1996). **(b)** Cairns, H., *The Acquisition of Language,* Pro-Ed, Austin, TX (USA), (1996).

LN-107 Bush, C., "On specifying a system for transcribing consonants in child language: A working paper with examples from American English and Mexican Spanish", Stanford University Child Language Project, Stanford, CA (USA), (1973).

LN-108 MacDaniel, D.; Cairns, H.; Hsu, J., "Binding principles in the grammars of young children", *Language and Acquisition* **1:4,** 121-38, (1990).

LN-109 Kuhl, P.; Williams, K.; Lacerda, F.; Stevens, K.; Lindblom, B., "Linguistic experience alters phonetic perception by 6 months of age", *Science* **255,** 606-8, (1992).

LN-110 Juscyk, P.; Frederici, A.; Wessels, J.; Svenkerud, V.; Jusczyk, A., "Infants' sensitivity to the sound patterns of native language words", *Journal of Memory and Language* **32,** 402-20, (1993).

LN-111 Fernald, A., "Four-month olds prefer to listen to motherese", *Infant Behavior and Development* **8,** 181-95, (1985).

PHo
(Phonetics)

Significant general, all-encompassing books:
PHo-1. O'Connor, J.D., *Phonetics,* Penguin Group, New York, NY (USA), (1973).

General primers, handbooks and manuals:
PHo-2. Hardcastle, W. J.; Laver, J. (Eds.), *The Handbook of Phonetic Sciences,* Blackwell, Oxford (England), (1997).
PHo-3. Ladefoged, P., *A Course in Phonetics, 3rd edition,* Harcourt Brace Jovanovich, New York (USA), (1993).
PHo-4. Ladefoged, P.; Maddieson, I., *The Sounds of the World's Languages,* Blackwell, Oxford (England), (1996).
PHo-5 Ladefoged, P., *Vowels and consonants,* Blackwell Publications, Malden, MA (USA), (2005).
PHo-6 Ladefoged, P., "The Classification of Vowels", *Lingua,* **5** 113-28, (1956).
PHo-7 Roca, I.; Johnson, W., *A Course in Phonology,* Blackwell Publishing Ltd, Malden, MA (USA), (1999).
PHo-8 Pickett, J., *The Sounds of Speech Communication: A Primer of Acoustic Phonetics and Speech Perception,* Pro-Ed, Austin, TX (USA), (1980).
PHo-9 Brosnahan, L. F., *Introduction to Phonetics,* Heffer, Cambridge (England), (1970), (ISBN: 0631201262).
PHo-10 Catford, J.C., *A practical introduction to phonetics, 2nd edition,* Oxford University Press, Oxford, (England), (2001).
PHo-11 Clark, J., *An introduction to phonetics and phonology,* Blackwell, Oxford (England), (1995).
PHo-12 Silverman, D., *A critical introduction to phonology: of sound, mind, and body,* Continuum, London (England), (2006).
PHo-13 Goldsmith, J. (Ed.), *The Handbook of Phonological Theory,* Blackwell Publishing Ltd, Malden, MA (USA), (1996), (ISBN: 063121478X).
PHo-14 Panconcelli-Calzia, G. in: Kaiser, L. (Ed.), *Manual of Phonetics,* North-Holland Publishing Co., Amsterdam (Netherlands), (1957).
PHo-15 Grammont, M.,*Traite de phonetique,* Delagrave, Paris (France), (1933).
PHo-16 Heffner, R.-M.S., *General Phonetics,* University of Wisconsin Press, Madison, WI (USA), (1949).
PHo-17 (a) Kaiser, L., *Manual of Phonetics,* North-Holland Publishing Co., Amsterdam (Netherlands), (1957). *For Cantonese reference, see p. 215 in this; for Nama reference, see p. 85 in this.* **(b)** *For Nama, see also:*

PART 4: GLOSSARY, LITERATURE CITED, INDEX, ABOUT THE AUTHOR

http://en.wikipedia.org/wiki/Khoekhoe_language **(c)** For Nama, see also: http://www.omniglot.com/writing/nama.htm

PHo-18 Malmberg, B., *Phonetics,* Dover Publications, Inc., NY (USA), (1963).
PHo-19 Abercrombie, D., *Elements of General Phonetics,* Aldine Publishing Company, Chicago, IL (USA), (1967).
PHo-20 Laver, J., *Principles of Phonetics,* Cambridge University Press, London (England), (1994).

Relating to Khosian (click) languages' phonology:
PHo-21 Traill, A., *Phonetic and Phonological Studies of !Xoo Bushman,* Helmut Buske Verlag, Hamburg (Germany), (1985).
PHo-22 Traill, A., "Agreement Systems in !Xoo", *Limi* **2**, (1974).
PHo-23 Van Reenen, J.F., "Dentition, jaws and palate of the Kalahari Bushman", *Journal of the Dental Association of South Africa* **19**, (1964), (ISBN: 0631222847).
PHo-24 Jakobson, R., "Extra-pulmonic consonants (ejectives, implosives, clicks)", *Quarterly Progress Report,* **90**, (1968), (ISBN: 978-0631214816).
PHo-25 Kagaya, R., "Soundspectrographic analysis of Naron clicks", *Ann. Bull. of the Research Institute of Logopedics and Phoniatrics,* (1984).
PHo-26 Beach, D.M., *Phonetics of the Hottentot Language,* W. Heffer & Sons, Ltd., Cambridge (England), (1938).
PHo-27 Westermann, D.; Ward, I.C., *Practical Phonetics for Students of African Languages,* Oxford University Press, London (England), (1933, 2nd ed.1949).

SCr
(Relating to scripts in general and to other scripts. Also, other scripts not technically part of Prior Art competing with Navlipi. e.g. Maya script. Also orthography.)

Significant general, all-encompassing works:

SCr-1. **(a)** Daniels, P.; Bright, W., (Eds.), *(The) World's Writing Systems,* Oxford University Press, Oxford (England), (1996).

(b) (i) Ostler, N., *Empires of the Word: A Language History of the World,* HarperCollins Publishers/Harper Perennial, London, UK and New York, NY, USA (2005). **(ii)** See also: Ostler, N., *The Last Lingua Franca: English Until the Return of Babel,* Walker & Company, New York, NY, USA (2010).

(c) Coulmas, F. (Ed.), *The Blackwell Encyclopedia of Writing Systems*, Blackwell Publishers, Oxford, UK, and Cambridge, MA, USA (1996).

(d) Rogers, H., *Writing Systems: A Linguistic Approach*, Blackwell Publishing, Malden, MA, USA (2005).

(e) Sampson, G., *Writing Systems*, Stanford University Press, Stanford, CA, USA (1985).

(f) Chandrasekhar, P., *NAVLIPI,* U.S. patent application N°. 12/764,094, dated 21 April 2010.

SCr-2. Albright, Robert, W.; Voegelin, C.F. (Eds), "The International Phonetic Alphabet: Its backgrounds and Development", *International J. Am. Linguistics Part III, Publication Seven of the Indiana University Research Center in Anthropology, Folklore, and Linguistics* **24**, (Jan. 1958), (ISBN: 0-521-63751-1).

SCr-3. *Handbook of the International Phonetic Association, A guide to the use of the International Phonetic Alphabet*, International Phonetic Association (IPA), Cambridge University Press, London (England), (2002).

SCr-4 For a very recent example of the continued but ad-hoc addition of glyphs to the IPA alphabet, see, e.g., Erard, M., "With Sound From Africa, the Phonetic Alphabet Expands", *The New York Times*, (13 December 2005).

General books and references:

SCr-5 Coulmas, F., *Writing systems: an introduction to their linguistic analysis,* Cambridge University Press, Cambridge (England), (2003).

SCr-6 Coulmas, F., *The Blackwell Encyclopedia of Writing Systems,* Blackwell, Oxford (England), (1996), (ISBN: 978-0195139778).

PART 4: GLOSSARY, LITERATURE CITED, INDEX, ABOUT THE AUTHOR

SCr-7 Coulmas, F., *Writing Systems of the World,* Blackwell Publishing, Oxford (England), (1989).
SCr-8 Senner, W. (Ed.), *Origins of Writing,* University of Nebraska Press, Lincoln, NE (USA), 203-37, (1989).
SCr-9 Campbell, G., *Handbook of scripts and alphabets,* Routledge, London (England) and New York (USA), (1997).
SCr-10 Sampson, G., *Writing Systems,* Stanford University Press, Stanford, CA (USA), (1985).
SCr-11 Oates, J. (Ed.), "Early Writing Systems [special issue]", *World Archaeology 17/3,* (1986).
SCr-12 Nakanishi, A., *Writing Systems of the World: Alphabets, Syllabaries, Pictograms,* Tuttle, Rutland, VT (USA), (1980).
SCr-13 Day, L., *Alphabets old & new, 3rd edition,* Omega, London (England), (1988).
SCr-14 Jensen, H., *Sign, Symbol and Script, 3rd edn. Tr. George Unwin,* George Allen and Unwin, London (England); Putnam's New York (USA), (1969).
SCr-15 Gelb, I.J., *A Study of Writing,* University of Chicago Press, Chicago, IL (USA), (1963), (ISBN 13: 978-0197259177).
SCr-16 Fevrier, J., *Histoire de l'ecriture, 2nd ed.,* Payot, Paris (France), (1959).
SCr-17 Gaur, A., *A History of Writing (Rev. Ed),* Crossriver Press, New York (USA), (1992).
SCr-18 Gelb, I.J., *A Study of Writing,* University of Chicago Press, Chicago, IL (USA), (1952).
SCr-19 Diringer, D., *The Alphabet: A Key to the History of Mankind,* Funk and Wagnalls, New York (USA), (1948).
SCr-20 Friedrich, J., *Geschichte der Schrift unter besonderer Berucksichtigung ihrer geistigen Entwicklung,* Heidelberg, Winter (Germany), (1966).

Primers on extinct scripts:
SCr-21 Gordon, C.H., *Forgotten Scripts: Their Ongoing Discovery and Decipherment,* Dorset Press, New York, NY (USA), (1982).

By region- Sumer:
SCr-22 Thureau-Dangin, F., *Die sumerischen und akkadischen inschriften,* Hinrich, Leipzig (Germany), (1907).

By region- Egypt:
SCr-23 Lichtheim, M., *Ancient Egyptian Literature: A Book of Readings 3 vols.,* University of California Press, Berkeley & Los Angeles (USA), (1980).

By region- Semitic to Greek:
SCr-24 Pope, M., *The Story of Archaeological Decipherment: From Egyptian Hieroglyphs to Linear B,* Scribner's, New York (USA), (1975).

By region- Chinese:
SCr-25 Boltz, W., "Early Chinese Writing", *World Archaeology,* **17,** 420-36, (1986).
SCr-26 Gao, M., *Gu wen zi lei bian [Tables of ancient characters],* Zhong hua, Peking (China), (1980).
SCr-27 Sampson, G., "Chinese Script and the Diversity of Writing Systems", *Linguistics,* **32,** 117-32, (1994).
SCr-28 Boltz, W., *Origin and Early Development of the Chinese Writing System [American Oriental Series 78], The,* American Oriental Society, New Haven, CT (USA), (1994).
SCr-29 (a) Chinese Labor Library, *Chinese Characters: Unsimplified, Simplified, plus Pinyin Romantization,* Foreign Languages Press, Beijing (China), (1985). **(b)** See also: *Mandarin for Beginners,* official Chinese Government publication, Beijing (China), (1978), which gives 23 elementary lessons in Mandarin, each including Chinese script, Romanization and word-for-word English translations. The passage shown is taken from Lesson 21, p. 121, of this book. The government printing office that published the book is no longer in existence under its original name, and is not traceable as of 2005.
SCr-30 Victor, H.; Mair, Hung-Kay, Bernard (ed.), "West Eurasian and North African Influences on the Origin of Chinese Writing." In *Contacts between Cultures: Selected papers from the 33rd International Congress of Asian and North African Studies*, Toronto, *Eastern Asia: Literature and Humanities,* Edwin Mellen, Lewiston, NY (USA), **3,** 335-38, (1990).
SCr-31 Cai, X., *Chuanyin kuaizi [Rapid graphs for transmitting sounds],* Hubei Guan Shuju: woodblock. Repr. Beijing: Wenzi Gaige Chubanshe, (1956). California Press, Berkeley & Los Angeles (USA), (1980).

By region- Mesoamerican:
SCr-32 Martinez, R.; Del Carmen, M.; Ceballas, P.O.; Coe, M.; Diehl, R.; Houston, S.D., Taube, K.; Calderón, A.D., "Oldest Writing in the New World", *Science* **313,** 1610-1614, American Association for the Advancement of Science, Washington, D.C. (USA), (15 September 2006).

SCr-33 Marcus, J., *Mesoamerican Writing Systems: Propaganda, Myth, and History in Four Ancient Civilizations,* Princeton University Press, Princeton, NJ (USA), (1992).
SCr-34 Saturno, W. et al., "Early Maya Writing at San Bartolo, Guatemala", *Science* **311,** 1281, (2006).
SCr-35 Houston, S., *Maya Glyphs [Reading in the Past],* British Museum, London (England) & University of California Press, Berkeley and Los Angeles, CA (USA), (1989),
SCr-36 Wilford, J.N., "Symbols on the Wall Push Maya Writing Back by Years", *The New York Times*, (10 January 2006).
SCr-37 Wilford, J.N., "Stone Said to Contain Earliest Writing in Western Hemisphere", *The New York Times International*, (15 September 2006).

SCr-38 (a) Brinton, D.G., *The ancient phonetic alphabet of Yucatan*, J. Sabin, New York (USA), (1870). (b) See also: "Cascajal Block", *Wikipedia*, http://en.wikipedia.org/wiki/Olmec_script#cite_ref-0 .

By region- Semitic to Greek, cont.:
SCr-38 Sass, B., *Studia Alphabetica: On the Origin and Early History of the Northwest Semitic, South Semitic and Greek Alphabets (orbiblicus et orientalis 102).* Universitatsverlag, Freiburg (Switzerland), (1991).
SCr-39 Bernall, M., *On the Transmission of the Alphabet to the Aegean before 1400 B.C. Bulletin of the American Schools of Oriental Research* **267,** 1-19, (1987).
SCr-40 Driver, G.R., *Semitic Writing: From Pictograph to Alphabet, New rev. ed.,* Oxford University Press, London (England), (1976), (ISBN: 978-08543-1180).
SCr-41 "The Decipherment of Minoan and Eteocretan", *Journal of the Royal Asiatic Society,* Cambridge University Press, London (England), 148-158, (1975), (ISBN: 0226286061).
SCr-42 Brice, W.C., *Inscriptions in the Minoan Linear Script of Class A.,* The Societies of Antiquaries, Oxford & London (England), (1961).
SCr-43 Albright, W., *Proto-Sinaitic Inscriptions and Their Decipherment, [Harvard Theological Studies 12),* Harvard University Press, MA (USA), (1999).
SCr-44 Gelb, I.J., *Old Akkadian Writing and Grammar, 2nd ed., Materials for the Assyrian Dictionary,* University of Chicago Press, Chicago, IL (USA), (1961).
SCr-45 *Webster's New Universal Unabridged Dictionary, Deluxe 2nd Edition*, Dorset & Baber, Cleveland, OH (USA), (1983).

By region- Korean/Haangul (Hangul):

SCr-46 For a general overview of Haangul, including its structure, see, e.g.:
http://www.zkorean.com/korean-alphabet-hangul

SCr-47 Kim-Renaud, Y-K. (Ed.), *Korean Writing System: Its History and Structure.* University of Hawaii Press, Honolulu, HI (USA), (1996).

SCr-48 Kim-Renaud Y.-K., (Ed.), *The Korean Alphabet,* University of Hawaii Press, Honolulu, HI (USA), (1997).

SCr-49 Ledyard, G., *Korean Language Reform of 1446: The Origin, Background and Early History of the Korean Alphabet, (Ph.D. dissertation),* University of California, Berkley & Los Angeles, CA (USA), (1966).

SCr-50 Kim, C. W., "On the origin and structure of the Korean script. Inaugural lecture as Chair of Linguistics, University of Illinois, Urbana-Champaign", *Sojourns in Language, Vol. 2. Collected Papers,* Tower Press, 1988, Seoul (South Korea), 721-34, (1980).

SCr-51 For a general overview of the history of Haangul, see, e.g.:
http://www.zkorean.com/hangul/history_of_hangul

SCr-52 For examples of Haangul glyphs suitable for the non-Korean, see, e.g.:
http://www.zkorean.com/hangul/appearance

SCr-53 Hope, E.R., "Letter Shapes in Korean Onmun and Mongol Phagspa Alphabets", *Oriens* **10:1**, 150-59 (1957).

SCr-54 *Mongolian alphabet, Wikipedia,* [http://en.wikipedia.org/wiki/Mongolian_script].

By region- Japanese:

SCr-55 Habein, Y., *History of the Japanese Written Language,* University of Tokyo Press, Tokyo (Japan), (1984).

Related to Pitman, Gregg, Evans and other shorthands:

SCr-56 Abercrombie, D., *Isaac Pitman [: A Pioneer in the Scientific Study of Language],* Pitman and Sons, London (England), (1937).

SCr-57 *Pitman Shorthand,* Sir Isaac Pitman & Sons, Ltd., Toronto (Canada), (1937).

SCr-58 Graham, A., *Handbook of Standard or American Phonography [In Five Parts],* A.J. Graham & Co., NY (USA), (1886).

SCr-59 Gregg, J.; Leslie, L.; Zoubek, C., *Gregg Shorthand Manual Simplified,* McGraw-Hill Book Company, NY (USA), (1949).

SCr-60 Gregg, J. R., *The Basic Principles of Gregg Shorthand,* Gregg, New York (USA), (1923).

SCr-61 Evans, J., *Shorthand,* Barnes & Noble, Inc., New York (USA), (1946).

PART 4: GLOSSARY, LITERATURE CITED, INDEX, ABOUT THE AUTHOR

By region- North American:
SCr-62 Chiltoskey, Mary U., *Cherokee Words With Pictures,* Cherokee Publishing, Cary, NC (USA), (1972).
SCr-63 Walker, W.; Sarbaugh, J., "The Early History of the Cherokee Syllabary", *Ethnohistory* **40,** 70-94, (1993).
SCr-64 King, D., & Chapman, J., *Sequoyah Legacy [Official Guide to the Sequoyah Birthplace Museum],* Cherokee Publishing, Cary, NC (USA), (1988). See also: "Cascajal Block", *Wikipedia,* [http://en.wikipedia.org/wiki/Olmec_script#cite_ref-0].

By region- European/Central Asian:
SCr-65 Nersoyan, G., "Why and When of the Armenian Alphabet", *Journal of the Society for Armenian Studies* **2**, 51-71, (1985-86).

By region- Vietnamese, Hmong and related:
SCr-66 For a description of native Vietnamese "alphabets", see, e.g.: Perlez, J., "Deciphering the Code to Vietnam's Old Literary Treasures", *The New York Times International*, (15 June 2006).
SCr-67 (a) Vang, C. K.; Yang, G. Y.; Smalley, W. A., *The Life of Shong Lue Yang: Hmong "Mother of Writing" (Keeb Kwm Soob Lwj Yaj: Hmoob 'Niam Ntawv'),* trans. by Mitt Moua and Yang See (Southeast Asian Refugee Studies Occasional Papers 9), University of Minnesota, Center for Urban and Regional Affairs, Minneapolis (USA), (1990). **(b)** See also: **(SCr-46).** Smalley, W. A.; Vang, C. K.; Yang, G. Y., *Mother of Writing: The Origin and Development of a Hmong Messianic Script,* University of Chicago Press, Chicago, IL (USA), (1990).

By region- African:
SCr-68 Whitney, W.D., "On Lepsius's Standard Alphabet", *American Oriental Society* **8**, 335-373, (1866).
SCr-69 Lepsius, R., *Standard Alphabet for Reducing Unwritten Languages and Foreign Graphic Systems to a Uniform Orthography in European Letters, 2nd ed.,* Williams & Norgate. Repr. Amsterdam: J. Benjamins, Amsterdam (Netherlands), (1981), (Original: London (England), (1863)).
SCr-70 (a) "Practical Orthography of the African Languages", *Suppl. To Le Maitre Phonetique,* Oxford University Press, Oxford (England), (1930). **(b)** See also: Bender, M. L.; Bowen J. D.; Cooper, R. C.; Ferguson, C. A. (Eds.) Bender, M. L.; Head, S. W.; Cowley, R., "The Ethiopian Writing System", *Language in Ethiopia,* Oxford University Press, London (England), 120-29, (1976).

SCr-71 Mafundikwa, S., *Afrikan alphabets: the story of writing in Afrika,* Mark Batty, West New York, NJ (USA), (2004).

Related to potential future methods of transcription, including direct brain-to-final-medium:
SCr-72 Bennett, J., "The Curse of Cursive: Penmanship, like hieroglyphics and the IBM Selectric, has lost its purpose. Let's erase it for good", *Newsweek,* 44, (23 February 2009).
SCr-73 "Mind Games: Brain-controlled games and other devices should soon be on sale", *The Economist,* 87-88, (17 March 2007).
SCr-74 Chistovich, L.A., et al, "Temporal processing of peripheral auditory patterns of speech", *The Representation of Speech in the Peripheral Auditory System,* Elsevier Biomedical Press, New York (USA), (1982).

Very significant, original world scripts, created over several millennia to ca. 2005. (Including older European works from ca. 1400 C.E. onwards as well as modern American ones.):
SCr-75 With respect to Indian *Modi,* see, e.g., Pai, P., "Decoding a Forgotten Script Fuels Property Claims", *India Abroad* **14**, March 1996.
SCr-76 Gamkrelidze, T. V., *Alphabetic Writing and the Old Georgian Script. A Typology and Provenance of Alphabetic Writing Systems,* Caravan Books, Delmar, NY (USA), (1994).
SCr-77 *Georgia alphabet, Wikipedia:* http://en.wikipedia.org/wiki/Georgian_alphabet
SCr-78 Harper, K., "Writing in Inuktitut: An Historical Perspective", *Inuktitut,* **53**, 3-35, (1983).
SCr-79 Harper, K., *Current Status of Writing Systems for Inuktitut, Inuinnaqtun and Inuvialuktun,* Northwest Territories Culture and Communications, Yellowknife (Canada), (1992).
SCr-80 Inuktikut Script image taken, with permission, from: http://en.wikipedia.org/wiki/Image:Inuktitut.png
SCr-81 **(a)** Tschihold, J., *Die neue Typographie, Ein Handbuch für zeitgemäss Schaffende,* Verlag des Bildungsverbandes der Deutschen Buchdrucker, Berlin, (1928). See also *Typografische Entwurfstechnik,* Akademischer Verlag Dr Fritz Wedekind & Co., Stuttgart (Germany), (1932). **(b)** See also: "Jan Tschichold", *Wikipedia,* http://en.wikipedia.org/wiki/Jan_Tschichold .
Scr-82 A useful summary of these European and North American contributions can be found in: Albright, R.W., "The International Phonetic Alphabet: Its Backgrounds and Development", *International J. American Linguistics,* **24:1**, i-viii and 1-78,

published by Indiana University Research Center in Anthropology, Folklore, and Linguistics, (Bloomington, IN, USA) (January 1958).

SCr-83 Hart, J., *Orthology*, William Seres, London, (1569).

SCr-84 Hart, J., *A Methode or Comfortable Beginning for all Unlearned*, Henrie Denham, London (England), (1570).

SCr-85 Robinson, R., *The Art of Pronunciation*, Nicholas Okes, London (England), (1617).

SCr-86 Wilkins, J., *An Essay Towards a Real Character and a Philosophical Language*, John Martin, London (England), (1668).

SCr-87 Mulcaster, R., *Elementarie*, Ed. by E.T. Campagnae, Oxford University Press, London (England), (1925).

SCr-88 Butler, C., *The English Grammar, or the Institution of Letters, Syllables, and Words in the English Tongue*, Ed. by A. Richler in *Neudrucke Frühneunglishcer Grammatiken*, **IV**, Akademie der Wissenschaften, Vienna, (1910).

SCr-89 Holder, W., *Elements of Speech: AN Essay of Inquiry into the Natural Production of Letters with an Appendix concerning Persons Deaf and Dumb*, John Martin, London (England), (1669).

SCr-90 Smith, T., *De Recta et Emendata Linguae Angelicae Scriptione Dialogue*, Ed. by O. Diebel in *Neudrucke Frühneunglishcer Grammatiken,* **VIII**, Akademie der Wissenschaften, Vienna, (1913).

SCr-91 Meigret, L., *Traité Touchant le Commun Usage de l'Ecriture Francoise*, Jeanne de Mernef, Paris (France), (1545).

SCr-92 For Latin shorthands, see, e.g.: Plutarch, "Cato the Younger", *Lives*, Trans. by John Dryden, (ca. 1660).

SCr-93 "Franz Xaver Gabelsberger", *Wikipedia*,
http://en.wikipedia.org/wiki/Franz_Xaver_Gabelsberger .

SCr-94 Ellis, A.J., *Alphabet of Nature; or Contributions Towards a more accurate Analysis and Symbolization of Spoken Words, with some Account of the Principle Phonetical Alphabets Hitherto Proposed*, S. Bagster and Sons, London (England), (1845).

SCr-95 Ellis, A.J., "On Glosik", *Trans. of Philol. Soc.*, 93, (1870-1872).

SCr-96 **(a)** Wintersteen, L.R., *A History of the Deseret Alphabet*, M.A. thesis, Brigham Young University, Provo, UT (USA), 1970). **(b)** For more on the Deseret alphabet, see, e.g.: http://www.utlm.org/images/deseretalphabet_englishequiv.gif

SCr-97 Bell, Alexander M., *Visible Speech: The Science of Universal Alphabetics; or Self-Interpreting Physiological Letters, for the Writing of All Languages in One Alphabet*, Marshall & Co., London (England), (1867).

SCr-98 Sweet, H., *A Primer of Phonetics*, 71-72 and 77-78, Clarendon Press, Oxford (UK), (1890). See also: *Collected Papers of Henry Sweet*, Clarendon Press, Oxford (UK), (1913).

SCr-99 Jespersen, O., *The Articulations of Speech Sounds Represented by Means of Analphabetic Symbols*, Elwert, Marburg (Germany), (1889). See also: Jespersen, O., *Phonetische Grundfragen*, Druck and Verlag bon B.G. Teubner, Leipzig and Berlin, (Germany), (1904).

SCr-100 Janvrin, F., "The Atomic Structure of Speech", *Archives Néerlandaises de Phonétique Expérimentale,* **VI**, 101-104, (1931).

SCr-101 Emsley, B. "The First Phonetic Dictionary", *Quarterly Journal of Speech*, **XXVIII**, (1942).

SCr-102 Story, C., *Fonetic Primer, [Offering the Universal Alfabet and the Science of Spelling], The,* Isaac H. Blanchard Company, New York, NY (USA), (1907), (ISBN: 0-340-05895-1).

SCr-103 Johnston, H., *Phonetic Spelling: A proposed Universal Alphabet for the rendering of English, French, German and all other forms of Speech,* Cambridge University Press. London (England), (1913).

SCr-104 Owen, R., *Global Alphabet [A Method of Teaching English to the World],* US Government Printing Office, Washington, D.C. (USA), (1944).

SCr-105 Pike, K., *Phonemics [A Technique for Reducing Languages to Writing],* University of Michigan Press, Ann Arbor, MI (USA), (1947).

SCr-106 Pike, K., *Phonetics [A Critical Analysis of Phonetic Theory and a Technic for the Practical Description of Sounds,* University of Michigan Press, London (England), (1943).

SCr-107 Dalby, D. "A Survey of the Indigenous Scripts of Liberia and Sierra Leone: Vai, Mende, Loma, Kpelle and Bassa", *African Language Studies* **8**, 1-51, (1967). See also: Hendrix, H. (Ed.), *The search for a new alphabet: a literary studies in a changing world: in honor of Douwe Fokkema,* J. Benjamins, Amsterdam (Netherlands) and Philadelphia, PA (USA), (1996).

SCr-108 Nyei, M. B., "A Three Script Literacy among the Vai: Arabic, English and Vai", *Liberian Studies Journal,* **9,** 13-22, (1981).

SCr-109 Welmers, W. E., *A Grammar of Vai,* University of California Press, Berkeley & Los Angeles (USA), (1976).

SCr-110 See: http://en.wikipedia.org/wiki/UNIFON . Unifon script image taken, with permission, therefrom.

SCr-111 Shavian or Shaw alphabet, see *Wikipedia*, http://en.wikipedia.org/wiki/Shaw_alphabet .

SCr-112 Ewing, J., *The Columbian alphabet,* Matthias Day, Trenton, NJ (USA), (1798).

PART 4: GLOSSARY, LITERATURE CITED, INDEX, ABOUT THE AUTHOR

SCr-113 Abulhab, S., "Method and Font for Representing Arabic Characters, and Articles Utilizing Them", *U.S. Patent # US 6,704,116 B1*, 9 March 2004.
SCr-114 (a) For the Fraser script, see, e.g.: http://en.wikipedia.org/wiki/Fraser_alphabet .
  (b) See also: http://unicode.org/mail-arch/unicode-ml/y2004-m05/0635.html
SCr-115 For the Pollard script, see, e.g.: http://en.wikipedia.org/wiki/Pollard_script
SCr-116 Noel, R. S., *The Languages of Tolkien's Middle Earth*, Houghton Mifflin, Boston (USA), (1980).
SCr-117 Bloquerst, A.J., *Nouvel abecedaire, ou, Alphabet syllabique*, Philadelphia, PA (USA), (1811).
SCr-118 Wilbur, J., *The grammatical alphabet*, H.C. Southwick, Albany ,NY (USA), (1815).
SCr-119 *Arthur's alphabet*, McLoughlin Bros., New York (USA), (1875).
SCr-120 Greenaway, K., *Kate Greenaway's Alphabet*, Routledge, London (England), (1885).
SCr-121 Weeks, R., *The N.E.A. phonetic alphabet with a review of the Whipple experiments*, The New Era Printing Company, Lancaster, PA (USA), (1912).
SCr-122 Thackeray, W.M., *The Thackeray Alphabet*, Harper & Brothers, New York (USA), (1930).
SCr-123 Herzog, G.; Newman, S.S.; Sapir, E.; Haas, M.; Swadesh, M.; Voegelin, C.F., "Some orthographic recommendations", *American Anthropologist* **36**, 629-31, (1934).
SCr124 Roudet, L., *Eléments de Phonétique Générale*, University Library, Paris (France), (1910).
SCr-125 For Unicode transcriptions of the world's scripts, see, e.g.: Erard, M., "For the World's A B C's, He Makes 1's and 0's: To Call Cyrillic, Chinese or Cherokee to the Screen, Typographer Helps Forge a Digital Lingua Franca", *The New York Times*, G1, (25 September 2003).
SCr-126 References drawn from relevant sections of *Wikipedia*, Where reproduced, reproductions are in accordance with *Wikipedia*'s use policy and with all relevant permissions.

Relating to the AMERICANIST (APA) "phonetic notation" (script):
SCr-127 Powell, J. W. , *Introduction to the Study of Indian languages, with words, phrases, and sentences to be collected*, 2nd Ed., Washington, D.C., USA: U.S. Government Printing Office. (1880).
SCr-128 Boas, F., "Introduction" (pp. 5–83), in Boas, F. (Ed.), *Handbook of American Indian languages*. Bureau of American Ethnology Bulletin, **40**. Washington, D.C., USA. (1911, Reprinted 1966).

LITERATURE CITED

SCr-129 American Anthropological Society, *Phonetic transcription of Indian languages: Report of committee of American Anthropological Association.* Smithsonian miscellaneous collections, **66**, 6 (1916). Smithsonian Institution/American Anthropological Society, Washington, D.C., USA.

SCr-130 Bloomfield, L.; Bolling G. M., "What symbols shall we use?" *Language, 3* (2), 123-129 (1927).

SCr-131 Herzog, G. ; Newman, S. S.; Sapir, E. ; Swadesh, M. H. ; Swadesh, M.; Voegelin, Charles F. "Some orthographic recommendations", *American Anthropologist, 36* (4), 629-631 (1934).

SCr-132 *Americanist* script figures reproduced, with permission, from the listings under the following websites:

(a) http://www.associatepublisher.com/e/a/am/americanist_phonetic_notation.htm

(b) http://en.wikipedia.org/wiki/Americanist_phonetic_notation

LAs
(Relating to specific languages, e.g. to Yoruba or Faarsi, etc., except Indian languages)

General:
LAs-1. Ruhlen, M., *A Guide to the World's Languages, Classification* Stanford University Press, Stanford, CA (USA), **1**, (1987).
LAs-2 *Hammond New Century World Atlas,* Hammond World Atlas, Corp. (Langenscheidt Publishing Group), 22-23, (2000).
LAs-3 *List of countries by populations, Wikipedia:*
 [http://en.wikipedia.org/wiki/list_of_countries_by_population].

Related to human migration, archaeology and related subjects:
LAs-4 For a concise summary of human migrations of the last 100,000 years and how they possibly relate to the isolated and unisolated development of languages, see, e.g., the several migration focal points shown in the figures in the following article: Stix, G., "Traces of a Distant Past", *Scientific American*, 56-63, (July 2008).
LAs-5 Ross, M.; Blench, I, R.; Spriggs, M., (Eds.), *Archaeology and Language,* Routledge, London (U.K.) 209-261, (1997).

Related to specific languages, language families or groups- African:
LAs-6 (a) Wade, N., "In Click Languages, an Echo of the Tongues of the Ancients", *The New York Times*, (18 March 2003).
 (b) Hahn, C.H.L.; Vedder, H.; Fourie, L., *The native tribes of South West Africa*, Cass Publishing, London, UK (1966).
LAs-7 (a) Sands, B., *Eastern and Southern African Khoisan: Evaluating Claims of Distant Linguistic Relationship,* Koppe, Cologne (Italy), (1998).
 (b) Kroenlein, J.G., *Wortschatz der Khoi-Khoin (Namaqua-Hottentotten)/Gesammelt, aufgeschrieben und verdeutscht von J.G. Kroenlein, herausgegeben mit unterstützung der Königl. Academie der Wissenschaften*, Dutsche Kolonialgesselschaft/ C. Heymanns Verlag, Berlin, Germany (1889).
LAs-8 Maingard, L.F., "The third bushman language", *African Studies* **17**, 100-115, (1958).
LAs-9 Welmers, W.E., *African Language Structures*, University of California Press, Berkeley, CA (USA), (1973).

LAs-10 Greenberg, J. H., *The Languages of Africa,* Indiana University, Bloomington, IN (USA), and Mouton, The Hague, (1963).
LAs-11 Greenberg, J., "Studies in African Linguistic Classification: IV. Hamito-Semitic *Southwestern Journal of Anthropology, - Article consists of 20 pgs, not accessible online.,* **6,** 47-63, (Spring 1950).
LAs-12 Ladefoged, P., *A Phonetic Study of West African Languages,* Cambridge University Press, London (England), (1964).
LAs-13 Diakonoff, I. M., *Afrasian Languages,* Akademika Nauka, Moscow (Russia), (1988).
LAs-14 Bendor-Samuel, J. (Ed.), *The Niger-Congo Languages,* University Press of America, Lanham, MD (USA), (1989).
LAs-15 Bamgbose, A., Yoruba, Dunstan, E. (Ed.), *Twelve Nigerian Languages: A Handbook on their Sound Systems for Teachers of English,* Longmans Green, London (England), 163-72 (1969).
LAs-16 Bender, M. L., *The Nilo-Saharan Languages: A Comparative Essay, 2nd edn.,* Lincom Europa, Munich (Germany), (1997).
LAs-17 Payne, D., "Maa Language Project: Kenyan Southern Maasai, Samburu", University of Oregon: http://pages.uoregon.edu/maasai/

Related to specific languages, language families or groups- Swedish:
LAs-18 Malmberg, B., "Observations on the Swedish Word Accent", *Haskings Laboratories Report,* (1955).

Related to specific languages, language families or groups- Ural-Altaic:
LAs-19 Attaoullah, F., *Beginner's Turkish,* Hippocrene Books, Inc., New York (USA), (1998), (ISBN: 81-206-1376-7).
LAs-20 Johanson, L.; Csato, E. (Eds.), *The Turkic Languages,* Routledge, London (England), (1998).
LAs-21 *Altaic languages, Wikipedia,* [http://en.wikipedia.org/wiki/Altaic].
LAs-22 Poppe, N., *Introduction to Altaic Linguistics,* Harrassowitz, Wiesbaden (Germany), (1965).
LAs-23 *Ural-Altaic languages, Wikipedia,* [http://en.wikipedia.org/wiki/Ural-Altaic].
LAs-24 Decsy, G. (Ed.), *Ural-Altaische Jahrbucher/Ural-Altaic Yearbook, 56, 1984,* Eurolingua, (1984), (ISBN-10: 0931922178, ISBN-13: 9788-0931922176).
LAs-25 Erdy, M., *The Sumerian, Ural-Altaic, Magyar relationship: a history of research,* Gilgamesh, New York (USA), (1974).
LAs-26 Abondolo, D. (Ed.), *The Uralic Languages,* Routledge, London (England), (1998).

PART 4: GLOSSARY, LITERATURE CITED, INDEX, ABOUT THE AUTHOR

Related to specific languages, language families or groups-   Altaic/Korean:
LAs-27 Brooke, J., "For Mongolians, E Is for English, and F Is for the Future", *The New York Times,* international pages, (15 February 2005).
LAs-28 Ju Won, K., *Materials of Spoken Manchu*, Seoul National University Press, Seoul (South Korea), (2008), (ISBN: 978-89-521-0947-7).
LAs-29 Lee, I.; Ramsey, R., *Korean Language,* State University of New York Press, Albany, NY (USA), (2000).
LAs-30 Korean National Commission for UNESCO (Ed.), *Korean Language,* Si-sayoung-o-sa Publishers, Inc. Seoul (South Korea), (ISBN: 0-7914-4831-2).

Related to specific languages, language families or groups-   Austronesian/Indonesian:
LAs-31 Robson, S.; Millie, J., *Instant Indonesian [How to Express 1,000 Different Ideas With Just 100 Key Words and Phrases!],* Tuttle Publishing, Boston, MA (USA), (2004).

Related to specific languages, language families or groups-   Swaahili (Swahili):
LAs-32 *Swahili, The Rough Guide, Phrasebook,* Rough Guides / Pearson PLC, London (England), (1998).

Related to extinct languages:
LAs-33 "Babel runs backwards", *The Economist*, 62-64, (1 January 2005).

Related to language isolates:
LAs-34 Catford, J.C., "Mountain of the tongues; the languages of the Caucasus", *Ann. Rev. Anthropology* **6**, 283-314, (1997).
LAs-35 Hewitt, B.,"Indigenous Languages of the Caucasus", The, *North West Caucasian Languages,* Caravan Books, Delmar, NY (USA), **2**, (1989).
LAs-36 Foley, W. A., *The Papuan Languages of New Guinea,* Cambridge University Press, Cambridge, (1986).
LAs-37 Dixon, R. M. W., *The Languages of Australia,* Cambridge University Press, Cambridge (England), (1980).
LAs-38 Bonfante, G.; Bonfante, L., *Etruscan Language: An Introduction, The,* Manchester University Press, NY (USA), (1983).
LAs-39 Hewitt, B.G. in collaboration with Z.K. Khiba, *Abkhaz. Lingua Descriptive Studies* **2**, North- Holland, Amsterdam (Netherlands), (1979).

Related to specific languages, language families or groups- Slavic:
LAs-40 Comrie, B.; Greville, G., *Slavonic Languages,* Routledge Press, London, (England), (1993).
LAs-41 Gardiner, S., *Old Church Slavonic: An Elementary Grammar,* Cambridge University Press, London (England), (1984).

Related to specific languages, language families or groups- Romance:
LAs-42 Posner, R., *Romance Languages,* Cambridge University Press, Cambridge (England), (1996).
LAs-43 Harris, M.; Vincent, N. (Eds.), *The Romance Languages,* Routledge, London (England), (1988).

Related to specific languages, language families or groups- Celtic/Scottish/Gaelic:
LAs-44 MacAulay, D., (Ed.), *Celtic Languages,* Cambridge University Press, Cambridge (England), (1993).
LAs-45 Renton, R.W.; MacDonald, J.A., *Scottish Gaelic-English / English-Scottish Gaelic*, Hippocrene Books, Inc., New York (USA), (1994).
LAs-46 Carmody, F.J., "*Is* in Modern Scottish Gaelic", *Word* **1**, 162-87, (1945).
LAs-47 Hamp, E.P., "Morphophonemes of the Keltic mutations, *Language* **27**, 230-47, (1951).

Related to specific languages, language families or groups- Sino-Bodic:
LAs-48 van Driem, G., "Sino-Bodic", *Bulletin of the School of Oriental and African Studies,* University of London, London (England), **60**, 455-88, (1997).

Related to specific languages, language families or groups- Chinese:
LAs-49 French, H.W., "Uniting China to Speak Mandarin, the One Official Language: Easier Said Than Done", *The New York Times International*, p. 4, (10 July 2005).
LAs-50 Chang, N T., "Tones and intonation in the Chengtu dialect", *Phonetica* **2,** 59-85, (1958).

Related to specific languages, language families or groups- Semitic/Afro-Asiatic:
LAs-51 Hetzron, R. (Ed.), *The Semitic Languages,* Routledge, London (England), (1997).
LAs-52 Loprieno, A., *Ancient Egyptian,* Cambridge University Press, Cambridge (England), (1995).

PART 4: GLOSSARY, LITERATURE CITED, INDEX, ABOUT THE AUTHOR

LAs-53 Versteegh, K., *The Arabic Language,* Columbia University Press, New York (USA), (1997).
LAs-54 Beeston, A.F.L., *Written Arabic*, Cambridge University Press, Cambridge (England), (1968).
LAs-55 Thornton, F.; Nicholson, R.A. (Eds.), *Elementary Arabic, A Grammar,* Asian Ed. Services, New Delhi (India), (2000).

Related to specific languages, language families or groups- Taiwanese
LAs-56 (a) Gluck, C., "Taiwan's aborigines find new voice", *BBC News*: http://news.bbc.co.uk/2/hi/asia-pacific/4649257.stm , (4 July 2005).
(b) Campbell, W., *A dictionary of the Amoy vernacular spoken throughout the prefectures of Chin-chiu, Chiang-chiu and Formosa,* Fukuin Printing Co., Yokohama, Japan (1913, reprint 1965).

Related to specific languages, language families or groups- Hawai'ian:
LAs-57 Hudson, M., *Ruins of Identity,* University of Hawaii Press, Honolulu, (HI), (USA), (1999).

Related to specific languages, language families or groups- Austronesian:
LAs-58 *Austronesian languages, Wikipedia,* [http://en.wikipedia.org/wiki/Austronesia].

Related to specific languages, language families or groups- Japanese:
LAs-59 Tsujimura, N. (Ed.), *The Handbook of Japanese Linguistics,* Blackwell Publishing Ltd, Malden, MA (USA), (1999).
LAs-60 Kuno, S., *The Structure of the Japanese Language,* M.I.T Press, Cambridge, MA (USA), (1973).
LAs-61 Nagase, O., Personal Communication, (2008).

Related to specific languages, language families or groups- Austro-Asiatic:
LAs-62 *Austro-Asiatic Languages, Wikipedia,* [http://en.wikipedia.org/wiki/Austro-Asiatic].

Related to specific languages, language families or groups- North/Meso-American:
LAs-63 Boas, F., Introduction in Boas, F. (Ed.), *Handbook of American Indian Languages, Vol. 1,* Bureau of American Ethnology, Washington (USA), (1911).
LAs-64 Campbell, L., *American Indian Linguistics: The Linguistic History of Native America,* Oxford University Press, New York (USA), (1997).
LAs-65 Hinton, L.; Munro, P. (Eds.), *Studies in American Indian Languages: Description and Theory,* University of California Publications in Linguistics **131** (USA), (1998).

LAs-66 Mithun, M., *The Languages of Native North America,* Cambridge University Press, Cambridge (England), (1999).
LAs-67 Campbell, A., *American Indian Languages,* Oxford University Press, New York, NY (USA), (1997).
LAs-68 Suarez. J. A., *The Mesoamerican Indian Languages,* Cambridge University Press, Cambridge (England), (1983).
LAs-69 Boas, F.; Swanton, J.R., *Siouan: Dakota (Teton and Santee dialects) with remarks on the Ponca and Winnebago*, 875-965, (1911).
LAs-70 (a) Hoogshagen, S.; Hoogshagen, H.H., "Mariano Silva y Aceves" in *Diccionario Mixe de Coatlán, Serie de Vocabularios Indigénas*, **32 SIL**, D.F., Mexico, (1993). **(b)** See also: Wichmann, S., *The Relationship Among the Mixe-Zoquean Languages of Mexico*, University of Utah Press, Salt Lake City, UT (USA), (1995), (ISBN 0-87480-487-6).
LAs-71 Spier, L., "Comparative Vocabularies and Parallel Texts in Two Yuman Languages of Arizona", *University of New Mexico Publications in Anthropology* **2**, University of New Mexico Press, Albuquerque (USA), (1946).
LAs-72 Gowan, G.M., "Mazateco whistle speech", *Language,* (1948).

Related to specific languages, language families or groups- South American:
LAs-73 McQuown, N.A.,"The indigenous languages of Latin America", *American Anthropologist, New Series*, **57:3**, 501-570, (June 1955).
LAs-74 Tax, S., "Aboriginal languages of Latin America", *Current Anthropology* **1**, (1960).
LAs-75 Kaufman, T., "Language history in South America: What we know and how to know more," In Payne, D. L. (Ed.), *Amazonian Linguistics: Studies in Lowland South American Languages,* University of Texas Press, Austin, TX (USA), 13-67, (1990).
LAs-76 Dixon, R. M. W.; Aikhenvald, A., *The Amazonian Languages,* Cambridge University Press, Cambridge (England), (1999).
LAs-77 Elson, B., *Studies in Peruvian Indian Languages: 1,* University of Oklahoma University Press, Norman, OK (USA), (1963).

Related to specific languages, language families or groups- "Nostratic":
LAs-78 Bomhard, A.R., *The Nostratic macrofamily: a study in distant linguistic relationship*, Mouton de Gruyter, Berlin (Germany), (1994).
LAs-79 Illic-Svityc, V. M., *Opyt sravnenija nostraticeskix jazykov, 3 vols.,* Akademika Nauka, Moscow (Russia), (1971-84).

PART 4: GLOSSARY, LITERATURE CITED, INDEX, ABOUT THE AUTHOR

LAi
(Relating to Indian languages)

Related to Sanskrit and comparative Indo-European grammar, phonology and etymology:

LAi-1 Halder, G., *Languages of India*, National Book Trust, New Delhi (India), (2000).

LAi-2 Misra, S.S., *A Comparative Grammar of Sanskrit, Greek and Hittite*, World Press, Calcutta (India), (1968).

LAi-3 Vasu, S.C., (Ed., Transl.), *Ashtadhyayi of Panini*, Motilal Banarsidass Publishers Pvt Ltd, Delhi (India), (2003).

LAi-4 Apte, V.S., *Practical Sanskrit-English Dictionary [Containing Appendices on Sanskrit Prosody & Important Literary & Geographical Names of Ancient India]*, Rev. Ed., Motilal Banarsidass Publishers Pvt Ltd, Delhi (India), (1965, reprint 1985).

LAi-5 Goldman, R.P.; Goldman, S.J.S., *Devavanipravesika: An Introduction to the Sanskrit Language*, University of California at Berkeley Press, Berkeley, CA (USA), (2002).

LAi-6 (a) *RgVeda Padapatha*, Sri Satguru Publications, Indian Books Centre, Delhi (India), (1992). **(b)** *RgWeda Samhita, Shrimatsaayanaaachaarya-wirachitabhaashyasameta* (RgVeda Samhita, with the Commentary of Saaynaachaarya). Published, in four volumes, by Vaidika Samshodhana Mandala (Vedic Research Institute), Pune, India (1978).

LAi-7 Jha, V.N., *A Linguistic Analysis of the Rgveda-Padapatha, [Sri Garib Dass Oriental Series No. 142, Pre-Paninian Grammatical Traditions (Pt.-1)*, Sri Satguru Publications, Delhi (India), (1992), (ISBN: 81-7030-320-6).

LAi-8 Dwivedi, K., *Sanskrit Saahitya Kaa Itihaas [A History of Sanskrit Literature]*, Raashtriya Sanskrit Saahitya Kendra (National Center for Sanskrit Literature), (2005).

LAi-9 Aggarwal, H.R.; Foreword by Sarup, L., *A Short History of Sanskrit Literature [Second Rev Ed.]*, Munshiram Manoharlal Publishers Pvt Ltd, New Delhi (India), (1963).

LAi-10 Gupta, D. K. (Ed.), *Recent Studies in Sanskrit and Indology [Felicitation Volume]*, Ajanta Publications, Delhi (India), (1982).

LAi-11 Gandhi D.N.; Kanade, R.J., *Dhaturupakosa, Sri Garib Das Oriental Series No.89, Compiled for the use of the Sanskrit Students*, Sri Satguru Publications, Delhi (India), (2005).

LAi-12 Yaaska (Author, est. before 1250 B.C.E.); Shaastri S., Sharmaa, S., (Eds.), *Shrimatyaaskamaharshi-Prakaashitam* **Niruktam***, Nighantu-Paathasamupetam*

[Niruktam of Yaaska], Shri Venkateshwara Steam Press, Mumbai (India), (1912), (ISBN: 81-7030-202-1).

Related to the Indus/Harappan script:
LAi-13 Mahadevan, I., Indus Script: Texts, Concordance and Tables [Memoirs of the Archaeologial Survey of India 77], The, Archaeological Survey of India, New Delhi (India), (1977).

LAi-14 Mahadevan, I., "S.R. Rao's Decipherment of the Indus Script", *Indian Historical Review* **8: 1-2,** 58-73, (1982).

LAi-15 (a) Mahadevan, I., "The Indus 'non-script' is a non-issue", *The Hindu*, Sunday Magazine, 3 May 2009. (The Hindu newspaper, Chennai, India) (2009). Viewable at:
http://www.hindu.com/mag/2009/05/03/stories/2009050350010100.htm
(b) See also: Mahadevan, I., "MELUHHA AND AGASTYA : ALPHA AND OMEGA OF THE INDUS SCRIPT", Publication of the Indus Research Centre, Roja Muthiah Research Library, Chennai, India (2009).

LAi-16 Archaeological Survey of India, *Corpus of Indus Seals and Inscriptions (Memoirs of the Archaeological Survey of India),* Suomalainen Tiedeakatemia, Mariankatu, Helsinki (Finland), (1987).

LAi-17 Parpola, A., *Deciphering the Indus script,* Cambridge University Press, London (England), (1994).

LAi-18. Mahadevan, I., "Agricultural Terms in the Indus Script", [http://www.harappa.com/arrow/indus-script-terms.html], (27 May 2007).

LAi-19 Kalyanaraman, S., "Inscribed terracotta seal at Vais'ali compared with inscribed stone celt of Sembiyan-kandiyur",
[http://kalyan96.googlepages.com/vaisaliseal.pdf], (3 May 2006).

LAi-20 Rao, S.R., *Decipherment of the Indus Script,* Asia Publishing House, Bombay (India), (1982).

LAi-21 Jha, N., *Indus Valley Seals Deciphered! Alphabet Writing Originated with the Ancient Hindus, Vedic Glossary on Indus Seals,* Ganga-Kaueri Publishing, Varanasi (India), (1996).

LAi-22 Punekar, S.M., *Mohenjodaro Seals, Read and Identified,* Caxton Publications, Delhi (India), (1984).

PART 4: GLOSSARY, LITERATURE CITED, INDEX, ABOUT THE AUTHOR

LAi-23 (a) *"Vikramkhol (Bikramkhol)", Regarding a possible "missing link" between the Harappan (Indus Valley) and Braahmi (Brahmi) scripts, see the descriptions of the Vikramkhol script, e.g. at:*
  http://en.wikipedia.org/wiki/Historic_sites_in_Orissa **(b)** *See also: "Significance of Mayiladuthurai find",*
  www.hindu.com/2006/05/01/stories/2006050101992000.htm *(2006).*

Related to Dravidian languages:

LAi-24 McAlpin, D., *Proto-Elamo-Dravidian: The Evidence and Its Implications [Transactions of the Am. Phil. Society, held at Phil. For Promoting Useful Knowledge, Volume 71, Part 3],* Am. Phil. Society, Philadelphia, PA (USA), (1981).

LAi-25 Damerow, P.; Englund, R., "The Proto-Elamite Texts from Tepe Yahya" American School of Prehistoric Research Bulletin, Cambridge University Press, London (England), **39,** (1989).

LAi-26 Amiet, P., "II y a 5000 ans les Elamites inventaient l'ecriture", *Archeologia* **12,** 20-22, (1966).

LAi-27 (a) Reiner, E., "The Elamite Language", *Altkleinasiatische Sprachen, (Handbuch der Orientalistik, div. 1),* **2,** 54-118, (1969).
  (b) Schmitt, R., *Meno-logium Bagistano-Persepolitanum: Studient zu den altpersischen Montasnamen und ihern elamischen Wiedergaben,* Verlag der Österreischischen Akademie der Wissenschaften, Vienna, Austria (2003).

LAi-28 Bush, F., *A Grammar of the Hurrian Language,* Brandeis University, Department of Mediterranean Studies Dissertation, Boston, MA (USA, (1964).

LAi-29 (a) Damerow, P.; Englund, R., *Die Zahlzeichensysteme der Archaischen Texte aus Uruk,* Mann, Berlin, (1987).
  (b) Damerow, P.; Englund, R.K., *The proto-Elamite texts from Tepe Yahya,* Harvard University Press, Cambridge, MA, USA (1989).

LAi-30 Krishnamurti, B., *Dravidian Languages,* Cambridge University Press, London (England), (2003).

LAi-31 Steever, S., *Dravidian Languages, (Routledge Language Family Descriptions),* Routledge Press, London, (England), (1998), (ISBN: 81-208-0290-x).

LAi-32 Varadarajan, Prof. M., "Tamil Language - A brief review of its history and features", *[http://www.TamilCanadian.com/]*.

LAi-33 Varadarajan, M.; Vralaaru, M., *The History of Tamil Language,* Madras (Chennai), India, (1954).

LAi-34 Iyengar, P.T.S., *History of Tamil from the Earliest Times to 600 A.D.,* Madras (Chennai), India, (1929).

LAi-35 Sastri, S., *Tolkappiyam-Collatikaram*, Annamalai University, Annamalainager (India), (1979).
LAi-36 Visalakshy, P., *The Grantha script,* Dravidian Linguistics Association, Thiruvananthapuram (India), (2003).
LAi-37 Marr, J.R., *The Early Dravidians* in Basham, A.L. (Ed.), *A Cultural History of India*, Oxford University Press, London (England), (1975).
LAi-38 Bray, D., *Brahui Language Introduction and Grammar,* Asian Ed. Services, New Delhi (India), (1986).

Related to Persian scripts:
LAi-39 Stronach, David, Vallat, Francois (Ed.), "On the Genesis of the Old Persian Cuneiform Scripts", In *Contributions a l'histoire d'Iran: Melanges offerts a Jean Perrot,* Editions Recherches sur les Civilisations, Paris (France), 195-203, (1990).
LAi-40 Schmitt, R., *Behistun Inscription of Darius the Great: Old Persian Text (Corpus Inscriptonum Iranicarum),* School of Oriental and African Studies, London (England), (1991).
LAi-41 Hincks, E., *On the Three Kinds of Persepolitan Writing, and on the Babylonian Lapidary Characters" [Transactions of the Royal Irish Academy 21 Polite Literature* H.Gill, Oxford (England), 249-56, (1846).
LAi-42 Hincks, E., *On the First and Second Kinds of Persepolitan Writing" [Transactions of the Royal Irish Academy 21 Polite Literature],* 114-31, (1846).
LAi-43 Windfuhr, G., "Notes on the Old Persian Signs", *Indo-Iranian Journal*, **12/2**, (June 1970).
LAi-44 Rawlinson, H., "The Persian Cuneiform Inscription at Behistun, Deciphered and Translated with a Memoir on Persian Cuneiform Inscriptions in General, and on That of Behistun in Particular:" *J. Royal Asiatic Society* **10**, (1846).

Related to Maraathi (Marathi), Hindi, etc.:
LAi-45. (a) See, e.g., the presentations by D.M. Mirajdar, A. Avachat and R.R. Borade, at *Vishwa Marathi Sahitya Sammelan 2009 (World Marathi Literature Convention)*, 14-196 February 2009, Cupertino, CA (USA). See also: http://wikibin.org/articles/vishwa-marathi-sahitya-sammelan.html.
(b) Jacobi, H., *Ausgewählte Erzählungen in Maharashtri. Zur Einführung in das Studium des Prakrit. Grammatik, Text, Wörterbuch*, S. Hirzel Press, Leipzig, Germany (1886).

PART 4: GLOSSARY, LITERATURE CITED, INDEX, ABOUT THE AUTHOR

LAi-46 Wiirkar (Virkar), K., *Subodh Maraathi-Ingrajii Shabdakosh [Wirkar, K., Elucidated Maraathi-English Dictionary]*, Anmol Pirakaashan, Pune (India), (2005).
LAi-47 Shapiro, M.; Garry, J.; Rubino, C. (Eds.), *Hindi: Facts about the world's languages* in: *An encyclopedia of the world's major languages, past and present*, New England Publishing Associates, Higganum, CT (USA), (2001)
LAi-48 Prasaad (Prasad), K.; Sahaaya (Sahaya), R.; Shriwaastawa (Shrivastava), M. (Compilers), *Brhat Hindi Kosh [Great Hindi Dictionary]*, Jnaana Mandal Ltd., Vaaraanasi, (India), (1989).
LAi-49 Harley, A.H., *Colloquial Hindustani*, Kegan Paul, Trench, Trubner and Co. Ltd., London (England), (1944).

Related to Praakrts (Prakrits):
LAi-50 Jain, B.D., *Ardha Magadhi Reader,* Sri Satguru Publications, Delhi (India), (1982).
LAi-51 Doshi, A.B.J., *Praakrta Maargopadeshikaa [Instructor for Praakrit], Trans. Into Hindi by Saadhvii, S. Suwrataajii, Saadhwii Shri Mrgaawatiijii, Saadhwii Shri Shiilawatijii and Shri Wijayawallabhbhasuurajii,* Motilal Banarsidass Publishers Pvt Ltd, Delhi (India), (1968).
LAi-52 Tagare, G.V., *Historical Grammar of Apabrahmsa,* Motilal Banarsidass Publishers Pvt Ltd, Delhi (India), (1987).
LAi-53 Law, B.M., *A History of Pali Literature,* Indica Books, New Delhi (India), (2002).
LAi-54 Kaashyapa (Kashyapa), B.J., *Paali-Mahaa Wyaakarana [Great Paali Grammar],* Motilal Banarsidass Publishers Pvt Ltd, Delhi (India), (1963),
LAi-55 Law Bimala, C.;Geiger, W. *A History of Pali Literature,* Kegan Paul Trench, Trubner & Co., London (England), (2000).
LAi-56 Gupta, K.M., *Linguistic Approach to Meaning in Pali,* Sundeep Prakashan, New Delhi (India), (2006), (ISBN:13 978-0415100236),
LAi-57 Hazra, K.L., *Pali Language and literature: a systematic survey and historical study,* D.K. Printworld, New Delhi (India), (1994).
LAi-58 Oberlies, T., *Pāli: A Grammar of the Language of the Theravāda Tipitaka",* Walter de Gruyter, Berlin (Germany), (2001).

Related to Dravidian languages, cont.:
LAi-59 Chhabra, B., *Expansion of Indo-Aryan Culture during Pallava Rule,* Munshiram Manoharlal Publishers Pvt Ltd, New Delhi (India), (1965).

LITERATURE CITED

Related to post-Harappan Indian scripts:
LAi-60 Sivapriyananda, "Brahmi, Kharoshthi, Telugu, Oriya, Kannada, Gurmukhi, Devanagari", *The India Magazine,* 36-45, (August 1982).
LAi-61 Upasak Chandrika, S., *History and Palaeography of Mauryan Brahmi Script,* Nava Nalanda Mahavihara, Nalanda (India), (1960).
LAi-62 Iyer, S. (Ed.), *Studies in Indian Epigraphy: Journal of the Epigraphical Society of India,* **Vol. XI**, Caxton Publishing, Delhi (India), (2008)
LAi-63 Salomon, R., *Indian Epigraphy: A Guide to the Study of Inscriptions in Sanskrit, Prakrit, and Other Indo-Aryan Languages*, Oxford University Press, Oxford (England), (1998). See esp. pp. 34 ff.
LAi-64 Dani, A., *Indian Palaeography, 2nd ed.,* Munshiram Manoharlal Publishers Pvt Ltd, New Delhi, (India), (1986).

Related to South-East Asian and Tibetan scripts:
LAi-65 Coedes, G.; Vella, W. (Eds.), (Trans. Cowing, S.), *The Indianized States of Southeast Asia,* University Press of Hawaii, Honolulu (HI), (1968).
LAi-66 Sarkar, K., *Early Indo-Cambodian Contacts, Literacy and Linguistics,* Visva-Bharati, Santiniketan, West Bengal (India), (1968).
LAi-67 Coedes, G., *The Making of South East Asia,* Routledge & Kegan Paul, London (England), (1966).
LAi-68 Nagaraju, S.; Ramesh K.V. et al, (Eds.), Palaeography of the Earliest Inscriptions of Burma, Thailand, Cambodia and Vietnam, Agam Kala Prakashan, Delhi (India), (Dr. B. Chhabra Felicitation) 67-80, (1984).
LAi-69 de Casparis, J. G., *Indonesian Palaeography (Handbuch der Orientalistik Division 3, Vol. 4, Part I),* Brill, Leiden (Netherlands), (1975).
LAi-70 Huffman, F. E., *Cambodian System of Writing and Beginning Reader,* Yale University Press, New Haven, CT (USA), (1970).
LAi-71 Danwiwat, N., *Thai Writing System,* Buske, Hamburg (Germany), (1987).
LAi-72 Chandra, L., *Indian Scripts in Tibet,* Sharada Rani, New Delhi (India), (1982).
LAi-73 Mair, V., "Cheng Chi'iao's Understanding of Sanskrit: The Concept of Spelling in China (re: Buddhist Influence in E. Asian Scripts), *A Festschrift in Honour of Professor Jao Tsung-I on the Occasion of His Seventy-fifth Anniversary,* Chinese University of Hong Kong, Hong Kong (China), 331-41, (1993).

Related to Western theories of the absence of writing in ancient India:
LAi-74 Farmer, S.; Sproat, R.; Witzel, M., "The Collapse of the Indus-Script Thesis: The Myth of a Literate Harappan Civilization", *Electronic J. Vedic Studies* **11:2** 19-57 (2004).

PART 4: GLOSSARY, LITERATURE CITED, INDEX, ABOUT THE AUTHOR

LAi-75 *See, e.g., some of the postings at* http://www.ancientscripts.com/.
LAi-76 See p. xiii in Preface in Deshpande, Madhav, M., *Samskrtasubodhini: A Sanskrit Primer,* University of Michigan Press, Ann Arbor, MI (USA), (2001).
LAi-77 Daniels, Peter; Harrak, Amir (Eds.), "Contacts between Semitic and Indic Scripts", [In *Contacts between Cultures: Selected Papers from the 33rd International Congress of Asian and North African Studies,* Toronto, *West Asia and North Africa* Edwin Mellen, Lewiston, NY (USA), **1**,146-52, (15-25 August 1990).
LAi-78 Bühler, G., "Indische Palaeographic von circa 350 Chr.- circa 1300 P. Chr.", *Grundriss der Indo-arischen Philologie und Alterumkunde,* Trubner, Strassburg (France), **1**, (1896).
LAi-79 Weber, A., "Uber den semitischen Ursprung des indischen Alphabets, *Zeitschrift der Deutschen Morgenlandischen Gesellschaft,* **10**, 389-406, (1856).

Related to Indian viewpoints on writing in ancient India:
LAi-80 Varma, K.C., *Annals of the Bhandarkar Oriental Research Institute, LXI,* Karve Nagar, Pune (India), (1980).
LAi-81 Dandekar, R.N. (Ed.), *Progress of Indic Studies, 1917-1942,* Bhandarkar Oriental Research Institute, Pune (India), (1942). See also: *Vedic Mythological Tracts,* Ajanta Publications, Delhi (India), (1979); *Insights into Hinduism,* Ajanta Publications, Delhi (India), (1979); *Exercises in Indology,* Ajanta Publications, Delhi (India), (1981).
LAi-82 Rao, R.P.N.; Yadav, N.; Vahia, M.N.; Joglekar, H.; Adhikari, R.; Mahadevan, I., "Entropic Evidence for Linguistic Structure in the Indus Script", *Science* DOI: 10.1126/science.11170391, (23 April 2009).

Related to Paanini and "spoken" Sanskrit vs. the literary language:
LAi-83 "Speaking fluency" in Classical (Paaninian, Paninian) Sanskrit merely implies sentence construction and articulation to express ideas, according to the strict grammatical rules of Paaninian Sanskrit. The jury is still out on whether Classical Sanskrit, as it has come down to us today, was truly a spoken language, or merely a refined, literature version of a spoken language. If it is merely the literary language that we have today, then what the spoken language was must be reconstructed. This author is of the opinion that Paanini (Panini) and his predecessor grammarians (of which he cites 63) effectively fossilized Sanskrit, and thus killed any record of earlier, spoken versions. At the time of Paanini, who certainly pre-dates Buddha and Mahaawiira (Mahavir) since there is no mention of anything even remotely related to Buddhism or Jainism in his works,

LITERATURE CITED

Sanskrit was already not a spoken language. Rather, it was like the language found at Boghaz-Koy in Anatolia (see Refs. [HIi-41, HIi-43 to HIi-47]), i.e. an *Apabrahmsa*. It is this author's hypothesis that the earlier, spoken versions of Sanskrit may have contained everyday words alluded to elsewhere in this book, such as *wadra*, *udra* ("water") or the verb *wir* ("to show courage; to contest"), which now appear to be lost forever, as well as familiar forms such as *tuu*, which is used for "you" in just about every Indo-European language, ancient and modern, including ones on the Indian subcontinent, in place of the formalized Paaninian *twam*, i.e. *tu-am*. This spoken Sanskrit may have also retained, in everyday use, grammatical forms such as the pluperfect, a tense which is now fossilized as the "7th aorist" of Classical Sanskrit. Earlier, spoken versions may also have had less formalized and compulsory use of *Sandhi*. Any linguist will admit that Sandhi is a mandatory construct for the literary language derived from natural euphony in the spoken language. In Paaninian Sanskrit, *Sandhi* is *compulsory*. That is much like making it compulsory to *always* pronounce *did you* and *want to* in American English as *didja* and *wanna* -- examples of *Sandhi* in American English.

PART 4: GLOSSARY, LITERATURE CITED, INDEX, ABOUT THE AUTHOR

HIh
(Relating to general human history, including migrations, except Indian history)

HIh-1. Cavalli-Sforza, L. L.; Cavalli-Sforza, F., *The Great Human Diasporas: The History of Diversity and Evolution,* Addison-Wesley, Reading, MA (USA), (1995).

HIh-2. Teresi, D., *Lost Discoveries: The Ancient Roots of Modern Science - From the Babylonians to the Maya,* Simon Schuster, New York, NY (USA), (2002).

HIh-3. Zohary, D.; Hopf, M., *Domestication of Plants in the Old World, (Re: migration into Mideast), Ed. # 3,* Clarendon Press, Oxford (England), (2000).

HIh-4. Bellwood, P., "Early Agriculturalist Population Diasporas? Farming, Languages, & Genes", *Ann. Rev. Anthropol.* **30**, 181, (2001).

HIh-5 For a concise summary of human migrations of the last 100,000 years, see, e.g.: Stix, G., "Traces of a Distant Past", *Scientific American*, 56-63, (July 2008).

HIh-6. Fleet, K., *The Cambridge History of Turkey*, Cambridge University Press, Cambridge (England), (2009).

HIh-7. Silverman, D. (Contributor), *Ancient Egypt*, Duncan Baird Publishers, London (England), (2003).

HIh-8 Wilford, J.N., "Archaeologists Unearth a War Zone 5,500 Years Old", *The New York Times International*, (16 December 2005).

LITERATURE CITED

HIi
(Relating to Indian history)

Recent, seminal references:
HIi-1. "Boring No More, a Trade-Savvy Indus Emerges", *Science* **320**, 1276-1285, (6 June 2008).

Significant references related to archaeology:
HIi-2. Archaeological Survery of India, "Excavations - Dholavira", http://www.asi.nic.in/asi_exca_2007_dholavira.asp .
HIi-3. Archaeological Survery of India, "Excavations- Adichchanallur, An Iron Age Urn Burial Site", http://www.asi.nic.in/asi_exec_adichchanallur.asp ,
HIi-4. Archaeological Survery of India, "Excavations - 2006-2007", http://www.asi.nic.in/asi_exca_2007_sanauli.asp , (2007).
HIi-5. Meadow, R. (Ed.), Harappa Excavations, 1986-1990: A multidisciplinary approach to 3rd millennium urbanism" *Monographs in World Archeology,* Prehistory Press **3**, (December 1991).
HIi-6. Whitehouse, D. (Ed.), *BBC News*, Science/Technology section, *"Earliest writing found",* http://news.bbc.co.uk/1/hi/science/nature/334517.stm .
HIi-7. *Harappa Excavations 1986-1990: A Multidisciplinary Approach to Third Millennium Urbanism,* Prehistory Press, Madison, WI (USA), (1991).
HIi-8. **(a)** Kenoyer, J.M.; Allchin, R. & B. (Eds.), "Excavations at Harappa 1994-1995: New Perspectives on the Indus Script, Craft Activities, and City Organisation", *South Asian Archaeology 1995,* Oxford & IBH, New Delhi (India), (1997). **(b)** See also: "Mehrgarh", http://en.wikipedia.org/wiki/Mehrgarh .
HIi-9 Bakliwal, P.C.; Grover, A.K., *Rec. Geol. Surv. India,* **116**, (1988).

Related to ancient landmarks, cities etc. (e.g. Saraswati river, Dwaarakaa (Dwarka, Dvarka):
HIi-10 (a) Hawthorne, M., "Dvaraka: Behold the Holy City Where Krishna Was Prince", *Hinduism Today, Jan/Feb/March 2008,* pp. 62-66, (2008). **(b)** See also: http://en.wikipedia.org/wiki/Dwarka
HIi-11 Francfort, H.-P., "Evidence for Harrapan Irrigation System in Haryana and Rajasthan", *Eastern Anthropologist* **45**, 87-103, (1992).
HIi-12 For studies and references on the original course and later, sudden drying up of the Saraswati river around 1900 B.C.E., and on the very large number of Harappan sites identified along the Saraswati's bed, and, more notably, some claims that the Saraswati river did not even exist, see, e.g.: **(a)** Bakliwal, P.C.;

PART 4: GLOSSARY, LITERATURE CITED, INDEX, ABOUT THE AUTHOR

Grover, A.K., "Signature and Migration of Sarasvati River in the Thar Desert, Western India", *Rec. Geol. Survey of India* **116**, 77-86, (1988). **(b)** LANDSAT at http://landsat.gsfc.nasa.gov **(c)** http://india.mapsofindia.com/culture/indian-rivers/saraswati-river.html **(d)** http://en.wikipedia.org/wiki/Sarasvati **(e)** http://en.wikipedia.org/wiki/Out_of_India_theory **(g)** Lawler, A., "News and Analysis: Archaeology In Indus Times, the River Didn't Run Through It", *Science*, **332**, 23 (1 April 2011).

HIi-13 Thappar, B.K., "Kalibangan: A Harappan Metropolis beyond the Indus Valley", *Expedition* **17:2**, 19-33, (1975).

HIi-14 Misra, S.S, *Fresh Light on Indo-European classification and chronology*, Ashutosh Prakashan Sansthan, Varanasi (India), (1980).

HIi-15 Sethna, K.D., *The Problem of Aryan Origins (from an Indian Point of View)*, Aditya Prakashan, Delhi (India), (1992).

HIi-16 Deo, S.; Surynath, K (Eds.), *The Aryan Problem*, Bharatiya Itihasa Sankalana Samiti, Pune (India), (1993).

HIi-17 Misra, S.S., *The Aryan Problem: A Linguistic Approach,* Munshiram Manoharlal Publishers Pvt Ltd, New Delhi (India), (1992).

HIi-18 Gupta, S.P., *The Indus-Saraswati Civilization*, Pratibha Prakashan, Delhi (India), (1996).

HIi-19 Singh, B., *The Vedic Harappans*, Aditya Prakashan, New Delhi (India), (1992).

HIi-20 Asimov, M.S., *Ethnic Problems of the History of Central Asia in the Early Period: Second Millenium B.C. In Greek and English*, Hayka, Moscow (Russia), (1981).

Related to South India:
HIi-21 Kishitar, V.R.R., *Pre-Historic South India*, Madras (Chennai), India, (1951).
HIi-22 Sastri, K.A.N., *A History of South India,* Oxford University Press, New Delhi (India), (2002).
HIi-23 See p.p 52ff., p.p 56ff. in Reference HIi-22.
HIi-24 See p.p. 78-80 in Reference Hii-22.

Related to origins of Tamil:
HIi-25 Gernot, W., *Hurrians*, Aris & Philips, Warminster (UK), (1989). Ltd, Delhi (India), 52ff, 56ff, (2006), (ISBN: 81-208-0164-4).
HIi-26 For ruminations on Tamil origins, see, e.g.: von Furer-Haimendorf, C., *Proc. 37th Indian Science Congress, Poona, 1950*, Part II: Presidential Addresses, 175-180, (1950). Also see: von Furer-Haimendorf, C., *Tamil Culture*, **2**, 127-135, (1953).

HIi-27 Lawler, A., "Central Asia's Lost Civilization", *Discover Magazine*, (30 November 2006). Available at: http://discovermagazine.com/2006/nov/ancient-towns-excavated-turkmenistan.

Related to ancient Indian theories of creation:
HIi-28:

> *RgWeda (RgVeda, Rig Veda)* **X.190**, **X.129**, widely considered to be the original Hindu creation hymns, upon which all Hindu theories of creation are technically based. In the opinion of many, they appear to convey profound intellectual contemplation on the part of their authors: They apparently come to conclusions coincidentally similar to theories of creation in modern physics, such as the Big Bang. And this is apparently done simply through powers of deduction (i.e. without the body of knowledge of modern physics). And in some cases they even appear to go further than these modern theories. For example, **X.190** posits that the Creator created the Laws of Physics (*Rta, Rita*) ***first*** [*Rtam cha Satyam chaabhiddhaat tapaso adhiajaayata*], and only *then* could the rest of Creation be born. The authors apparently and quite logically deduced that one needed a framework (*Rta*, the Laws of Physics) before one could even begin thinking of things like energy, space, the matter of heavenly bodies, and the other paraphernalia of Creation. It further posits that if a different set of Laws of Physics had been used by the Creator, one would have ended up with a different Universe! This hymn also envisions the concept of Nothingness (that is to say, *NO* matter, *NO* space, *NO* time, etc.) and, like all subsequent Hindu theories of creation, posits that *Existence*, i.e. the Universe as we know it, sprang from *Non-Existence*. (Indeed, in the other hymn (**X.129**, see below), it is said that "there was neither Existence nor Non-Existence" (*na asad aasiit na sad aasit tadaaniim*)!) That is to say, *even non-existence did not exist!* The theories also posit that Creation is recurring (*yathaa puurwam akalpayat*), always followed by Destruction, then Creation, then Destruction, then Creation, etc., with the universe existing in each cycle for tens of billions of years. And again, each cycle of Creation is said to start with an intense point of pure energy (*Tapas*), hauntingly anticipating the mathematical singularity in the origins of the Big Bang, although this is given a spiritual bent by saying that the Creator is responsible for this *Tapas*. More profoundly, **X.190** envisions that Time (*samwatsaras*) is a property that *needs to be created* (i.e. it is not something that we can assume always existed), and it is created *after* Space (*samudraadarnawaadadhi*) is created. **X.190** also gives a spiritual or moral bent to the Creation, saying that Truth (*Satyam*) was created

along with the Laws of Physics (*Rtam*), these being the *two pillars* of this particular Hindu theory of Creation; and of course that a Creator (here surprisingly, male, although in all later Hindu theology God is neuter) *is* responsible for the Creation! **X.129** goes a bit beyond **X.190** in the sense that it postulates that in the Beginning of All Beginnings, there was neither Existence nor Non-Existence (*Naasadaasiinno sadaasiit tadaaniim*)! **X.129** also gives an atheistic bent to the theory of Creation in its last two stanzas (#6, #7), saying "Who truly knows, who can here declare it, whence comes this Creation?...He (the Creator, masculine) alone truly knows, or perhaps even He knows not." (The Creator is here, again, surprisingly, male, although in later, mainstream monistic Hinduism, God is always neuter and may be considered inseparable from (*adwaita*) or separate from (*dwaita*) the Creation, according to two different schools of Indian philosophical thought, denoted *Adwaita* and *Dwaita*.)

Related to ancient Indian philosophy as represented in the Upanishads and other Vedaantic (Vedantic) writings:

HIi-29 (HIi-42a). See, e.g., Limaye, A.V.P.; Vadekar, R.D., *Eighteen Principle Upanisads*, Vaidika Samsodhana Mandala (Vedic Research Institute), Pune (India), (1958).

HIi-30 Gambhīrānanda, S., *Chāndogya Upaniṣad: With the Commentary of Śri Śankarācārya*, Advaita Ashrama, Calcutta (India), 1997.

HIi-31 Chinmayananda, *Discourses on Aitareya Upanisad*, Central Chinmaya Mission Trust, Mumbai (India), (2000).

HIi-32 Chinmayananda, *Discourses on Īśāvāsya Upanisad*, Central Chinmaya Mission Trust, Mumbai (India), (1997).

HIi-33 Chinmayananda, *Discourses on Mandukya Upanishad*, Central Chinmaya Mission Trust, Bombay (India), (1990).

HIi-34 Gambhīrānanda, S., *Taittirīya Upanisad: With the Commentary of Śankarācārya*, Advaita Ashrama Publication Department, Calcutta (India), (1998).

HIi-35 Mādhavānanda, *The Brhadāranyaka Upanisad: With the Commentary of Śankarācārya*, Advaita Ashrama Publication Department, Calcutta (India), (1993).

HIi-36 Chinmayananda, *Discourses on Kathopanisad*, Central Chinmaya Mission Trust, Mumbai (India), (2000).

HIi-37 Swaminathan, C.R., *Kanvasatapathabrahmanam*, **1**, Motilal Banarsidass Publishers Private Limited, New Delhi (India).

HIi-38 See p.p. 224-225, 258-263 in Reference LAi-9.

LITERATURE CITED

551

HIi-39 (a) *Taittiriiya Samhita* **VII.** 4. 8. **(b)** *Tandya Braahmana*, **V.** 9. **(c)** See also: Houben, J.E.B., *The Pravargya Brahmana of the Taittiriya Aranyaka: An Ancient Commentary on the Pravargya Ritual*, Motilal Banarsidass Publishers Private Limited, New Delhi (India), (1991). See also: Bali, S., *Sayana's Upodhata on Taittiriya Samhita and the Rgveda Samhita*, Motilal Banarsidass Publishers Private Limited, New Delhi (India).

Related to F. Max Müller:
HIi-40 (a) See, e.g., *Max Müller* http://en.wikipedia.org/wiki/Max_M%C3%BCller . **(b)** See also: http://en.wikipedia.org/wiki/Indo-Aryan_migration .
HIi-41 (a) Müller, F.M., *Lectures on the Science of Language: Delivered at the Royal Institution of Great Britain in April, May, & June 1861*, 5th Edition, Revised, Longmans, Green, and Co., London (England), (1866). **(b)** See also: Müller, F.M., *A History of Ancient Sanskrit Literature: So Far As It Illustrates the Primitive Religion of the Brahmans*, Bhuvaneshwari Ashrama (Allahabad), Asian Educational Services, New Delhi (India), (1993). **(c)** See also: Figulla, H.; Weber, O., *Keilschrifttexte aus Boghazkoi, Vol. 3*, Hinrichs, Liepizig (Germany), (1919).
HIi-42 Van Den Bosch, L., *Friedrich Max Müller: A Life Devoted to the Humanities*, Brill Academic Publishers, Boston, MA (USA), (2002).

Related to the excavations at Boghaz-koy:
HIi-43 Thieme, P., "The 'Aryan Gods' of the Mitanni Treaties", *Journal of the American Oriental Society*, **80,** 301-317, (1960).
HIi-44 Raulwing, P, "Zur etymologischen Beurtelung der Berufsbezeichnung Assussanni des Pferdetrainers Kikkuli von Mittani", ., in Anreiter et al, (Eds), *Man and the Animal World, Studies in Archaeozoology, Archaeology, Anthropology and Paleolinguistics in Memoriam Sandor Bokonyi, Archaeologia Main Series 8, Budapest*, 1-57, (1996).
HIi-45 Kammenhuber, A., *Hippologia hethitica*, Harrassowitz, Wiesbaden (Germany), (1962).
HIi-46 Ekrem, A., *Hattian and Hittite Civilizations*; Publication of the Republic of Turkey; Ministry of Culture, Ankara Publishing, Ankara, (Turkey), (2001), (ISBN: 975-17-2756-1). See also Ref. **HIi-41(c)** above.
HIi-47 Francfort, H.-P., *Eastern Anthropologist*, **45,** 87-103, (1992).

PART 4: GLOSSARY, LITERATURE CITED, INDEX, ABOUT THE AUTHOR

Relating to Indian viewpoints on ancient Indian history:
HIi-48 Misra, S.S., *New Lights on Indo-European comparative studies.* Varanasi: Manisha Prakashan, Manisha Oriental Research Series, (1975).
HIi-49 Misra, S.S., *The Old-Indo-Aryan, a historical and comparative analysis*, Ashutosh Prakashan Sansthan, Varanasi (India), (1993).
HIi-50 Kak, S., "Archaeoastronomy and Literature", *Current Science* **73**, 624-627, (10 October 1997).
HIi-51 Tripathi, R.S., *History of Ancient India,* Motilal Banarsidass Publishers Pvt Ltd, Delhi (India), (1999), (ISBN: 81-208-0018-4).
HIi-52. Frawley, D., "On the Banks of the Saraswati: The ancient history of India revised," *The Quest*, 22-30, (Autumn 1992).
HIi-53 Jacobi, H., *Indian Antiquary*, **Vol. XXIII**, 154, pp. 85 ff. (1895). Excerpts available at:
http://www.google.com/#hl=en&source=hp&q=Jacobi%2C+H.%2C+Indian+Antiquary%2C+Vol.+XXIII%2C+154&aq=f&aqi=&oq=&fp=2cca7b2e99206b9c

Related to ancient Indian astronomy:
HIi-54 Billard, R., *L'Astronomie Indienne,* Ecole Francaise d'Extreme Orient, Paris (France), (1971).
HIi-55 Thurston, H., *Early Astronomy,* Springer-Verlag, NY (USA), 188, (1994).
HIi-56 Kak, S.C., "The Astronomical Code of the Rigveda", *Puratattva: Bulletin of the Indian Archaeological Society* **25**, 1-20, (1994).

Indian and pro-Indian viewpoints on ancient Indian history, cont.:
HIi-57 Frawley D., *Gods, Sages and Kings: Vedic Secrets of Ancient Civilization*, Passage Press, Salt Lake City, UT (USA), (1991). See also: Feuerstein, G.; Kak, S.; Frawley, D., *In Search of the Cradle of Civilization: New Light on Ancient India*, Motilal Banarsidass Publishers Private Limited, Delhi (India), (2001).
HIi-58 Frawley, D., *The Myth of the Aryan Invasion of India*, Voice of India, New Delhi (India), (1994).
HIi-59 Panconcelli-Calcia, G., *Phonetik als Naturwissenschaft*, Wissenschaftliche Editionsgesellschaft mbH, Berlin, Germany (1948). pp. 51 ff.
HIi-60 Sastry, K., *Vedanga Jyotisa of Lagadha,* Indian National Science Academy, New Delhi (India), (1985).

LITERATURE CITED

553

Relating to ancient Indian works in engineering and mathematical sciences:
HIi-61 See introduction and discussion of predecessor works in *Natyasastra of Bharatamuni, with the Commentary of Abhinavabharati by Abhinavaguptacarya,* Parimal Publications, Delhi, (India), (1988) (ISBN: 81-7110-002-3). See also: *ibid.,* Vol. 1, Ch.'s 1-7.

HIi-62 *Natya Sastra of Bharatamuni [Raga Nrtya Series No. 2],* (Trans. Into English by a Board of Scholars), Sri Satguru Publications, Delhi (India), (1981), (ISBN: 81-7030-134-3).

HIi-63 Arya, R., *Vaastu, The Indian Art of Placement, Design and Decoration of Homes to Reflect Eternal Spiritual Principles,* Destiny Books, Rochester, VT (USA), (2000), (ISBN: 0-89281-885-9).

HIi-64. Maharaja, Jagadguru Swami Sri Bharati Krsna Tirthaji (Author); Agrawala, V.S. (Ed.), *Vedic Mathematics,* Motilal Banarsidass Publishers Pvt, (2006).

HIi-65 See, e.g., the references in: Mukhopadhyaya, G., *Surgical Instruments of the Hindus: A Comparative Study of the Surgical Instruments of the Greek, Roman, Arab and the Modern European Surgeons, with 396 Illustrations in 82 Plates,* R.K. Naahar & Co., New Delhi (India), (1977).

HIi-66 Sankalia, H.D., *Prehistoric and Historic Archaeology of Gujarat,* Munshiram Manoharlal Publishers Pvt Ltd, New Delhi (India), (1987), (ISBN: 81-215-0049-4).

Relating to ancient Indian works on politics and law:
HIi-66 Gairola, S.V. (Ed.), *Arthasastra of Kautilya and The Canakya Sutra [The Vidyabhawan Sanskrit Granthamala],* Chowkhamba Vidyabhawan, Varanasi (No. India), (1984).

HIi-67 Rangarajan, L.N., *The Arthashastra, [Kautilya],* Penguin Group, New York, NY (USA), (1992).

HIi-68 Bhatt, R., *Manusmrti [The Vrajajivan Pracyabharati Granthamala],* Chaukhamba Sanskrit Prathishthan, Delhi (India), (Reprint edition 1987).

Relating to ancient Indian works on philosophy:
HIi-69 See, e.g., Dutt, M.N.; Shastri, J.K.L. (Eds.), *Agni Mahapuranam, Sanskrit Text, English Translation and Index of Verses (Vol. 1),* Parimal Publications, Delhi (India), (2001), (ISBN: 81-7110-192-3).

PART 4: GLOSSARY, LITERATURE CITED, INDEX, ABOUT THE AUTHOR

IEu
(Relating to Indo-European languages, history, migration, etc.)

Relating to Indo-European linguistics:

IEu-1 Bopp, Franz, *A Comparative Grammar of the Sanscrit, Zend, Greek, Latin, Lithuanian, Gothic, German, & Sclavonic Languages,* (Translated into English from the German by Lt. Eastwick), Elibron Classics, Bibliobazaar, Charleston, SC (USA), (ISBN 1-4021-5370-8). (Originally published 1862; several reprints through 2006.) (1862)

IEu-2 Brugmann, K., *Kurze Vergleichende Grammatik der Indogermanischen Sprachen,* Karl J. Tubner, Strassburg (Strassbourg, Strasbourg, France), (1904).

IEu-3 Brugmann, K. (Trans. from the German by Wright, J.), *Elements of The Comparative Grammar of the Indo-Germanic Languages,* B. Westermann & Co., NY (USA), Reprint by Kessinger Publishing Legacy Reprints, (1888).

IEu-4 Osthoff, H.; Brugmann, K., *Morphologische Untersuchungen auf dem Gebiete der indogermanischen Sprachen,* S. Hirzel, Leipzig (Germany), (1878).

IEu-5 Pokorny, J., *Indogermanisches Etymologisches Woerterbuch,* Edition of French and European Publications, Paris (France), (1969).

IEu-6 Szemerenyi, O.J.L., *Introduction to Indo-European Linguistics [Translated from Einfuhrung in die vergleichende Sprachwissenschaft],* Oxford University Press, Oxford (England), (1999).

IEu-7 Lehmann, W., (Ed.), *A Reader in 19th Century Historical Indo-European Linguistics,* Indiana University Press, Bloomington, IN (USA), (1967).

IEu-8 Lehmann, W.P., *Theoretical Bases of Indo-European Linguistics,* Routledge Press, London (England), (1999).

IEu-9 Lehmann, W.P., *Proto-Indo-European syntax,* University of Texas Press, Austin, TX (USA), (1974).

IEu-10 Beekes, R., *Comparative Indo-European Linguistics,* John Benjamins Publishing Co., Amsterdam (Netherlands), (1959).

IEu-11 Rix, Hulmet, et al, *Lexicon der Indogermanischen Verben,* John Benjamins Publishing Co., Amsterdam (Netherlands), (1998).

IEu-12 Gamkrelidze, T. V.; Ivanov; V.V., *Indo-European and the Indo-Europeans, A Reconstruction & Historical Analysis of a Proto-Language and a Proto-Culture, Parts I & II, The Text,* Mouton de Gruyter, Berlin (Germany), (1995).

IEu-13 (a) von Schlegel, F., *The Philosophy of Life and Philosophy of Language in a Course of Lectures*, H.G. Bohn, London (England), (1847). **(b)** See also: "Out of India theory", http://en.wikipedia.org/wiki/Out_of_India_theory .

IEu-14 Kaul, R.K., *Studies in William Jones: An Interpreter of Oriental Literature*, South Asia Books, New Delhi (India), (1996).

Relating to "Proto-Indo-European" derivations:
IEu-15 (a) Mackey, Jake, Dept. of Classics, Princeton University, private communication, (2007).
(b) Sen, S.K.; Hamp, E.P., in *Encyclopedia of Indo-European Culture*, 503 (1997).
(c) Sen, S.K., "Proto-Indo-European, a Multiangular View", *J. Indo-European Studies,* **22**, 67-90 (1994).
(d) Sampson, G., "A reconstructed specimen of PIE", at: http://www.grsampson.net/Q_PIE.html
(e) See, e.g., http://en.wikipedia.org/wiki/The_king_and_the_god and http://simple.wikipedia.org/wiki/Proto-Indo-European_language

Relating to Indo-European linguistics, cont.:
IEu-16 Gimbutas, M.; Robbins Dexter, M.; Jones-Bley, K. (Eds.), *The Kurgan Culture and the Indo-Europeanization of Europe: Selected Articles From 1952 to 1993*, Institute for the Study of Man, Washington, D.C. (USA), (1997).

Relating to Germanic/Gothic:
IEu-17 Konig, E.; Van der Auwera, J. (Eds.), *The Germanic Languages,* Routledge, London (England), (1994).
IEu-18 Prokosch, E., *A Comparative Germanic Grammar*, University of Pennsylvania Linguistic Society of America, Philadelphia, PA (USA), (1939).
IEu-19 Wright, J., *Grammar of the Gothic Language*, Clarendon Press, Oxford (England), (1910).
IEu-20 Brauner, W., *Althochdeutsche Grammatik*, Henry Holt and Co., New York (USA), (1967).
IEu-21 Ellis, J., *An Elementary Old High German Grammar, Descriptive and Comparative*, Clarendon Press, Oxford (England), (1953).

Relating to Avestan:
IEu-23 Beekes, R., *A Grammar of Gatha-Avestan,* E.J. Brill, Leiden (Netherlands), (1988).
IEu-24 *[http://www.avesta.org/avesta.html], http://www.fas.harvard.edu/~iranian/,* (2008).

PART 4: GLOSSARY, LITERATURE CITED, INDEX, ABOUT THE AUTHOR

IEu-25 Jackson, A.V. W., *An Avesta Grammar in comparison with Sanskrit,* Wissenschaftliche Buchgesellschaft, Darmstadt (Germany) (1968).
IEu-26 Schmitt, R., *Altpersisch.* In *Compendium Linguarum Iranicarum,* Reichert, Wiesbaden (Germany), 56-85, (1989).
IEu-27 Geldner, K. F., *Avesta, the Sacred Book of the Parsis. 3 vols,* Kohlhammer, Stuttgart (Germany), (1896).
IEu-28 Hoffman, K. Avestan language, *Encyclopedia Iranica,* **3:1,** 47-62, (1988).

Relating to Classical and Homeric Greek:
IEu-29 Morwood, J., *Oxford Grammar of Classical Greek,* Oxford University Press, New York (USA), (2001).
IEu-30 Cunliffe, R., *Lexicon of the Homeric Dialect,* University of Oklahoma University Press, Norman, OK (USA), (1963).
IEu-31 Smyth, H., *Greek Grammar,* Harvard University Press, MA (USA), (1984).
IEu-32 Liddell, H.G.; Scott, R., *Greek-English Lexicon,* Oxford University Press, London (England), (1996).
IEu-33 Liddell, H.G.; Scott, R., *Intermediate Greek-English Lexicon,* Oxford University Press, London (England), (1995).

Relating to Russian:
IEu-34 Brown, N., *Russian Course,* Penguin Group, New York, NY (USA), (1996).
IEu-35 Cubberley, P., *Russian: A Linguistic Introduction,* Cambridge University Press, London (England), (2002).
IEu-36 Fairbanks, G.; Leed, R., *Basic Conversational Russian,* Holt, Rinehart & Winston, New York (USA), (1964).
IEu-37 Unbegaun, B.O., *Russian Grammar*, Oxford University Press, Oxford (England), (1957).

Relating to Anglo-Saxon (Old English), Including Effects on Modern English:
IEu-38 Sweet, H., *Sweet's Anglo-Saxon Primer*, Rev. by Norman Davis, Clarendon Press, Oxford (England), (1882).
IEu-39 Quirk, R.; Wrenn, C.L., *An Old English Grammar,* Methuen, London (England), (1957).
IEu-40 Moore, S.; Knott, T.A., *The Elements of Old English, 10th Edition*, Rev. by James R. Hulbert, George Wahr Publishing Co., Ann Arbor, MI (USA), (1955).
IEu-41 Bright, J.W., *Bright's Anglo-Saxon Reader,* Henry Holt and Co., New York (USA), (1959).

IEu-42 Jones, C., *An Introduction to Middle English*, Holt, Rinehart and Winston, New York (USA), (1972).

IEu-43 Jones, D., *An Outline of English Phonetics, 1st Edition*, W. Heffer and Sons, Cambridge, MA (USA), (1918).

Relating to Latin, Including Effects on Modern Romance Languages:

IEu-44 Palmer, L.R., *The Latin Language*, University of Oklahoma Press, Norman, OK (USA), (1988). Palmer notes in this book: "We have now examined the evidence bearing on the prehistory of the Latin language and come to the tentative conclusion that the proto-Latins were an IE tribe originating in central Europe which entered Italy towards the end of the second millennium B.C.. Arriving in Latium about the tenth century B.C., they settled Latium in scattered rural communitities (or populi) which combined in loose confederations. Rome itself originated in a synoecismus of *cremating* Latin and inhuming Sabine folk."

IEu-45 Verner, K., "Eine Ausnahme der ersten Lautverschiebung", Z. *fur vergleichende Sprachforschung*, **23**, 97-130, (1877).

IEu-46 Wheelock, F., *Latin, An Introductory Course Based on Ancient Authors [College Outline Series]*, Barnes & Noble, Inc., NY (USA), (1963).

IEu-47 Greenough, J.B. et al, *Allen and Greenough's New Latin Grammar*, Focus Publishing, Newburyport, MA (USA), (2001).

IEu-48 (a) Bennett, C., *New Latin Grammar*, Bolchazy-Carducci Publishers, Mundelein, IL (USA), (1998). (England), (1998). **(b)** Lewis, C.T., *Elementary Latin Dictionary*, Oxford University Press, London, (1998).

IEu-49 Caso, A., *The Kaso English to Italian Dictionary: With a Proposed One-to-One Relationship of Italian Graphemes (letters) and Phonemes (Sounds)*, Branden Books, Wellesley, MA, USA (2004) (ISBN 0-8283-2082-9).

Relating to Hittite:

IEu-50 Sturtevant, E., *A Comparative Grammar of the Hittite Language*, Linguistics Society of America, MD (USA), (1933).

IEu-51 Held, W.H.; Schmalstieg, W.R.; Gertz, J.E., *Beginning Hittite*, Slavica Publishers, Inc., (Indiana University Press), Bloomington, IN (USA), (1988).

PART 4: GLOSSARY, LITERATURE CITED, INDEX, ABOUT THE AUTHOR

GDn
(Relating to genetics, DNA, etc.)

General Genetics/DNA:
GDn-1. Cavalli-Sforza, L.L.; Menozzi, P.; Piazza, A., *The History and Geography of Human Genes,* Princeton University Press, Princeton, NJ (USA), (1994).
GDn-2 Wells, S., *Journey of Man: A Genetic Odyssey,* Princeton University Press, Princeton, NJ (USA), (2002).
GDn-3 Hedrick, P.; Waits, P., "What ancient DNA tells us", *Heredity* **94,** 463-4, (May 2005).
GDn-4 Ely, B., "How do researchers trace mitochondrial DNA over the centuries?", *Scientific American,* (January 2007).
GDn-5 Borman, S., "Mapping Human Genetic Variation", Genomics, *Chemical & Engineering News, [http://www.cen-online.org],* February 21 (2005); See also one of the original references cited in this article: Hinds, D.A., et al., *Science,* **307,** 1072-1079, (2005).
GDn-6 Henry, C. M., "Looking for Answers in Ancient DNA", *C&EN,* (29 March 2004).
GDn-7 Williamson, S.; Hubisz, M.; Clark, A.; Payseur, B.; Bustamante, C.; Nielsen, R., "Localizing Recent Adaptive Evolution in the Human Genome", *Public Library of Science (PLoS) Genetics,* **6,** e90, (3 June 2007).
GDn-8 Barreiro, L.; Laval, G.; Quach, H.; Patin, E.; Quintana-Murci, L., "Natural selection has driven population differentiation in modern humans", *Nat Genet* **40:3,** 340-345, (3 February 2008).
GDn-9 Knight, A.; Underhill, P.; Mortensen, H.; Zhivotovsky, L.; Lin, A.; Henn, B.; Louis, D.; Ruhlen, M.; Mountain, J., "African Y Chromosome and mtDNA Divergence Provides Insight into the History of Click Languages", *Current Biology* **31** 464-473, (18 March 2003).
GDn-10 Voight, B.; Kudaravalli, S.; Wen, W.; Pritchard, J., "A Map of Recent Positive Selection in the Human Genome", *Public Library of Science (PLoS) Biology* **4,** (2006).
GDn-11 Wade, N., "Still Evolving, Human Genes Tell New Story", *New York,* (7 March 2006).

Relating to the FOXP2 gene:
GDn-12 Itzhaki, J., "The FoxP2 story. A Tale of genes, language and human origins", http://genome.wellcome.ac.uk/doc_wtd020797.html (2003).

GDn-13 Enard, W.; Przeworski, M.; Fisher, S.; Lai Cecilia, S.L.; Wiebe, V.; Kitano, T.; Monaco, A.; Paabo, S., "Molecular evolution of FOXP2, a gene involved in speech and language", *Natur,* **418,** 869-872, (22 August 2002).

GDn-14 Lai, C; Fisher. S.; Hurst, J.; Levy, E.; Hodgson, S.; Fox, M.; Jeremiah, S.; Povey, S.; Jamison, D.; Green, E.; Vargha-Khadem, F.; Monaco, A. (Eds.), "The SPCH1 region on human 7q31: genomic characterization of the critical interval and localization of translocations associated with speech and language disorder". *Am J Hum Genet* **67,** 357-68, (2000).

GDn-15 Vargha-Khadem, F.; Gadian, DG; Copp, A.; Mishkin, M.; "FOXP2 and the neuroanatomy of speech and language", *Nature Reviews Neuroscience,* **6,** 131-137, (2005).

GDn-16 Haesler, S.; Rochefort, C.; Georgi, B; Licznerski, P.; Osten, P.; Scharff, C., "Incomplete and Inaccurate Vocal Imitation after Knockdown on FoxP2 in Songbird Basal Ganglia Nucleus Area X", *Public Library of Science (PLoS) Biology* **5,** e321, (2007).

General Genetics/DNA, cont.:

GDn-17 Macaulay, V.; Hill, C.; Achilli, A.; Rengo, C.; Clarke, D.; Meehan, W.; Blackburn, J.; Semino, O.; Scozzari, R.; Cruciani, F.; Taha A.; Shaari Norazila; Kassim, R.; Joseph, M.; Ismail, P.; Zainuddin, Z.; Goodwin, W.; Bulbeck, D.; Bandelt, H.; Oppenheimer, S.; Torroni, A.; Richards, M., "Single, Rapid Coastal Settlement of Asia Revealed by Analysis of Complete Mitochondrial Genomes" *Science* **308,** 1034-1036, (13 May 2005).

GDn-18 Melton, T. et al., "Genetic Evidence for the Proto-Austronesian Homeland in Asia: mtDNA and Nuclear DNA Variation in Taiwanese Aboriginal Tribes", *Am. J. Hum. Genet* **63,** 1807-1823, (1998).

Relating to littoral migrationof ancient H. sapiens from Africa:

GDn-19 Oppenheimer, S.; Richards, M., "Slow Boat to Melanesia", *Nature,* **410** 166, (2001).

GDn-20 Shang, H.; Tong, H.; Zhang, S.; Chen, F.; Trinkaus, E., "An early modern human from Tianyuan Cave, Zhoukoudian, China", *Proceedings of the National Academy of Science USA (PNAS),* **104,** 6573-6578, (17 April, 2007).

GDn-21 Wilford, J., "Kenya Fossils Challenge Linear Evolution to Homo Sapiens", *The New York Times,* (9 August 2007).

GDn-22 Fuku, N.; Nishigaki, Y.; Tanaka, M., "Human mitochondrial genome polymorphism database (mtSNP)", *Tanpakushitsu Kakusan Koso,* **50,** 1753-8, (2005).

GDn-23 Horai, S. et al., "mtDNA polymorphism in East Asian Populations, with special reference to the peopling of Japan", *Am. J. Hum. Genet.* **59,** 579, (1996).

General Genetics/DNA, cont.:
GDn-24 "Initial sequence of the chimpanzee genome and comparison with the human genome", *Nature* **437,** 69-87, (1 September 2005).

Relating to DNA-based ancestry determinations of Dravidians and Aaryans (Aryans):
GDn-25 Barnabas, S.; Apte, R.V.; Suresh, C.G., "Ancestry and interrelationships of the Indians and their relationship with other world populations: A study based on Mitochondiral DNA Polymorphisms", *Ann Hum Genet* **60,** 409-422, (September 1996).
GDn-26 Barnabas S., Shouche Y., Suresh C.G., "High-Resolution mtDNA Studies of the Indian Population: Implications for Palaeolithic Settlement of the Indian Subcontinent", *Ann Hum Genet.,* **70,** 42-58, (January 2006).
GDn-27 Barnabas S., Joshi B., Suresh GC., "Indian-Asian relationship: mtDNA reveals more," *Naturwissenschaften,* **87,** 180-3, (April 2000).
GDn-28 Barnabas S., Apte R.V., Suresh CG., "Human evolution: the study of the Indian mitochondrial DNA.", *Naturwissenschaften* **83,** 28-9, (January 1996).
GDn-29 Bamshad et al., "Genetic evidence on the origins of Indian caste populations", *Genome Research,* **11,** 994-1004, (2001).
GDn-30 Kivisild et al., "The Genetic Heritage of the Earliest Settlers Persist Both in Indian Tribal and Caste Populations", *Am. J. Human Genet,* (2003).
GDn-31 Mukherjee et al., "High-resolution analysis of Y-chromosomal polymorphisms reveals signatures of population movements from central Asia and West Asia to India", *J. Genetics* **80,** 125-135, (December 2001).
GDn-32 Anjana, S.; Swarkar, S.; Audesh, B.; Awadesh, P.; Ramesh, B., "Genetic among five different population groups in India reflecting a Y-chromosome gene flow.", *J.Hum Genet,* **50,** 49-51, (2005).
GDn-33 Sengupta, Sanghamitra et al., "Polarity and Temporality of High-Resolution Y-Chromosome Distributions in India Identify Both Indigenous and Exogenous Expansions and Reveal Minor Genetic Influence of Central Asian Pastoralists", *Am. J. Human Genet* **78,** 202-221, (2006).

Newer (1985-2009) references relating to DNA-based ancestry of peoples of the Indian subcontinent:
GDn-34 Sharma, S., et al., "The Indian origin of paternal haplogroup R1a1[*] substantiates the autochthonous origin of Brahmins and the caste system ", *J. Human*

Genetics **54**, 47–55 (2009); *doi:10.1038/jhg.2008.2;* (published online 9 January 2009*)*

GDn-35 Sharma, S., et al., "The Autochthonous Origin and a Tribal Link of Indian Brahmins: Evaluation Through Molecular Genetic Markers", Paper # 1344/T presented at the 57th Annual Meeting of The American Society of Human Genetics, October 23–27, 2007 • San Diego, CA, USA.

GDn-36 Sahoo, S., et al., "A prehistory of Indian Y chromosomes: Evaluating demic diffusion scenarios", *Proceedings of the National Academy of Sciences* 103 (4): 843–848, doi:10.1073/pnas.0507714103. (Published online January 13, 2006).

Related to DNA-based ancestry of Japanese:
GDn-37 Omoto, K.; Saito, N., "Genetic origins of the modern Japanese: A partial support for the dual structure hypothesis", *Am. J. Phys. Anthropology* **102**, 437, (1997).

General Genetics/DNA, cont.:
GDn-38 Bromham L., and Penny, D., "The Modern Molecular Clock", *Nature Reviews Genetics,* **4**, 216, (March 2003).

GDn-39 Fitch David, H.A., "Lecture Notes: Deviations From the Null Hypotheses: Finite populations sizes and genetic drift, mutation and gene flow"*:* http://www.nyu.edu/projects/fitch/courses/evolution/html/genetic_drift.html (1997).

Relating to the R1a and R1b haplogroups:
GDn-40 (a) Re the haplogroup R1a, see, e.g.: *Haplogroup R1a (Y-DNA), Wikipedia*, http://en.wikipedia.org/wiki/Haplogroup_R1a_%28Y-DNA%29 **(b)** Re the haplogroup R1b, see, e.g.: *Haplogroup R1b (Y-DNA), Wikipedia*, http://en.wikipedia.org/wiki/Haplogroup_R1b_(Y-DNA)].

Related to DNA-based ancestry of Europeans:
GDn-41 Arnaiz-Villena, A.; Gomez-Casado, E.; Martinez-Laso, J., "Population genetic relationships between Mediterranean populations determined by HLA allele distribution and a historic perspective" Hypothesis article, *Tissue Antigens,* **60**, 111, (August 2002).

GDn-42 (a) Cinnioglu, C. et al., "Excavating Y-chromosome Haplotype strata in Anatolia", *Hum Genet,* **114**, 127-48, (2004).

GDn-43 Maliarchuk, BA.; Czarny, J., "African DNA lineages in mitochondrial gene pool of Europeans", *Mol Biol (Mosk),* **39**, 806-12, (2005).

GDn-44 (a) Semino et al., "The Genetic Legacy of Paleolithic Homo sapiens sapiens in Extant Europeans: A Y Chromosome Perspective", *Science,* **290**, 1155-59,

(2000). **(b)** See also: Passarino et. al., "Different genetic components in the Norwegian population revealed by the analysis of mtDNA and Y chromosome polymorphisms", *Eur. J. Hum. Genet,* **10,** 521-9, (2002).

GDn-45 Achilli, A.; Rengo, C.; Battaglia. V.; Pala, M.; Olivieri, A.; Fornarion, S.; Magri, C.; Scozzari, R.; Babudri, N.; Santachiara-Benerecetti, A.; Bandelt, H.; Semino, O.;Torroni, A., "Saami and Berbers--an unexpected mitochondrial DNA link", *Am J Hum Genet* **76,** 883-6, (May 2005).

GDn-46 Ammerman, A.; Pinhasi, R.; Banffy, E., "Ancient DNA from the first European farmers in 7500-year-old Neolithic sites", *Science,* **312,** 1875, (2006).

GDn-47 Wells, S., "The Eurasian Heartland: A continental perspective on Y-chromosome diversity", *Proceedings of the National Academy of Science USA (PNAS),* **98,** 10244-10249, (28 August 2001).

GDn-48 Oppenheimer, S., *Origins of the British: A Genetic Detective Story*, Basic Books, New York (USA), (2006), (ISBN-10: 0786718900, ISBN-13: 978-0786718900).

GDn-49 Wade, N., "A United Kingdom? DNA Suggests the Possibility", *The New York Times*, (6 March 2007).

Selected "racist" and "anti-racist" references and articles:

GDn-50 Lewontin, R., *The Triple Helix*, Harvard University Press, Cambridge, MA (USA), (2000). See also: Lewontin, R.; Singh, R.S.; Uyenoyama, M., *The Evolution of Population Biology*, Cambridge University Press, Cambridge (England), (2004).

GDn-51 Wade, N, "In the Genome Race, the Sequel is Personal", *The New York Times Science*, (4 September 2007).

GDn-52 Leroi, A., "A Family Tree in Every Gene", *The New York Times Op-Ed,* (14 March 2005).

Related to convergent evolution:

GDn-53 Angier, N., "Independently, Two Frogs Blaze the Same Venomous Path", *The New York Times*, (9 August 2005).

GDn-54 Clark, V.; Raxworthy, C.; Rakotomalala, V.; Sierwald, P.; Fisher, B., "Convergent evolution of chemical defense in poison frogs and arthropod prey between Madagascar and the Neotropics", *Proceedings of the National Academy of Science USA (PNAS)*, **102,** 11517-11622, (16 August 2005).

LITERATURE CITED

563

Related to DNA-based ancestry of Europeans, cont.:
GDn-55 "Cowabunga: Tuscan cattle shed light on where the Etruscans came to Italy from", *The Economist*, 82, (17 February 2007).
GDn-56 Wade, N., "DNA Boosts Herodotus' Account of Etruscans as Migrants to Italy", *The New York Times,* F3, (3 April 2007).

Newer (post-2005) research or publications proposing new theories counter to older genetic theories:
GDn-57 Grine, F.E.; Bailey, R.M.; Harvati, K.; Nathan, R.P.; Morris, A.G.; Henderson, G.M.; Ribot, I.; Pike, A.W.G., "Late Pleistocene Human Skull from Hofmeyr, South Africa, and Modern Origins", *Science* **315**, 226-229 (12 January 2007).
GDn-58 Zielinski, S., "Interview: Fred Spoor", *Smithsonian Magazine,* (October 2007).
GDn-59 Reich, D., "The HLA-DRB1 shared epitope is associated with susceptibility to rheumatoid arthritis in African Americans through European genetic mixture", *Bioinfobank*, [http://lib.bioinfo.pl/auid:1635956], (31 January 2008).
GDn-60 Wang, S.; Ray, N.; Rojas, W.; Parra, M.V.; Bedoya, G. et al, "Geographic Patterns of Genome Admixture in Latin American Mestizos", *[http://www.plosgenetics.org]*, (2008).
GDn-61 Bush, E.; Lahn Bruce, T., "The Evolution of Word Composition in Metazoan Promoter Sequence", *Public Library of Science (PloS)* **2,** e150, (November 2006).

Related to mitochondrial-DNA:
GDn-62 Anderson, S.; Bankier, A.T.; Barrell, B.G.; de Bruijn, M.H.; Coulson, A.R.; Drouin, J.; Eperon, I.C.; Nierlich, D.P.; Roe, B.A.; Sanger, F.; Schreier, P.H.; Smith, A.J.; Staden, R.; Young, I.G., " Sequence and organization of the human mitochondrial genome", *Nature* **290: 5806**, 457–465, (9 April 1981).

Newer (post-2005) research or publications proposing new theories counter to older genetic theories, cont.:
GDn-63 "Convergent adaptation of human lactase persistence in Africa and Europe", *Nature Genetics* **39,** 31-40, (10 December 2006).
GDn-64 Wade, N., "Lactose Tolerance in East Africa Points to Recent Evolution", *The New York Times International*, A15, (11 December 2006).
GDn-65 Re the seminal work of Dmitri K. Belyaev in this regard, see, e.g.: Wade, N., "Nice Rats, Nasty Rats: Maybe It's All In the Genes", *The New York Times,* Science Times section, (25 July 2006).
GDn-66 Malhi, R.S., et al., "Native American mtDNA Prehistory in the American Southwest",

Am. J. Phys. Anthropol. **120,** 108, (2003).

Newer (1985-2009) references relating to DNA-based ancestry of peoples of the Indian subcontinent, cont.:
GDn-67 Indian Genome Variation Consortium, "Genetic landscape of the people of India: a canvas for disease gene exploration", *J. Genet.*, **87**. 3-20 (2008).
GDn-68 Zerjal, T. et al., "Y-chromosomal insights into the genetic impact of the caste system in India", *Hum. Genet.* **121**, 137–144 (2007).
GDn-69 Basu, A. et al. "Ethnic India: a genomic view, with special reference to peopling and structure", *Genome Res.* **13**, 2277–2290 (2003).
GDn-70 David Reich, D.; Thangaraj, K.; Patterson, N.; Price, A.L.; Singh, L., "Reconstructing Indian population history", *Nature*, **461**, 489-495 (2009).

Relating to the tree line during the peak of the last Ice Age ("Last Glacial Maximum", LGM):
GDn-71 See, e.g., http://en.wikipedia.org/wiki/File:Last_glacial_vegetation_map.png

INDEX

*A detailed Index is provided below.
This however does <u>not</u> include an author index.*

(NOTE: For all terms, see also definition and explanation in the GLOSSARY.)

Abulhab, S.D., *script* 261, 266
Accent, ictus, *in English, Spanish and other languages* 417-418
Accent, musical, *see* **Tone**
Accent, stress, *see* **Accent, ictus**
Algonquian, *script* 260
Alphabetical order, *of NAVLIPI, see* **Pedagogical**
AMERICANIST *Phonetic Notation (alphabet, script)* 279-282
Analphabetic *(script), see* **Jespersen, O.**
Arabic, *Transcription of, into NAVLIPI* 133-139
Arabic, *script, in NAVLIPI* 72-74
Arguments against *a new, universal script* 190-191
Arthur's alphabet, *(script)* 269
Articulation position, *see* **Artition**
Artition, *as variable* 218
Artitions, *in NAVLIPI defined* 11, 310-316
Artitions, *in NAVLIPI, summary table* 186, 311
Artitions, *unusual* 313-314
Audience (market) *addressed by NAVLIPI* xxxv, 167
AUTHOR, About the 575

Bell, A.M., *script* 233, 240-246
Bloquerst, A.J., *script* 269
Braahmi (Brahmi), *script* 196, 204-215
Brahmi *script, see* **Braahmi**
Braille, *for NAVLIPI,* xl
Bright, T., *script* 229
Bukele, M.D., *see* **Vai**
Burmese, *script* 196

PART 4: GLOSSARY, LITERATURE CITED, INDEX, ABOUT THE AUTHOR

Butler, C., *script* 226

Cantonese tones, *transcription of, in NAVLIPI* 408-411
Cashinahua tones, *transcription of, in NAVLIPI* 408-411
Centrals, *NAVLIPI glyphs for* 45-50
Chandrasekhar, P. *see* **Author, About the**
Cherokee, *script* 196, 260
Chinese, *script* 195
Classification, *systematic and scientific phonological (property of a new, universal script)* xxxiv, 179, 185
Classification, *systematic and scientific phonological, in Haangul (Hangul)* 198-200
Classification, *systematic and scientific phonological, in Indian scripts* 204-224
Clicks, *NAVLIPI glyphs for* 38-43
Columbian *alphabet (script)* 266
Combination phones, *transcription in NAVLIPI* 372
Compensation, *in NAVLIPI* 298
Completeness *(property of a new, universal script)* xxxiv, 179
Cree, *script* 260
Cursive writing, *amenability to, of NAVLIPI* 181-183
Cyrillic, *script, in NAVLIPI* 69-71

Deficiencies *of various world script* 283-285
Deseret *alphabet (script)* 238
Devanagari, *see* **Dewanaagari**
Dewanaagari (Devanagari, "refined urban"), *script, in NAVLIPI* 64-68, 204, 222
Dewanaagari, *script based on modified, new universal* 333-399
Discretization, *(property of a new, universal script)* xxxiv, 179, 188
Discretization, *of phonemic variables, as used in NAVLIPI* 382
Distinctiveness *(property of a new, universal script)* xxxiv, 179, 180

Ease of learning, *of NAVLIPI,* 8
Egyptian, demotic, *script* 195
Egyptian, hieroglyphic, *script* 195
Ejectives, *NAVLIPI glyphs for* 41-43
Ellis, A., *script* 234
Emsley, B., *script* 248, 269
English, *Transcription of, into NAVLIPI* xxxix, 127-129
Evans, J., *shorthand (script)* 230-231

INDEX

567

Ewing, J. 267-268

Flaps, *NAVLIPI glyphs for* 35-37
Formant frequencies, *of fundamental vowels* 214
Fraser, J.O., *script* 267
French, *Transcription of, into NAVLIPI* 140-142
Fricatives, *NAVLIPI glyphs for* 35-37

Gabelsberger, F., *script* 229
Gellius, A., *script* 229
Geometric symbols, *script based on, new, universal* 325-327
Georgian, *script* 195
German, *Transcription of, into NAVLIPI* 143-146
GLOSSARY 495 *ff.* (495-506)
Glossic *script* 235
Glottal stop, *in Indian phonology* 216-217
Glyphs (letters), *borrowed, in NAVLIPI* 380-381
Glyphs (letters), *for centrals' phonemic condensates*, *in NAVLIPI, selection of* 395
Glyphs (letters), *for laterals' phonemic condensates*, *in NAVLIPI, selection of* 396
Glyphs (letters), *for non-vowels*, *in NAVLIPI, selection of* 390-392
Glyphs (letters), *for semivowel phonemic condensates*, *in NAVLIPI, selection of* 393
Glyphs (letters), *for vowels*, *in NAVLIPI, selection of* 387-389
Glyphs (letters), *NAVLIPI , notation for* 385-386
Glyphs (letters), *new, in NAVLIPI* xxxviii, 380-381
Glyphs (letters), *redundant/reused, in NAVLIPI* xxxviii, 377
Glyphs (letters), *total number, in NAVLIPI* xxxviii, 8
Glyphs (letters), *transformed, in NAVLIPI* 380-381
Graham, A., *alphabet (script)* 235-237
Graham, A., *shorthand (script)* 231-234
Greek, *Homeric, tones, transcription of, in NAVLIPI* 412-416
Greek, *script* 195
Greenaway, *script* 270
Gregg, J., *shorthand (script)* 232-233

Haangul *script* 198-201
Hangul, *see* **Haangul**
Harappan, *script* 197
Hart, J., *script* 225-227

PART 4: GLOSSARY, LITERATURE CITED, INDEX, ABOUT THE AUTHOR

Hindi/Urdu, *Transcription*, *into NAVLIPI* xxxix, 121-126
Hmong *script* 202
Holder, W., *script* 226

Implosives, *NAVLIPI glyphs for* 41-43
India, scripts, *see* **Indian scripts**
Indian scripts 167, 204-224
Indian scripts, *inadequacies* 220
Indonesian, *script* 167
International Phonetic Association, *see* **IPA**
Intuitive nature *(property of a new, universal script)* xxxiv, 179, 180
Inuit, *script* 215, *see also* **Inuktikut**
Inuktikut, *script* 196, 260-261
IPA (International Phonetic Association), *Chart of* xxxiv, xxxv
IPA (International Phonetic Association), *alphabet (script) of* 270-278
IPA (International Phonetic Association), *alphabet (script) of, deficiencies in* 270-278

Janvrin, F., *script* 248
Japanese *script* 201-202
Jaw position, *in NAVLIPI,* 9
Jaw, *vertical and horizontal positions* 300
Jespersen, O., *script* 248
Johnston, H., *script* 249, 251-252

Kante, S., *see* **N'ko**
Keyboarding, *in NAVLIPI* xl, 77 *ff.* (77-115), 441 *ff.* (441-492)
Keyboarding, *in NAVLIPI, 4-part numerical (matrix) notation for* 445-450
Keyboarding, *in NAVLIPI, changes to QWERTY/AZERTY keyboard layout in* 452-453
Keyboarding, *in NAVLIPI, ease of* 183
Keyboarding, *in NAVLIPI, keys, major reassignments in* 455-458
Keyboarding, *in NAVLIPI, language specificity of* 441-444
Keyboarding, *in NAVLIPI, list of individual keys* 82-84
Keyboarding, *NAVLIPI, Unicode requirements for, see* **Unicode,** *NAVLIPI keyboarding*
Keyboarding, *in NAVLIPI, unused/leftover keys, inventory of* 490
Keys, *keyboard, in NAVLIPI, see* **Keyboarding**
Khmer, *script* 196
Kingsley, R., *script* 264-265

Lakota, *script* 196, 260
Laterals, *NAVLIPI glyphs for* 45-50
LeGuin, U.K., *script* 269
Lepsius, C.R., *script* 237, 239, 277, 283
Linear B, *script* 195
Lip position, *in NAVLIPI,* 9

Maagyaar (Magyar, Hungarian), *Transcription of, into NAVLIPI* 152-156
Magyar, *see* **Maagyaar**
Malaysian (Malay), *script* 167
Malone, J.R., *script* 264
Mandarin tones, *Chinese Government transcription system, difficulties with* 404
Mandarin, *Romanized, see* **Pinyin**
Mandarin, *Transcription of, into NAVLIPI* xxxviii, 117-120
Maraathi (Marathi), *Transcription of, into NAVLIPI* 147-151
Marathi, *see* **Maraathi**
Market (audience) *for NAVLIPI* xxxv, 167
Mason, W., *script* 229
Matrices, *non-vowel, of NAVLIPI, see* **Non-Vowel matrices**
Matrices, shell (templates), *for phonological classification, see* **Shell Matrix**
Matrices, *vowel, of NAVLIPI, see* **Vowel matrices**
Matrix elements, *of NAVLIPI, defined* 7
Matrix notation, *used by NAVLIPI* 318
Mayan, *script* 195
Meigret, *script* 226
Modi, *script* 201-202
Mongolian, *script, see* **Phagspa**
Mulcaster, R., *script* 226
Musical accent, *see* **Tone**

Naagari (Nagari, "urban"), *see* **Dewanaagari**
Nagari (Naagari, "urban"), *see* **Dewanaagari**
Nama tones, *transcription of, in NAVLIPI* 408-411
NAVLIPI, **meaning of the word** xli
Need, *for a new script* xxxiv, 166
Nirukta, *see* **Yaaska**
N'ko *script* 262
Nomic *script* 234

PART 4: GLOSSARY, LITERATURE CITED, INDEX, ABOUT THE AUTHOR

Non-vowel classification, *of NAVLIPI* 11
Non-vowel matrices, *of NAVLIPI* 31-50, 310-316
Non-vowel, *"silent", see* **Silent Non-vowel**
Non-vowels, *in NAVLIPI, selection of glyphs for* 390-391
North/South Indian languages, *divide, NAVLIPI as applied to* xxxv, 167
Notation for glyphs, *in NAVLIPI* 384-386

Objectives, *of NAVLIPI* xxxiv, 179-189
Ojibwe, *script* 260
Ol Ciki *script* 202
Olmec, *script* 197
Owen, R.L., *script* 253

Pahawh *script* 202-203
Palaeotype *script* 234
Pedagogical ("alphabetical") order, *of NAVLIPI* 60-63, 321
Pepys, S., *script* 229
Phagspa (Mongolian), *script* 196-198
Phoneme *(definitions, etc.)* xxxi-xxxii
Phonemic condensate, *for (semivowel + forward fricative)* 430
Phonemic condensate, *for (stop + flap)* 431
Phonemic condensate, *for (stop + forward fricative)* 430
Phonemic condensate, *for (stop + fricative)* 430
Phonemic condensate, *for (stop + semivowel)* 430
Phonemic condensate, *for (voiced + unvoiced)* 429
Phonemic condensate, *apico-alveolo-dental (flap+trill+semivowel), common "r"* 432
Phonemic condensate, *for aspirate/non-aspirate* 429
Phonemic condensate, *for retroflex (flap + trill + semivowel)* 433
Phonemic condensate, *for velar/uvular ([x]/[r]) combination* 433
Phonemic condensates, *complex* 176
Phonemic condensates, *definition and discussion of* 174, 429-438
Phonemic condensates, *various central/lateral/nasal combos, incl. significance* 434-438
Phonemic condensates, *of NAVLIPI, summary table of* 55-57
Phonemic condensation, *see* **Phonemic condensates, Phonemic condensate**
Phonemic idiosyncrasy xxxi-xxxiii, 169-176
Phonemic irrelevance 382
Phonemics, *practical (property of a new, universal script)* xxxiv, 179, 189
Phones, combination, *see* **Combination phones**

INDEX

Phones, *unusual, transcription of, in NAVLIPI*   397-399
Phonochromaticity, *see* **Phonochrome(s)**
Phonochromes ("colors" of the phone), *in NAVLIPI, defined*   12, 310-312, 315-316
Phonochromes ("colors" of the phone), *in NAVLIPI, summary table*   187, 312
Phonochromes ("colors" of the phone), *unusual*   315-316
Phonological classification, *ancient Indian*   204-224
Phonological classification, *ancient Indian, as basis for further expansion for a modern orthography*   223
Phonological classification, *as used by NAVLIPI,*   294 *ff.* (294-316), 377 *ff.* (377-397)
Phonological classification, *independent variables in*   215
Phonological variable, *discussion*   215
Phonotype *script*   233
Pike, K., *script*   253-259
Pinyin (Romanized Mandarin), *NAVLIPI as applied to*   xxxv, 161, 404
Pitch, *see* **Tone**
Pitman, I., *alphabet (script)*   233-237
Pitman, I., *shorthand (script)*   229-233
Pitman-Graham shorthand, script based on, new, universal   345-349
Plosives, *NAVLIPI glyphs for*   31-34
Pollard, S., *script*   266, 268
Post-ops (post-positional operators), *NAVLIPI, cursive writing of, quick examples*   184
Post-ops (post-positional operators), *NAVLIPI, presentation, discussion of*   xxxvii, 353 *ff.* (353-374)
Post-ops (post-positional operators), *NAVLIPI, Table of*   51-54
Post-ops, *script based on, new universal*   328-332
Post-positional operators   *See* **Post-ops**
Praakrts   204
Prakrit, *see* **Praakrts**

Recognizability *(property of a new, universal script)*   xxxiv, 179-180
Requirements, *ten, of a new script, discussion of*   xxxiv, 179-189
Robinson, R., *script*   225-226
Romic *script*   246
Roudet, *script*   268

Sanskrit, *Vedic, tones, transcription of, in NAVLIPI*   412-416
Sapir, E., *script*   269
Script, *new, universal, arguments against*   190-191

PART 4: GLOSSARY, LITERATURE CITED, INDEX, ABOUT THE AUTHOR

Script, *new, universal, based on Dewanaagari, see* **Dewanaagari, script based on**
Script, *new, universal, based on geometric symbols, see* **geometric symbols, script based on**
Script, *new, universal, based on Pitman-Graham shorthand, see* **Pitman-Graham shorthand,** *script based on*
Script, *new, universal, based on post-ops, see* **post-ops, script based on**
Script, *new, universal, exercises in making* 324 ff. (324-350)
Scripts, *various world, deficiencies of* 283-285
Scripts, world, *not covered in Prior Art discussion in this book* 195
Scripts, world, *Prior Art (prior work) in* 195 ff. (195-285)
Semitic, *script* 195
Semi-tonal languages, *definition* 412
Semivowels, *as derivatives of and in relation to vowels* 220, 305-309
Semivowels, *NAVLIPI glyphs for* 45-50
Shavian *script* 264-265
Shaw, G.B., *see* **Shavian**
Shell Matrix (Template), *for phonological classification* 291 ff. (291-321), 384-392
Shelton, T., *script* 229
Shorthands 229-232 *see also under the individual authors' names, e.g.* **Pitman**
Silent Non-vowel 373
Simplicity *(property of a new, universal script)* xxxiv, 179, 181
Smith, T., *script* 226
Sorang Sampeng *script* 202
Spanish, *Transcription of, into NAVLIPI* xxxix, 130-132
Story, C., *script* 248-250
Swadesh, *script* 269
Swedish, *tones, transcription of, in NAVLIPI* 412-416
Sweet, H., *script* 246

Tamil, *script, in NAVLIPI* 75-76
Tamil, *unique jaw articulation positions in* 300-301
Taps, *see* **Flaps**
Taylor, S., *script* 229
Teaching, *of NAVLIPI, see* **Pedagogical**
Template, Matrix, *for phonological classification, see* **Shell Matrix**
Tengwar, *script* 269
Thai, *script* 196
Tibetan, *script* 196

INDEX

573

Tiro, M.T., *script* 229
Tolkien, J.R.R., *script* 269
Tonal languages, *definition* 408, 412
Tones, *determinative, definition of* 412
Tones, *in Mandarin, Chinese Govt. system of transcription of, see* **Mandarin tones**
Tones, *in NAVLIPI, discussion of* 317
Tones, *in NAVLIPI, transcription of* 402 *ff.* (402-426)
Tones, *in Vietnamese, transcription of, see* **Vietnamese tones**
Tones, *IPA transcription of, difficulties with* 402-407
Tones, *of NAVLIPI, summary table of* 58
Tones, *significant, definition of* 412
Tongue articulation position, *in NAVLIPI,* 9
Transcription, *ease of (property of a new, universal script)* xxxiv, 179, 181
Transcription, *into NAVLIPI, of major world languages* 116 *ff.* (116-139); *see also under each language*
Trills, *NAVLIPI glyphs for* 35-37
Tschichold, *script* 196
Turkic languages, *NAVLIPI applied to* xxxv, 167
Turkic languages, *script* 167

Unicode 266
Unicode*, NAVLIPI keyboarding, requirements for* 454
Unifon *script* 264
Universality *(property of a new, universal script)* xxxiv, 179
Urdu*, Transcription, into NAVLIPI* xxxix, 121-126

Vai *script* 262
Varang Kshiti *script* 202
Vietnamese tones, *in Vietnamese, transcription of, difficulties with* 405
Vietnamese, *Transcription of, into NAVLIPI* 157-161
Visarga *see* **Wisarga**
Visible Speech *(script of A.M. Bell), see* **Bell, A.M.**
Voice recognition, *for NAVLIPI* xxxiv, xli
Vowel classification, *of NAVLIPI* 9-10, 294-302
Vowel classification, *of NAVLIPI , six variables in* 294-302
Vowel classification, *of NAVLIPI, 6 or 5 dimensions, reduction to 3 dimensions* 294-302
Vowel equations, *in Indian phonology and Dewanaagari (Devanagari)* 211
Vowel matrices, *of NAVLIPI* 14 *ff.* (14-30)

PART 4: GLOSSARY, LITERATURE CITED, INDEX, ABOUT THE AUTHOR

574

Vowel, *"mobile, generic"* 371
Vowels, *central ("vocalic centrals"), of NAVLIPI, glyphs for* 19, 23
Vowels, *derivative, in Dewanaagari (Devanagari)* 211, 216-218
Vowels, *fundamental and derivative, NAVLIPI glyphs for* 14-18
Vowels, *fundamental, in Dewanaagari (Devanagari)* 210, 214
Vowels, *in NAVLIPI, selection of glyphs for* 387-388
Vowels, *lateral ("vocalic laterals"), of NAVLIPI, glyphs for* 20, 22, 24, 26
Vowels, *nasal ("vocalic nasals"), of NAVLIPI, glyphs for* 27-28

Watt, G.D., *script* 237-238
Weeks, R., *script* 269
Wilbur, J., *script* 269 *ff.*
Wilkins, J., *script* 225 *ff.*
Willis, J., *script* 229 *ff.*
Wisarga, *probable original significance, in Dewanaagari* 216-218

Yaaska (Yaska), *(ancient Indian author of classic work on etymology, "Nirukta")* 229
Yoruba tones, *transcription of, in NAVLIPI* 408-411
Young, B., *script* 237-238

ABOUT THE AUTHOR

Education, Experience, Positions Held

Prasanna Chandrasekhar was born on 17 October 1957 in Mumbai, India. He received his B.Sc. (Honors) in Chemistry from the University of Delhi, Delhi, India in 1978, his M.S. in Inorganic Chemistry/X-Ray-Crystallography from Concordia University, Montréal, Canada in 1980, and his Ph.D. in Electro-analytical Chemistry from the State University of New York at Buffalo, Buffalo, NY, USA in 1984. He was a postdoctoral associate at the Department of Chemistry and Materials Science Center, Cornell University, Ithaca, NY, USA in 1984-5, and a Senior Research Scientist at Honeywell, Inc. in Minneapolis, MN, USA and Horsham, PA, USA from 1985-1987. From 1987-1992, he was Manager of Electrochemical Programs at Gumbs Associates, Inc., East Brunswick, NJ, USA. He founded Ashwin-Ushas Corporation, a small U.S. defense contractor (*see* http://www.ashwin-ushas.com), in October 1992, and has been President and CEO there since.

Current Scientific Interests and Work

Dr. Chandrasekhar's current scientific research interests and active research include conducting polymers, electrochemistry, materials science, solar energy, space sciences, bio-remediation, remediation of hazardous medical wastes and analytical microbiology.

Publications

Dr. Chandrasekhar is the author of over 90 peer-reviewed scientific papers. He has also authored several chapters in textbooks, and is the sole author of the widely acclaimed (non-edited) textbook *Conducting Polymers: Fundamentals and Applications. A Practical Approach* (Kluwer Academic Publishers/Springer Verlag, Boston, USA and Dordrecht, The Netherlands, 1999, ISBN 0-7923-8564-0); this is still used in graduate courses throughout the world. A current publication list is available on request.

PART 4: GLOSSARY, LITERATURE CITED, INDEX, ABOUT THE AUTHOR

LANGUAGE, PHONOLOGY, LINGUISTICS:
Work and Experience in These and Related Fields

While he had no formal training in the linguistics or related fields, a highly multi-lingual and multi-cultural environment during early childhood sparked a strong interest in these fields early on for Dr. Chandrasekhar. This was nurtured with active self-study of major languages and ancient literature, as well as linguistics, phonology, comparative philology and related subjects.

Dr. Chandrasekhar has *reading, writing and speaking fluency* in: English, French, German, Hindi/Urdu, Maraathii (Marathi), Tamil, and Classical and Vedic Sanskrit**.

He has *reading ability* in: Spanish, Italian, Portuguese, Romanian, Classical Greek, Anglo-Saxon (Old English), Nepaali (Nepali), and several other languages.

Dr. Chandrasekhar also has a basic, *"100-word street vocabulary"*, without reading or writing ability, in several other languages, as varied as Egyptian Arabic, Dutch and Mandarin common speech (*Putonghua*).

He also has a very strong grounding in English (including Old and Middle English) literature, in Sanskrit (including Vedic) literature, and in the grammar of Indo-European, Dravidian, and several other language families.

Dr. Chandrasekhar taught a non-credit course in Elementary Sanskrit and Dewanaagari Script to students of Latin and Greek in the Classics Department of Princeton University, Princeton, NJ, USA, in the Spring semester of 1989. He taught a similar course in 2005-6 to Indian-American children at a local Hindu temple (Sri Guruvayoorappan Temple, Marlboro, NJ) in New Jersey, USA.

Dr. Chandrasekhar is also currently working on a Sanskrit Primer especially targeted to students of Classics (Greek, Latin). This will use the *Navlipi* script, along with Dewanaagari, Roman and Greek transcriptions.

**[See footnote, Ref. [LAi-83], regarding "speaking fluency" in Sanskrit, and a discussion of whether what we know as Sanskrit today is merely a literary language, thanks to Paanini (Panini) and others, and, if so, what the spoken language might have been like.]*